EXPLICIT AND AUTHENTIC ACTS

EXPLICIT AND AUTHENTIC ACTS

Amending the U.S. Constitution, 1776–1995

David E. Kyvig

University Press of Kansas

Published by the University Press of Kansas (Lawrence, Kansas 66049), which was
organized by the Kansas Board of Regents and is operated and funded by Emporia State
University, Fort Hays State University, Kansas State University, Pittsburg State University,
the University of Kansas, and Wichita State University

Library of Congress Cataloging-in-Publication Data

Kyvig, David E.
Explicit and authentic acts : amending the
U.S. Constitution, 1776–1995 / by David E. Kyvig.
p.   cm.
Includes bibliographical references.
ISBN 0-7006-0792-7 (alk. paper)
1. United States—Constitutional law—Amendments—History.
I. Title.
KF4555.K98   1996
342.73′029—dc20
[347.30229]   96-7452

British Library Cataloguing in Publication Data is available.

Printed in the United States of America

10 9 8 7 6 5 4 3 2 1

The paper used in this publication meets the minimum requirements of the American
National Standard for Permanence of Paper for Printed Library Materials Z39.48-1984.

TO CHRISTINE

CONTENTS

PREFACE

IF REVOLUTION INVOLVES the sudden and fundamental transformation of basic conditions, then surely the most soft-spoken revolutions are those that occur without violence, disorder, or trauma. In Western political culture such revolutions were virtually unheard of prior to the late eighteenth century. Before that time political revolutions involved the forceful overthrow of regimes, the toppling of monarchies, and the often bloody removal of holders of power. During the English Civil War, however, the thought began to stir that such upheavals might be avoided if the sovereign power of the state could define and limit government through written constitutions. By the end of the eighteenth century, particularly in North America, optimism regarding human capacity for reason fostered the belief that fundamental changes could be wrought in otherwise enduring governments through a preordained and agreed-upon process that embodied republican values. The formal revision of constitutions by previously established methods could bring about revolutionary changes in governments while at the same time legitimizing their continued existence. In other words, constitutional amendment offered a means of successfully balancing competing desires for stability and change, tradition and innovation, the wisdom of accumulated experience and democratic preference for new definitions of government responsibility.

The United States of America, the first nation to incorporate amendment mechanisms into its constitutional system, has now operated under the same basic instrument for over 200 years. During those two centuries, however, it has undergone more than one revolutionary political transformation in which the terms of government were redrawn. Relationships between the states and the central authority were fundamentally altered, as were government controls over private property, government responsibilities to the individual, and mechanisms of republican rule. The individual changes, most notably articulation of civil rights and liberties, abolition of slavery, establishment of direct, progressive taxation, prohibition and reestablishment of the liquor trade, and repeated extensions of suffrage, have received considerable attention. The constitutional amending system, the process by which these and other momentous reforms were implemented, has attracted far less notice.

Creating an instrument to accommodate fundamental reform, the creators of the United States recognized, provided the best preparation for the changes that their society and its governmental needs would inevitably undergo. Article V of the 1787 Constitution, outlining an amending process, makes manifest that orderly constitutional revision from time to time was the "original intent" of the Founders. The repeated use of this amending mechanism during the early years of the republic while many of the Founders remained active in government underscores their intention. Altogether the Constitution has been amended twenty-seven times in slightly over two centuries of operation. The roughly 3,100 words in those amendments come fairly close to the 4,300 of the original instrument. Although most students of the Constitution have viewed this as minimal amending activity, the evidence seems incontrovertible that without its capacity for formal alteration, the Constitution on more than one occasion would have confronted a far more disruptive revolutionary process.

Explicit and Authentic Acts illuminates the creation of the American amending system, the manner in which it functioned each time a major effort was made to change the Constitution, the nature of attempts to modify it, and, ultimately, its role in American constitutional development. The book begins, as any comprehensive history of the amending process must, by examining thought about amendment at the time of the creation of the first American constitutions, those of the original states as well as of the United States. The replacement of the Articles of Confederation by the 1787 Constitution, itself a process of amendment, is considered in detail; arrangements for amendment by the Article V method merit particular attention. On that base is built the history of subsequent operation of the amendment system. The individual circumstances of successful amending efforts and notable failures, together with judicial as well as political discussions of the Article V mechanism, provide the historical context vital to a nuanced appraisal of the amending system. The result should recast understandings of American constitutionalism and the nation's political order.

In recent years scholars of constitutional law, politics, and philosophy have tended to discount or ignore altogether differences between formal constitutional alteration through the amending process and functional shifts achieved by judicial construction, unchallenged legislative initiative, or unchecked presidential embellishment. For instance, in 1992 political scientist John Vile asserted, "The more expansive role the courts take in interpreting and adapting the Constitution to new exigencies, the less need there is for constitutional amendment, except perhaps as a way of reversing overly broad judicial opinions."[1] Whether this argument is advanced by constitutional conservatives or liberals, and both have done so at times, the result is a blurring of the important distinction between a tentative, limited, and unstable process of constitutional elaboration and a fundamental definition of authority granted by sovereign power.

Bruce Ackerman of the Yale Law School minimized the differences between formal and informal change in his wide-ranging and stimulating 1991 discussion of constitutional development, *We the People*. He characterized the American tradition of higher lawmaking as constitutional change achieved by a clear mobilization of the sovereign popular will, however expressed, rather than by strict adherence to agreed-upon form. It began, he asserted, with the replacement of the Articles of Confederation by the Constitution and the Bill of Rights. The Civil War amendments he regarded as irregularly obtained but nonetheless legitimate for having been accepted by the three branches of the federal government. The alterations in the Supreme Court's interpretation of federal authority during the late 1930s he treated as the functional equivalent of constitutional amendment. Ackerman perceived constitutional amendment as an extraordinary enunciation of the will of the sovereign populace but regarded changes that presidents and Congress desired and the Supreme Court accepted as having similar "transformative" weight.[2]

Other historians, legal scholars, and political scientists, especially those preoccupied with short-term change, have often gone even further than Ackerman in according equivalence to judicial opinion and amendment. In so doing, they have recognized the political consensus-building inherent in constitutional change but neglected significant differences between ordinary political activity and decisions to reshape the fundamental terms of government, what Ackerman himself labels democratic "dualism." This approach pays insufficient attention to one of the principle American innovations in higher lawmaking. Simply put, it undervalues the singular role of formal amendment in American constitutionalism.

Challenging the interpretations of Ackerman, Vile, and their colleagues, this book offers a historical appraisal that finds unparalleled power in what George Washington called "an explicit and authentic act" of constitutional articulation. In the presence of formal amendment, constitutional revolutions endure; in their absence, their long-term fate remains insecure. Amendatory reforms of the 1780s, 1860s, and 1910s have persisted or even, as in the cases of the Bill of Rights, Fourteenth, Sixteenth, and Nineteenth Amendments, grown in significance. Meanwhile, the nonamendment "transformations" of federal government authority during the 1930s have been constantly challenged and, in recent decades, diminished. In the course

of more than two centuries, no fully adequate substitute for amendment
has emerged to ensure the durability of fundamental reforms in governmental structure and obligation.

One of the drafters of the 1787 Constitution, James Wilson of Pennsylvania, may have foreseen the reason that the amending process itself has attracted relatively little attention. This revolutionary principle, he said, "that
the sovereign power residing in the people, they may change their constitution and government whenever they please, is not a principle of discord, ran-
cor, or war: it is a principle of melioration, contentment, and peace."[3] In
other words, the eighteenth century's great innovation was to routinize revolution, not in the sense of making constitutional change easy or frequent but
in the sense of rendering it legitimate and affirmative of the existing order
when carried out in a specified, standard manner. A process that peaceably
channels and resolves conflict in human affairs, while no doubt highly beneficial, seldom draws much notice.

Generally speaking, studies of the creation of the 1787 Constitution and
its subsequent treatment by judicial interpreters have dominated the histori-
ography of American constitutional development. Although amendments repeatedly redrew the framework of American government, most notably in
the 1780s, the 1860s, and the 1910s, formal constitutional change has captured comparatively little attention. For over a century, however, a few
scholars have attempted to describe the history of American constitutional
amending. Generally, they restricted their attention to single amendments or
at most to a contemporary cluster of related measures such as the Bill of
Rights or the Reconstruction amendments. The closely connected national
prohibition and repeal amendments became the subject of my own initial
venture into amending history, for instance.[4] Over the years only a handful
of scholars attempted a more comprehensive look at the operation of the
amending process established by Article V of the Constitution. Their efforts,
for better or worse, have provided the basis for the contemporary understanding of amendments that exists in more general histories and in the
American political culture at large.

Shortly after the Constitution's centennial, Herman Ames undertook the
first substantial retrospective examination of the Article V process. Ames
carefully listed all proposals for amendment introduced in Congress in the
course of a century, treating the trivial and duplicative as seriously as the
substantial and original. He drew a sharp contrast between the more than
1,700 bills that individual legislators submitted and the mere fifteen amendments that they adopted. Writing near the time when the ratio of amendment
to the passage of time reached its nadir, Ames helped shape an image of Arti-

cle V's requirements placing "insurmountable constitutional obstacles" in the path of constitutional reform. Regarding the supermajorities for adoption and ratification of amendments as too great, he paid no attention to the question of whether a young constitution particularly needed amendment, much less whether, given the political culture of the nineteenth century, any alternative constitutional arrangements enjoyed even the most slender of majorities. Instead he characterized amendment as excessively difficult and warned of possible dire consequences. Ames reinforced the general historical view that scarcely distinguished the passage of the first ten amendments from the passage of the Constitution itself and treated the Reconstruction amendments as irregular, forced, and not entirely legitimate. Such a view left only the Eleventh Amendment of 1795 and the Twelfth Amendment of 1804 as independently and properly achieved Article V changes.[5]

Forty years later Michael Musmanno extended and reinforced Ames's analysis, cataloging all amendment proposals introduced in Congress in the intervening period. Although the early twentieth century had been a period of substantial Article V activity with seven amendments adopted by Congress and six ratified between 1913 and 1933, it also proved to be a period during which the number of reform proposals surged. Musmanno, like Ames, treated each congressman's bill as a separate amendment effort, although many were repetitious and most clustered around a few issues. As a consequence he enhanced the image of a vast number of failed amendment attempts. The Ames-Musmanno characterization of amendment as an exceptionally arduous and rarely successful procedure gained further credence, even though contemporary experience might have suggested an alternative interpretation.[6]

In 1942 University of Michigan law professor Lester Orfield brought together his extensive consideration of various relevant issues in the first legal treatise devoted specifically to the amending process. He possessed considerable insight on a century and a half of Article V history but employed individual amending incidents out of historical context in narrow, if useful, discussions of constitutional procedure.[7] Russell Caplan's 1988 look at state-initiated constitutional conventions was a capable extension of Orfield's approach. Caplan, too, used selected historical episodes merely to illuminate legal and political constitutional issues; his analysis paralleled that of Orfield. Both men represented the amendment mechanism as heavily laden with devices that could frustrate reform efforts.[8]

Attention to constitutional amending history increased in the 1960s and 1970s, a time during which more than a dozen amendment proposals received serious consideration. Charles Leedham's 1964 popular account provided a narrative history of Article V activity, but it was disappointingly shallow and error-ridden as well as attentive only to ratified amendments.[9] Political scientist Clement Vose in 1972 placed amendment in a broader framework of constitutional change that encompassed judicial review and wider currents of political reform. Vose, however, paid no attention to events that had transpired before 1900 and looked only episodically at twentieth-century developments, producing a truncated and uneven picture full of shrewd observations but far from comprehensive.[10] Six years later another political scientist, Alan Grimes, provided a narrative superior to Leedham's in terms of political detail but again one that focused narrowly on the legislative history of successful Article V actions. Grimes forced amendments into narrow categories emphasizing, indeed exaggerating, the regional origins of support for reform rather than fully acknowledging the national consensus required for its completion. He also took a limited view of the substance of amendments, analyzing each in terms of its contribution to participatory democracy rather than its bearing on a broader range of issues.[11] Neither Leedham, Vose, nor Grimes did much to alter the conventional view of amending as a rare and peripheral element in American constitutional development.

Thereafter, the failed ratification of the equal rights amendment (ERA) not only frustrated feminists but also further strengthened the orthodox view of the amending process. Mary Frances Berry made the most substantial effort to place the defeat of the ERA in historical perspective. Before examining the ERA battle itself, she reviewed Article V activities from 1789 to the 1970s. Though superficial in many respects, her survey placed amending in the mainstream of constitutional development and called attention to expectations of federal consensus for fundamental reform. The inability of ERA proponents fully to understand the amending process historically, in particular its consensus requirements, went a long way, in Berry's estimation, toward explaining their defeat, not to mention their subsequent discontent with the Article V system.[12]

Michael Kammen's seminal 1986 study of the Constitution in American culture stirred a fuller consideration of the role of amendments in the evolution of American constitutionalism. Breaking with the tradition of narrowly focused political and legal studies, Kammen examined popular perceptions and responses to the Founders, their handiwork, and the subsequent evolution of the Constitution. He set forth a compelling case for adjusting the balance of consideration between judicial and popular interpretations of the instrument. Calling attention to the American public's gradually evolving "Constitution worship" together with its limited understanding of the document's intended purposes and functions, Kammen suggested that resistance to amendment rested on much more than the mechanism of Article V. A political culture emotionally attached to the status quo and not particularly knowledgeable about constitutional matters was not inclined to favor frequent amendment. Kammen's pioneering cultural approach not only elevated understanding of constitutional history to a higher plateau but also offered a new methodological model.[13] The work set a standard that demanded that subsequent scholarship examine constitutional evolution with greater attention to its broader historical context as well as to the nuances of individual issues.

In the aftermath of Kammen's richly detailed cultural history, Bruce Ackerman provided his schema for considering the American constitutional experience. Distinguishing between normal majoritarianism and higher-consensus constitutional politics, Ackerman portrayed constitutional evolution as a combination of amendment and judicial interpretation in which the sovereign people gave final sanction, in one way or another, to acceptable arrangements. Ackerman's assessment was grounded more in political philosophy than in history. Yet his argument that a sovereign people continually shaped the Constitution, by either accepting existing arrangements or choosing change, underscored the need for more thorough examination of past successful and unsuccessful amending efforts.

Initial responses to Kammen's and Ackerman's recasting of American constitutional history came not from historians but from political scientists and legal scholars. John Vile surveyed eighteenth-century political theory to support his contention that the Founders intended amendment to be a difficult but not impossible mechanism for change. He extended his analysis to show that on balance the commentators of the next century embraced the Article V device that prevented easy, destabilizing alteration of the frame of government yet provided a workable alternative to revolution when a compelling need for fundamental reform arose. Richard Bernstein and Jerome Agel adopted something of Kammen's cultural perspective. They also embraced Ackerman's view that debate over constitutional issues represented a separate and vital element of American political life. However, Bernstein and Agel passed rapidly over much of American constitutional history, focusing instead on recent developments.[14] Although not contributing any striking new insights themselves, Vile, and Bernstein and Agel helped raise the profile of amendment as a phenomenon to be taken seriously, a significant element in two centuries of constitutional evolution. They effectively underscored the need for a closer and fuller examination of formal constitutional change over the entire sweep of American history.

Scholars have repeatedly noted that nearly half of all amendments were added to the Constitution within its first fifteen years. The ten amendments during the first three years have commonly been regarded more as steps completing the act of creation rather than as reforms of an existing structure. Amendments eleven and twelve quickly followed in the manner prescribed by the Founders. Then more than a century passed during which only three more amendments were approved. These three were in a sense irregular, emerging from the unusual circumstances of the aftermath of the Civil War. Otherwise, many constitutional discussions occurred and numerous proposals for reform were offered, but no amendments were made.

Not until the early twentieth century did constitutional amending resume functioning as the Founders had anticipated, achieving fundamental changes one at a time through a conventional process of political debate and decision. In the twenty years between 1913 and 1933, six amendments, each of major consequence, were adopted. Thereupon, however, the pace of amendment slowed once again, generating only one change in nearly three decades. Then in the 1960s another burst of reform produced four amendments. Thereafter, various amendment proposals attracted support but not consensus until 1992 when, in a curious anomaly, an amendment that James Madison had drafted and the First Congress approved in 1789 was finally ratified. If one assumes that, after its terms were settled, a well-drawn charter would need little alteration at first, the pattern of the Constitution's first century is hardly surprising. What is more striking, and in need of careful examination, is the sudden rise in the use of the amending mechanism during the first third of the twentieth century and the irregularity of its employment thereafter.

The era of the New Deal appears pivotal in any reappraisal of U.S. constitutional amendment history. Confidence in the political necessity and efficacy of constitutional amendment waxed in the early twentieth century but abruptly waned during the 1930s. The Great Depression, the culmination of decades of industrialization and urbanization, created the conditions for a new articulation of federal obligation and authority at a moment when a constitutional consensus regarding such matters appeared within reach. Instead a vague, incomplete, and insecure understanding of the desired nature and limits of the federal government emerged, one resting on judicial interpretation rather than on explicit constitutional statement. The political opportunity passed, and the potential of the New Deal to transform the United States remained unfulfilled.

Issues left unresolved by the 1930s remained in dispute during the rest of the twentieth century, provoking a draining post–World War II debate over the nature of federal authority, a debate that continued to distract the country from substantive problems. Constitutionally speaking, the New Deal appears to have been a misspent opportunity. In the six decades after 1933, amendments were fewer in number and notably less sweeping in their influence than those implemented during the previous two. In constitutional terms, as in so many other ways, the 1930s profoundly reshaped the political thought and practice of the United States. The question of whether these changes were for the good cannot be satisfactorily answered without setting the beliefs and behaviors of that period in the larger context of American history.

The New Deal raised the question of whether the constitutional amending process was a vestige of eighteenth-century political thought that no longer made sense a century and a half later. Since it emerged in the 1930s, Americans have confronted, but steadfastly ignored, a profoundly important issue: is the entire concept of constitutionalism outmoded? This is not an abstract philosophical problem but a matter of vital current importance in an age of uncertainty about the best manner for government to be organized and controlled to serve the needs of the society. To what extent should democratic majorities be served? What justification, if any, exists for demanding a greater degree of consensus to permit or prevent government action? To what degree should government be responsive to wishes of the moment and to what extent should it be resistant to change in order to ensure stability and to preserve less popular interests? Their present-day relevance should not obscure that these are timeless questions best dealt with by examining them in historical context. There is contemporary value in considering why and how the amending system came to be incorporated in Article V of the U.S. Constitution, evaluating how that system functioned at various times and under different circumstances, and appraising the views of its advocates and critics.

"Article V is *the* most fundamental text of our Constitution, since it seeks to tell us the conditions under which all other constitutional texts and principles may be legitimately transformed," Bruce Ackerman has observed. Therefore, he has insisted, "Rather than treating it as a part of the Constitution's code of good housekeeping, we should accord the text of Article V the kind of elaborate reflection we presently devote to the First and Fourteenth Amendments."[15] This book, responding to his call for reflection, ultimately locates the amending process at the very center of American constitutionalism. However, it disputes Ackerman's contention that there are functional equivalents to amendment, concluding that in practice as well as by design formal amendment has no equal in the American constitutional order.

Explicit and Authentic Acts examines the antecedents, creation, and operation of Article V within the broader context of American development from the 1770s to 1995. Its survey of amending efforts stretches well beyond the replacement of the Articles of Confederation with the 1787 Constitution and the twenty-seven amendments added since then. Constitutional reform proposals that failed to attract substantial political support, however inherently interesting, receive little attention. For instance, proposals for an amendment to authorize federal regulation of marriage and divorce, which dedicated advocates offered repeatedly in the late nineteenth and early twentieth century but never enlisted more than a handful of congressional supporters, fail this test. On the other hand, 1960s propositions to authorize prayer in schools that fell far short of congressional adoption but did muster majority support in the Senate meet the standard. Available devices for amendment are considered, namely constitutional conventions called by the states, that have not been employed since 1787 but that nevertheless exerted influence on amending efforts. Mainly, however, the work focuses on substantial attempts to alter the formal terms of U.S. government and the processes that produced either success or failure. Thus, this study seeks to enhance understanding of the distinctive constitutional characteristics of the republican culture of the United States as it actually evolved, the stable structure of government when principles were formally articulated, and the unsettled, even retrograde patterns when they were not.

This historical consideration of constitutional amending seeks not only to illuminate the past but also to enlighten current public policy discussions and future initiatives. Disagreement exists as to whether the U.S. Constitution today serves, or in the future can continue to serve, its declared purpose of expressing the sovereign will of the people as to the terms of their governance, checking the momentary whims and excesses of transitory holders of power, and providing for reasoned, consensual advances in the definition of governmental responsibility. In addressing these important civic questions, it is vital that the process and consequences of constitutional amendment, as well as the equally important results of the failure to amend, be well understood.

ACKNOWLEDGMENTS

MY RESEARCH AND WRITING about the amending process have given me a new sense of the constitutional term "privileges and immunities." I have been very privileged to have the support of individuals and institutions who have been generous with time, resources, and encouragement. At the same time, they deserve to be immune from responsibility for this book. They have been most helpful, but ultimately the judgments reached are mine alone. They are identified here with gratitude and in every case but one should be absolved of responsibility for what follows.

At various stages of my work on this project, I received financial support from the American Council of Learned Societies, the National Endowment for the Humanities, the University of Akron faculty research fund, the American Historical Association/American Political Science Association Project '87, the Fulbright program, and the University of Tromsø, Norway.

Librarians and archivists aided me at every stage of my work. Those to whom I am particularly indebted include the staffs of the University of Akron Bierce Library and Law Library, the Library of Congress, the National Archives, the Herbert Hoover Library, the Franklin D. Roosevelt Library, the Harry S Truman Library, the Dwight D. Eisenhower Library, the John F. Kennedy Library, the Massachusetts Historical Society, the Eleutherian Mills Historical Library, the University of Virginia Library, the University of Kentucky Library, the Ohio Historical Society, and the Wisconsin Historical Society.

As I began this project in 1980, the staff of the Subcommittee on the Constitution of the U.S. Senate's Committee on the Judiciary welcomed me into their offices and made a wealth of material available to me. The subcommittee, then chaired by Senator Birch Bayh of Indiana, had long devoted its efforts to questions with which I was just beginning to grapple. I appreciated their material assistance and, even more, their encouragement that the work I was embarking upon had public policy as well as historical importance. Furthermore, they helped me at the very time that most of them were clearing out their desks and looking for new positions. At the time, their chairman had just lost his Senate seat to a then little-known Republican, J. Danforth Quayle.

Three senior scholars gave freely of their time and insight as my work was taking shape. While I took too liberally of their time and squandered too much of their advice, I am grateful for the friendship and intellectual stimulation given me by William Leuchtenburg of the University of North Carolina, Walter Dellinger of Duke Law School, and the late Clement Vose of Wesleyan University.

I was able to try out some of my ideas on constitutional amending by presenting bits and pieces of my evolving study in different form over the years in *Ohio History, The Historian, American Quarterly, Prologue, Political Science Quarterly, The Public Historian,* and *Akron Law Review.* I appreciate the questions, suggestions, and encouragement of the editors of these journals as well as the exposure and feedback my work gained thereby.

I owe a considerable debt to friends and colleagues who have read and criticized this manuscript. They include my frequent collaborator Myron Marty, Ann G. and Sigurd E. Anderson University Professor and professor of history at Drake University; Professor Elizabeth Monroe of Indiana University–Purdue University at Indianapolis; Richard Aynes, John F. Seiberling Professor of Constitutional Law at the University of Akron School of Law; Dr. Allie Hixson of the Kentucky Pro ERA Alliance and the national ERA Summit; Catherine Murdock of the University of Pennsylvania; Dr. Paul Sheips; Professor Melvin I. Urofsky of Virginia Commonwealth University; Professor Donald S. Lutz of the University of Houston; and my University of Akron history department colleagues Don Gerlach, Walter Hixson, Jerome Mushkat, Daniel Nelson, and Robert Zangrando. Michael Briggs of the University Press of Kansas has been an unfailingly interested, helpful, and gracious editor.

The one person who cannot be absolved of responsibility for this book is Professor Christine Worobec of the Kent State University history department. She is my most valued academic colleague as well as my treasured spouse. Through the example of her dedication to her own work, as well as her cheerfulness about discussing topics and critiquing manuscripts no doubt of much less interest to her than nineteenth-century Russian peasants, she provided me the incentive and support to pursue this study to completion. Of all those who have assisted me, her contribution has been the greatest. Indeed, I cannot imagine finishing the book without her encouragement and, therefore, consider her partly responsible for it. With love and gratitude, I dedicate this book to her.

1

"HERE SHALL BE THY BOUNDS"

The Rise of Constitutionalism

The United States Constitution, George Washington told his fellow citizens as he bade farewell to the presidency in 1796, "till changed by an explicit and authentic act of the whole people, is sacredly obligatory upon all." The first president regarded the basis of the American political system to be "the right of the people to make and to alter their constitutions of government."[1] Washington made clear not only that he regarded the 1787 Constitution as a fixed and binding framework for the country's government worthy of respect but also that he believed it contained a well-defined and appropriate procedure for its own reform. "If in the opinion of the people the distribution or modification of the constitutional powers be in any particular wrong, let it be corrected by an amendment in the way the Constitution designates."[2] Nine years earlier, at the conclusion of the Philadelphia convention that drafted the Constitution, the Virginian had written, "The Constitution that is submitted is not free from imperfections, but . . . as a Constitutional door is opened for future amendments and alterations, I think it would be wise in the People to accept what is offered to them."[3] After nearly a decade of further reflection, Washington declared, "This Government, the offspring of our own choice, uninfluenced and unawed, adopted upon full investigation and mature deliberation, completely free in its principles, in the distribution of its power, uniting security with energy, and containing within itself a provision for its own amendment, has a just claim to your confidence and your support."[4]

The traumas of revolutionary change in government in 1776 and 1787 made Washington and his contemporaries eager to avoid a repetition of such upheavals when circumstances eventually again required some fundamental alteration of government. By the end of his term, the first president believed firmly in the constitutional amending process defined in Article V of the new federal Constitution. The amending article was a strikingly original political device based on recently evolved notions of written constitutionalism, popular sovereignty, and federal republicanism. Washington was convinced that the 1787 Constitution equipped with Article V would provide the United States with a stable yet flexible structure of government that could endure.

By 1796 American political culture embraced George Washington's perspective on constitutionalism, including his view of constitutional reform. The notion of routine constitutional change by specific, prearranged, extralegislative means was a particularly remarkable and new concept. It had emerged in America during the previous two decades as Washington was leading the military campaign to defend the American political decision for independence, chairing the Philadelphia convention, and serving as the first chief executive under the new Constitution. Washington bore little responsibility for the evolution of the means to avoid wholesale overthrow of governments by provision for their peaceful, consensual restructuring. Yet the first president's Farewell Address attested to the degree to which the concept of written constitutionalism and its corollary of formal amendment had become embedded in the minds of the founding generation of American political thinkers and practitioners.

In order to understand the operation of a system for constitutional revision over the subsequent two centuries as well as to evaluate the influence of that system in shaping or failing to shape the nature of American government, which are the purposes of this book, it is essential first to examine the evolution of the idea of constitutionalism and then to consider why and how the concept of constitutional amending arose. Only by confronting the assumptions on which written constitutionalism and amendment rested and investigating the circumstances of their creation can the performance of the amending system be properly evaluated. Thereafter it becomes possible to distinguish between the power of reform embodied in amendments and, conversely, the insecurity of change not formally embedded in a constitution. Both the purities of political thought and the impurities of political practice must be considered in order to grasp how Washington and his contemporaries could come to believe that only "an explicit and authentic act of the whole people" could and should alter constitutions.

CONSTITUTIONALISM, the authoritative articulation of the general principles, structures, and functions of government, is rooted in one of the oldest concerns of Western political culture: the felt need to define and limit the power of government so that it will carry out those tasks, and only those tasks, which the society wishes it to perform. Constitutions embody the agreements communities reached through one means or another as to the general form of their governments, the apportionment of power therein, and the acceptable boundaries of governmental practice. The Western concept of law underlies the constitutional approach. Law makes known the specific arrangements and requirements that the society will allow the government to enforce on the populace. Law provides for the standard treatment of similar circumstances rather than permitting varied and arbitrary governmental responses. Euripides wrote in the fifth century B.C.:

No worse foe than the despot hath a state,
Under whom, first can be no common laws,
But one rules, keeping in his private hands
The law: so is equality no more.
But where the laws are written, then the weak,
And wealthy have alike but equal right,
Yea, even the weaker may fling back the scoff
Against the prosperous, if he be reviled;
And, armed with right, the less o'ercomes the great.[5]

Other Greeks arrived at similar conclusions about government and law by different routes. Plato believed that the ideal form of government involved rule by philosopher-kings with no limits on their authority. "If a competent ruler should arise, they would have no need to be ruled by laws, 'for no law or ordinance is mightier than knowledge.'"[6] He eventually recognized, however, that such paragons of wisdom and virtue were not to be found. Grudgingly, he accepted as the best attainable alternative governments whose power was defined and limited by common agreement. Without law, Plato concluded, men "differ not at all from the most savage beasts."[7]

Aristotle saw the ideal government of Plato's *Republic* as dangerous and embraced his teacher's second-best alternative, constitutionalism, much more enthusiastically. Unrestricted arbitrary power in the hands of any individual or class led to despotism, he concluded. Freedom and equality could be maintained only when governments were constrained by laws that the citizenry had participated in establishing or otherwise willingly accepted. In *Politics*, Aristotle developed at length his conclusion that law, not unrestrained human will, was the best means of ensuring satisfactory government.

Concepts of law and constitutionalism evolved much further in the Roman Republic. Cicero, the foremost articulator of Roman legal thought, portrayed the state as a corporate body belonging to its citizens and existing to supply their need for mutual aid and just governance. The Romans regarded only direct enactments of the people as law; every other sort of governmental act, decrees of the Senate, proclamations of magistrates or consuls, later even decrees of the emperor, gained legitimacy and authority from its relation to the law. The letters SPQR on the standards of the Roman legions proclaimed the primacy of law. Roman legions marched, as

Romans lived, under the authority of *Senatus Populusque Romanus,* the
Senate of the People of Rome. In theory at least, the sanction of the populus
provided the foundation for the power of the state.

The onset of the Christian era brought to the fore the concept of natural
law, fundamental and unchanging principles of divine design that bound all
men and nations, and authority as derived from God. In the fifth century
Augustine articulated the Christian notion of a spiritual world superior to
the temporal world. For more than a millennium thereafter, Western political theory hinged on the assumption that the power to rule came from God,
who bestowed it upon monarchs or emperors as his agents. The higher
claims of the spirit limited the temporal authority of government and ruler;
the guidelines of scripture set the bounds of worldly power. The very vague-
ness of such concepts led inevitably to the expansion of the claims of monarchy as well as to concerns to restrain them.

English constitutionalism was rooted in a desire to limit the arbitrary
power of monarchs. The great gathering at Runnymeade in 1215 compelled
an unwilling King John to accept the principle that terms agreed upon by
peers of the realm set the bounds of royal authority. Furthermore, those terms
applied equally to all and had force only if publicly proclaimed so as to be
universally understood. Article thirty-nine of the great charter was the em-
bodiment of its constitutional approach: "No free man shall be taken or imprisoned or [deceased] or outlawed or exiled or in any way ruined, nor will
we go upon him nor send against him, except by the lawful judgment of his
peers or by the law of the land."[8] Magna Carta directly linked the Aristotelian
political philosophy of restricted power to the medieval English power struggle. The barons at Runnymeade, as they rejected the notion of the king's arbitrary rule and permanently limited his prerogative, were asserting their power
to act as society's spokesmen in setting the terms of government.

To gain sanction for their rule, English kings after Runnymeade gradually began summoning representatives from counties and boroughs as well
as the great lay and clerical barons to meet with them in Parliament. To ensure their authority, these representatives came with power of attorney to
bind their constituencies to whatever laws or taxes they agreed upon. From
this practice evolved the notion that Parliament had as much right to grant
and limit governmental power as if the people had acted in person.[9]

As constitutional authority began evolving from the theoretical to the
functional, its most obvious deficiency was its lack of means to deal with a
government indifferent to law. Given its power, how was a government that
chose not to obey the law to be restrained? In medieval theory, the church as
repository and defender of divine law stood as a check on secular authority.

Theologians found the issue of government troubling and reached different conclusions in regard to it. Augustine believed in unqualified obedience to the state, but by the time of Thomas Aquinas the view prevailed that government was obliged to behave in a just fashion. Both Martin Luther and John Calvin preached obedience to the authority of the state, counseling prayer or withdrawal in response to bad government. With the decline of the church's power following the Protestant Reformation, the only available means of combating a government that ignored the law appeared to be the threat or use of revolutionary violence.

Increasingly elaborate and modern theories of constitutionalism emerged during the seventeenth-century English Civil War. King James I began this tumultuous century arguing for royal absolutism, a monarchy based on divine authority, possessing all sovereignty, free from control by Parliament or law and empowered to provide for the welfare of the people as it saw fit. Then after 1625 as his son Charles I exercised power more and more arbitrarily, fears of uncontrollable royal absolutism spread throughout Britain. After the Parliament of 1628 pressed Charles to accept its Petition of Right, a declaration of individual legal rights and liberties, the king avoided summoning another Parliament for as long as possible. Finally forced by his need for revenues to call Parliament into session in 1640, Charles faced a highly charged opposition that reversed his initiatives, then defeated his forces on the field of battle. The Long Parliament, or more precisely the militant Puritan Rump that remained by 1649, rejected completely the notion that the king could do no wrong and asserted ultimate parliamentary control over a law-breaking monarch by ordering his execution.

The Levelers of the 1640s, one of the most radical factions on the English political landscape and an influential element within the ranks of the Puritan army, not only opposed the absolutism of the monarchy but also came to object to what they saw as the arbitrary tendencies of Parliament. These energetic middle-class pamphleteers interested in economic reform rejected the Long Parliament's inclination to support the status quo. Devoted Puritans, they resented what they saw as Parliament's unauthorized actions favoring Presbyterianism. Stirred by the particular events of recent years but taking constitutional theory seriously, the Levelers argued that sovereignty, the ultimate authority to define and direct government, rested with the people. They maintained that the best means for the sovereign power to establish the terms under which not only the monarch but also the Parliament would function was through a written constitution setting forth the terms of government for all to see, instead of the prevailing imprecise mix of natural law, custom, and statute.[10]

John Lilburne, the leader of the Levelers and a constant advocate of "the rights of the people," in 1647 offered the first written constitution for England. This Agreement of the People evolved through much discussion and several versions but rested upon bedrock Leveler principles. Most fundamental was the concept of sovereignty as belonging to the people, the entire community, rather than to the monarch as proponents of natural law proclaimed, or to Parliament as the Leveler's Puritan rivals asserted. From the outset the question of how the will of the people was to be articulated represented a major stumbling block for the theory of popular sovereignty.

The Levelers contended that Parliament possessed only delegated authority; the actual human beings who composed the nation had the natural right to determine the fundamental laws even if they normally allowed Parliament to act for them. Rejecting the traditional English notion that Parliament represented the great "interests" such as land, corporations, and church, the Levelers offered the new view that Parliament represented all Englishmen equally and directly. Such views led eventually to advocacy of universal manhood suffrage and equality of representation in Parliament. More immediately, however, they led toward the assertion of the power of the people themselves to establish a constitution that would define the individual's inalienable rights against his representatives.

The Leveler's Agreement of the People set forth a bill of fundamental individual rights that Parliament was not to infringe. Accordingly, Parliament was not to interfere with the operation of law, exercise power over religion, impress men for the army or navy, destroy rights of personal liberty or property, repudiate debts, or modify any of these rights. The Levelers wanted to convene a special body representing the sovereign people to refine the agreement, to act as a sort of constitutional convention to establish the foundation for government and to fix the limits of Parliament's legislative prerogative. Thereafter the agreement was to achieve regular sanction from the sovereign power by being endorsed and signed by voters and candidates at every election. Such a specific document would articulate and limit the powers of government, serving evermore as a measure of the government's legitimacy.

The Levelers quickly faded from the scene after 1649. While regicide needed their support (because of their standing among the army's rank-and-file), their agreement received a respectful hearing. Once Charles was dispatched, Puritan army leaders no longer regarded the Levelers as crucial. Yet their ideas of popular sovereignty, law as protection of individual rights against unrestrained government, and written constitutionalism did not fade with them. Soon the first written constitution, the 1653 Instrument of Government, was put into effect. And although written constitutionalism did not survive the Restoration in England, the open flow of political ideas across the Atlantic from the 1630s to the 1650s ensured that the Levelers' notions would not be altogether forgotten.

The Instrument of Government was created by leaders of the Puritan army after Oliver Cromwell forcibly dissolved the Rump Parliament in 1652 and the Barebones Parliament collapsed the following year. The forty-two numbered paragraphs of the instrument created three chief organs of government: the lord protector and a council of thirteen to twenty-one members were both to serve for life, and a 400-member unicameral Parliament, apportioned to the counties and boroughs of England, Wales, Scotland, and Ireland, was to be elected by property holders of £200 and meet triennially. The protector had a qualified veto over legislation, an absolute veto over acts of Parliament contrary to the instrument, and principal authority over the military, foreign relations, and domestic administration. Religious freedom was guaranteed, except to Catholics or "to such as, under the profession of Christ, hold forth and practise licentiousness."[11] It was, in all, a carefully crafted framework.

Although the rationale of the Instrument of Government was that sovereignty rested in the people, not even a modest ritual of popular formulation, acceptance, or endorsement of the document was performed. The army, asserting that it was acting for the people, simply imposed the unsanctioned and inflexible constitution upon Britain. Cromwell decreed the instrument to be in effect without any attempt to place it before a representative body, much less the people themselves. The instrument stipulated that Cromwell would be the lord protector and named the first sixteen counselors. Furthermore, the instrument was unchangeable: the protector could veto any legislation to amend it, and election returns were to specify that persons elected to Parliament had no power to alter the government

> to prevent a razing of those foundations of freedom that have been but newly laid; . . . it was high time, some power should pass a decree upon the wavering humors of the people, and say to the nation, as the Almighty Himself said once to the unruly sea; *Here shall be thy bounds, hitherto shalt thou come, and no further.*[12]

When the first Parliament to convene under the authority of the Instrument of Government met in 1654, however, Lord Protector Cromwell announced he would allow it to consider the terms of the instrument after all. When it proceeded to do so to the point of disputing the protector's control of the military, Cromwell dissolved this Parliament as soon as possible. The second Parliament, convened in 1656, went further, proposing the creation of a second House and making the protector into a king. Again acting as the possessor of full sovereign power to constitute government, Cromwell accepted most of the constitutional amendments embodied in the Humble Petition and Advice in May 1657, though not the kingship, and appointed the first members of the new "other House." The 1658 Parliament that convened under these reforms again proved troublesome to Cromwell, and it too was dissolved.

Repeated efforts at constitution-making failed to produce consensus, stability, or smooth governmental operation during the 1650s. Following the death of Oliver Cromwell in September 1658, constitutional disputes multiplied and soon produced a deadlock. In the convoluted and factional politics of the moment, the solution accepted by all parties and endorsed by the Parliament elected in 1660 that declared itself a convention competent to reconstitute government was restoration of the Stuart monarchy.

The ascension of Charles II momentarily abated constitutional turmoil. The specter of a Catholic monarchy, however, led to attempts to exclude Charles's brother and heir James from the succession and then provoked an uprising against him after he took the throne and fathered a son. The Revolution of 1688 brought William of Orange and James II's Protestant daughter Mary to the English throne on terms that made clear that Parliament would be the supreme authority in the realm. The newly elected Convention Parliament's 1689 Bill of Rights, which William accepted as the condition to receiving the crown, stipulated that the king could suspend no laws, taxes could be raised and armies maintained only through parliamentary consent, and no subject could be arrested or detained without legal process. Together with the 1701 Act of Settlement that barred Catholics from the English throne, the bill became a contract between king and Parliament. In concert with Magna Carta, the Petition of Right of 1628, and other great documents of English law, the revolutionary settlement achieved a clear and stable framework of government, a constitution of several independent parts, or as it is more commonly (if not altogether accurately) termed, an unwritten constitution.

The desire to justify the opposition of the new Whig political faction to the Restoration monarchs as well as to legitimate the government that emerged after 1688 from more than a half-century of tumult produced some of the most cogent and influential statements ever made about the nature of governments and constitutions. Much of late seventeenth-century political theory was, at least in part, a response to Thomas Hobbes. Writing in the 1640s, Hobbes had proceeded from a belief that in a state of nature people were selfish and brutish to the view that a government must be able to exercise force in order to restrain humanity's innately individualistic inclinations. To obtain the benefits of peace and protection, individuals must surrender the right of governing themselves to a person or assembly that would be sovereign in the use of force. Although Hobbes was seeking to justify monarchy, he was not taking the then-conventional position that royal authority was divinely granted. To Hobbes only individuals as the ultimate holders of power in a state of nature could bestow that power upon an agent and submit their will to the will of the agent. That agent, having become sovereign, must have unrestricted, indivisible power unless it failed to provide security, at which point humankind was thrown again into a state of nature and obliged to create a new government. Although offered in support of monarchy, Hobbes's arguments as to the nature of sovereignty could be, and soon were, used by the Levelers and thereafter the Whigs.

After the Restoration one Whig defended the sovereignty of the people so fiercely and eloquently that it ultimately cost him his life. According to Algernon Sidney, the people had a God-given power not only to establish government but also to judge the performance of that government. He rejected Hobbes's argument that, having formed a government, people were obliged to accept its rule. Sidney held that the people could exercise their sovereignty to change even just governments "to prevent or cure the mischiefs arising from them, or to advance a good that at the first was not thought on," in other words, to suit new tastes.[13] In his *Discourses Concerning Government,* Sidney declared that the people's power, "being eminently above that of all magistrates, was obliged to no other rule than that of their own will."[14] Such an opinion, whatever its logic, was not well received during the Restoration, and Sidney paid with his head in 1683.

The most influential as well as profound Whig intellectual, John Locke, apparently began writing his *Two Treatises of Government* at the time of the exclusion crisis but, perhaps because of Sidney's fate, thought better of publishing them until after the revolution of 1688.[15] Contrary to Hobbes, Locke believed that in their natural state men were happy, peaceful, tolerant, rational, and possessed of inherent rights to life, liberty, and property. Locke theorized that governments originated when unassociated individuals living in this state of nature came together to form a society for their mutual betterment, in his words, to make by their own consent a "social compact." Thereafter, Locke continued, this society would form a second compact, creating a government and agreeing to submit to its authority in return for its protection of life, liberty, and property. Furthermore, in the act of forming a government all consented to submit to the will of the majority, creating the fiction that the agreement of a majority was identical to the approval of the whole society. This second compact could be broken and the government altered or replaced, without the social compact being destroyed and the people thrown back into a state of nature. In other words, society, a cohesive community, came before government and thus could act to constitute or alter its government.

Locke took a more conservative view of sovereignty than Algernon Sidney. To Locke, once the society granted power to a government, that government had the right to retain power as long as it was faithful to its duties. The constitutive power, once exercised, bound the society until the government "dissolved." Not only Sidney but such an eighteenth-century democrat as Jean Jacques Rousseau would argue that such an obligation placed an unwarranted limitation on the perpetual power of the people to govern themselves as they saw fit. The more conservative Locke was not prepared to tolerate such flexibility in government, however. He could justify action against a ruler's clear violation of right but not the continual turmoil of the 1640s and 1650s.

The Revolution of 1688 proceeded along Lockean lines. After William's army landed and James II fled to France, a convention, elected in the manner of a parliament, met at William's call to settle the terms of government. With no king to veto its acts, the convention was in a position to exercise sovereignty and establish a new compact of government. This it did by granting the crown to William, declaring in the coronation oath it required him to swear that sovereignty would reside with the king in Parliament, and confirming the traditional authority of Parliament and laws rather than articulating any new set of structures and principles. The convention then proceeded to draw a Declaration of Rights. Yet not until William took the throne, the convention had been declared a Parliament, and the declaration had been adopted as statute was this fundamental instrument regarded as a fully sanctioned Bill of Rights.

The convention's decision to reconfirm old arrangements rather than to erect a new, explicit, unitary frame of government obscured the fact that a process of constitutional creation was carried out in 1689. Nevertheless, when Whigs and Tories in 1689 embraced a modified version of the traditional English constitution, they were conducting a process that had come to be regarded over the course of the seventeenth century as an act of constitutional formation. A body proclaiming itself to be exercising the sovereignty of the people set the terms of government anew. Clearly uncomfortable with their actions and unwilling to admit that in a legal sense they were making a break with the past, these late seventeenth-century Englishmen downplayed their role as constitutional innovators. Notably, in so doing they avoided, as had all prior generations, the issue of whether anything could be done short of another revolution if once again the established constitution proved unsatisfactory beyond parliamentary remedy.

ACROSS THE ATLANTIC in the British colonies of North America, the notion was present from the outset that a written framework should explicitly define and limit government. The authority to found and rule a colony originated in every case in a grant from the throne, the terms of which were made quite specific. The initial colonial enterprises developed as joint-stock ventures in which British sponsors such as the Virginia Company of London spelled out in some detail the terms of settlement. Their charters required proprietors of later colonies to obtain the consent of freemen to laws; they found that, in order to attract colonists, they needed to articulate arrangements for governance further.

The Virginia enterprise encountered immediate difficulty as the colonists of 1607 objected to the London company's specifications about the composition of their local government, directives revealed only upon their arrival in the Chesapeake. Thereafter the company proved willing to change the terms of colonial governance in order to shore up its shaky business prospects. Most notably, in 1619 the company provided the colony with a Charter of Grants and Liberties. This code of laws and rules of colonial government provided for a democratically chosen representative assembly, the House of Burgesses. When the first House of Burgesses asked for power to disapprove any law the company promulgated, the company's London directors granted the request, another noteworthy step in defining a framework of self-government, in the Ordinances and Constitutions of 1621. When the company failed in 1624 and Virginia became a royal colony, a period of uncertainty regarding the terms of government followed. Eventually, however, the established constitutional arrangements prevailed and became the model for other royal colonies.[16]

The contemporaneous Plymouth Company, begun as a joint-stock venture and seized upon by English separatists as a means of planting a New World foothold, carried the notion of a written frame of government a step further. Willing to extend to civil arrangements their firm theological commitment to covenants and believing that they were outside the jurisdiction of existing royal charters, the separatists, or Pilgrims as they styled themselves, before disembarking drew up and signed a civil covenant, an instrument of self-government. Forty-one adult colonists endorsed the Mayflower Compact, thereby pledging submission to a civil government and such laws as it might adopt.[17] The Mayflower Compact initiated North America's first self-defined, self-imposed constitution, a noteworthy development in the history of constitutionalism.

A similar desire to keep control of government in their own hands motivated the formation of the nonseparatist Puritan colony of Massachusetts Bay. The 1629 royal charter of the Massachusetts Bay Company granted company stockholders the right to govern the colony and to elect a governor, deputy governor, and eighteen assistants. Since nothing in the charter specifically required that it remain in England and since the physical location of the charter legally determined the meeting place of the stockholders, the Massachusetts Bay Puritans, by the unprecedented action of taking the charter with them to the New World, were able to ensure that they would retain control of the colony. Massachusetts Puritans thus took advantage of English legal doctrine to strengthen the sanctions for constitutional local self-government. Quick expansion of the right to participate in local government from stockholders to freemen, in other words church members, extended the notion of sovereignty. Permitting citizens to elect deputies to the General Court created a system of representative government. Dividing the General Court into an upper house containing the governor, lieutenant governor, and assistants and a lower house of deputies, each house with a veto on General Court actions, and publishing the General Lawes and Liberties, a 1636 articulation of the government's rules and concessions of authority, completed the process of transforming Massachusetts from a chartered company to a self-governing constitutional commonwealth.[18]

Enthusiasm for written frames of government, however derived, spread throughout Britain's American colonies especially as turmoil in the mother country created political uncertainty. The English Civil War forced the colonists to be more self-reliant and enabled their representative assemblies to be more self-assertive. As Thomas Hutchinson commented a century later, "They thought themselves at full liberty, without any charter from the crown, to establish such sort of government as they thought proper, and to form a new state as full to all intents and purposes as if they had been in a state of nature, and were making their first entrance into civil society."[19] In 1639 Connecticut used the General Lawes and Liberties of Massachusetts as a model when creating its Fundamental Orders, an instrument on which it based the legitimacy of its government until 1662. The royal charter granted Connecticut following the Restoration accepted this frame of government, providing that royal supremacy was fully acknowledged.[20] In similar fashion the towns of Rhode Island formed a colonywide government with the Acts and Orders of 1647, which in turn was affirmed by a 1663 royal charter.[21]

The value of an explicit framework for colonial government resting on some measure of popular approval had become well recognized.[22]

The articulation of constitutions grew common in the proprietary Restoration colonies. Nevertheless, these instruments were clearly concessions on the part of proprietors rather than compacts among people. The New Jersey proprietors' Concessions and Agreement of 1664 promised an elected representative assembly with the power to levy all taxes and to make laws for the colony. The principal proprietor of Carolina, Anthony Ashley Cooper, later the earl of Shaftesbury, sought the assistance of his secretary John Locke in drawing up the 1669 Fundamental Constitutions (which proved to be aristocratic and quite unwieldy). William Penn's 1682 Frame of Government for Pennsylvania, though extraordinarily liberal in its terms, was likewise the act of an authority willing to relinquish some power to encourage immigration.[23]

James II's 1686 decree establishing the Dominion of New England was most unwelcome in the affected colonies. It provided a stark reminder to the colonies that their constitutional arrangements rested on arbitrary authority. The upheavals of 1688 in Britain soon undid James II's changes. At the same time, the Glorious Revolution compelled all colonies to seek reconfirmation of their authority from Britain's new sovereign power. In some cases, notably Massachusetts and New York, the terms of government changed substantially. In every instance, the importance of constitutions was affirmed, as was the power of Crown and Parliament to determine them.

The events of the 1680s gave the colonies a ringing reminder that, in the eyes of Britain, they did not possess sovereignty. Accordingly, a sense of the importance of sovereign power, authority that could define the terms of government and from which there was no appeal, and a desire to exercise it grew steadily. In Pennsylvania, a new Charter of Liberties worked out between the proprietor, William Penn, and the colonial assembly in 1701 not only made a bold claim that they together possessed the colony's sovereignty but also that, once having exercised it to articulate a constitution, only an extraordinary consensus of themselves or their successors could alter the terms of government. "No Act, Law or Ordinance whatsoever, shall at any time hereafter be made or done, to alter, change or diminish the Form or Effect of this charter . . . without the Consent of the Governor . . . and Six Parts of Seven of the Assembly." The 1701 Pennsylvania Charter of Liberties culminated a century's quest by Americans for legal guarantees of personal liberty secured by written enactment beyond ordinary governmental control.[24]

The decades after the Glorious Revolution witnessed less overt constitutional turmoil in Britain's American colonies than had the decades before.

The practice of government for the most part evolved gradually and informally as colonial assemblies sought power at the expense of governors and councils. Time and again, royal authorities found that effective and profitable operation of the colonies could best, indeed sometimes only, be achieved by obtaining popular consent to their policies. Repeatedly this consent required the acknowledgment that some authority previously regarded as royal prerogative rested in the hands of representative assemblies. By the mid-eighteenth century long practice undergirded the American colonists' increasingly firm belief in the legitimacy of their claim to the type of sovereign power that John Locke envisioned.

Meanwhile, eighteenth-century French political philosophers such as Montesquieu and Rousseau, admirers of Locke, built on a foundation of respect for English constitutionalism even while they operated in a very different political environment of aristocratic absolutism. Montesquieu's *Spirit of the Laws* argued that constitutionalism, especially that which embodied a separation of powers, rather than reliance on the civic morality of leaders, was the most effective way to guarantee liberty.[25] Rousseau's *Social Contract* rejected a belief in the existence of natural law in favor of a concept of a general will, that is, a distinctive corporate personality in each community that determined its standards of right and justice. Government was merely the agent of the community's will. A government in which rights of liberty, equality, and property were protected resulted, not from substantially equal power among men as Hobbes had argued, but from the community's decision to establish those rights in its laws. Rousseau made clear that sovereignty rested in the people as a corporate body and that government merely served as their agent. Government, he held, operated on the basis of delegated powers that could be modified as the people chose.[26]

Though both Montesquieu and Rousseau offered complex and abstract political philosophies whose precise influence is difficult to assess, it is evident that they were being read in prerevolutionary America.[27] It is likely that they further enlarged and enriched the growing enthusiasm for constitutionalism among politically sophisticated Americans. Yet while lip service was being paid to the concept of constitutionalism in both Britain and its colonies, hard questions remained unanswered.

The extent to which constitutions were fixed and binding was an unsettled issue. Lord Bolingbroke, writing in 1733, took the view that a government acting contrary to its constitution was not good government, but he was not willing to say that such acts were illegitimate or could be disobeyed.[28] Twenty-five years later the Swiss philosopher Emmerich de Vattel held in *The Law of Nations* that the legislative power of assemblies and monarchs was subordinate: "For the *constitution* of the state ought to possess stability: and since that was first established by the nation, which afterwards intrusted certain persons with the legislative power, the *fundamental* laws are excepted from their commission."[29] By 1761 James Otis of Massachusetts was quoting Vattel as he argued, in the Writs of Assistance case, that acts of Parliament violating the constitution were void. The British constitution, in other words, limited Parliament and could not be redefined by it in the ordinary course of affairs. Yet at that point Otis saw parliamentary repeal of the offending act as the only solution. During the next decade and a half, however, Americans increasingly insisted that fixed fundamental principles of government constrained legitimate action.[30] Thomas Paine, for one, declared that "a government is only the creature of a constitution."[31]

Equally unsettled was the question of what determined that a constitution was no longer suitable. For Thomas Hobbes total calamity had been the necessary precondition; people in a state of nature having bestowed unrestricted, indivisible power on an agent in return for security could not reconstitute that power unless a failure of their agent to provide security threw them back into a state of nature. John Locke, despite his generally more benign views, took a similar position that once the society constituted a government, power remained in that government's hands as long as it faithfully performed its duties. Algernon Sidney, Jean Jacques Rousseau, and Emmerich de Vattel, on the other hand, considered that such a commitment placed an unwarranted limitation on the perpetual power of the people to govern themselves as they saw fit and to change the terms of government if they chose. The more conservative Locke could justify action against a ruler only in the case of a clear and substantial violation of obligation. Ultimately Locke's stricter standard had to be met before American colonial opinion broadly supported steps to make new constitutional arrangements, free of Great Britain.

An abstract concept of the sovereign people's power to set the terms of their constitution was one thing; how that power was actually to be exercised was quite another. Historian Edmund Morgan has suggested that popular sovereignty amounted to a fiction constructed by an elite seeking to wrest power from monarchs and needing an alternative to divine right as the source for the authority that they would exercise themselves. It is no doubt true, as Morgan says, that it is less difficult to imagine a king exercising sovereignty than to personify a whole people as a single body "capable of thinking, of acting, of making decisions and carrying them out, something quite apart from government, superior to government, and able to alter or remove a government at will, a collective entity more powerful and less fallible than a king or than any individual within it or than any group of individuals it singles out to govern it."[32] Although the notion of a whole people exercising sovereignty hardly mirrored the contemporary reality of effective power in the hands of a small elite, it is nevertheless true that the belief was widely shared that legitimate government rested on popular sovereignty. Furthermore, in practice the representative bodies of the American colonies came much closer to the ideal of the democratic republic than did Britain in the middle of the eighteenth century. Suffrage was more widespread in the American colonies than anywhere else and involved the majority of adult white males. Elections of representative assemblies were for the most part held annually, a sharp contrast to the normal seven-year term of British parliamentarians. And although it is true that members of the colonial elite dominated the election process, influenced its outcome, and most often became the legislators, it is also true that elections were often contested and that the electorate was in close contact with its representatives. Mid-eighteenth-century America did not operate with pure Lockean popular sovereignty, but the agreed-upon fiction that it did was closer to reality than fantasy.

A vital issue emerging from the theories of constitutionalism, one not resolved prior to the American Revolution, was how to carry out constitutional reform properly. As notions developed that constitutions ought to be devices that defined and limited parliaments as well as kings, the American colonists, if not the British, grew less comfortable with the idea of Parliament reforming the constitution by ordinary legislative process, especially when the sitting Parliament did not represent them. Innovations in constitution-making were soon to be offered, among them drafting of constitutions by bodies specially chosen for the purpose, direct approval of proposed constitutions by the sovereign people, and requirements for an extraordinary degree of consensus, supermajorities rather than simple majorities to implement constitutions. For the time being, however, other than parliamentary action, the only historical model for achieving constitutional change was seventeenth-century-style insurrection. That of course proved the necessary model when the colonies concluded that their constitutional arrangements within the British Empire had become intolerable.

By 1776 the leadership of the American colonies had come to believe that the British government intended to deprive them of various valued, long-standing constitutional arrangements, the sole authority to levy taxes upon themselves being paramount among them. A British government unwilling to respect its own constitution was cause for alarm. Defense of constitutional rights against such a government justified revolution.[33]

The declaration that Thomas Jefferson drafted and the Second Continental Congress adopted in Philadelphia during early summer 1776 was at

its core a summary of the concept of constitutionalism that had by then
emerged in America.

> We hold these truths to be self-evident: That all men are created equal;
> that they are endowed by their Creator with certain unalienable rights;
> that among these are life, liberty, and the pursuit of happiness; that, to
> secure these rights, governments are instituted among men, deriving their
> just powers from the consent of the governed; that whenever any form of
> government becomes destructive of those ends, it is the right of the peo-
> ple to alter or abolish it, and to institute new government, laying its
> foundations on such principles, and organizing its powers in such form,
> as to them shall seem most likely to effect their safety and happiness.
> Prudence, indeed, will dictate that governments long established should
> not be changed for light and transient causes, and accordingly all experi-
> ence hath shown that mankind are more disposed to suffer, while evils
> are sufferable, than to right themselves by abolishing the forms to which
> they are accustomed. But when a long train of abuses and usurpations,
> pursuing invariably the same object, evinces a design to reduce them
> under absolute despotism, it is their right, it is their duty, to throw off
> such government, and to provide new guards for their future security.

All the essential elements of eighteenth-century constitutionalism were present in Jefferson's spare prose: popular sovereignty, constitutions as devices to
define and limit the powers of government, and the propriety of altering
constitutions when conditions warrant.

The Declaration of Independence deserves to be regarded as much more
than a proclamation of revolution. It was the foundation block of the American Constitution, or as Daniel Webster would call it in 1830, "the title deed of
their liberties."[34] Joseph Story, one of the early nineteenth century's most careful and insightful writers on constitutionalism, observed that the Declaration

> was not an act done by the state governments then organized; nor by
> persons chosen by them. It was emphatically the act of the whole *people*
> of the united colonies, by the instrumentality of their representatives,
> chosen for that, among other purposes. . . . It was an act of original, in-
> herent sovereignty by the people themselves, resulting from their right to
> change the form of government, and to institute a new government,
> whenever necessary for their safety and happiness.[35]

Story concluded that from the moment the Second Continental Congress declared independence, if not even earlier when the First Continental Congress
began assuming powers and passing measures that were in their nature na-

tional, the colonies must be considered as being a nation de facto. A general government had been created. It functioned, furthermore, by the general consent of the people of all the colonies.[36]

Subsequent claims by states' rights advocates that the United States and its constitutions were creations and creatures of sovereign and independent states wither when placed in this light. Abraham Lincoln understood the circumstances of the country's founding when he declared that in 1776, not 1787, "four score and seven years ago," not three score and sixteen, "our fathers brought forth on this continent a new nation, conceived in liberty."[37] The Continental Congress in Philadelphia in summer 1776 made a fundamental commitment to an independent democratic republic based on popular sanction. The Declaration of Independence rested squarely upon a general conception that governments should be defined, limited, and bound by written agreements entered into by the people who ultimately established and validated them. A nation was brought into being in 1776 even though the task still loomed ahead of turning abstract concepts of constitutionalism, especially fixed yet flexible written constitutionalism, into a workable system of government.

2

"To Rectify the Errors That Will Creep In"

The Emergence of the Amending Corollary

The eighteenth-century rise of constitutionalism took place chiefly in the realm of political theory. Discussions of the nature of sovereignty, the bounds of government authority, and the process of government formulation were, for the first three-fourths of the century, animated but abstract. Although there was much talk of how societies freed of prior governmental arrangements might begin anew, no such circumstances presented themselves until the American colonies decided to sever their ties to Great Britain. Only then did people imbued with the ideas of Locke, Montesquieu, Rousseau, and other Enlightenment thinkers have an opportunity to translate philosophical concepts into functional government.

Throughout their first decade of separation from Britain, Americans engaged in a great continuous laboratory experiment in constitution-making. With each former colony drawing for itself a constitution that reflected its new status of independent statehood and some of the states undertaking the process more than once, much discussion took place concerning the translation of constitutional principles into functional government. The various perspectives of the new states engaged each other during the protracted effort of the Continental Congress to draw up satisfactory Articles of Confederation for what was being optimistically, if not entirely realistically, called the United States of America.

Against a backdrop of continuing bloody struggle with Britain, domestic discord, and considerable skepticism about the feasibility of republican government, the sustained experiment in constitution-making proceeded. Unitary, written constitutions immediately became the standard. A range of approaches to defining and limiting the scope and power of government was set forth. Various states tried different ventures to validate social contracts based upon concepts of popular sovereignty. With the evolution of fixed and specific written instruments to frame governments emerged a noteworthy new dimension of constitutionalism: the revolutionary generation began to recognize the need for agreed-upon procedures for altering the terms of constitutions to prevent their becoming ineffective or obsolete. A constitution to be effective could not afford to become oppressively restrictive or inadequately expressive of expectations for government. Establishing such procedures involved further contemplation of popular sovereignty. How flexible and responsive to democratic majorities should constitutions be? Should a simple majority be sufficient to establish or alter the basic framework of government? Or should such a step require an unusual degree of consensus within the community? And if so, what level of agreement would be consistent with a democratic philosophy? The nature of the answers to these fundamental questions would shape the character of the governments about to emerge.

The individuals who first addressed these basic components of constitution-making did not immediately perceive all the issues involved, much less agree on how they should be solved. Fundamental disputes over basic principles appeared at every turn. In the course of devising structures of government, however, abstract principles were transformed into workable procedures. Specific approaches were tested; found satisfactory or wanting; confirmed, revised, or abandoned. Constitutional thinking evolved rapidly to meet the demands of the moment. At the same time, a foundation was being created upon which later American constitutionalism would remain, for better or worse, firmly planted.

ONE MIGHT SAY that the American Revolution erupted over a question of who had authority to alter constitutional arrangements. The long-building tensions between Great Britain and its North American colonies finally broke into open conflict in April 1775 when British troops marched from Boston to Concord to enforce Parliament's 1774 Massachusetts Government Act, a measure abrogating the colony's charter and treating the Bay Colony as a conventional royal province. The British simply ignored the colonists' belief in their own exclusive right to alter the constitutional terms under which they lived. The redcoats fired upon by the Concord minutemen were the first representatives of the British government to discover just how seriously these Americans took their perceived constitutional rights.[1]

The British found it difficult to comprehend the American view of constitutionalism. Their thinking shaped by William Blackstone, mid-eighteenth-century Britons regarded a constitution as simply an assemblage of laws, customs, and institutions that collectively defined the proper form and functions of government. As the concept of parliamentary supremacy emerged from notions that sovereignty belonged to the people rather than to the monarch and that Parliament legitimately represented the sovereign will, any thought of limiting Parliament's power to alter the terms of government faded away. To the British, distinctions between constitutions and other laws seemed meaningless; in all cases an ordinary parliamentary majority was sufficient to decide an issue. The framework of government was simply part of the code of laws. If parliamentary majorities possessed the authority to make laws, they likewise had the power to set the terms of the constitution.[2]

Americans, because of their adherence to Lockean principles and because they were dealing with a Parliament in which they were not (and believed they could not be) adequately represented, considered a constitution to be higher law than ordinary legislation. As an expression of the sovereign will of the people, a constitution stood on a more elevated plane than an act of legislation. The higher constitutional law set the terms under which the government routinely functioned and which that government had no authority to alter. Thus, Americans came to believe that constitutions, if they were to define and limit government, must be explicit, written instruments. Only concrete, articulated constitutions provided the necessary clear standard against which to measure other laws.[3]

In British eyes any act of government that Parliament supported was, by definition, constitutional. From the American viewpoint, the Parliament as well as a government ministry was quite capable of overstepping its bounds and should properly be restrained by a constitution. The Declaration of Independence argued that the British monarch, by failing to stay within the bounds of his contract with his colonial subjects, had thereby nullified it. Parliamentary complicity in the long list of constitutional violations was implied, if unstated, in the Declaration.

In the months of escalating tension that followed the confrontations at Concord and Lexington in spring 1775, the American concept of constitutionalism took more concrete shape. Convinced that operative constitutional arrangements had broken down, delegates from Massachusetts, followed by New Hampshire, South Carolina, and Virginia, asked the Continental Congress how their provinces should proceed. Reluctant to take a step that would be seen as a clear assertion of independence, the Congress in June 1775 recommended that Massachusetts consider its 1691 charter still in force despite British violations of its terms. The Congress moved considerably further on November 3 in response to New Hampshire, which lacked a charter and operated on the basis of a royal commission that the crown granted to each new governor. Since the colony's governor had fled, the Continental Congress agreed that New Hampshire should have a "free and full" popular election of representatives to establish terms of government to remain in effect until the conflict with Britain was settled. The next day, Congress recommended the same steps to South Carolina and a month later advised that Virginia do likewise.[4]

By May 1776 the Continental Congress had moved much closer to an open and full break with Great Britain. In a resolution substantially adopted on May 10 but to which an explanatory preamble was added five days later, the Congress declared that all hope of reconciliation was gone. Henceforth, all power of government should be exercised under the authority of the people of each colony "for the preservation of internal peace, virtue, and good order, as well as for the defence of their lives, liberties, and properties." The resolution recommended that all colonies "where no government sufficient to the exigencies of their affairs have been hitherto established to adopt such Government as shall, in the Opinion of the Representatives of the People, best conduce to the Happiness and Safety of their Constituents in particular and America in general." The new constitutions that the Congress urged the colonies to create should derive their power, the resolution declared, from the authority of the people expressed through their representatives. To many of the members of the Congress, including both John Adams and Richard Henry Lee, the request that all states establish new constitutions announced the full and true independence of the thirteen American colonies six weeks before the formal declaration.[5]

New Hampshire on January 5, 1776, and South Carolina on March 26 had both already adopted written constitutions by action of popularly elected provincial congresses. Following Congress's May directive, the Virginia House of Burgesses in June adopted a bill of rights and then, separately, a constitution. New Jersey on July 2 likewise approved a constitution.[6] Even when couched in terms of having effect only until the conflict with Britain was resolved, these steps to establish republican charters were fundamental acts of revolution in advance of those moments that are conventionally thought of as decisive, the adoption of the Declaration of Independence by the Continental Congress on July 2 and its public pronouncement on July 4.

Finally having declared that "these United Colonies are, and of right ought to be, free and independent States," the Congress found itself temporarily unable to act further. Many delegates left Philadelphia for their home states before arrangements could be made for defending the newly proclaimed independence or for proceeding further with the establishment of a national government. Were these declarers of independence as totally irresponsible as they might seem? Not in their own eyes.

For the men who rushed home from Philadelphia in summer 1776, the most pressing need was to establish constitutions for those newly independent states that had not already acted. These Lockean thinkers believed that their states had been thrown back upon their basic social compact. Before anything else could legitimately occur, the sovereign people must form a fresh compact of government. Establishing constitutions "on wise and lasting principles," declared a New Yorker, "is the greatest work the mind of man can undertake." "A bare conquest over our enemy is not enough," one New Hampshirite explained. "Nothing short of a form of government fixed on genuine principles can preserve our liberties inviolate." The author of the Declaration of Independence himself gave highest priority to creating a new constitution for Virginia. "It is a work of the most interesting nature," Thomas Jefferson wrote, "and such as every individual would wish to have his voice in."[7]

The assemblies of Connecticut and Rhode Island simply stripped their royal charters of monarchical references and declared them to be republican constitutions. Elsewhere, provincial congresses soon established constitutions for Delaware, Pennsylvania, Maryland, and North Carolina. Thus, by the end of 1776, ten of the thirteen colonies had in hand written constitutions, all resting their claim of authority on popular sovereignty. Georgia in February 1777 and New York two months later followed suit. Only Massachusetts was slow to respond and certainly not because it failed to take constitutionalism seriously; on the contrary, it devoted the greatest attention to constitution-making. Protracted debate over a series of fundamental issues prevented Massachusetts from achieving an acceptable document before 1780. In the process, however, the Bay State perhaps did more than any of its peers to advance and mold constitutional thinking. Nevertheless, each of the thirteen state laboratories helped create the chemistry of the new American constitutionalism.

The initial burst of constitution-making by the American states reflected feelings of an urgent need to establish a legitimate basis of authority for the conduct of government. Despite the philosophizing in 1776 concerning government authority deriving from the consent of the people, none of the provincial congresses felt it necessary to seek public approval once they had drafted new constitutions. At first, popular election of the representatives who were to draw up the constitution was thought entirely sufficient. The New Hampshire provincial congress provoked no objections to its procedures when it quickly drew up a constitution and, by a 2-to-1 majority, adopted it as an ordinary act of legislation.[8] The South Carolina congress, which the Continental Congress authorized to act at the same time as New Hampshire but which moved more slowly, dismissed calls for prior elections, adopted the constitution as ordinary legislation by a bare majority, and then reconvened the same day as a duly constituted general assembly.[9] The New Jersey provincial congress likewise treated constitution-making as routine legislation when it acted on July 2.[10]

Legislative constitution-making did not go unopposed. Following the Continental Congress' May 15 call for provincial assembly action, one anonymous Pennsylvanian asserted that

> legislative bodies of men have no more the power of suppressing the authority they sit by, than they have of creating it, otherwise every legislative body would have the power of suppressing a constitution at will; it is an act which can only be *done to them,* but cannot be done *by them.* Were the present House of Assembly to be suffered by their own *act* to suppress the *old* authority derived from the Crown, they might afterwards suppress the *new* authority received from the people, and thus by continually making and unmaking themselves at pleasure, leave the people at last no right at all. . . . CONVENTIONS, my Fellow Countrymen, are the only proper bodies to form a Constitution, and Assemblies are the proper bodies to make Laws agreeable to that constitution.[11]

In Philadelphia on May 20 a public meeting attended by 4,000 persons demanded the holding of a provincial convention of popularly elected delegates to determine Pennsylvania's course of action.[12]

In New York City three weeks later a committee of workingmen, artisans, mechanics, butchers, cobblers, and carpenters, not comfortable with decision-making resting entirely in the hands of the upper class, went further to insist that any constitution drafted for the state be submitted to a popular referendum for ratification. In a letter to the provincial congress, the committee declared in part,

> We never can believe that you intended . . . to deny . . . that . . . right which God has given [the people of New York] in common with all men, to judge whether it be consistent with their interest to accept or reject a Constitution framed for that State of which they are members. This is the birthright of every man.[13]

The Virginia Declaration of Rights echoed those sentiments, stipulating that only "a majority of the community" had the right to reform, alter, or abolish government.[14] Nevertheless, the Virginia provincial congress instituted this bill of rights and established a new constitution in June without turning to the electorate. Thomas Jefferson objected, but he stood alone among the leading planters.[15] Under the pressure of the moment and lacking any experience with popular ratification procedures, provincial assemblies during spring 1776 adhered to the prevailing Anglo-American republican notion that elected representatives possessed complete authority to act for the people.

Desire for a more explicit popular sanctioning of new constitutions was stirring, however. It manifested itself in the decision of all states that delayed action until after July 4 to hold delegate elections before allowing representative bodies to formulate constitutions. Although the Pennsylvania assembly declared on May 22 that it was still functioning and competent, the following month a provincewide conference of delegates from county committees of inspection began discussing arrangements for elections with specific power to constitute a new government. Only those who swore allegiance to the new government were to be eligible to vote for delegates to design it. By mid-July, ninety-six delegates, most of them farmers and artisans, began their work, and on September 27 the convention agreed to a declaration of rights and a constitution to be effective immediately. This convention, controlled by radical democrats and committed to the idea that a constitution should be a popularly sanctioned higher law, produced an extremely democratic constitution. It featured strict proportional representation, a unicameral legislature whose acts had to be published and reapproved after the annual election before they could take effect, restricted executive authority, limited terms for judges, and a council of censors to review the constitution and propose modifications every seven years. Nevertheless, even this body considered itself empowered through the delegate election process to promulgate Pennsylvania's constitution without further popular action.[16]

No other constitution completed in 1776 was as innovative as Pennsylvania's, but two nearby states appeared to be influenced by its concern for obtaining specific popular sanction before undertaking constitution-making. Delaware, as it often had in the past, copied Pennsylvania's procedural model closely. The Delaware assembly voted on July 27 to hold elections for delegates to a convention to enact a constitution, following Pennsylvania's lead in distinguishing the creation of fundamental law from ordinary legislation. The Delaware convention met early in September, completed a declaration of rights by September 11, adopted a constitution on September 20, and then dissolved. Maryland chose not to create a separate constitutional convention but to hold elections for an assembly that would be empowered both to establish a constitution and attend to ordinary legislative business. Authorized on July 3 and convening on August 14, the Maryland assembly took until November 3 to adopt a declaration of rights and until November 8 to put a constitution into effect.[17]

North Carolina, the final state to act in 1776, had operated under an interim thirteen-member committee of safety since May. This body called for October elections to choose delegates to a congress that would draft both laws and a constitution. It met November 12, adopted a constitution and declaration of rights modeled after those of Virginia, Pennsylvania, and Maryland, and declared them in effect in mid-December. The North Carolina congress ignored advance requests from Orange and Mecklenburg counties that it recognize a distinction between its derivative power and primary power that remained with the people. The congress chose to disregard the implicit suggestion that it submit the proposed constitution to popular ratification, refusing to acknowledge that popular sovereignty might extend beyond the selection of delegates to the approval of their decisions. However, such ideas were in the air.[18]

Georgia did not receive news of the Declaration of Independence for more than a month after its proclamation in Philadelphia. Then, an interim committee of safety, much like North Carolina's, quickly called for elections of a new congress whose duties would include promulgating a constitution. Meeting in Savannah in October, this congress took until February 1777 to complete work on Georgia's constitution, which featured a unicameral legislature on the Pennsylvania model. Like its ten predecessors, this state constitution became operative upon the completion of legislative action.[19]

New York, where demands first surfaced in May 1776 that any constitution be submitted for popular approval, nevertheless followed the common pattern for the establishment of new governments. The provincial assembly called that month for new elections, and a congress of delegates met on July 9. Delayed by the military situation, this congress did not complete the drafting of a constitution until March 1777. The instrument, adopted April 20, took immediate effect. The previous year's calls for a popular referendum on the constitution were ignored.[20]

In Massachusetts the issue of authority for constitution-making came into sharpest focus. By May 1776 the Massachusetts General Court no longer considered its authority, based on the 1691 charter, to be fully legitimate. In June the house of representatives appointed a committee consisting of one delegate from each county to draw up a new constitution. That committee had not reported by September when the house had second thoughts about its approach. The representatives decided to ask town meetings for a mandate to draft a constitution that would be published so that it could be publicly inspected and discussed before the general court voted on it. All free adult males, not just the property owners to whom suffrage was ordinarily restricted, were declared eligible to vote in the town meetings on whether to grant constituent powers, reflecting the view that all parties to the social contract should be able to participate in formulating the constitution under which they must subsequently live.[21] Although providing for more popular involvement in initiating the process than had been the case elsewhere, the

Massachusetts house followed the universal 1776 pattern of placing actual constitutional decisionmaking in legislative hands.

Not everyone in Massachusetts embraced legislative constitution-making. Twenty-three of ninety-six Massachusetts towns objected to the procedure, many of them on the specific grounds that legislatures lacked authority to establish constitutions. The Pittsfield town meeting declared as early as May that "if this fundamental constitution is above the whole legislature, the legislature cannot certainly make it; it must be the approbation of the majority which gives life and being to it." Lexington repeated Pittsfield's call for ratification by town meetings, but Concord moved the discussion in a different direction.[22] The Concord town meeting argued that, since the function of a constitution was to protect individuals from arbitrary govern mental action, a governing body should not be able to define its constitution. A legislature that created a constitution, Concord reasoned, would retain the power to change it. Therefore, that constitution would provide no safeguard against legislative abuse. The Concord meeting asked for the establishment of a separate constitution-making body, a convention. Eight other town meetings, including Boston's, joined the call.[23]

The Massachusetts General Court decided in May 1777 to ask the towns to grant their representatives power to draft a constitution at the forthcoming town elections for delegates to a new house. The council grudgingly accepted after the house pointed out that the alternative would be the election of a constitutional convention. Once drafted by the general court, the constitution would be published and sent to the towns for discussion. Town meetings would then report back individual votes for and against the constitution so that the general court could determine whether two-thirds of the populace accepted it. Again property restrictions on voting were dropped, and all free males over twenty-one years old were allowed to take part.[24]

In June 1777 a new Massachusetts house of representatives convened, and by February 1778 it had agreed to a constitution. The following month for the first time in America a constitution was voted upon in an election open to all adult male citizens. In town meetings across Massachusetts, 2,083 voters cast ballots in favor of the proposed constitution, and 9,972 against it. Majorities in 147 towns disapproved, and only 31 accepted it. Many of the town election returns included detailed reports, which showed dissatisfaction with property qualifications for voting, distribution of seats in the house of representatives, the lack of a declaration of rights, and the drafting of the constitution by the general court instead of by a convention.[25]

After its initial effort at constitution-making was so emphatically rejected by the voters, the Massachusetts General Court hesitated for nearly a year before starting over. Then it asked town meetings whether they wanted a new constitution and, if so, whether they would empower their representatives to call a convention for the sole purpose of drafting one. A vote of 6,612 to 2,659 endorsed the new approach. With all free adult males again eligible to take part, town meetings then elected 293 delegates, distributed in proportion to legislative representation. On September 1, 1779, the Massachusetts constitutional convention convened in Cambridge.[26]

The convention that Massachusetts voters had insisted upon quickly turned the constitution-writing task over to a thirty-one-member drafting committee, which in turn gave the responsibility to three leaders of the independence movement, Samuel Adams, John Adams, and James Bowdoin. The convention had not, however, abandoned its duty. It proceeded to debate the draft proposal for four months and rejected features such as John Adams's proposal to grant the governor an absolute veto over legislative action.[27] The constitution that the convention adopted on March 2, 1780, created "a republican political system, created by and responsive to the wishes of the majority of the people, [with] a wide latitude of action in the pursuit of the public good."[28]

The Massachusetts convention sent its draft constitution to the towns for their approval. The general court in its initial authorization had recommended that the convention be allowed to put a new constitution into effect if approved by two-thirds of the people. Town meetings considered each article separately, rather than simply dealing with the document as a single piece. When the constitutional convention reconvened on June 7, 1780, it had a welter of responses to consider. Many towns had approved portions of the constitution and rejected others. The convention finally concluded that overall the instrument had been approved by more than the necessary two-thirds and declared it ratified.[29]

Although four years of struggle ended in some confusion, Massachusetts finally had an effective constitution, one that could claim to be a compact of the people, drawn by their specifically chosen representatives and then given their direct scrutiny and approval. It was a true Lockean constitution, a higher law by which the people defined and limited their government, and, although amended, it remains in effect over 200 years later, the longest enduring written constitution in history. The distinguished constitutional historian Andrew C. McLaughlin, reflecting on the 1780 Massachusetts constitution, found it "not quite appropriate to treat the compact origins of government and the body politic as if it were only a nebulous theory used for the purpose of war and revolution." McLaughlin perceived their constitutionalism as a "practical working theory" that was "part of the everyday thinking of the men of New England" and their "basis of state-making." It was not a pretense but "the basic principle of constructive statesmanship."[30]

By 1780 in Massachusetts, the notion had been fully developed and cast in concrete form that a constitution was the sovereign people's means to define their preferred system of government, authorizing or limiting that government's actions as they chose. The terms of the Massachusetts constitution furthered this vision of constitutionalism by specifying the particular tasks of the legislative, executive, and judicial components of the state's government. The delineation of executive and judicial functions gave these branches standing in conflicts with the legislature and restrained the representatives from doing what might please them or their constituents at the moment.[31] Using the constitution to confine government was certainly the intent of John Adams, its principal architect, but it also seemed the concern of those people who opposed the legislative construction of a constitution, sought popular review of the convention-designed instrument, and insisted upon more than a simple majority consensus for the implementation or alteration of the fundamental law.

New Hampshire, much influenced by Massachusetts, closely followed its neighbor's lead in matters constitutional. Although its assembly had adopted a constitution in 1776, two years later a convention of elected delegates received a mandate to draft a new instrument and submit it to town meetings for ratification. As in Massachusetts, this first effort failed badly; it came nowhere close to receiving the required two-thirds approval by the towns. In 1781 the assembly authorized another attempt. The constitutional convention's first proposal was rejected in 1782, but after the instrument was altered to reduce the power of the governor, it finally achieved ratification in 1784.[32] Specially elected conventions had been used only rarely and popular ratification not at all before Massachusetts took them up, but New Hampshire readily embraced both procedures. The perception that a constitution was distinguished from statute law and carried the higher authority of a social compact manifested itself as well in New Hampshire's confirmation of the notion that an extraordinary degree of approval was necessary before a constitution could take effect or, once ratified, then be changed.

A dramatic break from British ideas of sovereignty and constitutionalism, the Massachusetts model nevertheless made perfect sense to Americans. "There is an original, undivided, and incommunicable authority and supremacy in the collective body of the people, to whom all delegated power must submit, and from whom there is no appeal," declared the *Hartford Courant* in August 1783.[33] As state after state wrestled with constitution-making, methods emerged for turning popular sovereignty from a vague abstraction into a workable system for setting forth the terms of government. As a result, legislatures lost their status as absolute and therefore unrestrainable representatives of the people. Instead, the distinctively American notion of legislatures as finite powers operating within a defined framework emerged. If the ultimate authority of the people could be effectively expressed, then the power of government would always be limited.

IN THE COURSE of devising their constitutions, the newly independent American states wrestled with myriad problems. One was fundamental to the very notion of written constitutions. Given a dedication to concepts of higher law embodied in specific instruments endorsed by supermajorities, what was a sovereign people to do if it felt the need to change some or all of the basic terms of its government? Only by providing for a means of amending it, the Lexington, Massachusetts, town meeting declared in 1778, could a constitution "give satisfaction to the people; and be a happy means, under providence, of preventing popular commotions, mobs, bloodshed and civil war." A constitution, if it was to survive, must make provisions "to rectify the errors that will creep in through lapse of time, or alteration of situation," concluded the town meeting of Essex, Massachusetts, the same year. John Dickinson of Pennsylvania called attention to the advice of Machiavelli that "a state to be long lived, must be frequently corrected, and reduced to its first principles."[34]

Unwilling to accept the notion that the terms of government were unchangeable except by revolution yet indisposed to treat the fundamental directives to and limitations on government as ordinary law susceptible to reform by simple parliamentary majority, some states began working out arrangements by which their new constitutions could be changed. They sought amendment systems that would render revolution unnecessary yet avoid unstable government. Although methods varied, most states sought to ensure that amendment could be achieved only when a broad consensus, a supermajority of the sovereign people or their representatives, agreed to a change. Articulating a plan for amendment was increasingly seen as an essential part of defining a constitution as a higher law while avoiding its becoming a rigid and unduly confining structure.

The first references to amendment appeared in negative terms in the 1776 constitutions of New Jersey, Delaware, and North Carolina. Each listed provisions of their fundamental instrument, bills of rights being the most notable, that the legislature was specifically forbidden to alter. Delaware took the further step of stipulating that other provisions could be altered by vote of five-sevenths of the lower house and seven-ninths of the upper house. The Delaware reference to supermajorities was the only indication from these three states, other than their absolute prohibition on some amendments, that constitutional change was anything other than ordinary legislative action.

From his post in the Continental Congress in Philadelphia, Thomas Jefferson sent his ideas for the Virginia constitution to his friend and teacher George Wythe in Williamsburg. Among his proposals was a provision that the constitution could be amended by a majority vote of the inhabitants of two-thirds of Virginia's counties. The constitution that the Virginia assembly adopted in June 1776 contained no amendment provision, however. Later in *Notes on Virginia,* Jefferson characterized this constitution as insufficiently republican because the populace had no role in its adoption and because it lacked an amending procedure.[35]

Maryland and Pennsylvania in autumn 1776 and Georgia a few months later moved to address the amending issue. The Maryland constitution permitted its legislature to adopt constitutional amendments but required that they obtain a two-thirds majority in each house. Furthermore, the amendment would not take effect unless reapproved by a similar margin by a subsequent legislature. The intervening election was intended to function as a popular referendum on the amendment. Maryland's requirement of a supermajority for legislative action extended the higher-law conception of constitutions to their amendment; and the provision of a popular check on legislative action, as imperfect as it might be, affirmed the notion that constitutional decisions should involve a broad consensus of the sovereign people. Georgia's simpler system reflected similar ideas; its legislature was obliged to call a constitutional convention if petitioned to do so by a majority of voters in a majority of the state's counties.[36]

At almost the same time that Maryland was establishing the terms of its amendment procedure, Pennsylvania was creating the most elaborate and distinctive amending arrangement of the era. In the midst of designing a very democratic system of government with an annually elected unicameral legislature and a variety of devices to restrain executive and judicial authority, the delegates to the 1776 Pennsylvania constitutional convention established a separate political instrument solely for constitutional review. A Council of Censors, modeled loosely on Greek and Roman institutions recently praised by Montesquieu and Rousseau, was to be chosen every seven years beginning in October 1783. Each Pennsylvania city and country was to elect two representatives. Meeting in November and empowered to sit for one year, the council was "to enquire whether the constitution has been preserved inviolate in every part; and whether the legislature and executive branches of government have performed their duty as guardians of the people, or assumed to themselves, or exercised other or greater powers than they are entitled to by the constitution." The Council of Censors could subpoena persons, papers, and records in carrying out its review of government; censure misconduct; and initiate impeachment of public officials. Most significant, the council could recommend that the legislature repeal laws that appeared unconstitutional to the censors. Furthermore, it could "call a convention to meet within two years after their sitting, if there appear to them an absolute necessity of amending any article of the constitution which may be defective, explaining such as may be thought not clearly expressed, and of adding such as are necessary for the preservation of the rights and happiness of the people."[37]

The Pennsylvania Council of Censors was designed to allow the sovereign people to circumvent their sitting government in order to determine whether the power they had delegated was being properly exercised and whether the terms of delegation should be altered. The council's only duties were to examine whether the state's government was functioning according to its constitution, call attention to violations, and consider whether fundamental changes were necessary. By two-thirds vote the council could propose amendments, but after their publication six months would have to elapse before popularly elected and instructed convention delegates would determine their fate.[38] The Pennsylvania constitutional convention of 1776 assumed that constitutions and governments supposed to function under them needed frequent fundamental review and reconsideration. Legislatures were not suited to this task, since it would demand a large measure of self-examination. Special representatives should regularly be chosen to review the constitution and, if they reached a high degree of consensus, initiate revisions. Ultimately, constitutional changes needed to be approved by the people. The Pennsylvania plan sought to institutionalize and routinize constitutional reassessment.

Several other states appropriated or at least seriously considered the Pennsylvania model. Vermont, which lacked a royal charter and would not be fully recognized as an independent state until 1791, nevertheless established its own constitution in 1777. Modeled closely on the 1776 Pennsylvania constitution, Vermont's instrument also contained a council of censors.[39] A more vaguely stated plan appeared in the constitution New Hampshire finally ratified in 1784: a convention every seven years was to correct constitutional violations "as well as to make any alterations . . . found necessary." The unratified 1785 constitution for the territory then calling itself Franklin contained a council of censors, though the subsequent Tennessee constitution did not. Finally, in its 1789 constitution, Georgia moved from its 1777 constitutional-convention-on-petition system to an automatic amending convention to be held in 1794 and again in 1797.[40]

The 1779 Massachusetts constitutional convention's rejection of the Pennsylvania system of automatic constitutional reconsideration in favor of an amendment-on-demand approach greatly influenced the evolution of American constitutional thought. The failure of Massachusetts' earlier proposed constitution to contain any amendment provision was one reason for its defeat; Lexington's town meeting, for instance, had opposed it on those grounds.[41] The Stoughton town meeting appealed to the constitutional convention to provide for automatic election of a council of censors every three years. Instead the convention proposed that voters be asked every fifteen years if they wanted a constitutional convention. If a general consensus, a two-thirds majority of the electorate, favored one, it would be held. Over one-third of Massachusetts town meetings whose reactions to the 1780 constitution survive objected to the amendment provision. Most called for a more automatic and more frequent review, one occurring every five or seven years instead of every fifteen. This concern slipped from view, however, as the legislature declared that overall support for the constitution was sufficient to put it into effect. Opponents regarded the council of censors plan as too democratic and radical, and advocates failed to see it as essential and worth fighting for. So the Massachusetts constitution of 1780, innovative in many ways, turned in a conservative direction on the matter of amending procedure.[42]

Although most state constitutions created during the first decade of independence did not contain specific amendment provisions, the actions taken in Maryland, Pennsylvania, Vermont, New Hampshire, Georgia, and Massachusetts revealed the attention being given to the question. Some states were choosing to treat constitutional change as ordinary legislation, but consciousness was growing that so doing involved risks. Protesting the power of the Rhode Island legislature to change the state's constitution, a writer in the *Providence Gazette* complained, "We should have no remedy left us, but downright rebellion against that power we have vested them with."[43] The states' desire to have an acceptable amending system incorporated into the constitution for the confederation that the Continental Congress was creating offers evidence of the importance attached to this matter.

CREATING A NEW CENTRAL GOVERNMENT became the highest priority for the Continental Congress after it declared independence from Great Britain. The Articles of Confederation that the Congress eventually managed to fabricate took far longer to formulate and adopt than the state constitutions. A complex and unprecedented structure of multistate government needed to be designed. Conflicts between dissimilar states had to be resolved. Finally, the complicated result needed to be fitted into evolving notions of constitutionalism. Creating an amendment mechanism was a significant part of the undertaking, although certainly not the central focus.

Benjamin Franklin, one of the strongest voices in the Continental Congress in support of effective central authority, made the first serious effort to design a central government for the American colonies with his 1754 Albany Plan of Union. Despite its cold reception at the time, Franklin never abandoned his fundamental concept and offered it again after the colonies, slowly and reluctantly, came around to the view that a united voice, a Continental Congress, was necessary in dealing with Britain. In July 1775 he proposed "Articles of Confederation and Perpetual Union" to the Second Continental Congress; he offered a revised version in January 1776. Franklin's proposition that the articles be amendable by vote of a majority of the state assemblies epitomized his vision of cooperative states putting the national interest foremost. Although Franklin did specify that states would retain their laws, rights, privileges, and jurisdiction as they saw fit and might amend in the future, no doubt the specter of a bare majority of states, not necessarily the largest or most populous, imposing their will on the others helped account for the overall lack of interest in his plan.[44]

As separation with Britain became imminent, the Continental Congress gave more thought to constitutional matters. Silas Deane in 1775 and a group of Connecticut delegates headed by Roger Sherman in March 1776 put forth other draft proposals for confederation.[45] By mid-May 1776, the Congress directed all states that had not already done so to establish new constitutions for themselves based on the sovereign power of the people. Shortly thereafter, in another indication of its developing mood, the Congress on June 12 created a committee to draw up articles of confederation in the event, clearly anticipated, that they became independent. The committee, headed by John Dickinson of Pennsylvania, worked rapidly and was able to present a proposal to the Congress on July 12, only a month after its appointment and ten days after the critical vote to declare independence.

The Dickinson draft, and his it definitely was despite the vigorous debate on every detail within the committee, reflected the preference of the cautious majority of delegates for the retention of power in state hands. In light of their decision to declare independence, the label conservative is not altogether suitable, yet most of the delegates were not ready for Franklin's strong central government. The draft's provisions for ratification and later amendment mirrored this preference for state retention of authority but also displayed the latest thinking that constitutions should be written instruments of higher law, capable of restraining legislative bodies, and not merely reflections of current practices. According to the Dickinson draft, the articles were to be submitted to state legislatures for their consideration; if they approved, the legislatures were to authorize their congressional delegates to ratify; so ratified, the articles were to be perpetual. Any amendment would have to be agreed to by Congress and then confirmed by every state's legislatures. The requirement of state unanimity set an extraordinarily high standard of consensus for constitutional action. The revised draft of August 20, 1776, did not change this provision, nor did the much-debated, much-amended, and much-delayed version that Congress finally approved on November 17, 1777.[46]

The inevitability of amendment was evident to the congressional delegates who approved the Articles of Confederation. During their deliberations they had been unable to resolve fundamental disputes over the basis of congressional representation and apportionment of the confederation's expenses, by population or by states, as well as the question of contested rights to western lands. Wartime needs persuaded the Congress by late 1777 to adopt a recognizably imperfect constitution. Whatever its defects, a constitution was needed. Subsequent improvements were an unspoken necessity.[47] As delegate Charles Carroll of Maryland wrote, "I think it better to confederate even on these terms than not to confederate at all."[48] He told his father that "in my opinion an imperfect and somewhat unequal Confederacy is better than none."[49]

Many of the state legislatures found reasons to object to various provisions of the proposed Articles. South Carolina alone, however, expressed doubts about the amendment provisions. The South Carolina assembly sought no fewer than twenty-one modifications to the Articles, most tending to limit Congress and increase the power of the states. Nevertheless, it suggested that the Articles ought to be amendable by less than unanimous consent, arguing that the requirement of consensus ought to be high but not absolute. South Carolina was willing to make approval by eleven of the thirteen states sufficient to alter the Articles but instructed its delegates to ratify the instrument with or without its proposed changes.[50]

By July 1778 desire for a constitution was so strong that most states joined South Carolina in authorizing ratification of the Articles regardless of whether amendments and reservations were accepted. On July 9, delegates from ten states signed the Articles of Confederation. The following day, Congress wrote to the state legislatures of Delaware, Maryland, and New Jersey, the three states that had not acted, urging them to ratify. Congress appealed to their "patriotism and good sense [to trust] to future deliberations to make such alterations and amendments as experience may shew to be expedient and just."[51] The congressional appeal, with its suggestion that amendments offered the means of resolving remaining differences, convinced both New Jersey and Delaware to ratify.[52]

Even without the final ratification by Maryland, the Congress assumed that the Articles of Confederation had acquired a substantial degree of legitimacy. John Jay, the president of the Congress, in a September 8, 1779, circular letter to the states, declared, "For every purpose essential to the defense of these states in the progress of the present war, and necessary to the attainment of the objects of it, the States now are as fully, legally, and absolutely confederated as it is possible for them to be."[53] Jay no doubt concocted his claim out of eagerness to have the government seen as legitimate and awareness that the Articles did not specify the number of ratifications required for the instrument to take effect. He went so far as to assert that the delegates to the First and Second Continental Congresses had been authorized to establish a union to oppose Great Britain and that the Declaration of Independence had been a formal explicit act of confederation. Yet clearly Jay's letter was prompted by a recognition that the Articles would not be regarded as fully sanctioned without unanimous ratification. The amending provision of the Articles did specify that alterations required unanimous approval by the states, and that standard was presumed to apply to initial ratification as well. Given a general feeling that its authority needed full confirmation by the sovereign power, the Confederation remained in a constitutional limbo (although it continued to function in a weakened condition) until the final state endorsement.

Maryland continued to resist ratifying the Articles of Confederation. The unsympathetic treatment Congress accorded its claim to western lands underlay its dissatisfaction. By the time adjustments were made and Maryland agreed to ratify in 1781, discontent with the Articles had arisen in several quarters. In 1780 Congress discussed calling a national convention to reconstruct the confederation before the Articles could be formally put into effect. Yet most delegates felt an urgent need to secure a constitutional government. The war effort, the establishment of the nation's fiscal credit, and, not least, the restoration of the stature of Congress required ratification. Amendments could follow, but only implementation of the basic instrument could demonstrate the possibility of agreement on alterations.[54]

The confidence of some congressional delegates in 1781 that the "defective," "inadequate" Articles of Confederation would immediately be amended "to give vigour and authority to government" may have betrayed a lack of understanding of the depth of the divisions that would continue to plague the Congress.[55] Yet their thinking did reflect one reality. By the time the Articles of Confederation were finally formalized, constitutional thought and practice at the state and national level had evolved in a very short time to the point where providing for amendment of written constitutions was considered a realistic and necessary way of keeping fundamental laws vital and effective.

THE REQUIREMENT of unanimous state agreement to congressionally initiated proposals to amend the Articles of Confederation was, from the outset, the defining characteristic of the first government of the United States. As the Confederation proved unwieldy in practice from the very moment of its birth, changes in its structure were constantly being suggested. However, the unanimity requirement gave every state an absolute veto power over any alterations, encouraged each state to insist upon acceptance of its position rather than seek a compromise of differences, and ultimately frustrated several widely supported proposals for modification of the Articles. Consequently, the Confederation rapidly came to be seen as not only unsatisfactory in practice but also impossibly difficult to reform.

No sooner had the action of Maryland on March 1, 1781, completed ratification of the Articles of Confederation, than Congress appointed a committee to devise means to strengthen the central government's power over the states. Although committee members James Varnum, James Duane, and James Madison believed that confederation itself implied a general power of Congress to carry out its acts, the absence of a particular statement in the Articles to that effect convinced them of the need for a specific amendment. Their proposal would have allowed Congress to use the army and navy to enforce its decisions upon the states, seizing their vessels and prohibiting their trade if they did not comply. Such a heavy-handed expression of central authority did not appeal to most delegates, who referred the proposal to another committee and effectively buried it.[56]

Later the same year, however, Congress did approve and submit to the states an amendment to the Articles that would have strengthened its fiscal power. Abandoning a year-old paper money scheme, Congress endorsed a 5 percent import duty for an indefinite period. The legislatures of twelve states quickly ratified the amendment, but Rhode Island refused, regarding it as a grant of power to officials unaccountable to the state, an uneven tax that would fall most heavily on commercial states such as itself, and, finally, the establishment of undefined authority for an unlimited period that would render Congress independent of the states. In November 1782 the Congress, hopeful of persuading the lone dissenting state to reverse its position, sent a delegation to Rhode Island to discuss the matter. The effort collapsed on receipt of word that the Virginia general assembly had withdrawn its ratification. This first substantial attempt to amend the Articles of Confederation, although it failed, came so close to succeeding that a search quickly began for an alternative that would overcome the objections encountered.[57]

Within five months, Congress approved a new proposal to provide it with an adequate income. A legislative package of import duties, cession of remaining state-held western lands, state contributions of $1.5 million for twenty-five years, and congressional assumption of state war debts was to be accompanied by an amendment to the Articles making population (with slaves counted as three-fifths of free and indentured persons) rather than state-determined land values the basis for apportioning expenses among the states. This complex plan was designed to include something appealing to all sectors, in particular the unpaid Continental army. With the adoption of the legislative measures, soon followed by the signing of a peace treaty with Great Britain and the disbanding of the army, the sense of crisis and need for changes in the Articles eased. Thereafter the proposed amendment languished in the legislatures of the larger, negatively affected states.[58]

Once the war was over, Congress turned its attention to trade regulation and before long was considering yet another proposal to amend the Articles. In autumn 1783 it sought a limited fifteen-year grant of authority over imports that assertedly would not require constitutional action to implement. When this approach met resistance in some states, Congress, under growing pressure from merchant interests, began in 1784 to discuss an amendment giving it perpetual power to regulate foreign and interstate trade as well as to tax imports and exports. To ease state fears of centralized power, the amendment stipulated that Americans would not pay higher duties than citizens of foreign nations, that any state could prohibit export or import of any goods, and that each state would collect U.S. duties and put them to use locally. The amendment enjoyed substantial support, but, despite its concessions to state authority, some members of Congress opposed it as an increase of central power. With the certainty of rejection by some states, especially in the South, the Congress never offered the amendment for ratification.[59]

The discussion of amendments to improve the Articles of Confederation continued unabated, even as advocates of a stronger central government grew more impatient and vocal. Despite the frustration of early attempts to modify the Articles, the possibility of amendment was not regarded as hopeless. Efforts continued to find a formula acceptable to all concerned. Indeed, of all the endeavors to remedy perceived flaws in the Articles, the most broad-gauged occurred in 1786. That spring Congress appointed a committee to propose amendments to the Articles whose members offered a package of seven amendments to make the "federal government adequate to the ends for which it was constituted." The amendments dealt with the Confederation's most notable difficulties: the central government's inability to generate a dependable source of revenue, be taken seriously abroad in trade and other negotiations, enforce its laws, and, addressing perhaps Congress's most embarrassing problem, obtain the required quorum of delegates to conduct business.[60] The package of amendments would have significantly enhanced the central government's power and thereby the vitality of the Articles of Confederation. Congress discussed the proposal at length but in the end did not adopt it and submit it to the states for ratification because Virginia had called for a convention in Annapolis to discuss even more sweeping constitutional reform.[61]

In 1786 the quest for amendment of the Articles did not appear to be frustrated but rather redirected. Delegates from five states gathered in Annapolis the first Monday in September to address the problems of the Confederation but found themselves largely stymied. Neither the New England nor the lower South states had chosen to send delegates. Nor, most embarrassingly, had Maryland, with its state house a few minutes walk from Mann's Inn where the delegates lodged and met. Despite the insurmountable obstacles to immediate action posed by the lack of a sufficient quorum of states, the delegates who did attend the Annapolis convention displayed a continuing confidence that means could be found to deal with their constitutional difficulties. They realized that a broad range of issues, not merely matters of commerce, had to be taken into account in framing satisfactory amendments to the Articles. Unable to take substantive action themselves, the delegates called for a second convention to meet in Philadelphia the following May, this time with an explicit mandate to propose amendments to the Articles of Confederation. That the Congress reluctantly agreed was evident in its slow but decisive acceptance of the Annapolis convention's recommendation and its issuance of a call for the Philadelphia convention "for the sole and express purpose of revising the Articles of Confederation and reporting to Congress and the several legislatures such alterations and provisions therein as shall when agreed to by Congress and confirmed by the states render the federal constitution adequate to the exigencies of Government & the preservation of the Union."[62]

Not only did Congress deal almost continually during the 1780s with proposals for constitutional amendment, but at the same time states also discussed their fundamental laws. New Hampshire engaged in protracted constitutional debate before finally ratifying a new instrument in 1784. The territory that would eventually become Tennessee attempted to construct a constitution. The most central and visible constitutional review, however, occurred in the pivotal state of Pennsylvania.

The Pennsylvania constitution of 1776 had mandated its own regular reconsideration by a Council of Censors. Some prominent Pennsylvanians objected that the council would be a frequent destabilizing influence, "a jubilee of tyranny . . . when the foundation of government shall be torn up!"[63] In November 1778 the Pennsylvania legislature began action that could have led to abolition of the council but abandoned the effort three months later after 13,000 citizens signed a petition supporting it.[64] Without further dispute, the first Council of Censors was elected in October 1783 and convened a month later.

For nearly a year (interrupted by lengthy recesses), a sharply divided Council of Censors debated Pennsylvania's constitution. Complaints focused on the unicameral legislature, weaknesses in the executive and judiciary, frequency of elections, distribution of representation, and the amending process. Twelve censors voted to propose a set of drastic amendments, but nine opposed them. A protracted argument followed as to whether the amendments should be submitted to the people since they had not been endorsed by the two-thirds majority stipulated in Section 47 of the Pennsylvania constitution, the provision dealing with the Council of Censors. A slim majority of censors held that the constitution was defective and therefore remedies should be offered to the people. To the contrary, a large minority argued; constitutional changes should not be made lightly or by slender margins. The procedures of Section 47 had been agreed upon, and violating the two-thirds requirement would undermine the entire constitution. The majority declined to press further; instead both sides elaborated their views in published appeals to the public. Following an adjournment of several months, the balance of opinion had shifted. In September 1784, the council resolved, 14 to 8, not to call a constitutional convention.[65] Thus the first mandated review of the Pennsylvania constitution concluded with a formal decision to leave it untouched.

FORMULATING AND GAINING SANCTION for state constitutions and the Articles of Confederation was an important facet of the American Revolution. Thereafter, attempts to amend the Articles of Confederation provided American legislators and political thinkers of the 1780s with formative initial experiences in the process of revising a written constitution. Simultaneous consideration of state constitutional alteration, particularly in Pennsylvania where hot debate raged within the Council of Censors during 1783 and 1784, further shaped attitudes regarding constitutional change. In the course of these disputes, the tension between conservative Lockean constitutionalism with its resistance to revision and Rousseauesque responsiveness to the immediate democratic will came into sharper focus. The concept that constitutional terms could be modified acquired legitimacy, but Thomas Jefferson's assertion in the Declaration of Independence that constitutions should not be altered for "light and transient causes" gained wide acceptance. Mechanisms had been developed that required thorough deliberation and a high degree of agreement before changes could occur. Those individuals in the political ascendancy in 1787 and 1788 would draft and ratify new amendment procedures for the next national constitution. They would be able to draw on specific experience as well as on philosophical abstractions, something beyond their reach a mere decade earlier.

3

"A PEACEABLE PROCESS OF CURE"

Devising the American Amending System

The so-called Founding Fathers, the fifty-five men who met in Philadelphia between May and September 1787 and crafted a second constitution for the United States, were not, as the often-used collective label for them implies, engaged in an altogether original act of creation. Founders may be an appropriate honorific for these men who generated the Constitution that has since survived for more than two centuries, but they regarded themselves as reforming rather than as inventing a structure of government. The congressional mandate that brought the fifty-five to Philadelphia that summer directed them to consider amendments to the Articles of Confederation. Upon assembling, the Founders discussed constitutional matters not as if they were drawing on blank parchment but in terms of altering the details of their presently unsatisfactory governmental arrangements within an existing framework of sovereignty. The Philadelphia convention drew on the already substantial experience of American constitution-making and brought forth a plan of government, drastically revised in structural detail, to be sure, but not entirely new in its fundamental federal republicanism. In its preamble, the drafters of the 1787 Constitution acknowledged its revisionary character as they declared it an attempt "to form a *more perfect* union."

The Founders' rejection of the prescribed amendment procedure of the Articles of Confederation in favor of a less rigorous standard for implementing their proposed substitute helped to obscure the amendatory character of the 1787 convention. Indeed, the ratification plan for the new Constitution was arguably the most revolutionary act of the Philadelphia convention, overturning as it did the previously agreed-upon method of sanctioning constitutional change. A dozen years of experience with state and national written constitutions that specified procedures for their own amendment led to a consensus in Philadelphia on the sanctioning of constitutional arrangements significantly different from the process that had prevailed when the Articles were drafted and ratified. Both the ratification provision of the 1787 Constitution and the arrangements for its further amendment contained in Article V represented an adjustment of thinking about the process of constitutional change but by no means a complete abandonment of earlier ideas. The sub-

42

sequent approval of the new arrangements for constitutional alteration by the state conventions called upon to ratify the Constitution reflected the acceptance of these provisions. Ultimately every one of the thirteen states would embrace the new Constitution, meeting the strict standard of the Articles of Confederation for constitutional reform.

The Article V delineation of an amendment process reflected the Founding Fathers' quintessential thinking about constitutionalism: the necessity for written constitutions to define, direct, and delimit the powers and processes of government that were responsive to the sovereign power of the people, stable enough to endure through a crisis and yet flexible enough to adjust to new circumstance. While the arrangements specified for putting the proposed Constitution into effect represented a complex amalgam of principle and practical consideration, the proscribed method for further amendment was a purer statement of the Founders' ideal of constitutional change. The instrument embodied their concept of federalism. The national legislature could propose change, but any reform would have to be approved by the states; and if the national legislature declined to act when a substantial number of states wished it to do so, the latter could compel the calling of a convention to circumvent the former. Change binding on all required the assent of a preponderant majority of the states, though not their unanimous consent. The late eighteenth-century inclination toward representative government was likewise evident. Elected representatives, whether assembled in legislatures or conventions, were regarded as best equipped to draft proposed constitutional reforms. The final sanctioning of reforms in the name of the sovereign people could be carried out either by legislatures, where representatives were left to make their own judgments, or by conventions, where delegates chosen by voters to reflect particular principles would prevail. The Founders' beliefs led to the establishment of an instrument still in place after more than 200 years. Both its durability and the controversies that have frequently swirled around the employment of Article V in the course of those two centuries compel close scrutiny of the circumstances of its creation.

As DELEGATES summoned by Congress to a convention for considering amendments to the Articles of Confederation gathered in Philadelphia in May 1787, they immediately confronted the question of what "amendment" meant: was it confined to a limited adjustment of existing conditions, or did it encompass drastic change? Later, they would deal with the related but even thornier question of whether the rules for sanctioning change could themselves be altered. Did the original instrument set inflexible terms for implementing change, or did it not?

The Virginia delegation, one of only two to reach Philadelphia over rainsoaked, muddy roads by May 14, the date Congress set for the convention to convene, arrived seeking more than mere adjustment of the Articles of Confederation. James Madison, the most prepared and energetic of the Virginians, in particular believed that the decentralized Confederation needed to be replaced by an effective central government. As they waited for other delegations, the Virginians polished an elaborate set of proposals for a new, substantially different structure of national government.[1]

On May 25 a quorum of nine states assembled in the East Room of the Pennsylvania State House, the very room where the Continental Congress had met and signed the Declaration of Independence. The delegates first took care of preliminaries, the election of George Washington to preside and adoption of rules of voting, procedure, and secrecy designed to encourage open discussion and flexibility. Then on May 29 the convention, by now representing eleven states, heard Virginia's Governor Edmund Randolph introduce on behalf of his fellow delegates the resolutions that would come to be referred to as the Virginia plan.[2]

According to the fullest notes of convention debate, those recorded and preserved by James Madison, Randolph, early in his discussion of the defects of the Confederation and its need for reform, "professed a high respect for its authors, and considered them as having done all that patriots could do, in the then infancy of the science of constitutions & of confederacies." The drafters of the Articles had no experience with many problems that would plague the Confederation. Perhaps, Randolph suggested, nothing better than the terms of the Articles could have been obtained at the time from states jealously guarding their sovereignty. However, eleven years of experience now made possible the remedying of defects.[3]

The first of the Virginia resolutions presented by Randolph contended "that the Articles of Confederation ought to be so corrected & enlarged as to accomplish the objects proposed by their institution: Namely, 'common defense, security of liberty and general welfare.'" Randolph and those for whom he spoke possessed an expansive view of "corrected & enlarged." Their fourteen other resolutions called for, among other things, a bicameral national legislature (with one house popularly elected and the other house chosen by the first) apportioned according to population and possessing power superior to that of the states, a national executive, a national judiciary, and a council of revision to review legislative actions. These proposals, in particular the enhancement of the national legislature and the creation of a national executive and judiciary, would establish a radically different system of government for the United States. A strong centralized national government would replace the existing decentralized Confederation. Yet the Virginians regarded such changes as amendments.[4]

To call the Virginia resolutions amendments when they so obviously represented plans to change completely the structure of government has been called a "transparent subterfuge."[5] Charles Pinckney of South Carolina, who submitted a plan of similar character to Virginia's on the same day, believed that it was time to consider the subject "de novo" and "pay no further attention to the Confederation" rather than "attempt the repair of a system, not only radically defective in principle, but which, if it were possible to give it operation, would prove absurd and oppressive."[6] Yet Randolph, who was certainly making no effort to conceal the substance or effect of the proposals, did perceive them as within the meaning of amendments. The fullest account of the opening portion of Randolph's speech of May 29, that contained in the notes of delegate William McHenry of Maryland, records that the Virginia governor began by asserting that the Confederation fulfilled none of the objects for which it was framed: protection from foreign threats, creation of harmony among the states, provision of benefits, defense against encroachments on federal power, or establishment of a union paramount to the states. Randolph did not criticize the initial objectives, merely the power of individual states to frustrate them. He called the framers of the Articles wise and great men who were chiefly concerned with the protection of human rights and had no experience with requisitioning men and money. They could not foresee the flaws that had since been exposed. Therefore, the defects in the Articles were no reflection on their creators or their goals. Randolph seemed to be distinguishing between a thoroughgoing change in the declared objectives of government that would require a redrawing of the social contract with the sovereign people and a less consequential alteration of instruments and procedures that could be achieved by amendment.[7]

Resolving itself into a committee of the whole on May 30 to discuss the Virginia resolutions, the convention agreed to postpone discussion of whether the Articles should be corrected and enlarged in order to discuss the substantive proposals.[8] Gouverneur Morris of Pennsylvania treated the issue as irrelevant, believing that the proposed changes would go beyond amendment. Yet as they turned to the substantive resolutions, the issue of what constituted amendment remained on the delegates' minds. Two of the three resolutions next brought before the delegates so clearly rejected the Articles, C. C. Pinckney of South Carolina observed, that their passage must bring to an end a convention whose mandate was to revise the Articles of Confederation. The two stated that neither a "merely federal" union of states nor a treaty among sovereign states could accomplish the objectives of the Articles, "namely, common defense, security of liberty, and general welfare." The passage of these, Pinckney argued, would establish the "incapability of amendment or improvement" of the Articles and force the convention's dissolution. His remark led to the prompt dropping of the two resolutions. The third, "Resolved, That a national government ought to be established, consisting of a supreme judicial, legislative, and executive," although arguably the most radical of the convention and certainly the one from which subsequent decisions flowed, was, in the eyes of the delegates, not so clearly hostile to the Articles. It was promptly adopted, 6 to 1 with New York evenly divided.[9]

As discussion of the Virginia resolutions proceeded, the delegates vacillated as to whether they were amending the Articles or doing something other. On June 5, the committee of the whole considered the fifteenth Virginia resolution that this convention's recommendations should, having gained the assent of Congress, be submitted to popularly chosen assemblies in each state for their approval. Roger Sherman of Connecticut thought popular ratification unnecessary in light of the Articles of Confederation's provision for ratification of amendments by state legislatures. James Madison on the other hand considered the provision essential, summarizing his argument in his journal:

> The articles of Confedn. themselves were defective in this respect, resting in many of the States on the Legislative sanction only. Hence in conflicts between acts of the States, and of Congs. especially where the former are of posterior date, and the decision is to be made by State Tribunals, an uncertainty must necessarily prevail, or rather perhaps a certain decision in favor of the State authority. He suggested also that as far as the articles of Union were to be considered as a Treaty only of a particular sort, among the Governments of Independent States, the doctrine might be set up that a breach of any one article, by any of the parties, absolved the other parties from the whole obligation. For these reasons as well as others he thought it indispensable that the new Constitution should be ratified in the most unexceptionable form, and by the supreme authority of the people themselves.[10]

Elbridge Gerry, disdainful of popular judgment, disagreed, and Rufus King considered the legislative ratification provided in the Articles to be sufficient. King did concede that popular ratification might be good politics, with popular conventions less likely than legislatures to object to change. James Wil-

son and Charles Pinckney raised the issue of the Articles' unanimity requirement as they expressed hopes that the new arrangements could take effect
for the approving states when a plurality agreed. Pinckney suggested that
nine ratifications would be sufficient. Having heard all of the arguments, the
committee of the whole temporarily postponed further consideration of the
issue, then adopted the resolution on June 12.[11]

When the committee of the whole turned to the sensitive issue of
whether population or statehood should be the basis for apportioning representation in the national legislature, the question of whether the Articles
were being amended or superseded arose again. William Paterson of New
Jersey, a fervent advocate of the rights of smaller states, argued that the convention's basis of authority was its mandate from Congress and the states to
amend the Articles. Thus it was obliged to operate within the rules of the
Confederation. To him that meant, among other things, accepting the Confederation principle of one vote per state in the federal legislature. The convention's powers of amendment did not extend, he insisted, to the abolition
of state governments and the creation of a national government.[12]

Paterson's concerns took concrete form on June 15 when, on behalf of a
number of delegates from Connecticut, Delaware, New Jersey, and New
York, he presented an alternative plan to that of the Virginians. The New
Jersey plan, as it came to be known, asserted that "the articles of Confederation ought to be so revised, corrected & enlarged, as to render the federal
Constitution adequate to the exigencies of Government, & the preservation
of the Union." Specifically, the New Jersey plan continued, a number of additional powers should be vested in Congress, including the power to levy
and collect taxes from the states in proportion to their population, a federal
executive and judiciary should be created, and federal law should be made
supreme over state law.[13] In effect Paterson and his associates were saying
that, except for the change in the basis of state representation in Congress,
the Virginia proposals were acceptable and could be achieved through
amendment of the Articles.

New York delegate John Lansing soon observed the contrast between the
Virginia and New Jersey plans: "The one now offered is on the basis of
amending the federal government, and the other to be reported as a national
government, on propositions which exclude the propriety of amendment."
Lansing was "decidedly of opinion" that the convention had only been
granted the power to consider amendments within the framework of the
Confederation in being; that his state would never have sent delegates to
form a national government; and that states could not be expected to ratify
a scheme whose proposal they had not authorized and that exceeded what

they regarded as sufficient. He recalled that the committee of the whole had early on dismissed the second Virginia resolution that declared in substance that the federal government could not be satisfactorily amended, after C. C. Pinckney observed that to do otherwise would exceed the convention's mandate.[14] Clearly, with the convention deeply divided over the nature of constitutional change to be implemented, larger issues lay buried in the debate over the extent of amending power in the existing circumstances.

When the delegates reconvened on June 18, Alexander Hamilton took the floor for the first time to declare himself opposed to both plans. He began by acknowledging the concerns about the limits of amending power yet agreeing with Randolph that the convention must do whatever it deemed essential for the country's well-being. "The States sent us here to provide for the exigencies of the Union," Hamilton declared. As his New York colleague Robert Yates recorded, Hamilton went on to say:

> We are appointed for the *sole* and *express* purpose of revising the confederation, and to *alter* or *amend* it, so as to render it effectual for the purposes of a good government. Those who suppose it must be federal, lay great stress on the terms *sole* and *express,* as if these words intended a confinement to a federal government; when the manifest import is no more than that the institution of a good government must be the *sole* and *express* object of your deliberations.

Reviewing the mandate of the New York state assembly to its delegates, Hamilton concluded that it

> leaves us at liberty to form such a national government as we think best adapted for the good of the whole. I have therefore no difficulty as to the extent of our power, nor do I feel myself restrained in the exercise of my judgment under them. We can only propose and recommend—the power of ratifying or rejecting is still in the states.

Rufus King understood Hamilton's message to be that the delegates possessed the power to go to all lengths to accomplish the freedom and happiness of the country. If the legislatures lacked the power to ratify changes because doing so would diminish their own sovereignty, then the people possessed the right to do so.[15]

Although the plan of extreme centralization that Hamilton went on to propose did not win much support, his forceful argument that the convention's amendment powers were unrestricted, though entirely subject to approval or disapproval by the people, was persuasive. Thereafter debate proceeded on the merits of various proposals, not whether the convention possessed the power to consider them. The agreement already reached on June 12 that their work should be submitted to state conventions undermined further objections. Determining the proper method of sanctioning whatever reforms were decided upon, rather than assuming that the process specified in the Articles would be used, became the delegates' concern from that time onward.

After dealing with the most divisive issue before it, the basis of representation in the national legislature, and other major substantive matters such as the treatment of slavery, the nature of the national executive, and the creation of a federal judiciary, the convention returned on July 23 to the issue of validating constitutional reform. Virginia's proposal that the new Constitution be submitted for ratification to state conventions expressly chosen by the people for that purpose was taken up. Objections, similar to those raised on June 5 but more extended and forceful, immediately came from delegates who preferred to rest the ratification decision in the hands of state legislatures. The debate that followed blended philosophic and practical considerations. Delegates who favored the emerging plan of national government favored the resolution; those more comfortable with state-centered authority opposed it. Both sides clearly believed popularly chosen conventions more likely to approve the new arrangements and legislatures to resist the reduction of their own power.

Edmund Randolph complained in his initial May 29 speech that legislative ratification left the Articles inferior to state constitutions formed by delegates elected by the people. On July 23 Randolph's fellow Virginian George Mason declared that gaining the people's authorization of the convention's finished work was "essential." State legislatures, bound by their own constitutions, did not have authority to ratify; the people retained the power to do so. Randolph, reiterating that legislative approval was insufficient, argued that those people most likely to oppose the new system would be "the local demagogues who will be degraded by it from the importance they now hold. These will spare no efforts to impede that progress in the popular mind which will be necessary to the adoption of the plan. . . . It is of great importance therefore that the consideration of this subject should be transferred from the legislatures where this class of men have their full influence to a field in which their efforts can be less mischievous."[16]

Elbridge Gerry of Massachusetts and Oliver Ellsworth of Connecticut defended state legislative authority. Gerry thought that great confusion and disagreement would result from popular involvement. Furthermore, he did not believe that "the people will do what their rulers will not. The rulers will either conform to or influence the sense of the people." Ellsworth observed that convention ratification was a new idea since the establishment of the Articles. Legislatures had previously been regarded as competent to ratify the Articles and to consider amendments Congress proposed to them.[17]

As he had on June 5, Rufus King said that he agreed with Ellsworth. Yet now King indicated much more forcefully that he favored an expression of the people through conventions as most certain to dispel "all disputes and doubts concerning the legitimacy of the new constitution." Furthermore, a convention was "the most likely means of drawing forth the best men in the states to decide on it."[18]

James Madison disputed the belief of King and Ellsworth that state legislatures were competent to ratify changes. "It would be a novel and dangerous doctrine," he observed, "that a legislature could change the constitution under which it held its existence." All the reasons for holding the Philadelphia convention instead of having Congress propose constitutional reforms also favored its examination and adoption by state conventions rather than legislatures. Madison's most telling argument involved the distinction between a system based on legislative action and one based on popular sanction; this was, he held, "the true difference between a *league* or *treaty,* and a *constitution.*"

> The former in point of *moral obligation* might be as inviolable as the latter. In point of *political operation,* there were two important distinctions in favor of the latter. 1. A law violating a treaty ratified by a preexisting law might be respected by the Judges as a law, though an unwise or perfidious one. A law violating a constitution established by the people themselves would be considered by the Judges as null and void. 2. The doctrine laid down by the law of Nations in the case of treaties is that a breach of any one article by any of the parties frees the other parties from their engagements. In the case of a union of people under one constitution, the nature of the pact has always been understood to exclude such an interpretation.[19]

Whatever else they might have felt about the emerging plan of government, most delegates subscribed to the Lockean notion that a constitution rested on the sanction of the people and that the most direct expression of popular approval feasible was desirable. The proposal to submit the new Constitution to state legislatures went down to defeat 7 to 3. A resolution that the measure be sent to conventions chosen by the people then gained 9-to-1 approval, with only Delaware opposed.[20] It did not hurt that this approach also appeared the most likely path to success in the upcoming contest over ratification. Nevertheless, a convention that had already accepted indirect selection of senators and would soon authorize indirect presidential elections stood steadfastly for popular endorsement of the basic frame of government.

In discussing ratification, several delegates commented that it should be possible to put the new Constitution into effect without the unanimous consent of the states required by the Articles of Confederation.[21] One or two states should not be able to block the entire enterprise, as the delegates were well aware had happened to delay the initial ratification of the Articles and to stop altogether their proposed amendment in 1782. Rhode Island, which had on the latter occasion frustrated the action of the other twelve states, had not even sent delegates to Philadelphia and seemed likely to reject its results. North Carolina delegate Richard Dobbs Spaight was of a mind with many of his colleagues when he wrote privately that one or two states should not "prevent the Union from rising out of that contemptible situation to which it is at present reduced."[22] When the five-member committee on detail, assigned on July 26 the task of drafting a polished document from the resolutions approved, reported on August 6, it included the provision that "The ratifications of the conventions of ___ states shall be sufficient for organizing this Constitution."[23]

By the time the convention, in the course of reviewing the proposed draft clause by clause, got around to discussing ratification on the last two days of August, it was clear that support for the emerging Constitution was, though substantial, less than unanimous. James Wilson of Pennsylvania instantly proposed that ratification by seven states be deemed adequate to put the Constitution into effect, "that being a majority of the whole number & sufficient for the commencement of the plan." Gouverneur Morris suggested that if the ratifying states were contiguous a smaller number should be sufficient to introduce the new government than if they were dispersed. Roger Sherman, willing to accept less than unanimity, thought, however, that at least ten states should concur. Edmund Randolph proposed nine as "a respectable majority of the whole," and a level of concurrence frequently used in the Confederation. Wilson offered to compromise on eight.[24]

As the debate over state ratification went forward, James Madison worried that if seven, eight, or nine were the number agreed to, the Constitution could conceivably be put into operation "over the whole body of the people though less than a majority of them should ratify it." Wilson offered his understanding that only states that ratified could be bound by the new Constitution and appealed for feasible ratification arrangements in light of the urgency of the current situation. "We must," he said, "in this case go to the original powers of Society. The House on fire must be extinguished, without a scrupulous regard to ordinary rights."[25]

The debate continued into the next day. Pierce Butler of South Carolina, revolted by the idea that one or two states might restrain the rest, declared himself in favor of a minimum of nine ratifications. Rufus King moved to make specific that the new Constitution would apply only to those states ratifying it, and all but Maryland agreed. Only James Wilson and George Clymer of Pennsylvania supported Madison's formula requiring ratification not only by a majority of states but also by states that together contained a majority of the people. When the convention finally dealt with deciding how to fill in the blank on the number of states required for ratification, only Maryland voted for a unanimous thirteen. Connecticut, New Jersey, and Georgia joined Maryland in supporting ten, but seven states opposed. All, except for Virginia and the Carolinas who presumably preferred a lower number, accepted nine. By this process of groping toward compromise, the delegates agreed upon the ratification standard.[26]

The issue of whether ratification should be considered in state legislatures or conventions was also at issue on Friday, August 31. Gouverneur Morris moved to strike out the draft's requirement of conventions and leave the states to choose their own means of ratification. Rufus King equated giving up conventions with giving up the chance of gaining approval. "Conventions alone, which will avoid all the obstacles from the complicated formation of the Legislatures, will succeed," he predicted, "and if not positively required by the plan, its enemies will oppose that mode." Morris protested that he only meant to facilitate adoption of the Constitution. Madison agreed with King, noting that the power being given the central government was being taken from the state governments; state legislatures were more likely than conventions to oppose this, and, if so, "could devise modes apparently promoting, but really thwarting the ratification." In response to concerns that state constitutions already specified modes of ratification, Madison asserted that "the people were, in fact, the fountain of all power, and by resorting to them, all difficulties were got over. They could alter constitutions as they pleased." Morris's motion was put to a vote and defeated 6 to 4.[27]

The remaining issue was whether the sitting Confederation Congress should have any role in the adoption of the new Constitution. The original Virginia plan, as presented by Edmund Randolph on May 29, had called for amendments to be submitted to the states after "the approbation of Congress."[28] The committee on detail, reporting on August 6, was emphatic that "this Constitution shall be laid before the United States in Congress assembled, for their approbation" and was much more cautious in declaring "and it is the opinion of this Convention that it should be afterwards submitted to a Convention" in each state.[29] Some delegates believed that Congress would only be allowed to consider whether or not to attach its recommendation to the plan that "cannot remain long before them."[30] Yet others feared that Congress could scuttle the entire enterprise. No consideration of this requirement of obtaining the formal endorsement of Congress took place, or at least none was recorded, until August 31 when Gouverneur Morris and Charles Pinckney moved that the words "for their approbation" be stricken. Without discussion this was approved 8 to 3.[31]

The concerns previously expressed about state legislatures being unhappy with the proposed Constitution and seeking to thwart it did not have to be reiterated: Congress could be expected to be, at least in part, quite unhappy. Therefore the convention was prepared to do to the Congress what it had already agreed to do to each state legislature: appeal over its head directly to the people for approval of the new structure of government. The Framers took this action so quickly and with so little comment that its significance is easy to overlook. This step represented, as much as did the action declaring nine ratifications sufficient, a specific and overt rejection of the Articles of Confederation's procedure for constitutional change. Carl Van Doren properly called the adoption of these ratification arrangements "one of the most revolutionary decisions in the whole convention."[32]

On September 10, as the convention moved rapidly to settle small but significant final details and to polish its work, Elbridge Gerry sought to reinsert "the approbation of Congress" in the ratification procedure. He objected, he said, to changing the government without the sanction of Congress. It was "improper," would give "just umbrage" to Congress, and would annul the Confederation "with so little scruple or formality." Alexander Hamilton supported Gerry, adding that he thought it improper to allow nine states to institute a new government unless the Congress and the state legislatures agreed to that plan. Edmund Randolph added his voice to the chorus. Unhappy with the departures from the original Virginia plan, he wanted state conventions free to offer amendments that in turn a second general convention would consider. Hamilton then proposed, and Gerry seconded, a plan by which the new Constitution would be reviewed by Congress and then by the state legislatures before being submitted to popularly chosen state conventions, with the legislatures to decide whether approval of nine states would be sufficient to have the Constitution take effect.[33]

Other delegates, hitherto silent, now spoke out in strong opposition. James Wilson called it "worse than folly" to rely on Rhode Island to support the plan in Congress. On the basis of their actions in the Philadelphia convention, he was uncertain of the position in Congress of Maryland, New York, and perhaps other states. "After spending four or five months in the laborious & arduous task of forming a Government for our country," Wilson said, "we are ourselves at the close throwing insuperable obstacles in the way of its success." George Clymer, Rufus King, and John Rutledge agreed, King saying that with Hamilton's plan "every thing will go into confusion, and all our labor be lost." Put to a vote, the Hamilton motion met defeat 10 to 1.[34]

Edmund Randolph, supported by George Mason and Elbridge Gerry, made one final attempt on September 15 to alter the ratification procedure after the committee on style and arrangement put the penultimate draft of the Constitution before the delegates. The committee had settled on language that acknowledged Congress and the state legislatures but dealt somewhat ambiguously with their role in the ratification process. The Constitution would "be laid before the United States in Congress assembled," and "it is the opinion of this Convention that it should afterwards be submitted to a Convention of Delegates chosen in each State by the People thereof, under the recommendation of its Legislature, for their assent and ratification." Randolph proposed for a second time that the state conventions be authorized to propose amendments that another general convention would consider, a suggestion similar to a plan offered by Gouverneur Morris on July 23 that did not even receive a second. Without such a provision, Randolph said, he would be unable to endorse the current instrument. Mason, agreeing, complained that "this Constitution had been formed without the knowledge or idea of the people." He believed that a second convention would "know more of the sense of the people, and be able to provide a system more consonant to it." It would be improper, he concluded, "to say to the people, take this or nothing." Both Mason and Gerry indicated that they could sign the Constitution only if it provided for a second general convention.[35]

Charles Pinckney responded that the Randolph idea of allowing states to offer amendments would sow "nothing but confusion & contrariety." He predicted that "the States will never agree in their plans—And the Deputies to a second Convention, coming together under the discordant impressions of their Constituents, will never agree." In Pinckney's view, "Conventions are serious things, and ought not to be repeated."[36]

The delegates, at the end of their long and trying deliberations, overwhelmingly agreed with Pinckney's republican view that a second convention was a bad idea. The eleven states present voted against the Randolph motion. They then immediately agreed to the Constitution as it then stood and ordered it printed.[37] When the delegates gathered for a final time on September 17, Randolph, Mason, and Gerry were true to their pledge not to sign the document. Randolph again objected to the presentation of the plan to the people as a final alternative to be accepted or rejected in toto.[38] The other delegates signed, some with conflicted feelings, and the Constitution they had drafted was set on the path they had stipulated for its ratification.[39]

Throughout their long summer in Philadelphia, the delegates to the 1787 convention struggled with the fundamental issue of what would give legitimacy to the structure of government they were creating. Whatever their private thoughts, they never explicitly acknowledged that the Confederation had broken down. If they were to adhere strictly to a Lockean framework of thought, such an admission was required to free them to form a new compact of government, unbound by the rules of the old one. In its essentials—avoidance of congressional involvement, effective ratification with less than unanimity, and appeal through the device of popularly chosen conventions for the endorsement of the sovereign people—the 1787 Constitution broke cleanly with the Articles of Confederation. And although the delegates deliberately removed language suggesting that the Confederation Congress had any decisionmaking power over the instrument, they ultimately agreed to lay their handiwork before that body. By that action the Founders were, in effect, acknowledging that they had been called into being to initiate the amendment of the Articles of Confederation and had done so. Among their proposed changes was the system of amendment, both in the immediate circumstances of the ratification of their plan and, as will soon be evident, for the future. If the sovereign people sanctioned these revisions, the Philadelphia convention believed that it would have fulfilled its original mandate.

PROVISION FOR AMENDMENT, assumed from the outset to be a necessary part of the new Constitution but not settled until the end of the Philadelphia convention, evolved along with ideas about ratification procedure. Experience with the Articles of Confederation's unforeseen flaws reinforced the delegates' beliefs that the new Constitution should provide for further amendment. This same background persuaded them of the desirability of establishing amending rules different from the Articles' rigid requirements that Congress initiate amendments and the states unanimously approve them. The members of the Philadelphia convention clearly wanted to create an amending system that, without rendering the Constitution unstable, would allow generally agreed-upon change to take place. They did not wish ever to see repeated the combination of constitutional inadequacy and inflexibility that had produced the governmental crisis they were confronting.

The initial Virginia plan contained a resolution that "provision ought to be made for the amendment of the Articles of Union whensoever it shall seem necessary, and that the assent of the National Legislature ought not to be required thereto." Charles Pinckney seems to have proposed at the same time that "the assent of the Legislatures of ___ States shall be sufficient to invest future additional Powers in U.S. in C. ass. and shall bind the whole confederacy." Yet when the Virginia proposal first came up for discussion on June 5, Pinckney "doubted the propriety or necessity of it." Madison's cryptic notes left unclear whether Pinckney was expressing reservations about an amendment provision or merely the exclusion of Congress from it. Elbridge Gerry responded with a brief general appeal for an amendment provision. The delegates then postponed further consideration of the proposal.[40]

When the subject of an amendment provision came up again on June 11, several delegates, unidentified in Madison's notes, said they failed to see the necessity of it at all. Nor did they comprehend the propriety of making congressional consent to amendments unnecessary. George Mason, supported by Randolph, quickly rose to the defense of the Virginia proposal:

> The plan now to be formed will certainly be defective, as the Confederation has been found on trial to be. Amendments therefore will be necessary, and it will be better to provide for them in an easy, regular, and Constitutional way than to trust to chance and violence. It would be improper to require the consent of the Natl. Legislature, because they may abuse their power, and refuse their consent on that very account. The opportunity for such an abuse may be the fault of the Constitution calling for amendmt.

Without further discussion, the convention responded by approving the Virginia resolution without dissent, although postponing consideration of the congressional role in amendment.[41]

Little more was said about amending, not to mention the amendment process, until the waning days of the convention. Neither William Paterson nor Alexander Hamilton commented on the topic when they offered alternatives to the Virginia plan. The committee on detail, having been told to provide for amendment, drafted an extremely simple mechanism: "On the application of the Legislatures of two-thirds of the States in the Union for an amendment of this Constitution, the Legislature of the United States shall call a Convention for that purpose." When it came before the convention on August 30, Gouverneur Morris suggested that the Congress should be free to call a constitutional convention whenever it chose, but no more was said as delegates adopted the committee's proposal without dissent.[42] Procedures for initial ratification rather than subsequent amendment were still the focus of procedural discussions.

Not until September 10 did the convention specifically address the issue of amendment. On that day, Elbridge Gerry asked for reconsideration of the proposed amending article. He expressed concern that it would allow two-thirds of the states to obtain a convention that in turn could bind the Union to innovations that might subvert state constitutions altogether. Alexander Hamilton replied that he did not object to such a possibility, seeing no greater evil in making the people of the entire country subject to a majority than making the people of a particular state subject to one. He observed that many wished for an easier mode of amending the Articles of Confederation. An easy means of remedying defects in the new system was equally desirable. Under the proposed method, Hamilton believed, state legislatures would seek alterations only to increase their own powers. The national legislature would first perceive the need for amendments, and thus ought also to be empowered, whenever two-thirds of each branch concurred to call a constitutional convention. Hamilton saw no danger in this, if the people retained ratification power. After Madison added that he found the terms of the proposed article vague, the delegates voted 9 to 1 for Gerry's motion to reconsider the amending provision.[43]

Roger Sherman, responding to Hamilton's complaints, sought to overturn the Virginia and committee on detail plan excluding Congress from the amending process. He moved to add to the article "or the Legislature may propose amendments to the several States for their approbation, but no amendment shall be binding until consented to by the several States." James Wilson, conscious that this language would restore the Articles of Confederation's requirement of unanimous state ratification of amendments, promptly moved to specify two-thirds state approval. The two-thirds ratification standard, in effect the same requirement of approval by nine states that had already been agreed upon for the implementation of the new Constitution, was narrowly defeated by a vote of 6 states to 5. Wilson immediately proposed to raise the threshold to three-fourths, meaning that the endorsement of ten current states would be needed before the new Constitution could be altered. The delegates accepted without dissent this higher standard for change than for initial approval.

James Madison, having heard these expressions of support for allowing the Congress a role in amendments and a three-fourths level of state agreement on ratification, proposed the language that would become the essence of the final accord:

The Legislature of the U__S__ whenever two thirds of both Houses shall deem necessary, or on the application of two thirds of the Legislatures of the several States, shall propose amendments to this Constitution, which shall be valid to all intents and purposes as part thereof, when the same shall have been ratified by three fourths at least of the Legislatures of the several States, or by Conventions in three fourths thereof, as one or the other mode of ratification may be proposed by the Legislature of the U.S.[44]

Madison did not explain his addition of a provision whereby conventions could be employed as an alternative to legislatures in considering state ratifications. In doing so, however, he brought the amending mechanism more in line with the arrangement earlier adopted for initial state ratification of the Constitution.

South Carolina delegate John Rutledge instantly realized that this amending procedure could threaten the South's peculiar institution, the treatment of which in the Constitution had been settled upon with difficulty. "He could never agree," Rutledge said, "to give a power by which the articles relating to slaves might be altered by the States not interested in that property and prejudiced against it." Language was added to stipulate that no amendments "may be made prior to the year 1808" that would affect the terms already approved dealing with slavery. That having been agreed to, Madison's motion was approved 9 to 1.[45]

Discussion of the amending provision was hardly at an end, however. On Saturday, September 15, the amending article was one of the items with which delegates continued to tinker as they sought to conclude their work. Roger Sherman voiced concern that, as it stood, three-fourths of the states could combine to take actions fatal to other states, "abolishing them altogether or depriving them of their equality in the Senate." Small states had expressed fear of large state power throughout the convention. Sherman thought it reasonable that the specific protection of slave states be extended to prohibit amendments that would deprive states of their internal police power or equality in the Senate.[46]

George Mason expressed general unhappiness with the amending plan. It was, he charged, "exceptionable & dangerous." He pointed out that both means of proposing amendments required the approval of Congress and expressed his fear that "no amendment of the proper kind would ever be obtained by the people, if the Government should become oppressive, as he verily believed would be the case." Should Congress become oppressive, he had written in the margin of his copy of the September 12 printed draft, "the whole people of America can't make, or even propose alterations to it;

a doctrine utterly subversive of the fundamental principles of the rights and liberties of the people." Gouverneur Morris and Elbridge Gerry, sharing Mason's concern, proposed that the article be revised to require that a convention be held on the application of two-thirds of the states. Madison thought Congress would feel as compelled to propose amendments as to call a convention at the request of two-thirds of the states but did not object to providing for such a convention. Thereupon the delegates unanimously adopted the Morris-Gerry motion.[47]

Sherman then proposed to strike the three-fourths clause from the provision for ratification by state legislatures or conventions. This would, he said, leave future conventions free to act, as had the current convention, according to circumstances. Whether Sherman intended to loosen the ratification standard or to reimpose a unanimity requirement, as a strict reading of the proposed language would suggest, is not clear. In any case, the motion was defeated 7 to 3.[48]

Elbridge Gerry attempted to regain for state legislatures the exclusive right to ratify amendments, proposing that the provision for alternative ratification by conventions in three-fourths of the states be eliminated. Only Connecticut supported his motion; ten delegations opposed. Few doubts remained in this body that conventions provided an attractive alternative to legislatures when constitutional issues were to be decided.[49]

Sherman returned to his earlier idea, moving that amendments that would affect the internal police or equal Senate suffrage of a state without its consent should not be permitted. Madison, no doubt worried that the whole delicate constitutional balance achieved over the past four months could collapse in a rush to protect matters from amendment, declared, "Begin with these special provisos, and every State will insist on them for their boundaries, exports, &c." Others shared his concern with maintaining the convention's existing consensus, for the Sherman motion was defeated 8 to 3.[50]

Continuing to worry about the potential threat posed by amendment, Sherman immediately asked that the amending article be struck out altogether. Although this motion failed by a similar 8-to-2 margin, with Delaware divided, Sherman's point, which had support within the Connecticut, New Jersey, and Delaware delegations, was taken. Gouverneur Morris moved to add to the article that "no State without its consent shall be deprived of its equal suffrage in the Senate." According to Madison's journal, "This motion being dictated by the circulating murmurs of the small States was agreed to without debate, no one opposing it, or on the question, saying no."[51]

With this last important concession to the smaller states, the convention completed defining the amending system, and therewith, very nearly, its task.

At their next and final meeting two days later on September 17, all but a few delegates endorsed the result of their efforts. The Constitution that they offered the country incorporated its entire complex plan of government into only seven articles. Article V in its final form provided,

> The Congress, whenever two thirds of both Houses shall deem it necessary, shall propose Amendments to this Constitution, or, on the Application of the Legislatures of two thirds of the several States, shall call a Convention for proposing Amendments, which, in either Case, shall be valid to all Intents and Purposes, as Part of this Constitution, when ratified by the Legislatures of three fourths of the several States, or by Conventions in three fourths thereof, as the one or the other Mode of Ratification may be proposed by the Congress: Provided that no Amendment which may be made prior to the Year One thousand eight hundred and eight shall in any Manner affect the first and fourth Clauses in the Ninth Section of the first Article: and that no State, without its Consent, shall be deprived of its equal Suffrage in the Senate.[52]

The amending system worked out in the Philadelphia convention reflected the thinking of most of the delegates regarding a reasonable process of constitutional revision. Like the rest of their creation, Article V evinced the essential compromise struck between the proponents of a strong central government and the advocates of retained state power. Although Congress was granted a powerful role in the process, constitutional ratification and amendment were not to be achieved solely by the central government, nor merely with the concurrence of some majority of an undifferentiated national population. States, as distinct entities with separate populations and political institutions, occupied as significant and unavoidable a position in the process as did the national government; majorities in the legislatures or conventions of individual states would decide constitutional issues. The possibility of the states in concert initiating constitutional change as well as checking congressionally initiated reform were notable characteristics of the amending system. Although the Constitution proclaimed that "We the People of the United States" were ordaining and establishing a constitution, it was the people acting through their separate states who would do this and later revise the instrument. The federal compromise of the 1787 Constitution could be found in no more pure a form.

In the eyes of the Philadelphia delegates, it was not the general principal of concurrence between the central government and the states but rather the state unanimity requirement of the Articles of Confederation that represented the chief defect of the preceding amendment method. Their proposed alternative of three-fourths concurrence seemed to them to prevent a tiny minority of states from obstructing widely desired reform while establishing an adequate requirement of consensus to avoid the constitutional instability inherent in simple majoritarianism. Their experience with the Articles of Confederation had shaped their belief that a government with the support of two-thirds of the states could successfully be put into effect and that a constitutional reform with the endorsement of three-fourths of those states would not unreasonably endanger any individual state. After the previous decade, two-thirds state approval for ratification and three-fourths for amendment seemed a moderate standard, neither an unduly lax nor an impossibly difficult one.

Article V as finally set forth represented a compromise between the contending republican faiths of the era, often characterized as Whig versus Federalist.[53] Both rested squarely on the belief that authority ultimately lay with the sovereign people and, therefore, that government must operate by consent of the governed. They agreed that the people, holding final authority over the terms of their government, were free to set new terms if they wished. It seemed proper to Whigs and Federalists alike to ignore the existing framework of rules and appeal to the sovereign people to establish a new one, as the Philadelphia convention did in circumventing the Congress and state legislatures to submit the new Constitution with its altered set of ratification standards to popularly elected conventions. If the sovereign people approved, the Constitution would meet the highest standard of legitimacy.

Whigs and Federalists shared the Enlightenment's optimistic belief that it was possible to determine which course in human affairs was proper and virtuous, in other words, "the good." Whigs tended to be more sanguine than Federalists about the ease of perceiving the good, but both assumed that a high degree of community agreement could be eventually achieved in recognizing and supporting the good. They were not opposed, therefore, to requiring a high level of consensus on fundamental matters. They did not conceive of supermajorities as thwarting democracy; if only a slender majority could be formed, then the good was not yet in focus. Once the good had been distinguished, an overwhelming majority would choose to support it. On a matter as important as defining a constitution, a supermajority of two-thirds or three-fourths was not unreasonable, unattainable, or undemocratic.

However, Whig political theory in the 1780s rested on a belief in community homogeneity: people shared a capacity and willingness to identify and support the best interests of the community. Thus it was desirable to provide direct popular involvement in government through frequent election of representatives; so chosen, legislatures possessed great latitude in carrying out the popular will. Constitutions, devices that alone could define and limit legislatures, should be shaped and ratified by means most closely reflective of the public will, in other words, by popularly elected conventions. The Pennsylvania state convention of 1776 offered the purest expression of Whig values in eighteenth-century American constitution-making. The decision to require ratification of the 1787 Constitution by state conventions marked a triumph of this viewpoint, though it was obviously based on political practicalities as well as philosophy.

The Federalist view, in contrast, assumed that people's interests varied and that government served as an arbiter among them. In the presence of competing heterogeneous factions, deliberative mechanisms removed from popular passions were preferable. This approach meant entrusting constitution-making to legislatures, bodies composed of representatives with general responsibility, rather than to conventions with delegates chosen to pursue a specific action. The Massachusetts constitution of 1780, backing away from the Pennsylvania precedent, moved in this direction.

The evolution of Article V involved a balancing of Whig and Federalist preferences. The initial Virginia plan was vague on the mechanism to be employed but specific on the point that the national legislature should not be involved. Midway through the Philadelphia deliberations, the committee on detail proposed that a national constitutional convention be called when two-thirds of the state legislatures requested it. By September, however, the delegates were ready to give the Congress more power, first the right to call a convention on its own initiative, and then, at the last minute, to propose amendments itself. The compromise, allowing either the national legislature or a national convention to offer amendments, was then repeated in Madison's draft language providing for state ratification by either legislatures or conventions as the Congress chose. This maintained the balance between the Whig preference for conventions and the Federalist inclination toward legislatures and avoided undermining the already agreed-upon initial ratification method. Madison did, however, tilt the balance in the favor of legislatures by placing in the hands of Congress the crucial decision as to which ratification alternative would be used in the states.

The Philadelphia delegates apparently first thought to authorize constitutional action by conventions, but when a legislative role was suggested, no real resistance arose to its use at either the national or state level. The amending system as finally drawn with its legislative and supermajority elements contained Federalist checks on democratic impulses. It likewise possessed Whig features with its mechanisms to outflank legislatures at both state and national levels through the device of conventions. Though the convention approach would thereafter prove to be relatively little used, it was the system employed to design the amendment procedure and to give it the sanction of state ratification as well.

THE PHILADELPHIA CONVENTION OF 1787 did not by itself complete the process of constitutional reform. In their action stipulating a method for its completion, the delegates acknowledged that they had only begun the process. For all that historians from Charles Beard onward have claimed about the elite construction of the Constitution, the fact remains that its drafters did not regard their work as having legitimacy without the sanction of the sovereign people through the device of state convention ratification.

As its final act the Philadelphia convention sent its secretary, William Jackson, to deliver a copy of its handiwork to the Confederation Congress meeting in New York. Although in designing its ratification procedure the convention had avoided any stipulation for congressional approval, it now found it politic to gain a measure of congressional support, presumably because opposition had surfaced and some delegates had refused to sign.[54] In an accompanying letter to Congress over the signature of George Washington, the convention briefly declared that it was submitting to the consideration of Congress what it believed to be in the best interests of all, though it required the sacrifice of some state liberties: "The Constitution which we now present is the Result of a Spirit of Amity and of that mutual Deference & Concession which the Peculiarity of our political Situation rendered indispensable."[55] Concluding that the Constitution would not be entirely agreeable to every state, the letter left no doubt that its fate should nevertheless be left to the states to decide.

Ten of the Philadelphia delegates who were also members of Congress followed Secretary Jackson to New York. They took their seats on September 26 as Congress began consideration of the proposed Constitution. Comprising nearly one-third of those in attendance, they provided a counterweight to the vocal critics of the convention, most notably Richard Henry Lee of Virginia, who charged that it had exceeded its mandate to propose amendments to the Articles of Confederation. Led by James Madison, the ten explained and defended the convention's reasoning to their congressional colleagues. They failed to obtain an outright endorsement of the proposed charter and even had to fight off some of Lee's proposals to change it. The ten, however, did succeed within three days in persuading the twelve state delegations present to vote for virtually the same transmittal language contained in the Constitution itself. Were substantive changes made, the Constitution would become the creation of the Confederation Congress and subject to the unanimous ratification stipulation of the Articles. Left unaltered, the Constitution could be put into operation as it specified, by the ratification of nine states. The Congress, which had been unable to act on much of anything since it approved the Northwest Ordinance the previous July, readily agreed on September 28 to send the proposed Constitution to the state legislatures, which in turn were to submit it to popularly chosen delegate conventions.[56]

The September action of Congress represented a crucial step toward approval of the new Constitution. Henceforth, the contest would be fought on the terms that the Philadelphia convention had set. Even critics agreed to abide by the will of state conventions and implement the new system of government if nine states ratified. Not only did this agreement give proponents of the new instrument an obvious advantage, it indicated the willingness of others as well to acquiesce in results achieved by such means. The acceptance of this Constitution's legitimacy, should it be ratified, seemed thereby ensured.

The ultimate fate of the proposed Constitution remained in doubt after Congress's action. Since before the convention assembled, most American newspapers had been emphasizing the ills of the Confederation, the need for reform, and the wisdom of the delegates gathered in Philadelphia. On the whole the press conveyed a message that the work of the Framers should be accepted without question.[57] Nevertheless, with voices being raised in opposition, considerable debate on the wisdom of ratification could be anticipated. The rapid acquiescence of Congress to transmittal suggests that most representatives shared the predominant view of the press and the Philadelphia Founders that changing the current terms of government was essential if the United States was to be kept alive.

The Congress appears also to have shared with the convention an appreciation of the larger importance of their actions. They embodied the evolving eighteenth-century sense that a constitution assumed central importance in a republic. A constitution represented a "higher law" because it expressed the first principles of the sovereign people. Constantly changing conditions and desires posed the main obstacle to keeping a republican form of government functioning and vital. Developing a system whereby the citizens of a republic could establish, and, equally important, could alter the terms of their government in a way that preserved the crucial sense that the sovereign power of the people remained intact represented a great achievement for republicanism.

"The Americans of the Revolutionary generation believed that they had made a momentous contribution to the history of politics," Gordon Wood has observed. Specifically, "They had for the first time demonstrated to the world how a people could diagnose the ills of its society and work out a peaceable process of cure. They had, and what is more significant they knew they had, broken through the conception of political theory that had imprisoned men's minds for centuries and brilliantly reconstructed the framework for a new republican polity, a reconstruction that radically changed the future discussion of politics."[58] The concept of written constitutionalism lies at the heart of the republicanism that Wood and others have regarded as the eighteenth century's most notable political innovation. In turn, such constitutionalism had at its core the dynamic device whose presence enhanced the chances of republican agreements on government achieving lasting success: a mechanism for formal amendment.

4

"A REMEDY IN THE SYSTEM ITSELF"

Amending and the Adoption of the Constitution

A rticle V, the 1787 U.S. Constitution's provision for its own amendment, became the hinge upon which swung acceptance of the Philadelphia convention's proposal. In the state conventions that considered ratification, the existence of a clear and specific revision process armored defenders of the new charter and somewhat disarmed those assaulting it. Again and again the same argument could be heard: whatever defects the new structure of government proved to contain, remedies could be applied. The new amending arrangements would overcome the state unanimity obstacle to constitutional reform contained in the Articles of Confederation. While the ratification debate was intense, eleven states accepted the Constitution within ten months of its transmittal by Congress. Although much attention naturally focused on doubts expressed about the new charter, perhaps more notable was its remarkably rapid approval by conventions in states large and small, South and North, robust and fragile. All appeared to find the amending provision reassuring as they committed themselves to the new constitutional arrangements.

As soon as Congress placed the proposed Constitution before the states, public scrutiny and discussion of every clause commenced. The crucial debates took place within the state conventions held to decide upon ratification. Only partial convention records survive, but they provide insight into the central conflicts and accords. References to the amendment provision arose throughout the discussions. Collectively they suggest that Article V contributed in an important way to the achievement of ratification, particularly in the large, crucial states of Pennsylvania, Massachusetts, Virginia, and New York, where in three out of four cases the margin of victory was quite slender.

The long and often vitriolic campaigns preceding many of the delegate elections tended to reduce the perceived positions of the contending forces to the simplest of terms: they were, whatever their reasons, either friends or enemies of the proposed new form of government, either federalists or antifederalists. The reality, however, was more complex. Some federalists had reservations about various features of the new Constitution. Most antifederalists recognized the failings of the Confederation and the need to increase the power of the central government. Yet, for a variety of reasons, they feared the potential power of such a government. They saw great risk in adopting the plan approved at Philadelphia without setting clear limits on the powers that the federal government exercised over the states and individual citizens. Thus, for many, opposition to the Constitution was qualified rather than absolute. Despite the stark label applied to them and which they grudgingly accepted, these critics were not absolutely and irrevocably antifederal. If they could be convinced that the Constitution would be altered to assuage their concerns, many would accept it.

Several small states saw little choice but to ratify and, without much division or debate, quickly moved to do so.[1] In four such states, legislatures provided authorization, delegates were elected, and conventions convened within a matter of weeks after Congress forwarded the proposed Constitution to them. Delaware, convinced that under the new federal government its debt burden would be relieved by a stronger currency and its share of taxation would be reduced as a result of import duties and sales of western lands, was most eager to endorse the instrument. Its convention, of which no records survive, took only a few hours spread over four days to come to a unanimous agreement to be the first to ratify on December 7, 1787.[2] Likewise motivated by currency and taxation concerns, nearby New Jersey's convention discussed the matter for seven days at the Blazing Star Tavern in Trenton before ratifying, again unanimously, on December 18.[3] Georgia's convention became the third to achieve quick unanimity. After only one day of debate, the southernmost state voted in favor of ratification on January 2, 1788.[4]

Only Connecticut, among the small states taking prompt action, produced significant opposition to ratification.[5] Nearly one-fourth of its convention delegates voted in the negative when the ratification ballot was taken on January 9, 1788. At the end of the heated debate, delegate Richard Law observed, "As we have been a long time poring upon the defective parts of the Constitution, I think it will not be amiss to pay some attention to its excellences." He particularly admired Article V, "which provides a remedy for whatever defects it may have." In his estimation, "This is an easy and peaceable way of amending any parts of the Constitution which may be found inconvenient in practice."[6] Many Connecticut delegates, like those in Delaware, New Jersey, and Georgia who had already acted, concluded that their states had little choice but to embrace the new Constitution, but Law's comment helps explain their prompt and exceedingly positive responses.[7]

Pennsylvania was the first of the large, influential states to take up the ratification issue. Proponents of the new Constitution, who predominated in the eastern section of the state, were eager to take action before antifederalists, who seemed strongest in the more rural, scattered settlements of the central and western regions, could organize effective opposition. While the Congress in New York was still considering the convention's work on September 28, the Pennsylvania assembly adopted a resolution calling for a state ratification convention. The next day when the congressional transmittal resolution arrived, the antifederalist minority sought to block action by the only means available to them, staying away from the assembly and denying it a two-thirds quorum. The federalist majority ordered the sergeant-at-arms to round up the truants, and as soon as two were brought in, the assembly voted to hold delegate elections for a convention to meet November 20. When those elections produced a 2-to-1 federalist victory, the minority complained, with reason, that the process had been advanced with such haste that there had been little time for thoughtful public discussion of the proposed Constitution. This indeed proved to be the case, as federalists in Philadelphia and antifederalists further west spent more of their energy ridiculing and shouting down the local opposition than engaging in reasoned discourse.[8]

In the debates of the Pennsylvania convention itself, which were open to the public, the heavily outnumbered antifederalists sought vainly to forestall ratification. They used the by-now-old charge that the new Constitution exceeded the congressional mandate to propose amendments to the Articles and violated the amendment ratification process stipulated in them. James Wilson, Pennsylvania's only delegate to the federal convention who also sat in the state ratifying body, retorted:

> The truth is, that, in our governments, the supreme, absolute, and uncontrollable power *remains* in the people. As our constitutions are superior to our legislatures, so the people are superior to our constitutions. Indeed, the superiority, in this last instance, is much greater; for the people possess over our constitutions control in *act,* as well as right. The consequence is, that the people may change the constitutions whenever and however they please.

As a result, Wilson said, Americans showed the world an unparalleled scene: "a gentle, a peaceful, a voluntary, and a deliberate transition from one constitution of government to another." Elsewhere, revolutions in government were associated with war and calamity, but here they were progressive steps to increase the society's happiness.[9] Wilson's response dodged, as replies to such complaints usually did, the question of how a convention acting under a specific mandate became an agent of the unlimited prerogative of the people. Yet the antifederalists had no intention of challenging the view that ultimate power to define and change constitutions rested with the people. Even less assailable was Wilson's point that peaceful, deliberate reform was preferable to revolution and war.

The antifederalists then raised for the first time an issue that would become the common currency of the state ratification debate: the proposed Constitution's lack of a bill of rights. Wilson responded that "in a government of enumerated power, such a measure would be not only unnecessary, but preposterous and dangerous."[10] He argued that an imperfect enumeration of powers reserved to the people would throw all other powers into the hands of government, a far more dangerous situation. Not even petitions calling for a bill of rights and carrying hundreds of signatures persuaded Wilson and his fellow federalists to shift their views. On December 12, having heard enough objections, they pressed for a ratification vote. The convention debate did not influence one of the forty-six federalist delegates or the twenty-three antifederalists to alter the position on which he was elected. Antifederalists left grumbling about being treated in a heavy-handed fashion and refused the opportunity to offer amendments. Their unhappy supporters in Carlisle broke windows, fought in the streets, and burned James Wilson in effigy in response to the local federalist victory celebration. Meanwhile antifederalist calls for a bill of rights continued unabated.[11]

With five states having endorsed the Constitution, the struggle shifted to Massachusetts where the contest was more even, hard fought, and protracted. As in Pennsylvania, the state generally divided along east versus west, urban versus rural lines. In Massachusetts, however, the lingering discontents of the Shays uprising only two years before both energized the antifederalists and made the federalists more respectful of their opponents. Both sides listened attentively to the frank exchange of views in the state convention. Out of this dialogue came a compromise that contrasted sharply with the Pennsylvania result and made a substantive contribution to the ongoing ratification process.

Elected by town meetings throughout Massachusetts during the previous two months, over 350 delegates assembled in Boston on January 9, 1788, the same day that neighboring Connecticut completed its ratification. From the outset the Massachusetts convention appeared quite evenly divided between supporters and opponents of the proposed Constitution, though each side feared that the other held the balance of power. The better organized federalists were able to gather a slim majority for the selection of officers, establishment of rules, and formation of a committee to review election credentials (which in turn led to a shift of a few seats in the federalists' favor).

A decision to examine the Constitution paragraph by paragraph gave further advantage to the federalist delegates, many of whom were articulate, educated lawyers and businessmen in contrast to the more roughhewn antifederalist farmers.[12]

Able to explain and defend the Constitution skillfully, the federalists nevertheless did not wish to press for a ratification vote they were not sure they could win. The antifederalists likewise remained uncertain of the proper course to take, proposing at one point that the convention adjourn until other states had acted. Instead, the convention continued debating the merits of the Constitution for nearly a month.

The nature of the Massachusetts antifederalist critique was clear. They were indeed "men of little faith" regarding the prospects for a true republic surviving within this new framework of government.[13] The power of the federal government, particularly the Congress, and its freedom from popular control were their greatest concerns. In the convention the antifederalists talked at length about the infrequency of elections. Without annual elections, they worried aloud, representatives might become unresponsive to their constituents; the long terms of senators were even worse. Congressional independence concerned them, especially in light of expanded federal taxation and war powers. They also commented gravely and repeatedly on the proposed Constitution's protection of slavery and, redolent of Massachusetts' past, the lack of a religious test for officeholders.

In the course of the convention, Massachusetts federalist leaders came to realize that the best way to relieve apprehensions and win support for ratification was to propose the addition to the Constitution of specific protections of individual liberties and restraints on government power, a bill of rights. Given their precarious political position, they considered the matter in a much different light than had their Pennsylvania counterparts. The Massachusetts federalists did not wish to make adoption of a bill of rights a condition of ratification or a reason for calling a second federal convention, either of which could delay or destroy the chances for putting the new government into effect. But they did see that a convincing pledge to make creation of a bill of rights a priority of the new government would lay many constitutional anxieties to rest. The clear-cut and not overly onerous amending provision of Article V gave legitimacy to their assertion that adding a bill of rights would be possible, indeed relatively easy, once the new Constitution was ratified.

Federalist leaders shrewdly turned to Governor John Hancock to put such a proposal before the convention. Hancock, by most accounts an ambitious man of no strong views on the Constitution who was most concerned about retaining his statewide popularity and advancing his career, had been chosen chairman of the convention, but, claiming an attack of gout, had stayed away from its sessions. A proposal from Hancock was thought to stand the best chance of gaining antifederalist acceptance. Henry Knox, Nathaniel Gorham, Theophilus Parsons, and Rufus King helped persuade Hancock that the Constitution's ratification depended upon Massachusetts; that Hancock, by proposing that the convention accompany ratification with a set of suggested amendments, could ensure Massachusetts' approval; and that by doing so Hancock would become a leading candidate for vice-president or even, if George Washington declined or Virginia failed to ratify and he could not be chosen, president of the United States. The governor readily accepted the role offered him.[14]

James Bowdoin and Rufus King, earlier in the convention, had spoken favorably of the amending feature of the Constitution as a means to remedy its defects.[15] Shortly before Hancock addressed the delegates, Charles Jarvis and William Heath argued that if the Constitution failed to win approval, all thirteen states would have to agree to form a new convention to draw another instrument that would incorporate the desired changes. On the other hand, if it were ratified, adopting amendments would require the approval of only nine.[16] Hancock then went before the convention to present as his own idea the nine amendments that Parsons and others had prepared. Antifederalists from Samuel Adams to William Widgery responded to Hancock's proposal with praise, although a few doubted whether amendments would be adopted after ratification.[17]

The Massachusetts convention agreed to attach an appeal for consideration of the amendments Hancock advocated to an outright declaration of ratification. The convention then voted 187 to 168 on February 6 to ratify the Constitution. In by far the closest ratification vote thus far, a poll in which the switch of ten favorable ballots would have meant defeat, the federalist argument that a bill of rights could and would be added was pivotal. Nearly as important, the prospect of amendment calmed the fears of a number of antifederalists. He had opposed and fought the Constitution, said one of several who spoke in similar terms before the convention adjourned, but "In the hope that the amendments recommended by his excellency, the president [Hancock], will take place, I shall . . . go home and endeavor to satisfy those that have honored me by their choice, so that we may all live in peace."[18]

In their narrow Massachusetts victory, supporters of the Constitution discovered a weapon that would prove extremely valuable in nearly every battle yet to be fought over ratification. By holding out the prospect of amendments, the federalists found that they could allay fears and win over the undecided. Instead of having to convince skeptics of the absolute superiority of every aspect of their solution to the problems of U.S. government, they merely had to make a strong case for their central principles, argue persuasively that a workable method existed for repairing defects, and exhibit a willingness to consider immediate amendments. In the process, they presented an appealing image of the Constitution as genuinely republican, responsive to popular concerns, and flexible in adjusting the terms of government. As subsequently became apparent, the Massachusetts federalist strategy on amendments proved to be a masterful and decisive stroke in the battle to ratify the Constitution.

The Massachusetts victory, the sixth for the Constitution without a defeat, and the manner in which it had been won concerned antifederalists. "Philadelphiensis," one of the many pseudonymous pamphleteers on both sides of the struggle and in this case an unknown antifederalist, heaped such abuse on Hancock and his amendments as to suggest that they were seen as a serious threat. The amendments would be a "source of mischief," but the writer was confident that the people would not be "so ignorant as to be deceived by so pitiful a manoeuvre." Hancock, Philadelphiensis sneered, hopes to become "the *little king* if not the *big one*," but "knows or ought to know at least, that the liberties of the citizens of America are not to be trifled with: his schemes are too flimsy not to be seen through."[19]

The contest was far from over, as two antifederalist successes promptly demonstrated. When the New Hampshire convention met in Exeter in the middle of February, antifederalists appeared to have a slim but solid majority, and their leader, Joshua Atherton, refused to have anything to do with a Massachusetts-style scheme for ratification with recommendations for amendments. With difficulty, federalists managed to persuade a narrow majority to recess the convention until June. An outright defeat for the Constitution was thereby avoided, but federalists everywhere were shaken and antifederalists given renewed hope.[20] In Rhode Island shortly thereafter, where the idiosyncratic and antifederalist legislature had called for a direct poll on the Constitution in town meetings rather than in a state convention, gatherings boycotted by most federalists recorded a heavy antiratification vote. Rhode Island was expected to be hostile to the Constitution, having resisted strengthening the central government under the Articles of Confederation and having sent no delegates to the Philadelphia convention. However, Rhode Island and New Hampshire together dealt ratification an unwelcome blow.[21]

The next state to debate ratification was Maryland, a state that would find it difficult not to go along with its larger neighbors north and south but also a state that was home to one of the most skeptical Philadelphia convention delegates. Luther Martin, who left Philadelphia before the Constitution was completed and signed, wrote and spoke vigorously against its adoption. He exchanged a series of public letters in the *Maryland Journal* with Connecticut federalist Oliver Ellsworth (writing as "The Landholder"). Ellsworth's contributions were notable for their personal attacks on Martin as a long-winded, ignorant, contradictory, and foolish speaker who "exhausted the politeness of the Convention, which at length prepared to slumber when [Martin] rose to speak."[22] Martin's only slightly more restrained replies focused on his objections to the Constitution. He opposed legitimizing it by less than unanimous state ratification as "directly repugnant to our present articles of confederation," saying that "those who could advocate a contrary proposition ought never to be confided in and entrusted in public life." Furthermore, he declared the need for a complete bill of rights "as a barrier between the general government and the respective states and their citizens, because the more the system advanced the more clearly it appeared to me that the framers of it did not consider that either states or men had any rights at all." Martin, however, perceived little support in Philadelphia for such a bill of rights.[23]

Given Martin's leadership, Maryland antifederalists initially appeared to be a strong political force. In Anne Arundel (Annapolis), Baltimore, and Hartford counties, where Martin and other antifederalist lawyers were candidates for ratification convention delegates, they won majorities at the polls. Elsewhere, however, federalists achieved a landslide. When the ratifying convention met in Annapolis, the confident federalist majority enjoyed complete control. They allowed their opponents to speak at length, sat silently themselves, flatly rejected former governor William Paca's request merely to be allowed to read a list of proposed amendments, and then on April 24 ratified the Constitution by a vote of 63 to 11.

After Maryland's ratification vote was taken, Paca once again spoke, saying that he had voted for the Constitution "under the firm persuasion, and in full confidence that such amendments would be peaceably obtained." The convention, relaxed for the moment, voted overwhelmingly to form a committee with Paca as chair to consider amendments. But while the committee was discussing a substantial list of proposals, most designed to limit federal power over the states and the people, the federalists reconsidered, called the committee back, and discharged it without even permitting a recorded vote on amendments. They then promptly adjourned the convention, leaving an unhappy minority sputtering futilely. Afterward the federalists celebrated their victory by drinking toasts to "speedy ratification by the remaining six [states], without amendment."[24] Evidently they viewed any amendments as undermining the Constitution and saw no need, given their heavy majority, to sanction them.

News of Maryland's decision arrived in Charleston during the meeting of the South Carolina ratification convention. In January antifederalists in the state legislature, after an extended and heated debate over the proposed Constitution's merits, had come within one vote of blocking the convention call, but thereafter their strength faded. Delegate elections gave the federalists a 2-to-1 majority, with tidewater areas favoring and the Piedmont opposing ratification. The news from the Chesapeake weakened what remained of antifederalist resolve; in the convention itself no counterpoint was offered to Charles Pinckney's lengthy defense of the Constitution. After a motion to delay a decision until September was easily turned back, South Carolina ratified on May 23 by a vote of 149 to 73. Unlike their counterparts in Maryland, however, the triumphant federalists sought to conciliate the opposition by agreeing to offer a set of recommendatory amendments on the Massachusetts model.[25]

The suspended New Hampshire convention resumed as scheduled on June 18. Both sides, recognizing that an important victory was within their grasp in February, had canvassed and campaigned across the state. The tide of opinion had definitely turned in the federalists' favor. Conscious that their ratification would put the Constitution into effect, New Hampshire federalists listened to Joshua Atherton's shrill attacks for three days, beat back his attempt to make ratification conditional on the acceptance of amendments, then put the question of unqualified ratification to a vote and prevailed 57 to 47. Having at last achieved success, they carried through on the promise that had been made before the crucial votes and that accounted for their victory. They followed the increasingly common conciliatory practice of submitting a set of recommendations for immediate constitutional amendment to enumerate the rights of citizens and states.[26]

With the action of New Hampshire, nine states had ratified. The Constitution's minimum requirement for being placed in operation had been met. The Confederation was clearly dead, but the new government's viability was far from ensured. Virginia and New York, each crucial to its success, had yet to decide whether or not to ratify. In each state the battle had raged for months between articulate supporters and foes of the proposed plan of government.[27] Alexander Hamilton, John Jay, and James Madison, the authors who as "Publius" wrote the eighty-five essays known as *The Federalist*, hailed from New York and Virginia. So too did some of the most forceful and effective antifederalists such as George Clinton, Patrick Henry, Richard

Henry Lee, and George Mason. Which side would prevail was uncertain. In these climactic struggles, the amendment issue would play its most telling role.

As the ratification debate had progressed from state to state, the federalists enjoyed a considerable advantage in being able to state a positive case, while the antifederalists were forced to rely on negative arguments. The federalists could point to the Constitution as a concrete plan for a workable structure of government to replace the discredited Articles of Confederation. Their opponents, other than offering a shaky defense of the Confederation, were reduced to worrying about a stronger central government and complaining that the Constitution lacked a bill of rights to protect citizens against abusive government. The antifederalist position buckled under the weight of the counterargument, first made in Massachusetts and thereafter embraced in other closely divided conventions, that the best way to correct this problem was to employ the easier amending system offered by the Constitution once it was ratified. Nowhere was this more evident or influential than in Virginia and New York.

Hamilton, in the final *Federalist* essay published in May 1788, only weeks before the Virginia and New York conventions were to meet, devoted his principal attention to the opportunity for amendment of the Constitution. He admitted that the Constitution fell short of absolute perfection and acknowledged the questions of its opponents: "Why should we adopt an imperfect thing? Why not amend it and make it perfect before it is irrevocably established?" Though the questions were plausible, Hamilton wrote, they assumed that the endorsement of recommendatory amendments by state ratifying conventions amounted to a concession that the Constitution was radically defective. On the contrary, he argued, the conventions were affirming that the plan was a good one, "the best that the present views and circumstances of the country will permit," though in the future it might be improved. He regarded it as "the extreme of imprudence to prolong the precarious state of our national affairs, and to expose the Union to the jeopardy of successive experiments, in the chimerical pursuit of a perfect plan."

Hamilton stressed that "it will be far more easy to obtain subsequent than previous amendments to the Constitution." Changes at the moment required state unanimity, but once the Constitution was established, the concurrence of three-fourths of the states would be sufficient. He despaired of preratification amendments that would involve "the necessity of moulding and arranging all the particulars which are to compose the whole, in such a manner as to satisfy all the parties to the compact; and hence, also, an immense multiplication of difficulties and casualties in obtaining the collective assent to a final act." Once the Constitution was established, however, each amendment could be brought forth individually. "There would then be no necessity for management or compromise, in relation to any other point— no giving nor taking. The will of the requisite number would at once bring the matter to a decisive issue. And consequently, whenever . . . ten states were united in the desire of a particular amendment that amendment must infallibly take place." Even if the leaders of the national government were unwilling to yield any portion of their authority, which Hamilton doubted, Article V required the Congress to call a convention for the purpose of proposing amendments whenever two-thirds of the states requested.

Hamilton concluded his appeal for reliance on the possibility of amendment subsequent to the adoption of the Constitution by quoting David Hume's observation that "to balance a large state or society, whether monarchical or republican, on general laws, is a work of so great difficulty, that no human genius, however comprehensive, is able, by the mere dint of reason and reflection, to effect it." Hamilton subscribed to Hume's conclusion that "the judgments of many must unite in the work; experience must guide their labor; time must bring it to perfection, and the feeling of inconveniences must correct the mistakes which they *inevitably* fall into in their first trials and experiments." To Hamilton, establishing the Constitution and anticipating subsequent amendment was the course of moderation, the means for "all sincere lovers of the Union" to avoid the hazards of "anarchy, civil war, a perpetual alienation of the States from each other, and perhaps the military despotism of a victorious demagogue, in the pursuit of what they are not likely to obtain but from time and experience."[28] Whether Virginia or New York delegates were persuaded remained in doubt, however.

When it gathered in Richmond on June 2, the Virginia convention brought some of the Constitution's most ardent advocates face to face with its most articulate critics. James Madison, George Wythe, Edmund Pendleton, and the young John Marshall were among those who sought to defend the Constitution against an onslaught led by Patrick Henry and George Mason. Two of the most influential Virginians sympathetic to the federalist cause, the entirely committed George Washington and the more cautious Thomas Jefferson, were absent. Washington remained at Mount Vernon and Jefferson in Paris as the Confederation's ambassador to about-to-erupt France. Ironically, a future U.S. president, James Monroe, as well as the fathers of two others, Benjamin Harrison and John Tyler, bolstered the antifederalist cause in Richmond. In numbers as well as leadership, the forces arrayed for and against the Constitution were evenly balanced. The result was a full and cogent debate, a monumental three-week verbal struggle to win the allegiance of a few undecided delegates who would tip the balance for or against ratification.[29]

Opposition to ratification in Virginia centered on the Constitution's perceived lack of protection for the state and its citizens. As residents of the largest and wealthiest state, many Virginians naturally worried that the new central government might drain their assets and impose burdens upon them for the benefit of other states. Delegates repeatedly mentioned as troublesome federal power to tax, maintain an army, close the Mississippi to navigation, and interfere with slavery, but they most often expressed concern about the apparent lack of protection for individuals against the power of government. Virginians were mindful of the security their state's bill of rights afforded them and loath to weaken its explicit safeguards of trial by jury, freedom of speech, and other hard-won rights. Patrick Henry did not take long to conclude that his own complex reasons for opposing the Constitution could best be served by focusing his oratorical talent on the absence of a bill of rights and demanding amendments to the instrument before its acceptance.

As the convention began, Governor Edmund Randolph, perceived as an antifederalist stalwart after his refusal to sign the Constitution in Philadelphia the previous September and his lengthy explanation of his objections in a public letter to the speaker of the Virginia House, gave federalists an immediate boost.[30] He announced that the preservation of the Union outweighed his various reservations about the Constitution. "I will assent to the lopping of this limb," he declared with a dramatic flourish of his arm, "before I assent to the dissolution of the Union." At the end of the Philadelphia convention he had felt, Randolph explained, that immediate amendment of the Constitution was necessary. However, alteration of its terms before it was put into effect was no longer possible, he had since concluded. Too much time had passed. To insist now on amendment before ratification would bring "inevitable ruin to the Union." For Randolph, "The Union is the anchor of our political salvation," and its destruction must not be allowed. At the very outset of the convention, therefore, Randolph brought its most contentious issue into sharp focus.[31]

The Virginia convention divided, not over whether to accept the Constitution but over previous or subsequent amendment. Not even Patrick Henry chose to stand on the proposition that the Constitution should be rejected outright. He argued instead for Randolph's October 1787 view that it must be altered prior to ratification to ensure the protection of individual and states' rights. "Previous amendment" became his watchword. Federalists saw previous amendment as a clever device to destroy the Constitution in the course of protracted debates over revisions and, worst possibility of all, a second federal convention. They pointed to the relative ease of change under Article V once the Constitution was in force and called for "subsequent amendment."

Patrick Henry opened his assault on the Constitution by questioning why it should rest its power on "we the people" rather than "we the states," but quickly moved to his main argument. He declared that once the Constitution was ratified, "the way to amendments is, in my conception, shut." He doubted that two-thirds of Congress or state legislatures would willingly surrender power by initiating amendments, and the requirement of ratification by three-fourths of the states meant that a handful of states could block change. If the thirteen states ratified the Constitution, the four smallest, collectively less than 10 percent of the U.S. population, might prevent worthwhile amendment. Such power to obstruct would create "a most fearful situation, when the most contemptible minority can prevent the alteration of the most oppressive government; for it may, in many respects, prove to be such. Is this the spirit of republicanism?"[32]

Having listened to Henry go on at length about tax collections, standing armies, conduct of elections, and civil rights that might be lost to state control in an unamendable Constitution, James Madison stood to make the first of his many responses to Virginia's former governor over the course of the debate. In a voice so soft that the recorder had difficulty hearing it, Madison pointed out that Henry complained of a three-fourths rule for amendment but that the Articles of Confederation he wished to retain demanded state unanimity for reform. "Could any thing in theory be more perniciously improvident and injudicious than this submission of the will of the majority to the most trifling minority?" Madison asked. "Would the honorable gentleman agree to continue the most radical defects in the old system, because the petty state of Rhode Island would not agree to remove them?"[33] Madison shrewdly sought to link Henry with disliked, obstructionist Rhode Island in the delegates' minds while arguing that the Constitution's amending system was preferable to that of the Confederation.

George Nicholas continued the reply to Henry by challenging his argument that Congress would refuse to initiate amendments. Were the power to propose amendments to rest solely with Congress, a problem might arise, Nicholas admitted; however, he pointed out to the delegates, Article V required Congress to call a convention at the request of two-thirds of the states. Indeed it appeared to him that state action promised the fastest route to amendment.[34]

Henry was just beginning his assault. The best way to obtain a constitution to Virginia's liking was to insist on amendments by other states before ratifying: "If disunion will really result from Virginia's proposing amendments, will they not wish the reestablishment of the union and admit us, if not on such terms as we prescribe, yet on advantageous terms? Is not union as essential to their happiness as to ours?"[35] Henry scorned "the absurdity of adopting this system, and relying on the chance of getting it amended afterwards." He then unleashed his oratorical fury:

> Does it not insult your judgments to tell you, Adopt first, and then amend! Is your rage for novelty so great that you are first to sign and seal, and then to retract? Is it possible to conceive a greater solecism? I am at a loss what to say. You agree to bind yourselves hand and foot— for the sake of what? Of being unbound. You go into a dungeon—for what? To get out. Is there no danger, when you go in, that the bolts of federal authority shall shut you in? [36]

Federalist speakers disparaged Henry's demand for previous amendment, seeing in it "infinite dangers" leading to "total disunion."[37] Perhaps the most telling, not to mention calm, response came from the convention's chairman, Edmund Pendleton.

> When I sat down to read that paper, I did not read it with an expectation that it was perfect, and that no man would object to it. I had learned, sir, that an expectation of such perfection in any institute devised by *man,* was as vain as the search for the philosopher's stone. I discovered objections—I thought I saw there some sown seeds of disunion—not in the immediate operation of the government but which *might* happen in some future time. I wish amendments to remove these. But these remote possible errors may be eradicated by the amendatory clause in the Constitution. I see no danger in making the experiment, since the system itself points out an easy mode of removing any errors which shall have been experienced. . . . By previous amendments, we present a hostile countenance. If, on the contrary, we imitate the conduct of those states, our language will be conciliatory and friendly. Gentlemen, we put ourselves on the same ground that you are on.[38]

Henry fought back with an appeal to Virginia loyalism. The state's "weight and importance" will have "powerful influence," and its insistence will produce amendments, he argued. "Shall we forsake that importance and respectability that our station in America commands, in hopes that relief will come from an obscure part of the Union?"[39] He refused to abandon the view that the best, indeed perhaps the only, time that Virginia could press its case for amendments was while it retained the bargaining power of withheld ratification. Throughout the three-week section-by-section review of the Constitution, he continued to press this view with fervor and eloquence.

On June 24, George Wythe, who had chaired the committee of the whole in which the discussion had been carried out but who had himself remained silent, moved that Virginia ratify the Constitution without qualification. Highly respected as a jurist and as a Virginia delegate to Philadelphia in both 1776 and 1787, Wythe commanded the attention of his fellow delegates. His observation that "any amendments which might be thought necessary would be easily obtained *after ratification* in the manner proposed by the Constitution" no doubt carried weight. Yet what may have been most influential was the olive branch Wythe then extended to uncertain, wavering delegates. Pointing out that other states desired amendments and several had already suggested them, Wythe proposed that before dissolving, the Virginia convention could recommend amendments to the first Congress to assemble under the Constitution. The federalists had obviously discussed this offer in advance and responded to the suspicions of their opponents by pledging to remain in session to prepare amendment recommendations.[40]

Patrick Henry declared the proposal "an idea dreadful to me" and suggested that Wythe only meant to amuse the convention. "Evils admitted in order to be removed subsequently, and tyranny submitted to in order to be excluded by a subsequent alteration, are things totally new to me," he exclaimed. His last long appeal for previous amendment contained his prediction that to proceed otherwise invited civil discord.[41]

The amendment question consumed the final debates of the Virginia convention. Everything revolved around whether the amending system could and would work to produce the changes that some delegates thought essential and even James Madison, the strongest of federalists, now conceded as unobjectionable. Madison drew the line at Henry's previous amendments that he characterized as "pregnant with dreadful dangers." James Monroe responded with the prediction that if the Constitution was adopted unconditionally, "it will never be amended, not even when experience shall have proven its defects." Attorney General James Innes argued that the convention had been given only the power to vote yes or no, not to make alterations that might "radically change the paper on the table." Subsequent amendments, by contrast, could be considered by the people, Innes pointed out. Henry replied one more time, saying subsequent amendment talk was not serious. "If they are serious, why do they not join us, and ask, in a manly, firm, and resolute manner, for these amendments? Their view is to defeat every attempt to amend."[42]

Confidence in the possibility of amendment under the Constitution proved just strong enough in the Virginia convention to carry ratification. On June 25, the convention voted first on Patrick Henry's resolution to ratify with previous amendments. The motion failed 88 to 80. A shift of five votes would have given Henry his victory and thrown the Constitution into limbo. Without further debate, George Wythe's resolution for unqualified ratification was put to a vote; it carried 89 to 79. Immediately, the victorious side honored its pledge by appointing a committee to draft recommendations for amendments. When the committee returned two days later with a twenty-part bill of rights and a list of twenty-one other proposed amendments, the convention promptly agreed to everything but one of the amendments before it adjourned.[43] In one of the closest and most critical ratification decisions, delegates who elected to place their faith in the likelihood of constitutional amendment determined Virginia's choice.

Debate had been under way for more than two weeks at the courthouse in Poughkeepsie, New York, when news arrived on July 2 of Virginia's ratification. To that point, the New York convention appeared solidly opposed to ratification. Its sixty-five delegates had been chosen in May in an election in which "all free male citizens of the age of twenty-one years, and upwards" were eligible to vote, making it the most broadly representative of any state ratifying body. Observers calculated the upstate-based antifederalist majority at twice the size of the New York City, Long Island, and Westchester County–based federalist delegation. Yet as elsewhere, many antifederalists were far less than dead set against the Constitution; they merely wished to have their concerns addressed. In New York as in Virginia, the antifederalists were deeply suspicious of the federalists and doubted that their political rivals could be trusted to agree to amendments once the Constitution was adopted. Consequently, they too felt more comfortable with amendment prior to ratification.[44]

When the New York convention began on June 17, the antifederalist majority might have sought a quick vote to reject ratification and brought the proceedings to a prompt conclusion. Instead they indicated their willingness to consider the Constitution at length. The first of their leaders to speak, John Lansing, had been one of New York's delegates to the federal convention. He had been so unhappy with the emerging document that, together with his colleague Robert Yates, he left Philadelphia in the middle of the deliberations. Lansing now declared that he wished to preserve the Union but not at the price of lost civil liberty. He and his constituents were apprehensive about a central government failing to preserve the people's essential rights and liberties. Nevertheless, he did not reject the Constitution outright.

Instead Lansing invited accommodation by announcing that "every amendment which I am convinced will have the tendency to lessen the danger of
invasion of civil liberty by the central government will receive my sincere approbation." Melancton Smith, another antifederalist leader, followed by asserting that he was "disposed to make every reasonable concession and,
indeed, to sacrifice every thing for a union, except the liberties of his country, than which he could contemplate no greater misfortune." Smith said
that he hoped the convention would not be "reduced to the necessity of sacrificing, or even endangering our liberties, to preserve the Union."[45] These
were remarkably conciliatory statements from men apparently in control of
the convention. The New York antifederalists have been characterized as
confused and disorganized to the point of letting their chance to reject the
Constitution slip away. Yet a good many of them ought to be understood as
persons willing to accept the Constitution if persuaded that it could be
amended to deal with matters they considered vital.[46]

The Poughkeepsie convention plunged immediately into an intense para-
graph-by-paragraph discussion of the Constitution. Debate continued until
June 24 when word arrived that New Hampshire had become the ninth
state to ratify. Federalist leader Robert Livingston, the state chancellor, declared that the news made it evident that "the circumstances of the country
were greatly altered, and the ground of the present debate changed." The
Confederation had been dissolved; it no longer offered an alternative to the
Constitution. Melancton Smith replied, however, that the report from New
Hampshire "had not altered his feelings or wishes." John Lansing agreed,
adding, "It is still our duty to maintain our rights."[47] The delegates continued their detailed examination of the Constitution's provisions.

A week later news of Virginia's ratification had a far greater effect on the
delegates. New York antifederalists had anticipated that their Virginia counterparts would be able to insist on previous amendment as their price for
ratification. The news from Richmond forced them to reevaluate their own
position. Likewise, federalists were compelled to consider the bargain that
Madison and his colleagues struck to support recommendatory amendments. In Poughkeepsie intense negotiation began.[48] With Virginia included,
the new Union was much more substantial; the prospect of New York remaining outside the Union, with only Rhode Island and North Carolina for
company, was correspondingly less palatable.

New York antifederalist forces still hoped to compel amendment previous
to ratification. They continued, as they had done throughout the convention,
to propose specific revisions to almost every section of the Constitution. On
July 10, Lansing signaled antifederalist willingness to reduce their demands.

He proposed that the amendments be divided into categories: explanatory, conditional, and recommendatory. Only the second category, the most important, would be qualifications of New York's ratification. The following day John Jay offered the federalist counterproposal that the Constitution be ratified and all amendments be recommendatory. Four days later Melancton Smith proposed a further concession by which New York would ratify on condition that a long list of restrictions on federal power in the state would apply until a convention was called for proposing amendments. This marked a significant antifederalist compromise for it did not require acceptance of amendments but only their formal consideration as the price of ratification. As such, it demonstrated a growing acceptance of the view that, once the new Constitution began to function, amendment was a realistic possibility. On July 19 Lansing refined the offer, suggesting conditional ratification with a bill of rights and other amendments attached.[49]

On July 23 federalists moved, much like their Virginia counterparts, to thwart demands for previous or conditional amendment by pledging support for postratification amendment. They proposed that the ratification resolution be changed from "on condition" of amendment to "in full confidence" thereof. This critical change in language was approved by the slender margin of 31 to 29. Nevertheless, support for this expression of good faith held firm. The delegates rejected Lansing's subsequent motion that the state reserve the right to withdraw from the Union after a certain number of years unless the proposed amendments had been submitted to a general convention. At the same time, they reaffirmed that they were serious about pursuing amendments by authorizing Governor George Clinton to send a circular letter to the governors of other states urging support for such a general convention.[50]

The New York convention then approved the ratification resolution by a vote of 30 to 27. The delegates, who had seemed so decidedly opposed to the Constitution five weeks earlier, now endorsed it, if only by a narrow margin, without qualifications.[51] Their acceptance of the Constitution with a promised but uncertain set of amendments seems convincing proof that the so-called antifederalists were less than adamant foes of the proposed instrument. Their concerns about government power put them at odds with the federalists, but their disagreements did not mean that they were intransigent opponents. Their conversion to amendment subsequent to ratification represented the crucial element in the transformation of the New York antifederalists. It also serves as a key to understanding their essential nature. Doubtless influenced by the ratifications of ten other states and especially by that of Virginia, the shift reflected their conclusion that the Constitution's amending system could and would work.

Almost immediately, North Carolina provided a reminder of just how uncertain the process of ratification had been and even yet remained. When more than 260 North Carolina delegates convened in Hillsborough on July 21, they knew that at least ten states had approved the Constitution and that it would be going into operation. Nevertheless, opposition to the federal charter ran so high among the delegates that a move to reject ratification at once almost succeeded.[52] Instead, the convention proceeded with the customary clause-by-clause discussion of the Constitution and heard many of the standard concerns expressed about the dangers of central power.

The principal defenders of the Constitution in the North Carolina convention were Governor Samuel Johnston and former state attorney general James Iredell. Among Iredell's many explanations and defenses, perhaps none was more forceful than his effort to persuade the convention that by means of Article V flaws could be corrected without undue difficulty. "The misfortune attending most constitutions which have been deliberately formed," he asserted, "has been that those who formed them thought their wisdom equal to all possible contingencies, and that there could be no error in what they did." The men of Philadelphia were more modest, and through Article V, "one of the greatest beauties of the system," spared citizens the choice of submitting to oppression or resorting to civil war to achieve change. Iredell proclaimed,

> Happy this, the country we live in! The Constitution before us, if it be adopted, can be altered with as much regularity, and as little confusion, as any act of Assembly; not, indeed, quite so easily, which would be extremely impolitic; but it is a most happy circumstance, that there is a remedy in the system itself for its own fallibility, so that alterations can without difficulty be made, agreeable to the general sense of the people.[53]

Neither Iredell's arguments nor the example of ten other states (New York's ratification remained unknown in Hillsborough throughout the proceedings) proved persuasive to North Carolinians. Delegate after delegate expressed a preference for a second federal constitutional convention and amendment previous to ratification as the means of ensuring that their concerns would be met. They were unmoved by the argument of Richard Dobbs Spaight, one of North Carolina's representatives in Philadelphia the year before, that unless they ratified, "we are not more a part of the Union than any foreign power." By not ratifying, he said, North Carolina would throw away its opportunity to propose amendments and its weight in bringing them about. The convention turned aside Iredell's efforts to gain ratification with recommendatory amendments on the Virginia model and voted overwhelmingly, 184 to 84, not to ratify for the moment. Instead, a list of desired constitutional changes—a twenty-part declaration of rights and two dozen other amendments—would be placed before the new Congress. North Carolina would not rest its faith on the amending system as others had done but would wait to see whether indeed it worked.[54]

On the discordant note of North Carolina's rejection, the ten-month process of obtaining sufficient state ratifications to put the 1787 U.S. Constitution into operation came to an end. Some antifederalists, encouraged by New York governor George Clinton's circular letter calling for a second convention to consider amendments, held out hope throughout the autumn that immediate implementation of the Constitution could still be blocked. Such expectations proved fleeting, however.[55] The organizing of the new government proceeded. At least for the time being, it lacked the adherence of North Carolina and the even more leery Rhode Island. Whether the two states' hesitation was warranted or whether the greater confidence that the other eleven states placed in the Constitution was justified remained, for the moment, uncertain. That would not be determined until the new government began to function. Yet what was already clear was how ratification had come about.

At several crucial junctures in the struggle over ratification, most notably in the Massachusetts, Virginia, and New York conventions, the promise of amendment swung the balance in favor of acceptance. Given the previous experience of these states with efforts to achieve fundamental reform under the Articles of Confederation, their willingness to adopt the Constitution based on an unsecured pledge of immediate amendment is most significant. The presumption in these and other state conventions that an amendment process would go ahead promptly and smoothly reflects a level of optimism and good faith on the part of the antifederalists all too often overlooked. Confidence in the efficacy of Article V overcame demands for previous amendment or a second federal convention prior to ratification. Amendability, not any specific amendment, was the bedrock antifederalist concern. The presence of Article V helped reconcile most antifederalists to the new Constitution. After the strenuous objections and dire predictions voiced in the ratification debates, the lengthy persistence of vocal opposition might easily be assumed. In fact the months thereafter produced little of the sort.

As Gordon Wood has amply demonstrated, in the course of their revolutionary struggle Americans had accepted and institutionalized the concept that government rested on the sovereignty of the people. The process by which the new Constitution was adopted, as well as the provisions made in Article V for its further refinement, embodied this ideal. Allowing a return to the people for alteration of the terms of government and the healing of any ills of government represented the essence of republicanism.[56] Benjamin Franklin observed upon leaving the Philadelphia convention that what had been created there was "a republic, if you can keep it." The venerable Franklin's often-quoted remark exemplified not only the enthusiasm of the age for republican government but also the sense that its upkeep required constant vigilance and refinement. The manner in which the Constitution was ratified suggests that politically aware Americans of the late 1780s possessed a strong faith in constitutionalism and its amending corollary as the means to preserve republican government.

5

"THE MOST SATISFACTORY PROVISIONS FOR ALL ESSENTIAL RIGHTS"

Immediate Amendment as the Constitution's Price and Proof

Soon after the Constitution had been ratified but while skepticism about it still ran high, the process prescribed in Article V was used to add ten amendments to the original instrument. These ten closely related provisions established a bill of rights. Several states had made it clear in their ratification actions that they would not fully embrace the new Constitution unless such a bill of rights was attached to it. Without immediate amendment, the Constitution faced the prospect of being stillborn. The fledgling government quickly avoided such a fruitless outcome, however. James Madison initiated a package of amendments, based on proposals made in the course of the state ratification debates, in the House of Representatives in June 1789. Twelve won approval from Congress in September, and ten were ratified by December 1791. Not only did the first use of the amending system relieve many of the specific apprehensions surrounding the Constitution, but also it demonstrated that a workable method did in fact exist for making significant changes in the republic's fundamental law. Altered preferences and circumstances in the future could be dealt with in such a way as to keep the republic flourishing.

The state ratification conventions gave evidence that the 1787 Constitution probably would not have been ratified without its explicit provision for amendment. Even with the Constitution's adoption, the chances seem slight that it would have obtained a broad basis of public support without the immediate addition of a bill of rights. The extraordinary speed with which the Constitution gained wide backing was no doubt due to a variety of factors, including disenchantment with the Articles of Confederation and esteem for the new government's first head, President George Washington. Moreover, confidence built on the knowledge that a system existed for remedying errors and the experience of it having worked quickly and well certainly played an important role in the rapid and widespread acceptance of the Constitution by the American people following its more tentative and narrow ratification by their state conventions.

A concern for workable amendment procedures had accompanied the rapid emergence of written constitutionalism in the late eighteenth century.

Americans regarded constitutional change as more consequential than ordinary lawmaking and remained unwilling to leave it in the hands of mere parliamentary majorities, as did the British. In a number of early state constitutions as well as in the Articles of Confederation, Americans sought to create a satisfactory amending process. All provided stability but, at least in the case of the Articles, achieved it at a high cost in inflexibility. The 1787 Constitution attempted to strike a new balance. Yet it remained to be seen whether the new method would prove more satisfactory.

The adoption of the Bill of Rights represented the first successful amending of a written constitution. Indeed the process by which the Bill of Rights was added to the Constitution was arguably more innovative than its substance. Although it did not provoke a great deal of comment at the time and generated remarkably few records of state participation in the process, the method by which the Congress and state legislatures acted in concert to install the Bill of Rights in the Constitution was notable. The comparative ease of the amending system's operation reinforced the perception that, at last, satisfactory arrangements had been made for defining, empowering, and controlling republican government.

THE ENGLISH TRADITION of declarations of individual rights that governments were bound to respect originated in the Magna Carta nearly six centuries before the articulation of the U.S. Bill of Rights. It reached its fullest expression during the seventeenth century, in the parliamentary Petition of Right of 1628 and the Bill of Rights of 1689. From before the time of Magna Carta, the English had voiced concerns about the rights of individuals confronting the judicial power of the state to freedom from self-incrimination as well as to habeas corpus, reasonable bail, trial by jury, and the right to counsel. By 1689, English declarations of rights included protections of due process of law, freedom from excessive bail or fines and infliction of cruel or unusual punishment, protection against quartering of troops, and freedoms of the press, the bearing of arms, and, to a limited degree, religious practice.[1]

A number of colonial American charters echoed English statements of individual rights, notably the 1641 Massachusetts Body of Liberties, the 1676 West New Jersey Fundamental Laws, the 1683 Pennsylvania Frame of Government, and the 1701 Pennsylvania Charter of Privileges. When the newly convened Continental Congress chose in October 1774 to set forth a declaration of rights to which free men were entitled, it experienced little difficulty doing so. The delegates readily agreed that colonists had not forfeited by emigration any of the "rights, liberties, and immunities of free and natural born subjects, within the realm of England," that none should be deprived of life, liberty, or property without consent or due legal process, and that all retained the right of assembly, petition, and trial by jury.[2]

As the breech with Great Britain widened, colonial assemblies as well as the Continental Congress devoted considerable attention to the articulation of the rights of citizens. The Virginia Declaration of Rights of 1776, the most comprehensive statement of the revolutionary era's viewpoint on individual rights that needed to be guaranteed against government infringement, is justifiably famous for its clarity and the eminence of its architects, who included Patrick Henry, Edmund Randolph, James Madison, and, foremost, George Mason. Other states, in formulating their initial governments, itemized protected rights as well.[3] These lists were not standardized, in fact far from it. Some were incorporated into the state constitution; others stood separate. More important, their contents varied. In the twelve state bills of rights framed before 1788 (including Vermont and excepting Rhode Island and Connecticut), as Leonard Levy has pointed out,

> the only right universally secured was trial by jury in criminal cases, unless freedom of religion be added to the list even though some states guaranteed only religious toleration and others, no less than five, constitutionally permitted or provided for an establishment of religion in the form of tax supports for churches. Two states passed over a free press guarantee. Four neglected to ban excessive fines, excessive bail, compulsory self-incrimination, and general search warrants. Five ignored protections for the rights of assembly, petition, counsel, and trial by jury in civil cases. Seven omitted a prohibition on ex post facto laws, and eight skipped over the vital writ of habeas corpus. Nine failed to provide for grand jury proceedings and to condemn bills of attainder. Ten said nothing about freedom of speech while eleven—all but New Hampshire— were silent on the matter of double jeopardy.[4]

Nevertheless, by the 1770s, the American vision of the rights that should be secured had expanded to include rights of free assembly, speech, press, and religion as well as judicial process. Levy concluded, correctly, that "for all their faults, the state bills of rights adopted before the federal Bill of Rights were achievements of the first magnitude compared to anything in the past, on either side of the Atlantic."[5]

The Articles of Confederation did not contain a bill of rights. The delegates who gathered in Philadelphia during summer 1787 to revise or replace it as the framework of U.S. government did not regard the omission as among its defects. State constitutions, not the federal charter, were thought to be the place for declarations of individual rights since it was state government that dealt directly with the people. Only a few delegates, those most worried that a strong central government would reduce or eliminate the role of the states, believed that explicit statements of citizens' rights should be included in the Constitution. George Mason of Virginia stirred little response with his expressions of concern for a stipulation of rights.[6] Most delegates agreed with Rufus King of Massachusetts that no federal declaration of rights was necessary "as the fundamental rights of individuals are secured by express provisions in the State Constitutions."[7]

Only during the final days of the Philadelphia convention did the subject of a federal bill of rights arise. A few specific provisions regarding individual rights had earlier found their way into the Constitution. They included prohibitions on bills of attainder and ex post facto laws, guarantees of habeas corpus and trial by jury in criminal cases, and a ban of religious tests for officeholding. No general enumeration of rights had been discussed, however. On September 12, five days before the convention adjourned, Mason, the principal architect of Virginia's 1776 Declaration of Rights and one of the delegates most skeptical about the emerging plan, began arguing strenuously that a bill of rights was needed to check the potentially excessive power of the new federal government.[8] Elbridge Gerry quickly rose to support Mason's proposal that a committee be formed to prepare a bill of rights. After Roger Sherman reiterated the contention that a federal bill of rights was unnecessary, the convention rejected the Mason-Gerry proposal.

As a final effort, George Mason tried piecemeal insertion of statements of various rights into the Constitution. A few delegates supported him, but the effort failed. As the convention prepared to adjourn, Elbridge Gerry said he could overlook the Constitution's other defects, "if the rights of the Citizens were not rendered insecure."[9] Gerry, however, along with Mason and Edmund Randolph, decided he could not sign the Constitution as it stood. "Col. Mason left Philada. in an exceeding ill humour indeed," James Madison reported to Thomas Jefferson in Paris. "He returned to Virginia with a fixed disposition to prevent the adoption of the plan if possible. He considers the want of a Bill of Rights as a fatal objection."[10]

Upon adjournment of the Philadelphia convention, Mason wrote a fierce critique of the proposed Constitution. He began listing his "Objections to the Proposed Federal Constitution" with a ringing statement:

> There is no declaration of rights, and the laws of the general government being paramount to the laws and constitution of the several states, the

declarations of rights in the separate states are no security. Nor are the people secured even in the enjoyment of the benefits of the common law, which stands here upon no other foundation than its having been adopted by the respective acts forming the constitutions of the several states.[11]

Mason's "Objections" gained wide circulation. His lament that the Constitution lacked a declaration of rights quickly became the centerpiece of the antifederalist position. Robert Rutland, Mason's biographer and a careful student of the ratification battle, after pondering the question of whether the issue was a specious one raised simply to prevent the Constitution's ratification, ultimately rejected such a view and concluded that the omission of a bill of rights was the principal objection to the Constitution for many antifederalists.[12]

As soon as the Philadelphia convention transmitted the Constitution to the Continental Congress in New York, Mason's friend and fellow Virginian, Richard Henry Lee, took up the fight. Lee initially asked Congress to reject the Constitution as having exceeded the convention's mandate. He then proposed numerous amendments, first and foremost a bill of rights, before Congress sent the Constitution to the states for ratification. He wanted guarantees of freedom of religion and the press, trial by jury in civil as well as criminal cases, the right of assembly and petition, free and frequent elections, and an independent judiciary. He also sought bans on standing armies in peacetime, excessive bail or fines, and unreasonable government search and seizure of persons and property. The Congress, eager to pass responsibility for the fate of the Constitution along to the states, rejected Lee's amendments, but the issues he raised were far from dead. Although, like Mason, Lee enjoyed little support in the body in which he sat, he found much more backing for his position in his home state and elsewhere.[13]

The missing bill of rights drew more and more attention as the ratification debate moved to the states. The Delaware, New Jersey, and Georgia conventions said little or nothing on the subject as they rushed to ratify.[14] However, the issue soon came to the fore in Pennsylvania. James Wilson attempted to head off criticism regarding a bill of rights by observing that "such an idea never entered the mind of many" of the federal delegates. He could not remember it being mentioned until "within about three days of the time of our rising." More important, to Wilson a constitution of enumerated powers needed no bill of rights. Indeed it would be imprudent to include one since it would imply that all unenumerated powers had been left to the government.[15] After Wilson spoke, nothing swayed the Pennsylvania delegates from rapid, unconditional ratification.[16] Federalist leaders and Philadelphia delegates Oliver Ellsworth and Roger Sherman then used

sharper language but similar arguments with success in the Connecticut ratifying convention.[17]

The absence of a bill of rights was an objection to ratification seriously
raised and heeded in the evenly divided Massachusetts convention. The solution to the dilemma, John Hancock's recommendatory amendments, began
with a functional equivalent of a bill of rights, an explicit declaration that all
powers not expressly delegated by the Constitution were reserved to the
states. Samuel Adams declared that this first provision "appears, to my mind,
to be a summary of a bill of rights, which gentlemen are anxious to obtain. It
removes a doubt which many have entertained respecting the matter."[18]

The Massachusetts action altered Thomas Jefferson's thinking on the
Constitution. Earlier, he had much admired the form of the proposed government but was deeply concerned about its omission of a bill of rights.
From Paris he had written insistently to Madison that "a bill of rights is
what the people are entitled to against every government on earth, general
or particular, & what no just government should refuse or rest on infer-
ence."[19] Jefferson had suggested that nine states ratify and four states withhold ratification until changes were made by the first nine, using the easier
amendment system that Article V of the Constitution provided. After the
Massachusetts convention, however, he perceived improved prospects for
obtaining a bill of rights under the new government. His letters began to
support ratification wholeheartedly.[20]

The bill of rights question remained a centerpiece of later convention
debates. Now, however, the Massachusetts model existed for the accommodation of differences. In Maryland, federalists, with an overwhelming convention majority, saw no need to satisfy efforts to obtain amendments, the
most notable of which was an express limitation on congressional power in
order to protect state bills of rights.[21] As in Pennsylvania, their neighbor to
the north, Maryland antifederalists continued grumbling about the failure to
protect individual rights.[22] Elsewhere, where antifederalist delegates were
more numerous than in Maryland and at least as vocal on the absence of a
bill of rights, various recommendatory amendments were endorsed after the
Constitution had been ratified. South Carolina requested a constitutional expression that states retained all rights not explicitly relinquished to the federal government. New Hampshire appropriated the Massachusetts
proposals word for word, supplemented them with other appeals, and ex-
horted the state's representatives in Congress "until the alterations and provisions aforesaid have been considered agreeably to the fifth article of the
said Constitution, to exert all their influence, and use all reasonable and
legal methods, to obtain a ratification of the said alterations."[23] In Virginia

and New York as well, proponents of the Constitution also perceived that agreeing to recommend the addition of a bill of rights offered them the best chance of victory.

Two messages emerged from the ratification conventions that put the Constitution into effect by summer 1788. First, the promise of a bill of rights had secured the margin of victory in several critical states, among them Massachusetts, New York, and Virginia. Conceptions varied as to what a bill of rights should include, but the principle that the Constitution should contain an explicit statement of individual rights enjoyed wide support. Second, many people, perhaps a majority in a number of states, remained unpersuaded of the virtues of the new government. From South Carolina to New Hampshire, in states as large as Pennsylvania, Massachusetts, New York, and Virginia and as small as Maryland, substantial opposition remained. And of course, North Carolina and Rhode Island remained outside the new Union, unwilling to join without explicit guarantees of citizens' and states' rights.

The breadth of support for a bill of rights was evident; the uncertainty centered on whether the amending process of the new Constitution could function to implement one. Would leaders of the new government feel any obligation to pursue the matter since ratification of the Constitution had been achieved? Could critics who had talked about a bill of rights but wished to bring about more extensive alterations in the Constitution obstruct amendment that provided less change than they sought? Would the individuals who remained unconvinced of the need for a bill of rights undermine amending efforts? What would happen if the congressional and state supermajorities required for amendment turned out to be as unachievable as the higher standards that rendered the Articles of Confederation unworkable? In 1788 no one knew the answers to such questions.

As THE NEWBORN U.S. government began functioning in spring 1789, no American felt the need to add a bill of rights to the Constitution more strongly than James Madison. This short, intense, thirty-eight-year-old Virginian had worked as hard as any delegate to Philadelphia two summers earlier to create the Constitution and bore heavy burdens in the uphill ratification struggle in his home state the following year. He was utterly committed on both an intellectual and emotional level to seeing the new government succeed. In his initial conception of the federal Constitution, Madison had discerned no need for a bill of rights. Still, he paid close attention to each of the state ratification debates and was sensitive to their recur-

ring messages. His own constituents pushed him hardest to become a determined, indeed driven advocate of amendment, a relentless, undeflectable
force committed to using Article V to implement a bill of rights.[24] It is hard
to imagine the constitutional amending process moving forward so rapidly
without Madison or someone of equivalent stature (and such persons were
rare) at its head.[25]

The close contest in the June 1788 Virginia ratifying convention drove
Madison to revise his previous position concerning a federal bill of rights. As
Patrick Henry and George Mason rained criticism on the Constitution for its
failure to guarantee individual rights, Madison softened his contrary view
that federal protection was unnecessary. He made clear his belief that
Henry's insistence on amendment prior to ratification displayed neither
"confidence nor respect" for the states that had already, after free and full
consideration, ratified. Madison remained wary of attempts to enumerate
rights reserved to the people because an incomplete listing would grant increased power to the central government; also he considered some of Henry's
proposals "palpably and insuperably objectionable." Yet in his final words
to the convention, Madison endorsed the Massachusetts compromise approach of ratification with recommendations for amendment: "As far as his
amendments are not objectionable, or unsafe, so far they may be subsequently recommended—not because they are necessary, but because they can
produce no possible danger, and may gratify some gentlemen's wishes."[26] On
this basis, to Madison's great relief, the convention agreed to ratify. As its
final act, it drew up a twenty-item bill of rights based on the 1776 Virginia
Declaration as well as twenty other proposed alterations to the Constitution
for consideration by the first Congress.

Four months later, in mid-October 1788, Madison still did not see the
issue of a bill of rights as vital. Aware of Jefferson's concern for one, Madison wrote to his friend in Paris that although he personally had "always
been in favor of a bill of rights; provided it be so framed as not to imply
powers not meant to be included," he had never thought the omission of a
bill of rights from the Constitution "a material defect." He confessed he was
not "anxious to supply it even by subsequent amendment, for any other reason than that it is anxiously desired by others." He feared that a formal declaration of the most essential rights might lead to their being narrowed,
expressing particular concern about rights of conscience or religious belief.
State bills of rights had proven nothing more than "parchment barriers" unable to restrain the power of "overbearing majorities." The most that might
be gained from a federal bill of rights would be a check on "the impulses of
interest and passion" and a basis for appealing arbitrary acts of government

"to the sense of the community."[27] An encounter with Virginia voters soon changed his sense of priorities.

James Madison very nearly missed a chance to help breathe life into the structure of government he had toiled so hard to create. A resentful Patrick Henry maneuvered in the Virginia assembly to deny Madison one of the state's seats in the U.S. Senate. Then Madison's home county was gerrymandered into a heavily antifederalist congressional district to undermine his chances of being elected to the House of Representatives. In the winter of 1788–1789 when he came home to seek votes against his formidable antifederalist opponent James Monroe, Madison discovered that the greatest concern among voters was the protection of their rights under the new government. Rumors were circulating, fanned by Henry, that Madison saw no need for a single amendment to the Constitution. He found it necessary to go on record, in a widely circulated letter, that "it is my sincere opinion that the Constitution ought to be revised, and that the first Congress meeting under it, ought to prepare and recommend to the States for ratification, the most satisfactory provisions for all essential rights, particularly the rights of Conscience in the fullest latitude, the freedom of the press, trials by jury, security against general warrants &c."[28] This public pledge apparently won over influential Baptist leaders, among others, and accounted for Madison's narrow victory. Having so declared himself, the dedicated republican clearly felt obligated to pursue this goal when he went to New York to take his seat in the first Congress.[29]

When the House of Representatives convened on April 1, 1789, it faced a heavy agenda, headed, in many members' minds, by the need to settle the new government's finances. Despite the heated demands and earnest pledges of the previous year, amendment did not appear a priority to most members of the first Congress. Federalists seemed preoccupied with putting the new government in operation. Meanwhile, the staunchest antifederalists still clung to the notion that a second constitutional convention ought to be called to alter the instrument's terms. Despite the failure of most states to respond to New York governor George Clinton's appeal for a second convention, its endorsement by the Patrick Henry–led Virginia House of Delegates kept its backers' hopes afloat.

President George Washington in his inaugural address at the end of April made only vague and cautious references to amendments. He placed responsibility squarely on Congress, warning against radical changes that might weaken federal powers. Washington encouraged Congress to deliberate on how personal rights could be "impregnably fortified" and public harmony "safely and advantageously promoted," while at the same time "united and

effective" government was maintained.[30] The initiative clearly would not
come from the president.

Against this background, James Madison on May 4 announced to the
House his intention to bring up the subject of amendments in three weeks.
Madison no doubt wanted to counter any public impression that Congress
had forgotten the matter.[31] However, he may well have also had a more concrete objective in mind. Since Article V provided two means of initiating
amendments, Congress needed to take action to undercut the persistent demands for a second constitutional convention. Indeed the very next day,
Representative Theodorick Bland presented to the House the Virginia state
assembly's resolution asking Congress to call a convention for the purpose
of revising and amending the Constitution.

Congressman Bland asked that Virginia's request be referred to a committee of the whole House for consideration at the same time as Madison's
promised amendments. He sought to place Virginia's antifederalist amendment proposals on an equal footing with their rivals. He also may have
wished to entice Congress with the option of turning the drawing of amendments over to a convention rather than dealing with the issue itself. Bland's
ploy encountered opposition from New Jersey representative Elias Boudinot
and from Madison, who argued for tabling the Virginia application. Under
Article V, they contended, Congress had no power to debate such state applications: it must call a convention upon receipt of requests from two-thirds
of the states but had no option to do so in the face of fewer petitions. After
further debate, Virginia's application was entered on the House journal and
filed with the clerk.[32]

This very first congressional discussion of amendment established an important procedural precedent. State requests for constitutional revision conventions would not be considered matters that required congressional action
unless two-thirds of the states made the appeal. Congress could choose to
consider amendments on the initiative of its own members, but states could
not compel Congress to discuss amendments, much less act, unless they mo-
bilized the full two-thirds of their number required by Article V to force a
convention. The significance of this determination was easily overlooked at
the moment since it was clear that Congress would not ignore the issue but
would soon take up amendments. Thereafter, the balance of power in shaping the substance of amendments to be submitted for ratification would rest
with the Congress far more than with the states.

Five weeks later, after one postponement, Madison, "bound in honor
and duty to do [so]," sought House consideration of amendments he had
drafted.[33] In response, several representatives claimed that, though most

were sympathetic to amendment, other matters, especially finances, were more pressing. Discussion of amendments would require a great deal of time; the issue should be put off until they had launched the new government and gained experience with its operation. One proponent of delay, Congressman John Vining of Delaware, suggested that Article V required two-thirds of Congress to consent before amendment proposals could even be taken up.[34] For the first time, but definitely not the last, the view was put forth that addressing issues of constitutional reform would consume endless hours, hours that could not be spared from the more important consideration of immediate and pressing problems. Given the amount of energy devoted to constitutional discussion during the previous two years and repeated assertions throughout that establishing sound fundamental principles was vital, this seems a remarkable argument. Nevertheless it reflected the uncertainties of the moment regarding the difficulty of amendment.

Madison responded to his wary colleagues that further delay would suggest indifference to their constituents' wishes and incite public suspicion. "They may think we are not sincere in our desire to incorporate such amendments in the constitution as will secure those rights, which they consider as not sufficiently guarded." Madison was unconcerned as to whether a committee of the whole or a special committee would consider his proposals, but he wished that "those who have been friendly to the adoption of this constitution, may have the opportunity of proving to those who were opposed to it, that they were as sincerely devoted to liberty and a republican government as those who charged them with wishing the adoption of this constitution in order to lay the foundation of an aristocracy or despotism." He wished to reassure the people who had subscribed to the federal system but still had doubts about it, and he particularly sought to relieve the concerns of North Carolina and Rhode Island so that they would ratify the Constitution. Madison did not want a reconsideration of the governmental structure that had been adopted, but he did seek to incorporate provisions for the security of rights "to satisfy the public mind that their liberties will be perpetual."[35]

For all the resistance in the House to taking up the issue of amendments, Madison did not lack supporters. One representative, John Page of Virginia, went so far as to warn his colleagues that if they did not demonstrate that they were serious about considering amendments, those in the states who desired them would turn to the convention alternative offered by Article V. "How dangerous such an expedient would be, I need not mention, but I venture to affirm, that unless you take early notice of this subject, you will not have power to deliberate. The people will clamor for a new convention, they will not trust the house any longer."[36] The notion of a second convention to be held before the Constitution could be considered ratified, as George Clinton and other antifederalists had proposed earlier, now began to merge in Page's mind and no doubt in others with the prospect of an Article V convention for proposing amendments. The belief of Congress in the imprudence of allowing any other body to formulate constitutional amendments, which would grow into a deep conviction by the twentieth century, had its seeds already planted.

Madison, after hearing objections to his attempt to offer his package of proposed amendments for committee discussion, decided at the end of the June 8 debate to take the more direct and firm course of putting them forth as resolutions for adoption by the House.[37] Earlier in the debate he had presented and discussed his proposals, which consisted of a series of paragraphs to be inserted at various places in the Constitution.[38] Most, he explained, established a bill of rights, protections against the abuses of power, not merely by one or another branch of government but also by the majority of the people against the minority. Madison, convinced that some rights should be universal and anticipating the argument over whether the federal bill of rights applied to the states, included specific language to make the rights of conscience, freedom of the press, and trial by jury extend to state government as well. "I cannot see any reason against obtaining even a double security on those points," he said, "because it must be admitted, on all hands, that the state governments are as liable to attack these invaluable privileges as the general government is, and therefore ought to be as cautiously guarded against." Other amendments that Madison proposed would ensure that there would be no fewer than one representative in the House for every 30,000 people, prevent Congress from raising its own salary until an election had intervened, and declare that powers not delegated or denied by the Constitution would be reserved to the states. He also dealt shrewdly with his own strongest objection to a bill of rights: that any list of rights jeopardized rights not specifically mentioned. He included a provision that no stipulation of rights should be construed "as to diminish the just importance of other rights retained by the people; or as to enlarge the powers delegated by the constitution."[39]

Critics labeled Madison's amendments inadequate and suggested that he offered them merely to divert attention from more substantive issues. They repeatedly referred to them as "a tub to the whale," Jonathan Swift's term for an empty container that sailors threw overboard to distract a threatening behemoth.[40] Congressman Samuel Livermore of New Hampshire objected that Madison's proposals did not reflect all the amendments that various states had advanced in their ratification actions.[41] Livermore's home state had recommended twelve amendments. In addition, Massachusetts had offered nine, South Carolina four, Virginia forty, and New York fifty-seven, and North Carolina had stipulated a long list of necessary changes when it rejected ratification. Many of the proposals duplicated each other and most dealt with issues of individual rights, but others did not.

Madison had given thought to both the substance and symbolism of amendments and had thoroughly reviewed all the state proposals. He used them, along with his knowledge of state law and his own expansive ideas and phrasing, in putting together his enumeration of rights.[42] At the same time he deliberately ignored most of the state proposals that, instead of articulating rights, sought to alter the structure of the Constitution. This move was a calculated risk on Madison's part, predicated on his assumptions that the desire for a bill of rights was broadly based while antifederalist schemes to reduce the central government's power lacked equivalent appeal and that adoption of some harmless amendments would deflate the argument that others, more radical in character, were needed.[43] "I will not propose a single alteration which I do not wish to see take place, as intrinsically proper in itself, or proper because it is wished for by a respectable number of my fellow citizens; and therefore I shall not propose a single alteration but is likely to meet the concurrence required by the constitution," Madison insisted. Reiterating these standards for offering amendments, he concluded, "If we can make the constitution better in the opinion of those who are opposed to it, without weakening its frame, or abridging its usefulness, in the judgment of those who are attached to it, we act the part of wise and liberal men."[44]

Madison came closest to throwing "a tub to the whale" with the last two proposed amendments. First he offered the proposal that in amended form became the vague assurance of the Ninth Amendment: "The enunciation in the Constitution of certain rights, shall not be construed to deny or disparage others retained by the people." His second initiative had greater consequence. In several of the state ratification convention appeals for amendment, antifederalists included language taken from the Articles of Confederation restricting federal powers to those "expressly" listed in the Constitution. Madison's draft proposal, which occasioned little discussion or close scrutiny, conveyed the general idea of power limited to those enumerated but dropped the term "expressly."[45] Subsequently this language, which became the Tenth Amendment, was read as indicating that the federal government possessed unspecified but implied powers. This amendment may have been Madison's cleverest strategy for deflating antifederalist demands for restricting the new government. At the same time it created the greatest ambiguity in the Constitution regarding the nature and extent of federal authority.

After six weeks of silence on the matter, Madison again asked the House to address the question of amendments. Representatives immediately began to debate whether the entire body should take up the matter in a committee of the whole or should refer it to a select committee. The House, still working out procedures for the conduct of its business, was taking such questions very seriously. Some speakers contended that constitutional issues were so important as to require the undivided attention of the full House and that only through such a forum would the states that had appealed for amendment feel satisfied; in any case, the House would still have to consider a committee report. Others, some of whom treated the whole topic as a waste of time, anticipated endless, unfocused discussion in a committee of the whole on the wide variety of subjects involved and preferred to turn the matter over to a smaller body. The House eventually voted 34 to 15 to create a select committee of one member from each state to consider Madison's proposals and those from the states.[46]

Three weeks later, on August 13, when Richard Bland Lee moved that the House take up the report of the committee of eleven on amendments, the old arguments resurfaced once again. The judiciary bill, revenue and other financial matters, and western land sales were asserted to be more pressing matters than amendments. Madison and Page reminded their colleagues of the public concern for guarantees of rights and the likelihood of unhappiness in the face of further delay. At long last, the House agreed to begin immediate consideration of amendments.[47]

As soon as the House shifted its attention from procedure to substance, the debate took on far greater importance. The committee report, following Madison's proposal, called for amendments to be inserted at appropriate places throughout the text of the Constitution. Roger Sherman of Connecticut, who had steadfastly opposed taking up the amendment question, was immediately on his feet to object: "This is not the proper mode of amending the constitution. We ought not to interweave our propositions into the work itself, because it will be destructive of the whole fabric." Laws were properly altered by supplementary acts, not by rewriting the original. Furthermore, Sherman questioned whether Congress had the right to make changes in such fashion. "The constitution is the act of the people, and ought to remain entire. But the amendments will be the act of the state governments; again all the authority we possess, is derived from that instrument; if we mean to destroy the whole and establish a new constitution, we remove the basis on which we mean to build."[48]

Sherman moved that, instead of being inserted throughout the Constitution, amendments be appended to it. His objection to Madison's proposed approach addressed a fundamental question about the nature of constitutional amendment, and it provoked extensive discussion. Madison defended the "neatness and propriety" of interweaving amendments, keeping the Constitution "uniform and entire." If amendments were "separate and distinct," it would be possible to determine their meaning only by comparing relevant sections, "a very considerable embarrassment." Madison believed that with supplementary amendments "it will be difficult to ascertain to what part of the instrument the amendments particularly refer; they will create unfavorable comparisons, whereas if they are placed upon the footing here proposed, they will stand upon as good foundation as the original work."[49]

William Loughton Smith of South Carolina raised the specter of supplementary amendments making it difficult to know the law, as a result of "legislative obscurities that might easily be avoided." He offered the example of South Carolina, which, in revising its constitution, "instead of making acts in addition to acts, which is always attended with perplexity, . . . has incorporated them, and brought them forward as a complete system, repealing the old. This is what he understood was intended to be done by the committee, the present copy of the constitution was to be done away, and a new one substituted in its stead." John Vining of Delaware agreed with Smith, likening supplementary amendments to "a careless written letter, [with] more matter attached to it in a postscript than was contained in the original composition." He concluded, "The constitution, being a great and important work, ought all to be brought into one view, and made as intelligible as possible."[50]

Other representatives insisted on the need for amendments to stand separate from the original Constitution. The authority of the initial instrument and the intentions of its creators would otherwise be obscured. Michael Jenifer Stone of Maryland declared that interweaving amendments would make it appear that "George Washington, and the other worthy characters who composed the convention, signed an instrument which they never had in contemplation." Stone, like others, regarded the incorporation of amendments into the original text to be the equivalent of substituting a new constitution for the old one; this was beyond their authority and "set a precedent which in dangerous and turbulent times may unhinge the whole."[51]

Elbridge Gerry regarded the whole debate as "trifling about matters of little consequence." Amendments, if adopted, would be, in the words of the Constitution, wherever placed, "valid to all intents and purposes, as part of the constitution." As for the argument that incorporating amendments would virtually repeal the Constitution, the same could be said for supplementary amendments, "consequently the objection goes for nothing, or it goes against making any amendment whatever."[52]

After protracted discussion, the House defeated Sherman's motion to have amendments follow rather than interweave the Constitution, although more than one-third of the members supported it.[53] Six days later, however, after specific amendments had been thoroughly discussed, Sherman renewed his appeal. The question was taken up once more and the same arguments voiced again. This time, over three-fourths of the representatives present voted with Sherman.[54] Rejecting Madison's preference for once, the House established a basic format for amendments: they would follow the original text of the Constitution that would, in turn, be left untouched.

Although many of the arguments advanced for and against Sherman's motion may have been inconsequential, the decision was not the "trifle" that Elbridge Gerry termed it. Free-standing additions to the Constitution did not have to be reconciled with prevailing language to the same degree required of incorporations into the existing text. As Madison wrote five days later, "It is already apparent I think that some ambiguities will be produced by this change, as the question will often arise and sometimes be not easily solved, how far the original text is or is not necessarily superseded, by the supplemental act."[55] William Loughton Smith and others had worried as well about the increased potential for conflict between sections of the Constitution. The decision to make amendments supplementary increased the need for an arbiter of disputes over constitutional interpretation. The role of the judiciary in American constitutionalism would therefore grow larger.

In addition, the decision on placement of amendments shaped the subsequent image of the Constitution. The determination to treat the 1787 text as inviolate helped foster the later impression that it was a work of perfection. Amendments might properly deal with matters not addressed at the Philadelphia convention, but the core of the system articulated by the Founders was not to be touched. The conservatism of American constitutional arrangements rests, in some part, upon this perception.

Madison did see one advantage to the decision to make amendments supplementary rather than interwoven. It would allow amendments to be considered individually rather than together, "a single act to be adopted or rejected in the gross." He recognized that this method increased the likelihood of accomplishing much, if not all, of what he hoped. "The several propositions will be classed according to their affinity to each other, which will reduce them to the number of 5 or 6 in the while, to go forth as so many amendts. unconnected with one another."[56]

The House discussed the proposed amendments during the next nine days. Hot weather, bad tempers, and antifederalist objections led one representative to write, in the midst of the debate, "There has been more ill-humour & rudeness displayed today than has existed since the meeting of Congress."[57] The members divided over the necessity of adding language to the preamble, as three states requested, declaring that all power was originally vested in, derived from, and should be exercised for the benefit of the people who had "an indubitable, unalienable, and indefeasible right to reform or change their government, whenever it be found adverse or inadequate to the purposes of its institution."[58] After being approved by a majority in the committee of the whole, revision of the preamble to give explicit sanction to reform and revolution failed to receive the necessary two-thirds backing on final consideration by the House and so was dropped.[59]

Two other proposed amendments stirred debate but survived. Small states sought to limit the size of congressional districts. In extended discussion congressmen demonstrated limited comprehension of the possibilities of population growth, adopting a complex plan to control the population of districts and the House as a whole.[60] Virginia and New York wanted to prohibit Congress from adjusting its own salary.[61] Although Madison considered it a matter of lesser importance than most others, he incorporated this idea into his list of amendments as well.[62]

When attention turned to enumeration of a bill of rights, members seemed generally agreed as to the points that should be specified. First there were the general rights of citizens: freedom of religion, speech, press, assembly, and petition; participation in the militia by keeping and bearing arms; and protection against the quartering of troops in their homes. Then there were judicial rights: protections against unwarranted searches, double jeopardy, or compulsory witnessing against oneself. Due process of law, speedy and public trial by a jury of peers, specification of accusations, confrontation of witnesses, assistance of counsel, and freedom from excessive bail, fines, or cruel and unusual punishment were likewise guaranteed. Only a few members considered the stipulating of rights unwise. Samuel Livermore complained, "No cruel and unusual punishment is to be inflicted; it is sometimes necessary to hang a man, villains often deserve whipping, and perhaps having their ears cut off; but are we in future to be prevented from inflicting these punishments because they are cruel?" His concern stirred little sympathy.[63] One proposal, that the freedom of assembly and appeal to government for redress of grievances should be supplemented by the right to instruct one's representatives, led to prolonged discussion of the degree to which citizens should be able to bind their legislators. The clause was eventually rejected.[64] With few other objections but often in the simpler language of the select committee, the House embraced Madison's amendment proposals.

As House discussion of amendments came to a conclusion, a few members made efforts to bring forth other propositions advanced in the state ratifying conventions. Addition of amendments to block federal regulation of elections or imposition of direct taxes was suggested and rejected. The talk of limiting federal taxing power provided a brief echo of the debates in Philadelphia and the states, but the antifederalist argument was no more persuasive than before.[65] The House then gave the required two-thirds approval to its package of seventeen amendments on August 24 and sent them to the Senate for its consideration.[66]

The twenty-two members of the Senate met behind closed doors and kept no official record of their debates; it is therefore easier to determine the outcome than the course of their deliberations. The journal of Senator William Maclay of Pennsylvania records that when the House resolutions were read on August 25, senators Ralph Izard of South Carolina and John Langdon of New Hampshire sought to postpone their consideration until the next session. After defeating this delaying tactic, the Senate debated and amended the House resolutions between September 2 and 9 before approving them. In the process final efforts to add other state ratifying convention proposals not incorporated into Madison's resolutions were turned aside. The House Journal of September 14 contains the Senate resolutions that resulted from these proceedings.[67]

Though all but a few senators favored amendments, they did not find the House resolutions entirely satisfactory and set about reducing the wordiness of the other body's version. Separate articles dealing with religious freedom and with the rights of free speech, press, assembly, and petition were combined. Six articles dealing with judicial rights were compressed to four, their language simplified, and some minor provisions altered. The article Madison regarded most highly, the one prohibiting states from infringing trial, conscience, speech, or press rights, was, without explanation, dropped. Also deleted was a provision exempting those "religiously scrupulous of bearing arms" from military service and an article expressly separating legislative, executive, and judicial powers. On September 9, the Senate by two-thirds vote approved a revised package of twelve amendments.

A conference committee including congressmen Madison, Roger Sherman, and John Vining and senators Oliver Ellsworth, Charles Carroll, and William Paterson worked out differences between the House and Senate versions of the amendment package. Most of the Senate changes were minor and quickly agreed to. The only difficulty arose over the House's third article declaring that "Congress shall make no law establishing religion" and the Senate's preference for "no law establishing articles of faith, or a mode of worship." The committee eventually agreed upon "no law respecting an establishment of religion," a broader statement than either of those it replaced. On September 24 the House of Representatives by a vote of 37 to 14 and on September 26 the Senate by an unrecorded margin of at least two-thirds accepted the conference committee's report. Congress asked the president of the United States to submit the twelve amendments to the states for ratification and to send copies to Rhode Island and North Carolina as well.[68]

APPROVAL OF AMENDMENTS by two-thirds or more of Congress did not ensure their adoption, as anyone who remembered the difficulties of the Articles of Confederation era well knew. State legislatures' treatment of the proposed amendments would further test the mechanism for constitutional reform that Article V established. Over the next nine months, most states responded positively to the request for ratification. Foot-dragging by Massachusetts and Virginia, two states initially in the forefront of the call for a bill of rights, delayed ratification for another eighteen months. Even so, the entire amendment process, from Madison's introduction of resolutions in the House to the Virginia legislature's final action, consumed only two-and-a-half years.

Congressional passage of these amendments greatly encouraged the two states that had hitherto withheld approval of the Constitution. Even before the amendments gained ratification, both North Carolina and Rhode Island decided to join the young government. A North Carolina convention, meeting in Hillsborough, had declined to ratify in July 1788, choosing instead to request a bill of rights and other amendments. As the new federal government began taking shape, however, the consequences of remaining outside it became evident. At the same time, promises of and progress toward amendment provided desired reassurances. The process of reversing the Hillsborough decision began as early as November 1788 when the North Carolina general assembly arranged for another ratifying convention. Elections were held in August 1789 while the federal House was still considering the desired amendments. North Carolinians indicated their satisfaction with the course of events over the previous year and their confidence in the outcome by choosing an overwhelmingly federalist convention. Meeting in Fayetteville in November, this second convention, after three days of unrecorded debate, voted 194 to 77 in favor of the Constitution. A month later, the general assembly endorsed the twelve proposed amendments.[69]

The proposed amendments also won over the most recalcitrant of the original states. Granted an extremely democratic charter by Charles II, Rhode Island had, throughout the revolutionary era, fiercely protected its unusual degree of civil liberty and self-government. Subscribing to the Articles of Confederation in 1778, Rhode Island steadfastly blocked their amendment and declined even to attend the 1787 constitutional convention. The state's voters rejected the Constitution in a popular referendum in March 1788, and the general assembly thereafter repeatedly refused to call a state ratifying convention. The first sign of a softening antifederalist position appeared in October 1789 when the assembly decided to print and distribute copies of the proposed federal constitutional amendments. The following January the assembly finally agreed, by the narrowest of margins, to convene a ratifying convention.

The Rhode Island convention was unique in being able to consider both the Constitution and the proposed twelve amendments. Meeting in March 1790, it drew up a declaration of rights, essentially a restatement of the proposed federal bill of rights, and a list of additional constitutional amendments it wished to recommend. Among the latter were a revision of Article V to require the assent of eleven of the thirteen original states to any constitutional amendment; a prohibition of military drafts except in case of invasion; a ban on capitation taxes, poll taxes, standing armies, and slave importation; the requirement of two-thirds congressional vote to borrow money or declare war; and the establishment of the right to recall senators. The convention then recessed until May to give Rhode Island voters the opportunity to consider the recommendations and respond in the April general election. When the convention reconvened, five days of heated debate preceded the narrow 34 to 32 vote on May 29 to ratify the Constitution.

The emerging bill of rights as well as optimism about achieving more amendments assuaged Rhode Island's suspicions of the federal government, which centered upon debt, taxation, slavery, and civil liberties. Meanwhile, an increasingly impatient Congress posed the prospect of Rhode Island being commercially excluded from the United States as of July 1, subject to high tariffs and immediate payment of its revolutionary war debt. In this light, constitutional amendments provided a measure of face-saving as well as relief to a state that could ill-afford to remain outside the federal Union.[70] Only thirteen days after Rhode Island's convention approved the Constitution, its state assembly ratified eleven of the twelve proposed amendments, rejecting only the proposed restriction on congressional pay increases.[71]

Less is known about most other states' actions in ratifying the amendments Congress laid before them in September 1789. Records of roll-call votes, much less debates, do not appear to have been kept. Yet the pattern of rapid and uncontested approval suggests that most states, like North Carolina and Rhode Island, found these amendments at least unobjectionable and, more likely, reassuring. New Jersey and Maryland had already acted before North Carolina; South Carolina, New Hampshire, Delaware, New York, and Pennsylvania did so before Rhode Island. Thus the first nine ratifications were obtained even faster (by a margin of three days) than the original endorsements of the Constitution.

The first two proposed amendments, the only ones that did not focus on individual rights and about which congressional opinion seemed divided, stood alone in encountering difficulty. The first state legislature to consider ratification, New Jersey, declined to approve the second proposal, the one mandating delay of legislators' pay increases until after an election had occurred. Why New Jersey lawmakers found the measure unattractive is unclear. In any case, New Hampshire, New York, Pennsylvania, and Rhode Island followed suit in declining to approve it.[72]

Delaware, the sixth state legislature to consider amendment ratification, was the first to reject the first proposal, the measure dealing with the size of congressional districts. The result of discussions beginning during the Philadelphia convention, it called for restricting House districts to 30,000 residents until that body reached 100 members, then limiting districts to 40,000 until it reached 200, and thereafter holding districts to 50,000. Desires to keep congressional districts small in order to preserve a republican system contended with concerns that the House might become unworkably large. Viewpoints clearly were mixed, and consciousness that the population was growing rapidly further complicated matters.[73] Not only Delaware, the smallest state in terms of population, but also Pennsylvania, one of the largest, declined to ratify this amendment.[74] Taken together, the two rejections suggest that concern about the long-term implications of rigid definition of congressional district size, not just self-interest, was on legislators' minds.

With eight states having approved eleven amendments (though not the same eleven) and Pennsylvania having endorsed ten, the first Congress's propositions were within reach of enactment. Article V's three-fourths requirement meant that ten ratifications would be sufficient for adoption. Yet at this point the process slowed. The Virginia assembly, among the first to take up the issue, found itself immobilized by its usual evenly balanced federalist-antifederalist conflict. Georgia, whose leaders had consistently maintained that no amendments to the Constitution were necessary, took no action. Inexplicably neither did Massachusetts, the state whose ratifying convention had first appealed for a bill of rights. The Massachusetts legislature began but did not finish the ratification process. During January and February 1790 its senate approved all but the first and second proposed amendments; the house then rejected the twelfth as well, and the difference was not resolved. When Secretary of State Thomas Jefferson inquired a year later, he learned that the legislature had never completed action.[75] Connecticut followed a similar pattern as over the course of three sessions one house or the other approved most of the amendments but the other failed to concur. Unable to resolve its dispute over the first two amendments, the legislature postponed the matter until fall 1791 and then declined to take it up again.[76]

Yet no one charged that the amendment process had foundered or was impossibly difficult. Except for Patrick Henry and his colleagues grumbling that the amendments did not go far enough in protecting against government centralization, no serious opposition surfaced. Neither Massachusetts nor Connecticut seemed far from ratification of most, if not all, the amendments. Even the Virginians assuredly posed only a temporary obstruction since they had tentatively approved the first ten amendments before getting bogged down in internecine struggle. Confidence remained high that the amending process would soon be completed.

The next ratification came from an unexpected source. Vermont, which finally settled its territorial disputes with New York in October 1790 and thereby eliminated questions about its sovereignty, ratified the federal Constitution on January 10, 1791, and became the fourteenth state. Its general assembly then ratified the twelve amendments on November 3, 1791.[77] However, the addition of a state to the Union raised the three-fourths threshold to eleven, leaving ten amendments still one state short of ratification.

Six weeks later, the Virginia House of Delegates finally resolved its differences sufficiently to ratify the twelve amendments. The two Virginia U.S. senators initially reported that the amendments Congress had approved failed to fulfill the requirements of Virginia's 1788 petition and left them both apprehensive about civil liberty and republican government.[78] Richard Henry Lee told Patrick Henry that "a careless reader would be apt to suppose that the amendments desired by the States had been graciously granted. But when the thing done is compared with that desired, nothing can be more unlike."[79] Later he bemoaned, "The english language has been carefully culled to find words feeble in their Nature or doubtful in their meaning."[80] Such objections helped thwart quick action, leading the assembly to postpone consideration of the issue for one year and then another before it finally approved the amendments the state had done so much to initiate.

With Virginia's ratification on December 15, 1791, all except for the first two of the proposed amendments became part of the Constitution.[81] Discussion of further ratification ceased immediately. Action by Connecticut, Georgia, and Massachusetts could have put the other two amendments into effect, but none was taken. In fact, since the ten amendments, which quickly became known as the Bill of Rights, were legally in effect, none of the three states saw any need to add their approval. Not until the 150th anniversary of the adoption of the Bill of Rights did the three add their formal endorsement, a purely symbolic act.

Adoption of the first ten amendments achieved the immediate goal of relieving the anxieties of many antifederalists about their rights and liberties and it won them over to the new government. Thereafter the focus of political attention became how, not whether the federal government would proceed. Adoption of the Bill of Rights had additional important consequences. It began establishing the patterns by which the amending process would operate, and it offered proof that a workable system for constitutional reform had been established. Should the need arise, the mechanisms of Article V could be used to alter the Constitution within reasonable limits of time and effort. Neither congressional nor state approval by the required supermajorities posed impossible obstacles. The republic that the U.S. Constitution created could be kept vital and effective. The "new order" that had been established need not be only for the moment but might truly be "for the ages."

6

"Too Ticklish to Be Unnecessarily Multiplied"

Amendments and the Judicial Review Alternative

During the seventy years following the adoption of the Bill of Rights, the Article V amending process gradually fell into disuse. To be sure, after its striking initial success in dealing with demands for an enumeration of rights, the amending mechanism was soon employed again without difficulty. In 1798 and 1804 amendments were adopted to cope with other quick-to-appear flaws in the original plan of government. In 1810 an attempt to extend a constitutional restriction on public officials to cover all citizens stalled just one state short of completion. However, these efforts to adjust and fine-tune the Constitution during its first years of operation proved to be the last successful or near-successful formal alterations of the instrument until the Civil War.

After 1810 the force and frequency of amendment initiatives faded. James Madison, who took very seriously the need to respect the constitutional limits he had helped create even when he favored expanded federal activity, urged amendment to authorize federal spending on internal improvements in 1815 and 1816. The most practiced of amenders, Madison nonetheless failed to persuade Congress that new language was necessary to sanction canal and road building. State legislatures and individual members of Congress suggested other alterations, although few of them attracted substantial support. Two did gain Senate approval between 1813 and 1826, but neither won the endorsement of the House of Representatives. For more than three decades thereafter Congress paid scant attention to the stream of proposals that continued to flow. Not until faced with the impending collapse of the Union following the 1860 election did congressional and state leaders once again seriously consider amendment, and only after the breech in the Union had been dealt with did the amendment process again function successfully.[1]

Contributing to the limited use of amendment during the first half of the nineteenth century was a widespread, though hardly universal, feeling that once the Bill of Rights had been added, the Constitution provided an adequate structure of government. The job of constitution-making had been so well done that further amendment was unnecessary. Even the 1816 appeal for revision from James Madison, one of the document's most admired architects, could not shake that belief. Few people thought the framework itself needed major reform; indeed, most amendments to be offered suggested only slight alterations. The instrument may have meant different things to different sections and individuals, and eventually a dispute over who possessed the authority to interpret it would prove disruptive, but for most of these years Americans preferred to celebrate its virtues rather than deal with its imperfections, ambiguities, and outright contradictions.

The dark undercurrent of the deeply divisive and unresolvable conflict over slavery only occasionally disturbed the placid surface of constitutional well-being before midcentury. For the most part, a growing sense of national pride suffused the political culture. The belief spread that the United States benefited from divine preference and was being propelled toward a "manifest destiny." Americans came to revere the creators of the Constitution as persons of extraordinary wisdom who had found ways to balance competing interests in the course of creating a splendid system of government.[2] Admiration for and imitation of the U.S. Constitution by European and Latin American nations establishing their own governmental systems in the early nineteenth century reinforced this proud sense of national achievement and continued promise.[3] In such a climate it is no wonder that demands for amendment were seldom heard, much less heeded.

Amendment also receded because the less arduous use of judicial devices to resolve constitutional problems increased. Observing the creation of the Constitution from his vantage point in Paris, Thomas Jefferson had predicted that the judiciary would be called upon to resolve ambiguities and conflicts in the Constitution's meaning.[4] Though Jefferson would have preferred to see constitutional issues settled in republican conventions, judicial determination became commonplace. During Jefferson's presidency the Supreme Court laid firm claim to be the Constitution's arbiter in the landmark 1803 case *Marbury v. Madison*. Sixteen years later the importance of this role became clearer when the Court in *McCulloch v. Maryland* took an expansive view of the federal government's right to take actions judged "necessary and proper" to carry out explicit constitutional mandates. These steps toward less restrictive constitutionalism eroded the sense of amendment as the necessary solution to every uncertainty about governmental authority.

AS THE GOVERNMENT OF THE UNITED STATES began functioning, some of its provisions proved to be less well thought out than originally supposed. Without much difficulty, indeed in such a routine fashion that few comments were made or records kept, the Congress and the states twice employed Article V to take care of problems. The same approach to a perceived Founders' oversight brought less success a third time. Even though, as with the Bill of Rights, not every proposed amendment was ratified, the amendment process of resolving constitutional questions ever more firmly established its credibility during these years.

With the Constitution's judicial article its least-detailed provision, the operation of the courts required further definition. The Judiciary Act of 1789 accomplished some but not all of the task. The first case entered on the docket of the Supreme Court in 1791, and a total of seven cases within as many years, raised the question of whether a state could be sued in the federal courts by a citizen of another state or country. The Constitution stipulated that federal jurisdiction extended to controversies "between a state and citizens of another state," but it did not establish whether a state could be sued without its permission. The long-standing English common law doctrine of sovereign immunity, that the king could not be sued in the king's own courts even though he had a responsibility to redress valid legal claims through other means, created a complex legal problem. The issue was further complicated in the United States by the possibility of suit by a plaintiff from outside the state and the question of whether such suit should be tried in state or federal court. When they ratified the Constitution, Virginia, New York, North Carolina, and Rhode Island advocated an amendment denying federal courts jurisdiction in such cases. Not merely an abstract issue at a time when revolutionary war debt and property claims posed high risks for individual states, the question ended up before the Supreme Court.[5]

In *Chisholm v. Georgia,* the Court rejected a claim of state sovereign immunity. Alexander Chisholm, the executor of the estate of Robert Farquhar, a South Carolina merchant from whom a commissioner for the state of Georgia purchased war supplies, had asked the state to settle the unpaid bill. The Georgia legislature declined to pay, suggesting that Chisholm sue the commissioner. When Chisholm instead sued the state in federal court, Georgia claimed immunity. Furthermore, the state protested that the federal courts lacked jurisdiction. The Supreme Court, however, was persuaded to the contrary. Two of the Court's five justices, James Wilson and John Blair, along with Chisholm's attorney, Edmund Randolph, had helped draft the Constitution's judicial article at Philadelphia, and the other three justices, William Cushing, James Iredell, and John Jay, had sat in state ratifying conventions. Only Iredell supported Georgia, and the Court's judgment went against the state.[6]

In fall 1793 Georgia governor Edward Telfair called on his state legisla-ture to ask Georgia's congressional delegation to seek a constitutional amendment to guard against "civil discord and the impending danger." The Georgia house declared by a vote of 19 to 8 that anyone attempting to col-lect the Chisholm claim would be "guilty of felony, and shall suffer death, without the benefit of the clergy, by being hanged." State governments in New York, Virginia, and Massachusetts, which faced similar litigation, also reacted strongly against the Court's position. In September Governor John Hancock discussed several responses, including a quest for amendment, with a special session of the Massachusetts legislature. Later in 1793 the Virginia legislature joined Georgia and Massachusetts in asking its congressional del-egation to seek amendments clarifying state sovereignty.[7]

Amendments to limit the judicial power had already been laid before Congress. The First Congress declined to take up such a proposal by Repre-sentative Thomas Tucker of South Carolina. Two days after the Supreme Court announced its *Chisholm v. Georgia* decision, the Senate discussed a similar proposition but took no action. By the start of the Third Congress in December 1793, a majority of states were on record favoring amendment, the four that had declared their position in 1788, the three (two of them new) that had acted in fall 1793, and two others (Connecticut and New Hampshire) that had adopted legislative resolutions criticizing the Court's decision. On January 2, 1794, a resolution was introduced in the Senate call-ing for an amendment, to wit: "The judicial power of the United States shall not be construed to extend to any suit in law or equity, commenced or prose-cuted against one of the United States by citizens of another State, or by citi-zens or subjects of a foreign State." After little more than a day's debate, no record of which survives, the Senate adopted the resolution 23 to 2. After delaying for seven weeks, the House of Representatives took up the Senate resolution on March 4, 1794, and adopted it 81 to 9 the same day.[8]

With Kentucky having joined the original thirteen states and Vermont, the amendment required ratification by twelve states to take effect but was quickly achieved. The legislatures of New York and Rhode Island approved it within the month. Connecticut, New Hampshire, and Massachusetts acted before the end of June. Vermont, Virginia, Georgia, Kentucky, and Mary-land ratified during the fall, with Maryland alone reporting substantial op-position. Delaware and North Carolina completed the process in the first weeks of 1795. New Jersey and Pennsylvania were the only states to con-sider the amendment and refuse to ratify; South Carolina deferred action. Although the states completed ratification on February 7, 1795, the process of notifying federal officials proved slow and slipshod. Not until January 8,

1798, did President John Adams report to Congress the addition of the Eleventh Amendment to the Constitution.[9]

Although the Eleventh Amendment was unquestionably a declaration of states' rights, it appears to have been a narrow one in response to a specific problem that the Founders failed to resolve in the way most states wished. The fragmentary record does not show much division or dispute on the matter. Strong federalists as well as their critics supported the amendment in Congress. Nearly every state quickly and overwhelmingly ratified. Given the endorsement of the amendment by federalists committed to establishing strong credit and central power, it is hard to believe that those voting for the Eleventh Amendment saw it as either a debt avoidance measure or a major reclaiming of state authority. Even in the case that precipitated the amendment, the state of Georgia promptly paid the Chisholm claim. The amendment process appears to have been employed, not to address a major issue of political philosophy, but to settle a small constitutional oversight.[10]

The Eleventh Amendment did inadvertently clarify one aspect of the Article V amending process. Attorneys pressing an out-of-state claim against Virginia argued that the amendment was invalid because the congressional resolution proposing it had not been submitted to the president for approval before being sent to the states for ratification. Article I, section 7, of the Constitution required that, to become law, all bills adopted by Congress be approved by the president or passed once again, this time by a two-thirds margin, over his veto. The issue had not come up during the first use of the amendment process. U.S. Attorney General Charles Lee argued that amendments involved "a substantive act, unconnected with the ordinary business of legislation, and not within the policy, or term, of the policy investing the President with a qualified negative on the acts and resolutions of Congress." In other words, the president was to play no role whatsoever in the adoption of constitutional amendments. The Supreme Court, immediately and without comment, agreed, putting a quick end to what could have become an obstacle to the passage of future amendments, not to mention a blow to the viability of those already adopted, had the Court decided otherwise.[11]

Another oversight of the Founders soon generated an additional amendment. In creating the electoral college to choose a president and vice-president every four years, the Founders sought to deter simple national majoritarian democracy, maintain a measure of state identity and power in the selection process, and ensure deference to the political judgment of a leadership elite. Even before the 1796 electoral votes were counted, South Carolina representative William Smith called for amendment of the system, saying that "great inconveniences might arise." Four years later, the wisdom of Smith's warning became evident. The development of a national partisan network, the first flowering of what would eventually become a political party system, together with the unvarying loyalty of electors pledged to partisan candidates, meant that instead of a scattering of votes among various candidates, all seventy-three electors of the victorious majority cast their two votes apiece for Thomas Jefferson and Aaron Burr. Since the electoral college system made no provision for distinguishing between presidential and vice-presidential votes, the resulting tie vote suddenly presented the ambitious Burr with an opportunity to claim the presidency assumed to be Jefferson's. The electoral college tie sent the choice to the House of Representatives where each state had one vote. With Federalists supporting Burr in their eagerness to block Jefferson, the House deadlocked for a week. Representatives took thirty-six ballots before fears of a constitutional crisis and doubts about Burr led to a resolution. The election of Jefferson did not erase the possibility of similar conflicts in future elections. As the 1804 balloting approached, so did a sense of urgency about the need for reform of the electoral process.[12]

By 1802 the state legislatures of New York, North Carolina, and Vermont had called for amendment of the Constitution to correct this defect. Near the end of the congressional session, the House of Representatives by a 47-to-14 vote approved an amendment providing for choice of electors by district and division of the presidential and vice-presidential ballots. The measure failed by one vote to achieve the needed two-thirds in the Senate. As Congress considered various alternatives in fall 1803, New York senator DeWitt Clinton proposed a constitutional amendment that simply separated electoral college voting for president and vice-president. The Senate modified Clinton's measure, adding elaborate language to stipulate procedures to be used in the event that no candidate received a majority. The House of Representatives, voting by states, would choose a president from among the three highest vote-getters; the Senate would select a vice-president from among the top two.[13] It was immediately evident that the proposal would fundamentally alter the presidential selection process. Under the old system, the majority candidate would gain the presidency and his chief competitor the vice-presidency (as happened in 1796 when John Adams received 71 electoral votes and his rival Jefferson won 68). If the new approach was adopted, the majority would choose both. No doubt this procedure would further encourage the formation of electoral coalitions, those political parties that the Founders had viewed with such distaste and sought to avoid.

The stature of the vice-presidency would also be reduced. This official would no longer be thought of as the leader of the second most powerful political alliance in the country but as a secondary figure in the strongest bloc, a significant shift. The executive branch of the government would acquire a more unitary and partisan character. Within that branch the power of the presidency would face fewer challenges to its growth, and the vice-president would be reduced to presiding over the Senate, breaking tie votes in that body and awaiting presidential death or impeachment.

A full day's debate in the Senate on December 2 and another in the House on December 8 focused on the political consequences of the proposed changes. The Federalists, already in decline, were concerned about losing their chance of at least capturing a share of power through the vice-presidency. "In avoiding rocks," worried Connecticut representative James Hillhouse, the Federalists were "steering for quicksand." He saw the current executive system as giving each party "checks upon each other: our Government is composed of checks. . . . If we cannot destroy party we ought to place every check upon it." His Jeffersonian colleague, James Jackson of Georgia, on the other hand, foresaw the end of the intrigues he associated with Federalists. A number of speakers predicted that small states would lose influence in the choice of presidents and vice-presidents. Compelling the House to choose a president from among three candidates instead of five was both criticized and defended as requiring the choice to be more reflective of popular sentiment.[14]

Following Senate approval of the proposed amendment by 22 to 10 on December 2, opponents tried to stop further consideration by arguing that it had fallen one vote short of the two-thirds that Article V required. The House of Representatives agreed, however, that the standard should be two-thirds of the members present and voting, not two-thirds of the body's entire membership. After defeating this attempt to stiffen the requirements for congressional approval of amendments, the House endorsed the Senate proposal by exactly a two-thirds margin on a vote of 84 to 42.[15]

Federalist foes of the change in electoral method sought to prevent its ratification by three-fourths of the states. They sent letters and copies of Connecticut senator Uriah Tracy's speech against the amendment to influential politicians in every state. However, with Jeffersonian majorities ascendant in most states, ratification proceeded rapidly. North Carolina, Maryland, Kentucky, and Ohio ratified before year's end; Pennsylvania and Vermont in January; Virginia, New York, and New Jersey in February; and Rhode Island, South Carolina, Georgia, and New Hampshire by June 15. Federalist Delaware, Massachusetts, and Connecticut each rejected the amendment during the same brief period. Only twenty-seven weeks after its submission by Congress, the requisite number of states had ratified the Twelfth Amendment. As both supporters and opponents predicted, it fundamentally altered the nature of presidential elections and, as a result, stimulated the development of national political parties.[16]

More than six decades would pass before the Constitution was again amended, but in 1810 another attempt to remedy an alleged flaw in the original instrument came close to success. Article I, section 9 of the Constitution stipulated that "no Person holding any Office of Profit or Trust under [the United States], shall, without the Consent of the Congress, accept of any present, Emolument, Office, or Title, of any kind whatever, from any King, Prince, or foreign State." In 1810, with anti-European feeling running high because of the buffeting the United States was receiving from both sides in the Napoleonic Wars, the Eleventh Congress suggested extending the ban to all citizens. A proposed amendment to remove the citizenship of anyone who "shall accept, claim, receive, or retain any title of nobility or honour, or shall, without the consent of Congress, accept and retain any present, pension, office or emolument of any kind whatever, from any emperor, king, prince or foreign power" won Senate approval by a vote of 19 to 5 on April 27; the House concurred by a vote of 87 to 3 four days later. The reasons for extending to all citizens the restrictions already placed on some must have seemed self-evident because the measure generated no recorded debate. Twelve states promptly ratified, and the South Carolina senate likewise approved. Connecticut, New York, and Rhode Island rejected the amendment, however, and Virginia and the South Carolina lower house took no action, leaving the titles-of-nobility amendment stalled one ratification short of the necessary three-fourths of the states.[17] The feelings that moved Congress to its decisive action on the measure faded as quickly as they had arisen, and by the narrowest of margins the amendment was consigned to oblivion.

Never before or again would an amendment come so close to adoption and yet not gain approval. The titles-of-nobility amendment failed by the margin of one state; the 1789 amendment to limit congressional district size had failed by two. The other 1789 proposal to be defeated when first submitted for ratification, the amendment delaying congressional salary increases, fell four states short of acceptance at the time though it would eventually attain sanction two centuries later. Thereafter only the equal rights amendment of the 1970s would near ratification but fail to achieve it; it would fall three states short. In each of these cases, but particularly in the three early ones, the question arises as to whether a small minority of the U.S. population was able to block constitutional reform that a substantial majority desired. More particularly, given the Article V requirement of ratification by states, were states with small populations able to exercise undue influence on the amending process and place control of the decision in the hands of a tiny fragment of the nation?

In each of the early cases the outcome clearly did not distort the Founders' requirement that a three-fourths supermajority of states approve constitutional change. The same can be said of the equal rights amendment, which will be discussed in turn. The apportionment of legislatures carrying out ratification, an action that committed the entire state population, should also be considered. Until the Supreme Court insisted on "one man, one vote" in the 1960s, legislative malapportionment remained a factor. Yet at least at the level of aggregate state population, distribution of power in the amending process was not out of proportion to state size.

None of the failed amendments of the early national period passed the Founders' test for constitutional acceptability. States containing 66 percent of the nation's population ratified the congressional district amendment, states with 61 percent approved the titles-of-nobility amendment, and states with 49 percent endorsed the salary amendment. These results were well below the three-fourths level of consensus decreed by Article V. In each instance, more than one-third of the nation's population resided in the nonratifying states.

The contrary theoretical possibility that sparsely settled states could force an amendment upon a few states in which a large proportion of the population resided did not occur either. The Bill of Rights was ratified by states with 80 percent of the population, the Eleventh Amendment by states with 83 percent, and the Twelfth by states with 85 percent. Within the framework established by Article V, providing the states a voice in amendment and allowing legislatures to exercise that voice, the three early national-era defeats of proposed amendments, not to mention the twelve victories, seem consistent with the Founders' sense of the degree of consensus appropriate for fundamental change in the arrangements of governance. Differences in state population did not distort the amending system; as intended, substantial support or opposition determined outcomes.[18]

EVEN IN THIS ERA of infrequent constitutional alteration, amending initiatives never disappeared altogether. Individual inspiration regarding ways to perfect the Constitution led to the introduction of nearly 1,000 amendment resolutions between the 1790s and 1861. Most attracted little interest and did not receive as much as a congressional hearing.[19] Until the nation arrived on the threshold of civil war, none, other than those already mentioned, proceeded very far. Nevertheless, the mere fact that proposals for change were advanced at all suggests that Article V retained political vitality.

Calls for constitutional alteration flowed from the United States' first foreign relations crisis, the war between Great Britain and France set off by the
French Revolution. In the second Washington administration, maritime conflict severely strained relations with Britain. During the Adams administration, as U.S. fury concentrated on France because of the attacks of its
privateers on American merchant ships, antiforeign sentiment ran even
higher. In 1798 the Congress, dominated by the Federalist party and anticipating war with France, adopted a series of laws to restrict the rights of
aliens and to inhibit criticism of the government, not to mention to put the
"Gallic faction," their Jeffersonian opponents, at a disadvantage. In addition
to the Alien and Sedition Acts themselves, congressional Federalists approved a Naturalization Act to extend the waiting period for immigrants to
become citizens from five to fourteen years. Some legislators wished to restrict citizenship to native-born Americans. Compared to the suggestion of
Massachusetts Federalist Harrison Gray Otis that no further immigration be
allowed at all, this proposition seemed almost moderate.

The Massachusetts legislature, a Federalist stronghold, wanted to go further. It appealed for a constitutional amendment stipulating that only native-
born Americans would be eligible for public office. Connecticut, New York,
and three other states joined the call. Six states asking for amendment fell
below the two-thirds, or ten, needed to demand a constitutional convention,
and the Congress, having adopted the milder Naturalization Act and other
steps against aliens, declined to consider such an amendment.[20] The fairly
even balance between Federalists and Jeffersonian Republicans in Congress
and state legislative majorities made it unlikely that any meaningful amendment could be adopted. Yet to those people who wanted to make the
strongest possible declaration of public policy, calling for alteration of the
Constitution seemed an appropriate gesture under the circumstances.

The triumph of Thomas Jefferson in the election of 1800 alarmed many
New England Federalists. They blamed their region's decline in political influence largely on the constitutional provision providing that a slave be
counted as the equivalent of three-fifths of a white person for the purpose of
apportioning representation in Congress, votes in the electoral college, and
direct taxes. The three-fifths clause, a compromise necessary to gain southern support for the Constitution in 1787, had always been controversial.
Now Federalists perceived it as giving southern states disproportionate national weight, with the white electorate benefiting from the South's "peculiar
institution" while voters in nonslave states received no equivalent boost in
the value of their ballots. In 1804 the Massachusetts legislature appealed for
a constitutional amendment basing apportionment for representation and

direct taxes on the free population of each state. Congress ignored the request, and only Federalist Connecticut and Delaware indicated support. Meanwhile, the legislature of Georgia declared that the proposed amendment "has its origins in injustice and will disorganize the Union."[21] The brief episode foreshadowed the constitutional standoff on slavery that would continue until the 1860s.

Another Massachusetts appeal for amendment followed the 1808 election. Federalists, mightily upset by the trade embargoes that the Jefferson and Madison administration employed against Great Britain, began formulating plans for a convention of New England states to propose constitutional amendments. Although no other states responded, the Congress repealed the embargo early in 1809. The very threat of amendment seemed to the Federalists to have accomplished the desired result.[22]

The 1812 declaration of war against Great Britain renewed New England's unhappiness with the nation's leadership and revived the technique of calling a convention to respond. Twenty-six delegates from Connecticut, Massachusetts, New Hampshire, Rhode Island, and Vermont met in Hartford in December 1814. Extremists, particularly those such as Massachusetts' Timothy Pickering who were calling for secession, were absent, and somewhat more temperate voices prevailed. The deliberations of the Hartford convention remained secret but the outcome of the proceedings quickly became known. Once again the Federalists' preferred response to a political crisis was to propose constitutional amendments.[23]

Scarcely more moderate than Pickering in their principles though more cautious in their tactics, the Hartford Federalists adopted resolutions calling for eight amendments to the federal Constitution to restore national harmony. The first two provided for apportionment of representation and direct taxes on the basis of each state's free population, resolutions renewing earlier demands for elimination of the detested three-fifths clause. The third called for a two-thirds vote, rather than a simple majority, for Congress to admit new states, reflecting Federalist fears about power shifting to the West. The next three limited congressional power to impose embargoes, interdict commerce, or declare war, severely restricting the national government's authority in foreign affairs. Embargoes and interdictions would be limited to sixty days and, together with declarations of war, would require two-thirds approval by each house of Congress. The seventh revived a proposal to ban naturalized citizens from holding federal office. The final amendment limited the president to one term and prevented two successive presidents from the same state.[24]

Together these eight amendments summed up Federalist complaints about the political power of the South in general and Jeffersonian Virginia in particular. They also reflected on Federalist political acumen since they betrayed a total lack of realism that such amendments could attract sufficiently widespread support to survive the Article V adoption process. The state legislatures of Massachusetts and Connecticut endorsed the Hartford resolutions, but no other state concurred; indeed eight states specifically rejected them.[25] This fate signifies how out of touch with sentiment elsewhere the Federalists had become; yet the fact that they turned to amendment deserves notice. Although the Federalists were indeed radical dissidents, they displayed a noteworthy preference for playing politics by the established rules.

By the time the Hartford resolutions were introduced in Congress at the end of February 1815, Washington had received word of Andrew Jackson's military triumph in New Orleans and the signing of a U.S.-British peace treaty at Ghent. In the light of the victory celebration, the proposed amendments and the Federalists who offered them were judged harshly. Both faded from view promptly and permanently.[26]

Discontents of lesser magnitude, in particular unhappiness with the presidential elections system, stirred other amending efforts about the same time. In 1813 the Senate approved 22 to 9 a request from the North Carolina state legislature that presidential electors be chosen by district rather than on a statewide basis. This proposal revived an idea first broached during the discussion that led to the Twelfth Amendment. The measure for reducing the influence of state majorities in presidential voting got nowhere in the House of Representatives, and though the Senate adopted it again in 1818 and 1821, it never went any further. Likewise, a revived and modified version of a Hartford convention proposal, an amendment to bar a president from a third term in office, passed the Senate by wide margins (36 to 3 and 32 to 7) in 1824 and 1826 but found few endorsements in the House, where it died. The introduction of a wide variety of other plans for presidential electoral reform and restraints on the presidency continued in subsequent years. None obtained much support, suggesting that concern about constitutional issues was not accompanied by consensus on what should be done to improve the existing system of government.[27]

One significant electoral reform was suggested by repeated amendment proposals, though not achieved by that means. Initially, a state's representatives to Congress could be chosen at large rather than by districts, a system that enhanced the influence of a political majority at the expense of regional minorities. More than two dozen amendment proposals to require election of representatives by district were introduced in Congress from 1800 to the mid-1820s, but nothing came of them. Finally, in 1842 Congress exercised its clear constitutional power to make or alter the manner of federal elections so as to mandate district election of members of the House.[28] Although calling for a constitutional amendment was a way to focus attention on the issue, in this instance federal authority was clearly adequate to implement change through ordinary legislation. The amendment approach was hardly appealing when less strenuous political means proved sufficient.

The decrease in the number of successful amendments after the turn of the nineteenth century did not signal a disappearance of faith in amendment as a mechanism to deal with desires for change in a written constitution. However, neither much of the public nor many of their representatives perceived the need for amendment. The most serious unfulfilled demands for amendment during this period, those arising in New England in 1798 and 1814, may not have borne fruit, but the diplomatic situations that occasioned those demands were resolved quickly and satisfactorily. In neither case did advocates of change display bitterness that the amendment process had stalled far short of success. Their points had been made. It would take a more serious and protracted dispute, one concerning the rights of states to protect the institution of slavery, to produce a reconsideration of the fundamental tenets of constitutional reform.

THE DEVELOPMENT of a process by which courts adjudicated disputes over the meaning of constitutional terms and limits drastically reduced the need for amendment. Judicial review had been anticipated by the Founders and became firmly established during the new nation's early years. Although in no way as definitive a means of articulating constitutional requirements, judicial review offered a less complicated and arduous, and therefore often preferable, alternative to amendment.

With the purpose of constitutions being to define and limit the governments established under them, the possibility was ever present that such a government would take an action overstepping the restrictions upon it. The inevitable need to respond to such situations preoccupied constitutional theorists. Proponents of the British system of parliamentary supremacy held that a constitution allowed whatever a majority of Parliament, representing the people, condoned at the moment. Critics of this position argued that permitting a legislature to set or alter its own limits contradicted the very notion of restraints on government. Written constitutions emerged in reaction to concepts of parliamentary supremacy. In effect, they declared that legislatures should not have the last word on constitutionality. Methods to amend written constitutions developed in response to a persistent question:

what was to be done if a situation arose that the constitution-makers had failed to anticipate or where separate provisions gave conflicting guidance? Yet amendment offered what was at best a cumbersome system for dealing with questions of constitutional interpretation, small as well as large and technical as well as fundamental, that might develop. As the frequency of such questions grew, this awkwardness would become increasingly apparent. The establishment of a process of judicial review of disputes over the meaning of constitutional terms and limits provided a solution to the problem short of amendment.

The need for a definitive interpreter and arbiter of disputed language in a written constitution had been recognized from the outset of American constitution-making. The creation of a Council of Censors in Pennsylvania's first state constitution had been the most explicit response to the problem. The 1787 federal convention discussed establishing a council of revision composed of the president and members of the judiciary. The Virginia plan offered such a council as a means of reviewing the constitutionality of legislative actions.[29] Some of the Founders saw the council of revision blurring the separation of powers they were seeking. Likewise, most delegates opposed Madison's idea of granting Congress specific authority to review and veto state laws.[30] Instead the Founders decided to follow the more common state constitutional pattern of reliance on the judiciary to resolve the constitutional conflicts certain to arise. Rufus King encountered no disagreement from his fellow delegates when he declared that "judges will have the expounding of those Laws when they come before them; and they will no doubt stop the operation of such as shall appear repugnant to the constitution."[31]

Contemporary thinking regarding the rationale for turning to the judiciary had been articulated only a year before the Philadelphia convention by attorney and congressman James M. Varnum. The Rhode Island case of *Trevett v. Weeden* was apparently the first American case that advanced the argument that a law was unconstitutional and therefore void. Legislatures, Varnum asserted on behalf of his client, were subordinate to written constitutions, and when they "enact what they may call laws, and refer those to the judiciary Courts for determination, then (in the discharge of the great trust reposed in them, and to prevent the horrors of civil war, as in the present case), the judges can, and we trust Your Honors will, decide upon them."[32] The Rhode Island Superior Court, after hearing the arguments, declined to accept jurisdiction. By the time the federal convention met, pamphlets were circulating in Philadelphia containing Varnum's argument as well as those in the North Carolina case of *Bayard v. Singleton* in which judges voided legislative acts as unconstitutional.[33]

The Founders embraced the fundamental concept of judicial review when they declared in Article III, section 2:

> This judicial Power shall extend to all Cases, in Law and Equity, arising under this Constitution, the Laws of the United States, and Treaties made, or which shall be made, under their Authority

and stated in the supremacy clause of Article VI:

> This Constitution, and the Laws of the United States which shall be made in Pursuance thereof; and all Treaties made, or which shall be made, under the Authority of the United States, shall be the supreme Law of the Land; and the Judges in every State shall be bound thereby, any Thing in the Constitution or Laws of any State to the Contrary notwithstanding.

In neither the state ratification debates nor in the deliberations of the First Congress setting up the federal courts in the Judiciary Act of 1789 did any challenge emerge to the basic concept of judicial review of constitutionality.[34]

In both federal and state constitutions, concessions of judicial authority were tempered by provisions for amendment that could always be used to overrule unsatisfactory court decisions. Yet the understanding was widespread that courts served, among other things, as primary, and usually sufficient, means to resolve ambiguities and conflicts in constitutional law. Jefferson and Madison preferred that most issues of constitutional interpretation be worked out within the branch of government affected but conceded that the judiciary would arbitrate differences bound to arise. The decision to place amendments after the original Constitution rather than to interweave them throughout it would increase the possibility of conflict among provisions of the document. Jefferson wrote privately to Madison that an argument for a declaration of rights that had "great weight with me" was that it put a "legal check . . . into the hands of the judiciary."[35]

From the moment that the federal courts began to function, they found themselves called upon to resolve disputes over the meaning of constitutional language. In *Chisholm v. Georgia,* the Supreme Court reviewed the intent of Article III and decided that it conferred to the federal courts jurisdiction over suits against states by residents of other states. Even James Iredell, the one justice who agreed with Georgia on the issue at hand, considered it appropriate for the Supreme Court to deal with the question. In his dissenting opinion, Iredell declared that the Court was "not only bound to consult, but sworn to observe" the Constitution that was "superior in obligation." He had "no hesitation" in saying that acts inconsistent with the Constitution "would be utterly void."[36] Displeasure with the *Chisholm* decision did not provoke cries that the judiciary had overstepped its proper authority in rendering a decision; however, it did lead to a prompt and successful effort to amend the Constitution to overrule the decision.

On other occasions during the 1790s as well, the Court exercised judicial review without bothering to proclaim its power to do so. The right of Congress to impose a uniform federal tax on carriages, a tax clearly intended to fall on the wealthy, was upheld over objections that the Constitution required a "direct tax" to be levied in proportion to each state's population.[37] The Court declared void a Virginia law preventing British creditors from collecting debts owed them because it was contrary to the 1783 treaty of peace between the United States and Great Britain and because the Constitution's supremacy clause gave treaties higher standing than state laws.[38] Congress offered no objection to the judiciary addressing such matters, perhaps because the Court validated each action as within congressional tax-levying or treaty-making authority. Only later, when the Supreme Court ruled that an act of government violated the Constitution and thus was invalid, did the implications of the judiciary's role as constitutional arbiter come into sharper focus.

Not until its first decision under Chief Justice John Marshall in the case of *Marbury v. Madison* in 1803 did the Supreme Court itself explicitly articulate the principle of judicial review of the constitutionality of governmental acts. In a wave of judicial appointments just prior to leaving office, the same wave that brought Marshall to the chief justiceship, President John Adams named William Marbury a District of Columbia justice of the peace. Marshall, who continued to serve as secretary of state during the last month of Adams's term, was himself officially responsible for the oversight of not delivering signed and sealed commissions to Marbury and several other "midnight appointees." Once installed, the new administration of Thomas Jefferson, philosophically averse to authority residing with the judiciary and practically opposed to power resting in the hands of its political adversaries, refused to complete the process. Prevented from taking office, Marbury sued to compel Secretary of State James Madison to deliver his commission. Marshall, initiating a practice of enhancing the Court's authority by having it announce a consolidated decision rather than having each justice render an individual judgment, dealt with the politically sensitive *Marbury* case so as to gain support for judicial review. Marshall, speaking for the full Court, found provisions of the Judiciary Act of 1789 that served as the authority for Marbury's appointment to be constitutionally invalid. As a result, the Court could not order Madison to deliver Marbury's commission. This con-

clusion mollified the Jeffersonians. Yet in reaching it, the chief justice forcefully asserted the principle of judicial review.[39]

In *Marbury v. Madison* Chief Justice Marshall proceeded on the assumption that the right of the people to establish a written constitution was "the
basis on which the whole American fabric has been erected." However, he
said, "The exercise of this original right is a very great exertion; nor can it,
nor ought it, to be frequently repeated." Once a constitution had spelled out
the powers of government, its departments, including the legislature, were
bound by it. Marshall saw no middle ground.

> The constitution is either a superior paramount law, unchangeable by or-
> dinary means, or it is on a level with ordinary legislative acts, and, like
> other acts, is alterable when the legislature shall please to alter it. If the
> former part of the alternative be true, then a legislative act, contrary to
> the constitution, is not law; if the latter part be true, then written consti-
> tutions are absurd attempts, on the part of the people, to limit a power,
> in its own nature, illimitable.

Marshall left room only for formal acts of amendment as legitimate means
to change a written constitution. Meanwhile, he declared, "an act of the legislature, repugnant to the constitution, is void."

Judges were obliged, in Marshall's view, to determine what the Constitution required and to act on that basis.

> It is, emphatically, the province and duty of the judicial department, to
> say what the law is. . . . If two laws conflict with each other, the courts
> must decide on the operation of each. So, if a law be in opposition to the
> constitution; . . . the court must determine which of these conflicting
> rules governs the case: this is of the very essence of judicial duty. If
> then, . . . the constitution is superior to any ordinary act of the legisla-
> ture, the constitution, and not such ordinary act, must govern the case to
> which they both apply.
>
> Those, then, who controvert the principle, that the constitution is to
> be considered, in court, as a paramount law, are reduced to the necessity
> of maintaining that courts must close their eyes on the constitution, and
> see only the law. This doctrine would subvert the very foundation of all
> written constitutions.[40]

For judges to enforce unconstitutional laws would give legislatures "a practical and real omnipotence." They would, in effect, be able to adopt whatever
laws they chose and change the Constitution whenever they wished. Marshall considered such a situation clearly unacceptable.

The chief justice based his justification of judicial review on the inherent nature of written constitutions. Only after having made this point did Marshall turn to the Constitution itself to reinforce his argument. The Article VI supremacy clause and the Article III judicial oath to uphold the Constitution clarified the judicial obligation to declare void government acts contrary to the fundamental law. He made no direct reference to Article V but he well could have. The presence of a stipulated procedure for the legislature to initiate constitutional change could easily have been used as further evidence that it was otherwise to remain within the bounds of the existing framework.

Logically and vigorously presented, consistent with prevailing thought, and used to produce a result that even Marshall's political opponents approved, *Marbury v. Madison* stirred few open objections. In 1825 one critic, Pennsylvania state supreme court justice John Gibson, sneered that judicial review had become "a professional dogma" but was unable to convince his colleagues that it was inappropriate. Two decades later, even Gibson accepted the principle.[41] The Supreme Court's practice of interpreting the meaning of the Constitution grew and became entrenched during John Marshall's thirty-five-year tenure as chief justice. It continued thereafter. The lack of challenge to judicial review can no doubt be explained in part by the fact that more than a half century would pass before the Court once again found an act of Congress, the so-called Missouri Compromise, unconstitutional. The specific decision in *Dred Scott v. Sandford* provoked outrage, but by 1857 the Court's review of a question of constitutionality did not. Also important to the growing acceptance of judicial review was the fact that it reduced the need for resort to the amending process when, as repeatedly happened, the Constitution proved ambiguous.

Judicial review evolved as a complement to, not a substitute for, constitutional amendment. It emerged as a means for resolving conflict or uncertainty regarding the meaning of existing constitutional provisions in the light of imprecise language, unanticipated circumstances, or new legislation, not as a device to establish new constitutional requirements independent of what the instrument already contained. The Court did not use this power to overthrow the Constitution's accepted directives but to deal with such matters as its lack of clarity regarding the federal relationship between state and national authority or, later, the inexact declarations of protected individual rights. Judicial review simply provided a relatively uncomplicated means for determining what the Constitution required when that was in doubt. Often it mattered less what the Court's decision was than that a clear rule had been articulated, one that all could follow with confidence. James Bryce, a late-nineteenth-century English admirer of judicial review, wrote that "it has had the advantage of relegating questions not only intricate and delicate, but peculiarly liable to excite political passion, to the cool, dry atmosphere of judicial determination."[42]

A great deal of controversy over judicial review has arisen in the twentieth century, predicated on the assumption that it delivered absolute and final constitutional authority to the courts.[43] Constitutionally speaking, judicial review never became the last word. A judicial decision could always be appealed to the ultimate sovereignty of the people through the amendment process. The Founders most definitely intended it to be so. It is worth noting that they not only spelled out the amending procedure in Article V but placed it between Article III, establishing the judiciary, and Article VI, declaring the supremacy of the Constitution. Yet as long as the broad outlines of the Constitution remained acceptable, judicial review served a very useful purpose. It eliminated the need for constant resort to amendment in order to articulate the details of the Founders' plan.

STRICT ALLEGIANCE to constitutionalism, so much a part of revolutionary era thought, began to relax as the complexities and surprises of governing exposed the difficulties of adhering rigidly to a formal design. At first it was Federalists who strained against the perceived limits of the Constitution, but even Jefferson began to loosen his hitherto narrow view of what the charter permitted when faced with the opportunity to acquire the vast Louisiana Territory from France in 1803. Initially the president believed that a constitutional amendment would be required to allow the federal government to purchase land beyond its borders. However, Jefferson soon became worried that the delay involved in securing an amendment might doom the unexpected offer. It might be withdrawn as suddenly as it had been proposed. Acting on Secretary of the Treasury Albert Gallatin's suggestion, Jefferson determined that the Constitution's grant of treaty-making power to the government could be construed to permit immediate acquisition of the vast territory by treaty, assuming that two-thirds of the Senate agreed to ratify.[44] The quickly completed Louisiana Purchase marked a significant retreat from the initial conception of limited government.

Jefferson had long been a vigorous advocate of consulting the sovereign power of the people whenever constitutional questions arose.[45] In drafting a proposal for a new Virginia constitution in 1783, he had stipulated that whenever two of the three branches of state government, by a two-thirds vote, felt constitutional change necessary, a popular convention should be called to consider the matter.[46] Here Jefferson marched in step with his republican contemporaries who regarded conventions as the best expression of the sovereign popular will. The resort to conventions in 1787 to draft the Constitution itself, secure its state-by-state ratification, and provide for its future alteration met with Jefferson's approval. He expressed to Madison his belief that conventions should be held frequently to ascertain the constitutional wishes of an evolving society.[47] When he lent support during the state ratification battle to calls for a second convention to add a bill of rights to the document and eleven years later proposed in the Kentucky resolutions a convention to deal with the Alien and Sedition Acts crisis, Jefferson displayed his continuing commitment to the convention approach to constitutional change. The Louisiana Purchase therefore marked a shift in his constitutional thinking, a willingness to accept an expansive reading of the Constitution rather than to insist upon obtaining explicit sanction for an unprecedented governmental act.

James Madison's thinking about formal constitutional change also evolved, although along a somewhat different route from his fellow Virginian's. His views shaped by his participation in the strenuous experiences of the 1786 Annapolis convention, the 1787 Philadelphia constitutional convention, and the 1788 Virginia ratifying convention while his close friend sat in Paris, Madison as early as spring 1788 expressed a rare difference of opinion with Jefferson. In *Federalist* 49, Madison, not denying that the people were "the only legitimate fountain of power" for establishing constitutional meaning, nevertheless held that resort to such authority should be made only on "certain great and extraordinary occasions." Turning frequently to the public raised the prospect of tipping the delicate equilibrium of government toward the branch closest to the people, the legislative branch. More important, it might well undermine public faith in the Constitution to have its terms often brought into question. Implying that a continual discovery of defects might destroy the "veneration, which time bestows on every thing, and without which perhaps the wisest and freest governments would not possess the requisite stability," Madison feared that passion, not reason, might guide such a process of constitutional decisionmaking. Constitution writing, he declared, was "of too ticklish a nature to be unnecessarily multiplied."[48]

Although he expressed this caveat, Madison nevertheless repeatedly found circumstances that called for amendment. He took the lead in the battle for the Bill of Rights, having given his pledge to do so in order to ensure Virginia's ratification, and later stood alongside Jefferson in calling for amendments to deal with the Alien and Sedition Acts crisis. The caution displayed in *Federalist* 49 did not signal any wavering of Madison's basic commitment to constitutionalism; rather, it exhibited his belief that excessive and unnecessary resort to the formal process of amendment could possibly be counterproductive. This side of Madison's thought on amendment was again evident when, as Jefferson's secretary of state, he played a central role in the Louisiana Purchase. When Congressman John Quincy Adams posed the need for an amendment to sanction Louisiana's incorporation into the Union, Madison gave him no encouragement.[49] The secretary of state defended Jefferson's conclusion that in this case the Constitution was sufficient and that indeed it was best not to pursue amendment. Still, Madison's position did not indicate, any more than *Federalist 49,* that he had abandoned his fundamental support for clearly stated constitutionalism.

Near the end of his presidential term, Madison indicated anew his belief in the importance of having the terms of government set forth in fundamental law. In the aftermath of the Treaty of Ghent and the resultant upsurge of American nationalism, support became widespread for strengthening the country's economy, particularly its banking system and transportation network. In Congress Speaker of the House Henry Clay led the call for federal funding of internal improvements, the road and canal building that had hitherto been a local responsibility. In his December 1815 annual message to Congress, Madison demonstrated the continuing evolution of his republican ideas by embracing increased defense spending, a national bank, a protective tariff, and a national university. Yet in discussing internal improvements, the president indicated that he did not believe the Constitution as it stood permitted national spending for local purposes. Though he favored federally financed internal improvements to promote prosperity and bind the nation more tightly together, Madison suggested that, before this could be done, a constitutional amendment needed to be adopted. "It is a happy reflection," he concluded, "that any defect of constitutional authority which may be encountered can be supplied in a mode which the Constitution itself has providently pointed out."[50]

Although there was no response to his suggestion, the president did not drop the issue. A year later he spoke of the Constitution's virtues in his last annual message.[51] Then, just as Madison's term was drawing to a close, Congress adopted Clay's proposal to finance internal improvements with the $1.5 million federal bonus obtained from chartering a new Bank of the United States. On his last day in office, Madison vetoed the bonus bill, saying that "it does not appear that the power proposed to be exercised in the bill is among the enumerated powers, or that it falls by any just interpretation within the power to make the laws necessary and proper for carrying into execution those or other powers vested by the Constitution in the Government of the United States." In the president's view, the bonus bill violated the spirit of the Constitution, not to mention the specific terms of the Tenth Amendment. Such broad construction of congressional power to provide for the common defense and general welfare would in effect give Congress "a general power of legislation instead of a defined and limited one hitherto understood to belong to them." Constitutional amendment, Madison repeated, was needed for such an extension of federal powers beyond those enumerated. Otherwise Congress would be able to determine the constitutionality of its own acts on a standard of "policy and expediency." Although he saw the advantages of internal improvements, Madison chose to make a political last testament by standing steadfast for a scrupulous respect for constitutionalism. He cherished the hope, he declared, that "beneficial objects may be obtained by a resort for the necessary powers to the same wisdom and virtue in the nation which established the Constitution in its actual form and providently marked out in the instrument itself a safe and practicable mode of improving it as experience might suggest."[52]

Madison's veto of the bonus bill caught Speaker Clay by surprise. He could not persuade Congress to override it even after Madison's departure from office. Madison did not lack support for his continuing view that constitutional limits needed to be articulated to preserve republican government. Jefferson in particular applauded his friend's veto, agreeing that "strained constructions . . . would loosen all the bands of the constitution" and believing that "an application to the states for an extension of their powers to this object [will] be unanimously conceded." Jefferson went on to say that amendment "will be a better way of obtaining the end."[53] However, the departure from office of the last of the Founders to occupy the presidency marked the passing of such strict constitutionalism.

The emergence of a more generous view of governmental power, together with the increasing role of judicial review in resolving constitutional disputes, became evident in the 1819 Supreme Court decision in *McCulloch v. Maryland*. John Marshall articulated a view contrary to Madison's when he declared a constitution a flexible instrument sufficient to the "exigencies of the nation." He treated with scorn the view that a constitution should enumerate all powers of government and every means of their execution, saying that it would acquire "the prolixity of a legal code, and could scarcely be embraced by the human mind." Rather, the nature of a constitution requires that "only its great outlines should be marked, its important objects designated, and the minor ingredients which compose those objects be deduced from the nature of the objects themselves." When Marshall concluded this argument with his ringing declaration, "We must never forget that it is a *constitution* we are expounding," he was ignoring the Founders' understanding of the term and substituting a much broader reading.[54]

In *McCulloch,* Marshall took a far more expansive view than had Madison in 1817 of the powers of Congress to legislate in new areas without specific grants of expanded authority via amendment. The Court in *McCulloch* upheld the right of Congress to incorporate a national bank even though the Constitution did not explicitly give it the authority to do so. "To have prescribed the means by which government should, in all future time, execute its powers," declared Marshall, "would . . . have been an unwise attempt to provide, by immutable rules, for exigencies which, if foreseen at all, must have been seen dimly, and which can be best provided for as they occur." As Marshall boldly applied the Constitution's necessary and proper legislation clause, "Let the end be legitimate, let it be within the scope of the constitution, and all means which are appropriate, which are plainly adapted to that end, which are not prohibited, but consist with the letter and spirit of the constitution, are constitutional." Without the ability "to be adapted to the various crises of human affairs," the chief justice insisted, the Constitution would be reduced to a "splendid bauble" and not serve as a great charter of government "intended to endure for ages to come."[55] Marshall's doctrine, if accepted, would clearly give Congress a broad latitude and reduce the need to seek new constitutional language to justify legislative innovations.

Jefferson and Madison grumbled about *McCulloch v. Maryland* from their Virginia retirements. Jefferson, a consistent opponent of national banks, was most unhappy about John Marshall's latest assertion of judicial power to determine constitutional issues.[56] Madison accepted the constitutionality of the Bank of the United States that he had, after all, signed into law. Nevertheless, he was alarmed by Marshall's reasoning that he thought surrendered to Congress much too wide a latitude to determine its own limits. Expediency and constitutionality had become interchangeable terms, Madison feared. Echoing his bonus bill veto, he worried that the temptations of popular measures, such as internal improvements, would erode constitutional restraints on the legislative branch. Writing to Virginia chief justice Spencer Roane, Madison stressed that the United States was exceptional in being able to boast that its government had been "freely and deliberately established" by the people and could be "altered by the same authority only which established it." He continued, "It is a further boast, that a regular mode of making proper alterations has been providently inserted in the Constitution itself." Other means of innovation were unacceptable; amendment should be used to distinguish between ordinary legislative practice and the creation of fundamental law. "If the powers be deficient,"

Madison concluded, "the legitimate source of additional ones is always open, and ought to be resorted to."[57]

Despite these complaints and those of states' rights opponents of the Bank of the United States, however, *McCulloch* won the same general acceptance that Marshall's earlier great declaration in *Marbury v. Madison* had enjoyed. A constitution whose mandates to provide for the common defense and the general welfare as well as to take steps that were necessary and proper to carry out its obligations could be interpreted broadly, it was readily agreed. Such a constitution furnished a much more flexible governmental framework for an expanding nation than one that demanded frequent formal alteration to assume new tasks. Constitutionally based opposition to internal improvement gradually faded, for instance. As the role of judicial review came to be accepted and as the Marshall Court lent support to an expansive reading of the Constitution's terms, the perceived need for amendment declined. As the Constitution's founding generation passed from the American scene, so too did its understanding that a constitution defined narrow limits for government and that each new undertaking or altered practice required the sanction of formal constitutional amendment.

7

"In Pursuit of an Impracticable Theory"

States' Rights and Constitutional Amendment

Although no amendment was added to the U.S. Constitution between 1804 and 1865, the amending process continued to play a role in efforts to deal with constitutional difficulties during these years. Given the problems at hand and the array of political forces, amendment was repeatedly discussed and considered even though never achieved. Throughout this period, the core constitutional conflict remained the balance of state and national power in the federal relationship. The division of opinion on this delicate matter prevented the assembly of a stable majority in support of any settlement, much less the concurrent supermajorities of Congress and the states required to amend the Constitution. The obstacle blocking accommodation was invariably the uncompromisable issue of slavery.

The Founders themselves had discovered slavery to be an intractable problem. The delicate equilibrium of state and federal power they created in Philadelphia in 1787 served merely to defer, not to solve, the conflict between free and slaveholding cultures. Not surprisingly, the amendment process, a mechanism whose successful functioning was predicated on shared assumptions and goals, could not resolve a conflict so deep that it would eventually lead to civil war. Amendment declined during the antebellum era because most other problems could be dealt with by the lesser means of ordinary legislation, executive determination, or judicial review; the truly monumental constitutional problem of the age could be settled only by revolution.

The search for a path out of the constitutional swamp led some foiled and frustrated factions deeper into the quagmire. Unable to rely on judicial review from a nationalist-oriented Supreme Court to protect their interests, slavery's defenders were likewise unable to obtain a national majority, much less an amending supermajority, to rescue them. Consequently, they fastened upon a new concept of constitutional alteration. At different times and for different reasons various voices contributed to an evolving argument that each state retained a right to interpret, reform, or reject individual provisions of the Constitution. Furthermore, some Americans came to believe that it remained a state's right to withdraw or secede from the

Union if constitutional arrangements satisfactory to it could not be made. This theory evolved through a series of political battles in 1798, 1814, the early 1830s, and the entire decade of the 1850s. It offended the nationalists, who thought that the creation of 1787 required a singular verb, those who believed the United States *was,* not the United States *were.* They rejected the states' rights doctrine of constitutional change. Given the stakes involved and the determination of the people on both sides, it is hardly surprising that the struggle over the power to mold the Constitution did not end peacefully.

Even after the 1860 election of Abraham Lincoln convinced slave states that withdrawal from the Union was necessary, a search for constitutional accommodation continued. The last desperate efforts to prevent secession involved an attempt to craft a constitutional amendment that would satisfy all sides. In the most tension-filled of moments, Congress was able to fashion a conciliatory amendment acceptable to a two-thirds supermajority of those senators and representatives remaining in their seats. The proposed amendment was no doubt unrealistic. Only a handful of states chose to endorse it. Nevertheless, the turn to constitutionalism and the remedy of amendment in these circumstances was noteworthy. Congress regarded the Article V process as its last best hope of avoiding chaos. And when amendment failed, to use Lincoln's words, "One [section] would *make* war rather than let the nation survive, and the other would *accept* war rather than let it perish, and the war came."[1]

IN PHILADELPHIA during summer 1787, James Madison led a group of ardent supporters of the proposition that the federal government being created should be superior to the individual states.[2] The sixth of the Virginia resolutions that formed the basis for the delegates' discussion proposed that the national legislature ought to have the power "to negative all laws passed by the several States, contravening in the opinion of the National Legislature the articles of Union."[3] Charles C. Pinckney of South Carolina called this provision "indispensably necessary" if the Congress was to be effectual, saying "the States must be kept in due subordination to the nation." He went on to explain, "If the States were left to act of themselves in any case, it wd. be impossible to defend the national prerogatives, however extensive they might be on paper." A federal veto over the acts of individual states was, he concluded, "the corner stone of an efficient national Govt." Madison immediately took the floor to second Pinckney, terming the power to veto state acts "absolutely necessary to a perfect system." Both James Wilson and John

Dickinson quickly agreed, citing, as had Pinckney and Madison, the example of the unworkable alternative under the Articles of Confederation.[4]

This proposed clear statement of federal supremacy provoked strong opposition. Elbridge Gerry worried that "the Natl. Legislature with such a power may enslave the States." Gunning Bedford of Delaware expressed fear that small states such as his could thereby be crushed without recourse, a concern that appeared widespread. Every state delegation, except those of Massachusetts, Pennsylvania, and Virginia, voted against the proposal. Madison kept trying until the final days of the convention to have the decision reconsidered but without success.[5]

The 1787 convention instead made a much more vague declaration of federal supremacy, based on the language of the New Jersey plan as modified by the committees on detail and style and placed not in the articles listing federal legislative or judicial powers but among the miscellaneous provisions of Article VI.[6] Although it proclaimed that the Constitution together with laws and treaties made under it would be "the supreme Law of the Land" and that "Judges in every State shall be bound thereby, any Thing in the Constitution or Laws of any State to the Contrary notwithstanding," Article VI left dangling the question of who would determine whether the Constitution had been breached. The defeat of the original Virginia language meant that a specified power to decide such matters was not listed among those of Congress in Article II. Nor did Article III enumerate it among the powers of the federal judiciary.

The Founders, on this and other occasions when they had the opportunity to clarify the federal-state relationship as well as locate the authority to settle constitutional quarrels, left the door to dispute ajar. Though in many ways they created a framework of government with a clearly national focus, one that preempted many powers previously held by the states, they allowed the doctrine of federal supremacy to remain less than fully articulated. They proclaimed that "We the People" established the Constitution as the sovereign power, but at the same time they arranged for state-by-state ratification. Finally, they left an arbiter for constitutional disputes unspecified. They laid a strong foundation for the claim of federal judicial power to review constitutional disagreements that John Marshall soon asserted, but at the same time the door remained open for counterclaims of the right of states to interpret the Constitution.

The First Congress only made the situation murkier by proposing what became the Tenth Amendment. Its declaration that "the powers not delegated to the United States by the Constitution, nor prohibited by it to the States, are reserved to the States respectively, or to the people" left unanswered the question "What powers?" Against this background it is no wonder that when serious conflicts arose between the interests of individual states or groups of states and the federal government, the struggle would center on who had the authority to define or reform the Constitution. States' rights versus national rights became the primary issue of constitutional amendment, indeed the central question of nineteenth-century American government.

In summer 1798 the issue of the role of states in determining constitutional matters came to the fore for the first time since the Constitution had gone into effect. Domestic discord, stirred by the quasi-war with France and the increasingly bitter struggle between Federalists and Jeffersonian Republicans, led to the adoption of the Alien and Sedition Acts. These measures of the Federalist-dominated Congress seemed to many critics to alter the Constitution. They infringed upon the established electoral process, not to mention the First Amendment guarantees of free speech and press.[7] If unchallenged, the Alien and Sedition Acts would not only have the immediate political consequence of suppressing criticism of the Adams administration and thus Thomas Jefferson's campaign for the presidency in 1800, but also they would appear to set a precedent for Congress's revising the Constitution on its own.

During early autumn 1798 Jefferson and Madison conferred on a response and drew up resolutions for adoption by the legislatures of Kentucky and Virginia.[8] Jefferson's resolutions for Kentucky were more strident than Madison's for Virginia, but they made a similar central argument. Both contended that the Alien and Sedition Acts violated the terms of the federal Constitution, in particular the First Amendment's free speech and press protections. Congress must not, as it had in this case, exceed and thus alter its defined powers, construed exactly. Otherwise, as the Virginia legislation explained, "nothing could have been more frivolous than an enumeration of powers."[9]

Most significantly, Jefferson and Madison argued that the Constitution was a compact among the states that had ratified it and, therefore, the states could make the final determination as to what it required. "As in all other cases of compact among parties having no common Judge, each party has an equal right to judge for itself, as well of infractions as of the mode and measure of redress."[10] When the Congress overstepped and redefined its authority, the argument continued, the states possessed the right and responsibility to interpose themselves between the national government and their citizens, refusing to allow the offending law to be enforced within their borders. The states, said the Virginia resolution, "have the right, and are in duty bound, to interpose, for arresting the progress of the evil, and for maintaining, within their respective limits, the authorities, rights, and liberties, appertaining to them."[11] States were called upon to join in declaring the Alien and Sedition Acts unconstitutional and void. Kentucky, at Jefferson's urging, became more explicit in 1799 in a second set of resolutions that declared that "a nullification, by those sovereignties, of all unauthorized acts done under color of that instrument, is the rightful remedy."[12]

Much of the attention given to the Kentucky and Virginia resolutions has concentrated on their later use by John C. Calhoun in his argument that each individual state possessed the power to nullify a congressional act within its jurisdiction. However, a key element in Madison and Jefferson's position, one distinguishing it from Calhoun's, was the notion that states act together to overturn unconstitutional measures of Congress. By calling on other states to join them in declaring the Alien and Sedition Acts void, Kentucky and Virginia were implicitly following the Article V model for further definition of constitutional terms. The failure to follow its terms explicitly, calling for a constitutional convention and acknowledging that two-thirds of the states would need to concur, rendered the Kentucky and Virginia resolutions excessively vague. Furthermore, the hostile reaction of nine states, northern and Federalist in every case, made it clear that neither the voiding of Congress's actions nor specific constitutional change by the Article V process was possible at the moment.

No attempt to alter the Constitution by individual state action occurred in 1798. The states that formally responded to Virginia and Kentucky declared the claim of state legislative authority to proclaim an act of Congress unconstitutional "unwarrantable doctrine."[13] Madison, who was still living at the time that Calhoun advanced his doctrine that a single state could interpose itself between its people and Congress to nullify a federal law within its jurisdiction, said that he had never intended such a construction in the Alien and Sedition Acts crisis.[14] The Virginia and Kentucky initiatives went no further than legislative resolutions and unsuccessful appeals to other states. As both international and domestic tensions eased, the Alien and Sedition Acts were allowed to expire. Jefferson's 1800 electoral victory ended the immediate conflict, but the dispute over state constitutional authority lay dormant, not dead.

The next assertion of individual states' power to set constitutional bounds came from the opposite pole of the political compass, New England Federalism. As the Embargo of 1807 began inflicting serious economic damage upon New England, Federalists began to echo the constitutional theories of the Virginia and Kentucky resolutions they had not long before rejected out of hand. While their principal political effort involved a conventional quest for constitutional amendment, they also took up the claim that the United States was a confederation of independent republics, a league of sovereign states that had surrendered only limited powers to a central government. The states that had created the Constitution possessed the power to determine when their agreement had been violated. A state would be exercising its sovereignty, not committing treason, if it interposed its authority between its people and the national government to nullify a law or, in an extreme situation, to secede. Although both actions rested on the same constitutional theory of a compact of states, most Federalists preferred the vague but relatively moderate interposition approach to the radical alternative of secession.[15]

The Federalist argument for state interposition faded after the embargo's repeal but reemerged when the United States declared war on Great Britain in 1812. Not only did the Federalists fail to support the war and call for it to end, but by 1814, with an even stricter embargo in effect, some talked seriously of independence on the grounds that the Constitution had failed to protect New England's rights and provide it benefits. Among the delegates to the Hartford convention in December 1814 were a number of men, particularly from Massachusetts, who advocated secession. Though moderation, in the form of a call for amendments, triumphed at Hartford, the delegates scheduled a second meeting for Boston in June as an occasion for considering secession if the amendments were not adopted. The second meeting was never held. The almost immediate resolution of the war ended the discussion, stirred a great surge of nationalism, and essentially terminated the Federalists as a political force.[16]

The Supreme Court in its 1819 *McCulloch v. Maryland* decision struck a further serious blow to notions of state power. The immediate issue in *McCulloch* was whether the state of Maryland could tax the Bank of the United States established by Congress in 1816. John Marshall, speaking for a unanimous Court, declared that "the power to tax is the power to destroy" and insisted that no individual state had the right to thwart the exercise of legitimate federal authority within its borders.[17] *McCulloch* was the Marshall Court's most forthright statement of federal supremacy. It did not, however, lay the controversy to rest.

Nearly a decade passed before John C. Calhoun brought the issues of states' rights and constitutional change back to center stage in the course of expressing South Carolina's growing unhappiness with the extent of federal power. Although southern concern with protecting slavery underlay its actions, South Carolina's immediate preoccupation was federal tariff policy. Once an ardent nationalist who accepted tariffs as a means of paying for national defense, Calhoun now joined other South Carolinians who saw the high tariff that Congress adopted in 1828, the so-called Tariff of Abominations, inflicting serious and unreasonable damage on the state's economy. In the *South Carolina Exposition and Protest,* which the state legislature published anonymously in December 1828, Calhoun drew on the Virginia and Kentucky resolutions of three decades earlier and the views of other South Carolina leaders that had evolved therefrom. Echoing the argument that the Constitution was a compact of states and that states could judge the constitutionality of federal action, Calhoun articulated a plan by which this could be done and that went much further than Jefferson and Madison's.

Calhoun's means of dealing with constitutional disputes, which quickly gained the oversimplified label of "nullification" and the image of a single-state veto of federal action, was in reality more complex. In cases of serious state objection to a federal act, Calhoun proposed that a state convention be held to obtain a direct expression of the sovereign will of the people. If the delegates agreed, the convention should convey the state's protest to Congress, at which point Congress could either repeal the offending laws or, by a two-thirds vote, submit a constitutional amendment embodying them for all states to consider. If three-fourths of the states ratified the amendment, the complaining state would be obliged to acquiesce; if not, the disagreeable law would be annulled.

On its face neither a threat to secede nor a demand for state unanimity prior to federal action, Calhoun's plan would, nevertheless, have imposed Article V standards of congressional and state supermajority agreement upon every substantive federal initiative. In effect, every piece of federal legislation would have to meet the Founders' standard for constitutional change in order to be assured of adoption. One state could block a new federal law unless two-thirds of the Congress and three-fourths of the states agreed to uphold it; and indeed a single state could object to a previously constitutional measure and thereby alter the Constitution unless the requisite congressional and state supermajorities enforced the prior standard. To an insightful modern student of nullification, "Calhoun created a wildly revolutionary doctrine in the name of conserving the Union . . . a veritable snarl of contradictions. Calhoun stopped constitutional revisions by the federal government and then permitted constitutional alterations by single states; . . . he defended the consent of the governed at the expense of destroying the power to govern; he proposed conserving the Union with principles which would have destroyed it."[18]

By the 1850s southern states' rights extremists would come to recognize dangers in endorsing the power of constitutional amendment, but two decades earlier the South Carolina nullifiers relied heavily upon it. Calhoun acknowledged in his draft of the *Exposition* that "each State, by assenting to the Constitution with this provision, has modified its original right as a sovereign, of making its individual consent necessary to any change in its political condition; and, by becoming a member of the Union, has placed this important power in the hands of three fourths of the States—in whom the highest power known to the Constitution actually resides." The South Carolina legislature went even further in the printed *Exposition,* changing Calhoun's "has modified its original right as a sovereign" to "has surrendered its original right."[19] On its surface, this declaration conceded the power of the Union over individual states in matters of constitutional change. Yet by applying Article V standards to federal decisions, the nullification doctrine promised ample protection for the more than one-fourth of the states that defended slaveholding.

The national debate provoked by the *South Carolina Exposition and Protest* centered on the immediate political question of what should be done when one section of the country appeared to benefit at the expense of another, the same question that had arisen in 1798 and 1814. Nationalists asserted federal supremacy and the perpetual nature of the Union. Such views, articulated in the Senate by Daniel Webster and from the White House by Andrew Jackson, exposed the limits of Calhoun's support. Even most proponents of states' rights rejected the nullification doctrine. The general assembly of Kentucky declared that it could not recognize

> the right of a minority, either of the states or of the people, to set up their opinion not only in opposition, but to overrule that of the majority. . . . The consequences of such a principle, if practically enforced, would be alarming in the extreme. Scarcely any important measure of the general government is ever adopted, to which one or more of the States are not opposed. If one State have a right to obstruct and defeat the execution of a law of Congress because it deems it unconstitutional, then every State has a similar right. . . . If [in the objecting state the offending act is] enforced there is a civil war; if abandoned, without being repealed, a virtual dissolution of the Union.[20]

Little support appeared anywhere outside South Carolina for the doctrine of nullification.

In his famous reply to South Carolina senator Robert Hayne and other nullificationists in 1830, Daniel Webster pointed out that the Articles of Confederation had declared the United States to be a perpetual creation and that the 1787 Constitution's preamble declared that it was being established to form a more perfect Union. Such a charter could be amended but not dissolved. Senator Edward Livingston of Louisiana, soon to become Jackson's secretary of state, agreed with Webster and held that states believing a federal law to be unconstitutional did not have the right to nullify the law or to secede. Instead they could appeal to the Supreme Court or Congress, or they could seek an amendment to the Constitution. The president agreed wholeheartedly. "Perpetuity is stamped upon the Constitution by the blood of our Fathers," Jackson declared. "For this purpose was the principle of amendment inserted in the Constitution which all have sworn to support and in violation of which no state or states have the right to secede, much less dissolve the Union."[21] Jackson's vehement hostility to nullification overshadowed his willingness to point out a path of constitutional relief.

In 1832 South Carolina attempted to put the nullification doctrine into effect. By the required two-thirds vote, the state legislature called a convention that in turn proclaimed the tariff null and void in South Carolina and declared it "expedient that a convention of the States be called as early as practicable to consider and determine such questions of disputed powers as have arisen between the State of this Confederacy and the General Government." Only legislatures in neighboring Alabama and Georgia joined the South Carolina call for a convention, and even there a majority rejected South Carolina's act of nullification as "unsound in theory and dangerous in practice," not to mention "rash and revolutionary." Despite significant nullificationist minorities and great unhappiness about Jackson's threats to use force against South Carolina, Virginia, Mississippi, North Carolina, and Tennessee joined in condemning the doctrine. With a few qualms about the president's behavior, so did eleven northern and western states. James Madison, the last living Founder, objected strenuously to South Carolina's single-state-right-of-nullification interpretation.[22]

South Carolina's attempt to nullify the tariff enraged Andrew Jackson. Having recently made conciliatory gestures regarding tariff rates, public lands, and other matters, he issued a ringing proclamation denouncing South Carolina's claim of individual state power to annul a law of the United States as "incompatible with the existence of the Union, contradicted expressly by the letter of the Constitution, unauthorized by its spirit, inconsistent with every principle on which it was founded, and destructive of the great object for which it was formed." He heaped abuse on the idea of nullification, calling it an "impracticable absurdity," and a "metaphysical subtlety, in pursuit of an impracticable theory."[23] The president fully embraced a nationalist vision of the Constitution and left no doubt that he would use all the power at his disposal to enforce it.

South Carolina's retreat from nullification in 1833 is usually attributed to President Jackson's strident rejection of the compact theory in favor of indissoluble nationalism, the Congress's Force bill to compel collection of the tariff, and its peace offering of lower tariffs. However, the lack of support for South Carolina's amendment quest no doubt sent the message that, by its own declared standard, South Carolina had lost the battle for constitutional reform. The state would have to comply with federal policy or secede, an unrealistic alternative at the moment. As the most thorough historian of the crisis concluded, "Nullification had been irretrievably smashed. The . . . South would have to endure the anxiety being generated by a growing anti-slavery movement [and] could no longer hope to deal with the question indirectly."[24]

FROM THE NULLIFICATION CRISIS until the very eve of the Civil War, constitutional amendment remained a rarely discussed means of resolving the dispute over slavery. The delicate balance of the 1787 Constitution seemed difficult to improve upon at first. Then as both northern and southern discontent with the degree of protection afforded slavery grew, in different directions to be sure, there appeared less and less chance of effecting a change through the Article V process. By the time extreme abolitionist William Lloyd Garrison declared the Constitution "a covenant with death" and publicly set a copy afire in 1854, it seemed an unlikely platform on which to erect a settlement. Only when the tensions generated by the slavery conflict reached the fever pitch needed to prompt serious steps toward secession did discussion turn in desperation to achieving accommodation through constitutional revision. Then with fundamental issues of state versus federal rights as well as slavery in sharp focus, great energy was devoted to finding a solution that could be incorporated into the Constitution.

In 1805 and 1806 with the Constitution's initial twenty-year ban on tampering with the slave trade soon to expire, state legislatures in Massachusetts, Vermont, New Hampshire, Tennessee, and Maryland petitioned Congress for an amendment prohibiting further imports. Their objective was achieved through ordinary legislation. A dozen years later, Congress turned a deaf ear to a lone New Hampshire representative who proposed an amendment abolishing slavery, anticipating by a year the effort by Representative James Tallmadge of New York to end slavery in the new state of Missouri. With the Missouri Compromise having restored calm for the moment, the Georgia legislature in 1825 offered an amendment to reauthorize slave imports. Louisiana, Missouri, and Mississippi endorsed the idea, but Vermont, Maine, Ohio, New Jersey, Indiana, Connecticut, Delaware, and Kentucky indicated their disapproval.[25] Other than occasional proposals to tamper with the three-fifths compromise on counting slaves for apportioning representation, these were the only slavery-related amendments suggested during the Constitution's first half century.

In 1839, congressman and former president John Quincy Adams, who since his election to the House of Representatives in 1830 had become a steadily more outspoken opponent of slavery, proposed three antislavery amendments. At the moment Adams was particularly upset over the recent harsh treatment accorded the Africans who had taken over the Spanish slave ship *Amistad* and brought it into American waters. He also continued to be angry about the House of Representatives' "gag rule," its 1836 decision to table automatically and permanently all petitions on slavery. Adams's amendments would have abolished hereditary slavery after 1842, refused admission of slave states to the Union, and prohibited slavery and slave trading altogether in the District of Columbia after 1845. Adams, seeking to make the current generation of slaves the last, vigorously defended his plan against venomous attacks by southerners during ten days of House debate. The Adams initiative appears less a serious effort to amend the Constitution than an attempt to focus debate on the question of how long the United States was prepared to see slavery continue.[26]

The steady westward expansion of U.S. territory and concomitant pressure to admit new states to the Union made the specter of constitutional change ever more alarming for the slaveholding South. Unless a balance between slave and free states was maintained, the increasingly vocal antislavery forces of the North would come to dominate the constitutional process. Proposals such as those of John Quincy Adams could not then be turned aside. The South never held a majority in the House of Representatives and struggled to retain parity in the Senate. This mattered less, however, than the prospect of losing a constitutional margin, one-third of each house of Congress and one-fourth of the states, the proportion of votes that could block constitutional amendment. Following the annexation of Texas and the Mexican War, the Compromise of 1850 created an arrangement for the admission of new states from the Louisiana, Mexican, and Oregon accessions. This accommodation provided the South temporary relief by preserving not an absolute balance but at least a constitutional one. The growing northern opposition to slavery's extension voiced by the Free Soil and Republican parties magnified the possibility of a Union in which there would be too few proslavery states to prevent constitutional change destructive to the South's peculiar institution. A proslavery loss, as in the struggle to organize a government for Kansas, called the South's attention to this danger, and even a victory such as the *Dred Scott* decision failed to reduce it. As long as westward expansion continued with northern free soilers in the majority, the South had no difficulty comprehending that the day was drawing closer when it would be helpless to prevent distasteful constitutional reform.

Southern realization of the potential threat posed by the Article V amendment mechanism led its leaders to seek to erect new defenses. In 1850 one North Carolina congressman, recognizing the danger, proposed a constitutional amendment forbidding the abolition of slavery; he got nowhere.[27] South Carolina militants built upon the implications of Calhoun's nullification doctrine by developing a theory of implied consent to constitutional amendments. If a three-fourths majority of the states approved an amendment in the face of an individual state's objection, then, they argued, that state, by remaining in the Union, was giving its implied consent to the amendment. If on the other hand it chose to reject the amendment, it could exercise its sovereign power to withdraw from the Union.[28] John C. Calhoun himself resorted in his later years to a theory of "concurrent majority," constitutional decisionmaking by concurring majorities from each section. It was at heart an appeal for a measure of agreement on constitutional change that would protect the South from being forced against its will to accept an Article V standard of supermajority agreement for fundamental political decisions.[29] Both approaches reasserted individual states' rights in the process of constitutional reform, and both pointed to secession as an escape for a state that felt it could no longer accept the terms of the Constitution.

Secession from the United States, referred to ever since the Virginia and Kentucky resolutions as the ultimate alternative to acceptance of constitutional change, became a frequent subject of discussion in the 1850s. As the Wilmot Proviso, personal liberty laws, the battle over Kansas, the *Dred Scott* decision, and John Brown's raid on the Harper's Ferry arsenal ratcheted tensions ever higher, increasing numbers of southerners came to regard the Constitution as a trap into which they had innocently strayed. The Article V amending process was the hinge that could suddenly snap and crush their distinctive culture. The North only needed the will and the power to spring the trap: the former was great and growing while the latter appeared to nervous southerners to be nearly in hand. Increasingly, their only escape appeared to be secession. With the election of Republican Abraham Lincoln to the presidency, solely by the votes of northerners, in November 1860, uncertainty vanished. For the slaveholding South the time to leave the Union had arrived.

After Lincoln's victory, the legislature of South Carolina called for election of a state convention to consider secession from the United States. Prior to this time, the alteration of constitutional arrangements as a way of dealing with sectional tensions had remained in the realm of abstract political discussion. Actual proposals for constitutional amendment laid before Congress had fallen to an all-time low during the 1850s. Only one amendment had even been offered for consideration since March 1854, and it dealt merely with voter qualifications in the election of representatives. However, as soon as South Carolina signaled its intention to secede, the floodgates opened. Between the start of the second session of the Thirty-sixth Congress on December 3, 1860, and the inauguration of the new president on March 4, 1861, fifty-seven distinct amendment proposals, contained in over 200 individual resolutions, were laid before Congress.[30] With the nation teetering on the brink of collapse, some still thought disaster could be avoided. Restructuring the fundamental law had averted catastrophe in the 1780s; it seemed to offer the best chance of doing so again.

In December 1860 the about-to-depart president James Buchanan, who throughout his term in office had sought to mollify the South, undertook a final effort to find a compromise that would prevent secession. He had little prospect of success for he was, after all, "the retiring head of the minority wing of a divided party that had been repudiated at the polls."[31] Buchanan's State of the Union message opening the new congressional session was characteristically muddled. Secession was unconstitutional, he declared, but no branch of the national government had the authority to block it. The use of force to prevent illegal southern action was out of the question. "War would not only present the most effectual means of destroying [the Union]," he said, "but would banish all hope of its peaceable reconstruction."[32] Only goodwill could repair the breech, and that required a demonstration to the South that secession was unnecessary. The way to achieve such understanding, Buchanan believed, was to employ the normal constitutional procedure to obtain amendments.

President Buchanan offered three amendments that he hoped would resolve the crisis. The first expressly recognized the right to hold slaves as property and sought to reassure the South that slavery would be protected where it already existed. The second extended the right of slaveholding into the territories until they established state constitutions that did or did not allow slavery. The third proclaimed the validity of the 1850 fugitive slave law and voided state personal liberty laws that obstructed it. The first was consistent with the position then taken by Lincoln and most Republicans. The second flew in the face of northern efforts to bar slavery from areas not yet admitted to statehood. The third endorsed the southern demand that had most aggravated the North during the 1850s, the use of federal authority to return escaped blacks to slavery.[33] Buchanan either did not understand the extent of northern support necessary for the adoption of amendments, or, as seems more likely, he believed that the best chance of defusing the crisis lay in shifting discussion from secession to the terms of amendments that would keep the Union together.

Whatever Buchanan's intent, his proposals met instant rejection. By the end of 1860 northern Republicans were no longer willing, if they ever had been, to endorse a formal constitutional declaration of toleration for slavery, much less provisions that would abet it. If even the Founders of 1787 had avoided mentioning slavery by name, how could the Republicans, far more opposed to it, be expected to grant it official sanction? Ohio Republican Benjamin Wade protested to the Senate that the president was seeking to re verse the verdict of the recent election.[34] Although it is unclear whether the plan would have satisfied the South, a compromise unacceptable to the North was definitely unrealistic. Republicans might still be divided over whether to accept secession, compromise with the South, or crush it, but, most assuredly, none was ready to surrender altogether on the slavery issue. The Buchanan amendments could not enlist a congressional majority, far less the supermajority required for constitutional change. Buchanan's inability to provide constitutional reassurance to the South on terms acceptable to the North was merely the last of the long line of failures to reduce sectional tension that marked his presidency.

Although Buchanan's proposals fell flat, hopes for a solution to the secession crisis through constitutional amendment did not. Once the second session of the Thirty-sixth Congress began, both houses quickly established special ad hoc committees to explore the possibility of a compromise that could head off disaster. Committee attention would center on amendments because bitter experience had demonstrated that compromise arrangements expressed in legislative enactments could easily be upset by further legislation such as the Kansas-Nebraska Act of 1854 or judicial decisions such as *Dred Scott v. Sandford*. Stability required a constitutional settlement difficult or impossible to overturn.

A Senate committee of thirteen and a House committee of thirty-three each sifted through the many amendments being offered in hopes of finding one or a combination of several capable of resolving sectional conflict. The effort, which seems unrealistic in retrospect, may have been so recognized at the time. Yet to the legislators desperate to find a way of avoiding disunion and possible war, it possessed the appeal of a familiar mechanism for obtaining a widely acceptable settlement and the promise of a permanent resolution of the problem. Ultimately the leading seeker of compromise, Senator

John J. Crittenden of Kentucky, would confess, "We have done absolutely nothing." But he remained unwilling to concede this until the final hours of the Congress, after many people had expended a great deal of effort in the search for an amendment cure.[35]

The Senate committee, whose thirteen members included Crittenden, Jefferson Davis, Stephen Douglas, William Seward, Robert Toombs, and Benjamin Wade, devoted most of its attention to a package of amendments that Crittenden put forth. His earnest efforts to find a basis for North-South compromise reflected his political instincts, his border-state perspective, and his position as disciple of and successor to that earlier Kentucky mediator, Henry Clay. Crittenden offered a series of amendments that would have reestablished and extended the sectional compromises of 1820 and 1850. Slavery would have been permitted in territory that the United States possessed or thereafter acquired south of 36° 30' and would have been forbidden farther north. At the time of their admission, new states would have been allowed to choose whether or not to permit slavery. Slavery would have been preserved in states where it existed, and Congress would not be permitted to prohibit it in the District of Columbia as long as either Maryland or Virginia chose to retain it. The interstate slave trade would be allowed to continue, and the federal government would compensate owners of unreturned fugitive slaves. Finally, and most important, these provisions, together with the existing three-fifths slave representation and fugitive slave clauses, would become unamendable; the Congress would not have power to alter the Constitution to abolish or to interfere with slavery.[36] Less a true compromise than a concession to reassure the South, the Crittenden plan could succeed only if a broad political consensus could be assembled for such solution.

Before the committee of thirteen first met on December 22, a few prominent Republicans had expressed sympathy for the central features of Crittenden's plan, the extension to the Pacific of the Missouri Compromise dividing line of 36° 30' and the unamendable amendment. President-elect Lincoln, however, showered Congress with letters to let it know that he opposed any expansion of slave territory. The committee agreed at the outset that it would not endorse any proposal lacking the support of a majority of both its Democratic and Republican members. Therefore, the Crittenden plan, along with six others ranging from Jefferson Davis's and Robert Toombs's ringing proclamations of the legitimacy of slavery to William Seward's modest allowance of slavery where it currently stood, met with rejection. The Republicans voted solidly against every one of these stratagems. As 1860 ended, so did the committee's attempt to find a constitutional compromise.[37]

Senator Crittenden was not prepared to abandon his search for constitutional accommodation, however. He was urged on by both a wide range of political leaders and northern businessmen, fearful of the economic consequences of failure to resolve the conflict.[38] On January 3 he brought his plan before the full Senate, adding two measures, one put forth by Stephen Douglas and one of his own devising. Douglas suggested an amendment barring black suffrage and officeholding. Crittenden himself proposed that the amendment package be submitted to a national plebiscite.[39] Although his ideas on how such a referendum would be conducted were vague, the concept accorded with traditional American constitutional theory. If sovereignty ultimately lay with the people, then a settlement of the most troublesome constitutional issues should rest on their decision, thus ensuring its acceptability and durability. Answering criticism of the plebiscite, Crittenden found it consistent with the Constitution, unlike secession, a rash and lawless claim of states' rights. The package of amendments and its submission to the people quickly gained the endorsement of President Buchanan, among others.[40]

On January 16 opponents of Crittenden's revised plan carried 25 to 23 a resolution declaring constitutional amendment unnecessary. Six remaining southern senators joined Republicans in this maneuver to avoid a direct Senate vote on the Crittenden measures. Such a vote would present the embarrassing choice of standing by declared principles and denying the people the right to endorse a compromise or, on the other hand, allowing the public an opportunity to approve a compromise that would undermine fervently held principles.[41] Following this narrow Senate decision, the focus of attention shifted to the House of Representatives where the Crittenden compromise was again the most discussed approach.

The House committee of thirty-three considered gestures to the South other than amendments. For instance, it proposed admitting the New Mexico Territory (present-day Arizona and New Mexico) as a slave state, thinking this action would reassure the South but be acceptable to northern Republicans because slavery was unlikely to take hold there. Such measures roused little enthusiasm, and the committee returned to the consideration of constitutional alterations. Significant expressions of support for the Crittenden plan came from the North, the Midwest, and even the South as well as in state legislative resolutions from Delaware, Virginia, and Kentucky.[42]

Meanwhile, a parallel search for constitutional solutions went on outside the Congress. The legislature of Virginia, a state very much torn between southern and Unionist loyalties, sought to follow its own example from the 1780s by calling for a conference of the states. Since it was not convened according to the procedure outlined in Article V, this Peace Conference was of uncertain standing. Kentucky, New Jersey, Indiana, Illinois, and Ohio reacted by asking Congress to call an Article V convention. If two-thirds of the states joined in their request, such a meeting would have the power to propose constitutional amendments. Not prepared to wait, twenty-one states accepted Virginia's invitation and sent 132 delegates to the gathering that began in Washington's Willard Hotel on February 4. The seven secessionist states that were meeting in Montgomery, Alabama, the same day to draw up a constitution for the Confederacy sent no delegates; neither did distant California and Oregon or distrustful, Republican-dominated Michigan, Wisconsin, and Minnesota. After more than three weeks of debate, the Peace Conference, chaired by former president John Tyler, produced its own solution, again a set of constitutional amendments. They were based on Crittenden's package of sanctions and supports for slavery but would apply the 36° 30' line only to territory already held by the United States; acquisition of additional lands would not be allowed without the approval of congressional majorities from each section. Submitted first to the Senate, the Peace Conference amendments were soundly defeated. They never even came to a vote in the House.[43]

As Lincoln's inauguration drew closer, efforts to find a sectional compromise centered increasingly in the House of Representatives. The chairman of the committee of thirty-three, former-Whig-turned-Republican Thomas Corwin of Ohio, finally obtained committee agreement on a single amendment that would prohibit abolition of slavery where it then existed. Corwin's amendment was itself to be unamendable. Submitted to the House on the day that the Peace Conference adjourned, it took up an idea first proposed by Robert Toombs and subsequently incorporated into John Crittenden's plan. Corwin thought his proposal might be one measure that would win over the South while not provoking Republican objections. Guaranteeing slavery where it already stood did not controvert Republican policy. Furthermore, the Constitution already contained a feature—its provision for equal representation of states in the Senate—declared unamendable without unanimous consent. Thus he pressed for its adoption.[44]

The Corwin unamendable amendment was placed before Congress on February 27, after nearly every southern senator and representative had withdrawn. News of the enactment of a Confederate constitution had already reached Washington, and all thoughts that secession talk was not to be taken seriously had evaporated. A preponderant majority of those who remained in Congress were ready to clutch at whatever device they calculated best able to avert catastrophe. John Crittenden himself argued at the

last minute for setting aside his own plan and the Peace Conference proposals in favor of Corwin's amendment, the only measure that he felt could
send a conciliatory signal to the South quickly enough at this point.

As set before Congress, the Corwin amendment provided:

> No amendment shall be made to the Constitution which will authorize
> or give to Congress the power to abolish or interfere, within any State,
> with the domestic institutions thereof, including that of persons held to
> labor or service by the laws of said State.

The House adopted this measure by a vote of 133 to 65 and the Senate, rejecting all modifications that would need to be sent back for concurrence by
the House, followed suit by a vote of 24 to 12. This was the bare-minimum
constitutional majority, but it was, nevertheless, an impressive consensus of
two-thirds of the members of Congress who remained in their seats. On the
very last day of its term, the Thirty-sixth Congress threw the Article V mechanism into motion in a final attempt to avoid chaos.[45] Their support for an
unamendable acceptance of slavery provides a measure of how far a supermajority of the Congress was willing to go at that moment to avoid disunion.

Immediately sent to the states for ratification and endorsed by Abraham
Lincoln in his inaugural address, the Corwin amendment was nevertheless
quickly overtaken by events. The secessionist states were unwilling to await
northern state action or to participate in the ratification procedure themselves. Nor was Lincoln willing to delay asserting a federal presence in
places such as Charleston Harbor. On May 13, only ten weeks after the
Congress acted, the Ohio legislature became the first to ratify the proposed
Thirteenth Amendment. However, Ohio's action was already irrelevant because five weeks earlier on April 12 Confederate troops had begun shelling
Fort Sumter. All possibility that constitutional compromise might avert war
was shattered by the roar of those cannons. Only two other northern states
ever ratified the Corwin amendment, Maryland in January 1862 and Illinois,
in a questionable action by a state constitutional convention, a month later.[46]

How should the futile quest for amendment on the eve of the Civil War
be evaluated? Alabama fire-eater William L. Yancey, speaking to his state's
secession convention, sneered at the very idea. "No guarantees—no amendments of the Constitution—no compromises patched up to secure to the
North the benefits of Union yet a little longer, can reeducate that people on
the slavery issue, so as to induce them, having the majority, to withhold the
exercise of its power," he declared.[47] Yancey was an extremist, but by 1861
his words reflected southern distrust of amendment gestures.

At least one thoughtful historian of the era finds it difficult to take any of the amending efforts seriously. He points out the near impossibility of obtaining amendment by the time the Congress began to act in December 1860 and suggests that supporters were simply going through motions they knew to be hopeless. Amendment by the Article V methods always posed difficulties, but with seven of the thirty-four states having seceded by February 1, 1861, the obstacles were unusually formidable. Twenty-six of the remaining twenty-seven states would have to ratify to meet the three-fourths requirement, unless the number was lowered by acknowledging secession as a legal right and an accomplished fact, something "most Republicans and many northern Democrats were fiercely unwilling to do." Therefore, contrary action, or even inaction, by any two states could block amendment.[48] No doubt there is much merit in this argument; yet, before dismissing the amendment discussions out of hand, it ought to be remembered that Americans at the time could look back to the only comparable period of constitutional stress, the Articles of Confederation era, and see all but one state agreeing on constitutional reform when it was perceived necessary to rescue their union.

In the secession crisis, amendment was an unlikely solution but not an entirely implausible one and certainly no worse a course to pursue than most available alternatives. Furthermore, as even skeptics concede, Republican acceptance of the Crittenden plan, even without formal amendment ratification, would have had critical symbolic meaning under the circumstances. It would acknowledge the legitimacy of slavery, offer the prospect of constitutional protection, and renounce a Republican quest for abolition. Embracing such amendments would signify a great deal, even if in practical terms it could accomplish little.[49] No wonder so much hope was invested in this olive branch to the South and so much energy expended in battling over it. Yet it is also no wonder that most Republican leaders, in light of their party's 1860 election mandate, refused to support it. The Corwin amendment adopted as an alternative to the Crittenden plan was by itself too pallid a symbol of reassurance to the South. Furthermore, it was offered too late to have any impact. Consequently, amendment proved no more effective than any other strategy pursued in the futile hope of constitutional reconciliation during the last months before the war commenced.

At its heart, as Yancey's declaration makes apparent, the conflict between free and slave cultures was beyond the reach of a compromise that would allow both to exist in permanent comfort within the same constitutional framework. Resolution of the differences between the two incompatible systems might be put off, as it had been several times before, but ultimately no mutually satisfactory middle ground was to be found. The Founders recognized in 1787 that policy differences had to be resolved one way or another before stable constitutional arrangements could be made. Their insistence on supermajority agreement for the confirmation or alteration of constitutional terms reflected that understanding. The situation in which the United States found itself by early 1861 was not one that the Founders would have anticipated. It was certainly not one they designed the amendment system to handle. It should not be surprising, therefore, that the individuals who sought a compromise solution in the form of one or more constitutional amendments came up empty.

The force of arms crushed not only slavery but also the argument that individual states possessed the power to alter the Constitution. The states' rights claim, born in the Virginia and Kentucky resolutions, fostered by the Hartford convention, given its fullest statement in the nullification crisis, and put to the test by secession was finally brought to earth by the military power of unionism. No longer could a credible claim be made that the Constitution was a compact of the states, severable by any one of them. Indeed, the northern victory was, among other things, a victory for Article V. When the guns fell silent, it stood as the sole means of formally altering the Constitution.

8

"Consummated Amid Fiery Passions"

The Second American Constitutional Revolution

The Civil War produced a fundamental shift in American constitutional thought and practice, although hardly a complete break with the past. Previously, the Articles of Confederation and the Constitution had been regarded as confining statements of the restricted powers that the federal government was licensed to exercise. From its founding in 1776 until the Civil War, the national government actually performed relatively few functions compared to its counterparts abroad or its constituent states. Nevertheless, debate was ongoing as to whether actions of Congress, the president, or the courts overstepped strict constitutional boundaries. Whether the dispute focused on congressional and presidential power to levy taxes, establish banks, acquire territory, or undertake internal improvements, judicial authority to review questions of constitutionality, or the right of a state to dissent and withdraw from a federal consensus it deemed unsatisfactory, the issue invariably remained the precise extent of the narrow mandate permitted the U.S. government under the terms of its prevailing written framework.

American constitutionalism underwent subtle but profound changes in the course of the Civil War, propelled by intertwined desires to maintain the Union and eradicate slavery. The constitutional straitjacket of the antebellum period was exchanged for a more flexible and capacious garment. Instead of the issue being whether the Constitution specifically authorized an action, the question became whether the instrument's implied powers were sufficiently broad to condone it. The knowledge that the boundaries of permissible exercise of federal authority would have to be stretched in the war crisis if the Union was to be preserved encouraged relaxation of traditional beliefs. By argument and example, President Lincoln led the way in replacing the search for explicit sanction among the clauses and phrases of the Constitution with a hunt for plausible justification. The new standard of acceptability became the Constitution's adequacy to support such an interpretation of its powers.[1]

A vital consequence of the change from limited to broader construction of constitutional authority was the alteration of attitudes about amending the Constitution. Previous amendments, most of the many proposed as well as all of the few enacted, had been designed to construct additional curbs on federal power or further define limits and procedures already established. With the Civil War came a perceptible shift to amendments declaring new national policy or granting broader powers to the federal government. Furthermore, in the new environment of constitutional adequacy, amendments came to be thought of as necessary only if power to carry out a desired objective was clearly absent or if existing terms thwarted a preferred policy.

The impact of abstract developments in constitutional thought was less obvious at the time than the immediate effect of three crucially important amendments added to the Constitution. The Thirteenth Amendment abolishing slavery represented a dramatic statement of social policy placing the federal government on the side of human rights at the expense of private property rights as they were then understood. Of particular note, this amendment won approval less than five years after two-thirds of Congress approved, President Lincoln endorsed, and two states ratified a polar opposite Thirteenth Amendment permanently sanctioning slavery in states where it then existed. The Fourteenth and Fifteenth Amendments that soon followed carried forward a social as well as a political and legal transformation hardly imaginable a few years earlier. Together these three amendments established new federally enforceable standards of personal liberty and civil rights, the precise details of which were debatable but whose overall magnitude was undeniable. The epitome of Civil War change, these amendments were founded on the new philosophy of constitutionalism. Each markedly enlarged the federal government's mandate and reduced state authority, something no earlier amendment had done. Together the amendments and the ideas upon which they rested justified the label sometimes given the decade of the 1860s: "the second American revolution."

At the same time, traditional notions of federalism did not altogether disappear. Defense of states' rights remained a concern in many quarters during the effort to devise new constitutional provisions. Once the new amendments were ratified, they were interpreted in ways that preserved state power even at the expense of the civil rights their proponents thought they had advanced. Conservative Supreme Court decisions from 1873 to 1898 made clear that, at least in that era, the Civil War constitutional revolution had definite limits. Amendments might in theory express the sovereign power of the people regarding terms of government, but when the full implications of such declaration were not consistent with dominant political and racial beliefs, they could not by themselves immediately overturn the status quo. The Civil War amendments, adopted during a brief moment when political idealism and opportunity crested simultaneously, would thereafter lie dormant for decades before the political culture allowed their implementation.

Once the Civil War and Reconstruction were safely behind them, many American political and judicial leaders, together with constitutional scholars, quite naturally looked back on the period as an aberration, a time when the country veered from its chosen path. In the decades following their adoption, the Civil War amendments acquired the image of being extraordinary. They deviated from the federal-state balance previously maintained in the Constitution. Perhaps even more significant, they appeared to depart, at least in spirit, from the procedures laid out in 1787 for constitutional revision. Thus they came to be thought of as amendments that could not have been achieved in normal circumstances. In some minds it would follow that the Article V process was no longer viable if it had to be corrupted to obtain the Civil War amendments. This perception had lasting effects on regard for the Thirteenth, Fourteenth, and Fifteenth Amendments as well as on general attitudes toward the amending process and constitutionalism itself.

THE THIRTEENTH AMENDMENT, prohibiting slavery and involuntary servitude and giving Congress power of enforcement, grew out of an early application of the constitutional adequacy approach that, on second thought, was judged to need explicit sanction. Congress and the president used war powers granted by the Constitution to justify initial federal steps to free slaves. The abolition of slavery, however, represented a dramatic intrusion into the realm of individual state authority, not to mention a specific overturning of the Supreme Court's *Dred Scott v. Sandford* ruling that federal action in this regard was unconstitutional. Abolition also represented an unprecedented conversion of what previously had been considered private property. Therefore, it is hardly surprising that a constitutional amendment was believed necessary to ensure its legitimacy. Most notable, and indicative of how quickly the constitutional adequacy approach took hold in the war crisis, is that the process of slave emancipation advanced so far before obtaining the clear authority of an amendment.

When it became obvious in April 1861 that both North and South were prepared to defend their constitutional views by the force of arms, it also became apparent that President Lincoln was either going to have to take an expansive view of his constitutional powers or accept substantial, indeed probably fatal, restrictions on his ability to conduct the war. In ordering the blockade of Confederate ports, mobilizing state militias for federal service, authorizing the military arrest of allegedly disloyal citizens, and suspending habeas corpus in Maryland over the objections of Chief Justice Roger Taney, Lincoln left no question during the first weeks after the Fort Sumter attack as to which course he had chosen. He embraced the view that, under the Constitution, federal authority to preserve the Union was sufficiently broad to sanction these war powers. Both the president and Congress moved more cautiously to deal with the question of slavery, but they followed the identical line of constitutional reasoning.

The North clearly manifested willingness to tolerate slavery where it already existed in the March 1861 congressional vote on the Corwin amendment. A nearly unanimous new Congress reiterated this view four months later in a resolution declaring that the war's object was not to interfere with slavery or other states' rights. A Confiscation Act stripped slave owners of the right to the labor of slaves used in the rebellion but avoided the issue of seized slaves' legal status. For the time being the Republican majority clung to the party's 1860 platform that spoke out only against the extension of slavery into the territories. As the war continued, however, sentiment increased for making the abolition of slavery a victory goal.

A year after the war started, Congress began to take steps, cautious at first, then increasingly bold, to attack slavery. In April 1862 it abolished slaveholding in the District of Columbia, with slave owners who had remained loyal to the Union compensated for their lost property. Two months later federal legislators went further, abolishing slavery in the territories without compensating owners of the small number of slaves held there. In July Congress took steps affecting many more slaves and slave owners. It repealed the Fugitive Slave Act that the North so detested and adopted a second Confiscation Act, declaring that all slaves belonging to persons engaged in the rebellion who escaped to Union lines or were seized by the Union army would be "deemed captives of war, and shall be forever free of their servitude, and not again held as slaves." At the same time Congress agreed, in the Militia Act, that any slave who rendered military service would be free, together with his mother, wife, and children.[2]

Lincoln followed the lead of Congress in justifying and using abolition as an instrument of war. In September 1862 he issued a preliminary proclamation of emancipation, warning that slavery would be abolished in those states still in rebellion by the start of the new year. Lincoln also recommended that Congress compensate the property loss of slave owners in defiant states who remained loyal to the Union or in loyal slave states that abolished slavery on their own initiative. The president cited his constitutional authority to suppress the insurrection as justification for both this proclamation and the final emancipation decree of January 1, 1863.

Lincoln held that the war powers granted by the Constitution provided adequate authority for the steps taken. Yet his discomfort with the constitutionality of congressional and presidential emancipation was obvious, revealed in private conversation, correspondence, and public statement. Furthermore, Lincoln made it clear that he believed the Constitution allowed the federal government to take action only against rebellious states. The total abolition of slavery, calls for which were increasingly heard in the North, could not, in the president's view, be constitutionally imposed on loyal states such as Delaware and Kentucky against their will. Other means than war powers, specifically constitutional amendment, would have to be used to achieve comprehensive abolition.[3]

More than two months after the preliminary emancipation proclamation and only weeks before the final edict, the president, in his annual message to Congress, presented a detailed proposal for ending slavery through a series of three constitutional amendments. Primarily, Lincoln sought to induce states themselves to take action against slavery. He proposed an unspecified amount of federal compensation to slave owners in states abolishing slavery by January 1, 1900. The terms of the federal offer, even the amount and interest rates of the U.S. bonds to be delivered to the states, were to be made explicit by Congress. The decision on whether to enter into the bargain was to be left to each state, however. Additionally, Lincoln proposed an amendment declaring that slaves who had "enjoyed actual freedom by the chances of the war at any time before the end of the rebellion shall be forever free," their owners, if they had remained loyal, to be compensated at the same rate. This measure would give specific constitutional sanction to the Emancipation Proclamation and other steps already taken. A final amendment would specifically authorize Congress to appropriate money and otherwise provide for the colonization of free blacks outside the United States by their own consent, an old, often proposed remedy for the country's racial dilemma. This gradual, compensated emancipation, argued Lincoln, would "greatly mitigate" the dissatisfaction of proponents of perpetual slavery by delaying the freeing of slaves until states chose to act and by avoiding the destruction of property acquired by inheritance or purchase.[4]

His quest for constitutional sanction revealed, among other things, Lincoln's concern about the legitimacy of the federal initiatives already under way against slavery. The explicit authorization to be provided by these amendments would erase any questions. His desire to place the emancipation decision so largely in state hands reflected the president's conservative views on the federal-state relationship. He had serious doubts as to whether the federal government, even with the approval of an amending supermajority, could force an individual state to alter its internal arrangements regarding slavery. Under his plan, states, which collectively possessed the right to ratify or reject the amendment itself, would also individually retain the subsequent right to accept or refuse its inducement to end slavery. After nearly two years in office, most of it spent exercising expanded wartime power, Lincoln was still sensitive to the Constitution's circumscription of federal authority and, as a consequence, was willing to settle for less than certain, total abolition of slavery.

The Emancipation Proclamation, designed and justified as an act of war, sought to end slavery only in territory beyond the grasp of the Union at the moment. As the Union army advanced, the proclamation began to take effect in captured regions. The status of slaves in areas previously occupied as well as in border states and elsewhere, however, remained a complex and tangled issue. During the House debate over the second Confiscation Act in 1862, Missouri representative John Noell took up the argument that although seizing slaves as enemy property was a legitimate war measure, Congress had no power to alter the standing of persons in loyal states. Noell contended that the definition of personal status was, constitutionally speaking, the right of states, not of the federal government.[5] Northern criticism of presidential emancipation, continuous though not massive, centered on the lack of federal authority over a state's internal policy regarding slavery.[6] In offering incentives for abolishing slavery but not compelling loyal slave states to do so, Lincoln made clear in the preliminary and final emancipation proclamations as well as through his December amendment proposals that he believed there to be substance in this constrained view of federal constitutional authority.

While the war and with it the political fate of the Republican party hung in the balance, the constitutional issue of slavery abolition remained unresolved. Yet as the fortunes of war turned in the North's favor on the fields of Gettysburg and the bluffs of Vicksburg, northern desire increased for resolution of the slavery question in a complete and constitutional manner. When the Thirty-eighth Congress convened in December 1863, several radical Republicans proposed to abolish slavery by statute. Doubting Congress' authority to take such action, Ohio representative James Ashley offered a simple and straightforward constitutional amendment "prohibiting slavery or involuntary servitude in all of the States and Territories now owned or which may be hereafter acquired by the United States." Together with a simultaneous and similar proposal from Iowa representative James Wilson and four subsequent propositions of the same sort, the Ashley resolution was referred to the House Committee on the Judiciary. For five months, the measures languished, not even debated.[7]

An amendment resolution for the abolition of slavery was also introduced in the Senate in January 1864. Its sponsor, John Henderson of Missouri, argued the need for a constitutional amendment; otherwise, Congress lacked authority to mandate universal abolition. The Senate Judiciary Committee agreed, saying that an amendment would "secure to us future peace" by bringing an end to conflict between the states over slavery. However, the committee rejected the effort by Charles Sumner of Massachusetts to broaden the amendment to include the phrase "All persons are equal before the law" on the grounds that its effects were unpredictable. It might do more than prohibit slavery, some senators worried. It might cause other legal and civil rights such as citizenship and suffrage to be bestowed on blacks. It might even lead to women being treated as legal equals to men. Clearly, some legislators opposed to slavery lacked enthusiasm for any of these further possibilities. Instead, the Judiciary Committee favored compromise language drafted by Chairman Lyman Trumbull of Illinois and patterned after the Northwest Ordinance of 1787: "Neither slavery nor involuntary servitude, except as a punishment for crime whereof the party shall have been duly convicted, shall exist within the United States, or any place subject to their jurisdiction." Trumbull's version incorporated Sumner's provision that "Congress shall have power to enforce this article by appropriate legislation" into the amendment as a second section; this simple terminology embodied a critically important assertion of federal authority.[8]

The Senate debated the amendment resolution briefly but heatedly. Sumner and others asserted the need to bring the Constitution into harmony with the solemn promises of equality in the Declaration of Independence. Other Republican senators, less ardent abolitionists, nevertheless viewed the end of slavery as necessary to a stable, restored Union. Opponents, six of the Senate's ten Democrats, argued not for slavery but for the rights of states to determine the issue for themselves. The power of amendment, they contended, did not extend to such fundamental changes in the federal relationship. "I deny that the power of amendment carries the power of revolution," exclaimed Senator Garrett Davis of Kentucky. "It is an absurdity to say that this power of amendment will impart the power to change the government and to establish a monarchy if the different departments and authorities authorized to enact the amendment choose to adopt it. It cannot be done, legitimately at any rate." Davis, his Kentucky colleague Lazarus Powell, and Willard Saulsbury of Delaware offered between them nearly three dozen amendments to alter or undermine the Judiciary Committee's proposal. Unpersuaded, the Senate promptly and decisively adopted the Trumbull resolution on April 8, 1864, by a vote of 36 to 6.[9]

The House of Representatives bore heavy burdens of concern about border-state reaction, constitutional proprieties, and amendment politics when it finally took up the matter of amendment at the end of May 1864. Not coincidentally, the Democratic minority was numerically more significant in the House than in the Senate following the 1862 elections. The Senate's resolution failed to win the necessary two-thirds, passing in the House by only 93 to 65 on June 15. The House contained a substantial majority for abolition but, unless thirteen votes shifted from opposition to support, not a constitutionally sufficient one. For the moment, House Republicans turned their attention to legislative measures, in particular the Wade-Davis bill they adopted less than three weeks later. Among other things, Wade-Davis required Confederate states to abolish slavery as a condition of their return to the Union. Lincoln pocket vetoed the Wade-Davis bill, believing that Congress could not abolish slavery by statute. So doing would make the fatal admission that states had left and legitimately could leave the Union. Only constitutional amendment, Lincoln insisted, could properly bring a total end to slavery.[10] Later in the summer, the Republican platform took up the call for an abolition amendment.

Once the 1864 election secured Republican power and manifested the increasing strength of northern antislavery sentiment, momentum for a constitutional solution quickly accelerated. Enough Democrats had been defeated to ensure the Republicans a three-fourths majority in the next House, but for the moment the minority party continued to resist. Peace Democrat Fernando Wood of New York took the extreme position that slavery was a positive good. Many of his Democratic colleagues expressed the more moderate view that constitutional change in the midst of a war was simply inappropriate. Indiana representative Daniel Voorhees argued, "Such an act should not be consummated amid the fiery passions and vehement hates engendered by civil war. It should be the work of calmness and of peace." Still others worried about the consequences of amendment: the possibility of Negro suffrage and the diminution of state power. A few, such as George Pendleton of Ohio, contended that, as a new and independent exercise of power unrelated to any provision of the existing Constitution, the proposed amendment exceeded the bounds of Article V that sanctioned only modification of existing constitutional authority.[11]

President Lincoln appealed to Democrats to support immediate bipartisan action on the slavery abolition amendment as a gesture of unity.

Whether responding to Republican appeals or their own sense of their party's best interests, sixteen Democrats, fourteen of them lame ducks, abandoned the official Democratic opposition position to vote for the amendment. Eight other Democrats remained absent during the roll call. On January 31, 1865, the House approved the April 1864 Senate resolution by 119 to 56. This time the necessary two-thirds vote was achieved, if only by a small margin; a shift of three votes could have blocked passage. When the result was announced, the galleries cheered, outside the Capitol cannons boomed a 100-gun salute, and on the floor of the House, wrote Representative George Julian of Indiana in his diary, "Members joined in the shouting and kept it up for some minutes. Some embraced one another, others wept like children. I have felt, ever since the vote, as if I were in a new country."[12]

After the House action, the amendment resolution was sent to Lincoln, who immediately added his signature. In 1798, while reviewing the adoption of the Eleventh Amendment, the Supreme Court had ruled that presidential action was not intended to be a part of the Article V process.[13] Senator Trumbull immediately introduced and the Senate quickly passed a resolution declaring the president's approval of the amendment was unnecessary and should not be regarded as any sort of precedent.[14]

State ratification of the Thirteenth Amendment proceeded rapidly. Within a week eight states, Illinois, Rhode Island, Michigan, Maryland, New York, Pennsylvania, West Virginia, and Missouri, had endorsed it. Ten more completed action before the end of February. By July 1, nineteen northern states and four secessionist states had approved the amendment. Four more southern states acted between November 13 and December 6, when the process was declared completed. Five more states, four of them northern, added their endorsements within the next seven weeks, bringing all loyal states except for slaveholding Delaware and Kentucky into the fold.

The Thirteenth Amendment's ratification stirred controversy. In announcing on December 18, 1865, that the antislavery amendment had been adopted, Secretary of State William Seward proclaimed that the necessary three-fourths approval had been achieved by the action of twenty-seven of the thirty-six states. That very month Congress refused to seat representatives of formerly secessionist states, declaring those states had forfeited their privileges of government. How could states not competent to conduct elections and legislative affairs have authority to approve federal amendments? If the eleven secessionist states and their eight favorable votes were removed from the equation, nineteen of the twenty-five unquestionably legitimate state governments, again a three-fourths margin, had sanctioned the Thirteenth Amendment. Even though the new amendment met Article V's standard of validity by either of these measures, there was no way it could have achieved ratification by three-fourths of all states without the inclusion of the votes of those whose legitimacy was under challenge.

Lincoln's unwavering insistence from the moment of his inauguration that the Union remain unbroken, that states could not leave and had not left it, led directly to this problem of the ratification majority. The difficulty that this posed for obtaining three-fourths state approval for constitutional change had been foreseen. Indeed, one of the antislavery amendments offered at the start of the Thirty-eighth Congress proposed the lowering of Article V supermajority requirements. It would have allowed amendments to be offered by congressional majorities or by conventions requested by a majority of state legislatures rather than require a two-thirds vote in either case to initiate proceedings; positive action on the part of legislatures or convention in two-thirds rather than three-fourths of the states would complete the adoption process. The Senate Judiciary Committee did not pursue the proposal.[15] Subsequently, both the dominant Republicans and most northern Democrats ignored the delicate question of amending procedures. The body politic was determined to have the slavery issue settled and confident that it could do so within existing bounds. The attitude prevailed that the legitimacy of the Thirteenth Amendment's ratification was within the power of the secretary of state and Congress to confirm. Nevertheless, the irregularity of the process foreshadowed more amending problems just over the horizon.[16]

THE SPEEDY ADOPTION of the Thirteenth Amendment might well have augured a smooth and rapid return to a normally functioning government. At the time of Robert E. Lee's surrender at Appomattox, many historians agree, a majority of northerners would have welcomed mild treatment of the South leading to an early restoration of conventional government. A few radical voices called for severe punishment, but most of the victors were inclined to leniency. The South simply had to acknowledge its defeat and demonstrate its assent to the sort of Union for which the North had fought. More than anything else, considerate southern treatment of the former slaves would signal its acceptance of Union victory. "Given the strong desire for 'normalcy,' " writes one respected modern scholar, "it is most likely that the South could have satisfied northern opinion by ratifying the Thirteenth Amendment, repudiating secession, and acquiescing in the exercise by blacks of civil, but not political, rights."[17]

Instead, the South conceded no more than ratification of the Thirteenth Amendment. Several state legislatures did even that with obvious reluctance,

and Mississippi flatly refused to do so at all. Then, rather than repudiate secession as inherently wrong in the first place, most states merely repealed
their secession ordinances and declared them no longer in effect. Furthermore, the recalcitrant states moved immediately to adopt legal codes severely
restricting the freedmen, black codes that appeared to be a reimposition of
slaverylike conditions. The South was responding to the impression being
given by Lincoln's successor, Andrew Johnson, as to what was expected, but
its actions infuriated much of the North. Defeat, the North believed, was
being snatched from the jaws of victory, notwithstanding the achievement of
the Thirteenth Amendment. Johnson's refusal to require southern reform and
his insistence that the national government had no power to compel state action led frustrated northerners into protracted conflict with the president and
to the conclusion that further constitutional reform was definitely required to
preserve their triumph.[18]

By the time the Congress elected in November 1864 first met in December 1865, the war had been over for eight months and President Johnson
had presided over the establishment of provisional southern governments.
Generous presidential grants of amnesty and pardon allowed former supporters of the Confederacy to take leading roles in the formation of the new
southern governments. In every one of these states, the legislature promptly
adopted a legal code pertaining only to blacks that segregated the races,
banned political participation, restricted social conduct, established severe
vagrancy and labor laws that in turn created a peonage system, and provided harsh criminal punishments. The northern feeling of achievement had
been swiftly replaced by a sense of alarm.

Upon convening, the Thirty-ninth Congress immediately took issue with
presidential restoration and southern state behavior and began exploring
means, including constitutional amendment, to protect the North's victory.
The House and Senate alike refused to seat the new southern representatives. Federal legislators quickly sought to strengthen the Freedmen's Bureau
and to give the army responsibility for protecting black civil rights but failed
by a margin of two votes in the Senate to overcome a presidential veto. By
March, Congress, aroused by the South, was ready to accept federal responsibility for guarding individual rights to make and enforce contracts, sue and
give evidence, and own property. Despite some hesitancy about intruding
into what had traditionally been an area of state authority, it approved a
Civil Rights Act. When President Johnson sought to block this legislation,
the increasingly combative Congress overrode his veto.

The battle over the Civil Rights Act of 1866 led directly to a campaign
for a new constitutional amendment. The North recognized that the freshly

minted Thirteenth Amendment had not ensured blacks the range of protections they required. Prohibiting slavery itself was not enough to guarantee civil freedom to blacks in the face of southern white hostility. Congress quickly began considering additional constitutional protections. Consciousness that a hostile president, not to mention unrepentant southern states, would seek to undermine legislative measures gave urgency to the discussion. It gained additional momentum from doubts about whether the Supreme Court would concede that Congress possessed the authority to supplant a state in setting the terms of individual rights.

The Joint Committee on Reconstruction's first amendment proposal, set before the House in January 1866, sought to reduce proportionally the congressional representation of states that denied the right to vote on the basis of race. First offered by the committee's powerful senior Republican representative, Thaddeus Stevens of Pennsylvania, the measure drew criticism from radicals for conceding that states had the power to deny black suffrage. The plan also gained the outspoken opposition of President Johnson. He preferred no amendment at all but was willing to accept one simply basing representation on each state's number of legal voters. The Johnson plan would have encouraged border states not to disenfranchise rebel sympathizers and would have benefited western states with relatively few women. The presidential proposal unified his Republican opponents in the House around the joint committee's amendment. In the Senate, however, where conservative Republicans sided with Johnson and radicals led by Charles Sumner wanted explicit protection for black voting, the resolution fell far short of the required two-thirds.[19]

At the same time he advanced his proposal for representation reduction, Stevens had set forth three other amendment resolutions. At the very start of the Thirty-ninth Congress, he introduced a measure to protect black civil rights by declaring that "all national and state laws shall be equally applicable to every citizen, and no discrimination shall be made on account of race or color." Simultaneously, Stevens sought to punish the southern insurrection through amendments authorizing duties on exports and prohibiting payment of Confederate debts.[20]

Congressman John Bingham of Ohio, a prominent moderate on the Joint Committee on Reconstruction, took a different approach to the issue of freedmen's rights once the new Congress convened in December 1865. He proposed an amendment granting Congress the power to pass all laws necessary and proper to secure equal rights to all persons. On January 9, 1866, Bingham disparaged claims of independent state authority in this regard, insisting that "the spirit, the intent, the purpose of our Constitution is to secure equal and exact justice to all men." States had ignored the "guarantee of your Constitution [that] applies to every citizen of every State of the Union; there is not a guarantee more sacred, and none more vital in that great instrument." Therefore, he proposed explicit language to treat the privileges and immunities of all citizens as a national matter. "Hereafter there shall not be any disregard of the essential guarantee of your Constitution in any State of the Union."[21] While others offered civil rights amendments, Bingham's direct approach to a grant of federal authority, together with his forceful oratory and influential position, brought his proposal to the fore.

Stevens's and Bingham's resolutions, together with others submitted since the opening of the Congress, received serious consideration by the Joint Committee on Reconstruction after its first amendment attempt failed on March 9. The passage of the Civil Rights Act the same month followed by the overriding of the presidential veto in early April convinced amendment advocates that, despite philosophical differences among Republicans, they were sufficiently united to muster the House and Senate votes needed to pass some reasonable and effective measure.[22] The challenge lay in deciding what to choose from a plethora of propositions dealing with citizenship, suffrage, civil rights, and the punishment of Confederate leaders, supporters, and financial backers. As problematic as the choice of reforms was the strategy for ensuring their ultimate installation in the Constitution.

Near the end of April, the joint committee adopted a political tactic suggested to Stevens by Robert Dale Owen, binding a variety of measures inextricably together in a single amendment. Designed to enlist the broadest possible coalition of support, this tactic increased the likelihood of congressional adoption and state ratification of a reconstruction amendment. The committee fashioned a five-part amendment that incorporated the Stevens and Bingham initiatives into Owen's framework. At the same time that he proposed his plan, Owen suggested an enabling act that would restore rebellious states to the Union once they ratified the omnibus amendment and altered their own laws to conform to it. The amendment process would in effect permit a northern gesture of forgiveness in return for the much-desired southern acknowledgment of defeat and apology. At the moment, however, the joint committee was not prepared to offer such an automatic quid pro quo.[23]

The Owen single-amendment approach departed significantly from earlier amending practice. In the only previous episode of simultaneous amendment, the Bill of Rights, various propositions were offered as separate amendments to be decided upon individually. Some were adopted; others were not. To combine a number of proposals into a single measure subtly but perceptibly shifted critical decisionmaking from the ratifiers to the initial adopters of an amendment resolution. Unlike the 1790s experience, states would confront a take-it-or-leave-it, all-or-nothing choice. Owen's tactic would also encourage the construction of an amendment around a coalition of interests. Instead of demanding a supermajority committed to a single measure, the Owen approach brokered inclusion of individual elements for willingness to accept the other parts of the package. Whether because of the difficulty of assembling such a coalition, failure to recognize it as an effective strategy, or perceived undesirability of an approach that compromised the terms of amendment, the Owen method of designing an amendment has not been used again, despite its effectiveness when first employed. Its sole application did, however, produce the longest, most complex, and arguably the most influential of the U.S. Constitution's amendments.

The joint committee's deliberations leading to its drafting of the Fourteenth Amendment were long and difficult. Unfortunately, the debate was not recorded. As a result, there has been much discussion but little consensus on the arguments that led to the final choice of language. The record of committee votes reveals that provisions were added, altered, dropped, restored, and rearranged. Ambiguities were created, inadvertently or deliberately. A combination of intellectual persuasion, political strategy, and compromise may have been involved.[24] What is clear is that the statement that emerged from the committee process revolved around the principle of nationally guaranteed equality before the law for all citizens, a principle that more than two-thirds of Republicans could agree upon. As legal historian William Nelson has argued,

> the resolution of specific legal issues, such as who should possess the right to vote, was not the *raison d'etre* of the Fourteenth Amendment. While many Americans cared deeply about the suffrage issue, its resolution in 1866 was not mandatory. What was politically essential was that the North's victory in the Civil War be rendered permanent and the principles for which the war had been fought rendered secure, so that the South, upon readmission to full participation in the Union, could not undo them. The Fourteenth Amendment must be understood as the Republican party's plan for securing the fruits both of the war and of the three decades of antislavery agitation preceding it.[25]

The first section of the proposed amendment that the House of Representatives considered only slightly modified Bingham's original language banning state abridgement of individual rights and denial of equal protection or due process. Significantly, rather than merely give Congress authority to protect citizens' rights if it chose to do so, those rights were proclaimed as absolute. The guarantees of citizens' privileges and immunities, due process of law in matters of life, liberty, and property, and equal protection of the laws gave specific meaning to American citizenship. The drafter of this provision believed it did one thing more. During the House floor debate and again in an 1871 speech to Congress, Bingham asserted that he had drawn this sentence so as to make the Constitution's first eight amendments binding on the states, explicitly reversing John Marshall's 1833 opinion in *Barron v. Baltimore* that they were not.[26]

In Bingham's mind there was no reason for later disputes as to whether the Fourteenth Amendment incorporated the Bill of Rights into the equal protection and due process obligations placed upon the states; it certainly did. Modern arguments that the Fourteenth Amendment should be interpreted narrowly because many who voted for it were negrophobic dwell on statements made early in the legislative process as well as outside it. They fail to account for Bingham's clearly stated and widely apprehended ultimate declarations.[27] Further, and more important, the constitutional amending process had always been grounded on the idea that an addition or alteration became associated with those provisions of the instrument not explicitly changed. Amenders did not have to link their reform specifically to existing features of the Constitution for this to be so. The Founders who designed Article V would doubtless have regarded the first eight amendments and the fourteenth as bearing on each other.

The proposed amendment's second section revived Stevens's previously defeated plan for reducing congressional representation if states denied the franchise to any male citizens over the age of twenty-one. Without directly challenging state claims of authority to set the terms for voting, claims that the 1787 Founders had respected, the provision gave the federal government the power to penalize states that restricted this right. Women's rights advocates vigorously protested the misogyny of this measure, the first explicit reference to male-only rights in the Constitution, but the architects of the amendment, absorbed with the question of black voting rights, were unmoved.[28] Fifty years would pass before Congress addressed woman suffrage, an entire century before it dealt with full gender equality.

The remaining sections of the proposed amendment addressed even more specifically northern unhappiness with the current state of reconstruction. The third section disfranchised all who had supported the Confederacy, in other words, nearly all southern whites. The fourth section, which likewise originated in Thaddeus Stevens's December resolutions, forbade payment of Confederate debts or compensation of former slave owners for their emancipated property. These statements were the clearest expression of the northern view that the South should pay for its sins and not be allowed to repeat them. The final section, mirroring section two of the Thirteenth Amendment and seeking to ensure that the constitutional reforms would have effect, empowered Congress to enforce the new amendment.

Despite so much revision that Owen's initial proposal was all but unrecognizable in the joint committee's ultimate creation, the strategy of combining the provisions into one amendment survived in the resolution that Stevens finally presented to the House and William Fessenden to the Senate. Criticism of the proposed amendment was immediate and widespread: it focused particularly on the Confederate disfranchisement section. Protests came from the White House, the northern press, the South, and the floor of both houses of Congress. Yet among those who would have to vote, the objections were regularly followed by a concession that it was as good an amendment as it was possible to obtain. Not surprisingly, the House approved the amendment 128 to 37 on May 11 after only three days of debate.[29]

The Senate did not agree so readily. A sentence guaranteeing citizenship to all persons born or naturalized in the United States was added to the first section in order to avoid executive or judicial determination of citizenship. This first sentence resolved, in favor of the former slaves, lingering questions as to whether the Thirteenth Amendment granted full citizenship to freedmen. The Senate also reduced the third section's broad disfranchisement to a bar on officeholding by those who had sworn a public oath to uphold the Constitution and subsequently supported the Confederacy. The senators were clearly uncomfortable with a sweeping denial of political participation, particularly one that would leave political power in the South in the hands of the freedmen. The lesser disqualification they approved may have applied only to a few thousand people, mainly former military officers and state legislators, but it dealt directly with northern concern about renewed political authority by unrecalcitrant former rebel leaders. Unless blocked, it was felt, their restoration would have incalculable, but certainly distasteful, consequences. In a pointed reference to President Johnson's liberal pardoning of former Confederates, Congress gave itself sole power, by two-thirds vote, to remove such a disability. After nearly three weeks of debate, the Republican caucus, having agreed to these changes, voted to support the amendment. The Senate then adopted it 33 to 11 on June 8. Five days later, after brief discussion, the House concurred 120 to 32, sending the amendment to the states for ratification.[30]

Congressional Republicans were pleased to put the proposed Fourteenth Amendment before the country in advance of the 1866 elections. Their widening differences with President Johnson, not to mention the Democrats, were fundamental, and the amendment gave them a rallying point. They could compose their own disagreements and fight the election contest on the issue of support or opposition to the amendment as the basis of Reconstruction. In that respect, state ratification of the amendment, which remained problematic, was less crucial than its submission by a partisan vote of Congress.

Unmoved, Andrew Johnson responded to the transmittal of the proposed amendment to the states with a statement disputing whether a Congress that represented only twenty-five of the thirty-six states could legitimately propose constitutional reform. Congress had not, in his opinion, met the Article V standard of two-thirds congressional approval. At the same time the president declared war against the proposed amendment, he sought to revive a procedural issue.[31] However, adoption of the Twelfth Amendment in 1803 established that two-thirds of the quorum present and voting was sufficient. A quorum of the Thirty-ninth Congress had no doubt been present even in the absence of Confederate state representatives. Thus Johnson's complaint provoked little response.

Soon after its delivery into their hands, the legislatures of Connecticut on June 25 and New Hampshire on July 6 ratified the amendment by wide margins. Most other northern states, with the exceptions of slaveholding Delaware and Kentucky, could be expected to follow suit, but even if all did, Article V's three-fourths requirement still presented an obstacle to ratification. Radicals such as Charles Sumner and Thaddeus Stevens favored ruling the Confederate states out of the process, as had been contemplated with the Thirteenth Amendment, but sympathetic moderates feared that to do so would cast doubts on the amendment's validity. Instead, their attention focused on inducing southern states to ratify.[32]

Owen's quid pro quo of readmission in return for the southern states' acceptance of the amendment remained fixed in many minds although Congress tabled it. In July 1866 Tennessee's provisional governor told a special session of the state legislature that approval of the amendment was a small but expected price for the state's restoration to the Union. Opponents hid to deny a two-thirds legislative quorum, but some absent house members were located, arrested, and declared present even though they refused to answer a roll call. These unorthodox means produced the first Confederate state's ratification. Congress immediately recognized Tennessee's action, saying it had been taken by a majority of a full house despite the controversial measures used to assemble the required quorum, and voted to seat its delegation.[33]

Without formally committing itself, Congress, by admitting Tennessee's representatives, conveyed a clear implication that ratification would lead likewise to the restoration of other states' standing in the federal legislature. The northern press, as well as Republicans from Lyman Trumbull to Benjamin Butler to John Sherman, said as much. Not everyone agreed, however. Charles Sumner and Thaddeus Stevens were prominent among those desiring to evaluate southern behavior and perhaps require other actions, especially if the rebellious states denied black suffrage. They were certainly not prepared to grant automatic readmission.[34] Yet Tennessee's reinstatement and the bulk of Republican statements during the fall election campaign indicated that at the moment the congressional balance of power favored restoration of the South in return for prompt ratification.[35] During the same period, however, Andrew Johnson was making ever more clear his opposition to the amendment, and southern states chose to cast their fate with his.

During autumn 1866 and the first months of 1867, southern state legislatures, one after another, rejected ratification. The leaders of the former Confederate states recognized that approving the amendment would help them regain northern support, but at the same time they had received no pledge that agreeing to this measure they found so distasteful would satisfy the North. In a letter to the *Columbia Phoenix* South Carolina provisional governor B. F. Perry asked, "What security has the South that worse terms will not be imposed if the Amendment is adopted?"[36] Furthermore, southerners were convinced that withholding their assent would prevent the amendment from being ratified. Of course the result might be the imposition of harsher northern terms, but it seemed to them as likely to lead to a more moderate settlement. Thus they made a calculated political choice.

Texas was the first state to reject the amendment on October 27, 1866, and Georgia followed on November 9. Florida voted no December 3. Despite the governor's recommendation that the state would benefit from ratification, the Arkansas legislature on December 17 refused to ratify, four days after North Carolina had taken similar action and three days before South Carolina did likewise. Virginia rejected in early January 1867 and Alabama, after longer debate than in any other southern legislature, followed suit. Mississippi, which had refused to ratify the Thirteenth Amendment, did so again on January 30 and Louisiana added its rejection February 6. A number of these southern votes were unanimous; the closest votes for approval, if they could be called that, came in the lower houses of North Carolina, where the amendment was disapproved 93 to 10, and in Alabama, where the tally was 69 to 8 against ratification.[37]

Several themes ran throughout the extensive discussions that preceded these legislative actions. Opposition to black suffrage was clearly at the fore-front. Serving as a counterbalance was distaste at the prospect of reduced southern representation should black voting be barred. Southern legislators did not concede black equality, nor did they feel that they should be made to suffer for denying it. The prospect of disfranchisement of former Confeder-ate leaders provoked further unhappiness; such action was decried as an ex post facto law. In reacting to the proposed amendment, southerners retained their belief that in matters of political participation states should enjoy their pre–Civil War autonomy. The repeated complaint that the amendment was improper because the Congress framing it did not contain all the states also displayed the South's reluctance to accept the North's battlefield triumph or to acknowledge that the outcome of the war had altered the balance of fed-eralism.[38]

While the South dug in its heels, northern states rapidly endorsed the amendment. In close votes, New Jersey ratified September 11, 1866, and Oregon eight days later. Vermont overwhelmingly approved on October 26. The November congressional elections, in which Reconstruction policy was the central issue, produced a formidable Republican victory regarded as a popular mandate for pressing forward. With the coming of the new year and the convening of northern state legislatures, ratifications came quickly and by consistently wide margins. New York, Ohio, Illinois, West Virginia, Kansas, Maine, Nevada, Missouri, and Indiana acted in January. Minnesota, Rhode Island, Wisconsin, Pennsylvania, and Michigan followed in February, and Massachusetts did so in March. Only northern border states with a tra-dition of slavery rejected the amendment, Kentucky on January 7, Delaware exactly one month later, and Maryland on March 22.[39] Thus by March 1867, battle lines had been drawn between Tennessee and the twenty north-ern free states that had sanctioned the amendment and the ten southern and three loyal slave states that had formally rejected it.

The Thirty-ninth Congress, which reconvened after the November elec-tions knowing that Republican dominance of the body would continue, did not take long to confront southern intransigence. During its final session, the aroused and determined Congress constructed a bill to strip the provisional southern governments of all power and to place authority in the hands of the military until the former Confederate states established acceptable gov-ernments and embraced the Fourteenth Amendment. In part the Supreme Court motivated the bill with its December *ex parte Milligan* decision that military tribunals lacked authority over civilians while regular state courts were open and functioning. Still, southern refusal to acquiesce in constitutional change lay at the heart of the matter. Passed over President Johnson's veto on March 2, 1867, the Military Reconstruction Act reopened the issue of southern ratification of the amendment.[40]

Massachusetts senator Charles Sumner maintained that the rebellious southern states had committed "state suicide" and thus had no authority of any sort until granted by the Congress. By his standard, the Fourteenth Amendment would become effective when three-fourths of the loyal states ratified it, a threshold reached on March 20 when the legislature of his own state became the twenty-first to approve.[41] Yet for most northerners, not to mention southerners, the arguments that had pertained when the Thirteenth Amendment was under consideration still applied. The Article V requirement would have to be met on the basis of three-fourths of all states.

The Military Reconstruction Act became the instrument for achieving southern ratification of the Fourteenth Amendment. The act and a supplementary measure that the new Fortieth Congress adopted within weeks directed the military to register voters, including former slaves but excluding Confederate leaders, and to conduct elections for delegates to state conventions. The conventions were to draft constitutions that the new electorate had to endorse in order for them to become effective. If Congress approved the new constitutions and, of great importance, if the new governments ratified the Fourteenth Amendment, then, and only then, would the rebellious states be restored to full self-government and representation in the national legislature. Southern compulsion to ratify, not clearly in evidence earlier, was now quite explicit.

Faced with these unambiguous requirements and simultaneously able to watch Andrew Johnson, their strongest supporter in the federal government, being reduced to political impotence and subjected to impeachment, most southern states moved ahead quickly to comply with the terms of military reconstruction. All but Texas rewrote their suffrage requirements and allowed the redefined electorate to choose constitutional convention delegates before the end of 1867. Soon reconstructed state governments began functioning. Containing black members but predominantly white, the new southern legislatures were most notable for the absence of traditional state leaders. As these legislatures assembled in spring 1868, consideration of the proposed Fourteenth Amendment became their first priority.

During the previous year, two more northern states, Nebraska on June 15, 1867, and Iowa on March 16, 1868, had added their ratifications. With every non-Confederate state except Democratically controlled California now having acted, the outcome depended upon the South. Five more state ratifications were needed to reach the Article V threshold. Because of military reconstruction, a conclusion was not long delayed. The new legislatures of Arkansas on April 6, Florida on June 9, North Carolina on July 2, and both Louisiana and South Carolina on July 9 approved the amendment, by wide margins in every instance. With these last two actions twenty-eight of the thirty-seven states, or three-fourths, had assented to the Fourteenth Amendment. Alabama on July 13 and Georgia on July 21 soon contributed their endorsements to comply with Reconstruction requirements.[42] Some disgruntled southerners were outspoken in criticizing these actions. "If we are to wear manacles," said former governor Benjamin Perry of South Carolina, "let them be put on by our tyrants, not by ourselves."[43] Yet more people within the state and across the South seemed to agree with the *Charlotte News* that the consequences of defeat finally had to be accepted. "Do they desire to see the present agitation indefinitely prolonged, industry clogged, commerce checked, credit and confidence altogether destroyed?" the paper asked editorially.[44] Georgia governor Joseph E. Brown grudgingly conceded, "We shall never get better terms."[45]

Meanwhile, northern state actions complicated the ratification process. In 1867 Ohio Democrats won a majority in fall elections for the state legislature in which black suffrage was a dominant campaign issue. Upon convening, the new legislature voted on January 15, 1868, to repeal the state's ratification of the Fourteenth Amendment. New Jersey was the scene of another Democratic victory in state legislative elections in November 1867. That body voted on February 20 to rescind its ratification, but Governor Marcus Ward vetoed the resolution, asserting that New Jersey's initial 1867 endorsement had completed the amending process and bound the state to a federal contract. Unpersuaded, the legislature overrode the governor's veto.[46] As a result of the Ohio and New Jersey actions, opinion divided as to whether the Article V process had been completed on July 9 by the actions of Louisiana and South Carolina. Had the three-fourths standard indeed been met?

Congress, on the day that Louisiana and South Carolina acted, asked Secretary of State William Seward, the federal official responsible for receiving the formal certificates of state endorsement, to provide a list of states whose legislatures had ratified. On July 20 Seward named every state that had taken positive action, including Ohio and New Jersey, as well as those that had reversed earlier rejections, Louisiana, North Carolina, and South Carolina. He indicated that it was "a matter of doubt and uncertainty whether such resolutions are not irregular, invalid, and therefore ineffectual," pointedly leaving Congress to resolve the issue. Congress, the very next day, adopted a concurrent resolution declaring the Fourteenth Amendment to be a valid part of the Constitution and listing the states about which Seward raised questions as among those having ratified.[47]

This was the first time, though scarcely the last, that the question arose of a state's power to reverse its decision to ratify a constitutional amendment. The secretary of state and Congress held, and seventy years later the Supreme Court would formally agree, that this question was for the Congress to settle.[48] Certainly the explicit terms of Article V did not resolve the issue; they went no further than to give Congress power to decide whether state legislatures or conventions were to be the agents of state ratification. In summer 1868, the Fortieth Congress, its Republican majority eager to achieve southern Reconstruction on a basis upon which the party's various factions could agree and battered by the recent bitter struggle over the impeachment of President Johnson, favored the procedural interpretation that would immediately certify the Fourteenth Amendment as valid. Thus the Congress held that states could continue to consider an amendment until they approved it but thereafter could not rescind that act. Constitutional amendment was a specific procedure, not an ordinary legislative process, and therefore conventional practices of reconsideration did not apply. Perhaps under different circumstances other considerations would have prevailed, but in 1868 Congress viewed the amendment ratification process as a ratchet wheel that could move ahead but not backward. The Fourteenth Amendment's adoption established a principle that courts and Congress have since left untouched.

At the time, congressional refusal to recognize southern state governments as legitimate and seat their delegates until after they had ratified the Fourteenth Amendment proved even more controversial. This order of events raised anew the question initially posed when the Thirteenth Amendment was ratified by provisional southern state governments later held incompetent in other matters: were amendment ratifications valid if provided by governments not in good standing at the moment? Once again Congress asserted the authority to determine the means that constituted a lawful state ratification, and at the time its claim was not seriously challenged.

The Fourteenth Amendment offers perhaps the best demonstration of the fundamental changes in American constitutionalism wrought by the Civil War: the adequacy of the Constitution, in this case Article V, to provide for unspecified circumstances and the shift of authority from the states to the central government to set the terms of the federal relationship, including amendment ratification procedures. Eventually, nearly ninety years later, the Fourteenth Amendment would provide the legal basis for a federally directed end to racial segregation, not a result its framers discussed or apparently anticipated but one consistent with its terms and the notion of constitutional adequacy. A powerful northern desire to obtain a symbol of acceptance of the values for which it had fought shaped the manner in which the amending process was conducted. Had the South conceded defeat at the end of the war instead of continuing to resist, much might have been different, not merely the course of reconstruction but the evolution of amending procedures and the installation in the Constitution of one of its most significant amendments.

THE QUESTION OF black suffrage repeatedly arose as the Thirteenth and Fourteenth Amendments were being formulated and adopted. At first northern Republicans were largely indifferent to political rights for the freedmen. Subsequently they wavered between reluctance to have blacks voting in their own states and eagerness for them to have a political role in a reconstructed South. Continually torn between desires to protect state authority and interest in establishing minimum national standards of justice, most Republicans eventually came to regard suffrage as a vital issue. Though radicals such as Charles Sumner advocated black suffrage guarantees from the outset, more and more of their comparatively cautious colleagues came to favor it as they observed the South's resistance to more modest protections for former slaves. Some historians have interpreted the effort to ensure black suffrage as a maneuver to secure continued Republican political control of the reconstructed South.[49] Others have viewed it as a scheme to retain power in the North.[50] However, it may come closer to the truth to argue that the Fifteenth Amendment, guaranteeing that the right to vote "shall not be denied or abridged by the United States or by any State on account of race, color, or previous condition of servitude," was a direct outcome of the battles over the two previous amendments. Discussion of their substance and observance of southern resistance to them moved a congressional supermajority as well as state legislators in both the North and the reconstructed South to conclude that further constitutional protection of freedmen's rights was a logical and necessary fulfillment of their declared political principles. Experience with the Thirteenth and Fourteenth Amendments led proponents of suffrage rights gradually to overcome qualms about altering the federal relationship and to seek national standards in this area.[51]

During the formulation of the Thirteenth Amendment in 1865, the question of black suffrage was already an issue. A year earlier, a measure requiring southern states to grant black voting rights had been considered but not included in the Wade-Davis bill, a District of Columbia voting bill, and a resolution to admit Montana as a state. The belief that states, not the federal government, should set the terms of suffrage outweighed the spreading belief that blacks should be allowed to vote. The same notion prevailed during the drafting of the Thirteenth Amendment.[52] Referendums in 1865 in Connecticut, Minnesota, Wisconsin, Colorado Territory, and the District of Columbia demonstrated that two-thirds to three-fourths of Republicans, though a minority of voters overall, favored black suffrage.[53]

Adoption of the Thirteenth Amendment increased the urgency of the suffrage question for the North. Ending slavery voided the provision of the 1787 Constitution that counted slaves as three-fifths of persons in the apportionment of representation in Congress and presidential elections. If southern blacks were included in the census but not allowed to vote, southern white voters would thereby gain exaggerated political influence in national affairs. Granting blacks the right to vote in northern states was not generally popular, but, given the small black populations residing there, the denial of suffrage did not significantly benefit whites. Disfranchising blacks in the South, on the other hand, would enhance the power of the very people considered responsible for the Civil War. The North was reminded of the possible consequences as the provisional southern governments of 1865, populated by former Confederate leaders, quickly adopted restrictive and discriminatory black codes.

Endorsing and safeguarding black suffrage was again discussed during formulation of the Fourteenth Amendment. Once more the view held that the establishment of voting requirements fell into the realm of state authority.[54] The equal protection guarantee, furthermore, seemed to obviate the need for specific assurances. But as Democrats railed against black suffrage during the election campaign of 1866 and as the provisional southern legislatures thumbed their noses at the proposed amendment during fall 1866 and winter 1867, the North became increasingly aware that the South would do no more for blacks than explicitly compelled to do. Uncertainty as to whether the broad protections of the Fourteenth Amendment expressly defended suffrage or whether its grant of congressional enforcement power authorized voting rights legislation heightened awareness that the newly adopted amendment might prove insufficient.

Initial southern rejection of the Fourteenth Amendment reinforced radical Republican opinion that black suffrage must be specifically ensured, a case not convincingly made in spring 1866. Thus in adopting the Military Reconstruction Act in early 1867, congressional Republicans required southern states to provide for black voting as part of the process of rehabilitating themselves. Yet concern lingered that, once southern states ratified the

Fourteenth Amendment and were restored to full self-government, they would erect new barriers to black political participation. By summer 1867, Charles Sumner was demanding a federal statute to protect black voting rights while more moderate and conservative Republicans had begun calling for a constitutional amendment to that effect.[55] Once again southern intransigence persuaded the North that further steps must be taken to warrant that its battlefield victory had not been achieved in vain.

Supporters of black suffrage included individuals such as Sumner who believed that the bold assertion of the Declaration of Independence that "all men are created equal" would not be fulfilled until there was a universal right to vote. Other suffrage proponents believed that certain franchise restrictions had merit as long as impartially applied. Universalists wanted to eliminate racial and property-holding limitations and, in some cases, desired the removal of gender restrictions and the lowering of age barriers. One even called for voting by all citizens over the age of twelve.[56] Impartial suffrage advocates, on the other hand, argued that, as long as they were fairly and evenly applied, property-holding and literacy requirements were reasonable devices for ensuring an electorate with ties to the community, a stake in decisions, and a capacity to comprehend the political debate. This legitimate philosophical debate complicated the discussion of an appropriate response to the denial of suffrage in the South and the southern rejoinder that the North also limited the franchise to whites.

The suffrage issue began to come into sharper focus during the northern state elections of autumn 1867. Ohio voters defeated a constitutional referendum to enfranchise blacks while at the same time they elected a Democratic majority to the legislature. New Jersey Democrats, likewise opposed to black suffrage, gained control of that state's legislature. In Kansas and Minnesota as well black suffrage amendments met defeat, though by lesser margins than in Ohio. The specter of a revitalized Democratic party naturally concerned Republicans, and the fact that the resurgence gained its momentum from a policy most Republicans had come to oppose made it especially galling. Realization that southern Democratic majorities, once in command of their state governments, would quite likely retreat from commitments to enfranchise freedmen added to Republican concerns. The 1868 elections reinforced these worries, because even though Republicans retained control of the Congress and regained their hold on the presidency, they lost ground to the Democrats.[57]

A sense of urgency about the suffrage question gripped the Republican majority of the Fortieth Congress as it returned for its final session following the 1868 election. Many of these Republicans harbored a long-standing, deeply felt concern for racial justice, even at the cost of political popularity. Senator Edmund Ross of Kansas was speaking not only for himself when he declared, "The first great and sufficient reason why the negro should be admitted to the right of suffrage in all the States is that it is right."[58] Recent developments, including emergence of the Ku Klux Klan, intimidation of black voters in Louisiana, and maneuvers by Georgia's Conservative party to unseat black legislators, furthered Republican feelings of alarm.[59] If a solution could be found quickly, before a Congress with a smaller and more cautious Republican majority took office and before a number of safely Republican state legislatures adjourned, perhaps black voting rights could be safeguarded. As a result, the final session of the Fortieth Congress saw the introduction of more than sixty resolutions for a constitutional amendment dealing with suffrage in one way or another.[60]

The desire for a constitutional amendment to protect black suffrage was linked to an understanding of both the political process of obtaining an amendment and the consequences of achieving one. Congress and state legislatures, both in Republican hands by the required Article V supermajorities at the moment, could secure an amendment. Moreover, once adopted, such a constitutional protection could be removed only with the consent of equivalent supermajorities. Any amendment would be difficult if not impossible to overturn. Thus the Democratic upsurge, perceived as unprincipled, self-serving, and opportunistic, could be waited out; transient electoral victories and referendum results, not to mention southern backsliding, could be resisted. An amendment seemed to Republicans a proper way to secure those larger purposes for which the Civil War had been fought against the petty politics of the moment. "This constitutional amendment," declared Senator Oliver Morton of Indiana, "will forever withdraw the subject from politics, and will strike down that prejudice to which the Democratic party has appealed for years."[61]

Agreement on the need for a constitutional amendment did not automatically produce consensus on the substance of that amendment. Congressman George Boutwell of Pennsylvania introduced amendment language almost identical to what finally emerged. Critics who argued that the South could circumvent mere protection of impartial suffrage by imposing race-neutral criteria such as education or property-holding immediately challenged Boutwell's resolution. After gaining their state delegation's support at a caucus, Ohioans Samuel Shellabarger and John Bingham called on the House to guarantee universal male suffrage. Shellabarger preferred to exclude former rebels, but Bingham included even them. In the Senate a resolution similar to Boutwell's but protecting the right to hold office as well as the franchise emerged from the Judiciary Committee and likewise ran into demands for universal suffrage. Senator Henry Wilson of Massachusetts sought specifically to bar discrimination on access to the ballot based on race, color, nativity, property, education, or creed. Other senators questioned universal suffrage, favoring an educational requirement or preferring to leave standards to the states. The division between impartial and universal suffrage provisions became evident as the House adopted Boutwell's resolution on January 30 by 150 to 42, and the Senate approved Wilson's 39 to 16 ten days later.[62]

After complex parliamentary maneuvers in both the House and Senate, the two bodies convened a conference committee, which then agreed to an amendment resolution that made no mention of the right to hold office or prohibitions of discrimination on any basis other than race, color, or previous servitude. It did contain a grant of authority to Congress to enforce the amendment identical to those in the Thirteenth and Fourteenth Amendments. Some of the radicals expressed unhappiness with this compromise, but the House, without debate, endorsed it by a vote of 144 to 44. After some further discussion, the Senate did likewise by 39 to 13. Final congressional action on February 26 testified more to the rapidly approaching end of the term and the felt need to find a basis for agreement to overcome the dilatory and obstructionist tactics of the Democratic opposition than to universal satisfaction with the exact terms. The outcome can be attributed to those Republicans who concluded that it was more important to obtain a suffrage guarantee that states would ratify than to hold out for other protections they themselves would have liked but that might encounter fatal opposition. They believed that black voting would inevitably lead to black officeholding and so chose not to be held hostage by those who opposed the latter right. Henry Wilson probably spoke for the mainstream when he admitted, "I have asked always for what was right and taken on all occasions what I could get. I have acted upon the idea that one step taken in the right direction made the next step easier to be taken. I suppose, sir, I must act upon that idea now: and I do so with more sincere regret than ever."[63]

Senator James Dixon of Connecticut, a conservative opponent of the suffrage amendment, proposed that, as allowed by Article V, it be sent for ratification to state conventions rather than legislatures.[64] Republicans such as Dixon who had allied with President Johnson and the Democrats reasoned that black suffrage would be unpopular among the white-only northern electorate, as several state suffrage referendums had already shown. Dixon reasoned that conventions of delegates specifically chosen on this one issue would be less likely to approve the amendment than state legislators elected on a variety of positions. When the Senate rejected the convention ratification option, Dixon and his colleagues shifted to a strategy that Article V neither offered nor foreclosed. They sought to require that the amendment be ratified by state legislatures elected after it was put forth for consideration, notwithstanding the abject failure of earlier efforts by Pennsylvania senator Charles Buckalew to block the Fourteenth Amendment using the same tactic.[65] Dixon and his supporters argued that debate on the merits of the amendment and the selection of legislators who reflected the sovereign will of their constituents should precede action. They hoped that current Republican majorities, expected to ratify, would be reduced or eliminated before the crucial vote was taken. Recognizing this shrewd and legitimate effort to set the terms of the ratification process as a crafty political ploy, the Republican majority defeated it.

Not only was the suffrage amendment submitted to the same approval process as its fourteen predecessors, but unreconstructed states faced the same pressure to ratify as had accompanied the last two. Mississippi, Texas, and Virginia remained under military control, not having complied with the terms of congressional reconstruction, and Georgia had been returned to military government after its restored state legislature blatantly disregarded those terms. The Forty-first Congress notified these states that their rehabilitation required ratification of the suffrage amendment as well as the Fourteenth.[66]

Submitted for ratification at a time when many state legislatures were meeting and when Republican majorities were firmly ensconced in most of them, the suffrage amendment won rapid approval. A dozen states, Nevada, West Virginia, Louisiana, North Carolina, Wisconsin, Illinois, Michigan, Maine, South Carolina, Massachusetts, Arkansas, and Pennsylvania, ratified within a month. Five more, New York, Connecticut, Indiana, Florida, and New Hampshire, acted during the spring. By July 1 seventeen of the needed twenty-eight ratifications had been secured. Two more, Vermont and Virginia, followed in October, and Alabama concurred in November. The remaining eight were completed in January and early February, soon after legislatures convened in Missouri, Minnesota, Mississippi, Rhode Island, Kansas, Ohio, Iowa, and Georgia. Ratification of the Fifteenth Amendment was completed February 3, 1870, less than a year after it began. Texas and Nebraska added their endorsements the same month, and New Jersey did so one year later.[67]

All of the reconstructed southern states ratified promptly, with the exception of Tennessee, the only such state to avoid military rule. The four states that had not yet fulfilled the requirements of military reconstruction did so with simultaneous approval of the Fourteenth and Fifteenth Amendments. Virginia acted on October 8, 1869, Mississippi on January 17, 1870, Georgia on February 2, and Texas on February 18. These ratifications of the Fourteenth Amendment and the Texas endorsement of the Fifteenth occurred after completion of the Article V process, but they were carried out by the legislatures to demonstrate that the states accepted the national consensus and were worthy of restoration to self-government. Once again, a legitimate question arises as to whether the southern states ratified in a manner consistent with the Philadelphia Framers' desire for an expression of sovereign sanction. And again the answer is problematic. The four unreconstructed states did seem compelled to act. The other states, observing how Georgia had regained self-government, then lost it a second time by ignoring Reconstruction mandates, no doubt felt pressure to ratify. Yet in each state, legislative bodies could consider alternatives and, with the exception of Tennessee, chose, after debate and with dissenting voices raised, to accept the amendment. Southern state legislatures, predominantly white in every case, contemplated the Fifteenth Amendment on its merits and concluded that opposition, while possible, was not worth its costs.

Every northern state where Republicans held a majority in the legislature ratified, but where Democrats were ascendant the outcome proved different. The border states of Kentucky, Maryland, Tennessee, and Delaware, together with the Pacific coast Democratic strongholds of Oregon and California, declined to ratify. Ohio refused its approval in April 1869 while Democrats controlled the legislature but changed its position in January 1870 once Republicans regained control. New Jersey followed the same pattern as a Democratic legislature rejected the amendment in February 1870 and its Republican successor approved it one year later. The reverse occurred in New York where a Republican majority ratified in April 1869 and the new Democratic majority voted to withdraw consent the following January.[68] Partisan differences did not slow, indeed probably speeded the ratification process to completion within forty-nine weeks. The Republicans' desire to complete a Reconstruction agenda to which they had a principled commitment while they still had power to enact it proved central to the emergence of the Fifteenth Amendment.

EACH OF THE THREE Civil War amendments represented an effort to define the rights of freed slaves and to give those rights constitutional protection. Each provided less protection than intended, whether as a result of sloppy draftsmanship, deliberate compromises that produced ambiguous perceptions, or determined resistance. Section one of the Fourteenth Amendment, for instance, had supporters who believed that spelling out what specific rights were protected was unnecessary, watchful bystanders uncertain about what rights were covered, and opponents eager to see rights narrowly construed. The consequences of differences in understanding came quickly to light. Thus experience with the Fourteenth Amendment immediately begat the Fifteenth, just as the Thirteenth begat the Fourteenth. The story did not end there, for the Supreme Court proceeded to interpret the Civil War amendments in ways unanticipated by their drafters. The entire episode speaks to the difficulty of designing amendments that achieve the results their architects intend.

As it dealt with cases coming before it as a result of the Civil War and Reconstruction, the Supreme Court contended with both constitutional innovations and persistent traditions of government restraint and federalism. Especially as passions stirred by the war and the struggle over Reconstruction policy began to cool, the Court was willing to acknowledge that specific constitutional alterations had occurred yet repeatedly ruled that their effect had narrow limits. Throughout the late nineteenth century, the Court acted in ways that minimized the impact of the Civil War amendments but satisfied the dominant conservative and racist political-legal community.

At first the Court had no trouble supporting the concept of constitutional adequacy. In an 1869 case involving a dispute over Texas state bonds, the justices addressed fundamental issues of secession and Reconstruction in terms supportive of Lincoln and the Republican Congress. Chief Justice Salmon Chase wrote that rebellious states had abdicated their responsibility in a perpetual Union. The Constitution, he declared, "looks to an indestructible Union, composed of indestructible States." It followed, Chase said, that states refusing to carry out their obligations would have their rights suspended. The federal government had the duty to rehabilitate those states. The president during wartime and thereafter Congress enjoyed "discretion in the choice of means" to work out policies to do so.[69] *Texas v. White* broadly confirmed the legitimacy of congressional Reconstruction, from the refusal to seat southern delegates in December 1865 to military rule to insistence on amendment ratification as the price for reinstatement.

Having indirectly affirmed the propriety of the Civil War amendments, the Supreme Court found ways to construe them narrowly. The first cases directly involving the Thirteenth and Fourteenth Amendments came before the Court in 1873. A group of white butchers challenged a Louisiana statute that granted a limited local monopoly to one New Orleans livestock slaughterhouse; they claimed it violated their privileges and immunities and denied them due process and equal protection of the laws. A 4 to 3 majority of the Court, however, held that the amendments had been written specifically to protect former slaves and otherwise had not altered the relationship between a state and its citizens. The ruling in the *Slaughterhouse Cases* drew an important and sharp distinction between state and federal citizenship, determined that the Fourteenth Amendment applied only to a limited set of federal rights, and decided that the amendment had not incorporated the Bill of Rights into the obligations of state governments. The vague wording of the amendment's first section, particularly its "privileges and immunities" clause, allowed the Court's majority, eager to retain traditional federalism, to conclude that Congress had not intended to go beyond very limited guarantees to freedmen.[70] Rejecting the notion that the Fourteenth Amendment incorporated the Bill of Rights required the Court to ignore the claims of amendment sponsors such as John Bingham to the contrary. A majority of the justices did so without hesitation, preferring to confine themselves to the words of the amendment before them.

Three years later, Court rulings limited the scope of the 1860s amendments even more. In *United States v. Reese* the enforcement section of the Fifteenth Amendment was held only to pertain to denial of suffrage specifically because of race, color, or previous servitude and not to its denial on other grounds. By invalidating a broadly worded voting law, the Court chose to ignore that the discrimination at issue was precisely on the basis of race.[71] In *United States v. Cruikshank* the Court went further yet. William Cruikshank was a member of a white mob that attacked and killed more than 100 blacks gathered to support local Republican elected officials in Colfax, Louisiana, in April 1873. Charged with violating the victims' civil rights in the course of this massacre, Cruikshank and two others appealed their federal convictions. The logic of the *Slaughterhouse Cases* was extended to hold that federal constitutional rights were limitations on the power of the national government and did not apply to states or to private citizens; it was up to states to protect individual citizens.[72] The Court again refused to recognize desires on the part of the Reconstruction Congress or the ratifying states to guarantee rights beyond what had been explicitly articulated.

In 1883 the Supreme Court tightened its reading of the Civil War amendments again. First, in *United States v. Harris,* justices invalidated the 1871 federal law on which rested the conviction of a Tennessee Ku Klux Klan lynch mob member. They said that a federal law that applied no matter how well states performed their duties to provide equal protection went beyond the Fourteenth Amendment's authorization of congressional action when states failed to enforce its provisions.[73] Then in cases from five states grouped as the *Civil Rights Cases,* the Court held that the Thirteenth Amendment banned slavery and the "badges of slavery" but did not, nor could it, bar racial prejudice. Furthermore, the Fourteenth Amendment's enforcement provision only allowed Congress to legislate to reverse state actions violating the amendment's protections. Congress did not gain authority to deal with private discrimination exercised by hotels, theaters, restaurants, streetcars, and citizens. Justice John Marshall Harlan dissented, declaring that in this ruling the Supreme Court stripped the Fourteenth Amendment of most of its meaning.[74] Together with *Cruikshank,* these 1883 decisions severely inhibited states from ensuring the enforcement of civil rights within their borders, surely not an outcome anticipated by Reconstruction legislators seeking to compel southern states to respect freedmen's rights.

The most famous of late-nineteenth-century cases interpreting the Fourteenth Amendment further exposed the ambiguities of its language. In earlier cases the Supreme Court had failed to find racial segregation discriminatory under the Fourteenth Amendment. The Court first ruled that states could not prohibit segregation, then later held that they could require it.[75] In 1896 *Plessy v. Ferguson* clarified and expanded the Court's views of segregation. A New Orleans black organization, the American Citizens Equal Rights Association, sought to prevent Judge John Ferguson from enforcing an 1890 Louisiana law requiring railroads to provide "separate but equal" accommodations for blacks and whites. Their plaintiff, Homer A. Plessy, arrested for boarding a whites-only rail coach, had, ironically, only one black great-grandparent and was not discernibly black. The association's attorney, Albion Tourgee, himself an active participant in Reconstruction, argued that the purpose of the Civil War amendments was to establish a colorblind Constitution. Segregation, he explained, stigmatized blacks, furthered discrimination, perpetuated a caste system, and patently violated the Fourteenth Amendment.

The Supreme Court, however, saw no evidence that the creators of the Fourteenth Amendment opposed segregation of the races. In the Court's view, they sought merely to guarantee legal equality, not social intermingling. Louisiana's requirement of separate but equal facilities satisfied the mandate of the amendment. Most justices, finding nothing specifically contrary in the record of the 1860s, readily embraced the scientific racism of their own day and ignored the growing reality of racial hatred, violence, and abuse that oppressed its victims. Justice John Marshall Harlan, in a strong but lonely dissent from the *Plessy* decision, declared that segregation was "conceived in hostility to, and enacted for the purpose of humiliating citizens of the United States of a particular race." It defeated, he said, the entire purpose of the Civil War amendments.[76]

The Court dealt black rights another serious blow two years after *Plessy* in the case of *Williams v. Mississippi*. It found a state law imposing a literacy test for voters as well as a poll tax to be racially neutral on its face. Justice Joseph McKenna's opinion acknowledged that the Mississippi Supreme Court had openly admitted that the law was designed to disfranchise blacks, but nothing in its terms specifically denied anyone the right to vote on the basis of their race. In effect, the Court was declaring that the Fifteenth Amendment, like the Thirteenth and Fourteenth, imposed no constitutional obligations beyond those clearly visible in its formal language.[77] Advocates of impartial as opposed to universal suffrage had triumphed, first in the limited language of the amendment itself and three decades later in the strict construction placed upon it. Southern states would erect all sorts of barriers to voting, not on racial grounds but on educational and economic terms that denied large numbers of poor whites as well as almost all blacks access to the ballot.

Not every Court decision during the late nineteenth century, however, constricted the effect of the Civil War amendments. In two 1880 cases and a third the following year the Court ruled that restricting jury service to white men violated the Fourteenth Amendment's equal protection clause. Whether carried out by statute, a judge, or state officials, this practice constituted hostile action against which the Fourteenth Amendment was designed to protect former slaves.[78] The Court's assertion that participation in grand and petit juries was exactly what the Fourteenth Amendment meant by equal protection and due process highlights how closely the justices felt bound by the language of the amendment.

When race was not at issue, the Supreme Court took a far less restrictive view of the potentially most far-reaching of the Civil War constitutional innovations, the Fourteenth Amendment. Indeed, late-nineteenth-century judicial decisions repeatedly expanded understandings of this amendment, increasing its impact. From two particularly important rulings flowed a great body of law concerning the powers of states and corporations. In *Munn v. Illinois*, an 1877 case dealing with laws governing the operation of grain elevators, the Court held that a state had power to regulate private property in order to protect the lives, liberty, and property of its citizens.[79] Nine years later a more probusiness Court casually agreed that a corporation was a person in the sense of the Fourteenth Amendment and thus was entitled to its protections of due process and equality under the law. This judgment, expanding and formalizing the common law understanding of corporations, conferred substantial legal advantages upon them. The Court did not base its position on any clear evidence of the intent of the amendment's drafters but on self-interested recollections twenty years afterward by a congressman turned corporate lawyer, Roscoe Conkling.[80] Clearly the Court did not devote all of its energies to reducing the impact of the Civil War amendments.

Ultimately, however, the late-nineteenth-century Supreme Court, reflecting the dominant social-political consensus of the day, treated the Civil War constitutional revolution as a modest one indeed. From its first consideration of the Civil War amendments in the 1873 *Slaughterhouse Cases,* the Supreme Court set forth its belief that federal power over states remained quite limited. The 1883 *Civil Rights Cases* decision spoke directly of restricted federal power for the protection of black civil rights. The *Plessy* and *Williams* rulings of the 1890s interpreted the amendments to allow construction of segregationist racial barriers and thinly veiled denials of black opportunity.

To many observers these judicial developments signified that the Civil War amendments had failed. They did not override an earlier constitutional commitment to federalism and immediately produce a new constitutional order based on equality. However, while there is truth in the harsh verdict that freedom was sold out to federalism in the late-nineteenth-century climate of American racism, the Civil War amendments did enter the fabric of the Constitution. They did enlarge the Constitution's authority and, as the South remained acutely aware, retained at least the potential for sanctioning change as long as the doctrine of constitutional adequacy prevailed. Thus historian Eric Foner properly characterized Reconstruction when he declined to declare it a failed revolution but instead entitled it "America's unfinished revolution." Eventually, during the 1930s and 1950s in particular, the Civil War amendments would be reconsidered. They then served as the legal foundation for a new structure of federalism and civil rights that would have been much harder, indeed perhaps impossible, to establish without them.

9

"No Force Less Than the Force of Revolution"

Resurrecting the Amending Remedy

Constitution worship was flourishing by the time the United States observed the centennial of the Philadelphia convention in 1887. The design of the nation's fundamental political instrument had come to be widely regarded as inspired; its Framers won accolades as geniuses. How else to explain the country's capacity to emerge whole from the Civil War and to develop so rapidly thereafter? Americans referred to the Constitution as "the Ark of the Covenant," Independence Hall as "the holiest spot of American earth," and visitors to it as "pilgrims" in "the spirit of worshippers before a shrine"; terms such as "reverence," "sacredness," and "hallowed ground of its birthplace" were used constantly. They proudly and, it seems, endlessly quoted William Gladstone's 1878 characterization of the Constitution as "the most wonderful work ever struck off at a given time by the brain and purpose of man." Most Americans forgot, or never knew, that Gladstone's comment was merely part of a larger statement expressing his greater admiration for the unwritten British constitution as a "subtle organism" able to evolve to meet changing needs. Though Gladstone happily agreed that the American Constitution had been a splendid creation, he shared with far less enthusiasm the common perception that it was now entrenched and impossible to alter.[1]

Reconstruction left many Americans believing that all major constitutional problems had been solved. Moreover, the emergent worshipful attitude toward the Constitution fostered resistance to any notion that it might deserve further reform. In 1900 one conservative legal writer cautioned judges that even improper decisions were irreversible, explaining, "A constitutional amendment is so remote a possibility as scarcely to be worth consideration."[2] Writing in the *North American Review* near the end of the century, North Carolina Supreme Court justice Walter Clark drew a telling parallel between American constitutional close-mindedness and the rigid, thoughtless traditionalism of the Imperial Russian Guard that stationed a soldier at the spot where Catherine the Great had asked that a flower be protected from being plucked. Since no direct order came for the guard's removal, one continued to be posted on the spot for 150 years. Justice Clark implied that American reverence and rigidity regarding the Constitution was no more enlightened.[3]

In the two decades after adoption of the Thirteenth, Fourteenth, and Fifteenth Amendments, members of Congress submitted over 400 amendment resolutions, but none came close to upsetting the constitutional status quo. Few enjoyed any significant support or received serious attention. In some cases, the proposed alteration appeared of consequence. In others, a belief in constitutional adequacy undermined any perceived need for amendment; the problem could be solved by ordinary statute. In even more instances, the suggested change simply stirred little enthusiasm. Advocates of substantial reforms, including direct election of presidents and senators, woman suffrage, national standards for marriage and divorce, and prohibition of alcohol, offered many proposals but generated scant response. In an era when partisan forces were evenly divided, mundane political issues of civil service and tariff reform occupied center stage, aspirants for office usually displayed caution, and the belief was widespread that most authority should be exercised by the states, it is no wonder the amending process lay dormant.

On the few occasions when some interest in amendment displayed itself, the proposed reforms seemed constitutionally peripheral if not altogether unnecessary. In December 1875 President Ulysses Grant's call for support of public schools included a recommendation that no school taxes be used for religious education. Congressman James G. Blaine immediately introduced an amendment to extend to the states the First Amendment bar on making laws respecting an establishment of religion and, furthermore, prohibiting state appropriation of money to sectarian schools. In August 1876 the House adopted the Blaine amendment by 180 to 71; then, on a vote of 28 to 16, it fell just short of two-thirds approval in the Senate. Despite the near success, nothing more came of this initiative even though it was reintroduced no fewer than twenty times. Congressional committees generally ignored it but on one occasion recommended against its passage. They regarded state constitutions as adequate in this area, and concerns with federalism, always strong in the Senate, mitigated against further intrusion into state affairs.[4]

Christian fundamentalists responded to the secularization of American government, a development in which the Grant-Blaine initiative appeared to them only the latest stage, with their own call for an amendment declaring that "Almighty God [is] the Author of National Existence and the source of all power and authority in Civil Government, Jesus Christ [is] the Ruler of Nations, and the Bible [is] the formation of law and supreme rule for the conduct of nations." The National Reform Association, founded in 1863 in

Xenia, Ohio, by eleven fundamentalist churches, led the campaign for a Christian amendment. The association considered the Civil War a divine retribution on a godless nation.[5] Complete lack of success did not halt the effort. Between 1894 and 1910 Congress received at least nine proposals to alter the Constitution's preamble to express trust in or acknowledge the authority of a Christian God.[6]

The constitutional delicacy of religious issues and political caution in dealing with them became most evident when theological opinions were decidedly one-sided. Desire to deal with religious customs centered in a single state, a task that could be achieved by amendment, was more than balanced by concerns for the constitutional rights of states in general. Antipathy towards the Church of Jesus Christ of Latter-day Saints had existed since its founding in the 1830s. Not even the withdrawal of most Mormons to the region of the Great Salt Lake during the late 1840s had dampened hostility toward their unconventional beliefs. Indeed ill-will increased with their establishment of a theocratic government and sanctioning of polygamy, which eventually perhaps 10 percent of church members practiced. For example, the 1856 Republican party platform linked slavery and polygamy as twin evils. Through legislation and criminal proceedings, the federal government actively sought to suppress plural marriage, notwithstanding the Latter-day Saints' claims of First Amendment protection of their free exercise of religion. Recognizing that if Mormon-dominated Utah Territory achieved statehood, it would be in a position to establish its own marriage laws, President Grant in his 1875 State of the Union message recommended a constitutional amendment prohibiting polygamy. Resolutions for such an amendment were introduced in the next several Congresses. In 1882 Congress attempted to settle the issue with strong antipolygamy legislation. Congress and later President Benjamin Harrison also told Utah it could not hope for statehood until it banned polygamy. In 1890 Mormon leaders finally declared that they would submit to federal laws against polygamy. Thereafter Utah was allowed to begin the transition from territory to state that it completed in January 1896.[7]

Utah's failure to enforce the ban on polygamy in its state constitution soon revived the controversy. When Utah elected Brigham H. Roberts, an alleged polygamist, to Congress in 1898, a Rhode Island congressman proposed an amendment disqualifying polygamists from Congress and establishing a national ban on polygamy. The House of Representatives did not vote on the proposal but instead unseated Roberts by a vote of 268 to 50. Subsequent House discussion of renewed calls for amendment revealed that representatives overwhelmingly believed authority over marriage should remain with states, that existing laws could be used to deal with the specific problem of polygamy, and that polygamy was not a subject of sufficient importance to address in the Constitution. Disagreement with this view eventually provoked twenty-six states at one time or another before World War I to request a federal convention to launch an antipolygamy amendment. Yet distaste for what Grant called Utah's "anomalous, not to say scandalous, condition," though widespread and lasting, never became so intense as to precipitate constitutional action.[8]

Two other matters generated calls for amendment and eventually did stir some congressional activity. Although the Fourteenth Amendment prohibited payment of the Confederacy's public debts, the issue of private claims for destruction of property led to the introduction of more than a dozen amendment resolutions. In June 1878 the House voted 145 to 61 for an amendment prohibiting payment of war claims to disloyal persons, but it never came to a vote in the Senate where the influence of reconstructed states weighed more heavily.[9] Dissatisfaction with the dates for presidential inauguration and commencement of congressional terms produced proposals for amendment as early as 1795 and with frequency after 1876. In 1886 and 1887, efforts to move the commencement of presidential and congressional terms to the end of April to correspond with the centennials of George Washington's inauguration and the First Congress's assembly led to unanimous Senate passage of amendment resolutions. Both died in the House, the first in committee, the second on an almost evenly divided vote far short of the necessary two-thirds margin.[10] In 1898 the Senate again approved such a measure, but it too expired in the House.[11] In neither of these instances did the need for constitutional amendment appear to be strongly felt.

As the twentieth century approached, glorification of the Constitution and contentment with its existing terms had become a formidable foe to advocates of political reform in the United States. Increasingly, they perceived the Constitution as an obstacle to change they desired. Although Article V had been used to make a dozen additions or refinements in the 1787 instrument during its first fifteen years of operation, complaints centered on the fact that constitutional amendment had not occurred by the normal process since 1804. While over 1,700 resolutions of amendment had been introduced in Congress during its first century, only nineteen ultimately obtained the necessary two-thirds congressional approval. Four of these then failed to win the required three-fourths state endorsement, two falling only one state short. Altogether only fifteen amendments to the Constitution had been adopted in a century, only five since 1791. Furthermore, the most recent three, the Civil War amendments, had been achieved under the extraordinary circumstances of Reconstruction that compelled the supine southern states to ratify in order to regain their seats in Congress. Thus the very achievement of these amendments contributed to a growing belief that under normal circumstances the Constitution was unamendable.

Historian Herman Ames, the compiler in the 1890s of this legislative record, helped shape views of the amending process. Ames decided that amendments generally failed "in part because some were suggested as cures for temporary evils, others were trivial or impracticable, still others found a place in that unwritten constitution which has grown up side by side with the written document; but the real reason for the failure of those other amendments which have been called for repeatedly by the general public has been due to the insurmountable constitutional obstacles in their way." Ames discounted the lack of demand for or agreement upon amendments in concluding that the system Article V created was responsible for so few being adopted.[12] He quoted the complaint of the prominent Princeton constitutional scholar Professor Woodrow Wilson that "no impulse short of the impulse of self-preservation; no force less than the force of revolution, can nowadays be expected to move the cumbrous machinery of Article V."[13] Other observers shared this view.[14] The British writer James Bryce, in his classic assessment of U.S. political life, *The American Commonwealth,* stressed the difficulty of constitutional alteration. Lord Bryce attributed it to the problem of assembling the bipartisan majorities necessary to meet amending requirements as well as to the disinclination of most American statesmen to see amendment as improvement.[15]

With agitation increasing for various substantial political, economic, and social reforms, criticism of the amending process grew apace. The sectional, class, and economic differences within the modern continental republic appeared to present far greater barriers to amendment than had existed when first the Constitution and then the Bill of Rights were approved. Progressives of various types expressed growing impatience with obstacles to constitutional change. The congressional supermajorities necessary even to propose an amendment to the states were hard to achieve in an era of political balance. Thereafter, the three-fourths state ratification requirement made it possible for a dozen sparsely populated states, and sometimes even disproportionately powerful small factions within those states, to block an amendment. Frustration with the requirements of constitutional reform was understandable though perhaps unreasonable at a time when even ordinary legislation was often difficult to obtain.

"The Constitution," declared Justice William P. Potter of the Pennsylvania Supreme Court, "ought not to be regarded as though it were the last will and testament of the only body capable of making a plan of government for the American people." Nevertheless, Potter concurred with a speaker at the 1907 meeting of the American Bar Association that "we are taught by a century of our history that the Constitution can no longer be . . . amended."[16] Following a visit to the United States, Australian parliamentarian Henry Bournes Higgins observed that Americans regarded the Constitution as "practically unalterable."[17] Scholars such as John W. Burgess declared the amendment process "ordinarily unworkable," permanently preventing "the will of the undoubted majority of the whole people in a democratic republic from realizing its well considered and well determined purposes in its organic law."[18] Frederic Bruce Johnstone complained, "So far as the Constitution is concerned, we are proceeding today on the theory that conditions of life and property are as they were before the commencement of the 19th century."[19] Monroe Smith asked readers of the *North American Review,* "In what other Federal union would a vote of two-thirds of the constituent States, including nearly three-fourths of the population, be insufficient to change the law? In what other nation, possessing representative institutions, would a measure supported by so large a majority of the people fail of effect?"[20]

Several early-twentieth-century critics of the constitutional status quo concluded that no remedy was possible unless Article V was itself amended to make the obtaining of other amendments easier. William Potter and Monroe Smith, following a suggestion made by John W. Burgess twenty years earlier, proposed amendment by simple majorities of both houses in two successive Congresses and ratification by a majority of states, providing that they contained a majority of the population.[21] Wisconsin senator Robert La Follette, eager to make the federal government more responsive to simple democratic majorities, introduced an amendment along these lines in 1912. The Progressive party platform of the same year simply called for amendments when approved by a popular majority in a majority of states.[22]

Just when appraisals of the Article V process were at their most negative, however, events forced their reconsideration. Demands for constitutional reform that had been stirring at least since the 1890s finally bore fruit. Two crusades, one for reform of federal tax policy, the other to democratize the selection of U.S. senators, catalyzed the amending system. The adoption of two amendments in 1913 reawakened faith in the viability of Article V for making changes in the Constitution when a broad consensus agreed that reform was imperative. The Sixteenth and Seventeenth Amendments provided a long-absent demonstration that, despite the difficulty of assembling a two-thirds majority in each house of Congress and obtaining ratification votes in three-fourths of the states, constitutional relief could be obtained through

Article V. This was a vital message in an age of substantial political discontent and doubt in some quarters as to whether the 1787 Constitution would be adequate to the needs of a rapidly modernizing society.

A FUNDAMENTAL REDIRECTION of American constitutional development certainly appeared unlikely in the circumstances of the late nineteenth century. Nevertheless, one began in the course of efforts to establish a federal tax on incomes. Although it did not bear fruit until 1913, the income tax crusade resurrected the amending process as a viable remedy for significant political discontent. It stirred other amendment efforts, one almost simultaneously and several in the years that followed. Moreover, it gave Americans a reminder that the power of the Supreme Court to define the meaning of the Constitution was not absolute. Because of its pivotal importance in the longer history of American constitutional reform, not to mention the complicated circumstances of its adoption, the genesis of the Sixteenth Amendment deserves particular attention.

Farmers and workers, southerners and westerners had been calling for an income tax since the 1870s. By the 1890s depression a tax on incomes appeared to most of the Democratic majority in Congress to offer the best solution to the twin problems of falling federal revenues and rising resentment against concentrated wealth, privilege, and power in an industrializing society. Article I of the Constitution authorized Congress "to lay and collect taxes, duties, imposts and excises to pay the debts and provide for the common defense and general welfare" so long as "all duties, imposts and excises" were uniform throughout the country and "capitation or other direct taxes" were apportioned according to the population of the states. The Founders had not clearly defined "direct tax," allowing some people to argue that the term referred only to land or capitation taxes, whereas others claimed that it applied to any levy on persons or property. The Supreme Court had repeatedly taken a broad view of the federal taxing power, defining uniformity and direct taxation narrowly. In 1796 it upheld a tax on carriages, obviously a levy on wealthy property holders.[23] A federal income tax adopted by Congress in 1861 and not allowed to expire until 1872 had met much of the cost of the Civil War. The high court had declared this tax both uniform and indirect in a case decided as recently as 1881.[24] Thus in 1894 debate over a new federal income tax centered not on its constitutionality, which was assumed, but on whether it was good public policy.

In December 1893 President Grover Cleveland bowed to party sentiment and, in his annual message to Congress, gave a surprise endorsement to "a small tax" on corporate income. House Ways and Means chairman William Wilson soon adopted the same position. Both men apparently had favored an income tax in principle but had feared its political consequences. Speaking for the president as well as himself, Wilson argued that the "one class of our citizens who own and control a very large and increasing part of the property of the country [and] who enjoy public franchises of a very substantial character" have no right to object to a small tax upon their incomes.[25] The wealthy had not carried a fair share of the tax burden, Wilson charged repeatedly. Instead, tariffs and excises, taxes on consumption, bore most heavily on the poor. A federal income tax would strike a better balance.

Congressman William Jennings Bryan, on behalf of the Ways and Means Committee's Internal Revenue Subcommittee, drafted income tax legislation. At first Cleveland and Wilson balked at Bryan's insistence that individual as well as corporate income be taxed and that the tax proposal be attached to the pending tariff revision. Eventually, however, the House Democratic caucus supported Bryan. The caucus agreed that no distinctions should be drawn between sources of income; the income tax, a burden to eastern industrialists and a benefit to farmers and workers, was best linked to higher tariffs that would benefit industry but burden consumers. As it emerged from the subcommittee, Bryan's income tax proposal placed a flat 2 percent tax on individual and corporate incomes over $4,000. Bryan himself favored a graduated tax on all incomes over $2,500, but more cautious politicians prevailed.[26]

House debate was heated, even by the standards of the conflict-ridden 1890s. Both supporters and opponents acknowledged that the impact of the tax would be uneven. The Treasury Department estimated that only about 85,000 of the 65 million Americans had annual incomes large enough to be affected. The *New York Tribune* identified 4,000 American millionaires and noted that three-fourths of them lived in seven states (New York, Pennsylvania, Illinois, Massachusetts, Ohio, California, and New Jersey). Opponents of the tax, Republicans and northeastern Democrats, notably Tammany spokesman Bourke Cockran, called it discrimination against thrift and industry, an assault on democracy, an act of vengeance against the northeastern states and the creators of the nation's wealth, and a specter of socialism. Bryan responded with passion, eloquence, and biblical allusions, insisting that those who derived the greatest benefit from economic and political arrangements should provide the most support rather than, as had been the case, shifting the burden to poor consumers. After the House agreed to add the tax plan, the Wilson-Gorman tariff bill won approval by 204 to 140 in the House and 39 to 34 in the Senate. No Republican voted for the bill in either chamber; of the seventeen Democrats in the House and one in the Senate who broke ranks, most came from New York, Connecticut, Rhode Island, New Jersey, or Pennsylvania.[27]

With the adoption of the income tax, the tide in Congress appeared to be turning against the laissez-faire business culture. Desperate business leaders looked to the judiciary as a last line of defense. The business counterattack was swift, shrewd, and successful. And in the literal sense, it was outrageous. When their legislative victory was negated almost before they could savor it, proponents of the income tax were rendered absolutely furious. They felt victimized by undemocratic forces, betrayed by unfair albeit constitutional means. Given the manner in which the counterattack unfolded, their outrage was understandable.

Congress in 1867 prohibited legal challenges to tax assessments prior to their collection. Nevertheless, two extremely conservative New York attorneys, Joseph H. Choate and William D. Guthrie, quickly found a way to circumvent this obstacle. Choate, long a prominent member of New York City's legal elite, was once described as "effectively quarantined from the Great Unwashed" and "so well bathed that his words virtually smelled of soap." A colleague characterized Choate as having "an abiding doubt as to the validity of the claims of social reforms." Choate provided effective legal arguments after Guthrie, whose legal reputation would approach Choate's as a result of this case, devised the litigation strategy.[28]

Guthrie arranged for Charles Pollock, a resident of Massachusetts who held $5,000 in stock in the New York Farmers Loan and Trust Company, to sue the company's directors to block their payment of the income tax. He also arranged for another attorney to defend Farmers Loan and Trust. Because of its interstate character and the sums involved, Pollock's suit was eligible for immediate admission into federal court. The lack of a legitimate basis for the suit (since both parties desired the same outcome) remained concealed. The suit was filed eighteen days after the tax law took effect on January 1, 1895. Within nine days Guthrie had convinced Solicitor General Lawrence Maxwell to avoid lengthy lower court proceedings, consolidate the Pollock case with two other challenges to the income tax, and set the earliest possible date for arguments before the Supreme Court. The high court heard *Pollock* on March 7, 1895, a mere forty-seven days after its filing. As a consequence, the government had little time to prepare and of course no opportunity to rehearse its arguments or to hear those of the plaintiffs in the lower courts. Attorney General Richard Olney and President Cleveland, already unhappy with the solicitor general for his weak and much-criticized defense of the Sherman Anti-Trust Act in the *United States v.*

E. C. *Knight* case, the government's loss of which was announced on January 21, were furious. They forced Maxwell's resignation, but the damage had been done.[29]

A battery of eminent attorneys presented the case against the income tax to the Supreme Court. William Guthrie began by arguing that the tax violated the constitutional requirement of uniformity since it would fall only on the 2 percent of the population with incomes over $4,000. Clarence A. Seward carried this argument further, calling the tax a clear violation of the equal protection clause of the Fourteenth Amendment. George Edmunds then challenged previous Court rulings on the nature of a direct tax, insisting that an income tax was a direct tax requiring apportionment. Otherwise, "one evil step will lead to another . . . until by and by we will have revolution, then anarchy and then a tyrant to rule us." Joseph Choate reasoned that there was no difference between a tax on property and a tax on the income from property. He then turned up the rhetorical heat as he concluded for the plaintiff: "This Act . . . is communistic in its purposes and tendencies, and is defended here upon principles as communistic, socialistic—what shall I call them—populistic as ever have been addressed to any political assembly in the world." The Court, he said, must act "now or never. . . . You cannot hereafter exercise any check if you now say that Congress is untrammeled and uncontrollable. . . . I have thought that one of the fundamental objects of all civilized government was the preservation of the rights of private property. I have thought that it was the very keystone of the arch upon which all civilized government rests, and that this once abandoned, everything was at stake and in danger."[30]

Defenders of the income tax appeared to have an easier task given the Court's past decisions. Farmers Loan and Trust attorney James C. Carter conceded that the tax would fall on only 2 percent of the population but pointed out that this 2 percent received a majority of the nation's income. The levy could be termed class and sectional legislation only because wealth had become class and sectional. Taxation was a question of politics, not law, and a matter the courts should leave to Congress. Assistant Attorney General Edward B. Whitney argued that the definitions of uniformity and direct taxation were settled matters. Richard Olney then summed up saying that Congress acted within its powers when it classified people reasonably for tax purposes, levied the same rate on all within a classification, and applied the same classifications and rates throughout the country. To reverse a century's holdings on the government's taxing powers, Olney concluded, "would go far to prove that government by written constitution is not a thing of stable principles, but of the fluctuating views and wishes of the particular period and the particular judges when and from whom its interpretation happens to be called for."[31]

Within a month, the Supreme Court announced that it found a tax on income from land to be a direct tax, requiring apportionment among the states, and the tax on income from municipal bonds likewise unconstitutional. Justices John Marshall Harlan and Edward White dissented. Because Justice Howell Jackson had been absent due to illness and the other justices had divided four to four on several questions, the Court called for a second round of argument on a number of issues. Olney and Choate rehearsed their previous arguments. The attorney general now addressed the direct tax issue in detail, still insisting that taxes on land rents were legitimate. After further consideration, five justices declared income taxes on personal property as well as land to be direct and therefore unconstitutional. Four members of the Court disagreed. Since the returned Justice Jackson was among the four, it was apparent that one of the unidentified justices in the earlier even division had switched sides. Not only had a single vote decided the fate of the federal income tax, but also an uncertain, vacillating justice apparently had provided the margin.[32]

While at least one modern scholar regards the *Pollock* decision as narrow and centrist and as an open door to progressive taxation of wealth, at the time most observers would have regarded such claims as preposterous.[33] The strident language and intemperate tone of the *Pollock* decision and dissents added to their impact. Writing for the majority, Chief Justice Melville Fuller called earlier decisions defining direct taxation narrowly "a century of error." Fuller held that the rule of uniformity in the levying of federal taxes protected unequal wealth in the manner that the provision of two Senate seats for every state protected small states. Both were provisions demanded and accepted as conditions for adoption of the Constitution. They could be changed only by amendment, said the Chief Justice. Associate Justice Stephen Field, a champion of property rights throughout his forty years on the Court, went further than Fuller in an emotional concurring opinion that echoed Joseph Choate. Field called the income tax an "assault on capital," a "stepping stone" toward "a war of the poor against the rich." An angry John Marshall Harlan pounded his desk and shook his finger at Fuller and Field while delivering a strong dissent against a class decision that overturned well-settled precedent and made the Constitution "a most dangerous instrument to the rights and liberties of the people." Another dissenter, Justice Henry Brown, declared the decision "a national calamity" and called it "a surrender of the taxing power to the moneyed class."[34]

The Court announced its *Pollock* decision soon after it destroyed the

Sherman Anti-Trust Act in *United States v. E. C. Knight* and shortly before it approved injunctions against labor strikes in its ruling *in re Debs*. Together these decisions focused public attention on judicial review and the high court's determined defense of an unrestricted laissez-faire economy. The questionable means that Guthrie had used to get *Pollock* so quickly before the Court and the narrow yet decisive result raised a specter of arbitrary judicial power. The arguments Choate employed and the Court majority favored manifested an extreme and rigid defense of privilege.

The *Pollock* decision provoked immediate and extreme reaction. No high court decision since *Dred Scott* had been so widely condemned, observed one legal scholar twenty years later. "It took hold of the popular imagination," he concluded, and fostered the impression that the rich were escaping the burden of paying taxes.[35] The Populist-Democratic former governor of Oregon, Sylvester Pennoyer, denounced the whole system of judicial review as an oligarchy's "usurpation" of the legislative prerogative and called for the impeachment of the majority justices. The slender and apparently mercurial nature of the Court majority that fashioned the *Pollock* outcome infuriated Pennoyer.[36]

Most reaction was more temperate, but criticism of the Court was nevertheless intense. Although major eastern and midwestern newspapers rushed to applaud the decision, leading some historians to conclude that the Supreme Court was in step with public opinion, there is ample evidence of widespread and deep dissatisfaction with the *Pollock* decision. Bryan immediately echoed Harlan's dissent, declaring that the Court had taken the side of the wealthy against the poor. Newspapers throughout the Midwest, South, and West also portrayed *Pollock* as an unjust and selfish class decision. The *Augusta* [Georgia] *Chronicle* claimed it "robs the masses . . . for the few who own the wealth of the country," and the *St. Louis Post-Dispatch* editorialized that the decision showed "the corporations and plutocrats" to be "securely intrenched in the Supreme Court." Even some eastern papers took up the cry. The *Springfield Republican* found the decision intolerable, and the *New York World* termed it "a triumph of selfishness over patriotism." The *World* continued, "Great and rich corporations, by hiring the ablest lawyers in the land and fighting against a petty tax upon superfluity as other men have fought for their liberties and their lives, have secured the exemption of wealth from paying its just share toward the support of the government that protects it." Before the end of 1895 a constitutional amendment to legitimize an income tax and overturn *Pollock* was introduced in Congress.[37]

General concern with the income tax and the rare spectacle of the Supreme Court overturning an act of Congress focused public attention on judicial review. The narrow vote on *Pollock* and the apparent vacillation of the pivotal judge heightened doubts about the Court's power. The traditional justification for judicial review, that the Court merely clarified the Constitution, seemed to fly in the face of a decision that ignored *stare decisis,* the principle of following judicial precedent. Great unhappiness was expressed about the ability of the Court to frustrate a legislative or popular majority and the inability of that majority to overcome the Court's objections unless it could muster two-thirds of the Congress and three-fourths of the states. If amendment was impossible, the Court was beyond all restraint. *Pollock* stimulated numerous proposals between 1895 and 1912 to reduce the power of the courts, make judges subject to popular election and recall, limit judicial terms of office, give Congress power to override Court decisions, and make it easier to amend the Constitution.[38]

The extent of discontent with the *Pollock* decision became evident within a year as the income tax became a major 1896 election issue. The Democratic platform contained planks bluntly criticizing *Pollock* and hinting that, to secure its reversal, the Court should be packed with contrary-minded justices. It also called for equal and impartial taxes "to the end that wealth may bear its due proportion of the expenses of the government." The Populist platform took an even bolder position, urging a graduated income tax and calling *Pollock* "a misinterpretation of the Constitution and an invasion of the rightful powers of Congress." Bryan devoted a substantial portion of his convention "Cross of Gold" speech to the income tax and during the campaign kept calling for a reversal of *Pollock* either by changing the personnel of the Court or by amending the Constitution. When he spoke before large crowds during his September eastern campaign tour, Bryan focused on labor injunction reform and the income tax.[39]

Desire for an income tax no more died with Bryan's defeat than it had been born with his campaign. Though income tax advocates continued to criticize *Pollock,* they found themselves at a political disadvantage for the moment. Furthermore, the rapid return of prosperity, together with conservative McKinley administration budgets, eliminated, for the time being, pressure for additional federal revenue. When congressional Republicans proposed to finance the war with Spain by issuing bonds, Democrats complained that this approach would create an investment opportunity for the rich and an ongoing burden for the poor. However, the Republican majority rejected Democratic efforts to substitute an income tax; instead, they approved a modestly graduated inheritance tax, characterizing it as an excise tax determined by the size of the inheritance. The Court soon agreed that this was a legal tax, suggesting that both the Republican majority in Congress and the Court wanted to assuage the unhappiness that the *Pollock* decision created by agreeing to a limited tax on unearned as opposed to earned wealth.[40]

In the early twentieth century the concern of many Democrats and increasing numbers of Republicans with highly concentrated wealth and its power kept the income tax issue alive. Southern and western Democrats, including Bryan, fought for an income tax plank in their party's 1904 platform, finally bowing to fears of appearing to flout the courts and eastern objections by accepting a strong antitrust plank instead. In his April 1906 speech attacking "the man with the muck-rake," President Theodore Roosevelt hastened to demonstrate that he stood on the side of genuine, meaningful reform by suggesting that a federal income tax might someday be desirable. In several messages to Congress between 1906 and 1908, Roosevelt recommended taxation of income and inheritance, and in June 1907 he declared that "most great civilized countries have an income tax and an inheritance tax. In my judgment both should be part of our system of federal taxation." As early as August 1907, William Howard Taft joined Roosevelt in calling for an income tax. Taft, however, disassociated himself from Roosevelt's view that a constitutional amendment would be required, suggesting instead that the Court might have revised its thinking. In accepting the 1908 Republican presidential nomination Taft reiterated this view. Thus by 1908 not only did the Democratic, Socialist, and Prohibition platforms call for an income tax but the Roosevelt-Taft wing of the Republican party had also expressed sympathy. The tax issue increasingly appeared to pit the will of a popular majority against a tiny privileged minority fortified by the Supreme Court's interpretation of the Constitution.[41]

When Congress took up the Payne-Aldrich tariff bill in 1909, the income tax soon emerged as a central issue. On March 29 Tennessee representative Cordell Hull appealed for immediate adoption of an income tax as "the fairest, the most equitable system of taxation that has yet been devised." Overturning *Pollock* by constitutional amendment was impractical, said Hull; a tiny minority of the American people concentrated in a few states could thwart the amending process. Instead, he proposed that Congress reenact the 1894 income tax and force the Supreme Court to reconsider its erroneous decision. Pessimistic about amendment, Hull was ready to employ the pressure of public opinion and legislative action to force the Court to reverse itself. Speaker Joe Cannon's opposition stymied Hull in the House, so he urged Democratic senator Joseph W. Bailey of North Carolina to take up the fight. Bailey, a longtime ally of Bryan and an income tax advocate, needed little encouragement. The bill he introduced on April 15 copied the 1894 act except for stipulating a 3 percent tax on incomes over $5,000 and exempting state and municipal bonds. Bailey demanded that the Court reverse *Pollock* "in behalf of justice to all the people and not to help the greedy rich escape the law's just tribute."[42]

Insurgent Republican senators, led by Albert B. Cummins of Iowa, soon offered a more radical proposal, a graduated tax ranging from 2 percent on $5,000 incomes to 6 percent on those over $100,000. Senator William Borah gave a ringing speech in support of the Cummins proposal, and other reform-minded Republicans also endorsed it. In mid-May Republican insurgents and Democrats agreed to unite behind a compromise plan close to Bailey's original proposal. Cummins and Borah told Taft that nineteen Republicans and all the Democrats, together a sizable majority of the Senate, were prepared "to pass a regular income tax exactly in the teeth of the decision of the Supreme Court" in order to have it brought before the Court again.

The impending addition of the Bailey-Cummins income tax to the tariff bill troubled Taft. Not merely did it expose a fundamental division within his party, it also seriously threatened the judiciary about which he cared deeply. Taft had reconsidered his earlier endorsement of an income tax and concluded that only with the prior passage of an authorizing constitutional amendment could a federal income tax be adopted without damage to the Court. Otherwise, the Court would be humiliated and reduced in stature if it conceded that *Pollock* had been in error, subjected to further scorn and abuse if it did not.

Senate Republican leader Nelson Aldrich, one of the Senate's numerous conservative millionaires, a staunch defender of business interests, and a determined opponent of the income tax, sought to thwart the Bailey-Cummins plan. He calculated that his best opportunity lay in linking veneration for the Constitution with the difficulty of amendment. He prepared to play off against each other Taft's desire to protect the Court by securing an amendment and the political obstacles to amendment. Aldrich went to Taft with a proposal. He had previously opposed Taft's suggestion of federal inheritance and corporation excise taxes, but if Taft would support these far less objectionable levies and oppose the Cummins plan, Aldrich would seek passage of an income tax amendment. Aldrich obviously thought it a safe bet that after the pending legislation had been defeated, the income tax amendment would fail to win ratification. Furthermore, the failure of an amendment to win approval would strengthen future arguments that an income tax was constitutionally unacceptable.

The shrewd Aldrich judged Taft correctly. The president sent a message to Congress advocating the compromise and stressing the danger of a direct congressional challenge to the Supreme Court. Public confidence in the stability of the judiciary might be dangerously shaken. The Taft-Aldrich proposal stunned Democratic and insurgent Republican leaders, who saw it as insincere, a ploy to deflect an immediate income tax and run it aground on the rocks of constitutional amendment. They were well aware of the history of amending efforts. Aldrich's strategy became even more apparent in his manifest indifference to the extremely broad taxing power incorporated in the language that the Senate Finance Committee devised for the proposed amendment. In the face of certain defeat, it hardly mattered that the amendment would give Congress power "to lay and collect taxes on incomes, from whatever source derived, without apportionment among the several States, and without regard to any census or enumeration."

Aldrich placed income tax supporters in an awkward position. Bailey summed up their dilemma when he told his colleagues that he would have to vote for the amendment although "I do not think it necessary and I know the submission of it is fraught with extreme danger." Cummins and Borah joined him in suggesting that the proposers of the amendment were insincere and would seek to defeat it in state legislatures. Borah pointed out that the defenders of wealth would have to hold only twelve state legislatures to prevent an amendment's ratification. Bailey proposed that the amendment be submitted to state conventions rather than the more easily manipulated state legislatures. Aldrich, however, had boxed in his foes and would retreat no further. Even when they despaired of its ratification, they could hardly vote against an amendment that would, in a constitutionally proper fashion, give them exactly what they sought.

Although Bailey continued to call for immediate adoption of an income tax, Aldrich's scheme and Taft's appeal won over a number of Republican insurgents. Indiana senator Albert Beveridge was typical. As he explained to an Indianapolis friend,

> If it were not for the fact that to pass an income tax precisely like the one that the Supreme Court declared unconstitutional would be the hardest imaginable blow to the respect which the people ought to retain for the Courts, I should, of course, vote for an income tax. I believe heartily in the principle, but I believe even more in the maintenance of respect for the courts and for their authority. If we do not look out we are going to tumble the courts into the ash barrel.[43]

Even insurgents who continued to oppose the Aldrich compromise admitted its shrewdness. Jonathan Dolliver wrote to Robert La Follette, "I am glad we are recorded against it, though I do not under-estimate the political peril of being against the president."[44]

Aldrich maneuvered cleverly so that senators would have to vote on the constitutional amendment before the Bailey-Cummins bill came to the floor. As the debate neared its end, the widely respected Elihu Root made an eloquent appeal for the amendment as "the most dignified, the most wise, the most patriotic way to deal with the subject." He wanted Congress to have the power to levy an income tax in time of need, the former secretary of war said. Although he would have decided *Pollock* differently, Root did not favor putting the exact question before the Court once more. If the Court yielded in the face of legislative and executive pressure, "where then would be the confidence of our people in the justice of their judgment?" And if the Court refused to yield, a dangerous and destructive breach would open between Congress and the Court.[45]

The powerful appeal of Aldrich's strategy was soon evident. The Senate approved the constitutional amendment 77 to 0 on July 5, 1909. The House, after reiterating all the arguments, followed suit 318 to 14 on July 12. Thereafter, by narrow margins the Payne-Aldrich tariff bill, with the corporation tax but without the income tax, was approved as well. The test was now whether Aldrich had accomplished a brilliant political maneuver or had allowed his position to be overrun. The answer depended on whether state legislatures would or would not ratify the proposed amendment. Aldrich did not conceal his preferences. Unlike Taft and Root, who appealed to their home state Ohio and New York legislatures to ratify the amendment, Aldrich remained silent. Rhode Island, where Aldrich was the undisputed political leader, promptly rejected the amendment in 1910 and thereafter steadfastly refused to reconsider.[46]

In that the amendment directly challenged a decision of the Supreme Court, efforts to frustrate the amending process might be expected from the Court. Within days of congressional passage of the amendment, David J. Brewer, one of two surviving justices from the *Pollock* majority, spoke out against ratification. Those who sought the amendment, said Brewer, were "demagogues and revolutionaries" who, given the power to tax incomes, would have the power to tax the states "not out of their existence, but out of their vitality."[47] Amendment supporters' immediate and vigorous rebuttal suggested how nervous they were about the possible impact of Justice Brewer's remarks.

State ratification of the proposed amendment got off to a slow start.[48] When Congress approved it, very few state legislatures were in session. Only Alabama, on August 17, ratified in 1909. As legislatures began to reconvene in January 1910, a formidable obstacle arose. New York governor Charles Evans Hughes, one of the nation's most highly regarded political leaders, strongly urged the New York General Assembly to reject the amendment. He favored a personal and corporate income tax, explained Hughes, but authorizing taxes on incomes "from whatever sources derived" would allow taxation of state and municipal bond income and place state and local government at the mercy of federal taxing power.[49] Hughes, perceived as thoughtful, moderate, and free of self-interest, offered a rallying point for opposition to the amendment. Several governors, conservative legal scholars, many newspapers, and prominent attorneys, including the ever-present Choate and Guthrie, embraced Hughes's position.[50]

Amendment advocates immediately responded to Hughes. New Jersey governor John Franklin Fort soon called the income tax "the most just and equitable tax that can be devised" and scoffed at Hughes's objection. With a 1 percent income tax, the holder of a $1,000 bond paying 4 percent interest (these were, as unlikely as it might seem today, reasonable figures in 1910) would pay 40 cents a year. He did not expect such a levy to affect the securities market, said Fort. Nor did he believe that voters would ever elect a Congress that would lay taxes to destroy states.[51] Senator William Borah took the Senate floor to argue that the amendment would not increase Congress's taxing power but merely remove the uniform apportionment requirement. He reminded his audience that during the century before *Pollock* when it had the power to levy income taxes Congress had been restrained from taxing state and local government.[52]

The most telling rebuttal to Hughes came from his fellow New York Republican, Senator Elihu Root, who wrote a public letter to a New York state senator essentially repeating Borah's argument. Root emphasized that the effect of the amendment would only be to overturn the disastrous *Pollock* decision. Root concluded with an appeal for New York to support the income tax because it had become America's financial and commercial center. "We have the wealth because behind the city stands the country. We ought to be willing to share the burdens of the National Government in the same proportion in which we share the benefits."[53] Despite Root's rebuttal, Hughes's argument helped persuade the New York State Assembly to reject the amendment in spring 1910.

Even though eight southern and western states ratified between February and August 1910, supporters of the amendment feared that Hughes's stature might make his opposition fatal.[54] In addition to the New York setback, during the spring legislatures defeated ratification in Virginia, Louisiana, Rhode Island, and Massachusetts. The November 1910 elections, however, manifested such an outpouring of support for progressive reform that prospects brightened considerably. Twenty state legislatures ratified the amendment, in most cases by overwhelming margins, in the first six months of 1911. All were midwestern, southern, or western; but two of them, Ohio and California, were, like New York, states that would bear a heavy portion of any income tax burden. In 1910 Illinois had been the only state with a concentration of wealth to ratify. Ratification by these states upon which any income tax could be expected to fall most heavily improved the prospect that no bloc of such states would defeat the amendment. Still, the amendment was rejected or postponed in ten states, mostly in the Northeast but also occasionally in the South, where conservative senates offset highly favorable votes in lower houses more responsive to public opinion. Southern senators frequently balked, not in opposition to taxing incomes but because they objected to the expansion of federal authority at the expense of states' rights.[55]

In 1910 New York Democrats, with a campaign built around an appeal for ratification of the income tax amendment, won the governorship and majorities in both houses of the state legislature. John Dix, the new governor, confronted Hughes's argument head on, saying that exemption of bond interest from taxation was contrary to the American tradition of equality for all and special privilege for none. He embraced the argument of many progressives in Congress and other parts of the country that no form of wealth should escape taxation.[56] Dix fanned the resentment stirred by *Pollock* that the rich were avoiding taxation. When the New York senate approved the amendment in April 1911 and the house followed suit in July, an important symbolic hurdle was crossed. New York was not only the first wealthy, industrial northeastern state to ratify, it was also home for much of the most effective opposition, including the influential *New York Times*. The prospect of one region, much less a conservative minority within it, blocking ratification began to evaporate.

The Supreme Court followed Charles Evans Hughes in casting doubt on the proposed amendment. Moving quickly to address the constitutionality of the 1909 corporation tax, the Court weakened the argument that an amendment was essential. Corporations had immediately challenged the 1909 act on the basis that the corporation tax was an income tax, therefore a direct tax and unconstitutional unless apportioned among the states. Fifteen cases, consolidated as *Flint v. Stone Tracy Co.*, were scheduled for argument in March 1910 and subsequently reargued in January 1911.[57] *Pollock* veterans Joseph Choate and William Guthrie were prominent among the attorneys raising myriad objections to the tax. In March 1911 the Court ruled unanimously that the 1909 tax was not a direct tax but an excise upon the particular privilege of doing business in a corporate capacity and that the excise was properly measured by the income of the parties subject to the tax. It was less clear that the 1909 tax differed from the 1894 one than that the personnel and attitude of the Court had changed under the barrage of *Pollock* criticism and the progress of the effort to amend the Constitution. The Court now seemed to be saying that an unaltered Constitution could justify a broad interpretation of the taxing power.[58] Nevertheless, popular support for the income tax amendment had progressed beyond the point where an apparent change of heart on the Court's part, even one reflected in a unanimous decision, provided an acceptable resolution of the issue.

Four more state ratifications in spring 1912 left the amendment only two short of approval. When they reconvened following the sweeping Democratic-Progressive victories in the 1912 elections, eight state legislatures acted promptly. Delaware, New Mexico, and Wyoming on February 3 provided the necessary minimum. Within the next five weeks, four northeastern states, New Hampshire, New Jersey, Massachusetts, and Vermont, all of which had earlier rejected the amendment, joined the consensus. By March 1913 forty-two states had ratified, six more than the required thirty-six. States in the Midwest, West, and South, where agriculture predominated and very few residents had large incomes, moved most rapidly to embrace the amendment, but by the time the constitutional process was completed most states primarily involved in manufacturing and commerce had also ratified. In the end neither partisan, sectional, nor economic divisions thwarted the broad popular appeal of the income tax amendment that translated into large legislative majorities for ratification in most states.

As soon as the necessary ratification was obtained, Congress began discussions that within seven months led to the adoption of a graduated income tax as a part of the Underwood-Simmons tariff. Soon called upon to review this new tax, the Supreme Court, in a transparent effort to save face, declared that the Sixteenth Amendment conferred no new taxing power on Congress; it merely restored a power that the Congress had held before 1895. Appropriately, Chief Justice Edward White, the sole *Pollock* dissenter remaining on the high court, announced the decision.[59]

The attainment of the income tax amendment had clearly not been anticipated by many political observers and constitutional scholars, much less the man who, ironically, received much of the credit for its adoption, Senator Nelson Aldrich. Yet solid reasons existed for the Sixteenth Amendment's achievement. First, a broad-based consensus developed that a basic governmental change was required. Outside a small, well-to-do elite, public preference for taxation based on income became unmistakable. A congressional majority for an income tax already existed by 1894, and it widened beyond partisan or regional boundaries during the next two decades, especially as a result of the 1910 and 1912 elections. Second, proponents of an income tax generally agreed that their goal could be satisfactorily reached only through constitutional change. The Court defeated the 1894 income tax with its *Pollock* decision, but at the same time it created the belief that a constitutional amendment offered the only responsible way to secure such a tax. The alternative that frustrated tax reformers had suggested in 1909, legislating an income tax and challenging the Court to reverse *Pollock*, troubled even its advocates. They had complained about the capriciousness of judicial review ever since 1895. To them, an amendment would provide a legitimacy and stability that a more expedient approach lacked. Having argued that in *Pollock* the Court abused judicial review and undermined confidence in the constitutional system, how could they sanction a solution that relied upon raw political power to compel further judicial review and reversal of constitutional doctrine? Respect for the Constitution required use of the Article V process if it was to be altered.

THE SIXTEENTH AMENDMENT, one of the most fundamental and crucial reforms of the Progressive era, wrought a revolution in constitutional thinking even before its ratification was complete. "The supreme significance of the amendment," one constitutional scholar soon declared, "is that its adoption proved that the constitution could be peaceably amended if the people really so desired."[60] When ratification of the income tax amendment moved steadily ahead despite substantial objections raised by Charles Evans Hughes and others, the notion that the Constitution was unamendable quickly evaporated, and public pressure for other amendments escalated. The Senate provided the first evidence of a changed constitutional climate when its resistance finally crumbled to long-standing demands for an amendment requiring direct election of senators.

Proponents of expanded popular participation in government had long advocated having voters rather than state legislators choose U.S. senators, as specified in the 1787 Constitution. James Wilson had suggested direct election at the Philadelphia convention, but only his home state of Pennsylvania had supported his motion. In 1826 Representative Henry Storrs of New York became the first to offer a direct election constitutional amendment. Other representatives, though no senators, broached the idea in 1835 and the 1850s. Andrew Johnson of Tennessee advanced the same notion as a congressman in 1851 and 1852, as a senator in 1860, and as president in 1868. From the 1870s onward, the number of resolutions on the subject increased gradually and by the 1890s had become substantial. Twenty-five direct election amendment resolutions were introduced during the 1892–1893 first session of the Fifty-second Congress alone.[61]

Increasing unhappiness with the U.S. Senate by the 1890s centered on the growing impression that its members formed an unrepresentative, unresponsive "millionaires club," high in partisanship but low in integrity. Senators were perceived often to have gained their seats as the result of financial influences within the political parties and state legislatures that selected them; they kept their positions by heeding the wishes of party leaders and corporate sponsors rather than of their constituents. Overall, the Senate seemed to embody the most self-serving and undemocratic aspects of political parties.[62] Occasional allegations or disclosures of bribery of state legislators in connection with senatorial elections stirred suspicion that the practice was widespread. Legislative deadlocks over the choice of a senator furthered the image of a defective electoral system. In no fewer than forty-five instances in twenty states between 1891 and 1905, legislatures, unable to reach agreement on candidates, delayed filling Senate seats. Fourteen seats remained empty for an entire legislative session or more. In the worst case, Delaware was represented by only one senator in three Congresses and none at all from 1901 until 1908.[63] "The Senate ranks lower in popular estimation today than it has at any time in the history of the country," declared the *Seattle Post Intelligencer* in January 1897. Two months later the *Louisville Courier Journal* proclaimed, "To be a Senator is to be a suspect."[64]

During the 1890s Congress was deluged with petitions and published appeals for direct popular election of senators as a remedy for the upper house's perceived flaws. Beginning in 1892 the People's party platform regularly demanded direct election; the Democratic platform did likewise starting in 1900. The House of Representatives, the most sensitive national barometer of mass political opinion, first approved, by a two-thirds voice vote, a constitutional amendment resolution providing for direct election of senators on January 16, 1893. On July 21 of the following year a similar measure passed 141 to 50. Fifteen state legislatures joined the call for an amendment by 1897. Three subsequent Houses endorsed similar resolutions, on January 12, 1898, by 185 to 11; on April 13, 1900, by 242 to 15; and on January 21, 1902, without a recorded vote.[65]

These actions were for naught because the Senate itself steadfastly refused to countenance direct election. The resolutions of the House were referred to the Senate's committee on privileges and elections from which they never emerged, except once in 1896; even then, the measure was not brought to a vote. In every case, the Senate allowed the resolution to expire quietly despite the rising clamor for reform outside the chamber.[66]

The perceived impossibility of overcoming Senate resistance to constitutional change affecting its own circumstances served to confirm disparaging opinions of the normal amending process. Stymied by five setbacks in Congress, reformers turned to other solutions. In 1893 the Nebraska legislature, which eighteen years earlier had established the first and for years the only senatorial primary election, again assumed leadership. It sought to employ Article V's alternative process for initiating amendments by requesting that a constitutional convention be called to submit a direct election amendment to the states for ratification. States had applied for a convention before but on no occasion in influential numbers. In 1900 a committee of the Pennsylvania legislature suggested a coordinated effort of states to demand a convention. The Senate would not act, the committee believed, until two-thirds of the states forced it to do so. Pennsylvania sent every other state a copy of its convention petition to encourage them likewise to submit one. A number did, while others, nervous about what else might occur at a constitutional convention, followed the lead of Georgia and Arkansas in passing memorials "most respectfully" requesting Congress to propose a direct election amendment. By 1903 thirteen state legislatures had taken one action or the other. The number grew to thirty-one by 1912. Even though the total was only one less than two-thirds of the states, the fact that some states sought a convention while others wanted Congress to act on its own left room for the argument that the point was not even close to being reached at which Article V required the amending process to be set in motion.[67]

Senate resistance to House resolutions and state appeals led reformers to explore still other avenues. If the Constitution could not be formally altered, perhaps electoral practice could be changed by more circuitous legal means. Oregon, a pioneer in the progressive campaign for direct democracy through initiative and referendum laws, improvised a system for de facto direct election of senators. In 1904 Oregon provided that petitions of candidacy for the state legislature include a statement as to whether or not the candidate felt bound to support the senatorial candidate receiving the highest popular vote in a state primary election. Most candidates of course pledged to respect the popular preference, and bribery and deadlocks quickly became a thing of the past. In 1907 a local news report exulted, "On the first ballot, in twenty minutes, we elected two Senators, without boodle, or booze, or even a cigar!" By 1909, when Oregon's Republican legislature elected a Democratic senator who had won the popular contest, the system's effectiveness was demonstrated. By 1911 over half of all states had adopted the Oregon system or some similar method approximating direct election.[68] The number of senators popularly chosen and inclined to insist that their colleagues be selected by the same means was rapidly escalating.

Although the Oregon approach reduced the problem, it did not altogether eliminate it. Senatorial contests in Wisconsin and Rhode Island in 1907 and Kentucky in 1908 produced taint and deadlock. A prolonged scandal surrounding the 1909 selection of Illinois's senator vividly personalized the continuing difficulty. At the start of that year the Illinois legislature deadlocked for five months before finally settling on William Lorimer of Chicago. Charges of bribery and corruption swirled around the proceeding. A year later an investigation revealed that a $100,000 corporate "slush-fund" had been used in Lorimer's behalf and identified four legislators as having accepted large payments to vote for him. A Senate inquiry into Lorimer's election led eventually to his expulsion in 1912.[69]

The Senate began to confront the Lorimer case while simultaneously debating the income tax issue. Unexpectedly, on July 5, 1909, insurgent progressive Joseph L. Bristow proposed that a provision for direct election of senators be added to the income tax amendment resolution. New to the Senate, Bristow had the previous year won Kansas's first senatorial primary, partly on his pledge to support direct election nationally. Republican majority leader Nelson Aldrich, in the midst of his already complicated maneuvering over the income tax, objected to Bristow's motion. The Senate agreed that it was out of order, not pertinent to the original resolution. Once again, defenders of the senatorial status quo had dodged a bullet.[70]

Bristow did not abandon the fight. At the start of the next session, he submitted a direct election amendment resolution, asking that it be considered by the Judiciary Committee of which his ally, Idaho senator William Borah, was a member, rather than by the committee on privileges and elections that had repeatedly buried similar measures. After more than a year's delay, the Judiciary Committee finally gave the Senate a favorable report on the measure that Borah had revised and championed. Growing demands for reform, manifested throughout the nation in the November 1910 elections, no doubt had more to do with the committee's decision than Bristow's repeated impatient calls for action. Eighteen years after the initial House vote on a direct election amendment, the Senate took its first roll call on the issue February 28, 1911. The vote of 54 to 33 fell short of the two-thirds required for passage. Though a switch of only five votes would have brought success, complicating factors prevented contemporary observers from concluding that victory was close at hand.[71]

From the outset of the battle over a direct election amendment, race had been a sub rosa issue, complicating what appeared on the surface to be a straightforward political power struggle. Lingering southern resentment over the Fourteenth and Fifteenth Amendments prompted a search for ways around their requirements. Literacy tests and poll taxes proved to be effective devices for disfranchising black voters. These instruments, however, provoked an 1890 federal elections bill to standardize voting rights that the South called a Force Bill and effectively filibustered to death. Thereafter, southerners remained nervous about control of elections and sought constitutional protection. Massachusetts representative Henry Cabot Lodge was quick to note in 1893 that the first direct election amendment brought before the House provided that "the times, places, and manner of holding elections for Senators shall be as prescribed in each State by the Legislature thereof." Lodge expressed alarm that the provision radically reduced federal power to regulate elections; he did not nor did he need to refer to racial exclusion as the likely outcome of giving states full control over elections.[72]

Whenever the direct election amendment was put forth, southern Democrats indicated that the price of their support was inclusion of a state-regulation-of-elections provision. When a three-member subcommittee of the Senate Judiciary Committee took up the issue in 1910, the swing member, Maryland Democrat Isidore Rayner, insisted upon removal of federal power to regulate elections. Borah, as chairman of the subcommittee, accepted this means of obtaining Democratic support. When Borah's resolution came before the full Senate, however, some Republicans objected. Henry Cabot Lodge, now a senator, spoke against surrendering national power to the states, and his colleague Chauncey Depew of New York bluntly opposed "deliberately voting to undo the results of the Civil War." This question posed a dilemma for northern supporters of direct election who could not abide the prospect of unrestrained southern states. It also provided a convenient disguise for northern senators such as Elihu Root of New York, who thought direct election too populist and preferred to have growing governmental power placed in the hands of an experienced elite of elder statesmen such as himself unwilling to endure public campaigning for office.[73] Senator George Sutherland's motion to retain federal authority over elections was approved 50 to 37, but thereafter the direct election amendment itself fell short, with twenty-three Sutherland supporters voting against final passage.[74]

Although the Borah resolution failed at the close of the Sixty-first Congress, the defeat in the 1910 elections of ten senators who voted against it encouraged direct election advocates to press forward when a special session of the next Congress convened shortly thereafter. Joseph Bristow believed that the uncompromised amendment could now pass the Senate by three or four votes, but the House acted first, adopting a direct election amendment on April 13 that eliminated federal control of elections. This version went before the Senate, once again bearing the endorsement of Borah's committee. Bristow led a fight to preserve a measure of federal control by retaining the ambiguous language of Article I, section 2 of the Constitution, requiring that federal voting qualifications be the same as for the largest branch of each state's legislature. The Bristow revision won by the narrowest of margins when the Senate divided 44 to 44 and Vice-President James Sherman broke the tie. The Senate then adopted Bristow's version of the direct election amendment by 64 to 24, well above the required two-thirds.[75]

The Senate's action on June 12, 1911, did not end the matter because its version of the amendment differed from that of the House. A conference committee struggled for nearly a year to resolve the conflict, meeting sixteen times without success. The racially fraught issue of state or federal control of elections blocked agreement. Finally in April 1912 the frustrated Senate voted to insist that the House accept its version, and House Democratic leaders grudgingly agreed that it was better to do so than sacrifice the entire measure. On May 12, 1912, the House voted 238 to 39 to concur with the Senate resolution and send the amendment to the states. Every Republican and over three-quarters of the Democrats gave their approval; the remaining opposition came from southern Democrats.[76]

State ratification of the direct election amendment appeared almost a foregone conclusion. By the time Congress approved the amendment, thirty-one states had requested that a convention be called to propose one. A careful scholar of the Article V convention mechanism found no evidence that the threat of a constitutional convention if it did not act itself was crucial in moving Congress.[77] Yet the number of state legislatures appealing for an amendment was only five fewer than the number needed to ratify since Arizona and New Mexico achieved statehood earlier in the year.

Massachusetts, Arizona, and Minnesota ratified within four weeks after Congress submitted the amendment. Other state legislatures were either not in session or preferred to await the outcome of the fall elections. Once new legislatures began to convene, ratification came with remarkable speed. Nine states ratified in January 1913, seventeen in February, four in March, and three during the first eight days of April. Only Utah rejected the amendment. When Connecticut became the thirty-sixth state to ratify on April 8, 1913, less than eleven months had elapsed.[78] Once the dam of congressional resistance broke, the great reservoir of enthusiasm for direct election of senators swept all before it.

THE ACHIEVEMENT of the Sixteenth and Seventeenth Amendments led at least some scholars to reconsider the previous history of the amending process. Writing in the *Yale Law Journal,* Joseph R. Long pointed out that while thousands of amendment proposals had been offered to Congress, the bulk of them dealt over and over with the same few subjects: slavery, elections, terms of office, and presidential veto powers. Many others dealt with temporary conditions, trivial matters, or unexamined ideas. Even on the few issues of wide and lasting interest, there was little agreement as to what might be appropriate solutions. Thus the amending system had been seriously called upon only infrequently. Views of the amending process were inadequately informed and overly pessimistic, Long implied. The reasonably prompt adoption of the Sixteenth and Seventeenth Amendments after the emergence of sentiment in their favor demonstrated, he concluded, that "there is no great difficulty in securing the adoption of any amendment that a decided majority of the people of the United States really want." Article V did not need to be changed. "When the ratification of the required three-fourths of the states can be obtained within twelve months there is little room to complain."[79]

The optimism regarding constitutional amending that the Sixteenth and Seventeenth Amendments spawned may have been as unbalanced as earlier pessimism about the likelihood of change. Both viewpoints were certainly grounded on limited evidence. Nevertheless, in each case assumptions about the prospects for success created a distinctive political dynamic. The Sixteenth Amendment ended a century that witnessed few serious attempts to change the Constitution. It was a profoundly important reform, one that sanctioned a fundamental shift of tax burdens and ultimately the distribution of wealth as well as one that provided the federal government funds for entirely new military, social service, and economic policies. The Seventeenth Amendment altered political decisionmaking both substantially and symbolically as it replaced the Founders' system of vesting power in an elite insulated from the masses with one that rendered the Senate more directly responsive to the public.

Together the Sixteenth and Seventeenth Amendments initiated an era during which constitutional change was thought of and pursued as a solution to a number of major political problems, not only structural matters of elections but also social issues such as alcohol use, women's rights, and child labor. In an age of increasing urbanization, industrialization, bureaucratization, and social diversification, the central questions of government no longer represented issues of whether the republic would cohere or sunder, live or die. The circumstances of a nation moving ever further from the conditions of its founding called for less ultimately fateful but nevertheless important decisions to alter or perpetuate governmental arrangements so that they would be suitable to a modern situation. A new agenda for government produced a fresh approach toward the constitutional role of amendment.

Increasing resort to amendment was consistent with high regard for the Constitution. How else was the United States' "Ark of the Covenant" to be preserved inviolate? Despite the difficulty of amendment, Americans in the early twentieth century definitely preferred it when the constitutional structure seemed to require change and acceptable alternatives, moderate judicial review in particular, appeared unavailable or unsuitable. Thus constitutional amendment was viable when necessary and if, though probably only if, all else had failed. In retrospect, contemporaries concluded, the absence of such conditions went a long way toward explaining the barren history of amending in the nineteenth century. The same reasoning would lead them to turn with increasing frequency to the amending remedy in the years just ahead.

10

An Era of Constitutional Activity and Faith

A doption of the Sixteenth and Seventeenth Amendments in spring 1913 ignited other constitutional reform initiatives. Before the year ended separate drives were under way to obtain amendments on two long-discussed matters. Reformers' pessimism about the capacity of the Article V process to function as the Founders intended had evaporated. After the almost simultaneous achievement of the income tax and direct election amendments, constitutional alteration no longer appeared impossibly difficult. The advantages of winning an amendment became ever more evident as Congress soon implemented a graduated income tax and a number of long-resistant states for the first time conducted popular elections for the Senate. A constitutional amendment could, in fact, produce prompt and profound change. Opponents of reform likewise began taking more seriously the prospect of constitutional alteration. As a result, the image of the Constitution as merely an antique to be admired began to fade, replaced by the vision of a workable tool ready for use.

Since shortly after the Civil War, Congress had been receiving proposals for amendments to banish alcoholic beverages and to ensure women the right to vote. Not until 1913, however, did crusades for such amendments begin in earnest. Within seven years both campaigns attained their objectives. The rapid triumph of these prohibition and suffrage quests reinforced the sense that amending the Constitution was, under certain circumstances, not only a desirable but also a realistic, achievable political goal. The adoption of four amendments, each through a separate initiative, in less than a decade thoroughly dispelled at least for the moment prior notions of an inflexible, unamendable Constitution.

The prohibition and suffrage crusades affected views of the Article V process in other respects as well. The first amendments to take shape outside the national political establishment, they represented demands for government action initiated by popular constituencies rather than proposals arising within governing bodies for solutions to acknowledged problems. From Madison's draft of a Bill of Rights in response to concerns expressed in ratification conventions to congressional responses to the need to reconstruct the Union to legislatively crafted measures to deal with tax and election problems, the governing consensus continued to spawn amendments. Grassroots public crusades to deal with perceived social problems and inequities, led by persons outside government, were hardly new, but it was unprecedented for their efforts to focus on obtaining constitutional amendments. The success of both the antialcohol and woman suffrage crusades stirred further thought as to how the public could define what it wanted its government to do or not do.

These amendments proved distinctive not only in their origins but also in their purposes. Each sought to involve the federal government in a matter with which it previously had little or nothing to do. Expanding the federal government's constitutional mandate to embrace alcohol and gender policies had obvious specific consequences. Yet their result was also to encourage thinking about further redefinition or expansion of federal obligations. If the federal government could be given authority over something as personal as alcohol use, could and should it be given responsibility for other matters as well? If gender discrimination in voting could be barred, should the federal government intervene in other areas, such as labor, where society drew distinctions between citizens? Whereas legislative or executive efforts to increase federal activity could be blocked by the judiciary, constitutional change provided a definitive means of reshaping the government's role. When substantive constitutional amendment became a realistic possibility, debates over what duties should be given the federal government took on fresh meaning.

The prohibition and suffrage amendments had another significant effect. They illuminated the capacity of single-minded reformers to mobilize the amending process. They were achieved without lowering supermajority standards for adoption, as some reformers had suspected might be necessary. The Article V standards no longer appeared too formidable to overcome. Each of these amendments demonstrated the ability of well-organized and vocal citizens' groups to press their elected representatives to sanction constitutional change. Both amendments shed light on the inherent possibilities and limitations of the Article V amending system within a democratic republic. Thus the battles over what would become the Eighteenth and Nineteenth Amendments were not only consequential in their own right but also in terms of the larger history of U.S. constitutionalism.

National prohibition and woman suffrage were separate but intertwined reform movements. The effort to banish alcohol was the older of the two, but it developed such strong linkages with the suffrage crusade that it is hardly surprising that they reached fruition at nearly the same moment. Although the two amendment episodes deserve to be examined individually, the ties between them, as well as their relationship to their two immediate predecessors, must also be understood. The connectedness of amending efforts throughout the 1910s helped make that decade a prolific era for constitutional change.

THE TEMPERANCE CRUSADE stood alongside the antislavery and women's rights movements as one of the widely popular reform impulses of the nineteenth century. Prior to the 1830s, Americans were heavy consumers of alcoholic beverages. Given the alternatives of impure water, unpasteurized milk, and more expensive coffee and tea, many Americans routinely sipped alcohol throughout the day. Each year in the early nineteenth century those over fifteen managed, on the average, to imbibe some 28 gallons of beer and hard cider, 4 gallons of wine, and 9.5 gallons of distilled spirits.[1] A sharp decline in drinking followed the first large-scale temperance agitation by religious and social reformers in the 1820s and 1830s. Pleased by the wave of voluntary pledges to abstain from drink yet not entirely satisfied, temperance advocates reasoned that the continued presence of liquor tempted individuals and perpetuated social problems. Preferring a total to a partial solution, these so-called "drys" concluded that if prudent people could voluntarily give up liquor, it made good sense to help weaker-willed persons and their victims by outlawing "the liquor traffic." Coercing people into giving up alcohol would serve their ultimate best interests. Scattered local liquor restrictions in the 1840s preceded the decision of Maine, ten other states, and two territories during the 1850s to ban the manufacture and sale of distilled spirits. The Civil War slowed and in some places reversed the drive to outlaw alcohol but did not bring it to an end.[2]

Failing to win major party support after the Civil War, prohibitionists formed independent political organizations to press for liquor restriction. The Prohibition party was founded in Chicago in September 1869 by drys who, encouraged by the Republican example, believed that a party devoted to a moral issue could gain control of the federal government. Five years later in November 1874, Protestant women concerned with home and family protection gathered in Cleveland to establish the Woman's Christian Temperance Union (WCTU). For both the party and the union, alcohol prohibition came to serve as the centerpiece of extensive social reform agendas. "Home Protection" and "Do Everything" became WCTU slogans under its second president, Frances Willard, and the Prohibition party advocated woman suffrage, a federal income tax, and direct election of senators as well as alcohol restriction. The party made little progress at first, but in 1884 its presidential candidate, buoyed by a WCTU endorsement, drew enough votes from dry Republicans in New York to enable Democrat Grover Cleveland to win the presidency in an extremely close national contest. Growing dry sentiment during the 1880s manifested itself further in a resurgence of state and local liquor restrictions. The Prohibition party won an additional 100,000 votes in 1888 and 1892, accumulating more than 250,000 votes each time, but never again held the electoral balance of power it enjoyed in 1884. Thereafter its vote totals declined, and its membership divided over tactical issues.[3]

Abandoning hope of achieving independent political power, the temperance movement nevertheless moved forward. The ranks of the WCTU swelled to 150,000 by 1892, making it by far the largest women's organization of the day. Even more significantly, in the 1890s a single-issue organization, the Anti-Saloon League of America, arose to pressure political candidates to support liquor bans in return for its support. Founded in Ohio in 1893 and organized nationally two years later, the Anti-Saloon League grew rapidly. Soliciting pledges from office seekers and making election endorsements on the principle of "he who is not with me is against me," it soon became a potent political force. Its capacity to remain indifferent to other issues while rallying a significant minority of voters to cast their ballots on the basis of a single issue gave it disproportionate influence in closely divided races. Although its antidrink objectives were national, even international, the league's rhetoric emphasized "home rule," and its politics were purely local. The league sought to dry up towns, townships, and counties by obtaining local option laws and then winning local elections. When the opportunity appeared, it pursued statewide prohibition as a broader form of local option. Anti-Saloon League tactics proved extremely effective and helped stimulate an increase in state and local antialcohol legislation.[4]

By 1912, one-half of the American people lived under some type of alcoholic beverage restriction although everywhere liquor for private consumption could be imported from out of state or made at home. However, the piecemeal approach of the temperance crusade seemed to have reached the limits of its effectiveness. In some areas the battle to place and then keep a liquor ban in force had to be fought constantly. Important sections of the country, particularly the most urbanized areas, remained for the most part untouched. This situation was unsatisfactory to a reform movement that increasingly viewed the urban saloon as a source of social problems, an encouragement to family neglect, a contributor to worker inefficiency and incompetence, a center of political corruption, and a shelter for immigrant cultures against pressures to assimilate. Furthermore, Anti-Saloon League leaders felt they were at risk of losing control of the temperance movement. The growing use of popular referendums to decide liquor issues reduced the potential of a single-issue pressure group to influence state and local decisions. Between 1909 and 1913 four state legislatures adopted prohibition laws, but eight of twelve state referendums rejected them. Turning the antialcohol focus toward national prohibition allowed the league to concentrate on congressional elections, the very sort of contests where it was most effective. This approach seemed the best way to regain the initiative and advance the cause.[5]

Ever since the 1851 Maine law, state prohibition statutes had allowed citizens to import liquor from outside the state for personal use. In 1889 and 1898 the Supreme Court struck down Iowa's attempts to bar shipments into the state on the grounds that only Congress was empowered to regulate interstate commerce.[6] Complaining that it was impossible for states to enforce prohibition laws in the face of a flood of liquor from beyond their borders, the Anti-Saloon League pressed Congress to forbid transportation of intoxicants into a state in violation of "bone-dry" laws. In February 1913 Congress complied by passing the Webb-Kenyon Act. Departing president William Howard Taft vetoed the act as unconstitutional, but Congress immediately overrode his action with a Senate vote of 63 to 21 and a House ballot of 244 to 95.[7] Achievement of this first significant national victory by a congressional supermajority larger than required for passage of a constitutional amendment exhilarated prohibitionists and naturally shaped their thoughts about an appropriate next step. Completion of ratification of the Sixteenth Amendment earlier that same month and the Seventeenth little more than two months later made it evident to antialcohol crusaders what that step should be.

A constitutional amendment prohibiting alcoholic beverages had first been offered in Congress in 1876, and sessions since then had averaged about one such proposal each. None received serious consideration.[8] The Anti-Saloon League had long spoken of a national solution without offering a specific proposal and certainly not advocating constitutional reform. In 1913 the situation changed. "The Time Has Come," proclaimed the league's newspaper, _The American Issue,_ immediately after the Webb-Kenyon victory.[9] League general superintendent Purley A. Baker proposed to his headquarters committee in April that "the next and final step" be a campaign for a constitutional amendment. This move would follow Anti-Saloon League policy always "to go just as fast and just as far as public sentiment would justify."[10] With committee and board of directors' approval, the League announced its new strategy at its Twenty Year Jubilee Convention in November. In Washington on December 13 a Committee of 1,000, together with a similar WCTU committee and representatives of nearly 100 other organizations, marched down Pennsylvania Avenue to the Capitol. On its steps they presented a resolution calling for an amendment to prohibit the "sale, manufacture for sale, and importation for sale of beverages containing alcohol" to Representative Richmond Hobson of Alabama and Senator Morris Sheppard of Texas, who would introduce it in their respective houses.[11]

The Anti-Saloon League pursued a national solution, believing that centers of resistance could be dealt with in no other way; otherwise, liquor would continue to invade dry territory. The crucial decision to seek an amendment rather than an ordinary statute reflected long experience with temperance backsliding. Drinkers would pledge to abstain, then fall off the wagon. Reform crusades would win converts, then succumb to liquor industry counterattacks or a changed electorate. Local or state restrictions would be adopted, then overturned. Drys had become acutely aware that a statute approved by a simple congressional majority, with the shift of relatively few votes, could likewise be toppled. On the other hand, a constitutional amendment, while difficult to obtain given the supermajority requirements for congressional approval and state ratification, seemed, once adopted, impervious to change. An immense political turnabout, not merely a marginal shift, would have to take place. A second amendment, one requiring approval by similar supermajorities, would be needed to neutralize the first. No such reversal had ever occurred; indeed, none had apparently even been seriously contemplated. Once installed, an amendment would appear to be secure against future human weakness. Senator Sheppard expressed the perception of amendment advocates as, years later, he gloated, "There is as much chance of repealing the Eighteenth Amendment as there is for a hummingbird to fly to the planet Mars with the Washington Monument tied to its tail!"[12]

A year after Hobson and Sheppard introduced it, the Anti-Saloon League's amendment resolution first came to the floor of the House. Proponents spoke with emotion regarding the evils of the liquor traffic. Critics used different arguments against the plan to secure temperance by constitutional amendment. Congressmen J. Charles Linthicum of Maryland, James Parker of New York, Robert Henry of Texas, and Oscar Underwood of Alabama took a states' rights position that having the central government police alcohol use was contrary to the federal design of the Founders. Absolute opposition came from representatives Edward Browne of Wisconsin and Richard Bartholdt of Missouri. Bartholdt, a particularly vigorous critic, contended that "prohibition is a deathblow to the liberty of the individual because it prohibits what is not wrong in itself." However, neither argument reached the rhetorical heights scaled by Henry Vollmer of Iowa, who invoked "George Washington the brewer; Thomas Jefferson the distiller; Abraham Lincoln the saloon keeper; and Jesus of Nazareth who turned water into wine." When the speeches ended, the amendment received 197 yea votes to 190 nays, well short of the required two-thirds approval.[13]

Encouraged at having gained a majority, if not a victory, in a first effort to pass an amendment, the Anti-Saloon League and its allies immediately sought to elect more sympathizers to Congress. Brewers and distillers, perennially disorganized and divided among themselves, provided ineffective opposition.[14] Single-mindedly endorsing candidates who supported prohibition and opposing those who did not, the Anti-Saloon League appeared to hold the balance of power in many close contests. Enough candidates embraced prohibition on its merits or for political advantage to ensure that drys in 1916 won a bipartisan majority of more than two-thirds in each house of Congress.[15]

Two months later prohibitionists received further good news. Shortly after the passage of the Webb-Kenyon Act, a distillery had sued to compel a railroad to accept a liquor shipment into West Virginia despite a state injunction. Anti-Saloon League general counsel Wayne Wheeler defended the Webb-Kenyon law before the Supreme Court when the Justice Department declined to do so. After two rounds of oral argument, the Court in January 1917 validated the law as a legitimate regulation of interstate commerce.[16] This confirmation of the power of their 1913 supermajority bolstered dry forces on the eve of the congressional battle over adoption of a prohibition amendment.

When the Sixty-fifth Congress convened in special session to declare war in April 1917, drys wasted little time pressing the advantages conferred by their electoral victory and the emotional climate surrounding American entry into World War I. Wartime acts to keep intoxicants from soldiers by banning sales near military bases and to conserve grain by banning production of distilled spirits won prompt approval. A notably stricter Anti-Saloon League amendment resolution, introduced on the third day of the session, sought to prohibit not merely sale but also manufacture, transportation, importation, and exportation of intoxicating liquors for beverage purposes. This language would outlaw not only commercial traffic but all exchange of alcoholic beverages.

With so many members of Congress committed to vote for a prohibition amendment, discussion was limited and action, by legislative standards, prompt. The Senate rehearsed familiar arguments for three days while the House did so for a single afternoon. Four issues received most of the attention: property rights, revenue, the wisdom of increasing federal power, and the feasibility of prohibition. Destroying an industry without compensation was excoriated as unjust and stoutly defended as both principled and precedented to protect society's welfare. Elimination of the source of about one-third of federal tax revenue brought forecasts of increases in other taxation, warnings undercut by the new federal income tax and the prevailing prosperity. Southern conservatives found themselves generally ignored when they repeated states' rights arguments about the dangers of expanded federal power and intervention into local affairs. Doubts about whether the law would be observed faced the assertion that violations had never been a sufficient reason for abandoning laws.[17]

Those who sought to stop what increasingly appeared to be an Anti-Saloon League juggernaut chose to do so by seeking to make the amendment's ratification less likely rather than by openly opposing it. When the amendment first came before the House in 1900, Representative James Mann of Illinois proposed that it be sent to state conventions for ratification, a procedure authorized by Article V but never used. Mann was well aware that recent state referendums had often rejected prohibition laws while state legislatures, susceptible to Anti-Saloon League pressure, usually supported them. Ratification conventions with delegates popularly elected on the basis of their position on a single issue would function as referendums and, he reasoned, be more likely to thwart prohibition. The dry majority recognized and rejected Mann's maneuver.[18]

When the Senate took up the amendment in 1917, another subtle attempt was made to derail it. Ohio senator Warren Harding, sensitive to his large WCTU and Anti-Saloon League constituency but by no means a prohibition enthusiast, devised a plan that would permit him and others to vote for the amendment, thus avoiding the wrath of the drys, yet ensure that it would fail of ratification. He saw an opportunity to play on both the drys' desire to secure every possible congressional vote and the widespread wish of his colleagues to eliminate "this unending prohibition contest in the halls of Congress." He acknowledged that he opposed prohibition but said that his primary objective was to get the issue resolved one way or the other.[19] Harding proposed that language be added to the amendment requiring that it be ratified within five years in order to be valid. Realizing that at the moment only twenty-six states had adopted bone-dry or limited prohibition, he calculated that the ten additional states necessary to meet Article V's three-fourths requirement could not be secured within that time. Negotiations with Anti-Saloon League general counsel Wayne Wheeler and later with House leaders increased the time limit, first to six years, and eventually to seven. Wheeler agreed to gain additional Senate votes, since he believed that ratification could be achieved within the time limit. Never before had any such restriction been imposed on the amending process, but the Senate, its members no doubt acting from a variety of motives, endorsed it 55 to 23 on August 1. Immediately thereafter the Senate approved the amendment 65 to 20.[20]

Two weeks after Congress reconvened in December, the House of Representatives considered the amendment resolution. As it had in December 1914, the House added language specifically granting the federal and state governments concurrent power to enforce prohibition. To deal with complaints that the liquor industry was being given no time to wind up its affairs, an agreement was reached that delayed the amendment's effective date for one year after ratification in return for extending the ratification limit from six years to seven. These alterations having been approved, the House passed the resolution 282 to 128. On the following day the Senate concurred 47 to 8 in the House changes, sending the amendment on to the states.[21]

State ratification proceeded at a pace that surprised even the Anti-Saloon League, not to mention the calculating Warren Harding. The temperance sympathies of many delegates together with the pressure that the Anti-Saloon League endorsement strategy exerted on the uncommitted produced overwhelmingly favorable state legislatures. Five states ratified during January 1918, eight more before summer, and two later in the year. Then in January 1919 newly elected legislatures gave their approval in no fewer than twenty-seven states. Within thirteen months of congressional action, the Eighteenth Amendment had been endorsed by the necessary thirty-six states. After seventeen months forty-four states had given their sanction. New Jersey's subsequent ratification in March 1922 meant that every state in the Union, except Illinois, Indiana (where it was never brought to a vote), and Rhode Island (whose legislature rejected it), ratified national prohibition well within the seven-year limit.[22]

The subsequent decline in prohibition's popularity has obscured the extent of its support in 1919. Traditional temperance crusaders with roots in the evangelical Protestant denominations and the women's crusade had been joined by a broad spectrum of Progressive reformers interested in uplifting the urban poor, eradicating the political influence of saloon-based political machines, and improving the efficiency of industrial workers. Racist and nativist desires to take drink away from blacks and recent immigrants from southern and eastern Europe were also widespread. The entry of the United States into World War I, which was accompanied by a spirit of patriotic self-denial and the reviling of all things German, including beer and schnapps, swelled the dry ranks.[23]

Since the political tactics of the Anti-Saloon League could exaggerate the influence of a small but determined segment of the electorate in congressional and state legislative vote tallies, the assessment of prohibition sentiment is incomplete without a comparison of outcomes in representative bodies with direct measurements of popular attitudes. Referendums on statewide prohibition measures in twenty-three states during the five years preceding ratification of the Eighteenth Amendment showed a preponderance of dry sentiment. Only in California and Missouri did voters reject liquor bans by wide margins, in both states doing so more than once. In Iowa and Vermont state prohibition was narrowly defeated; in Ohio it was twice turned down before being adopted. In the eighteen other states, however, majorities ranging from 52 percent in Colorado to 73 percent in Utah and 76 percent in Wyoming approved antialcohol laws of varying severity.[24] Although votes on state measures should not be considered identical to endorsements of a national law, nevertheless, these results suggest that those who voted for the amendment in Congress or state legislatures were not altogether out of step with their constituents. Perhaps enthusiasm for prohibition was not always great, but acceptance of it was broad.

Congress in 1919 perceived the mood of the country as determinedly prohibitionist. The Eighteenth Amendment declared a ban on "intoxicating beverages," leaving it to Congress to define as well as implement national prohibition. Without hesitation, Congress overwhelmingly chose to interpret the new amendment in a strict fashion by adopting a prohibition enforcement act drafted by Wayne Wheeler and introduced by Minnesota representative Andrew Volstead. The Volstead Act, as it became known, focused on the liquor industry. It did not explicitly bar consumption, and it exempted medicinal, sacramental, and home-fermented beverages. More important, however, it defined a beverage as intoxicating whenever it contained more than one-half of 1 percent alcohol. This sweeping definition banned not only distilled spirits, as universally expected, but also beer and light wine, which many people had anticipated would be tolerated. Whether the Volstead Act reflected or exaggerated the dry mood is impossible to determine. However, in October 1919 a Congress normally sensitive to public preferences left no doubt as to its reading of the popular will when it overrode Woodrow Wilson's veto of the Volstead Act by 176 to 55 in the House and 65 to 20 in the Senate.[25]

In 1919 national prohibition appeared to be a widely supported innovation in public policy and constitutionalism. It had, after all, met the demanding congressional and state supermajority requirements necessary for a constitutional amendment. It had attained, indeed exceeded, the degree of support mustered for the Bill of Rights and the constitutional abolition of slavery, not to mention every other change in the Constitution. Like the Thirteenth Amendment, the Eighteenth altered private property rights, ended a vast and profitable business activity, and fundamentally transformed American society. Moreover, the alcohol prohibition amendment gave the national government direct responsibility over the routine activities of ordinary citizens, a notable extension of its authority. Although states were to share concurrent enforcement power, the federal relationship had been significantly reshaped. No wonder then that the adoption of the Eighteenth Amendment reinforced a growing sense of the Article V process as a readily available tool for accomplishing basic reform of American government.

WHEN EARNEST young temperance crusader Susan B. Anthony rose to discuss a motion at the Albany convention of the New York Sons of Temperance in 1852, she was denied the floor and told, "Women were not invited there to speak but to listen and learn." Anthony, just beginning to awaken to American society's denial of women's rights, responded instantly to the hitherto unchallenged misogyny of the organized antialcohol movement. She left the hall and proceeded to found a separate women's antidrink organization. Nevertheless, when the New York State Temperance Society met in Syracuse in June 1852 Anthony was again turned away. At the Whole World's Temperance Convention in New York City the following year, she and other women were once more excluded. At this point Anthony abandoned the antiliquor cause. She joined Elizabeth Cady Stanton, organizer of the 1848 Seneca Falls women's rights convention, in devoting their considerable energies to the quest for what was at the time thought to be the most radical of women's demands, the right to vote.[26]

Such inauspicious early relations between the temperance and women's rights crusades did not, however, create an unbridgeable gulf. By the 1870s, with both causes regaining the momentum lost during the Civil War, greater understanding and mutual support developed. Women seized the initiative in the temperance movement, first with grass-roots protests against liquor dealers in Washington Court House, Ohio, in winter 1873–1874, and soon thereafter with the founding of the Women's Christian Temperance Union.[27] With Frances Willard's ascendancy to the WCTU presidency in 1879, the union not only became a powerful political force but also moved from a narrow focus on liquor to a broad campaign for women's rights, including woman suffrage. Thereafter the temperance crusade became closely identified with the women's movement.

The pursuit of women's rights seemed poised to go in a variety of directions after the Civil War. The causes of temperance and family protection, marriage and property law reform, education and employment access, worker protection, and health reform competed for attention with the quest for the vote. Suffrage proved to be about the only goal that otherwise divided reformers could agree upon, and thus it became the centerpiece of women's rights efforts during the next half century. The positions taken by two organizations founded in 1869, the National Woman Suffrage Association (NWSA) and the American Woman Suffrage Association (AWSA), reflected the divisions within women's ranks. The NWSA, under the leadership of Stanton and Anthony, took a broad and aggressive approach toward women's rights while the AWSA, headed by Lucy Stone and Elizabeth Blackwell, concentrated on obtaining the vote and downplayed other agendas. Initially the NWSA objected to the Fifteenth Amendment unless it enfranchised women as well as blacks; the AWSA, by contrast, refused to jeopardize the opportunities of black males. Thereafter NWSA pursued a national strategy for obtaining suffrage, but AWSA believed it better to work state by state. Two decades passed before the gulf between the two organizations began to narrow. In 1890 younger women's rights advocates fostered a merger of the two into the National American Women Suffrage Association (NAWSA). Fundamental differences remained, however, as the first two presidents, Stanton and then Anthony, preferred to work for a federal suffrage amendment, although many NAWSA members still agitated for state suffrage referendums and laws.[28]

State suffrage campaigns built organizational membership but otherwise did little to advance the cause. Between 1870 and 1910 a total of 480 campaigns in thirty-three states to place woman suffrage on the ballot produced only seventeen referendums. Even more disheartening, only two victories were achieved, in Colorado in 1893 and Idaho three years later.[29] In addition, Wyoming and Utah retained the woman suffrage of their territorial charters when they entered the Union in 1890 and 1896 respectively. The two territories had adopted woman suffrage less to support women's rights than as a strategy to keep political power in the hands of settled families in the face of an influx of largely male miners and drifters.[30] Even after encouraging referendum victories in Washington in 1910, California in 1911, and Arizona, Kansas, and Oregon in 1912, the nine western states remained the only success stories of the state-by-state campaign for woman suffrage.

The alternative, a national guarantee, faired no better. In fact, when Representative James Brooks of New York first proposed penalizing states for denying suffrage on the basis of gender as an element of the Fourteenth

Amendment in 1866, he was engaged in a cynical attempt to divide and embarrass advocates of women's and black rights. Undeterred by defeat, Brooks repeated the tactic, seeking to insert language banning gender discrimination in suffrage, when the Fifteenth Amendment was being drafted in January 1869. A sincere and separate woman suffrage amendment was initially suggested by Kansas senator Samuel C. Pomeroy less than two weeks later. Nine years afterward, a Senate committee first gave consideration to the so-called Susan B. Anthony amendment proposed by California senator Aaron A. Sargent. In language eventually adopted in 1920, it simply stated: "The right of citizens of the United States to vote shall not be denied or abridged by the United States or by any State on account of sex." Not until January 1887, however, did Congress vote on any amendment resolution. At that time the Senate rejected the Anthony amendment 34 to 16. Thereafter, Congress would not vote on the issue again for more than thirty years. Although nearly every Congress after the Civil War received a woman suffrage amendment, little support surfaced in the all-male body until the 1910s. Then the new environment of constitutional reform helped lift the suffrage crusade out of the doldrums.[31]

In January 1913 an imaginative and impatient young Quaker social worker arrived in Washington determined to press for the apparently moribund Anthony amendment. Alice Paul had become involved in the militant British suffrage movement while pursuing her University of Pennsylvania doctoral studies in London. In 1912 she persuaded NAWSA leaders to put her in charge of their congressional committee. With the help of a small cadre of like-minded women, Paul quickly found a way to dramatize their cause. In March 1913 5,000 suffrage advocates paraded down Pennsylvania Avenue on the day before Woodrow Wilson's inauguration. Facing a large, abusive crowd with little protection from an indifferent District of Columbia police force, the beleaguered marchers focused considerable attention on their demands for a suffrage amendment.[32]

The March 1913 Washington parade served as an amendment campaign catalyst for suffragists as well as for prohibitionists, who would stage their own Pennsylvania Avenue parade before the end of the year. Within months Alice Paul's Congressional Union split off from the NAWSA to become an independent, rival body. Adopting single-issue tactics similar to the Anti-Saloon League as well as to the British suffrage movement's policy of concentrating pressure on political incumbents, the militant Congressional Union demanded action on the Anthony amendment first proposed thirty-five years earlier. The Senate responded by rejecting the amendment 34 to 35 in March 1914, and a year later the House did likewise by a wider margin of 174 to 207.[33] Paul turned to a strategy of holding "the party in power" responsible for inaction on the suffrage amendment and campaigning against the reelection of incumbent Democratic congressmen. Despite some Women's party successes in the West in 1914, the House turned down the Anthony amendment 174 to 204 the following January.[34] Meanwhile, Alice Paul's tactics offended though did not completely alienate some western congressional Democrats who supported woman suffrage.[35]

National American Woman Suffrage Association leaders briefly pursued an alternative tactic. They persuaded Senator John Shafroth of Colorado and Representative A. Mitchell Palmer of Pennsylvania to propose an amendment requiring any state to hold a binding referendum on whether to provide woman suffrage upon petition by 8 percent of the voters in the previous election. This would not only make it easier to secure referendums, they argued, but would gain the support of those who claimed to be sympathetic but insisted on the right of states to determine suffrage requirements. Though consistent with progressive democratic enthusiasms, the Shafroth-Palmer amendment seemed complicated, confusing, and ultimately of limited value to many suffragists who were becoming exasperated with NAWSA. The loss of five midwestern state referendums in 1914, against only two western state victories, underscored the point. The Shafroth-Palmer amendment's principal effect was to signal the NAWSA leadership's strategic confusion over how best to use the Article V process to achieve their goals.[36]

In 1915 state suffrage referendums lost again, in Massachusetts, New Jersey, New York, and Pennsylvania. Nevertheless, the example of Congressional Union aggressiveness together with their own reassessment of the political climate led new NAWSA leaders finally to drop the Shafroth-Palmer plan and to campaign wholeheartedly for the Anthony amendment. Resuming the presidency of NAWSA in December 1915 after a thirteen-year absence, Carrie Chapman Catt spent the next several months revitalizing the organization and developing a strategy for achieving a federal suffrage amendment. She concluded that not only did justice demand equal suffrage for women but that a federal amendment offered the simplest way to obtain it. State constitutions and laws were more difficult to alter, she decided. Not hesitant to play on nativist, anti-Catholic, and class sentiments, she insisted, "A referendum in many of our states means to defer woman suffrage until the most ignorant, most narrow-minded, most un-American, are ready for it." By contrast, Catt declared, "The removal of the question to the higher court of the Congress and the Legislatures of the several states means that it will be established when the intelligent, Americanized, progressive people of the country are ready for it."[37]

Catt's Winning Plan, which in 1916 NAWSA and its state affiliates secretly committed themselves to pursue, recognized the two levels of approval required by the Article V process and shrewdly set forth to win both congressional and thirty-six state victories. In states where women could vote, congressional delegations would be pressed to seek passage of an amendment. In states where referendums on suffrage could be obtained, they would be pursued to increase the number of legislators sensitive to women voters. Where plebiscites were unlikely, suffragists would seek the right to vote in party primaries or other circumscribed circumstances. Catt believed that much resistance to suffrage would crumble once victories were won in an eastern and a southern state. The East was concerned about new immigrants and the South worried about black women voters and federally supervised elections. The opposition, particularly liquor interests financing antisuffrage campaigns out of fear of women's dry votes, needed to be kept off-balance, she thought. Thus NAWSA must, she said, in the manner of a military campaign with its feints and deceptions, "keep so much 'suffrage noise' going all over the country that neither the enemy nor friends will discover where the real battle is."[38]

Organized opposition to woman suffrage made its presence felt throughout the struggle. Widespread male aversion to women's participation in government had been manifest for centuries and clearly so in the legislative and referendum contests of the late nineteenth and early twentieth centuries. Men had little need for new agencies to wage the battle since they could easily express their negative views through the existing political, business, and social bodies that they dominated. Antisuffrage women, on the other hand, lacked established means to present their views. Many of them shared the common male view that woman's proper place was in the home functioning as wife and mother; political involvement would only undermine their moral virtue and influence. Unhappy with the emerging feminist movement, a few traditionalist women, often with male encouragement, began in the 1880s to engage in organized political activity to discount and resist the notion that women should have the right to engage in politics.[39]

The Massachusetts Association Opposed to the Further Extension of Suffrage to Women, founded in 1895, was the first and eventually the largest women's organization against suffrage. It grew out of a committee formed in 1882 by wealthy, well-educated, socially prominent Boston women to discourage the state legislature, which had allowed women to vote in school elections, from granting them the right to participate in municipal elections. Unwilling to speak publicly themselves, these women arranged to have males represent them. In January 1884, for instance, federal judge John

Lowell, attorney Louis Brandeis, and Harvard history professor Francis Parkman appeared in their behalf before a state legislative committee.[40] From 1890 to 1920 the Boston antisuffragists published a periodical, *The Remonstrance,* that proclaimed that "the great majority of their sex do not want the ballot, and that to force it upon them would not only be an injustice to women, but would lessen their influence for good." In 1911 the Massachusetts Association, which had grown to more than 12,000 members, led similar groups that had been established in about two dozen other states, most notably New York and Illinois, to form a National Association Opposed to Woman Suffrage.[41]

Although their numbers were uncertain and probably modest, the antisuffrage women constituted a worrisome opponent for supporters of the Anthony amendment. As they lobbied state legislative committees, distributed brochures, pamphlets, periodicals, and books, and campaigned in state referendums, the antisuffragists provided men of unsettled views with reasons for voting against enfranchisement. Women voted in the eleven states where the Mormon church was entrenched, a 1915 Pennsylvania Association pamphlet alleged, because polygamous Mormon priests knew that the more wives they had the more votes they controlled.[42] In another pamphlet Dolly Blount Lamar, vice-president of the Georgia Association, wrote that woman suffrage would jeopardize white control of southern politics. She steadfastly maintained that most women did not want the vote.[43] Another Georgia opponent, Mildred Rutherford, told the legislature that "the women who are working for this measure are striking at the principle for which their fathers fought during the Civil War. [They] do not believe in state rights and . . . wish to see negro women using the ballot. I do not believe that the State of Georgia has sunk so low that her good men can not legislate for the woman."[44] Once the United States entered World War I, foes of woman suffrage linked it to the "pro-German, pacifist, and socialist vote."[45]

The National Association Opposed to Woman Suffrage, furthermore, formed or encouraged other organizations, male as well as female, to make it appear as if a wide variety of groups with different motivations objected to the amendment.[46] The Maryland League for State Defense pushed a states' rights message. The American Constitutional League, founded by Everett P. Wheeler as a successor to his earlier Man Suffrage Association, likewise argued that individual states should retain control over suffrage.[47] It also aimed at southern states with a blatantly racist argument. Since women outnumbered men in the black population, while the reverse was the case among whites, woman suffrage would increase black political influence "even *if every white woman in the South* was willing to be *crowded into the polling places with negroes of both sexes.*" The National League for the Civic Education of Women proclaimed that women needed to learn more about government; otherwise, "Woman Suffrage could not have gained the headway that it has and many of them would very clearly see how the movement is strongly allied with Socialism."[48] Though these organizations were small, their skill in publicizing their views makes their influence difficult to calculate.

The liquor industry played an important behind-the-scenes role in the antisuffrage movement. Fearing that women voters would support prohibition laws, brewers, distillers, and saloon keepers from the 1880s onward quietly made large contributions to campaigns against state suffrage referendums. While no doubt helpful at the time, the donations proved an embarrassment to suffrage opponents as the battle over votes for women moved into its final phase. Accused by the Anti-Saloon League and Attorney General A. Mitchell Palmer of unpatriotic wartime activities, the United States Brewers Association was investigated by the Senate Judiciary Committee in 1918. Not only were the brewers found to have financed pro-German publicity, their other political contributions to defeat woman suffrage as well as prohibition stood revealed.[49] Laid low also by the adoption of the Eighteenth Amendment, the liquor industry was of little help to the antisuffrage forces when the battle over the Anthony amendment reached the states.

While antisuffragists objected to any support for the Anthony amendment and, from an entirely different perspective, Alice Paul sought to punish Democrats as "the party in power," Carrie Chapman Catt strove to win all possible friends for the cause. Her search for support in both major parties contrasted sharply with Paul's British-inspired treatment of political parties as monolithic. In 1916 Catt's attention focused on Woodrow Wilson, who by temperament and practice had long opposed allowing women a role in public affairs. Avoiding taking a position on suffrage and calling it a state issue during his 1912 presidential campaign, Wilson gradually reconsidered. After carefully weighing the political advantages and costs, he announced without warning in October 1915 that he would vote for woman suffrage in a New Jersey referendum the next month. The following year he was persuaded to support a Democratic platform plank favoring woman suffrage but maintaining that granting the vote was a state right. The Republican platform took the same position. When its nominee, Charles Evans Hughes, went further and endorsed a federal suffrage amendment, Catt encouraged Wilson to do likewise. Though he refused to go that far, he did agree to address the NAWSA convention in September 1916. There he spoke of how rapidly the suffrage cause had progressed and in gracious but general terms indicated his support, declining to quarrel over methods.⁵⁰ Despite Alice Paul's opposition, peace-motivated women in the twelve states where they exercised the suffrage in 1916 helped bring about the president's narrow re-election. Wilson carried ten of those states.⁵¹

Alice Paul's followers, reorganizing as the National Woman's party, did not relent from criticizing Wilson and "the party in power." They began picketing the White House in January 1917, proclaiming the lack of American democracy. Picketing continued after the United States declared war on Germany. Arrests began in June, and as longer and longer jail sentences were handed out, hunger strikes followed, met in turn with forced feeding. By the autumn the situation and the resulting public outcry had become serious embarrassments to the administration. In late November the pickets were released, with their arrests, convictions, and sentences subsequently invalidated. When a suffrage amendment began moving ahead shortly thereafter, the Woman's party naturally claimed responsibility.⁵² Yet while they certainly drew attention to their cause, the pickets may have stiffened resistance to it as well. Other efforts simultaneously in motion probably contributed more to the building of the broad political consensus required for a constitutional amendment.

Carrie Chapman Catt and the NAWSA took the position, contrary to the Woman's party, that displays of women's cooperation and patriotism, together with persistent grass-roots agitation, ought to be rewarded with full enfranchisement. As they hoped, President Wilson began acknowledging the importance of women's contribution to the war effort as soon as the United States entered World War I, and he continued to do so regularly. Furthermore, responding to NAWSA suggestions, Wilson in May 1917 encouraged the House of Representatives to establish a committee on woman suffrage. Although the president was unwilling to designate suffrage as a war emergency measure to expedite its consideration by Congress, he did endorse a New York state suffrage referendum for which NAWSA was campaigning strenuously. The passage of the New York measure represented the first victory for suffrage in the Northeast, not to mention a significant shift of opinion in the largest state. Two years earlier only 42 percent of New York voters had favored granting the ballot to women.

As the House prepared to vote on the Anthony amendment on January 10, 1918, Wilson took the further step of advocating a federal solution. He issued a public statement "frankly and earnestly" advising representatives to support the amendment "as an act of right and justice."⁵³ As he explained to a House delegation, he was departing from the details of the Democratic platform because holding to its state action provision would thwart its pledge to support woman suffrage. "The difference in form is not sufficient reason for voting against it," he said, a view disputed by many southern Democrats.[54] Although most House support came from Republicans while Democrats divided along sectional lines, Wilson's intervention no doubt helped the measure achieve the necessary two-thirds vote by a slim margin of 274 to 136. Clearly "the war to make the world safe for democracy" led Wilson to revise his position on woman suffrage. The war, congressional passage the previous month of the prohibition amendment that removed a motivation for antiprohibitionists to oppose votes for presumably dry women, and changing public opinion also help explain the shifting votes of fifty-six congressmen who had opposed woman suffrage in 1915 but who now helped bring about this important first national victory.[55]

Despite the conversion of the House of Representatives, Senate resistance continued. Senators acted less concerned about apparent shifts in public opinion, perhaps because of their longer terms and the fact that, only four years after adoption of the Seventeenth Amendment, some had little or no experience facing the voters. Moreover, the distribution of Senate seats by state rather than population gave the South greater influence in the upper chamber. Opposition to a suffrage amendment was strongest in the South, where it was seen as yet another potential threat to the region's system of excluding blacks from elections. The Fourteenth and Fifteenth Amendments remained sore points to many southern whites. Just as the possibility of federal intrusion into the South's racial practices fueled its senators' resistance to the Seventeenth Amendment, it provoked their opposition to woman suffrage.[56] The battle of women and an increasingly engaged President Wilson to convert southern senators went on outside public view throughout spring and summer 1918.

On September 30, with a Senate vote looming and suffrage supporters still short of the needed two-thirds, Wilson took a step unprecedented in the history of amendment politics and, indeed, of the upper house. Giving but thirty minutes notice, he appeared in the Senate chamber, accompanied by his cabinet, to urge passage of the Anthony amendment. The war served as the centerpiece of his argument. Having made women partners in the war, he said, the nation needed to enfranchise them to demonstrate its commitment to democracy. Suffrage was "necessary to the successful prosecution of the war" and "vital to the right solution of the great problems which we must settle, and settle immediately, when the war is over."[57]

Since presidents had no formal role in the Article V process, Wilson's visit was nothing more or less than a dramatic effort at political persuasion, one in character for someone who more than any previous chief executive actively sought to direct the legislative process. No president had ever entered so directly into debate taking place on the Senate floor, whether on an amendment or any other issue. While his legislative tactics may have served Wilson well in the past, they did not in this case, at least in the short run. His son-in-law, Treasury secretary William McAdoo, who had urged him to make the speech, observed that it was "bitterly resented by all those opposed to the amendment and that even those who favored it were influenced by senatorial tradition and the feeling that the Chief Executive should not plead for any particular measure which the Senate had under consideration."[58] The president was scarcely out of the room before Alabama senator Oscar Underwood rose to speak against the amendment. When the Senate voted 53 to 31 in favor of the amendment the following day, it denied Wilson victory. Had all senators been present and voted as announced, the tally would have been 61 to 35, leaving the measure three votes short of adoption.[59]

The Senate's action occurred only a month before congressional elections. Wilson's advocacy of woman suffrage had no doubt been stirred by the sense he shared with other partisans that universal female voting was only a matter of time and that the Democratic party should court, and certainly not alienate, the mass of new voters. Southern Democrats who provided the bulk of the Senate opposition undermined Wilson's efforts. Women furious with the result of the Senate vote turned their efforts against those who had opposed them, regardless of party. Suffragist attention concentrated on four apparently well-entrenched but possibly vulnerable senators. Republican John Weeks of Massachusetts and Democrat Willard Saulsbury of Delaware both met defeat in November; Republicans George Moses of New Hampshire nearly lost and David Baird of New Jersey had his victory margin sharply reduced. These Republican setbacks stood out in an election where in general the Democratic party suffered, losing its congressional majorities. Referendum victories for woman suffrage in Michigan, Oklahoma, and South Dakota, together with a near-success in the Deep South state of Louisiana, provide further evidence of the importance to the 1918 electorate of votes for women.[60]

During the lame duck session of the Sixty-fifth Congress, senators held their ground and on February 10, 1919, again rejected the Anthony amendment. This time, because of the death of South Carolina's Benjamin Tillman and his replacement by a suffrage supporter, the margin of defeat was a single vote. Nine negative votes came from senators whose state legislatures had just sent appeals for passage.[61] Forced to wait for the next Congress to convene, suffrage advocates mounted a barrage of petitions. Encouraged by completion of the Eighteenth Amendment's ratification on January 16, they remained hopeful but nervous about overcoming the obstacles to a federal amendment.

On May 21, 1919, the third day of a special session, the new House of Representatives readopted the amendment resolution, this time by the enlarged margin of 304 to 90. The departure of Weeks and Saulsbury and the announcement of three former opponents that they would now support the amendment appeared to alter the balance in the Senate, but diehard antisuffragists such as William Borah of Idaho and James W. Wadsworth, Jr., of New York continued their oratory. Senator Underwood, one of the most determined opponents, sought to amend the resolution to require ratification by state conventions rather than legislatures. On its face a call for a popular vote on the issue through the election of convention delegates, it was at heart a maneuver calculated to sidestep legislatures expected to favor the amendment. The imposition of a seven-year time limit on ratification had proven so ineffectual in blocking the prohibition amendment that it generated little enthusiasm. Not willing to sacrifice perceived advantages, suffragists turned back the Underwood measure 55 to 28 as well as all other last-minute desperation attempts to modify the amendment resolution. On June 4, the Senate finally approved the Anthony amendment 56 to 25, sending it on to the states where the battle to achieve the necessary Article V victory margin was also expected to be close.[62]

Despite rapid advances in recent years, not enough states had given women voting rights to ensure ratification of the Anthony amendment. The rapid adoption of the prohibition amendment encouraged but did not altogether reassure suffragists. The prospect of southern opposition, not faced by the prohibitionists, hung ominously over the campaign. Article V's three-fourths approval requirement meant that a few states held the power of rejection. States especially sensitive about federal control of voting, the eleven states of the old Confederacy together with border states with segregationist traditions such as Delaware, Maryland, and Kentucky, held a veto if they acted together. Rejection of the woman suffrage amendment by thirteen states would prevent its addition to the Constitution. Suffrage supporters would have to win the endorsement of virtually every state outside the South as well as at least a couple in that region, more if necessary to make up for defections elsewhere. Despite the growing belief of both national political parties that woman suffrage was inevitable and thus to be supported so as not to offend vast numbers of potential voters, the Article V equation rendered the outcome uncertain.

Both the National Woman's party and the National American Woman Suffrage Association understood the challenge remaining. Both had created state-level organizations, whether to wage referendum or legislative battles for state reform, as NAWSA had often done for years, or to press a state's congressional delegation for federal action, a tactic of the Woman's party since 1915. Carrie Chapman Catt sought to keep NAWSA affiliates functioning even after a state adopted woman suffrage, anticipating that they might be needed again in the ratification struggle.[63] Whatever their background, these bodies did give suffragists an effective means of agitating for state legislative action.

On June 10, 1919, less than a week after Congress sent it to them, Illinois, Michigan, and Wisconsin, states where women already voted, ratified the suffrage amendment. Eight more states acted before a month had passed. An additional eleven approved during the next six months. Though a number of other legislatures could be expected to ratify once they convened, the issue remained in doubt because of southern recalcitrance. Texas had been among the first to ratify and Arkansas had followed suit, but the legislatures of Georgia and Alabama just as quickly rejected the amendment.[64] "If you pass this Nineteenth Amendment you ratify the Fifteenth," explained J. M. Jones, a Georgia representative, "and any Southerner . . . [so doing] is a traitor to his section."[65]

The coming of the new year and the convening of many legislatures brought a burst of ratification but not an end to uncertainty. Five states approved in January, six more in February. An even and bitter struggle in West Virginia ended with ratification on March 10 when state senator Jesse Bloch rushed home from a trip to California to break a tie in the upper house. When Washington approved on March 22, the Anthony amendment stood only one state away from adoption. However, southern rejections had begun to pile up as well. Legislatures in South Carolina in January, Virginia and Maryland in February, and Mississippi in March registered their disapproval; North Carolina and Florida declined even to address the issue. Delaware's conservative, rural-dominated lower house rejected the amendment 23 to 9 on April 1, and although the state senate later approved ratification and the Republican governor urged the house to reconsider, a final ballot on June 2 confirmed the original decision.[66]

Legislatures in Republican Vermont and Connecticut appeared ready to ratify but were temporarily thwarted as antisuffragist governors refused to call special sessions, citing the expense involved and counseling delay until voters could express their preferences at the next election. Republicans did not appear too upset by this turn of events. They seemed happy to let states' rights southern Democrats feud with suffrage supporters, publicly embarrass their party, and offend a national audience of women with their refusal to ratify. Eventually Republicans, who had overwhelmingly supported the amendment, would be able to gather the political rewards of completing ratification. When Louisiana's Democratic legislature rejected the amendment on July 1, Republican tactics appeared to be working. At their national party conventions, Republicans proclaimed their support of suffrage and gloated over Democratic disarray. Meanwhile, Democrats remained divided on the issue itself, with southerners steadfastly opposed and the national party desperate to avoid being viewed as antiwoman. Some suffragists grew increasingly fearful that the 1920 election would pass with the amendment unratified, and thereafter their opportunity for success would disappear.[67]

By midsummer 1920 only Tennessee had not spoken on the Anthony amendment. Pressed by Wilson and others, Governor Albert H. Roberts overcame his own doubts about state constitutional requirements and called the Tennessee legislature into special session on August 9. Supporters and opponents of suffrage descended upon Nashville as on no other state capitol during the battle. Carrie Chapman Catt remained for six weeks, while antisuffrage forces were bolstered by the arrival of Kate Gordon of Louisiana and Laura Clay of Kentucky, former NAWSA officers who insisted that suffrage should be achieved only by state action. Every argument that had been offered by one side or the other was voiced once again. After brief debate, the state senate voted 25 to 4 to ratify on August 13. A different story unfolded in the lower house where opinion was divided. Opponents, led by Democratic house speaker Seth Walker, thought they had a one-vote margin to table the measure until a Democratic friend of the governor changed his mind at the last minute. Then the youngest member of the house, Republican Harry Burns, added his vote for ratification, fulfilling a promise to his suffragist mother that he would ignore the preferences of his rural east Tennessee district if his support was needed to carry the resolution. Walker himself added one more vote in order to be in a position to request reconsideration. Unable to gain a majority for reconsideration within the three days allowed, the speaker persuaded thirty-eight members to leave the state in a last desperate effort to prevent a quorum from being assembled on August 21 to complete action. Governor Roberts, however, certified that ratification had been accomplished with the initial house vote and notified Washington. Secretary of State Bainbridge Colby promptly declared that the Nineteenth Amendment had been ratified as of August 18, 1920, making women eligible to vote nationwide in the federal election of 1920.[68]

When Republican presidential candidate Warren Harding pointed out that four-fifths of ratifications came from Republican-controlled states, and a special session of the Connecticut legislature was at last summoned to add its ratification in September, concern over how women voters would regard party roles in the adoption of the Nineteenth Amendment was evident. Possibly because partisan responsibility for both success and delay was divided, or perhaps because Democrats so thoroughly controlled the ten states that failed to ratify, all of them except Delaware members of the Confederacy, neither party was particularly rewarded or punished. The female vote in 1920 and after split along roughly the same lines as the male vote. The Nineteenth Amendment wrought a revolution in women's status but not in the immediate political circumstances of American life.

THE YEAR 1920 marked a high point of progressive enthusiasm about achieving fundamental change through explicit and authentic acts of constitutional amendment. By then income taxation and direct election were functioning smoothly and successfully. National prohibition took effect in January with the *New York Times* proclaiming the peaceful death of John Barleycorn.[69] Woman suffrage gained ratification in time for female voters throughout the country to participate in the November balloting. The addition of this large bloc of new voters raised expectations that women's particular viewpoints would move politics onto a higher plane.[70] As the decade of constitutional innovation came to a close, some advanced reformers were already thinking about additional structural alterations to improve American government further. Yet those less enamored of some or all of the events that had taken place were also giving thought to the situation. In retrospect, it would become evident that 1920 did not represent an incoming flood tide of constitutional change but the crest of a wave soon to dissipate.

11

"Like the Ratchet on a Cog Wheel"

Second Thoughts About Amendment

The Eighteenth and Nineteenth Amendments accelerated a reevaluation of the constitutional amending process. "The view as to the difficulty of amending the federal Constitution is now quite different from the view which existed ten or twelve years ago," observed William F. Dodd of Yale Law School in 1920. "This changed attitude has, to some extent, made the federal amending process easier," he decided, "for a part of the difficulty, at least before the ratification of the Sixteenth Amendment, was due to the feeling that the amending machinery was unworkable rather than to the unworkability of that machinery."[1]

A neutral spectator such as the once and future Supreme Court justice Charles Evans Hughes could call the amending power "our essential means of adaptation, our answer to the inciters of violence, our assurance of meeting peacefully—without any good reason for resort to revolution—all demands to which new exigencies may give rise," while at the same time cautioning against putting too much trust in the system.[2] Reform-minded monitors, however, who not too long before had despaired of achieving constitutional change, started to think of the Article V process as a facile method to reverse unsatisfactory Supreme Court rulings and to complete other agendas. Meanwhile, opponents of reforms completed or contemplated no longer felt secure behind the unscalable obstacle that they had thought Article V represented. They began to worry that the amending mechanism was itself flawed.[3]

Controversy about the process of constitutional amendment grew directly from the experiences of national prohibition and woman suffrage. These new fundamental rules for social behavior and gender relationships had been discussed for at least seven decades without any national action being taken. Then in rapid fashion both reforms had been installed in the Constitution amid questions about the procedures used to obtain ratification. The fact that the two amendments were adopted during a period of extraordinary tumult and dislocation brought about by World War I added to the sense that traditional bounds had been broken. More than a few Americans exulted, but others questioned whether this was the way to carry out constitutional revision.

Circumstances surrounding the adoption of the two amendments heightened the attention given them. The aggressive role of organized advocates of national prohibition and woman suffrage in obtaining congressional and legislative sanction for the two reforms led some observers to believe that such tactics could produce other reforms. Those who were having difficulty accepting one or both of the amendments concluded that a skillful, manipulative minority had overridden the preferences of most citizens. Such suspicions were strengthened by legal challenges to the amendments' adoption and subsequently kept alive despite, indeed perhaps because of, the Supreme Court's dismissal of the complaints.

The Eighteenth and Nineteenth Amendments together provoked a reconsideration of the merits of Article V. Indeed the 1920s produced the most sustained and substantial discussion of the amending mechanism by the courts, the Congress, and the public since the adoption of the Constitution. A host of essays, not only in law journals but in general circulation magazines as well, considered a topic that until recently had stirred almost no interest in either forum. Was the amending process able to respond properly to the public will? Could momentary whim sway it too easily? Did state legislatures and Congress respect their constituents' preferences sufficiently in such matters? Did certain well-placed minority interests wield excessive influence? Should the Constitution be more difficult to alter, or less so? Basic issues of republicanism and federalism as they applied to constitutional change had not received such attention since at least the Civil War and perhaps the nation's founding.

Criticism of the Eighteenth Amendment proved particularly severe. Not only did it continue after national prohibition took effect on January 17, 1920, it steadily increased. Unhappiness with prohibition spilled over onto the mechanism by which it had been brought into being. Furthermore, disenchantment with the antiliquor amendment obstructed other movements for constitutional reform, not stopping them completely in every case but contributing to their being regarded skeptically, scrutinized carefully, and treated cautiously. The 1920s did not become a decade of accelerating constitutional change, despite the hopes of advocates of new amendments to guarantee women's full legal equality and to use federal power to prevent children's employment. Rather, it proved to be an era of second thoughts about the process as well as the substance of reform.

WHEREVER CONTESTS over constitutional amendments were close and fiercely fought, the Article V process itself came under close scrutiny in the search for political advantage. This certainly held true in Ohio, birthplace of the American Woman Suffrage Association, the Women's Christian Temperance Union, and the Anti-Saloon League as well as a major battlefield in the struggles over national prohibition and woman suffrage. Since the state was a leading beer and liquor producer, opposition to the two amendments was correspondingly strong within its borders. From the Civil War onward political loyalties were evenly divided in Ohio. The state's vital role in national victory constantly led Republicans and Democrats to seek national candidates and wage vigorous campaigns there. Wets and drys as well as suffragists and their opponents regarded the state in similar fashion. Ohio's heated amendment struggles produced important if sometimes unanticipated consequences.

Ohio, like many other states during the early twentieth century, began using popular referendums to resolve controversial public policy issues. Various proposals on alcohol prohibition as well as woman suffrage were placed before the state's roughly 1 million active voters. In 1912 woman suffrage was one of only eight of forty-one constitutional proposals that voters rejected. In 1914 it again met defeat by a substantial margin, as did state prohibition, after a campaign in which liquor interests actively opposed both. In 1915 a prohibition amendment to the state constitution lost by 55,408 votes. When the same measure reappeared on the ballot in 1917, however, it failed by only 1,137. At the same time voters rejected woman suffrage in presidential elections. A third prohibition referendum in 1918 produced a 25,759 victory for a state constitutional amendment.[4]

In the same election in which Ohio voters approved state prohibition, they endorsed another state constitutional change. Well aware that a national prohibition amendment was soon likely to be placed before the states and that the Anti-Saloon League wielded great influence in Columbus in a legislature with disproportionate rural representation, the state's voters decided by the wide majority of 508,283 to 315,030 to allow referendums on the ratification of federal amendments. This plan, initiated by opponents of national prohibition but supported more broadly, stipulated that no ratification by the legislature should go into effect for ninety days. During that time, a petition signed by 6 percent of the state's voters would force a referendum, and the legislature's action would then not take effect unless approved by a majority of those voting.

On January 7, 1919, the Ohio General Assembly, by a vote of 20 to 12 in the senate and 85 to 29 in the house, ratified the national prohibition amendment. Secretary of State Robert Lansing counted Ohio among the thirty-six ratifying states when he proclaimed the Eighteenth Amendment adopted as of January 16. Opponents responded swiftly. On March 11, they filed a referendum petition bearing more than the necessary 60,000 signatures with Ohio secretary of state Harvey C. Smith. Thereupon Smith ordered a referendum on the state's ratification of national prohibition to be held at the November general election.

George S. Hawke, a Cincinnati attorney and prohibitionist, sought an injunction to prevent Smith from spending public funds for a referendum Hawke considered was unconstitutional. The Franklin County Court of Common Pleas refused Hawke's request, as did the Court of Appeals and eventually the Ohio Supreme Court. On November 4, 1919, the referendum was held. Ohio voters rejected the national prohibition amendment by 500,450 to 499,971, a mere 479 votes out of 1 million cast.[5] Despite the narrow margin, the first state referendum ever held to consider ratification of a federal constitutional amendment overturned the state legislature's action, or so it appeared.

Undaunted, George Hawke asked the U.S. Supreme Court to uphold the general assembly's ratification and invalidate the referendum. By this time, Congress had placed the woman suffrage amendment before the states. When the Ohio legislature ratified it, a referendum petition had once again been filed. Hawke's suit was expanded to ask the Court to block the scheduled November 1920 suffrage amendment referendum. Both of Hawke's requests rested squarely on Article V and contended that its language was clear: amendments that Congress proposed were valid "when ratified by the legislatures of three-fourths of the several states, or by conventions in three-fourths thereof, *as the one or the other mode of ratification may be proposed by the Congress.*"[6] Hawke and his attorneys, who included Anti-Saloon League general counsel Wayne B. Wheeler, contended that Ohio's referendums were unconstitutional. The state could not impose any limitation upon the ratification process chosen by Congress.[7]

Ohio attorney general John G. Price and former U.S. solicitor general Lawrence Maxwell of Cincinnati, the referendum provision's author, defended it before the Supreme Court, contending that the Constitution did not require states to have any particular form of legislature. Indeed the people of a state had the right, if they wished, to dissolve their representative assemblies and take all legislative matters into their own hands. More practically, the people had the power, affirmed by the Supreme Court in 1916, to suspend legislative acts pending a referendum vote to accept or reject them. In other words, the argument ran, the term "legislature" included the entire lawmaking power of the state, not only the two houses of the general assembly but also the popular will as expressed in a referendum. This progressive argument for democratic authority rested squarely on the notion that constitutional sovereignty derived from the people.[8]

The outcome of *Hawke v. Smith* concerned everyone involved in the battles over national prohibition and woman suffrage. Referendums on the prohibition amendment had been sought in other states besides Ohio. In Maine and Oregon courts had refused to sanction them, and in California a referendum bill had failed in the legislature. In Washington, the maneuvering became even more complex: the legislature unanimously ratified national prohibition; opponents obtained a *mandamus* order from the state supreme court ordering acceptance of a referendum petition; the secretary of state then found the petition lacking sufficient signatures to place the question on the ballot. If the U.S. Supreme Court upheld the Ohio referendum, antiprohibitionists indicated they would seek referendums in several states in the hope of invalidating enough legislative ratifications to bring the total below the required three-fourths. The Ohio voting encouraged their belief that a chance still existed to overturn the Eighteenth Amendment.[9]

Suffragists allied themselves with prohibitionists to oppose ratification referendums, fearing that these might doom women's quest for the ballot. Thirty-five states had ratified the suffrage amendment by the time the Supreme Court heard arguments on *Hawke,* but that total could slip if Ohio was permitted to hold its referendum in November and other states followed suit. In recent popular votes, statewide woman suffrage had been defeated in the Dakotas, Massachusetts, Maine, Missouri, Nebraska, New Jersey, Pennsylvania, and Texas, not to mention three times in Ohio. In several of these states, legislatures had nonetheless proceeded to grant women the vote (the most recent Ohio referendum overturned such an act) as well as to ratify the federal amendment. Court authorization of ratification referendums would clearly jeopardize these steps. Efforts to secure popular votes on the federal suffrage amendment were already under way in Maine, Massachusetts, Missouri, Oklahoma, and Texas. Therefore, not only wets and drys but also suffragists and their opponents waited nervously for the Supreme Court ruling in *Hawke v. Smith.*[10]

On June 1, 1920, a unanimous Supreme Court upheld the Ohio General Assembly's ratifications of the Eighteenth and Nineteenth Amendments. In Article V, the Court said, the people granted amending authority to Congress, including power to choose one of the two specified ratification processes. "The framers of the Constitution might have adopted a different method," the Court conceded. "Ratification might have been left to a vote of the people, or to some authority of government other than that selected." However, "the language of the article is plain, and admits of no doubt in its interpretation."

The Supreme Court went on to declare that the Founders used the term legislature in the common sense of representative body. When they approved amendments, legislatures were simply designated instruments for carrying out a federal function. "Ratification by a State of a constitutional amendment is not an act of legislation within the proper sense of the word. It is but the expression of the assent of the State to a proposed amendment." On the basis of this distinction, the Court supported George Hawke's appeal, concluding,

> It is true that the power to legislate in the enactment of the laws of a State is derived from the people of the State. But the power to ratify a proposed amendment to the Federal Constitution has its source in the Federal Constitution. The act of ratification derives its authority from the Federal Constitution to which the State and its people have alike assented.[11]

In the Court's opinion, the language of Article V was determinative and should be read narrowly. When Congress stipulated that state legislatures were to ratify, it did not authorize a referendum. Six days later, in deciding a series of prohibition-related cases, the Court reiterated that state referendum provisions could not constitutionally be applied to the ratification process.[12]

The *Hawke v. Smith* decision invalidated Ohio's 1919 national prohibition referendum and relieved prohibitionists throughout the country. Never again, they thought, would they have to wage an electoral battle over the place of their reform in the Constitution. Suffragists were, if anything, more relieved. Not only did *Hawke* remove the specter of referendums upsetting state ratifications, but also it brightened the situation in Tennessee. The Tennessee constitution required that its legislature stand for election before ratifying any amendment submitted by Congress. As with the Ohio referendum provision, the requirement was designed to provide the public with a voice in constitutional decisions. Tennessee governor Albert H. Roberts had declined to call a special session of the legislature to provide the suffragists with their desperately sought thirty-sixth ratification, believing that he must await the 1920 election. When the Supreme Court declared flatly that the federal, not the state, Constitution controlled the method of amendment, Roberts summoned the legislature to complete action on the Nineteenth Amendment.[13]

Regardless of logic and legal soundness, *Hawke v. Smith* left a large and lasting impression that the Article V amending process denied democratic choice in the case of national prohibition. The disparity between the lopsided legislative action and the contrary, albeit close, popular vote in Ohio raised questions about the validity of other legislative ratifications. Earlier referendums in other states for the most part approving state prohibition were generally overlooked. Instead, the disallowed 1919 Ohio referendum, the only specific test of national prohibition's public acceptability, became a cause of resentment. Ignored as well was the fact that the Eighteenth Amendment had been ratified by the same procedure used for all previous constitutional changes.

The *New York Times,* no enthusiast for referendums, called the *Hawke v. Smith* decision a "shocking" failure to represent the will of the people of Ohio. The *Times* believed that "if the principles laid down in this decision and their application in this particular case had been present in the minds of the members of the Convention and of the people 130 years ago, the Constitution itself would not have been ratified."[14] Substituting wry humor for outrage, Will Rogers observed, "Ohio was voted wet by the people and dry by their misrepresentatives."[15] Not to be outdone, H. L. Mencken later commented, "A free people, asked to give up their ancient liberties, ought to have a fair chance to say yes or no, and not be rooked of them by a process suggesting that whereby a three-card monte man operates upon the husbandmen at a county fair."[16]

A week after announcing its *Hawke v. Smith* decision, the Supreme Court commented further on the amending process. The *National Prohibition Cases* consolidated seven challenges to the Eighteenth Amendment; two concentrated on Article V. The array of legal counsel arguing these cases included two dozen state attorneys general and, by one scholarly estimate, was the most notable since the 1866 *Milligan* case.[17] The Court scheduled an extraordinary five days for oral argument.

Rhode Island attorney general Herbert A. Rice began by arguing that the Eighteenth Amendment invaded the sovereignty of his nonratifying state in a manner not intended by Article V. The amending power, he contended, was not a substantive power but merely a precautionary safeguard to ensure the intended ends of the Constitution against oversights and errors in its creation. To Rice, amendment ought to be limited to the remedy of error in the document itself. The first ten amendments were adopted, for instance, to correct flaws in the original instrument to which Rhode Island had been sensitive. The ten ensured against encroachment upon state functions and individual rights. If amending power was construed as allowing any type of change, novelties subversive of fundamental principles could be introduced in the guise of amendments. Boundaries between federal and state authority could be shifted at will. The people of a state would be at the mercy of others in matters of political institutions and personal rights. New Jersey attorney general Thomas F. McCran followed up along the same lines, stressing that the Tenth Amendment reserved all unenumerated powers to the states and to the people. The right to surrender such rights and powers, McCran contended, belonged exclusively to the sovereign people and not to their legislative representatives.[18]

Elihu Root, the former secretary of war, secretary of state, and senator from New York, carried the argument further. He declared the Eighteenth Amendment unconstitutional. The substantive portion of the so-called amendment did not relate to the structure or authority of government, as constitutional provisions ordinarily do, he contended. Instead of empowering Congress to prohibit the use of intoxicating liquor, the amendment required such a prohibition. That made it a direct act of legislation, one whose repeal could perpetually be prevented by a minority since it could be accomplished only by passage of another constitutional amendment with its supermajority requirements. Root denied that Article V authorized amendment to thwart the democratic process. Furthermore, he contended, the Eighteenth Amendment would subvert the federal system by directly invading the police powers of the states and encroaching upon local self-government. The states would no longer be indestructible if this amendment were upheld. "Your Honors will have discovered a new legislative authority hitherto unknown to the Constitution and quite untrammelled by any of its limitations," Root perorated ominously; "In that case, Your Honors, John Marshall need never have sat upon that bench."[19]

Reviewing the *National Prohibition Cases,* law professor William F. Dodd scoffed, "The briefs presented against the validity of the Eighteenth Amendment are addressed more to what the opposing interests thought ought to be, than to any issue which may properly be termed legal in character."[20] Even Root's equally conservative co-counsel William D. Guthrie, who had successfully argued *Pollock v. Farmers Loan and Trust* in 1895, thought the argument weak.[21] So too did the Supreme Court. On June 7, 1920, it unanimously upheld the Eighteenth Amendment against all claims.

The Court, no doubt aware that nearly every state except Rice's Rhode Island and McCran's New Jersey had already ratified national prohibition, accepted both the substance of the amendment and the method by which it had been adopted. Although they differed on the meaning of concurrent power of enforcement, the justices let stand the government's assertion that the prohibition embodied in the amendment was constitutional. The solicitor general had told the Court, "It has always been understood that there is no limitation upon the character of amendments which may be adopted, except such limitations as are imposed by Article V itself." Furthermore, he continued, "The fact that the Eighteenth Amendment confers upon Congress a power which had previously belonged exclusively to the States does not prevent that Amendment from being within the amending power conferred by Article V of the Constitution. . . . Many of the amendments heretofore adopted have taken away from the States powers previously reserved to them."[22]

A further challenge to the Eighteenth Amendment centered on its seven-year ratification time limit. A convicted bootlegger's suit argued that without the time limit, Congress would not have adopted the amendment resolution. The seven-year limit in turn increased pressure for immediate ratification and "tended to destroy any deliberation by the States." The very speed with which they approved the amendment underscored the fact that some states acted without awaiting the election of legislators chosen by voters aware of the proposal. The Supreme Court, however, found nothing in Article V or the records of the 1787 convention to prohibit time limits on ratification. Justice Willis Van Devanter indicated that linking in time amendment proposals and their ratification, "succeeding steps in a single endeavor," might be wise. State actions of ratification ought to be "sufficiently contemporaneous . . . to reflect the will of the people in all sections at relatively the same period." Nevertheless, the justice wrote in *Dillon v. Gloss,* judging what was "sufficiently contemporaneous" remained an open question and a political rather than a judicial one at that. He noted that four amendments proposed by Congress without a ratification time limit, two in 1789, one in 1810, and one in 1861, were still pending and might someday still receive enough state endorsements to gain three-fourths. Few people, Van Devanter thought, would find such amendments tenable. He did not indicate what should be done in the unlikely situation that one was ratified, an event that, however implausible, did occur seventy years later. Van Devanter contented himself with finding a seven-year time limit reasonable.[23]

Other aspects of the ratification process came under scrutiny soon afterward in an objection to the Nineteenth Amendment. On behalf of the Maryland League for State Defense and the American Constitutional League, allies of the National Association Opposed to Woman Suffrage, Oscar Leser sued Baltimore's voting registrar to block the enrollment of women voters. Unsuccessful in state courts, *Leser v. Garnett* came before the Supreme Court on the grounds that the constitution of Maryland limited the suffrage to males. Since Maryland had not ratified the Nineteenth Amendment, the plaintiffs argued, it should be exempt from federal woman suffrage. Attorney William L. Marbury contended that the Constitution established, in Lincoln's words, "an indestructible Union of indestructible States" and that therefore no amendment that destroyed a state could be forced upon it without its consent. An amendment that so substantially altered the electorate in effect destroyed the original state and created a new one.[24] Marbury, an unrelenting reactionary and states' rights advocate, had cast the same argument in racial terms in 1915 when he unsuccessfully attempted to overturn the Fifteenth Amendment.[25] Writing for a unanimous Court, Justice Brandeis, who had long since abandoned the antisuffrage position, found no merit whatsoever in Marbury's argument. He accepted the comparison of the Nineteenth Amendment to the Fifteenth; both expanded the suffrage and were rejected by several states, including Maryland. "One cannot be valid and the other invalid," said Brandeis, and the validity of the Fifteenth had been "recognized and acted upon for a half century." In response to Leser's claims that state rules of procedure had been violated, the justice added that official state notices of ratification were binding upon the U.S. secretary of state and, in turn, his proclamation that the amendment was in effect conclusively settled the issue of its validity.[26]

Leser v. Garnett forcefully reasserted the Court's *Hawke v. Smith* ruling twenty-one months earlier that states did not control the terms of amendment ratification. *Leser,* like *Dillon,* dealt with a narrow issue, but *Hawke* stated the terms of Article V in a broad fashion. *Hawke* stirred, in some minds at least, an image of an amending process beyond citizen control. It became the principle justification for complaints that something was wrong with the amending system and needed to be changed.

LIMITED AND LARGELY INCONSEQUENTIAL discussions of altering Article V had taken place long before the 1920s. When it ratified the Constitution in 1790, Rhode Island proposed that amendments require the approval of eleven of the original thirteen states. In 1826 a Maine congressman, unhappy with a deluge of schemes to change the presidential election system following the 1824 Adams-Clay-Crawford-Jackson debacle, suggested that amendments be considered only every tenth year. The Civil War brought a variety of propositions to require direct popular approval of amendments as well as to reduce or eliminate the supermajorities for proposing and ratifying them.[27]

Progressive reformers early in the twentieth century brought forth a host of ideas to render amendment easier and more reflective of the preferences of simple majorities in Congress and the states. The most notable of these was undoubtedly Senator Robert La Follette's, which allowed amendments to be proposed either by a majority of both houses of Congress, state legislatures, or presidential electors from ten states. Ratification would depend upon popular majorities in a majority of states. Throughout, majoritarianism was the crucial element. The La Follette plan became a plank in the 1912 Progressive party platform but, along with other progressive proposals, faded in popularity with the progress of the Sixteenth and Seventeenth Amendments. Reintroduced by Oklahoma senator Robert Owen in 1919, it provoked little interest at a time when the Eighteenth and Nineteenth Amendments were winning adoption.[28]

La Follette himself gradually became more concerned with judicial ability to thwart progressive reform. In 1922 he began advocating an amendment to permit Congress by a two-thirds vote to override the Court and readopt legislation. La Follette's proposal became a conspicuous feature of his 1924 presidential campaign.[29] Prominent constitutional scholar Charles Warren worried that the senator's plan would fundamentally alter U.S. constitutional arrangements. Congress could, by a two-thirds vote, ignore Court rulings and set constitutional terms with no need for state ratification. "This plan," he warned, "makes Congress the supreme and, in the last resort, the sole power in this country. For by a twice-passed statute, Congress could alter or abolish any of the powers of the president or of the Court, granted by the Constitution; alter or destroy any of the reserved powers of the States; deprive individuals of any or all of the rights guaranteed by the Bill of Rights."[30] Any remaining progressive enthusiasm for new methods of constitutional reform withered in light of such reasoning.

In the 1920s expressions of concern about Article V tended to come not from those who feared that amendment was too difficult but from those who worried that it was too easy. The Supreme Court's interpretation of Article V troubled those who were unhappy with the Eighteenth and Nineteenth Amendments. Most notable among them was Elihu Root's successor in the U.S. Senate, aristocratic, conservative New York Republican James W. Wadsworth, Jr. Speaking out against national prohibition on grounds that such a law should not be a federal responsibility, Wadsworth was one of only ten Republican senators to vote against the amendment. He became even more vocal in criticizing the woman suffrage amendment as a violation of state sovereignty. Even after his constituents endorsed suffrage in a 1917 state referendum and the 1918 election produced a Senate alignment in favor of the amendment, he and Senator John Weeks of Massachusetts blocked requests for unanimous consent to bring it to a vote. His wife, Alice Hay Wadsworth, daughter of former secretary of state John Hay, shared and bolstered the senator's position. In July 1917, she became president of the National Association Opposed to Woman Suffrage and for the following two years proved to be one of the most vocal and influential female antisuffragists. When the suffrage amendment came before the Senate in June

1919, James Wadsworth took the floor for a final impassioned speech against its approval. "The tendencies of the day, without any question," he warned, "are traveling fast along the road which, if followed to its ultimate goal, will mean [the Constitution's] destruction or its alteration to such a degree in spirit, if not in letter, that it will be scarcely recognizable." He then cast one of only ten nonsouthern votes against the amendment resolution. Outraged prohibitionists and suffragists campaigned against him in New York in 1920, but he won reelection by nearly .5 million votes in the Republican landslide.[31]

Wadsworth's displeasure with recent amendments and others being proposed drew his attention to the amending process itself. In April 1921, shortly after the inauguration of President Warren Harding, the New York senator joined Democratic congressman Finis J. Garrett of Tennessee, another critic of woman suffrage, in proposing revision of Article V. Their declared objective was to prevent repetition of the Ohio and Tennessee debacles but their design was to add barriers to constitutional change. The Wadsworth-Garrett resolution sought to slow the process and limit the independent judgment of state legislatures by stipulating, as had the Tennessee state constitution, that the members of at least one house of ratifying legislatures be elected after Congress had proposed the amendment. Second, any state would be free to require, as Ohio had attempted to do, that ratification by its legislature be subject to confirmation by popular referendum. Finally, the Wadsworth-Garrett resolution reached back to deal with a controversy that had first arisen when the Fourteenth and Fifteenth Amendments were pending in the late 1860s and Congress refused to allow Ohio, New Jersey, and New York to withdraw ratifications. The Wadsworth-Garrett measure permitted states to change their votes until three-fourths of the states had ratified or more than one-fourth had rejected a proposed amendment.[32] Though agreeing that a case could be made for each provision of the plan and noting that its supporters called it the "back to the people amendment," one contemporary constitutional scholar found that Wadsworth-Garrett proponents hoped "to remove the constitution even farther from the control of the people by making it infinitely more difficult to amend."[33]

Senator Wadsworth and Congressman Garrett made no attempt to alter the provisions of Article V dealing with congressional or convention submission of amendments, nor did they tamper with the arrangements by which Congress might stipulate convention ratification of amendments. They were preoccupied entirely with what they declared to be undemocratic methods used in the past, especially the recent past, to ratify amendments to the Constitution. "The story of the ratification of the 18th and 19th Amendments contains so many extraordinary incidents," Wadsworth explained, "that no sane, thinking man can fail to realize the necessity for guarding the Constitution against such methods of ratifying amendments in the future."[34] Yet the Wadsworth-Garrett plan did not simply render the amending process more directly responsive to the popular will. Instead it added one more step to the process by ensuring that if a legislature took action, the electorate would have an opportunity to object.

In a 1923 Lincoln Day dinner speech to the National Republican Club, Senator Wadsworth expressed concern about the accelerating pace of constitutional change. He observed that of nineteen amendments to the Constitution, ten were virtually a part of the original document but four of the remaining nine had been adopted since 1913. The senator conveyed alarm over the number of amendments proposing "revolutionary" change in government currently before Congress, especially in light of "recent events comparatively unnoticed." Wadsworth referred in particular to the manner in which Ohio's 1919 antiprohibition referendum had been ignored. He also expressed concern that thirty-four states had acted on the federal woman suffrage proposal without the issue having been raised in an election of state legislators, thirteen contrary to recent state suffrage referendum results. Wadsworth, who earlier in his career had spoken out against direct primaries as well as woman suffrage and who continually placed faith in the judgment of leadership elites, nevertheless insisted that the people must have the power to approve or disapprove constitutional amendments. "We cannot afford," he concluded, "to have some future amendment, destructive of our whole theory of government, manipulated through the requisite number of legislatures, with the people standing helpless to prevent it."[35]

Opponents of recent constitutional reforms praised the Wadsworth-Garrett resolution before the Senate Judiciary Committee in 1923.[36] Critics, however, quickly pointed out that it offered only limited and one-sided public participation in the amendment process. Only if a legislature ratified an amendment and had previously approved a referendum system could one be called. The state's electorate could defeat an amendment, but it could not compel an inactive or hostile legislature to ratify one. Therefore, while blocking an amendment would be made easier, adoption would become even more difficult. Moved by this reasoning, the Judiciary Committee endorsed a substitute, offered by Democrat Thomas J. Walsh of Montana, that required that, in every instance, congressionally approved amendments be referred directly to the people of each state for a ratification vote. Contrary to the Wadsworth-Garrett measure, the Walsh substitute would make direct democracy an obligatory feature of constitutional amendment. Wadsworth, showing himself an obstructionist rather than a populist, grumbled that Walsh's version once again had the central government telling the states exactly what they must do.[37]

The delicate and complicated balance of factors in the amending process became even more apparent when the full Senate considered the measure. Senator Wesley L. Jones of Washington, observing that Walsh's substitute eliminated state legislatures from the consideration of amendments, offered a compromise between the Wadsworth-Garrett and Walsh plans in which legislatures would act but a binding referendum would follow. In effect the legislature's function would be merely advisory. Seen by some as an assault on legislative dignity and by others as a device to delay or even defeat an amendment, if legislatures declined to vote, the Jones compromise nevertheless provided both a legislative role and a public decision. The Senate at first agreed to substitute the Jones plan for the Judiciary Committee's proposal, 34 to 29, then reversed itself 39 to 35. Indecision led inevitably to the conclusion that it was best to do nothing; the Senate eventually voted 41 to 28 to send the entire measure back to committee.[38]

The House of Representatives followed the Senate in holding hearings on the Wadsworth-Garrett resolution but never brought any version to a determinative vote.[39] An effort by Democratic minority leader Garrett and Speaker Nicholas Longworth to rush it through during the post-1924 election session met the opposition of the League of Women Voters, the American Federation of Labor, the Women's Trade Union League, and the railroad unions, all of whom demanded open committee hearings before the full House acted. At that point the measure was set aside.[40] Changing the rules for changing the rules was either of too little interest or too fraught with peril to stir congressional action. Calls for revising Article V ended, for the most part, with James Wadsworth's defeat for reelection in 1926 and Finis Garrett's departure from the House two years later.[41] Yet the unhappiness with recent constitutional developments manifested in the battle over the Wadsworth-Garrett resolution found other means of expressions.

THE PEOPLE WHO drew encouragement from the new amendments proved to be as active as the critics. Most noteworthy were feminists who had at least partially submerged philosophical differences among themselves to seek woman suffrage. Buoyed by the adoption of the Nineteenth Amendment, they understandably kept Article V in mind as they turned their attention to other issues. No longer able to avoid or conceal fundamental discord within their own ranks, however, they set off in quite different directions. The coalition that provided the core of support for suffrage split irrevocably once the right to vote was gained. One element embarked on an effort to protect children and the other on a quest for equal rights for women. In their divided and weakened condition, feminists in the 1920s were unable to surmount skepticism toward constitutional amendment equal to or greater than any doubts they had previously confronted.[42]

Most early-twentieth-century feminists had seen suffrage as an end in itself. It would, they believed, empower women to carry out what they perceived to be their roles as mothers, nurturers, and social consciences. The membership of the National American Woman Suffrage Association generally had no trouble reorganizing itself in 1920 into the League of Women Voters for work within the traditional political and social system. Those who combined a traditional sense of women's role with an aggressive determination to bring their influence to bear on problems of the family, the community, the workplace, and the wider world, women since labeled social feminists, devoted a great deal of attention to maternal and childhood issues. A constitutional amendment prohibiting child labor became one of their prime objectives.

Some women regarded as unacceptable persistent gender inequalities the Supreme Court sanctioned in *Muller v. Oregon* to justify protective legislation for female workers.[43] A portion of the National Woman's party believed that all legal restrictions specific to women, even if enacted with the intent of protecting them, were detrimental. These so-called radical feminists such as Alice Paul could not be content with suffrage alone. Only removal of all legal disabilities for women, they became convinced, would alleviate an uneven and destructive gender relationship. The best means to achieve this comprehensive goal, they believed on the basis of their recent experience, would be another federal constitutional amendment. In December 1923 an equal rights amendment resolution that Alice Paul drafted was introduced in Congress. A simple declaration, "Men and women shall have equal rights throughout the United States and every place subject to its jurisdiction," the amendment attracted little support at first, even among women.[44]

Equal rights advocates may have analyzed women's problems shrewdly, but they confronted enormous resistance in a society used to thinking of women in terms of confined roles and status. Indeed social feminists led the criticism, believing that women needed special legal protection. Despite its policy against publicly fighting other women's groups, the League of Women Voters so strongly opposed the equal rights amendment that it waged a concerted and vocal campaign against the proposal. Closely linked advocates of protectionism, the General Federation of Women's Clubs, the National Consumers League, the Women's Bureau of the U.S. Department of Labor, the Women's Trade Union League (WTUL), and the Young Women's Christian Association (YWCA), joined the attack. Florence Kelley of the WTUL became especially outspoken about the equal rights amendment's threat to laws affording women marital, sexual, labor, and health protection.[45] Men in general and male politicians in particular accepted the social feminist position as more congenial. Radical feminists, aware of the long struggle to achieve suffrage, did not find this initial reception daunting. They would, however, have to encourage and await fundamental changes in their society's attitudes toward women.

The social feminists made greater immediate progress with the amendment crusade in which they took a leading part, no doubt because they were dealing with a long-visible, much-discussed issue rather than a new and unconventional concept. Ever since the great increase in industrialization during the nineteenth century, observers had lamented and fought the employment of women and especially that of children as machine tenders for long hours at low wages under dreary and dangerous factory conditions. *Muller v. Oregon,* which equal rights advocates regarded with such disdain, represented a great victory in the campaign to protect women and children. The *Muller* decision helped lead reformers to focus attention on southern textile mills, the most visible and notorious employers of children, although nine-tenths of the 280,000 industrially employed children counted in the 1900 census lived elsewhere.[46]

A long reform crusade produced the first federal child labor law, the Owen-Keating Act, in August 1916. It prohibited interstate shipment of goods produced by children under fourteen years of age and those between fourteen and sixteen who worked more than eight hours a day or forty hours per week. Hailed as a great progressive achievement, the Owen-Keating law was immediately challenged in the courts by southern textile manufacturers. In June 1918 the Supreme Court in a controversial 5 to 4 decision declared the law an unconstitutional extension of Congress's authority over interstate commerce and an interference with state power to regulate manufacturing.[47]

The National Child Labor Committee (NCLC), unprepared for the Court's *Hammer v. Dagenhart* decision, likened it to *Dred Scott v. Sandford* or *Pollock v. Farmers Loan and Trust.* As had been done in those cases and as some child labor reformers already advocated, the committee immediately considered seeking a constitutional amendment. In 1913 the Massachusetts legislature petitioned Congress to initiate such an amendment, and two of the state's representatives, James Michael Curley and John J. Rogers, introduced resolutions for one. Upon reflection, however, the NCLC decided constitutional change was unnecessary. A new legislative approach, one based on congressional authority to tax rather than to regulate commerce, could be achieved more simply, quickly, and certainly. Whether this cautious choice was wise at a time when congressional support for child labor restriction was overwhelming and when other amendments were winning prompt ratification has been questioned.[48]

Before year's end Congress approved a 10 percent profits tax on employers of child labor. This time it took textile manufacturers longer to mount a successful judicial challenge, but, aided by U.S. solicitor general James M. Beck's unenthusiastic defense of the measure, they eventually won again. In May 1922 the Supreme Court held in the case of *Bailey v. Drexel Furniture* that the tax was only nominally a revenue measure but fundamentally an effort to restrain commerce, thus again unconstitutional.[49]

After their second Supreme Court defeat, advocates of federal child labor reform lacked any practical alternative to a constitutional amendment.[50] Despite strong congressional support and endorsements from presidents Wilson and Harding, the Court had twice deemed child labor restriction beyond the limits of federal authority. Article V offered the most straightforward means of overcoming judicial review. Predictably, congressmen began offering amendment resolutions within days of the *Bailey v. Drexel Furniture* decision. The House first held hearings on such proposals in January 1923, but Congress adjourned before reaching agreement on the wording of an amendment.[51]

With a few exceptions, members of the NCLC board favored seeking an amendment. However, they were at first uncertain about its phrasing. Florence Kelley, the National Consumers League representative on the board, became its strongest proponent of immediate action to give Congress broad power to legislate in the area of child labor. When sympathetic groups tried to work out differences, her inflexibility and impatience led her to see every attempt at compromise or delay to broaden support as a sellout. Kelley worried particularly that efforts to defuse states' rights opposition would weaken an amendment. She resisted language granting concurrent state and federal power to legislate. Although concurrent enforcement had been specified in the Eighteenth Amendment, the Supreme Court had left its meaning somewhat uncertain in the *National Prohibition Cases*. The NCLC thought concurrent power specification essential to building state support and obtaining ratification, but Kelley remained doubtful. Debate also swirled around the question of the age limit for child protection, with the more cautious favoring sixteen and Kelley advocating eighteen.

After more than a year of discussion, the need to put a resolution before Congress that could be dealt with before the 1924 election led to a settlement. The NCLC-endorsed amendment authorized Congress "to limit, regulate and prohibit the labor of persons under eighteen years of age." The term "labor" was used instead of "employment" in order to prevent maneuvers to evade the law by not paying direct cash wages. A political gesture to reassure states was contained in a second section declaring that "the power of the several States is unimpaired by the article except that the operation of State laws shall be suspended to the extent necessary to give effect to legislation enacted by the Congress." Florence Kelley's influence was reflected in the eighteen-year age limit, the absence of the term "concurrent," and language that permitted states to establish higher standards.[52]

Once the NCLC coalition agreed on resolution language with two influential senators, Pennsylvania Republican George Wharton Pepper and Montana Democrat Thomas J. Walsh, their many supporters in Congress moved quickly to approve it. Social feminists from the YWCA, the General Federation of Women's Clubs, and the American Association of University Women, as well as the Women's Trade Union League and the National Consumers League were well received when they presented their case to Congress. The amendment drew a broad spectrum of support, ranging from conservative Massachusetts Republican senator Henry Cabot Lodge to liberal Republican secretary of commerce Herbert Hoover to Wilsonian cabinet member Newton D. Baker to Progressive senator Robert La Follette.[53] James Wadsworth, one of the few dissenters, told the Senate that it represented a step toward "establishing here at Washington an imperial government whose territory will be divided into what might be termed provinces, instead of what we have known as sovereign States. We are whittling at the structure established by the fathers." Ignoring such forecasts, dismissing 58 to 22 Delaware senator Thomas F. Bayard's proposal for use of the Article V provision for state convention ratification, and rejecting time limits on ratification, the Senate on the evening of June 2 adopted the child labor amendment resolution 61 to 23. Five weeks earlier on April 26, 1924, the House of Representatives had overwhelmingly endorsed it 297 to 69.[54]

Florence Kelley confidently assumed prompt state ratification, as had been the case with recent amendments after long battles on Capitol Hill. Her lament was that few state legislatures were meeting in 1924, thus delaying ratification by the necessary three-fourths until 1925. That meant that no federal implementing legislation could be expected before 1926.[55] Though some of Kelley's NCLC colleagues were less sanguine, neither they nor she had prepared for the ratification battle that awaited them. Indeed, three-and-a-half months would pass before groups supporting the amendment assembled to discuss a unified ratification campaign. Since the amendment's merits seemed so self-evident, they assumed that opposition would give way as soon as misunderstandings and false impressions were corrected. Planning only modest activities and a limited budget, they clearly were not prepared for the resistance beginning to surface.[56]

Opposition to the child labor amendment varied from state to state and region to region. Industrialists' groups such as the National Association of Manufacturers often provided leadership. Southern textile manufacturers, led by *Southern Textile Bulletin* editor David Clark, had mounted the two successful court challenges to federal legislation. Newspaper publishers, employers of young boys for sales and delivery, joined in the attack. Farmers' organizations, in particular the American Farm Bureau Federation but also the Grange and various farm journals, became vociferous critics. Also important were veterans of the battles against the Eighteenth and Nineteenth Amendment, such as the National Association Opposed to Woman Suffrage, now calling itself the Woman Patriots, and the American Constitutional League. Everett P. Wheeler of the latter group joined with other prominent constitutional conservatives including former Treasury secretary Louis A. Coolidge of Boston, Columbia University president Nicholas Murray Butler, William L. Marbury, Oscar Leser, James and Alice Wadsworth, and others in a new organization, the Sentinels of the Republic, to fight further constitutional amendment.[57]

The Sentinels of the Republic, who looked back unhappily at every amendment from the Fourteenth onward, regarded the child labor amendment as a reprehensible violation of local self-government. "The Amendment seeks to transfer to Federal control the domestic relations between parents and their children—a matter peculiarly and exclusively within the jurisdiction of the 48 separate States," the Sentinels charged. Furthermore, it "set up a *National* standard as to the work which minors under the age of 18 years may do—and to subject every State to that standard regardless of the varying conditions of agriculture, industry and education,—the differences of sentiment and development prevailing in those 48 States." They worried about "another constantly expanding bureau to the many already existing in Washington" and "a new swarm of federal inspectors" to add to "the thousands of such Federal inquisitors already buzzing into and out of their homes and offices to the injury of their family life and the conduct of their daily vocations."[58] The Sentinels declared that the amendment was the most far-reaching ever proposed, seeking to "substitute national control, directed from Washington, for local and parental control, to bring about the nationalization of the children, and to make the child the ward of the Nation." Furthermore, it was "a highly socialistic measure—an assault against individual liberty."[59]

Several southern legislatures quickly demonstrated the unhappiness of the region's politically influential with the child labor amendment. Although Arkansas immediately ratified, both Louisiana and Georgia soundly rejected the amendment within a month of its congressional passage, and North Carolina followed suit a few weeks later. The Georgia legislature declared that the amendment "would destroy parental authority and responsibility throughout America, would give irrevocable support to a rebellion of childhood which menaces our civilization, would give Congress, not only parental authority, but all state authority over education, would destroy local self-government, would eviscerate the states and change our plan of government from a federal union to a consolidated republic and create a centralized government far removed from the power of the people." Displaying their continuing resentment against the Civil War amendments, the Georgians went so far as to characterize the child labor amendment as a reestablishment of "a system of slavery, with public ownership substituted for private ownership."[60] These southern fulminations were not as devastating to the amendment, however, as the events that occurred shortly thereafter in New England.

The Massachusetts legislature asked for an advisory referendum on the child labor amendment at the November 1924 election. Legislators, buffeted by well-organized, vocal groups on both sides of the question, had become sensitive to accumulating complaints, particularly from antiprohibitionists, that amending was being done without concern for public preference. A Sentinels of the Republic spokesman contended the legislatures could too easily be stampeded to "adopt any kind of an amendment no matter how destructive of American principles." He revived the charge that "there is grave doubt whether the 18th and 19th Amendments were sanctioned by the will of the American people."[61] Under such an assault, the Massachusetts legislature found it easy to justify a referendum.

As soon as the referendum was authorized, opponents launched a fierce attack on the child labor amendment. Supporters, they themselves later acknowledged, were slow to fight back.[62] The Sentinels and their allies claimed that the amendment would invade states' rights, produce a mass of federal laws regulating marriage, divorce, maternity, and education, and prohibit children from doing household chores. A WCTU lecturer observed, "As I met the working people, especially women, I found they had been told the most amazing things and were afraid the government was going to step in and take their children from them, that children were to be prevented from working in the home or on the farm, that no child under eighteen was to be allowed to do any thing but school work, that parents were to be deprived of the authority over their children, and much more of the same kind."[63] A speaker for the Citizens Committee to Protect Our Homes and Children, rekindling the postwar red scare, went so far as to call the amendment the keystone in the Communist program, conceived in the brain of Lenin's mistress.[64]

A month before the Massachusetts referendum, William Cardinal O'Connell directed every priest in Boston's large Roman Catholic archdiocese to warn parishioners against the amendment. O'Connell's pastoral letter accompanied a series of articles in the archdiocesan newspaper, *The Pilot,* that, among other things, charged that the amendment would "commit this country forever to the communistic system of the nationalization of her children" and "would certainly impose involuntary servitude."[65] Such attacks helped prompt two influential Irish Catholic Democrats who had previously supported the amendment, Boston mayoral candidate James Michael Curley and Senator David I. Walsh, to turn against it. Harvard University president A. Lawrence Lowell joined this powerful chorus. Amendment supporters remained on the defensive throughout the campaign, and when the votes were counted, they were on the short end of a 700,000 to 230,000 tally.[66] Faced with a three-to-one negative public verdict, the Massachusetts legislature, which as recently as February 1924 had petitioned Congress to propose a child labor amendment, declined one year later to ratify.

Another blow to prospects for ratification soon followed. New York governor Alfred E. Smith, previously an advocate of child labor reform but also a leading critic of national prohibition and the method of its adoption, called for a state referendum on the proposed amendment in his January 7, 1925, annual message to the legislature. A bitter Florence Kelley believed that Smith had abandoned his strong record on behalf of social reform because of pressure from the Catholic hierarchy. Kelley and other amendment proponents, still reeling from the Massachusetts campaign and convinced that they could not match a similar expensive campaign in New York, asked the legislature to table both the referendum proposal and the amendment itself.[67]

When New York suspended consideration of the child labor amendment, the ratification campaign ended, at least for the moment. Only three states had completed ratification; one or both houses of twenty-one state legislatures had rejected the amendment.[68] Child labor reform advocates had hoped that New York would turn the tide, but defeat rendered prospects bleak. Barring reversals, enough states had already rejected the amendment to prevent ratification. Proponents tried to put the best face on the situation by asserting that rejection was "a temporary setback, not a final defeat" and quoting Finis Garrett that although ratification of a constitutional amendment was final, rejection was not. Such bravado could not conceal their disappointment and defeat.[69] Critics of the amendment, on the other hand, breathed a sigh of relief at "the turning of the tide against the whole idea of centralizing power in the federal government."[70]

Only three more states ratified the child labor amendment during the next five years. The National Child Labor Committee, celebrating its twenty-fifth anniversary in December 1929, talked only of legislative progress. Not one word was uttered about the amendment.[71] Fear of negative public sentiment appeared crucial in the abandonment of the campaign. Reformers did not anticipate referendums moving legislatures to favor ratification. Complaints about the process that produced prohibition had clearly touched a public nerve and affected calculations of amendment opponents and supporters alike.

No DOUBT RESISTANCE to further amendment was linked to the unhappiness with national prohibition that continued to grow throughout the 1920s. A significant minority of Americans, perhaps as much as one-third of the adult population, continued to drink. Cost, risk, or unwillingness to break even a law with which they disagreed deterred others. The illegal manufacturing and distribution system that grew up to meet the demand for alcohol needed to operate in a fairly visible and widespread fashion to reach its clientele. A small federal enforcement bureau together with overburdened state and local police forces proved incapable of staunching the flow of liquor. The result was an image that national prohibition neither worked nor enjoyed broad popular support.[72]

Organized opposition to national prohibition independent of the brewing and distilling industry emerged even after Eighteenth Amendment ratification. Of the dozens of groups established, the Association Against the Prohibition Amendment (AAPA) led by retired navy captain and attorney William H. Stayton of Baltimore quickly became the strongest.[73] From the outset, the AAPA appealed to constitutional conservatism and traditions of local self-government. "The Constitution inherited from our Fathers has been amended and mutilated," an association pamphlet proclaimed. "The right to govern ourselves in local affairs—a right won by our ancestors in three generations of struggle—is ignored."[74] In 1922 Stayton told a Carnegie Hall audience, "This prohibition business is only a symptom of a disease, the desire of fanatics to meddle in the other man's affairs and to regulate the details of your lives and mine."[75] Those who joined the AAPA, including veterans of the American Constitutional League and the Sentinels of the Republic, shared Stayton's feeling that prohibition did not belong in the Constitution. One lamented, "We have indolently permitted a well-organized and enormously financed body composed of zealots, fanatics, and bigots . . . to insert a Draconian statute in the great charter of our liberties."[76]

Critics of prohibition found themselves stymied, however, by obstacles to overturning a constitutional amendment. Belief was pervasive that no amendment could ever be repealed. The supermajority support assembled to adopt it would have to evaporate nearly completely in order for a contrary supermajority to assemble, which seemed highly unlikely. "The mechanism controlling the amending power of the Federal Constitution is very much like the ratchet on a cog wheel," New York attorney Archibald Stevenson complained. Even if the twelve largest states, containing over 60 percent of the nation's population, wished to end prohibition, they faced a constitutional majority of thirty-six states. Moreover, even if a large majority of states had second thoughts, the thirteen smallest, with a combined population at the previous census of only 5 million, could prevent repeal. "The wheel may be turned conveniently in one direction, but it cannot be reversed," Stevenson concluded.[77] Civil liberties lawyer Clarence Darrow declared repeal "well-nigh inconceivable."[78] Samuel Gompers of the American Federation of Labor considered it "utterly hopeless," as did Walter Lippmann, a vociferous critic of the law.[79] The *New York Times* concluded, "The Amendment is beyond effective attack."[80]

For a time in the early 1920s, antiprohibitionists concentrated on reform of the Volstead Act to modify its strict definition of intoxicating beverages. Raising the legal alcohol content of beverages to allow beer could be achieved by legislation, they reasoned, and that would ease the impact of the Eighteenth Amendment. After fifty-nine congressmen cosponsored a bill to permit 2.75 percent alcohol-content beverages, the House held hearings in April and May 1924. The Anti-Saloon League and other prohibitionists dismissed all modification proposals as contrary to the Eighteenth Amendment rather than as legitimate steps to refine its terms.[81] They again refused to budge when the Senate held modification hearings in 1926.[82] Thereafter, modification, which the American Federation of Labor advocated and which might have led workers and others to accept prohibition of high-alcohol-content beverages, was abandoned.[83]

Disappointed hopes for modification and beliefs that amendment repeal was even more unlikely led to suggestions for another type of constitutional change: nullification. Simple nonobservance and nonenforcement of a law remaining on the books seemed to some critics of the liquor ban to offer the only escape from national prohibition. Arthur R. Hadley, president emeritus of Yale University, made the first serious nullification proposal in a 1925 *Harper's Magazine* article. Laws were observed, Hadley contended, because the vast majority of people voluntarily accepted them, not because police compelled obedience. "Conscience and public opinion enforce the laws," he argued, "the police suppress the exceptions." Voluntary law observance was essential to self-government; without it anarchy would result. Hadley saw tyranny replacing democracy when a government went beyond what public sentiment would support to adopt laws at the demand of pressure groups. When an unsatisfactory law could not be removed, the remedy lay with the people. "If any considerable number of citizens who are habitually law-abiding think that some particular statute is bad enough in itself or danger-ous enough in its indirect effects to make it worthwhile to block its enforcement, it can do so." The antebellum North ignored the fugitive slave laws while nullification persisted in the post-Reconstruction South. In the face of unwise legislation, Hadley concluded, nullification might be the only remedy. "It is the safety valve which helps a self-governing community avoid the alternative between tyranny and revolution. It reduces the tension; it gives a warning to those in authority which they disregard at their peril."[84]

Hadley's suggestion was taken up by other responsible, law-respecting, but troubled people. Walter Lippmann, for example, thought nullification of-fered a way out of an impossible situation in which a majority opposed but could not repeal a law. "This is a normal and traditional American method of circumventing the inflexibility of the Constitution," he declared. "When the Constitution has come into conflict with the living needs of the nation, and when amendment was impossible, the method of changing the Constitu-tion has been to change it and then get the very human Supreme Court to sanction it." The majority will of the South had, with judicial acquiescence, effectively nullified the Fourteenth and Fifteenth Amendments, Lippmann pointed out. The same could be done with prohibition.[85] Others, from pro-gressive reformers such as Clarence Darrow and Brand Whitlock to Catholic theologian John A. Ryan, joined Lippmann in distinguishing between law-breaking and orderly, principled, majoritarian nullification of a law.[86]

The tortured logic of nullificationists reflected their frustration with a disliked but apparently untouchable constitutional amendment. Lippmann, Darrow, Whitlock, and Ryan viewed law as an instrument for social better-ment. They shared a progressive faith that the adoption of laws could cause people to behave in a manner more noble than they would otherwise choose. They were not happy with the argument that only laws that reflected a social consensus were enforceable. The cynical use of the South as a model in nullifying the Fourteenth and Fifteenth Amendments was, at least for some of them, a painful admission. Nullification was a response to the dilemma created when a political situation believed to be unacceptable to a substantial majority of the people remained beyond constitutional remedy. The idea never took hold as a formal means to deal with national prohibition, although proponents continued to emerge.[87] As an individual approach, on the other hand, it appeared to have many practitioners.

The modification and nullification discussions revealed dissatisfaction with the process that had brought national prohibition about and apparently prevented its removal. Writers such as H. L. Mencken and Clarence Darrow, along with journalists and scholars, regularly reminded the public that national prohibition had been installed in the Constitution without a direct popular vote in most states and despite a hostile majority in its only direct test of public acceptability.[88] Results from seventeen state referendums during the 1920s reinforced the image of prohibition's unpopularity. Nine of those polls, held in California, Illinois, Massachusetts, Montana, and Wisconsin, found voters opposed to continued enforcement of state laws adopted to complement the Volstead Act. Furthermore, large majorities in Illinois and New York in 1926 appealed to Congress to modify the Volstead Act, and voters in Nevada the same year, Massachusetts in 1928, and Rhode Island and Illinois in 1930 asked for the Eighteenth Amendment's repeal.[89] These polls did little to alter prohibition, but they served as reminders of the futile 1919 Ohio referendum and reinforced beliefs that prohibition existed contrary to the wishes of a majority.

In 1930 antiprohibitionists again challenged the manner of the Eighteenth Amendment's ratification. Ten years earlier in *Hawke v. Smith* and the *National Prohibition Cases,* the Supreme Court had not answered every query about amending procedure. At that time, several constitutional scholars questioned the relationship between the amending process and the sovereign power of the people. Could Article V be used to take legislative or political functions away from states without the direct assent of the people? If so, they argued, amendments approved by legislative majorities in three-fourths of the states but not by the people could destroy state government.[90] After the Supreme Court failed to deal with these issues, they faded for the time being.

Late in 1927 the New York County Lawyers' Association had begun to reexamine the constitutionality of the Eighteenth Amendment. In March 1930 an association committee released a report by one of its members, Selden Bacon, contending that the Tenth Amendment limited Article V by reserving powers not delegated or prohibited to the federal government "to the states respectively, or to the people." This meant, Bacon said, that the choice of amendment ratification methods—state legislatures or conventions of the people—ought to be determined not by congressional whim but on the basis of whether the proposal affected the functions of the state or the rights and powers of citizens. Unlimited amending power, Bacon said, permitted two-thirds of Congress and majorities of the legislatures in three-fourths of the states to wipe out all individual rights protected by the first eight amendments. When adopted, those amendments were assumed to be beyond federal usurpation. Only the people themselves had authority to surrender them. Yet the Supreme Court had ruled in *Hawke v. Smith* that a legislature's ratification of an amendment was a federal function, not subject to any limitation imposed by the people of a state. If so, concluded Bacon, all rights guaranteed the individual could be voted away without citizen consent by people exercising federal functions. The Founders had clearly not intended this. Bacon's dire hypothesis assumed that a large majority of Congress and the states would endorse the destruction of existing constitutional terms contrary to popular interest and desire, a logical leap of some distance but one in keeping with the constitutional pessimism he shared with other critics of the Eighteenth Amendment.

Bacon pointed out that conventions, not state legislatures, had ratified the original Constitution. This demonstrated, he argued, that the Founders recognized that authority lay with the people. Concern with limiting the powers of the federal government over the individual led to the adoption of the first ten amendments. The Ninth Amendment sought to prevent the informal extension of federal powers. The Tenth Amendment was designed to block their extension through constitutional amendment. Ratification of amendments by state legislatures was appropriate only when merely the rights of the states themselves were involved; popularly elected constitutional conventions were necessary when individual rights were affected. Bacon concluded that the Eighteenth Amendment, since it involved individual rights, had been improperly ratified.[91]

The committee issuing Bacon's report urged that the issue be presented to the Supreme Court in a test case, but the Lawyers' Association took no action. Selden Bacon, however, also belonged to the Association Against the Prohibition Amendment. That organization enthusiastically supported him, quickly printing and distributing 250,000 copies of his report in pamphlet form. Within a few months, Bacon and several colleagues appeared in federal district court in Newark, New Jersey, on behalf of William Sprague, who had been caught transporting beer in clear violation of the prohibition law.[92]

On December 16, 1930, federal judge William Clark startled the nation by declaring the Eighteenth Amendment void. It had not been properly ratified by the convention method, Clark said. Therefore he ordered the indictment of William Sprague quashed. The young judge possessed a reputation for independence. Advised by Princeton professor Edward S. Corwin, he did not employ the same reasoning as Bacon. Instead of relying on the Tenth Amendment, Clark resorted to historical and theoretical claims of principles of local self-government and popular sovereignty. These required, he held, that when amendments transferring powers reserved to the states or the people were being considered, the method of ratification that most directly represented the people must be used. A constitutional convention, elected on the basis of one issue and devoting its deliberations entirely to that question, was satisfactorily representative. The members of a state legislature, elected on a variety of issues, perhaps not even including the proposed amendment, did not necessarily reflect the popular will regarding such an amendment and, therefore, were not competent to act for the people in such a matter.[93] The morning after it was announced, Clark's decision merited a four-column, page-one story in the *New York Times,* and his lengthy opinion was printed in its entirety.[94]

Although elated antiprohibitionists hailed Judge Clark's decision, a unanimous Supreme Court took only ten weeks to reverse it. Not wishing to leave an important constitutional provision in limbo, the Court heard arguments on January 21, 1931, and issued its opinion on February 24. The justices completely rejected Clark's argument and Bacon's as well. Justice Owen Roberts's opinion scolded Clark for abandoning accepted judicial practices and "resorting to 'political science' and 'political thought' of the times." Congress's right under Article V to choose the method of amendment ratification was unqualified, Roberts wrote. Neither the Tenth Amendment nor a reasonable interpretation of Article V placed any limitation on the amending power. The Eighteenth Amendment had been legally adopted, the Supreme Court once again emphatically proclaimed.[95]

"Even if this opinion meets with a cold reception in the appellate courts," wrote Judge Clark in clear anticipation of the Supreme Court's response to his decision, "we hope that it will at least have the effect of focusing the country's thought upon the neglected method of considering constitutional amendments in conventions."[96] Selden Bacon believed that Clark "has so widely advertised the subject that almost any lawyer now who can get a copy of it will really study our brief."[97] Together Clark and Bacon drew new attention to the significance of the method by which amendments were ratified and did so in a far more effective fashion than the scholars who had advocated convention ratification in legal journals.[98] Bacon and his allies may not have presented a persuasive case to the Supreme Court that the Eighteenth Amendment was fatally flawed, but they did point out an available remedy to those who found *Hawke v. Smith* troubling. In the nearly century and a half since state conventions adopted the Constitution, only the legislative method of ratification had been used. *United States v. Sprague* served as a reminder that the Article V provision for ratification of amendments by elected state conventions was available as a form of referendum. As such, *Sprague* provided a fitting conclusion to a decade of scrutiny of Article V, especially by those critics wary of the ways it had been put to use and proposals for its further employment.

THE PECULIAR CIRCUMSTANCES of the Eighteenth and Nineteenth Amendments helped shape a notion that direct popular participation in the amending process was more than a means of determining the sovereign people's constitutional preference. The *Hawke v. Smith* case sowed the idea that popular referendum represented a means to block amendments. The proreferendum arguments of amendment critics such as James Wadsworth reinforced this viewpoint, as did the Massachusetts and New York episodes in the child labor amendment campaign.

More than a touch of irony could be found in evolving attitudes about constitutional amendment during the 1920s. Conservatives came to argue that an amendment's validation required direct popular participation in its approval. Meanwhile, progressive reformers, usually the advocates of participatory democracy, grew leery of its application to the amendment process. Constitutional referendums became popular with conservatives and developed a bad reputation in reform circles because of their association with antiamendment crusades over liquor, woman suffrage, and child labor. Article V's supermajority requirements, giving great influence over ratification to well-located national minorities, affected thinking on both sides. The discussions of the 1920s, followed by an actual constitutional amendment referendum early in the following decade, would influence subsequent thinking about the amending process.

12

"WHERE THE PEOPLE THEMSELVES EXPRESS THEIR WILL"

Altering Established Constitutional Provisions and Practices

The national prohibition experience stirred unprecedented doubts about the wisdom of constitutional amendment and reservations about the process to change the fundamental terms of government. Throughout the 1920s the Eighteenth Amendment fostered the impression that a measure, once installed in the Constitution, became immovable. Senator Thomas Walsh confidently wrote to a Montana friend and constituent in 1926, "A sojourn of only a brief period about the corridors of the capitol would disclose that there was not the faintest ground for hope that any material alteration would be made in the law, or that the idea of repealing the amendment would be entertained at all."[1] Walsh's viewpoint was widespread, and yet two separate movements to alter existing provisions of the Constitution were already gathering momentum.

Unhappiness with the Eighteenth Amendment did not bring efforts at constitutional change to an end. Two amendments ratified within eleven months of each other in 1933 displayed the continuing vitality of the Article V mechanism. One, a superficially modest but actually quite important reform, bore little relation to the constitutional controversies of the previous decade. This so-called lame duck amendment sped up the transfer of power to newly elected presidents and legislators while it significantly reduced the potential of representatives who had been defeated for reelection to abuse authority. The other, an amendment repealing national prohibition, went to the core of the 1920s discussions. Extraordinary in substance and unparalleled in process, prohibition repeal illuminated as never before the possibilities inherent in Article V.

At the heart of both amendments lay the question of the degree to which citizens should control the legislative process. This issue always had been delicate for republican governments. The drafters of the Constitution favored choices made by indirectly elected elites well insulated from the public, but early-twentieth-century progressives preferred to put their faith in directly elected officials further checked by referendums. In the early 1930s the need to place confidence in elected representatives clashed in various ways with evidence that federal and state legislators had attended to self-interest or special pressures rather than responded to majority needs or preferences. A constitutional remedy was constructed to deal with one such problem; and the terms of Article V proved ready-made to solve another. Both problems were inherently structural, and thus it was appropriate that they be dealt with in constitutional terms.

"WITH THE EXCEPTION of Members of Congress and their families, and instructors in civics and constitutional lawyers, I do not believe there are 2 percent of the American People who know that a Member of Congress is elected one year and does not take his office until 13 months afterwards," Representative Fiorello LaGuardia observed in 1927.[2] He spoke on behalf of an amendment to the Constitution that the Senate had already approved three times but that House leaders continued to thwart. Involving subtle alterations in the calendar of government rather than dramatic political or social change, the proposed lame duck amendment was, nevertheless, a significant reform as well as one that could be dealt with only by using the Article V process.

The lame duck amendment was both necessitated and made possible, its proponents believed, by circumstances that the Founders failed to anticipate. To begin with, the Philadelphia convention could not predict when the new Constitution might be ratified and therefore could not establish a schedule for putting it into effect. The Founders could and did, however, set the annual meeting date of Congress as well as the length of terms for federal officers. Soon after completion of the necessary ratifications in summer 1788, the last Congress under the Articles of Confederation determined that the new government would begin to function on the first Wednesday in March of the following year, March 4, 1789. Thus the two-, four-, and six-year constitutional terms of representatives, presidents, and senators began on that date. The combination of starting date and constitutional requirements produced a governmental calendar that proved no hindrance at first but by the twentieth century created serious problems.

Under the calendar established in 1789, officials elected in even-numbered years commenced their terms the following March. Most states soon settled on the first Tuesday after the first Monday in November for federal elections, believing that in the four months before new terms of office were to begin, presidential electors would have ample time to make their choice as would state legislatures charged with selecting senators. Given the eighteenth-century pace of communications and politics, the arrangement seemed reasonable. Its wisdom appeared to be affirmed by the time needed to resolve the choice of president following the elections of 1800, 1824, and 1876, not to mention frequent state legislative difficulties in selecting senators. Such justification evaporated, however, as the electoral college became little more than a quaint device for acknowledging a popular choice and especially once the Seventeenth Amendment provided for direct election of senators as well. The changes in electoral mechanisms together with the transformation of communication and transportation by the 1910s shifted attention to the negative features of the calendar.

With Congress scheduled to meet annually on the first Monday in December, thirteen months would elapse between its election and first meeting; only eleven months remained before legislators faced another election. Presidents had often summoned special sessions, and expiring Congresses could arrange for their successors to convene early, as had been done during Reconstruction to prevent Andrew Johnson from having a free hand to act without congressional supervision. Setting an earlier annual date for Congress to meet, March 4 for instance, could have been accomplished fairly easily. Ever since 1795 members of Congress uncomfortable with the long delay between elections and the required meeting date of the new Congress had been offering amendments to revise the calendar. Others pointed out that a change in the routine starting date of congressional sessions could be achieved legislatively, without amendment.[3]

More serious than the delayed start of a Congress was its continuation beyond the next national election. Indeed, the second session of each Congress did not even begin until after its successor had been elected. It became known as the "short session" because it began on the first Monday in December and necessarily ended by March 4. In comparison, the first, or "long session" could continue indefinitely. During the short session pressure to complete actions before the term expired encouraged hasty, ill-considered adoption of bills. The short session gave minorities powerful tactical weapons of delay or filibuster to defeat legislation or to force compromise. Moreover, since the short session was not constitutionally terminated until four months after an election, officials guaranteed their full term of office continued to exercise authority from November to March even after being repudiated at the polls. Defeated officeholders, about to leave their positions, might be unusually susceptible to improper inducements. If a disputed presidential election were left to Congress to decide, the old Congress, potentially one with a discredited majority, rather than the newly elected one would select the new president and vice-president. Complicating the situation further, no constitutionally specified term of office could be shortened without an amendment.

The congressional lame duck session following the 1922 election raised awareness of this constitutional problem. Republicans, defeated for reelection and hoping for appointment to an executive or judicial position, appeared ready to curry favor with the Harding administration by voting for its merchant marine construction proposal, the "ship subsidy bill," that was highly unpopular with the public and theretofore with a majority of Congress. Outraged, Democratic senator Thaddeus Caraway of Arkansas quickly introduced a sense of the Senate resolution that members defeated for reelection should abstain from voting on all but routine, nonpolicy matters during the short session. Senators dismissively referred Caraway's resolution to the Committee on Agriculture and Forestry since it was a "lame duck" bill.[4]

Within the agriculture committee, however, progressive Nebraska Republican George W. Norris took the matter seriously. A veteran of the House of Representatives before his move to the Senate in 1913, Norris had actively supported the income tax, direct election of senators, national prohibition, and woman suffrage amendments.[5] Within a month his committee reported that the Caraway resolution would unconstitutionally restrict elected members of Congress. Instead of dropping the matter, Norris offered a constitutional amendment built on past proposals to eliminate the lame duck session, advance the commencement of congressional and presidential terms, and provide for direct election of the president. After Norris withdrew the last provision, a separate and distracting issue that threatened to delay action on the main question, the Senate promptly and with little debate passed his resolution 63 to 6 on February 13, 1923. The House, however, did not consider the measure in the waning days of the session.[6]

Norris's first lame duck amendment resolution provided that congressional terms would begin the first Monday in January. The same date would be used for convening the annual meeting of Congress. Presidential terms would commence two weeks later, leaving the newly elected Congress time to resolve any disputed election. In each of the two subsequent Congresses, the Senate adopted slightly revised versions but the House again failed to bring the measure to the floor.

Senator Norris thought there was "no valid argument against the proposal."[7] He believed that, while the public focused its discontent upon the "archaic and uncivilized" continuation of defeated legislators in office "contrary to the very fundamental principle of a Republic or a Democracy," political resistance to change stemmed from other, less obvious reasons. In the short session, it was impossible for either house of Congress to consider all legislation proposed, allowing the party in power to choose what would be considered. Further, he explained,

> Every Member of Congress knows that the enactment of any particular bill is surrounded by very grave doubt if the machine is against it. As the fourth of March approaches, this tension increases its strength in a wonderful degree. Members of Congress who are trying to prevent the passage of what they believe to be obnoxious legislation, very often remain silent because they think other legislation in which they are deeply interested may stand some show if they do not take up the time of the Senate or the House in debating what is to have consideration. It therefore often happens that half-baked legislation is enacted. Jokers creep into the laws, because those who would guard the public interest are anxious to get consideration for other important legislation which Congress will not have time to consider unless expedition is made.[8]

In addition, Norris believed that presidents could improperly influence lame ducks hoping for an appointment. "Machine politicians," he concluded, "want to utilize the votes of those who have been defeated to put thru legislation that could not be put thru in any other way, and they do this by means of giving public office to the subservient ones."[9]

The lame duck amendment appeared to escape the phenomenon that an American Bar Association (ABA) spokesman described to a 1926 House hearing: "Constitutional amendment is becoming unpopular in the United States, apparently. We are all aware that the child-labor amendment has failed in the States, due, I am informed, to a growing feeling among the States that too much changing of the Constitution of the United States is dangerous." A lame duck amendment, something the ABA had endorsed for eleven years, possessed a different character, he pointed out. This amendment dealt only with the operation of the federal government without extending its powers. The public did not understand the technical reasons why an amendment was necessary to accomplish this reform, but lawyers who did, he assured the House, considered it vital.[10]

After January 1928 when the Senate approved a lame duck amendment for the fourth time, House leaders began to confirm Norris's assessment of their objections. The bill that emerged from the House Elections Committee provided that, while annual sessions of Congress should all begin on January 4, in election years they should end on May 4; thus the short session with its fixed termination date would be preserved. House leaders were willing to abandon the post-election lame duck session but clearly wanted to retain tactical opportunities inherent in the short legislative session.

When the full House of Representatives discussed the lame duck amendment for the first time in March 1928, every one of its complicated features was considered at length. Recent thinking about the amending process in general also entered into the debate. Congressman Henry St. George Tucker of Virginia gained considerable support when he sought to have the amendment referred to state conventions for ratification. His motion was narrowly defeated 90 to 107. Shortly thereafter, Finis Garrett proposed a seven-year time limit on ratification and a requirement that at least one branch of ratifying legislatures be elected subsequent to the amendment's submission to the states. Garrett's motion, less a device to ensure direct democracy than a continuation of the earlier Wadsworth-Garrett effort to render amendment more difficult, received overwhelming House endorsement 187 to 23. Nevertheless, on final passage, the revised lame duck amendment obtained only 209 aye votes to 157 nays, well short of the needed two-thirds, and died once again.[11] A House Republican told Norris that the leadership had not even allowed the amendment to be discussed until they obtained enough pledged votes to ensure its defeat. The frustrated Norris, who found the existing calendar "absolutely indefensible," thought the House "silly to make the argument that we ought not make any change because the Constitution is sacred and we cannot improve upon the work of our fathers."[12]

In the next Congress, House Speaker Nicholas Longworth held up referring Norris's proposal to committee for nearly a year after the Senate gave its usual strong endorsement to it. Then on February 24, 1931, the about-to-adjourn Republican-dominated House finally adopted a lame duck amendment. However, this measure, a substitute introduced by Speaker Longworth, was almost identical to the previous House resolution providing a short session ending on May 4 in even-numbered years.[13] "By such a provision the biennial threat of a filibuster which now occurs just before March 4 would merely be shifted to the beginning of May," observed the *Cleveland Plain Dealer*. "Better postpone the Norris resolution again—after its many postponements—than pass it with the Longworth amendment."[14] When a conference committee was unable to resolve differences between the Norris and Longworth versions, the measure died for the fifth time.

The congressional tide turned after the 1930 elections when, for the first time since 1916, the Democrats obtained a majority in the House of Representatives. Liberals lamented a system that allowed President Hoover to avoid confronting the new Congress until December 1931. Meanwhile Norris hoped in vain that the Republican defeat might cause Longworth to have a change of heart.[15] The new Speaker, John Nance Garner of Texas, favored Norris's amendment, however. As usual, the Senate acted first, adopting the measure 63 to 7 on January 6, 1932, after Senator Bingham could muster only 18 votes to substitute the Longworth version. Garner promptly brought it before the House. The opposition, never able to mount principled objections, found itself reduced to complaining about wasting time on such matters in the midst of a serious depression. A New York congressman grumbled that the amendment had been "conceived by crackaloos, propagated by crackpots, and supported by thoughtless demagogues." Nevertheless, the House embraced the Norris amendment 336 to 56 on March 2.[16]

As finally approved, the Twentieth Amendment provided that congressional terms would begin on January 3 following an election and presidential terms on January 20. Congress would meet annually on January 3 unless it appointed a different day. Qualms about being compelled to convene on Sunday two or three times each century had been expressed in the course of congressional debate, leading to the addition of the device to alter the meeting date. Complicated provisions were made for presidential succession in the event of death between election and inauguration. A seven-year time limit on ratification, virtually identical to the one in the Eighteenth Amendment, was included.

Senator Norris made no effort to prepare the way for state ratification by communicating with governors or others.[17] Nevertheless, nine states ratified within thirty days. Eight more did so during the rest of the year. When newly elected legislatures, believing that they carried a mandate from the electorate, convened in 1933, they promptly completed action. Seventeen states approved within the first three weeks of January. Then on January 23 four more added their sanction to conclude the Article V process. Six more states concurred before January came to an end, and when Florida ratified on April 26, every state had endorsed the lame duck amendment.[18] Never before had an amendment been unanimously approved on initial consideration, even in the days of a much smaller Union. To say that states welcomed the lame duck amendment would be an understatement.

Ratification of the Twentieth Amendment was completed in the midst of perhaps the most memorable lame duck session of Congress ever held. In the depression election of November 1932, eighty-one congressmen, mainly Republicans, together with President Herbert Hoover, had been turned out of office. Because Franklin Roosevelt would not be sworn in until March 4 and the new Congress with its large Democratic majority could not be convened until then, a discredited government remained in office incapable of action during the bleakest winter of the Great Depression. Lame duck votes in the House and a Huey Long filibuster in the Senate brought Congress to a near standstill. The hostile and long-drawn-out transfer of presidential power rendered the federal government almost completely powerless at a moment of national crisis. The only comparable situation had occurred between the election and inauguration of Abraham Lincoln on the eve of the Civil War. The Twentieth Amendment was completed too late to avoid the long interregnum of 1932–1933 and at the moment offered little consolation that there would never again be an equivalent episode. Yet the important consequences of even apparently minor, nonheadline-grabbing constitutional arrangements were clearly demonstrated. Ironically, the value of the amendment's least-discussed section, providing for replacement of a president or vice-president-elect who died or did not qualify to take office before inauguration, was vividly illustrated three weeks after ratification. An assassin's bullet narrowly missed Franklin Roosevelt and fatally wounded Chicago mayor Anton Cermak as the two men sat in a car in Miami. Fortunately, the amendment provision did not have to be called upon, but the chaos that would have resulted had it not been in place was obvious to all. The lame duck amendment produced fundamental change, increased the stability of presidential transitions, and, altogether, amounted to far more than a needless diversion by "crackaloos, crackpots, and thoughtless demagogues."

CONSTITUTIONAL OBJECTIONS to national prohibition loomed larger than desire for legal access to alcohol among enlistees in the organized antiprohibition movement as the 1920s wore on. Members of the Association Against the Prohibition Amendment and the Women's Organization for National Prohibition Reform expressed concern that public dissatisfaction with the Eighteenth Amendment was eroding respect for the Constitution and law in general. Furthermore, they complained, efforts to uphold prohibition damaged other constitutional principles. These objections were assuredly not the primary ones among the general public, but they were highly important to those devoting money and time to changing the law. Many members of the antiprohibition societies had earlier belonged to Everett P. Wheeler and William L. Marbury's American Constitutional League, Alice Wadsworth's National Association Opposed to Woman Suffrage, or Louis Coolidge and Alexander Lincoln's Sentinels of the Republic. James Wadsworth, involved with them all, personified the close ties among the various antiamendment organizations.

The business and social elites that William Stayton attracted to the AAPA shared his feeling of danger in the growing power of the federal government. They feared the loss of local control over what they believed to be essentially community matters, such as standards of acceptable behavior. In many cases they faced a personal loss of influence if decisionmaking shifted from the local to the national level. Some worried that increased government regulation of business would follow. They recognized, furthermore, that expanded federal activity meant larger government budgets, the burden of which would most likely fall on them. Already national prohibition had raised federal expenses and reduced revenues. Stayton reported in 1926 that a Wisconsin business group had become "tremendously interested in the question of the form of government under which they shall live. They realize that prohibition is not a real disease, but merely a symptom of a very great and deep-seated disease—the disease of plutocracy, of centralization of government from Washington in public affairs that extends now in to the home and to the dinner table."[19]

Constitutional concerns were common among the AAPA leaders whom Stayton recruited. New York investment banker Grayson M.-P. Murphy told a congressional committee in 1930 that the Eighteenth Amendment was "absolutely contrary to the spirit of the rest of the Constitution" and had "materially weakened" respect for it.[20] Pierre du Pont of Delaware, former president of General Motors and the Du Pont Corporation, saw nothing wrong with moderate drinking and was alarmed by the expansion of federal authority. His closest business associate, John J. Raskob, agreed, concluding that a lack of respect for property rights was only a short step from bolshevism.[21] Together with Stayton, Wadsworth, and others, Murphy, Du Pont, and Raskob endorsed a 1928 AAPA declaration blaming prohibition for "the distortion of our Federal Constitution by compelling it to carry the burden of a task which is an affair for the police power of each of our forty-eight separate and sovereign states, and never should be the business of the Federal Government."[22]

A series of Supreme Court decisions accounted in part for the apprehensions of the antiprohibition movement. Under the leadership of Chief Justice William Howard Taft, the Court throughout the 1920s regularly decided conflicts between various provisions of the Constitution in such a way as to bolster the Eighteenth Amendment. In 1922 the justices held that the Fifth Amendment guarantee against double jeopardy was not violated when Vito Lanza, convicted of bootlegging under a Washington State statute, subsequently faced federal prosecution for the same offense. The Eighteenth Amendment authorized such dual prosecutions by granting concurrent state and federal enforcement power.[23] In 1925, the Court permitted warrantless searches of automobiles thought to be transporting concealed alcohol. Police did not conduct an "unreasonable search and seizure," the Court ruled, because the vehicle of two Michigan men suspected but never convicted of bootlegging could otherwise depart before a warrant was obtained.[24] Finally, the Court upheld the conviction of a Seattle bootlegger on the basis of evidence obtained by wiretapping his telephone. Likening the wiretap at telephone company headquarters to overhearing a public conversation, the justices ruled that no search violating the Fourth Amendment had occurred. Neither was the Fifth Amendment protection against self-incrimination infringed since the defendant had been speaking voluntarily when overheard.[25] Each of these judicial decisions increased apprehensions that prohibition enforcement had far-reaching negative consequences for constitutionally protected rights.[26]

Spreading signs of public unhappiness with national prohibition and increasing problems with its enforcement led President Herbert Hoover, shortly after his inauguration in March 1929, to appoint a national commission to study the law. Hoover had supported national prohibition during his tenure as secretary of commerce under Warren Harding and Calvin Coolidge. He defended it as "a great social and economic experiment, noble in motive and far-reaching in purpose" during his 1928 campaign for the presidency against antiprohibitionist Democrat Alfred E. Smith. In his inaugural address, Hoover called for compliance with prohibition to avoid the "most malign" danger of undermining respect for all law. His National Commission on Law Observance and Enforcement reflected his engineering background and progressive mentality. Thoughtful examination of a problem by a panel of experts should produce realistic plans for appropriate solutions. Hoover assumed that the Eighteenth Amendment was an unshakable reality and chose his commissioners, starting with former attorney general George W. Wickersham as chairman, for their ability to find ways of securing compliance with it. The Wickersham Commission spent twenty months collecting testimony, conducting studies, and otherwise carrying out its mandate for a thorough investigation of national prohibition.

When the Wickersham Commission completed its work in January 1932, Hoover characterized its summary recommendations as supportive of national prohibition. Once the commission's full 162-page report became public, however, a close reading revealed that the commissioners agreed that prohibition was not working well. Furthermore, nine of the eleven perceived a lack of public support for the law, most found the current system unworkable or unwise, six wanted immediate modification, and two favored outright repeal. Indeed, five commissioners endorsed establishment of a Swedish-style, government-regulated liquor monopoly, and two others favored such a solution if further trial of prohibition proved unsuccessful. In other words, a majority of the Wickersham Commission was either ready to abandon the Eighteenth Amendment or close to it. Only one commissioner remained an unequivocal supporter of continued national prohibition.[27]

One striking judgment of the Wickersham Commission bore directly upon the amending process. Prohibition enforcement difficulties, the commission report concluded, stemmed in part from the manner of the law's adoption. Rather than referring to the *Hawke v. Smith* dispute, the report observed that ratifying legislatures had not been elected on the basis of the alcohol issue. Furthermore, many of those bodies were malapportioned and over-represented rural voters. In addition, they were chosen while many voters were absent for military service. Thus, legislatures exaggerated prohibitionist sentiment. "These circumstances gave grounds for resentment which has been reflected in the public attitude toward the law and has thus raised additional obstacles to observance and enforcement," the report concluded. Three commissioners, including the chairman, suggested a national referendum on whether national prohibition should be continued. The device they proposed for conducting such a poll was a repeal amendment that Congress would submit for ratification to popularly elected state conventions.[28]

The Wickersham Commission report encouraged, even inspired, the antiprohibition movement. Chairman of the AAPA's executive committee, Pierre S. du Pont thought his organization could have written the body of the report. "The facts certainly track your citation of facts, and, in most cases, could not have been put in better words for our purposes," he told AAPA president Henry Curran.[29] Repeal of the Eighteenth Amendment, the declared AAPA objective, no longer seemed utterly impossible.

By the time the Wickersham Commission's report was released, the organized antiprohibition movement had become a substantial political force, though one that mainstream political leaders from Hoover to New York governor Franklin D. Roosevelt still regarded as quixotic. Captain William Stayton's initial small band had not only swelled, it had also acquired important allies, most notably the Woman's Organization for National Prohibition Reform (WONPR). Like the AAPA, it consisted largely of well-to-do social and political conservatives who regarded prohibition as less an obstacle to their life-style than as a danger to a satisfactory political order. Established in 1929 by Pauline Sabin, a former member of the Republican National Committee from New York, it eventually claimed over 1 million members and shattered the image of women as unalterably committed to the Eighteenth Amendment.[30] James Wadsworth later recalled that the WONPR "made a lot of men wake up and realize that, 'By heavens, there is a chance of getting repeal if the women are going to join with us!'"[31]

The Eighteenth Amendment became increasingly vulnerable in the early 1930s as complaints about the spreading economic depression swelled the chorus of criticism. During the 1920s prohibitionists attributed the decade's prosperity to the liquor ban. However, joblessness, agricultural surpluses, and shortages of government revenue gave an immediacy to charges that prohibition had destroyed a legitimate industry employing many workers, using a great deal of grain, and paying large taxes. Public opinion polls, crude by modern standards but providing nonelectoral measures of popular sentiment not previously available, showed growing discontent with national prohibition.[32]

Antiprohibition organizations, convinced after the Supreme Court's *Sprague* ruling that no judicial solution was likely, stepped up their political efforts. While the AAPA and WONPR membership was bipartisan, the Democratic party gave them a much warmer reception than the Republicans. Antiprohibitionist activity, therefore, became most visible within the Democratic party. As the party in power since 1921, the Republicans bore the responsibility for law enforcement and enjoyed the support of temperance groups. Democrats, on the other hand, although initially as supportive of the adoption of the Eighteenth Amendment as Republicans, had since seen their ranks swelled by urban voters, often Catholics and immigrants, who considered prohibition an attack on their culture.[33] In 1928 Democratic presidential nominee Alfred E. Smith, himself of urban, Catholic, immigrant stock, appealed to these voters with a campaign that incorporated opposition to prohibition. Smith proved anathema to conservative, dry, rural, white southern Democrats and probably had no chance anyway in a race against the well-respected Hoover in a time of prosperity, but Smith's antiprohibitionism did not go unnoticed. The 1928 election reinforced the Republican belief that retaining dry support was vital. At the same time it persuaded many advocates of repeal that the road to their goal ran through the Democratic party.

Partisan divergence on prohibition in 1928 was symbolized and subsequently shaped by Smith's choice of AAPA leader John Raskob as Democratic national chairman. Raskob retained control of the Democratic National Committee after the election, spoke out against the liquor ban, and further identified the Democrats with the repeal movement. In 1930 the Republicans, embarrassed that their own party chairman had been exposed as a well-paid lobbyist for private business interests, sought to turn the tables by publicizing Raskob's AAPA connection. The Democratic chairman boldly seized the opportunity to advocate repeal and link his party more closely with antiprohibitionism.[34] Early in 1931, when the Wickersham Commission report was released and Hoover characterized it as endorsing continued enforcement, Raskob drew attention by seeking Democratic National Committee support for an amendment allowing states to exempt themselves from national prohibition.

As partisan battles became heated, antiprohibition organizations, stirred by the *Sprague* decision and the Wickersham report, demanded that any new amendment regarding prohibition be submitted to state conventions for ratification. They argued that constitutional change should reflect public opinion and avoid repetition of the 1919 Ohio fiasco. In May 1931, Raskob asked the Democratic National Committee, "Can any patriotic citizen deny the people opportunity to vote on this important and vital question and properly call himself a Democrat?"[35]

A resolution for repeal of the Eighteenth Amendment "when ratified by conventions in three-fourths of the several states" had first been introduced in Congress in June 1926 by Senator Edward I. Edwards of New Jersey and Representative John J. Cochran of Missouri, both Democrats. Representative Patrick O'Sullivan of Connecticut had said nothing about which Article V ratification mechanism should be used when offering the first proposal for the amendment's repeal in May 1924. In any case, Congress totally ignored both.[36] It did not hold hearings on a repeal amendment until February 1930.[37] In March 1932, however, the House came close to mustering a majority for an amendment, along the lines of Raskob's proposal, permitting states to set up their own system of liquor control. For the first time, antiprohibitionists rallied enough support to force a congressional roll call on a version of repeal, and, significantly, their resolution provided for state convention ratification.[38] The following month, James Wadsworth, on behalf of the AAPA, urged a Senate Judiciary Subcommittee to submit any repeal resolution to state conventions rather than to legislatures.[39] Journals that had earlier favored a nationwide referendum on prohibition but had seen no possibility of obtaining one, now called for use of the convention ratification provision.[40]

When the national party conventions met in Chicago in June 1932, wets called upon both Republicans and Democrats to allow the people to decide the prohibition issue. Henry Curran, president of AAPA, asked each Republican delegate to declare for repeal or at least pledge to submit the question to popularly elected state conventions.[41] A similar plea to Democratic delegates came from the Women's Organization for National Prohibition Reform.[42] The drink issue stirred intense debate at both conventions. Hoover and his lieutenants felt that abandoning prohibition would be politically disastrous, but other Republicans urged repeal. The plank eventually adopted contended that prohibition was not a partisan issue and suggested that any change should be effected by submitting a new amendment to state conventions so that the people might decide the matter.[43] Wets remained unhappy over Republican insistence that the federal government should retain power to deal with "the evils inherent in the liquor trade," protect states where prohibition existed, and prevent "the return of the saloon and attendant abuses," but they had won a concession on the issue of ratification procedure that would later prove important.

The Democratic convention witnessed an even more heated contest over repeal. Party chairman John Raskob had been its advocate for years. On the other hand, the leading candidate for the party's presidential nomination, New York governor Franklin D. Roosevelt, thought it a mistake to take any position that might divide the party's wet, liberal, urban wing from its dry, conservative southern and western wing, in the process possibly costing the Democrats the election over what he regarded as a minor issue. Personal rivalry heightened the conflict between Roosevelt and Raskob, a close ally of Al Smith. A resolutions subcommittee, heavily weighted with Roosevelt supporters, drafted a plank similar to the Republican's, merely endorsing submission of the repeal question to state conventions. The full resolutions committee, however, noting the convention's warm reception to calls for repeal from Raskob and keynote speaker Alben Barkley, approved by a wide margin a strong antiprohibition plank: "We advocate the repeal of the Eighteenth Amendment. To effect such repeal we demand that Congress immediately propose a constitutional amendment to truly representative conventions in the states called to act solely on that subject." The reading of the plank to the delegates provoked a twenty-five minute demonstration, the most raucous of the convention. After a brief debate, the repeal plank was adopted 934 ¾ to 212 ¼, the most one-sided roll call of the convention.[44]

One of the most clear-cut party differences in 1932 involved the forthright Democratic call for repeal and Republican equivocation on the issue. The contrast immediately led the WONPR to endorse Roosevelt, a step the editors of *Time* magazine regarded as sufficiently noteworthy to justify putting Pauline Sabin's picture on its cover.[45] New York senator Robert Wagner subsequently observed, "These were no ordinary run-of-the-mill party planks. The attention of the entire country was riveted on each of the conventions, eagerly awaiting the formulation of its prohibition views. These declarations were thoroughly debated and the proceedings were broadcast through press and radio to the entire country." Once the parties had taken their positions, he continued, "Throughout the campaign they were minutely discussed by spokesmen for both parties. If there be any who contend that the American people did not thoroughly comprehend the issue so sharply joined on prohibition, they must ascribe to the voters a degree of incompetence which would make a democracy a farce and a byword. I do not hold that view." Wagner concluded that the electorate should be credited "with full and ripe understanding of the prohibition issue. And upon that issue they expressed their preference by giving an overwhelming victory to the Democratic candidates."[46]

On November 8 Roosevelt carried forty-two states to Hoover's six, and Democrats turned an evenly divided Congress into a 310 to 117 House majority and a 60 to 35 Senate margin. The landslide Democratic victory, no doubt due primarily to the depression, was nevertheless widely regarded as a mandate for Eighteenth Amendment repeal. Eleven state referendums on prohibition issues, all won by wets by large margins, reinforced the image of an electorate demanding repeal.[47] Pennsylvania congressman James Beck expressed the view of many House members when he declared the election results "a clear mandate to Congress to end, as soon as possible, the tragic folly of Federal prohibition."[48]

Many congressmen who previously supported national prohibition quickly reversed their position during the postelection final session of the Seventy-second Congress. On the first day, House Democratic majority leader Henry T. Rainey introduced a resolution for a new constitutional amendment to repeal the Eighteenth that Speaker (and Vice-President-elect) John Nance Garner had drafted. It fell six votes short of the two-thirds required for adoption. Only the votes of eighty-one lame duck congressmen kept the measure from passing.[49] Ironically, the very situation that the Twentieth Amendment was designed to correct arose to block another constitutional change during the last session before the lame duck amendment would take effect.

On January 9, 1933, the Senate Judiciary Committee, still in the hands of a Republican majority, reported out a repeal resolution. Drafted by Republican senator John J. Blaine of Wisconsin, this resolution followed his party's platform. It obligated the federal government to protect states against liquor imports in violation of state laws, in effect reviving the 1913 Webb-Kenyon Act. It also granted Congress concurrent power with states to forbid saloons by preventing the sale of intoxicants for consumption on the premises. The Blaine resolution provided for ratification of the proposed amendment by state legislatures. Blaine explained that over forty state legislatures were then in session, and if Congress acted promptly, the legislatures could ratify quickly. The convention method, he warned, might take four years or more and involve heavy expenses for campaigns, delegate elections, and conventions. The senator implied that repeal was inevitable and conventions unnecessary; privately he predicted that drys could more likely block repeal in them.[50]

Antiprohibition leaders disagreed with Blaine's view that ratifying conventions posed more problems than they were worth and that state legislatures could be depended upon to approve repeal. With their memories of *Hawke v. Smith, Sprague v. U.S.*, the Wickersham report, and their own strenuous efforts to persuade both parties to endorse convention ratification, they were not prepared to back down. The AAPA's new president Jouett Shouse assailed Blaine's plan as stopping short of repeal and according undue influence to rural supporters of prohibition in malapportioned state legislatures. Recalling that the victorious Democrats had campaigned for outright repeal and that both party platforms had endorsed convention ratification, Shouse in a nationwide radio address insisted that such pledges be kept.[51] Pauline Sabin meanwhile declared that the WONPR would accept nothing less than complete repeal of the Eighteenth Amendment.[52]

For more than a month, repeal efforts were stalemated, making it appear that action would have to await the new Congress. The situation changed abruptly when Senator Joseph T. Robinson, the Democrat's floor leader and formerly a staunch defender of national prohibition, decided to support repeal by state ratification conventions. Senators promptly voted 45 to 15 to provide for convention ratification. The antisaloon provision was struck down by a single vote. On the other hand, since it removed a cause for complaint and permitted local self-determination, federal enforcement of state transportation or importation restrictions was allowed to stand. These matters settled, the Senate adopted the resolution 63 to 23. Four days later on February 20, the House agreed to the Senate's language 289 to 121 and sent the amendment to the states.[53]

Never having held conventions to ratify a federal amendment, the states seemed uncertain how to proceed. Constitutional scholars disagreed as to whether Congress or the individual states legislatures had authority to set up conventions.[54] In January, the California legislature asked Congress to enact a law covering delegate selection, scheduling and conduct of elections and conventions, and payment of expenses incurred. New Mexico, on the other hand, declared that any attempt by Congress to prescribe the details governing conventions would be null and void in that state. When Congress failed to reach a consensus after much debate, observers anticipated a long delay while the Supreme Court resolved the procedural issue.[55]

Repeal advocates understood that many state legislatures then in session would not meet again for a year or more. If they adjourned without providing for conventions, repeal might be postponed by as much as two years. Fear of delay as much as certainty of state prerogatives led officials of the AAPA and the Voluntary Committee of Lawyers (VCL), a New York–based repeal association of 4,000 attorneys formed in 1927, to work feverishly through January and February to prepare a model bill that any state legislature could use to create a ratification convention.[56] Joseph H. Choate, Jr., VCL chairman and son of the successful *Pollock v. Farmers Loan and Trust* attorney, and Columbia University law professor Noel T. Dowling drafted the bill. It provided for an at-large election of convention delegates with one slate pledged to repeal and another opposed so that a referendum on prohibition could, in effect, be conducted.

Choate knew that with so many legislators eager to act and yet uncertain about procedure, the first convention system established was likely to set the terms for others. A draft plan providing for a convention delegate elected from every state assembly district, sent to him by a Milwaukee VCL member, alarmed Choate. The plan might be perfectly safe in a state such as Wisconsin that was certain to favor repeal, he believed, but it might prove disastrous in a narrowly divided state where malapportionment gave extra weight to dry rural districts. Instead, Choate sought to ensure that a statewide majority prevailed.[57] While pressing for at-large elections, Choate also prepared an alternative plan for delegate selection by legislative districts to mollify critics. And in case Congress subsequently stipulated how conventions were to operate, both VCL model bills contained an escape clause so that states could easily abandon their own arrangements.[58]

Completed only days before Congress passed the repeal resolution, the model convention bills were quickly circulated to state legislatures by AAPA and VCL representatives. Choate wrote every governor urging use of one of the model bills, preferably the at-large version. The provision of detailed plans for creating ratification conventions along with well-marshaled arguments on the right of states to go ahead rather than await congressional action reduced legislative indecision and delay to a minimum. By the time Congress approved the amendment resolution on February 20, one state had adopted and twenty-eight others were proceeding with convention legislation. By the end of the month a dozen more states were doing likewise. Congress ceased work on a state conventions bill because it no longer seemed necessary.[59] Every state but Georgia, Kansas, Louisiana, Mississippi, and North Dakota soon completed the necessary arrangements, generally along lines that the AAPA and VCL suggested.

Of the forty-three states that established conventions, thirty-nine acted within four months of the repeal amendment's submission by Congress. Twenty-five states decided to choose their convention delegates at large and fourteen by districts; four states combined the methods. Twelve followed the model bill almost exactly. At least eight others used it with some modification, and several more adapted portions. In the absence of congressional directives, the VCL measure provided guidelines with which the states felt comfortable, although in the federal tradition practically every state gave its own convention a few peculiar features.[60]

So that the election of delegates would serve as the widely desired popular referendum on prohibition, nearly every state arranged for separate slates of delegates pledged to favor or oppose amendment ratification. Eight states provided for the election of an unpledged slate as well, but only Wyoming made no mention of delegate preference, leaving its convention free to act as a truly deliberative body. Delegates in Alabama, Arkansas, and Oregon were required to vote in accordance with a referendum on the amendment to be held simultaneous to the delegate election. The surest sign that the convention was expected to reflect popular preference came from New Mexico. There, if a delegate failed to vote in accordance with the position stated on his nominating petition, he would "be guilty of a misdemeanor, his vote not considered, and his office deemed vacant."[61]

Once mechanisms were formulated, delegate selection and state conventions themselves proceeded smoothly and rapidly. Michigan, the first state to act, elected delegates on April 3, 1933, convened its convention on April 10, and in less than three-and-one-half hours ratified the amendment 99 to 1.[62] By the end of June, sixteen states had voted for delegates, with the results all favoring repeal. During July and August, eight other states did likewise, and by mid-October voters in nine additional states had cast ballots for repeal. On November 7 six more states voted and ensured the repeal of the Eighteenth Amendment when conventions met on December 5.

Nearly 21 million voters participated in repeal convention elections in thirty-seven states (Nebraska and Wyoming selected delegates in precinct-level open meetings and county conventions). Fifteen million, or 73 percent, favored repeal, and slightly more than 5.5 million, or 27 percent, opposed it. Only in South Carolina, where 52 percent rejected repeal; North Carolina, where 71 percent voted against holding a convention; and Tennessee, where repeal was approved by a mere 51 percent, was the result less than 57 percent for repeal. In most states the margin was much greater. Whatever the status of public opinion had been in 1919, this nationwide referendum made it clear that in 1933 an overwhelming majority approved the Twenty-first Amendment.[63]

The conventions proved to be brief, nondeliberative affairs merely to confirm the voters' decisions. None lasted more than a day, and in the New England tradition of few wasted words, New Hampshire managed to conduct its proceedings in seventeen minutes. In only eight of the conventions that approved the new amendment were negative votes cast. Indiana, which chose its delegates by county and where 83 of the 329 so elected favored prohibition, stood alone in manifesting any significant opposition. So perfunctory were the conventions that questions arose as to whether a simple, direct referendum would not have been more sensible and economical. Nevertheless, with the action of state conventions in Pennsylvania, Ohio, and finally Utah on the afternoon of December 5, 1933, the Twenty-first Amendment achieved ratification.[64] For the first time in the Constitution's history, an amendment had been overturned.

The use of state conventions proved no more time-consuming than legislative action. In fact, the nine-and-one-half months or 288 days between its submission to the states on February 21 and its adoption on December 5 made the Twenty-first among the most rapidly ratified amendments. The Twelfth was ratified in 190 days but required the approval of only twelve states in 1804. Other amendments had taken from eleven to forty-seven months to gain endorsement.[65]

In the course of the state conventions in 1933, delegates commented on the process. Vermont governor Stanley C. Wilson congratulated the nation for "finding a way by which the people themselves may determine whether they want an amendment to the Federal Constitution." New Jersey senate president Emerson L. Richards found it significant that "in righting a wrong that we have done to our government and ourselves we should return to this ancient form of popular expression—the convention." The chairman of the Maryland convention's resolutions committee, Leonard Weinberg, declared, "In this day of Fascism and Sovietism and the subjugation of peoples to the domination of the State or of a man," the state ratifying convention "marks the return to that form of government, a pure democracy, which was the ideal on which this government was founded, where the people themselves express their will by their own votes."[66]

Speaker after speaker insisted that individual freedoms could not be altered through constitutional amendment except with the direct concurrence of the people—possible only through convention ratification of amendments. No direct reference was made to the Ohio ratification controversy of 1919, the *Hawke v. Smith,* or *United States v. Sprague* decisions, but Sidney Stricker, Ohio VCL leader and chairman of his state ratification convention's resolutions committee, alluded to them. He told the convention that "tyranny and intolerance" could not be imposed by a minority and that America now enjoyed "a government of free institutions responsive to the will of the people."[67] To Stricker and many other delegates, the conventions of 1933 represented the discovery of a better, more democratic method of revising the Constitution.

EVEN AMONG a body of constitutional amendments small enough to be considered unusual in every case, the Twenty-first Amendment was extraordinary. It overturned a previous amendment, a step never before taken. Furthermore, it employed Article V's alternative ratification method, also a unique episode in amending history. The Twentieth Amendment was less exceptional, but it too was notable in its alteration of entrenched constitutional arrangements.

Taking a stand in support of the lame duck amendment posed no problem for the vast majority of federal and state legislators but doing so in the case of national prohibition repeal proved quite another matter. They found themselves in an awkward position between well-organized and intense pressures placed on them by the Anti-Saloon League, the Women's Christian Temperance Union, and other prohibition supporters on one side, and the Association Against the Prohibition Amendment, the Women's Organization for National Prohibition Reform, and other antiprohibitionists on the opposing side. Turning the issue over to voters to decide for themselves allowed a painless escape. A member of Congress could say, without taking either side, that the people should have the right to decide. A state legislator could hide even more effectively behind the congressional mandate for convention ratification and the popular election of delegates. Very few responded to the appeal of desperate prohibitionists to block legislation to set up the state's ratifying convention. As a way to avoid a discomforting constitutional issue, submission to state conventions was a legislator's godsend. It would have served Warren Harding's purposes much better than a seven-year ratification time limit, if only he had thought of it in 1917 in his quest for a way to avoid offending either side in the national prohibition debate.

Although the fact was often overlooked then and since, the Twenty-first Amendment did not simply and completely repeal the Eighteenth. The second section of the Twenty-first established a constitutional prohibition on imports of alcoholic beverages into states in violation of their laws. In due course, the validity of the provision was challenged. Liquor dealers objected to a California import license tax on the grounds that it did not prohibit but merely burdened interstate commerce in violation of the commerce clause.

"To say that would involve, not a construction of the amendment, but a rewriting of it," responded Justice Brandeis. The liquor dealers also claimed that their right to equal protection under the law had been violated. To this Brandeis replied, "A classification recognized by the Twenty-first Amendment cannot be deemed forbidden by the Fourteenth."[68] In other words, the Twenty-first defined a federal power equivalent to any other in the document. This affirmation of the Twenty-first Amendment's second section encouraged states to erect trade barriers in the isolated alcoholic beverage market where there was an interstate commerce loophole.[69] The Court has continued to regard this small afterthought in the drafting of the prohibition repeal amendment as determinative, using it in the 1970s, for instance, to sanction regulation of nude dancing in places where alcoholic beverages were sold.[70] If nothing more, such decisions provide a reminder of how amendments reshape the Constitution in small ways as well as large.

The two 1933 amendments, one ratified in January, the other in December, climaxed a remarkable twenty-one-year period of Article V activity. In just over two decades, six amendments were added to the Constitution and another endorsed by Congress, although it failed of ratification. A great deal had been learned about the amending process, not the least that it could be highly volatile and unpredictable. Not only opponents of change but reformers as well came to be wary of it. The constitutional consequences of this acquired caution soon became apparent.

13

Forgoing Amendment in the Third American Constitutional Revolution

Unlike the eras of the American Revolution and the Civil War, the only previous crisis periods of similar magnitude in the history of the United States, the New Deal did not produce formal constitutional change. New understandings of the federal government's authority and responsibility took concrete shape in the 1780s in the language of the Constitution and the Bill of Rights and in the 1860s in the terms of the Thirteenth, Fourteenth, and Fifteenth Amendments. No similar explicit and authentic constitutional statement of a revised consensus concerning the obligations of government emerged from the 1930s, although it seems clear that in the aftermath of the 1936 election a new notion of what was expected from government enjoyed widespread national support.

The New Deal's political values not only gained sufficient popularity to generate a legislative program but also enough political currency to win eventual judicial endorsement. For many individuals, from President Franklin Roosevelt himself to subsequent scholars, such shifts represented the equivalent of constitutional amendment. Constitutional objections to the New Deal that marked Roosevelt's first four years in office disappeared during his second term, in part because of sitting justices changing their minds and in part because of new appointments to the bench. "Transformative" opinions of the Supreme Court, supported by a broad political consensus, altered the character of the American government.[1] Yet the changes that occurred in the 1930s lacked the clarity and specificity of constitutional amendments. Debate over the nature and limits of federal responsibility for domestic social conditions would continue, almost unabated, and serve as a focus for political contention over the subsequent half century. The failure of the New Deal to articulate itself in specific constitutional terms would have ongoing consequences.

The lack of constitutional redefinition during the New Deal stemmed from President Franklin D. Roosevelt's 1935 to 1937 confrontation with the Supreme Court. In the course of that dramatic clash, Roosevelt considered and rejected constitutional amendment as a means of resolving the immediate fundamental dispute over the extent and limits of federal power. His perception of the amending process as impossibly difficult and amendment it-self as unnecessary outweighed any evidence or argument to the contrary. Consequently, no effort was made to chisel the New Deal conception of gov-ernment into the rock of the Constitution. For the moment at least, other paths seemed easier and more direct routes to political success. A chastened and changed Court allowed simple legislation to accomplish reforms, such as child labor regulation, which earlier, in its opinion, had required constitu-tional amendment. The Court also conceded authority to Congress in other areas, including the prerogative to regulate the amending power itself.

Notwithstanding the lack of amendment, the New Deal did represent a rudimentary change of direction, constitutionally speaking. Observers have focused on the sharp turn in the direction of judicial review.[2] After 1937 the Supreme Court shifted its attention away from restricting the economic and social legislative prerogatives of Congress and began to concentrate on the protection of civil liberties and civil rights. Notice should also be taken, however, of the abandonment of the use of Article V to work out major new understandings of government's responsibilities. With the nature of Ameri-can government evolving rapidly and substantially in the 1930s and the decades immediately thereafter, forgoing the practice of articulating basic changes in principles of government through constitutional amendments marked a turning point of fundamental importance.

THE OUTLINES of Franklin D. Roosevelt's battle with the Supreme Court are fairly well known. From the moment that the justices began to rule on New Deal legislation in January 1935, the Court made clear its restrictive view of federal power, one that clashed with the approach adopted by Roosevelt and Congress.[3] When a unanimous Court restricted legislative delegation of power to the executive and narrowly construed the commerce clause in May 1935, Roosevelt angrily retorted that the issue of federal government authority over the national economy, "the biggest question that has come before this country outside of time of war," had to be decided. The Court, he protested, was employing a "horse-and-buggy definition of interstate commerce."[4]

Further decisions during the next year raised doubts about whether any federal wage, hours, or other regulation of labor conditions could survive a court test, not to mention whether the Social Security Act, the Tennessee Valley Authority, and other New Deal innovations would be allowed to stand.[5] A number of the Court's decisions appeared as sweeping as earlier rulings on the income tax and child labor regulation that had led reformers to conclude that their goals could be obtained only through constitutional amendment.

By early 1936 several proposals for a New Deal constitutional amendment had been set forth. The House of Representatives received an amendment resolution that would grant Congress power to enact uniform laws to regulate commerce, business, industry, finance, banking, insurance, manufactures, transportation, agriculture, and the production of national resources. In the Senate, Edward Costigan of Colorado proposed an amendment giving Congress power to regulate prices, wages, hours of labor, and unfair practices affecting the general welfare of the United States. The dean of the University of Wisconsin Law School suggested consideration of language providing that "Congress shall have power to promote the economic welfare of the United States by such laws as in its judgment are appropriate, and to delegate such a power in whole or in part to the states. Existing state powers are not affected by this article, except as Congress may occupy a particular field."[6] Each of these measures offered a different approach to the complex issues of federal power over commerce and social welfare, but all of them acknowledged a need for constitutional revision if the New Deal was to be secured against judicial review.

Roosevelt fumed privately at the Supreme Court's rulings but declined to take public action before the 1936 elections.[7] Meanwhile, the New Deal's political opponents, conservative Democrats such as former presidential nominees Alfred E. Smith and John W. Davis, as well as Republicans, echoed the Supreme Court's criticisms. No doubt Roosevelt's discomfort was increased by the knowledge that his defeats often came by the narrowest of margins in a Court divided five to four and by the realization that he was fast becoming the first president since James Monroe to serve a full term without naming even one new justice to the high court.

FDR had to believe that the November 1936 election results secured his political position and vindicated his policies. In the most one-sided electoral triumph in the history of American presidential elections, not only did Roosevelt amass 61 percent of the vote and carry every state except Maine and Vermont, but he also drew into the Congress an unprecedented Democratic majority of 331 Democrats (to 89 Republicans and 13 others) in the House and 76 Democrats (to 16 Republicans and 4 others) in the Senate. This better than three-fourths majority in Congress meant that the Democrats, if they held together, could easily cut off debate, adopt legislation, and even approve constitutional amendments without one vote from outside party ranks. In fact, almost as soon as the new Congress assembled, Roosevelt sought its aid in dealing with the Supreme Court.

On February 5, 1937, Roosevelt sent Congress a plan to reorganize the federal judiciary that he and Attorney General Homer Cummings had developed in great secrecy. Although it contained several provisions for streamlining federal judicial procedure, the heart of the bill was its proposal to add an additional member to every federal bench whenever a sitting judge failed to retire within six months of his seventieth birthday. The plan allowed for as many as forty-four additional federal district judges, but its core—and quickly the focus of attention—was its creation of up to six additional Supreme Court justiceships. The bill was widely perceived as a sly attempt to evade the Constitution's provision of lifetime tenure for members of the Court, to diminish their influence by permitting the president to "pack the Court" with sympathetic justices.

In the course of a battle that raged fiercely until midsummer, the administration insisted that its proposal represented normal legislative action to bring the Court in step with the needs of modern society, but opponents decried the plan as a duplicitous evasion of the Constitution and a dangerous usurpation of power by the president. Meanwhile the Court began announcing decisions that narrowly sustained the National Labor Relations and Social Security Acts, and at the end of the spring term conservative Justice Willis Van Devanter announced his retirement. The administration sought to salvage judicial reform with a revised, more modest Court bill, but that strategy collapsed as well when its chief Senate sponsor, majority leader Joseph Robinson, suffered a fatal heart attack in the oppressive heat of a Washington summer.[8]

Roosevelt tried to put the best face on the outcome of the Court fight, asserting that even though battles had been lost, the war had been won. A fundamental political shift had indeed taken place, with the Court abandoning efforts to restrict New Deal legislative initiatives. Still, Roosevelt had experienced heavy losses, some not immediately apparent. Opponents of the Court bills discovered that a coalition of Democratic and Republican conservatives could be assembled in Congress to block a major New Deal legislative initiative.[9] Thereafter the administration enjoyed few of the legislative successes that had been so frequent before the Court fight. Roosevelt's huge 1936 electoral triumph was dissipated, its congressional majority never to produce the legislation that had seemed so easily within reach. In many respects, the New Deal had come to its end.

The drama of the Court battle itself has obscured Roosevelt's alternatives in dealing with the Supreme Court. Yet at the time much of the criticism leveled at the president centered on his choice of tactics for resolving his differences with the Court. Time and time again, his plan to enlarge the Court was characterized as a devious political maneuver to circumvent constitutional obstacles that FDR was unwilling to confront. Not only opponents of the president but also a number of his supporters expressed the belief that a more forthright and defensible approach would have been to seek one or more amendments to the Constitution to give the New Deal's federal initiatives an unquestionable and lasting legitimacy.[10] A debate on amending the Constitution would directly address the issue of the proper role of the federal government rather than treat it obliquely in a discussion of the antimodernistic tendencies of aged judges. A stronger, more durable political statement would give measurable evidence of the constitutional preferences of the current generation. A New Deal amendment, however phrased, would send the Court the clearest message possible regarding the need to adopt a new view of federal responsibility. Furthermore, the amending requirements of two-thirds congressional approval and ratification by three-fourths of the states should pose no obstacle to a political leader who had just achieved one of the greatest electoral victories of all time, built a partisan congressional majority in excess of 75 percent, and carried 46 of 48 states.

Roosevelt did in fact seriously consider seeking a constitutional amendment before deciding on another course of action. In his February 5 message to Congress, FDR acknowledged, then specifically rejected, the possibility of amendment. He explained, "If these measures achieve their aim, we may be relieved of the necessity of considering any fundamental changes in the powers of the courts or the constitution of our Government—changes which involve consequences so far-reaching as to cause uncertainty as to the wisdom of such course."[11] As was often the case with Roosevelt's pronouncements, this simple assertion obscured a more complex reality.

Franklin Roosevelt was no stranger to amendment politics. One of his first acts in the New York state senate was to introduce a resolution calling on New York's congressional delegation to support an amendment for the direct election of U.S. senators. He achieved his first political prominence leading upstate Democratic dissidents against Tammany Hall's choice for a U.S. Senate seat; the bruising experience made him increasingly appreciative of direct election. Conservative opponents of the income tax amendment actively courted the young state senator. Roosevelt, however, voted to ratify it and also endorsed woman suffrage.[12] He served in Wilson's cabinet as national prohibition and woman suffrage made their way through Congress and the states. While he recuperated from polio in the 1920s, his wife became actively involved in the child labor amendment campaign.[13] These experiences left him well aware that constitutional amendment, though certainly not easy and not invariably successful, was politically viable even in the face of strenuous opposition. Furthermore, it could move ahead rapidly. His most substantial experience with amendment politics vividly confirmed these observations.

National prohibition caused problems for FDR from the time he tried to win support from both wets and drys by supporting local option in his first campaign for a New York state senate seat. Once the Eighteenth Amendment was adopted, he continued to try to straddle the issue and more than once advised Al Smith to do the same. But Smith and his closest associates, particularly Democratic national chairman John J. Raskob, were determined to bring an end to prohibition. In his quest for the 1932 Democratic presidential nomination, Roosevelt regarded this emphasis on prohibition as potentially damaging to his chances and those of his party. More than any other issue, he felt, prohibition threatened to drive a wedge between conservative rural southern and western Democrats and northern urban party members. Viewing repeal as highly unlikely, FDR considered prohibition merely a distraction. Raskob disagreed and worked tirelessly to commit the party to prohibition repeal. The Roosevelt forces managed to stymie Raskob during preconvention maneuvering but finally surrendered on the issue at the Chicago convention when they discovered that prohibition repeal was the principal unifying point for their rivals. Continuing to oppose repeal might conceivably cost the New York governor the hotly contested presidential nomination. The overwhelming convention vote to include an outright prohibition-repeal plank in the platform could only have reinforced FDR's impression that on constitutional issues Raskob and his Association Against the Prohibition Amendment allies were politically well attuned.[14]

The 1932 election gave the Democrats their greatest victory since before the Civil War, following a campaign in which to some observers prohibition provided the most clear-cut policy distinction between the two parties. Thereafter, prohibition repeal moved ahead rapidly with the AAPA and its allies pressing Congress to approve state convention ratification and then working quickly and effectively to get thirty-seven state legislatures to hold conventions before year's end. Repeal of national prohibition, something that many experienced politicians including Roosevelt had believed impossible, was achieved with extraordinary speed.

The conclusion of the constitutional struggle over prohibition did not end Roosevelt's confrontation with the forces who had led the repeal battle. The Association Against the Prohibition Amendment and the Women's Organization for National Prohibition Reform, which had consistently argued that national prohibition's major error was putting too much regulatory power over individual affairs in the hands of the federal government, were soon reincarnated as the American Liberty League. The transmogrification was superficial and transparent. The Liberty League's national advisory board, its contributors list, doctrine, organizational structure, and even its letterhead bore a striking resemblance to the AAPA. Three former WONPR leaders, including Pauline Sabin, were quickly added to the eleven-member executive committee.[15] Just as the AAPA had itself built on earlier anti-amendment groups such as the Sentinels of the Republic, now the Liberty League extended an ongoing tradition of organized opposition to constitutional change.

From the moment of its founding, the Liberty League declared that its purpose was to defend the Constitution. It began a steady drumbeat of criticism of the New Deal with a weekly barrage of pamphlets, radio broadcasts, and press releases. The league concentrated its attack on programs such as the National Recovery Administration (NRA) and the Agricultural Adjustment Administration (AAA) that, it said, usurped power by shifting congressional functions to executive-controlled bureaucratic structures. When the Supreme Court declared the NRA and AAA unconstitutional, the league expressed delight; and when Roosevelt criticized the decisions, the league charged that he was seeking to build an omnipotent presidency.[16]

Rather than dismissing and ignoring the American Liberty League, as he often did his opponents, Roosevelt fought back fiercely. In his January 1936 State of the Union address, the president described his critics as "unscrupulous money-changers [who] steal the livery of great national constitutional ideals to serve special interests."[17] At the Democratic convention in June he declared, "These economic royalists complain that we seek to overthrow the institutions of America. What they really complain of is that we seek to take away their power. In vain they seek to hide behind the Flag and the Constitution."[18] With the election looming and the Liberty League's strength untested, a nervous James Farley, the Democratic national chairman, hired a full-time publicist to do nothing but plan attacks on the League, or, as he called it, "the millionaire's union."[19]

Although historians, their perspective no doubt influenced by the November election results, have usually dismissed the Liberty League and treated FDR's attacks upon it as a clever straw-man tactic, Roosevelt appears to have been genuinely concerned about these foes.[20] He made many oblique references to them, presumably remembering their previous successes and wondering whether they might surprise him again. Roosevelt's landslide 1936 victory shattered the Liberty League and left its leaders silent, but FDR apparently did not dismiss the possibility that they might return to fight if they could do so on their favorite constitutional battlefield, employing their impressive skills with the amendment process. When he received word that the Supreme Court had upheld the National Labor Relations Act in April 1937, a relieved and ebullient FDR showed how much the Liberty League had been on his mind by immediately pointing out to the press that the Court's decision refuted the league's September 1935 claim, which he quoted precisely, that the act was "thoroughly and completely unconstitutional."[21]

Roosevelt was casting around for a solution to his problems with the Court at the same time he was contending with the American Liberty League. The president and his inner circle began considering what to do about the Court in January 1935. FDR discussed with Interior Secretary Harold Ickes the possibility of expanding the Court and adding sympathetic justices if the next decision also went against the administration. The following day, Attorney General Homer Cummings suggested the same possibility at a cabinet meeting.[22] As usual, however, Roosevelt was simultaneously exploring various ways of dealing with an issue. He discussed a number of specific amendment proposals with senators, cabinet members, informal legal advisers from Felix Frankfurter to the American Federation of Labor's chief counsel, Charlton Ogburn, and Attorney General Cummings. FDR appears neither to have chosen nor ruled out a wide variety of legislative or amendment solutions to the Court problem.[23]

In late January 1935, Roosevelt indicated to Senate Judiciary Committee chairman George Norris his favorable opinion of a constitutional amendment to require more than a simple majority of justices to declare an act of Congress unconstitutional. Republican senator William Borah had proposed as early as 1923 that a 7 to 2 vote be mandatory for the Court to overturn legislation.[24] Norris, whose Article V experience included the successful fight for the lame duck amendment, had long desired such a reform and believed that with FDR's support it could be adopted. The Nebraska senator urged the president to make the attempt and offered his "hearty cooperation."[25] Enthusiasm for Norris's proposal that a two-thirds vote of the Supreme Court be required to set aside an act of Congress as unconstitutional soon cooled, however, when it became clear that such a requirement could lead to the awkward situation where a 5-to-4 majority of the Court would declare a law unconstitutional but the law would remain in force.

The administration's narrow victory in the gold cases apparently ended talk of Court reform for the moment. However, in May 1935 Attorney General Cummings noted in his diary that the *Schechter* decision had revived talk of amending the Constitution. Roosevelt began gathering advice from Cummings, NRA general counsel Donald Richberg, and others.[26] Senator

Edward Costigan of Colorado urged the president to seek an amendment empowering Congress to legislate for the general welfare where states could not effectively do so and suggested that a conference of governors be called to help obtain its adoption.[27] FDR thought enough of the proposal to want to discuss it further with Costigan in a White House meeting.[28]

Roosevelt aide Thomas Corcoran and NRA attorney Jack Scott looked further into the possibility of amplifying the general welfare clause. Between January and September 1935, Scott worked on the idea of employing the language of the 1787 Virginia resolutions. The Virginia delegation had asked the Constitutional Convention to provide for the national legislature to "legislate in all cases for the general interests of the union, and also in those to which the states are separately incompetent, or in which the harmony of the United States may be interrupted by the exercise of individual legislation." The convention had accepted this definition of congressional authority, Scott explained, but the committee on drafting had obscured it. An amendment employing language specifically endorsed by George Washington, James Madison, and their Virginia colleagues would gain ready public approval and be awkward to oppose, he thought. Scott concluded that such an amendment would legitimate the NRA and other legislation pending before the Court and yet not be seen as a reaching for new power.[29]

Meanwhile, however, Felix Frankfurter, one of the president's most trusted advisers on law and legislation, cautioned Roosevelt. Professor Frankfurter, cool to the amendment approach from the outset, counseled delay in proposing an amendment until public support materialized. Instead, he urged going forward with legislation such as the Social Security bill and the Wagner labor relations bill, putting them up to the Supreme Court. If the Court struck them down, the problem would be sharply defined in ways that the common man could understand and against which opponents could not use vague arguments based upon traditionalist loyalties to the Court. Besides, Frankfurter concluded, the Court might in the meantime change its mind.[30] FDR's May 31 press conference outburst about "the horse-and-buggy Court" was widely interpreted as signaling an impending initiative against the Court; however, Roosevelt adopted Frankfurter's view that action was premature. He was not yet certain how to proceed and was unhappy at the criticism that merely hinting at reform had provoked. The president wrote a friend: "Time alone can tell what constitutional procedure can accomplish the results or whether constitutional amendment is advisable, as it has been in a number of cases in the past. After all, Abraham Lincoln was not called a traitor when he suggested an amendment abolishing slavery; neither were other Americans, great and small, anathematized when they recommended a constitutional amendment repealing the Eighteenth Amendment!"[31] Meanwhile, a public opinion survey showing that over three-fourths of New Jersey voters would support constitutional change to make the New Deal effective caught Roosevelt's eye.[32]

The American Liberty League, however, appeared willing, even eager, to confront the New Deal on a constitutional battlefield. In July 1935 at a league-sponsored University of Virginia conference, James Wadsworth applauded recent Supreme Court decisions and declared that any expansion of federal authority would have to be sanctioned by amendment. "So when the President says that the people must decide," Wadsworth asserted, "he must mean that they must make the decision through the ratification or the rejection of an appropriate amendment submitted and passed upon in accordance with the amendatory article of the Constitution. While the President refrained from urging the adoption of an amendment, the plain fact is the vast program of planned economy under the New Deal cannot be put into effect without an amendment. That's all there is to it and we might just as well face it." Wadsworth practically goaded FDR to seek constitutional reform, saying, "If this Administration is to be consistent it must press for such an amendment. Failure to do so would mean abandonment of the New Deal program by its own champions."[33] The Liberty League could scarcely have made more clear its readiness to take on the administration in an amendment contest.

Charlton Ogburn, AFL general counsel, advised Roosevelt in August that his office was drafting for the AFL executive committee an amendment "which, if enacted, would, I believe, give the power to Congress needed to carry out your policies and prevent their being nullified by the Supreme Court."[34] The president quickly professed to be "very anxious" to see what Ogburn had come up with.[35] By autumn, Roosevelt was exploring yet another possibility. Over lunch with Harold Ickes, FDR talked of seeking an amendment to reduce the long wait for Court decisions and to curb the Court's absolute power to declare laws unconstitutional. The amendment he had in mind would allow the attorney general to seek an immediate ruling from the Court on just-passed legislation and give the Congress the right to override any finding of unconstitutionality by again approving the legislation in its next session. The power of judicial review would be made explicit but final authority would be shifted to the legislative branch. Roosevelt presented the same proposal to a cabinet meeting six weeks later. On both occasions he specifically expressed distaste for the British practice of reversing constitutional rulings by simply adding members to the House of Lords. The president told the cabinet he preferred either a substantive amendment or one permitting Congress to override the Court. Ickes, the old progressive, saw particular merit in the latter plan.[36]

During 1935 FDR proceeded slowly, apparently uncertain about how to deal with the Court but inclined to think that some amendment would be necessary. It was typical of Roosevelt to mull over several possible solutions before committing himself to any one. After another Supreme Court jolt in January 1936, Charlton Ogburn anticipated that some amendment would shortly be forthcoming and talked to FDR of the need to make amendment ratification easier and more democratic.[37] A few days later, Ogburn discussed with Attorney General Cummings a judicial retirement amendment. Cummings, eager to eliminate lifetime judicial tenure, talked of requiring federal judges to retire at age seventy. The AFL counsel pointed out that before he became chief justice William Howard Taft favored mandatory judicial retirement at that age.[38] Cummings passed the retirement amendment idea and the Taft quotation along to Roosevelt, cautioning that he did not offer this solution "as an immediate proposition, but as one which we should have seriously in mind should conditions develop to that point."[39]

Attorney General Cummings, not very familiar with the amending process, displayed a pronounced wariness about it.[40] When FDR asked him on January 29, 1936, whether the time had come to revise the Constitution, Cummings thought not. He saw "enormous difficulties" presented by amendment, though least by a judicial retirement amendment that "would have the advantage of not changing in the least degree the structure of our Government, nor would it impair the power of the Court. It would merely insure the exercise of the powers of Court by Judges less likely to be horrified by new ideas." The attorney general told the president, "The real difficulty is not with the Constitution but with the judges who interpret it." Cummings was beginning to frame his preferred solution to the Court crisis. It is significant, however, that at the outset he thought it necessary to cast his plan in the form of an amendment, despite his clear discomfort with that approach.[41]

In a series of speeches during 1936, Donald Richberg, former NRA general counsel who frequently conferred with FDR and Cummings on the Court, offered perhaps the clearest view of evolving administration thinking on constitutional change. Richberg moved from describing amendment as a possible solution to the New Deal's judicial problems through an increasingly alarmist contemplation of the consequences of amendment to the conclusion, echoing Cummings, that a transient majority of justices represented the problem. Richberg eventually decided that constitutional amendment was not only dangerous but unnecessary.

On the day after the *Butler* decision, Richberg reminded an audience that the Constitution could be changed rapidly. "The prohibition amendment," he pointed out, "was ratified within thirteen months after it was submitted by the Congress and the repeal amendment in less than one year. Every one of the last five amendments was ratified within two years of its submission to the States." He continued: "Constitutional amendment has been indeed difficult—and . . . not one revision has been made—in a period of tranquil progress, when conflicting economic and political interests were being wisely compromised. But . . . [in] periods of great national strain constitutional amendments have been rapidly effected by mass movements of irresistible force . . . against which the arguments of lawyers and the warnings of political scientists . . . have the gallant futility of soap bubbles blown into a hurricane." Richberg's uneasiness about the effect, not the difficulty, of amendment came through clearly as he warned in conclusion: "Efforts to thwart the public will through stretching the judicial power to nullify legislative acts and to evade statutory prohibitions are practically certain in the long run to result in extensions of legislative power and curtailment of judicial power through constitutional amendment that may work infinitely more radical changes in our institutions and render individual rights and property rights much less valuable and secure than if there had been greater toleration of legislative action in the beginning."[42]

Richberg advanced the argument that only a slender and temporary majority of Supreme Court justices, disregarding an impressive body of lower court opinion, was rejecting the New Deal.[43] Responding to Al Smith's Liberty League dinner speech in which the former presidential candidate charged that the New Deal was ignoring the Constitution, Richberg pointed to the 1787 Virginia plan for the Constitution. It offered a sufficiently broad view of congressional responsibility for the general welfare to deal with modern circumstances. What was needed, said Richberg, was not a change in the Constitution but a change in the construction placed upon it by a Supreme Court majority. In the face of judicial autocracy, Richberg indicated he would favor the provision of congressional power to override the Court.[44]

Requiring amendment to reverse Court action gave the judiciary an unintended dominance over the legislature, Richberg argued. "Why should words of the Constitution be amended merely in order to change the construction placed upon those words, when equally able, high-minded and disinterested students of the law believe that the Constitution, as it now reads, should be construed that the law will be held valid?" he asked.[45] Richberg's speeches increasingly emphasized the difficulty of phrasing amendments that would enhance federal power without seriously curtailing local self-government.[46] "The people have a right to demand that the Constitution should be interpreted to express the will of the people and not the personal opinions of the justices of the Supreme Court," he declared repeatedly.[47]

Roosevelt consulted with Richberg and Cummings before approving a statement for the 1936 Democratic platform. It presented amendment more as a threat than a solution: "If these problems cannot be effectively solved within the Constitution, we shall seek such clarifying amendment as will assure the power to enact those laws, adequately to regulate commerce, protect public health and safety and safeguard economic security."[48]

During 1936, Richberg came to view amendment as a possible but not mandatory—or even desirable—solution to the New Deal's problems. Observing that in the past amendments occurred most often during a crisis, he assumed that amendment could be achieved in the present circumstances. He concluded, however, that the Constitution contained adequate justification for New Deal actions and that amendment was unnecessary. Only an out-of-step element on the Supreme Court, a slender majority, refused to embrace what most judicial opinion accepted. The time had come for the Court majority to heed the popular voice. Franklin Roosevelt soon embraced the argument.

WITH VOTERS DEMONSTRATING overwhelming support for the president and his party in November 1936, many New Deal partisans assumed that FDR would proceed with an amendment. At its December annual meeting, the National Consumers' League, which had been soliciting the views of leading attorneys since midsummer, announced that it supported an amendment clarifying federal power under the general welfare clause.[49] A group of government and labor leaders from fifteen states headed by the New York State industrial commissioner began organizing a campaign for an amendment granting Congress specific power to regulate hours, wages, working conditions, labor relations, and social security.[50] Democratic National Committee vice-chairman Mollie Dewson encouraged both groups. She enlisted support around the country for a New Deal amendment, declaring, "Personally, I can't see any substitute for an amendment and I believe a satisfactory one can be worked out."[51] As 1937 dawned, liberals and party loyalists were gearing up for an amendment campaign with notable enthusiasm and optimism.

Meanwhile, Roosevelt and Attorney General Cummings were making up their minds to proceed in another direction. Shortly after the election, Cummings noted in his diary that "the president thoroughly understands my attitude which is in substance that there is nothing the matter with the

Constitution but that the entire difficulty has grown out of a reactionary misinterpretation of it." The attorney general preferred a legislative solution, worrying that "the path to an amendment to the Constitution is a thorny one and would necessitate a delay of at least two years before anything tangible could be done."[52] During the next month, Cummings gained confirmation of his view by consulting with such constitutional experts as Edward Corwin of Princeton and Charles Clark of Yale.

By Christmas Eve, Cummings had abandoned as hopeless the quest for a satisfactory amendment. "Many of the schemes that have been suggested are fantastic and some of them, if adopted, would pretty well wipe out any check on legislative authority. Herein lies the chief danger of tinkering with the so-called welfare clause of the Constitution," the attorney general concluded. Other possibilities, such as altering the commerce or due process clause presented similar dangers. "If the amendment goes as far as some desire, it would let down all the barriers, and, on the other hand, unless drastic provision is taken, might be the subject of subsequent devitalization by interpretations at the hands of an ultra-conservative court." The adoption process as well as the substance of an amendment drove Cummings toward other solutions. He concluded, "The Administration cannot very well let its social program bog down because of adverse Supreme Court decisions, and, on the other hand, the delays incident to amendment are rather appalling."[53]

On the day after Christmas, FDR, who had been reading Richberg's latest memorandum disparaging amendment, listened as Cummings did likewise. When the attorney general then offered the court-packing alternative, by all appearances a relatively simple concept to articulate and implement, the president gave the go-ahead to draft legislation. Over the next six weeks, both Cummings and Richberg met repeatedly with Roosevelt as the bill and the message presenting it to Congress were polished.[54]

FDR, having made his choice, began to build a public case against amendment in his January 6, 1937, State of the Union message. Reviewing the problems of depression and the New Deal's efforts to meet them, FDR embraced the Richberg-Cummings view as his own: "During the past year there has been a growing belief that there is little fault to be found with the Constitution of the United States as it stands today. The vital need is not an alteration of our fundamental law, but an increasingly enlightened view with reference to it." Furthermore, he told reporters, too much time was required to win agreement on an amendment from among the many different proposals put forth and to overcome obstacles to ratification.[55]

Roosevelt explained his choice to intimates more bluntly. He told his cabinet that he understood that the Liberty League had already collected a large sum of money in New York to block an amendment.[56] In a letter to Felix Frankfurter on which he handwrote "Privatissimo," Roosevelt explained that he felt it would be impossible to get two-thirds of both houses to agree on amendment language "which would cover all of the social and economic legislation, but at the same time, not go too far." FDR put the chances of success in Congress at fifty-fifty and then gave ratification little chance. Despite his recent electoral triumph, the political challenge of amendment seemed formidable to Roosevelt. It appeared to daunt him more than the problem of choosing appropriate New Deal–affirming language. The president told Frankfurter, "If I were in private practice and without a conscience, I would gladly undertake for a drawing account of fifteen or twenty million dollars (easy enough to raise) to guarantee that an amendment would not be ratified prior to the 1940 elections. In other words, I think I could prevent ratification in thirteen states."[57]

Roosevelt again stressed the political difficulty of amendment to another intimate, Charles Burlingham, a few days later. Burlingham, a leader in the ongoing effort to ratify the child labor amendment, required little convincing, but the child labor episode no doubt weighed on FDR's mind. The president declared,

> Those people in the Nation who are opposed to the modern trend of social and economic legislation realize this and are, therefore, howling their heads off in favor of the amendment process. . . . You and I know perfectly well that the same forces which are now calling for the amendment process would turn around and fight ratification on the simple ground that they do not like the particular amendment adopted by the Congress. If you were not as scrupulous and ethical as you happen to be, you could make five million dollars as easy as rolling off a log by undertaking a campaign to prevent ratification by one house of the legislature, or even the summoning of a constitutional convention in thirteen states for the next four years. Easy money.[58]

In a fireside chat radio broadcast on March 9, FDR, facing intense reaction against his plan, criticized the Court's treatment of the New Deal and argued that the Constitution gave the Congress ample powers. He cited minority opinions from recent decisions to demonstrate that "there is no basis for the claim made by some members of the Court that something in the Constitution has compelled them regretfully to thwart the will of the people." He then described the court plan as the only solution "short of amendment." After presenting his plan in the most reassuring light, FDR declared that many amendments had been proposed and that it would take months or years to get substantial agreement upon the type and language of an amendment. It would take months and years thereafter to get a two-thirds majority in favor of that amendment in both Houses of the Congress. Then would come the long course of ratification by three-fourths of all the States. No amendment which any powerful economic interests or the leaders of any powerful political party have had reason to oppose has ever been ratified within anything like a reasonable time. And thirteen States which contain only five per cent of the voting population can block ratification even though the thirty-five states with ninety-five per cent of the population are in favor of it.[59]

The president made no mention of recent episodes that suggested otherwise about the time needed to achieve an amendment. The lame duck and prohibition repeal amendments of 1933 did less to stir confidence than the thwarted child labor amendment did to provoke contrary expectations.

Roosevelt hinted at his concern with the Liberty League to his radio audience:

Two groups oppose my plan on the ground that they favor a constitutional amendment. The first includes those who fundamentally object to social and economic legislation along modern lines. This is the same group who during the campaign last Fall tried to block the mandate of the people. Now they are making a last stand. And the strategy of that last stand is to suggest the time-consuming process of amendment in order to kill off by delay the legislation demanded by the mandate. To them I say—I do not think you will be able long to fool the American people as to your purposes.

He continued, "The other group is composed of those who honestly believe the amendment process is the best and who would be willing to support a reasonable amendment if they could agree on one." However, FDR warned against relying on an amendment as the answer to the problem. "When the time comes for action, you will find that many of those who pretend to support you will sabotage any constructive amendment which is proposed. Look at these strange bed-fellows of yours. When before have you found them really at your side in your fights for progress?"[60]

Roosevelt loyalists such as Mollie Dewson, Charlton Ogburn, and Harold Ickes dropped their amendment schemes and rushed to support the president.[61] Aides James Farley, Thomas Corcoran, and Benjamin Cohen, who had not helped develop the proposal, went to work pushing the president's plan and arguing against the need for amendment.[62] The battle, thus joined, produced congressional stalemate as well as the shift of Court decisions that allowed FDR to claim victory.

Roosevelt's argument that amendment was just too difficult has generally been taken at face value. Failed efforts to win ratification of the child labor amendment, especially in FDR's home state of New York where a hostile senate committee chairman kept it from coming to a vote, gave plausibility to the explanation.[63] Yet the evidence suggests a more complex reality. The six most recent amendments, all but one of which involved major constitutional change and the last five of which were ratified within fifteen months of passage by Congress, together with the 1936 election results supported George Norris's opinion that an FDR-led amendment effort would have had a good chance of success. Roosevelt, however, was clearly quite apprehensive about the amending process, even as he stood at the very peak of political popularity and strength in late 1936. Having looked at possible amendments for a year and a half, he had not found one to his liking. Recasting the general welfare clause, perhaps the most viable approach to undergirding the New Deal but one that would not guarantee satisfactory Supreme Court rulings, failed to capture his enthusiasm. All other proposals carried liabilities as well. It is not surprising then that he would jump at an alternative that promised desirable results, that his legal advisers regarded as constitutionally permissible, and that seemed more within reach. Despite his forty-six-state, 61 percent presidential victory and three-fourths Democratic Congress, FDR was leery of amendment politics. He obviously feared that his sophisticated and moneyed Liberty League foes, however discredited at the polls, retained the support and skills to block an amendment. Roosevelt wanted to avoid battle with those who had surprised him before in the prohibition repeal struggle.

The argument that thirteen state legislatures would have frustrated a New Deal amendment rings hollow, and not only in light of the 1936 election returns. A Justice Department memorandum showing that Congress could establish ratification conventions such as those used in 1933 undercut the notion that state legislatures would ever need to be involved.[64] Yet neither Roosevelt, his attorney general, nor those close to them appear to have carefully thought through the workings of the amendment process.[65] Their attention centered on the language of amendments and the worst possibilities of obstructionism, not on the realistic political mechanics of their passage. The president and his circle downplayed the adoption of Amendments Sixteen through Twenty-one since 1913 and worried about the problems encountered by the child labor amendment. They simply did not understand very much about how advocates of amendments had achieved their goals in the past and how they themselves might manage the process to get an amendment through the Congress and states in rapid order. The infrequency of amendment left normally skilled politicians with relatively few of the experiences that could have helped them see the way to obtain additional amendments.

It is well worth contemplating that Roosevelt came to view the Constitution itself as fundamentally irrelevant to his immediate problem. The Constitution was clearly to be worshiped from afar, but at close range it presented a stumbling block to be circumvented, not a structure to be lived in and remodeled to suit. Devising constitutional language to sanctify the New Deal concept of government did not seem essential. On the other hand, maneuvering judicial appointments to win approval of a reformulated definition of federal government powers made sense. Fear of the unanticipated consequences of an amendment that the Court might interpret more broadly or more narrowly than intended outweighed the sense of obligation to bring the language of the Constitution into conformity with current or desired governmental practice.

Observing the 150th anniversary of the conclusion of the Philadelphia convention, the president in September 1937 spoke of his reverence for the Constitution. Then, with no sense of contradiction, FDR expressed frustration with its inflexibility. Pointing to the time it had taken to adjust the Constitution's terms on income taxes and women's and children's labor issues, Roosevelt declared, "We can no longer afford the luxury of twenty-year lags."[66]

FDR had immediate political success, not permanence of policy foremost in mind. His attitude made George Norris, a longtime student of the Constitution who was strongly sympathetic to the New Deal, clearly uncomfortable. He went along grudgingly with the Court bill. The Nebraskan wrote: "I do not like the president's proposal, not because it is unconstitutional, but because I doubt the wisdom of proceeding in that way and because it is not, in my judgment, fundamental, and will only be a temporary remedy."[67] Norris used even stronger language to AFL president William Green, warning that there was "great danger in the method he has proposed" that will "plague our descendants" because "it does not strike permanently at the evil we want to remedy."[68] New Deal loyalists such as Interior Secretary Ickes and Representative D. Worth Clark agreed with Norris. Ickes believed that "in the end we must have an amendment. We can't depend upon a liberal majority of the court in the future any more than we can now."[69] Clark addressed his fears bluntly: "The weapon which the president has chosen to achieve his end is a two edged sword. It may serve the cause of liberty today but tomorrow it could prove just as effective in the hands of a despotic reactionary."[70]

THE RESURRECTION and redirection of child labor reform during the 1930s provided a prime means to evaluate the opportunity for constitutional amendment during the New Deal and the resort instead to legislative solutions. Twists and turns continued in the effort to empower the federal government to regulate the employment of children. The reform drive that began with legislation in the 1910s, suffered two setbacks at the hands of the Supreme Court, prompted congressional passage of a constitutional amendment in 1934, and then shortly thereafter fell apart as states declined to ratify, resumed in the 1930s. Determined child protection advocates eventually obtained not a constitutional but rather a legislative solution, one in keeping with the pattern of the New Deal. Along the way, the quest for child labor reform contributed coincidentally to further delineation of Article V.

The election of Franklin Roosevelt, a Democratic congressional majority, and many new state legislators in 1932 revived the apparently moribund child labor amendment. Since its submission to the states by Congress in 1924, it had won only six ratifications and had been formally rejected by at least one house in no fewer than thirty-eight legislatures.[71] The tide turned dramatically in 1933, the year of so many New Deal initiatives to revive, reform, and regulate the American economy. Between February 1 and July 15, nine state legislatures ratified the amendment. Five more approved it during December special sessions, bringing the total to twenty, more than half the number needed for adoption. A once-discouraged National Child Labor Committee, busy seeking other solutions to the growing exploitation of child labor during the depression, regained hope. Joining with the American Legion and the American Federation of Labor as well as traditional allies, it renewed efforts on behalf of the amendment.[72]

The 1933 turn in child labor's fortunes was more immediately apparent in early New Deal legislation and its implementation. The National Industrial Recovery Act provided for industry-by-industry creation of codes of fair competition. The NRA sought to restrain destructive competition and to revive capitalism by establishing uniform and reasonable standards on prices, wages, and business practices. The first NRA code, adopted in July by the cotton textile industry, contained a provision, sought by the NCLC, agreeing to ban employment of children under sixteen in cotton textile mills. Later the same month, Roosevelt promulgated a blanket code to operate until the end of the year or until other industries adopted their own; it also incorporated a minimum employment age of sixteen, except for nonmining, non-manufacturing industries where fourteen- to sixteen-year-olds could work three hours a day when school was not in session. Overnight a national child labor ban had been established.

By the end of 1933, over 100 industry codes had been enacted, all but 6 banning all employment under sixteen and nearly half barring workers below eighteen. A year later more than 500 such codes were established, with only 13 allowing sub-sixteen-year-old employment. During the last half of 1933, over 100,000 children under sixteen were banished from the work force, and large numbers of sixteen- to eighteen-year-olds were removed from hazardous jobs; the numbers grew during the following year. National Child Labor Committee general secretary Courtney Dinwiddie exulted in November 1933, "We have done more to eliminate child labor in the last three or four months than we were able to do in the preceding ten years."[73] Two months later, in his State of the Union message, Roosevelt declared that "child labor is abolished."[74] His proud claim, though understandable, was exaggerated, since 500,000 children engaged in agriculture, home work, and some other categories of labor were not affected by the NRA codes.

The NRA attack on child labor generally benefited the depressed economy by eliminating the lowest paid workers and increasing opportunity for unemployed older workers, usually at higher wages. The fragile nature of administratively obtained reform became starkly evident, however, when the Supreme Court in May 1935 proclaimed the National Industrial Recovery Act unconstitutional. The *Schechter v. U.S.* decision rendered child labor restrictions, along with the other features of the codes, unenforceable. Almost immediately, the hiring of workers younger than sixteen, often for long hours and at wages lower than their elders, shot up again.[75]

Always aware of the NRA's limited and transitory nature, the National Child Labor Committee kept pressing for the adoption of the child labor amendment.[76] The NCLC public education campaign, together with evidence generated by the NRA experience, proved effective in stimulating support for the measure. A May 1936 Gallup poll discovered that 61 percent of the American people and majorities in forty-five states favored the amendment. Nine months later, a follow-up poll found that support had increased to 76 percent overall with majorities in every state. The NCLC crusade was boosted further in January 1937 when both Roosevelt and former president Herbert Hoover, in his first public statement since the bitter 1936 election campaign, called for ratification.[77]

By 1938 twenty-eight states, located in the North, Midwest, and West, had ratified the child labor amendment, four of them during the previous year. In a number of states, however, legislatures continued to respond to influential opposition minorities. This proved particularly true in the South, the poorest region and the one with the worst record of exploiting children in agriculture and textile mills. The South remained a solid holdout against the amendment. Legislatures also rejected it in Nevada, despite the fact that 69 percent of the public favored ratification; New York, where 83 percent did so; and Rhode Island, where 88 percent approved.[78] Whenever Franklin Roosevelt needed evidence that a minority could effectively resist adoption of a constitutional amendment, he had to look no further.

The rejuvenated child labor amendment brought veteran antiamendment crusaders to life. The American Liberty League was a vocal enemy until it faded after the 1936 election. The Sentinels of the Republic reemerged as opponents of constitutional change, and prominent individual foes of previous amendments reappeared as well. Sterling Edmunds, a St. Louis attorney and board member of both the Sentinels and the Association Against the Prohibition Amendment, organized a National Committee for the Protection of Child, Family, School, and Church (NCPCFSC) in January 1934. Linked as well with the Woman Patriots, the successor to the National Association Opposed to Woman Suffrage, the NCPCFSC sent out literature and lobbyists charging that the amendment would put youth under national control, send federal bureaucrats into every home, and lead to compulsory military training in the schools. The frightening new image of Hitler Youth overshadowed older assertions of Communist-inspired, central government control of children.[79]

Another attack on the amendment originated with the American Bar Association. In 1933 the ABA decried the amendment as an unwarranted federal invasion of the rights of states and families after its president called it "a communist effort to nationalize children, making them primarily responsible to the government instead of to their parents. It strikes at the home. It appears to be a definite positive plan to destroy the Republic and substitute a social democracy."[80] The ABA in 1934 appointed William D. Guthrie to chair a special committee to oppose the amendment. Guthrie, a veteran of both *Pollock v. Farmers Loan and Trust* and the *National Prohibition Cases,* argued that the child labor amendment was dead. He pointed to the Supreme Court's 1921 finding in *Dillon v. Gloss* that a seven-year ratification limit was reasonable. In his *Dillon* opinion, Justice Van Devanter commented that after some long but unspecified period ratification would no longer be valid. Guthrie's committee contended that "more than a reasonable time had elapsed" since Congress had proposed the amendment in June 1924. Furthermore, long after more than one-fourth of all state legislatures had rejected a proposed amendment, a legislature could not "validly annul, withdraw, or revoke its prior rejection." Under the circumstances, the child labor amendment would have to be proposed a second time if Congress still deemed it necessary.[81]

James Wadsworth renewed his calls for alteration of Article V, alleging its defects with arguments similar to Guthrie's and seeking prompt state decisions regarding ratification, preferably through the process used to approve prohibition repeal. Wadsworth had returned to Congress as a member of the House of Representatives with a rare 1932 Republican victory and subsequently become a leader of the Liberty League. He did not specifically attack the child labor amendment, as much as he disliked its furtherance of federal authority, seeming to recognize that he might drive undecided votes to the opposite position. Instead he kept repeating in speeches and correspondence that once having rejected an amendment, states should not be able to reverse their position and ratify, as an increasing number of states were doing with the child labor amendment. It frustrated Wadsworth that the Democratic Congress showed no interest in taking up his latest version of the Wadsworth-Garrett resolution to modify Article V, and he took hope when a court challenge was mounted to child labor amendment ratification.[82]

As the campaign for the child labor amendment accelerated with four state ratifications in 1937, judicial challenges in two states sought to test the Guthrie theory of limited ratification authority. Guthrie himself died in 1935, but child labor opponents in the Kansas and Kentucky legislatures subsequently used his arguments in seeking to overturn their states' ratifications. The Kansas legislature had formally rejected the child labor amendment in 1925 and sent notice of its action to the U.S. secretary of state. Twelve years later, the Kansas senate divided 20 to 20 on a new ratification resolution, and the lieutenant governor cast a tiebreaking vote in favor of approval. The state house of representatives then concurred. Eighteen senators and three representatives from the losing side appealed unsuccessfully to the state supreme court and then to the federal Supreme Court, arguing that the lieutenant governor had no right to break the tie. Moreover, they said, prior rejection and the passage of time had cost the proposed amendment its vitality.[83] Meanwhile, Kentucky's supreme court endorsed the Guthrie theory, holding that the legislature's 1926 rejection of the child labor amendment had exhausted its vitality and invalidated the governor's certification of ratification in 1937.[84] If the Kansas ruling was sustained, the amendment might yet be adopted, but if the Kentucky decision was allowed to stand, it most certainly was dead.[85]

After oral arguments in October 1938 in the cases of *Coleman et al. v. Miller, Secretary of the Senate of the State of Kansas* and *Chandler, Governor of Kentucky, v. Wise,* the Supreme Court was forced by the death of Justice Benjamin Cardozo and the retirement of Justice Brandeis to delay a decision until June 1939. The justices then further clarified the Article V process along lines consistent with the earlier decision in *Dillon v. Gloss.* Speaking for the Court, Chief Justice Charles Evans Hughes first announced a 4-to-4 division on the question of whether the lieutenant governor of Kansas was a member of the legislature within the meaning of Article V; therefore, the justices would express no opinion on that point. On the major issues, however, they were in agreement.

Article V made no mention of rejection of amendments, only of ratification when approved by three-fourths of the states; thus a state legislature's power to ratify remained open despite previous rejections. Hughes acknowledged the argument that if Congress stipulated state convention ratification, once those conventions met, rejected it, and went out of existence, they could not reassemble and ratify. He did not, however, extend that logic to an ongoing legislative body. Instead he noted that when the issue had come up with the Fourteenth Amendment, Secretary of State William Seward and Congress found the amendment valid. The Court believed, Hughes concluded, "that in accordance with this historic precedent the question of the efficacy of ratifications by state legislatures, in the light of previous rejection or attempted withdrawal, should be regarded as a political question pertaining to the political departments, with the ultimate authority in the Congress in the exercise of its control over the promulgation of the adoption of the amendment."[86]

On the question of whether the proposed amendment had lost vitality through the passage of time, Chief Justice Hughes noted that Congress had not set a time limit for its ratification. Referring to the *Dillon v. Gloss* holding that time limits were reasonable, he said that it did not follow that the Court should set one when Congress had not done so. There were no constitutional or statutory criteria for judicial determination of time limits. "The question of a reasonable time in many cases would involve, as in this case it does involve, an appraisal of a great variety of relevant conditions, political, social and economic," wrote Hughes. These were political, not judicial questions, open for Congress to decide and not reviewable by the courts regardless of whether determined when an amendment was submitted or when ratifications by three-fourths of the states had been completed.[87]

Justice Hugo Black, in a concurring opinion signed by the three recent Roosevelt appointees to the Supreme Court, Felix Frankfurter, William O.

Douglas, and himself, as well as by Justice Owen Roberts, went even further. "The Constitution grants Congress exclusive power to control submission of constitutional amendments," Black wrote. "Final determination by Congress that ratification by three-fourths of the States has taken place 'is conclusive upon the courts.'" Insofar as *Dillon v. Gloss* implied that the judiciary had the right to impose limits, he declared, it should be overturned. "If Congressional determination that an amendment has been completed and become a part of the Constitution is final and removed from examination by the courts, as the Court's present opinion recognizes, surely the steps leading to that condition must be subject to the scrutiny, control, and appraisal of none save the Congress, the body having exclusive power to make that final determination."[88]

The *Coleman v. Miller* decision provided the Supreme Court's most sweeping statement on Article V. The related Kentucky decision, announced the same day, added little to the *Coleman* opinion.[89] The complex, technical arguments to restrict the amending process made by opponents of change were set aside at one time. Contentions that the Tenth Amendment limited the subject of amendments and that amendments had to be demonstrably necessary were dismissed as was the Kentucky contention that courts could restrain the amending process. The Court held that Congress, the element of the federal government closest to the sovereign authority of the people, possessed unrestrained authority to determine whether an amendment was appropriate and whether a proper process of sanctioning it had been employed. As implied in Hughes's opinion but stated most forthrightly in Black's concurrence, Article V "grants power over the amending of the Constitution to Congress alone." The message of *Coleman v. Miller* was summarized in Black's final sentence: "Any judicial expression amounting to more than mere acknowledgment of exclusive Congressional power over the political process of amendment is a mere admonition to the Congress in the nature of an advisory opinion, given wholly without constitutional authority."[90]

Coleman v. Miller kept alive the possibility that the child labor amendment would be ratified. Meanwhile, however, states had ceased considering the amendment. The states that could still ratify, *Coleman* affirmed, were the very ones where resistance was greatest. Meanwhile the possibility of a federal legislative solution improved in the aftermath of changes in the Supreme Court. Once the Court upheld the constitutionality of the National Labor Relations Act and the Ashurst-Sumners Act, a federal statute prohibiting shipment of prison-made goods into states barring their sale, prospects seemed bright that new federal child labor legislation would be judicially acceptable. Congress deliberated dozens of proposals and eventually combined features of several in the Fair Labor Standards Act. The legislation included, in addition to minimum-wage and maximum-work-hours regulations, provisions for a minimum working age of sixteen, except in particularly hazardous occupations where it was raised to eighteen.[91]

Quite similar to the first child labor act of 1916, the Fair Labor Standards Act of June 1938 still left an estimated 800,000 to 1 million children under sixteen legally employed, mainly in agriculture, but also as newsboys and in industries not engaged in interstate commerce.[92] However, it diminished the sense of urgency regarding ratification of the child labor amendment.[93] When the Supreme Court, now dominated by Roosevelt appointees, upheld the constitutionality of the Fair Labor Standards Act in *U.S. v. Darby* in February 1941, explicitly overruling *Hammer v. Dagenhart,* any remaining feeling of need for the still-unratified amendment evaporated.[94] The Congress was now regarded as possessing ample power to regulate labor and protect children. Even more than in 1937, resort to Article V to ensure federal government reform seemed a waste of political energy.

THE CONSTITUTIONAL CRISIS of the mid-1930s forced the three branches of the federal government, not to mention the American public, to consider the role of the Constitution in defining and limiting governmental responsibility and activity. At the point when amendment might have entered more than ever into the mainstream of the political process, confronting fundamental issues and encouraging the articulation of basic understandings, it was instead relegated to the periphery. After a quarter century of frequent resort to Article V to deal with central issues of the extent and nature of federal authority, a period during which both the political and technical aspects of amendment methods came to be better understood than ever before, the American political system reached a turning point. Confronted by resistance of uncertain, though probably overestimated strength, the leaders of the day chose to accept what could be achieved by simple legislative majority and justified to a subdued and agreeable judiciary. Assertions in the Constitution of the federal government's basic obligations, with all the implications of lasting commitment that such declarations involved, were abandoned. Potentially broader and clearer statements of the reach of governmental obligation remained unrealized.

Franklin Roosevelt's New Deal raised the notion of collective responsibility for the social welfare of the individual to a higher level than ever before reached in the United States. The belief achieved broad support that government, in particular the federal government, was the proper agency to discharge community obligations. At its pinnacle in the 1936 election, this viewpoint was endorsed by as close to a consensus as the American electorate achieved in the twentieth century.

Yet the New Deal vision of government was not formally incorporated into the Constitution by amendment. Complex reasons stood in the way, not the least of which was the perceived skill in amendment politics of Roosevelt's most vocal conservative opponents. At a time when legislative agreement, executive cooperation, and judicial assent appeared secure, the importance of installing the New Deal formulation of civic obligation in the Constitution was discounted. The New Deal generated a sense that constitutional obstacles had been overcome and that new possibilities were opening up rather than a belief that a philosophy of government ought to be ensured durability by being articulated in constitutional instruments. The consequences of this view were not immediately apparent, indeed would not be so for decades. Failure to pursue amendment meant, however, that the New Deal was not erected on as strong and solid a constitutional foundation as might well have been possible at the time.

14

"THE SHARP ANGER OF A MOMENT"

Attempted Counterrevolution by Amendment

During the twenty years following the 1937 battle over the Supreme Court, attempts to amend the Constitution did not slacken. The nature of the efforts, however, shifted sharply from previous decades. After the Court's change in direction, advocates of the New Deal perceived no need to press for further constitutional sanction. The proponents of change, however, possessed a notably different agenda. Rather than endeavoring to enhance the electorate, either in its size or its direct influence on government as in Amendments Seventeen, Nineteen, and Twenty, or to expand federal authority as in Amendments Sixteen, Eighteen, and the nearly successful child labor amendment, post–Court-fight proposals for constitutional change sought to restrain federal, particularly presidential, power. The anomalous Twenty-first Amendment, rescinding federal authority to prohibit alcoholic beverages, offered the only precedent for the wave of restrictive propositions that crested in the years following World War II.

Although not necessarily mere reactions to the performance of Franklin D. Roosevelt, most significant amendment initiatives during this era bore a pronounced anti–New Deal cast. Despite the downturn in the New Deal's fortunes following the 1937 Court battle, FDR's political strength while he lived and his powerful legacy thereafter helped to keep all but one proposed constitutional reform from being implemented. Nevertheless, an ongoing series of amendment debates, especially during the late 1940s and early 1950s, vividly demonstrated the New Deal's failure to secure an unchallengeable constitutional position.

Although alteration of the U.S. Constitution occurred only once in the two decades after 1937, other amendments received serious consideration and substantial support. Instead of affirming a 1930s constitutional transformation, each of these proposals challenged some aspect of the New Deal or Franklin Roosevelt's leadership. Attempts to reduce presidential authority in foreign affairs twice gained significant backing, even though both fell short of their goal. Less success greeted a variety of measures designed to restrict taxation, restrain federal domestic initiatives, buttress the independence of the Supreme Court, and shift power over the amending process to

315

the states. However, presidential term limitation, a measure aimed squarely at FDR, the only president ever elected more than twice, achieved the level of endorsement that Article V mandated. The New Deal was not overturned by amending activity, but neither did it obtain confirmation. Instead the unsettled nature of American policies regarding government revealed itself.

Conflict over the power of the federal government to deal with two of the most sensitive political issues of the day, foreign affairs and race relations, lay at the heart of many amendment discussions from the late 1930s through the 1950s. Either concern with the presidential authority to make international commitments or sensitivity to the federal government's potential to reshape domestic social arrangements motivated several amending efforts during this era. These initiatives can hardly be considered politically peripheral. They dealt with central concerns of presidential power, the cold war, and civil rights. Furthermore, they elicited impressive support for fundamental change in U.S. constitutional arrangements. Though only one amendment scheme succeeded during this era, the fate of others as well revealed the political temper of the times.

THE STRENGTH OF an attempt to restrict presidential and congressional capacity to commit the United States to war provided an early signal of the rapid shift in the political atmosphere following the 1937 battle over the Supreme Court. Within the year, conservative congressmen forced the House of Representatives to give serious attention to a long-standing but previously little-noticed proposal. The constitutional amendment, championed since 1935 by Democratic congressman Louis Ludlow of Indiana and favored by a growing contingent of international isolationists, would restrict presidential and congressional warmaking authority. Declarations of war, except in the case of a direct attack upon the United States, would require voter approval in a national referendum.

Reflecting a distrust of existing arrangements for the conduct of foreign relations, Ludlow's measure sought to reduce dramatically the authority of the federal government, in particular that of the president. Historians have generally treated the measure as a narrowly drawn, foolhardy scheme, overlooking the broader constitutional implications of the war referendum amendment. They perceive the Ludlow amendment as growing out of what Charles Beard labeled "the devil theory of war," the mid-1930s belief that selfish bankers and businessmen, so-called "merchants of death," had maneuvered the United States into World War I. In this view, the war referendum amendment, like the 1935 and 1937 neutrality laws, merely sought to block a repeat performance on the assumption that most Americans would never choose a war option.[1] This interpretation discounts the larger post–Court-fight context of constitutional concerns. Passage of the Ludlow amendment would unquestionably have reversed the accumulation of power in federal hands manifest during the New Deal.

The question of whether decisions on war could wisely be made democratically had intrigued philosophers from Aristophanes to Condorcet and Kant. In the United States, war referendums, first suggested after the Spanish-American War, gained more serious consideration in 1914. A month before fighting erupted in Europe, Republican congressman Richard Bartholdt, who represented a heavily German-American St. Louis district, introduced a war referendum amendment in the House. Bartholdt's resolution provided that Congress not declare war, except in circumstances calling for self-defense, until after a national plebiscite on the matter. While embraced by a few prominent reformers, most notably Jane Addams, William Jennings Bryan, and Robert La Follette, and endorsed in 1916 by the Socialist party, the idea was otherwise generally ignored at first. As anxieties about U.S. involvement in the war increased, so too did advocacy of war referendums. Once the United States entered the conflict, however, the only further mention of the idea came in a mild August 31, 1917, amendment resolution requiring an advisory referendum on future wars introduced by Oklahoma senator Thomas P. Gore, an industrious seeker of means to avoid involvement.[2]

After World War I, the idea of a democratic decision on declaring war remained alive, although just barely. During debate over the League of Nations covenant a few senators suggested that the United States reserve the right to conduct a war referendum. In 1924, both the Democratic and Progressive platforms endorsed war referendums, due to the efforts of Bryan and La Follette. Amendment resolutions continued to be offered in Congress on an average of about two per year from the early 1920s to the mid-1930s. William Borah, Republican chairman of the Senate Foreign Relations Committee and a persistent critic of traditional diplomacy, became an advocate. Rising disillusionment with U.S. participation in World War I ensured that the idea would at least continue to be discussed, if not widely endorsed.[3]

In 1935 Congressman Ludlow took up the war referendum cause. An Indiana journalist and respected Washington correspondent since 1901, Ludlow was elected to Congress from an Indianapolis district in 1928. Long a proponent of popular control of government, he had first been introduced to the war referendum idea during World War I by Bryan and Vice-President Thomas Marshall, a fellow Hoosier. Ludlow, becoming increasingly committed to isolationism, began advocating the war referendum in 1924. He became its principal sponsor with the retirement of Wisconsin congressman James A. Frear in 1934.[4]

In January 1935, Ludlow, moved by Senator Gerald Nye's investigation of the World War I munitions industry, offered a constitutional amendment resolution providing for both a plebiscite on declaring war and government wartime takeover of the munitions industry to eliminate private business profits from war. In a letter to House Judiciary Committee chairman Hatton Sumners, Ludlow explained his pursuit of an amendment rather than legislation. "A statute might be repealed by the next congress, or the next day by the same congress," he said. More specifically, "The same forces that maneuver the country into war would override or repeal all statutes that stood in their way. Only a constitutional amendment would have permanency and stability enough to accomplish the purpose."[5] To the president, Ludlow put it more simply: "A statute might temporarily curb the war profiteers but a constitutional amendment will remove that menace permanently and forever."[6] The recent overturning of the alcohol prohibition amendment, that supporters initially justified on the same grounds, failed to diminish Ludlow's enthusiasm for an amendment.

The aftershocks of the Nye investigation included a brief three-hour June 1935 hearing on the Ludlow resolution. The failure of the House Judiciary Committee to take any further action frustrated the measure's sponsor. By 1936, Ludlow, in the face of growing German, Italian, and Japanese aggressiveness, ever more fervently advocated completing "the democratic processes by democratizing the war power." He had become convinced that, if it were brought to a vote of the full House, public pressure would ensure the amendment's approval. Ludlow saw no conflict between a war referendum and adequate national security. "It has no reference to the size of the Army and Navy but only to the method of declaring war," he asserted as he urged Roosevelt to embrace the idea. Ludlow hastened to add, "I am personally a believer in strong national defense."[7]

Ludlow, who received only a brief, perfunctory acknowledgment of his appeal for presidential support, came to believe that the opposition of the administration and congressional leadership represented the sole obstacle to a constitutional amendment.[8] If his resolution could only be pried out of committee, it would triumph. Under House of Representatives rules, the device for achieving such a result was a discharge petition. Once signed by a majority of House members, such a petition compelled a vote on whether to bring a measure to the floor.

Ludlow's first discharge petition circulated in 1936 and obtained only 72 signatures, far short of the 218 required. Before the next Congress convened, Ludlow decided to drop his provision relating to the munitions industry and concentrate exclusively on the referendum measure. He introduced his new amendment resolution on February 5, 1937, the same day Roosevelt announced the court reorganization plan. Amid the flood of reaction to FDR's perceived attempt to increase presidential power, the discharge petition began circulating on April 6. It obtained 120 signatures within two months and 185 by the time the congressional session ended in August. The outbreak of war between Japan and China, increased press attention to Ludlow's measure, and rising apprehension about presidential authority stirred by the Court fight appear to have encouraged House members to sign.[9]

Franklin Roosevelt's first major foreign policy address, his October 1937 Chicago speech vaguely advocating a quarantine of nations which threatened the health of the international community, alarmed opponents of foreign intervention with its hint of American overseas military involvement. The war referendum amendment gained further support. The National Council for Prevention of War, a leading pacifist group that had participated in the 1935 hearings and sponsored publication of Ludlow's book, *Hell or Heaven,* devoted much time and money to the petition campaign.[10] Following Roosevelt's speech, a national public opinion poll conducted by George Gallup found that at that moment 73 percent of respondents favored a referendum on declaring war.[11] A score of congressmen added their names to Ludlow's petition soon after Congress reconvened in November for a special session. Japan's December 12 attack on the U.S. Navy gunboat *Panay* in China's Yangtze River near Nanking provided further incentive for representatives fearful of impending war. Two days later, the discharge petition had acquired thirteen additional signatures to give it the necessary 218 to force a vote on the Ludlow amendment on January 10, 1938.[12]

The historian responsible for the most thorough study of the war referendum movement, Ernest C. Bolt, Jr., maintains that Louis Ludlow was concerned with democratic control of foreign affairs rather than with a specific policy objective. Bolt calls attention to the lengthy history of the war referendum idea and Ludlow's long involvement with it. Nevertheless, as Bolt acknowledges, the completion of the discharge petition in the immediate aftermath of the *Panay* incident, amid rising demands for the United States to isolate itself from foreign conflicts, tied the Ludlow amendment to the isolationist campaign in many minds. Advocates of the view that the United States should concern itself only with defense of its national territory reinforced the linkage by endorsing the amendment. Yet Ludlow's draft language, which merely required approval of such activity by a national popular majority, did not preclude foreign involvement as much as remove the choice from presidential and congressional hands.[13]

The Roosevelt administration, for the most part, ignored the Ludlow amendment before completion of the discharge petition. Thereafter it attacked the resolution as vigorously as it felt it could in the unsettled political climate of foreign policy debate at the moment. In a December 15 press conference, Secretary of State Cordell Hull called it a peace measure without "wisdom or practicability." Two days later Roosevelt, responding to a reporter's question as to whether a war referendum was consistent with representative government, replied "with a sharpness not characteristic of him" and without elaboration, "No!"[14]

More strident criticism of the war referendum came from other quarters. Journalists such as Walter Lippmann and Arthur Krock, Republican leaders including Henry Stimson, Alfred Landon, and Frank Knox, and such internationalists as Clark Eichelberger of the League of Nations Association contended that presidential diplomacy to avoid war would be paralyzed. A speech prepared by Eichelberger, reviewed and approved by State Department officials, including Hull, and given by House Foreign Affairs Committee chairman Samuel D. McReynolds, argued that Ludlow's plan would frustrate international cooperation against aggressors. Implying that the nation would be left defenseless, this critique avoided pointing out that the referendum provision would not apply in event of an attack upon the United States.[15]

Organized grass-roots support for the Ludlow amendment was limited. Among the host of active peace groups, sentiment remained divided, with the pacifist Fellowship for Reconciliation, the Women's International League for Peace and Freedom, and the National Council for Prevention of War notable among advocates and the League of Nations Association, which favored international cooperation to discourage aggression, prominent among opponents. On December 22, 1937, Ludlow himself announced vague plans for the formation of a National Committee for the War Referendum to stimulate and coordinate public endorsements. He had apparently given scant thought to the task of generating mass support for a constitutional amendment, much less to winning state ratification should it gain congressional approval. The group, chaired by retired general William C. Rivers, proved to be of little consequence.[16]

Most Americans, opinion polls suggested, liked the idea of a plebiscite on war. Yet few stirred themselves, either on their own initiative or because of any orchestrated campaign, to act on such a belief. Without a broad-based expression of active concern, such as Father Charles Coughlin generated against the World Court in 1935, congressmen were unlikely to be swayed from their own judgments.

As the House prepared to vote on Ludlow's discharge petition, proponents moved to strengthen their case. A January 7 caucus of about sixty House members supporting Ludlow accepted proposals offered by Representative Hamilton Fish to tighten the terms of the amendment and incorporate into it the Monroe Doctrine.[17] Fish's version, the language ultimately considered by the House on January 10, read:

> Except in case of attack by armed forces, actual or immediately threatened, upon the United States or its Territorial possessions, or by any non-American nation against any country in the Western Hemisphere, the people shall have the sole power by a national referendum to declare war or to engage in warfare overseas. Congress, when it deems a national crisis to exist in conformity with this article, shall by concurrent resolution refer the question to the people.[18]

Although some of the amendment's proponents thought these modifications improved their prospects, others believed their chances were weakened by last-minute changes to eliminate a referendum if attack was "immediately threatened" or "any non-American nation" attacked "any country in the Western Hemisphere."[19]

Congress formally debated the Ludlow amendment only briefly but did so quite vigorously. Ohio Democrat Bryan Harlan complained that forcing a committee to discharge a bill violated good legislative procedure and merely represented a ploy to embarrass the administration. The resolution had no chance of winning a majority, much less the necessary two-thirds, he said, but the discharge petition gave members the opportunity to "demagog with impunity." A frustrated Harlan went on to call the referendum itself "a crackpot, balmy suggestion . . . that is so hard to argue against because the people who make the proposal mean so well and as a class are such fine citizens."[20]

A more subdued Hatton Sumners, in whose committee the resolution was being held, contended that the referendum would "create an erroneous impression in the world as to what they can do to us without our fighting." Furthermore, it would give a prospective antagonist an advantage from the time a referendum was called until it was decided. "It is a resolution calculated to provoke war and to handicap us in its prosecution," he concluded.[21]

On the other side of the issue, Everett Dirksen, a conservative Illinois Republican and a World War I veteran with strong doubts about the wisdom of U.S. involvement, spoke at length about "presidential dictatorship," "rubber-stamp Congresses," and the need for the people to take back power over government. "What was the most convincing argument against enlarging the Court?" he asked, answering that "if the people desire changes in the highest judicial tribunal of the land, the people can speak through their power to amend their own Constitution." Dirksen regarded the discharge vote as "nothing more than a proposal to let the people speak through representatives of their choice in the legislatures or in special conventions as to whether they want their Constitution amended with respect to the power of Congress to declare war." He scoffed at another congressman's characterization of the war referendum as holding a town council meeting to decide whether to put out a fire. Instead, he said, the proper comparison would be with calling a meeting of the fire department to decide on impressing civilians into service to put out a fire in another country. His remarks provoked supportive comments from other isolationists.[22]

On January 10, 1938, final debate began with the Speaker of the House, William Bankhead of Alabama, reading a letter from Franklin Roosevelt. It bluntly opposed the amendment as "impracticable in its application and incompatible with our representative form of government." Expanding on his press conference statement, Roosevelt focused on long-term constitutional implications of the proposed amendment. "Our Government is conducted by the people through representatives of their own choosing," he said. "It was with singular unanimity that the founders of the Republic agreed upon such free and representative form of government as the only practical means of government by the people." Next, he objected that the amendment "would cripple any President in his conduct of our foreign relations" and "encourage other nations to believe that they could violate American rights with impunity." Roosevelt said that he realized proponents "sincerely believe that it would be helpful in keeping the United States out of war." However, he bluntly concluded, "I am convinced it would have the opposite effect."[23]

Roosevelt's letter shaped the balance of the discussion. Vigorous arguments for the maintenance of representative government were pitted against equally passionate calls for direct democracy on the issue of going to war. Although the substance of the debate was constitutional, it was interspersed with discussions of the East Asian crisis. Advocates characterized the amendment as necessary to avoid the carnage of a foreign war in which, it was implied, an administration unchecked by the obligation to obtain popular consent would involve the country.[24]

Both Speaker Bankhead and majority leader Sam Rayburn declared the vote the most crucial of their lengthy congressional service. In an unsubtle summoning of party loyalty, Rayburn termed a discharge vote "the most tremendous blunder . . . since the formation of our Government under the

Constitution."[25] Meanwhile on the morning of the vote, Democratic national chairman James Farley telephoned seventy-eight Democrats, most of them petition signers, urging loyalty to the administration. About half of them were firmly committed to Ludlow, but rhetoric and political pleading persuaded the others to switch.[26]

On a roll-call vote, the discharge motion failed 188 to 209.[27] Democrats opposed discharge 188 to 111 while Republicans supported it 64 to 21. Progressives gave it their 8 votes and Farmer-Laborites their 5. Fifty-five signers of the discharge petition, all but three of them Democrats, reversed themselves to vote against the motion.[28]

The Ludlow vote revealed substantial resistance to involvement in the current international situation and shaped Roosevelt's cautious approach to foreign affairs during the next four years. Presidential aides kept watch on war referendum advocates, although their fears of renewed efforts on behalf of the amendment quickly faded.[29] Lost in the attention given isolationism was the possibility that some votes, Ludlow's own among them, may have been cast as much from concern with general issues of authority as with a specific foreign policy. Furthermore, obscured in the talk of the isolationists' near majority was the reality that the two-thirds support required for submission of a constitutional amendment remained far beyond their reach. Attention focused on the fact that a switch of eleven votes would have provided the majority to bring the resolution before the House. Lost from sight was the need for considerably greater support to meet the Article V requirement. The further challenges of Senate endorsement and state ratification remained unmentioned. Roosevelt had reason to worry about the political strength of the isolationists but little cause to fear a new constitutional restraint.

The central constitutional issue in the Ludlow battle was clearly understood inside and outside Congress.[30] Roosevelt himself drew attention to the question of representative versus direct democracy. Speaker Bankhead pointedly termed the war referendum "a radical—and I use that word in the proper sense of course—and revolutionary—and I use that in its usually accepted sense—attack upon the fundamental basic principle of a representative democracy for a free people."[31] Ludlow disparaged this argument as "fallacious and ridiculous." The measure would alter nothing, he said, except "that in respect to the great and most tragic of all issues the people comprising our great American Democracy have themselves chosen to make the decision."[32] In the final moments of debate, however, Ludlow supporters Robert Crosser of Ohio, Edouard Izac of California, Knute Hill of Washington, and Gerald Boileau of Wisconsin each expressed reservations about representative governance and declared their preference for direct choice. A skeptical John O'Connor of New York ended debate with the retort, "Once you have this 'pure democracy,' the next step is a dictatorship."[33]

The congressional vote not to discharge the Ludlow resolution bore a marked contrast to apparent public sentiment. A November 1935 American Institute of Public Opinion survey showed nearly three out of four Americans favoring a popular vote on declarations of war. After FDR's December 1937 press conference during which he criticized the idea, public approval fell but still stood at 64 percent, nearly a 2-to-1 margin. Although this represented passive support, it could not be considered insignificant. Even after Congress rejected the Ludlow amendment, opinion surveys in March 1938 and March 1939 showed that 58 percent of the public continued to favor war referendums.[34]

Most members of the House on January 10 ignored this consensus. With the issue explicitly stated as one of constitutional republicanism versus democracy, representative versus popular government, a majority of members put aside, at least for the moment, differences with the president to assert traditional republican arrangements. Few joined in the debate, no doubt finding it awkward to explain for the record their preference for the independent judgment of elected officials as opposed to the immediate will of the people. Some surely felt relief that they could vote against discharging the resolution from committee instead of the substantive issue. Yet the outcome probably would have been similar in a vote on the amendment itself rather than on a parliamentary maneuver. As they came to understand the constitutional implications of the Ludlow amendment, representatives were not generally prepared to reduce their own authority or that of the president. Even Democrats initially sympathetic to isolationist appeals reversed themselves when the issue was thus defined. After Ludlow's defeat, Roosevelt, in correspondence with his son, through a State Department paper, and even in a press conference a year later, reiterated the danger of crippling presidential power in foreign affairs.[35]

Louis Ludlow continued his efforts to win approval of a war referendum but with little success. Despite further committee hearings in May 1939, he never again came anywhere near even a limited victory as in January 1938. Although supporters continued to rain petitions and letters upon Congress, La Follette's attempt to get the Senate to add a referendum provision to neutrality law revision in October 1939 failed 73 to 17.[36] Once Germany invaded Poland in September 1939, discussion of Ludlow's idea virtually ceased, even in areas where isolationist sentiment remained strong.[37]

In retrospect, it is understandable and appropriate that historians have treated the Ludlow amendment as a high-water mark of isolationist sentiment and a warning to the president rather than as an indication of fundamental desire to recast the constitutional balance between the people and their chosen representatives.[38] It is questionable, however, whether the war referendum debate should be viewed strictly in terms of U.S. foreign policy. In the larger context of the ongoing debate over republicanism, the competing claims of leadership authority and popular sovereignty, Louis Ludlow's constitutional amendment stands in a different light. As such, it appears a significant backlash against presidential power, the possibility of Franklin Roosevelt or a successor exercising authority in an even less restrained fashion than did Woodrow Wilson in leading the country into World War I. The broad support for a constitutional amendment as a vehicle to rein in the federal government in 1938 testifies to the vitality of constitutional conservatism in the political thought of the day.

THE 1937 COURT BATTLE stirred other reactions against the expanding role of the president in the American constitutional structure. Efforts to reduce this power by means of a constitutional amendment limiting a president to two terms had a long history, but they became much more serious following the Court fight. Court reform opponents from both parties, Democratic senators Rush Holt of West Virginia and Edward R. Burke of Nebraska prominent among them, then began talking about presidential term limitation. Burke went so far as to hold sixteen days of hearings in September and October 1940 after his defeat for renomination and endorsement of the Republican presidential nominee. The Burke hearings, highly political and intensely anti–New Deal, foreshadowed more substantial efforts to obtain a presidential term-limit amendment.[39]

Franklin Roosevelt's decision to run for a third presidential term in 1940 broke a pattern voluntarily established by George Washington, reinforced by Thomas Jefferson, and observed for one reason or another by the seven other once-reelected chief executives. Not even the two vice-presidents elevated to the office and thereafter elected in their own right, Theodore Roosevelt and Calvin Coolidge, defied the eight-year limit (though TR, once out of office, had second thoughts and attempted unsuccessfully in 1912 to do so). Conscious of the tradition, FDR engaged in an elaborate charade of not running and only accepting a Democratic draft. He was still justifying himself in his final campaign speech, saying, "There is a great storm raging now, a storm that makes things harder for the world. And that storm, which did not start in this land of ours, is the true reason that I would like to stick by these people of ours until we reach the clear, sure footing ahead."[40]

Roosevelt's 1940 opponents were furious. Democrats whose own advancement was blocked or who preferred a more conservative candidate generally muted their criticism. One who did not, Representative Elmer J. Ryan of Minnesota, was shouted down when he proposed a no-third-term platform plank on the floor of the Democratic convention.[41] Republicans proved less reticent. In New York, New Jersey, and Rhode Island, Republican-dominated legislatures adopted anti–third-term resolutions in strict partisan voting.[42] The Republican national convention pledged to seek a constitutional two-term limit "to insure against the overthrow of our American system of government," and their nominee Wendell Wilkie declared that, if elected, such a measure would be his first request of Congress.[43]

Republican unhappiness grew with Roosevelt's third consecutive victory. A month after Democratic leaders in February 1943 began calling for a fourth Roosevelt term, Republican-controlled state legislatures in Michigan, Indiana, Illinois, Wisconsin, and Iowa adopted term-restriction resolutions. By May of the following year, Republican governors, congressmen, and senators from thirty states had declared opposition to third terms. Spontaneous applause from the convention floor greeted Robert Taft's reading of the Republican platform demand for a two-term limit. After FDR won once again, fifteen members of Congress, including House Republican minority leader Joseph Martin, introduced term-limit amendment resolutions. The Republican legislature of Oregon on April 1, 1945, added its voice to the chorus urging a curb on presidential service.[44]

Inability to defeat Roosevelt made the notion of restricting presidential terms, an idea considered but rejected in Philadelphia in 1787, attractive to his political opponents. They reviewed limits proposed to Congress, most commonly a single six-year term or two four-year terms, more than 200 times since the first in 1803. Amendment resolutions had in fact been approved in the House in 1824 and 1826 and the Senate in 1875 and 1928 but died each time in the other chamber.[45] Interest surged in the early 1940s, then flagged after Roosevelt's death; a Senate subcommittee hearing five months later aroused almost no interest.[46]

Circumstances changed, however, in the months that followed. The unsteady, unpopular performance of FDR's successor, Harry Truman, exposed the political vulnerability of the Democrats. Economic difficulties undermined the party nationally, and Truman's appointment of a President's Committee on Civil Rights as well as his advocacy of a permanent Fair Employment Practices Commission and the abolition of poll taxes alarmed southern white

Democrats. The election of Republican majorities in both houses of Congress in 1946, not seen since 1928 and widely regarded as a rejection of the New Deal legacy, provided an outlet for accumulated frustration.[47]

The moment that Republicans regained control of the House of Representatives, they put forth a presidential term-limit amendment. On January 3, 1947, the first day of the Eightieth Congress, new House Judiciary Committee chairman Earl C. Michener of Michigan introduced an amendment resolution identical to the one offered two years earlier by Joseph Martin, now Speaker of the House. Exactly one month later a Judiciary subcommittee endorsed the Martin-Michener proposal for a strict two-term limit, and within two days the full committee did likewise. The following day, February 6, the measure came before the House under a rule allowing only two hours of debate. When the roll was called, every one of the 238 Republicans present voted for the amendment. They were joined by 47 Democrats, 37 of whom came from the South. The resolution carried 285 to 121, well in excess of the Article V two-thirds requirement.[48]

Shortly after its introduction, Speaker Martin predicted that the term-limit amendment would be the "first important measure" enacted by the Eightieth Congress. Georgia congressman E. E. Cox indicated that at least ninety southern Democrats would support quick passage.[49] The prospect of immediate ratification by the many newly elected Republican state legislatures if the amendment reached them while they were still in session provided a powerful incentive. Judiciary Committee leaders shared Martin's sense of urgency, judging from their brief and perfunctory deliberations. Karl Mundt of South Dakota, a strong amendment proponent, embodied the anti-Roosevelt animus as he told the House that the amendment "grows directly out of the unfortunate experience we had in this country in 1940 and again in 1944 when a President who had entrenched himself in power by use of patronage and the public purse refused to vacate the office at the conclusion of two terms, but used the great powers of the Presidency to perpetuate himself in office." Mundt warned darkly that Americans might lose the freedom to vote officials out of office, as had Germans under Hitler.[50]

Republicans argued that, although law had not been transgressed, established constitutional tradition had been. An amendment would merely restore intention that had been understood, if unspoken. Otherwise the vital balance of power among the three branches of government could be lost. Custom, once violated, would no longer serve as a sufficient check. Mundt's colleague, Louis Graham of Pennsylvania, typified the more pointed and personal view of many Republicans. "We have seen the evil of perpetuation of centralization of government, of control through great bureaucracies, appointment of courts and control of our foreign relations," Graham said, "all due to the built-up, accumulated potency and power of one man remaining too long in public office."[51] Other Republicans kept up a drumbeat of disparaging comments about FDR's long tenure in office.

Outnumbered Democrats charged that Republicans were seeking to reduce the extent of political free choice and restrict the rights of the electorate. Neither Washington nor Jefferson, they tried to demonstrate, was irrevocably committed to the two-term standard. A majority in thirty-eight states in 1940 and thirty-six in 1944 had already shown their acceptance of more than two terms for a president, Texan John Lyle and other Democrats observed. South Carolina's Joseph Bryson insisted, "If the people of the United States can be trusted to elect a President for one term, or two terms, they also can be trusted to determine whether he should be continued in office for a third one." Previous amendments to the Constitution had expanded democratic practice, said Frank Chelf of Kentucky, but this one "seeks to impede and curtail the fundamental democratic power of the voter." Reminding his listeners of the world crisis in 1940 when Roosevelt stood for a third term, John McCormick of Massachusetts asserted that this measure would prevent "Americans in the future from exercising in a great emergency the judgment which they may deem is for the best interests of our country."[52]

The people themselves gave no evidence of concern for limiting presidential terms. Various congressmen acknowledged receiving little or no mail on the subject. The press paid little attention. Gallup polls found it did not even register among public political concerns.[53] Democratic senator Scott Lucas of Illinois claimed to have received only eight letters on the subject; his colleague, Lister Hill of Alabama, said he had received "no letter, no telegram, no telephone call, not one word from anyone about such a constitutional amendment." Hill observed, "If there be any real support among the people for such a constitutional amendment, it is so small that not even one person has been able to get himself a job as a lobbyist to come before the Congress and try to have it pass the joint resolution."[54] Political scientist Paul Appleby later observed that "the amendment was achieved so quietly as almost to suggest a conspiracy of inattention."[55] One does not need to resort to conspiracy theories to conclude that presidential term limitation mattered to few Americans other than disgruntled anti–New Deal politicians, mainly frustrated Republicans whom Franklin Roosevelt had repeatedly defeated and southern Democrats out of step with their party's national leadership.

The overriding force of partisanship became most evident in discussions of amending procedure. Both sides paid lip service to the principle that the people should decide the fate of any amendment, but they took quite different positions on the ratification methods that Article V provided. Republicans, who had gained control of twenty-six state legislatures in 1946 and were clearly confident of their support, proposed the usual method of legislative ratification. "That has always been construed, and is today construed," claimed Judiciary subcommittee chair Raymond Springer of Indiana, "as submitting the question to the people themselves."[56] Democrats immediately challenged this view, contending it would put the decision in the hands of legislators elected on the basis of other considerations. A far more accurate measure of public preference could be obtained, they suggested, through ratification by convention.

Whether moved by partisanship or faulty memory, several Republicans equated legislative ratification with popular endorsement, declining to acknowledge any difference between the two Article V procedures. Lack of understanding of the amending process proved bipartisan, however. Democratic congressman William Colmer of Mississippi, moving to alter the amendment resolution to require convention ratification, considered it "the only vehicle through which we can get a clear-cut and unequivocal decision of the people" but thought it had been used to obtain the Eighteenth Amendment. In any case, his motion was defeated 134 to 74 just before the House approved the amendment itself.[57]

The rush to expedite a presidential term-limit amendment continued as the measure moved to the Senate. The Senate Judiciary Committee, like its House counterpart, heard no outside testimony, deliberated only briefly, and promptly sent the measure to the floor. The committee did, however, reconsider the issue of ratification method after Democratic senator J. Howard McGrath of Rhode Island and Republican John Sherman Cooper of Kentucky made effective appeals for use of conventions. Missouri Republican Forrest Donnell, at first inclined to favor legislative ratification because of its prior use, reconsidered after Cooper pointed out that legislators would not be chosen for their position on this issue. The convention method would, Donnell decided, "afford opportunity for further and adequate consideration by the country, even if it results in some cooling off in the process of consideration, even though it involves some delay in the consideration of and action upon the amendment."[58] Committee chair Alexander Wiley, concerned about getting the amendment to the Senate floor, did not resist.

Senate debate demonstrated that members had given little thought to the implications of Article V procedural alternatives. Senator Wiley voiced doubts as to whether convention ratification would bring the amendment decision closer to the people. He believed, he said, that legislatures could simply resolve themselves into conventions to carry out the ratification process. However, Senator Donnell, the recent convert, suggested that such legislative action would violate the Founders' intention to provide two distinct alternative methods. After some debate, Democrats agreed that voters could simultaneously elect persons as delegates and legislators. No sense emerged that this procedure condoned circumventing the 1787 effort to provide a means of ratification in which legislatures would not be involved.[59]

Minority leader Alben Barkley and his deputies, Lister Hill and Scott Lucas, further undercut the change in ratification method that their Judiciary Committee colleagues had obtained. Seeing no popular concern for presidential term limitation, they argued that legislatures would reflect public opinion as well as conventions. Barkley and Lucas took the position that convention-delegate elections would be dominated by a relatively few vitally interested citizens, an unsatisfactory arrangement. They concluded that legislators, even if elected without regard to their position on this issue, would be more representative of the people than convention delegates.[60]

Confusion as to how the convention ratification system ought to function recalled congressional debate over the Twenty-first Amendment. This time, however, no strong advocate of convention ratification, such as the Association Against the Prohibition Amendment or Voluntary Committee of Lawyers, emerged to demonstrate how it could be done speedily, simply, and directly reflective of public opinion. Displaying more legislative self-esteem and desire to control the outcome than logic or historical awareness, the Senate on March 10 overwhelmingly rejected convention ratification 63 to 20.[61]

The Senate Judiciary Committee had also sought to modify the strict two-term limit of the Martin-Michener resolution on the principle that someone briefly elevated to the presidency due to death or removal of an incumbent should not be barred from being twice elected in his own right. The committee proposed that only after a year or more of service in each of two terms should a president become ineligible for reelection. When the resolution reached the Senate floor, Washington Democrat Warren Magnuson offered the simpler and more generous substitute: "No person shall be elected to the office of President more than twice." Thereafter Magnuson tried once more to reduce the limitation to two successive terms so that, conceivably, a young former president might run again after being out of office, but that proposal failed as well. After Ohio Republican Robert Taft raised the perennial suggestion of a single six-year presidential term, an idea already discussed at length in the House before being rejected, a compromise was struck that limited a president to two elected terms plus two years of a term to which someone else had been elected. Responding to comments that Republicans were concerned about Truman's eligibility for two more terms, Taft proposed that Truman be specifically exempted from the amendment. This would, Senator Wiley said, take the issue "out of politics." On that doubtful premise, the Taft compromise was adopted by voice vote.[62]

Late on the evening of March 12, after devoting portions of five days to discussing the matter, the Senate approved the revised term-limit resolution 59 to 23. As in the House, not one single Republican cast a ballot against the amendment. In contrast, thirteen of forty-five Senate Democrats, nine of them southerners, abandoned their party's position against it.[63] Rather than insist on its own version of the amendment, the House quickly accepted the Senate changes concerning the length of nonelective presidential service. On March 21, by a recorded vote of only 81 to 29 the House sent the amendment to the states for ratification.[64]

The partisan character of the presidential term-limit amendment stands out. Every Republican who cast a ballot in either house of Congress approved the measure. The additional votes needed to secure the two-thirds margin for acceptance came overwhelmingly from conservative, anti–New Deal, southern Democrats. Only ten House Democrats outside the Old South supported the amendment. One of only two northern urban liberal Democratic members to vote for it was freshman representative John Kennedy of Massachusetts, whose father had become a bitter foe of Franklin Roosevelt.[65] This pattern of Republican solidarity and Democratic division continued as state legislatures took up the question.

Republican-dominated legislatures rushed to ratify the term-limit amendment in spring 1947. Nineteen of the twenty-six where Republicans held majorities in both houses were meeting when Congress submitted the amendment; all but one ratified within eight weeks.[66] Where roll calls were recorded, a cumulative 358 Republican state senators voted for the amendment and only 3 opposed it. This powerful and remarkably unified partisan behavior was even more pronounced in lower houses as 1,213 Republican members voted yea and only 8 voted nay. In contrast, minority Democrats opposed the amendment 85 to 9 in the eighteen senates and 294 to 46 in the lower houses. The sole nonratifying Republican state was Massachusetts, where legislators agreed to submit the measure to an advisory referendum, thus reviving the notion first expressed in the Bay State in the 1770s that constitutional change should be directly approved by the people. In 1948, Massachusetts voters not only rejected the amendment but also turned out the legislative Republicans, ensuring that the state would remain nonratifying.[67] New York reasserted the more typical pattern in 1948 when Republicans voted to ratify by 37 to 0 in the senate and 103 to 1 in the assembly;

they easily outweighed Democrats who opposed the measure 12 to 3 in the senate and 43 to 0 in the assembly.[68]

By the time New York acted, nineteen Republican-dominated legislatures had ratified, but only seven more existed to add support. All but Massachusetts did so, the Dakotas after the 1948 election and Indiana, Idaho, Montana, and Wyoming following the 1950 election.[69] Despite their best partisan efforts, however, Republicans could not by themselves bring about the amendment's adoption. They could produce a majority of state ratifications but not the required three-fourths.

In state ratification as in congressional adoption, southern Democrats provided the margin of victory for the presidential term-limit amendment. When it was sent to the states and every sitting Republican legislature promptly took action, legislatures controlled by Democrats either did nothing or, in the case of Texas, rejected it. Circumstances changed, however, soon after Truman's Committee on Civil Rights recommended a broad program of action. Southern Democrats, determined to protect the racial status quo and already uncomfortable with much of the New Deal, began to look with greater favor upon the amendment, a measure they perceived as reducing presidential and federal power. On January 28, 1948, the overwhelmingly Democratic Virginia legislature voted unanimously in the senate and with only six dissents in the house to ratify, the first southern and first Democratic state to do so. On February 2 Truman sent Congress a civil rights message, and ten days later the Mississippi legislature, where every seat in both houses was held by a Democrat, ratified by 36 to 6 in the senate and 123 to 4 in the house.[70] Although few southern legislatures met in 1948, anger with Truman was evident at the Southern Governors' Conference in March and in the subsequent Dixiecrat revolt.

Truman's 1948 victory momentarily subdued the southern rebellion. Only North Carolina took up the term-limit amendment in 1949 and soundly defeated it. Not until 1950 did another southern state ratify, and once again it was a segregationist stronghold concerned about the Truman administration's civil rights initiatives. Louisiana, which the Dixiecrats carried in 1948, gave unanimous approval in May. As in Mississippi, Democrats held every seat in the Louisiana legislature.[71]

A flood of southern ratifications followed the 1950 election with its further erosion of liberal Democratic strength. Speculation that Truman might run for another term provided added motivation. Eight southern states endorsed the amendment in little more than eleven weeks between mid-February and early May 1951. In the Arkansas legislature, where Democrats held all but two seats, members expressed concern that Truman had developed "a civil rights complex" and created "nearly a dictatorship"; on February 15 they approved ratification by 24 to 9 in the senate and 63 to 17 in the house. Two days later Georgia ratified, Tennessee followed suit three days thereafter, and Texas did so two days after that, all under similar circumstances. North Carolina Democrats, who in 1949 rejected the amendment as had Texans in 1947, now favored it by a substantial margin; they were joined by every member of the small Republican minority. The all-but-totally Democratic legislatures of South Carolina, Florida, and Alabama ratified in one-sided votes in March, April, and May, thus completing the embrace of the amendment by every state of the Confederacy. Equally striking, southern Democrats had overwhelmingly abandoned their national party's position.[72]

Four other states where Democrats possessed legislative power also agreed to ratify in early 1951. In each, resistance to federal initiatives on race and other matters was increasing. In New Mexico and Maryland, where Democratic majorities prevailed, most Democrats joined all Republicans in supporting the amendment. In closely divided Utah and Nevada, Democrats split fairly evenly; Republicans approved with only one exception.[73] These states were not critical, considering that forty-one states ratified by May 1951, five more than required. Yet they provided added evidence that the Twenty-second Amendment was achieved through a combination of virtually absolute Republican support and substantial backing from conservative Democrats.

Desire to impose restraints upon presidential power pervaded term-limit discussions. "If you will look back through history, you will see that dictatorships occur by one man assuming office indefinitely," declared a Tennessee state senator in a comment typical of the debate. Constitutional amendment seemed the appropriate remedy to most, but not all, sympathetic to this concern. A Maine representative disparaged "an ill-considered and hasty step" that would affect "the fundamental law of the country" and "the ruler of this nation in time of crisis in the future." A North Carolina legislator predicted, "The time may come again when we will need another third termer. Personally I think that if we pass this amendment we would be saying to our people that we don't have any confidence in their judgment."[74]

Although his patron, Franklin Roosevelt, and his office were the targets of the presidential term-limit amendment, Harry Truman remained remarkably silent during the battle over its congressional passage and state ratification. Whether from recognition that presidents had no formal role in the amending process or shrewd appraisal of the likely negative impact of his intervention, Truman chose to distance himself from the issue. Not even Representative Adolph Sabath's lament that the amendment represented "a pitiful victory over a great man now sleeping on the banks of the Hudson" roused Truman, the normally feisty partisan, to enter the fray.[75] With neither the administration, the Democratic National Committee, nor any other opponent of the measure coordinating resistance, the Twenty-second Amendment, a liberal journal observed, "glided through legislatures in a fog of silence—passed by men whose election in no way involved their stand on the question—without hearings, without publicity, without any of that popular participation that should have accompanied a change in the organic law of the country."[76]

Before long, Republicans began having second thoughts about the amendment their determination and unity had produced. In July 1956 resolutions to repeal the Twenty-second Amendment began to be introduced in Congress. In October Dwight Eisenhower told reporters that the electorate "ought to be able to choose for its President anybody that it wants, regardless of the number of terms he has served." Eisenhower's reelection as president a month later made him the first chief executive to whom the Twenty-second Amendment would apply. Predictably, Republicans soon submitted more repeal resolutions. The author of one, Oregon senator Richard Neuberger, acknowledged that a plan "conceived primarily by the political opponents" of Franklin Roosevelt now blocked another Eisenhower term. When Eisenhower immediately declared his lack of interest in a third term, even if the amendment was repealed, discussion slowed.[77]

In 1959 both houses of Congress held hearings on presidential term limitation. Former president Truman appeared before a Senate Judiciary subcommittee to advocate repeal of "a bad amendment." While FDR's leadership in World War II demonstrated the value of his continued reelection, Truman declared, "Roosevelt haters got busy and sold the country a bill of goods." In their spiteful desire to get Roosevelt, they actually made "a 'lame duck' out of every second term President for all time in the future." Outspoken as usual, the former president called the presidency the hardest job in the world under the best of circumstances and said, "You do not have to be very smart to know that an officeholder who is not eligible for reelection loses a lot of influence." The way to get rid of someone who was not a good president was to not reelect him, Truman believed, and that "does not require a constitutional amendment."[78] Several members of the subcommittee, including Everett Dirksen, who had voted for the amendment in 1947 and since recanted, hurried to agree with Truman that term limits, like national prohibition, represented an undemocratic restriction and that the people could be trusted to make wise choices.[79] Truman later told the committee counsel that if his appearance helped accomplish the amendment's repeal, he "will be very happy, indeed."[80] Eisenhower, reflexively at odds with his predecessor, immediately recanted his earlier criticism of the Twenty-second Amendment and called for its further trial.[81]

Following the Truman-Eisenhower exchange, repeal efforts largely died. They were renewed momentarily after Richard Nixon's election to a second term in 1972 and Ronald Reagan's in 1984. The first revival was quickly stillborn as Watergate scandal revelations began emerging. The second took shape when Reagan himself told a group of state legislators in September 1985 that limiting presidents to two terms was "ridiculous" if voters wanted them to serve longer. The American people "ought to have a right to decide who their leadership would be." A few months later Reagan declared, "We ought to take a serious look and see if we haven't interfered with the democratic rights of the people." He assumed, he said with his typical disarming modesty, that no president could ever advocate repeal of the Twenty-second Amendment "with himself in mind." This may have been mere pose because within months Representative Guy Vander Jagt of Michigan, chairman of the National Republican Congressional Committee, was calling the Twenty-second Amendment a mistake, introducing a repeal resolution with sixty-five cosponsors, and advocating yet another term for Reagan. The effort was widely considered a clever Republican fund-raising gimmick, a device to keep attention focused on the Republicans' greatest political asset, who after all would be seventy-seven years old at the end of his second term. Yet the highly partisan Vander Jagt was unlikely to have raised the issue unless he assumed that Republicans were certain to dominate the presidency for the foreseeable future. Not able to stir support beyond the ranks of the Republican faithful, term-limit repeal talk declined rapidly as the Iran-Contra scandal began to expose Reagan's liabilities.[82]

Reexamination of the Twenty-second Amendment has occurred whenever a president has won reelection. Concerns have been voiced about the amendment's negative influence on a second-term president's power and effectiveness at home and abroad, not to mention the people's sovereign right to their choice of leaders. Yet to date every effort to initiate repeal has collapsed in the face of perceived partisan benefit and the obstacles of Article V. What one distinguished constitutional scholar called "a tainted amendment," a measure "based on the sharp anger of a moment rather than the studied wisdom of a generation," remained, nevertheless, entrenched in the Constitution.[83] Conservatives who engineered the amendment, were, for the ensuing forty years, its repeated and indeed sole victims. The amendment, adopted more from animosity toward the New Deal and fear of federal civil rights initiatives than as a result of thoughtful consideration of presidential functions, achieved the restraint on the executive that its proponents sought but at a political price they did not anticipate.

SUCCESS IN OBTAINING the Twenty-second Amendment gave birth or new life to other midcentury conservative efforts to reverse the New Deal and rein in the presidency through constitutional reform. Amendments, after all, could be obtained by exclusively legislative action at the federal and state level. Thus they particularly appealed to persons politically alienated from an executive and judiciary shaped by the New Deal. Most such retrograde amendment initiatives found limited support, but the strength of one provided a reminder that these crusades were not inconsequential.

The New Deal's expansion of government spending and taxation came under attack as soon as conservatives began regaining their voices. In 1938 the American Taxpayer Association proposed a constitutional amendment limiting federal taxing power to 25 percent of income. Frustrated when Congress took no action, the association turned to Article V's seldom employed and never successful alternative means of offering an amendment, state requests for a constitutional convention. Tax limitation advocates hoped to "put the fear of God," or at least concern about an uncontrollable constitutional convention, in Congress and thus compel it to propose the amendment. By 1953 they had obtained convention applications from twenty-eight states and stirred Congress to hold hearings.[84]

Congressman Wright Patman, a Texas Democrat, vigorously attacked the "millionaire's amendment." He called one sponsor, the Committee for Constitutional Government, the "outstanding fascist group in America" and warned that, as in 1787, a convention could "rewrite the whole Constitution." Patman's outburst helped blunt the movement for the amendment. Although a few more states submitted convention requests, a dozen others rescinded theirs, and ultimately Congress ignored the lot.[85] Returning to more traditional approaches, Illinois congressman Chauncey Reed and Senator Everett Dirksen introduced a joint resolution for an income-tax-limitation amendment, but it went nowhere either.[86]

Another attempt to reform New Deal fiscal practices was launched by Democratic senator Harry F. Byrd of Virginia and his Republican colleague Styles Bridges of New Hampshire. They offered an amendment to require the federal budget be balanced annually by limiting congressional appropriations to estimated government receipts. Only by a three-fourths vote could Congress avoid the stricture in an emergency.[87] The Byrd-Bridges balanced-budget amendment enlisted little congressional support at the time and never came to a vote. It did, however, acquire some steadfast proponents who would bring it forth again twenty years later as a means of restoring fiscal responsibility allegedly abandoned in the 1930s.

Two other amendment resolutions represented symbolic opposition to the Roosevelt and Truman administrations more than consequential reform efforts. Republican senator John Marshall Butler of Maryland suggested an amendment to fix the size of the Supreme Court at nine and the retirement age of justices at seventy-five. He clearly intended a further rebuke to FDR's court reorganization efforts, though in attempting to sanction existing arrangements such an amendment would have introduced age limits on judicial tenure. Another proposal, one prohibiting a president from seizing private property under the guise of war powers, displayed a similar character. It would merely confirm the Supreme Court's rejection of Truman's 1952 federal seizure of control over the strike-paralyzed steel industry.[88]

Republican senator Karl Mundt of South Dakota and Representative Frederic Coudert of New York took a more political approach to reversing the New Deal's legacy. They proposed to revise the electoral college system of presidential election by providing for the choice of electors in the same manner as senators and representatives. This deceptively simple reform would produce two electors chosen at large and others by congressional district, altering the winner-take-all pattern in each state's presidential contest. Mundt and Coudert argued that the measure would increase harmony between presidents and members of Congress. It would, however, sharply reduce the electoral influence of large cities and heavily populated states. Such areas, with their concentrations of working class, ethnic, and black voters, formed the core of the New Deal coalition. Mundt admitted his intentions when he proclaimed that "those who would push our country leftward toward totalitarian centralized control and toward national socialism would not be able to exert pressures on our presidential candidates and our party platforms and policies at all commensurate with their present power."[89] Expressing concern that a candidate with a minority of the vote might win the presidency, Senator Henry Cabot Lodge, Jr., of Massachusetts and Representative Ed Gossett of Texas renewed their proposal for a proportional division of popular votes within each state. It had gained two-thirds Senate endorsement in 1950, but, challenged as a threat to state power and the two-party political system, had been defeated in the House. Reintroduced in the Senate by Democrats Price Daniel of Texas and Estes Kefauver of Tennessee, proportional voting drew less support when reconsidered.[90] Minnesota Democrat Hubert Humphrey complicated matters when he suggested a simple national popular vote to choose the president. The various amendment resolutions divided whatever support existed for electoral college reform, and they met defeat in the Senate in March 1956.[91]

When none of their amendment ideas made any headway in the Article V process, frustrated conservatives offered yet another, this one to make proposing amendments easier. Unlike Progressive Era efforts to place amending power in the hands of simple democratic majorities, or the Wadsworth-Garrett attempt of the 1920s to use popular referendums to erect additional obstacles to change, this measure would allow smaller numbers of state legislators to put forth amendments for ratification. Oregon attorney John Ebinger established the Committee for the Preservation of State and Local Government to promote a plan of his own devising; it would allow twelve states by two-thirds vote of their legislatures to initiate amendments. Reducing from two-thirds to one-fourth or less the number of states needed to demand that an amendment be offered for ratification could dramatically alter the nature of constitutional revision, sharply diminish the influence of Congress in the process, and increase the power of state legislators desirous of protecting states' rights or interests. Five states requested the amendment between 1953 and 1955. Not surprisingly, however, when Chauncey Reed and Francis Walter of Pennsylvania introduced the Ebinger plan in 1954 and again in 1955, the House made no move to reduce its own power.[92]

Together with the Twenty-second Amendment, these proposals were recognized at the time as departing from the previous pattern of using the amending mechanism. Constitutional scholars noted that a process hitherto used by liberal forces to expand government authority was now being employed by conservatives to restrict that power. Many of these amendment efforts involved sleight-of-hand maneuvers to gain fundamental changes with a minimum of public discussion, political scientist Clement Vose observed. "It seems clear at the moment," he wrote, "that a substantial part of the American public is completely in the dark about the issues at stake." He, for one, was clearly relieved that the Article V process presented apparently insurmountable obstacles to the wave of amendment initiatives.[93]

An exception to the pattern of easily thwarted conservative proposals involved the so-called Bricker amendment to restrict presidential authority in foreign affairs. Its advocates claimed that Franklin Roosevelt's wartime diplomacy revealed its need, even though their concern took root a quarter of a century earlier. In 1920 the Supreme Court had reviewed a treaty with Great Britain (acting for Canada) concerning migratory birds and a congressional act for its enforcement. The treaty and statute circumvented a 1914 district court decision finding a previous federal law protecting migratory birds to be an unconstitutional invasion of state powers. Properly enacted treaties, Justice Oliver Wendell Holmes declared for the Court, had status as supreme law; they overrode rights reserved to states under the Tenth Amendment.[94] In 1936 the justices allowed far more executive latitude in foreign affairs than they were conceding in domestic matters when they upheld a Roosevelt-imposed arms embargo.[95] The following year the Court affirmed the validity of executive agreements with foreign nations, specifically the 1933 Roosevelt-Litvinov agreements settling American property claims against the Soviet Union, even in the absence of treaty ratification.[96] These decisions were widely regarded as enhancing presidential authority in the foreign arena and conceivably in domestic affairs as well.

The initial 1945 congressional action in response to these concerns was easily mistaken for House of Representatives' unhappiness with its exclusion from the treaty-making process. House Judiciary Committee chairman Hatton Sumners proposed a constitutional amendment requiring that treaties be ratified by House and Senate majorities. Discussion of the measure centered less on the House role in foreign affairs than on whether Sumners's proposal would further enhance presidential power. Some representatives saw action by simple majorities as more susceptible to presidential influence than the prevailing two-thirds Senate supermajority requirement. With treaties having the functional authority of constitutional amendments, opponents declared, the Sumner plan offered the prospect of a new system of amendment by treaty and posed a threat to state power. The House approved the amendment resolution 288 to 88 on May 9, but, not surprisingly, the Senate gave it no consideration.[97]

The Yalta agreements and the United Nations Treaty stirred growing conservative fears about federal treaty-making and executive-agreement power undermining specific domestic arrangements, state authority, and even national sovereignty. Disquieting indications continued to surface. In 1946 the National Lawyers Guild suggested that the UN Charter could be employed to force the federal government to take action against lynching and segregation. Court decisions in 1948 and 1950 used the charter to invalidate a California law prohibiting land ownership by Japanese ineligible for citizenship. Conservative apprehensions that the pending UN Covenant on Human Rights and Genocide Convention could force revolutionary social change provoked a reaction that Dwight Eisenhower later described as a crusade to "save the United States from [UN delegate] Eleanor Roosevelt." In 1948 American Bar Association president Frank Holman, who regarded the New Deal as a long step toward socialism, launched an ABA campaign against UN treaties and executive agreements in general.[98] Holman eventually told a Senate Judiciary subcommittee that he opposed treaties declaring a universal human right to "food, clothing, housing, and medical care, and necessary social services, and the right to security in the event of unemployment, sickness, disability, widowhood, [or] old age." He explained his worry that such treaties would transform the United States "into a completely socialistic state."[99]

Still shrouded in secrecy, the Yalta agreements between Franklin Roosevelt and Joseph Stalin took on added significance to conservatives in the late 1940s as the Soviet Union increased its domination of Eastern Europe, the Soviets detonated an atomic bomb, a communist insurgency achieved a revolution in China, and challenges to the loyalty of Roosevelt's Yalta aide, Alger Hiss, created a cause célèbre. Not only Republican extremists such as Joseph McCarthy but mainstream partisans as well charged that FDR, acting without consultation or restraint, had set these steps in motion at Yalta. When the Korean War erupted, the Yalta accords again were blamed. Throughout the 1952 campaign, the dangers of treaties and secret executive agreements exemplified by Yalta provided a constant Republican refrain in its litany of criticism of Roosevelt and Truman. Fiercely anti-Communist Notre Dame Law School dean Clarence Manion railed against Secretary of State Dean Acheson's "conspiratorial Communism" and warned that State Department–negotiated treaties undermining American government were "ominously continuous."[100]

For more than a decade Ohio Republican senator John W. Bricker, the party's 1944 vice-presidential candidate and a pillar of its conservative wing, had linked the New Deal with radicalism and communism. He also became an outspoken critic of Roosevelt and Truman diplomacy and what he saw as a growing presidential tendency to act without consulting Congress. In particular, the UN's 1948 Declaration on Human Rights and subsequent efforts to draft an enforceable covenant defining political, civil, social, economic, and cultural rights struck Bricker as a devious attempt to impose New Deal and European socialist policies upon the United States.[101] In July 1951, therefore, he introduced a congressional resolution labeling the latest version of the UN Covenant on Human Rights an unacceptable restriction of individual liberty and ordering the president to withdraw from further negotiations. A number of Republicans and southern Democrats endorsed Bricker's warning that, given current judicial understanding of the treaty power, UN agreements threatened to override American domestic policies. They feared the undermining of constitutional protections that states used to defend their racial practices against federal pressure for change.[102]

Acknowledging that his UN covenant resolution was merely a stopgap measure, Bricker two months later proposed a lengthy, complex constitutional amendment that stirred the interest and support of many of his Senate colleagues.[103] Discounting existing requirements that treaties be approved not only by the president but also by a two-thirds majority of the Senate, the Ohio senator sought to make treaties subject to judicial acceptance as well. His amendment would require treaties to be consistent with the Constitution and would likewise limit executive agreements. He discussed the matter with Holman and other American Bar Association leaders who shared his view that socialist measures and civil rights legislation not otherwise possible might be enacted through diplomatic devices. Although he and the ABA did not fully agree on means to achieve their goals, the senator was eager to hold hearings and advance the amendment process.

The ABA Committee on Peace and Law Through United Nations, far from the internationalist group its name implied, quickly concurred that an amendment offered "the only effective answer to the extension of federal power." Preoccupied with limiting the domestic effect of treaties, the committee drew its own amendment declaring, "A provision of a treaty which conflicts with any provision of this Constitution shall not be of any force or effect. A treaty shall become effective as internal law in the United States only through legislation by Congress which it could enact under its delegated powers in the absence of such treaty." Bricker had doubts about the final clause, soon labeled the *which* clause, preferring a specific, self-executing constitutional limitation on the treaty power rather than a requirement that legislation be adopted if a treaty was to have domestic effect. Bricker wished to assert judicial authority to invalidate treaties and executive agreements inconsistent with the Constitution; the ABA would block them from taking effect unless endorsed by legislative action, in practice a far more severe restriction. Early in 1952 Bricker reintroduced his own amendment, this time with all but one of his forty-five Republican colleagues together with fourteen conservative Democrats as cosponsors.[104]

The text of the Bricker amendment engendered controversy, given the ABA alternative and the statements of several of Bricker's Senate cosponsors that they supported the general idea of treaty power limitation but not necessarily his approach. Nevertheless, although conservatives found it difficult to agree on terms, they shared an antipathy for the not-forgotten Roosevelt as well as for Truman's conduct of foreign affairs, his commitment of troops to Europe, his firing of Korean commander Douglas MacArthur, his refusal to disclose agreements reached in meetings with British prime minister Winston Churchill, and, in April 1952, his seizure of control of strike-threatened

American steel mills as a war measure. Supreme Court rejection of presidential authority to carry out the steel seizure failed to calm them, especially since three justices approved Truman's action.[105] The following month, initial Senate hearings on the Bricker amendment served primarily as a platform for critiques of recent developments. With 1952 being a presidential election year, desire to express concern about presidential conduct outweighed feelings of need to reach an immediate solution. With the ABA's states' rights focus not entirely in step with Bricker's anti-UN preoccupation and with neither endorsed by the Eisenhower campaign, the Republican victory did not produce a clear mandate on how to implement the party's vague platform pledge to "wage war against secret covenants."[106]

The Republican party in 1952 captured control of Congress as well as the presidency for the first time since before the New Deal. Sensing their opportunity in the Eighty-third Congress, Bricker and ABA amendment advocates sought common ground.[107] The senator immediately introduced a revised amendment resolution closer in form and substance to the ABA version. It did not, however, contain an equivalent to the *which* clause granting legislative power to block the operation of treaties. In February 1953 the ABA likewise revised its draft amendment, adding a clause to regulate executive agreements as if they were treaties and modifying the *which* clause. The latter read, "A treaty shall become effective as internal law in the United States only through legislation which would be valid in the absence of treaty." Senator Bricker observed that this softer language, though it might permit judicial resolution of disputes, would still place international negotiations at the mercy of state legislatures and grant them "what amounts to a veto power over foreign policy."[108]

After making the questionable claim at a February Senate hearing that the amendment's objectives were "too important . . . for any words to stand in the way of ratification," Bricker in May struck a compromise with the ABA. Merely adding a statement that "a provision of a treaty which conflicts with this Constitution shall not be of any force or effect," the compromise remained close to the earlier ABA version with its *which* clause. Bricker tacitly acknowledged that ABA support was vital to any amendment's chance of advancing. Most Senate Judiciary Committee Republicans and southern Democrats promptly endorsed the compromise, sending the revised amendment to the Senate floor by a vote of 9 to 5 on June 4.[109]

Prior to the convening of the Eighty-third Congress, most opposition to the Bricker amendment came from the Truman administration, internationalist-minded lawyers in the ABA and the Bar of the City of New York, and liberal organizations, who warned that it would handicap the conduct of the nation's foreign affairs.[110] The Eisenhower administration immediately perceived as much; it hesitated, however, to say so bluntly and risk alienating conservative Republicans. Initially, Senator Bricker thought he enjoyed the new president's support.[111]

When first asked about the Bricker amendment by a *Chicago Tribune* reporter, Eisenhower observed that advocates were not really out to change the Constitution but to prevent its being altered by international agreement. "Now that seems to me to have a little bit of an anomaly, right in that kind of reasoning: you amend it in order to show that it is going to remain the same." He quickly pointed out that the president had no formal role in the amending process.[112] A week later he was more forthright, saying, "An analysis for me by the Secretary of State" determined that the amendment would "as I understand it, in certain ways restrict the authority that the President must have, if he is to conduct the foreign affairs of the Nation effectively." He respected the intent of its proponents but believed "certain features . . . would work to the disadvantage of our country, particularly in making it impossible for the President to work with the flexibility that he needs in this highly complicated and difficult situation."[113] Even though Eisenhower privately wrote his brother Edgar that the amendment would "cripple the executive power to the point that we become helpless in world affairs," his restrained public remarks left the impression with Bricker and others that John Foster Dulles rather than the president was the measure's principal opponent. Secretary of State Dulles and Attorney General Herbert Brownell reinforced this image as they presented the administration's case at April 1953 hearings. Eisenhower's careful coaching of his spokesmen was overlooked.[114]

Opposition to the Bricker amendment stayed strong but partially submerged. Foes ranging from the Republican chairman of the Senate Foreign Relations Committee, Alexander Wiley of Wisconsin, to the Democratic minority leader, Lyndon Johnson of Texas, appeared to believe that the measure, though unwise, was popular.[115] The same factors may explain why support remained visible but in many cases shallow. Forty-four Republicans and nineteen Democrats ultimately listed themselves as cosponsors of Bricker's amendment resolution. The sixty-four votes represented the two-thirds of the Senate necessary to approve an amendment. Yet not all of these senators felt equally strongly about the measure, nor did all subscribe to language as restrictive as the ABA's.

The country at large did not press Congress on the Bricker amendment. As late as October 1953, only 19 percent of the public indicated they were conscious of the issue, and they held varied opinions. Even when congressional debate crested in early 1954, at which time public awareness had risen to 28 percent, only a few small groups indicated deep concern. Conservative ideologues, including Frank Holman, Clarence Manion, Robert E. Wood of Sears, Roebuck, and newspaper publisher Frank Gannett, were vocal supporters. Liberal and labor organizations spoke in opposition. Divided views within its own ranks immobilized the American Bar Association. Elsewhere few signs of interest appeared.[116]

In June 1953, Eisenhower and his deputies decided to explore compromise with Bricker. The president told reporters that he was open to an amendment but not "anything that interferes with the constitutional and traditional separation of powers between the departments."[117] The senator proved unwilling to drop the *which* clause, anathema to the administration, and thereby lose ABA support. Eisenhower then decided a prudent tactic would be to offer an alternative amendment specifying only that treaties and executive agreements could not violate the Constitution. He could thereby satisfy enough Bricker supporters to thwart those insisting on the restrictions of the *which* clause or congressional regulation of executive agreements. Eisenhower's July 1953 decisive success in overcoming Bricker's opposition to ratification of a NATO treaty concerning the legal status of troops stationed abroad encouraged the administration. Its alternative amendment was set before the Senate by majority leader William Knowland just before Congress adjourned for the year in August.[118] A combative Bricker labeled it "ridiculous."[119]

Congress fought the climactic battle over treaty powers after reconvening in January 1954. Following autumn discussions in which Bricker wavered and then stood by the *which* clause, an angry Eisenhower characterized the Ohioan's amendment as intending to return American foreign affairs to the paralyzing state independence of the Articles of Confederation.[120] Ten days later in a public letter, Bricker responded that it was "highly improper of the President of the United States to employ extra-legal pressures in an effort to defeat the amendment. . . . The President has no constitutional role to play in the amending process."[121] As Eisenhower and Bricker pointedly criticized each other, the division within Republican ranks over presidential authority grew more obvious. Although the nuances of language and the subtleties of objective made the debate complex and difficult for outsiders to follow, the issue for Republican senators increasingly became one of supporting the president or the party's most conservative traditions. For a time Eisenhower hoped that an alternative amendment, if not the Knowland measure then one brought forth by Democratic senator Walter George of Georgia, would at least camouflage, if not repair, the interparty discord, but ultimately it could not.

As a showdown neared in the Senate, John Bricker decided to abandon the *which* clause, though not other provisions of his amendment, to improve chances of obtaining a two-thirds majority. Senator George, in collaboration with Democratic minority leader Lyndon Johnson, offered a substitute requiring treaties and other international agreements to be consistent with the Constitution and stipulating that international agreements other than treaties would become "internal law in the United States only by an act of the Congress." The administration, after initially admiring the George measure, concluded that congressional approval of executive agreements would unduly restrict a president. It then put forth its own substitute, through Knowland, eliminating even this provision.[122]

When the Senate finally addressed the various amendment proposals in February 1954, it quickly endorsed, 62 to 20, the provision common to all of them that treaties and agreements must conform to the Constitution. Fewer than one-fourth of those voting appeared staunchly opposed to any sort of amendment. Bricker's own often-revised proposal, in final form requiring congressional approval for either treaties or executive agreements to have domestic effect, received only 42 votes. Fifty senators opposed it on February 25. The next day Senator George's provision to require that executive agreements obtain congressional approval in order to gain internal effect was inserted in the resolution. Bricker's hard-core supporters joined southern Democrats to create a 61 to 30 majority for the substitution. At this point the administration abandoned any hope of a face-saving compromise. Opting to protect presidential authority, it firmly opposed the George executive-agreement provision. Abandoning the administration, majority leader Knowland announced he would vote for the George resolution and depend on the House of Representatives to modify it. However, Republicans Homer Ferguson of Michigan and Prescott Bush of Connecticut countered that they preferred no amendment to a badly flawed one. The final vote of 60 to 31 on February 27 left the amendment resolution one vote short of the two-thirds needed for passage.[123]

Although the outcome clearly relieved Eisenhower, it disappointed conservatives who believed victory to be within their grasp.[124] Bricker complained endlessly about the last-minute arrival of an inebriated Harley Kilgore, Democrat of West Virginia, to cast the deciding vote against passage of the amendment. The narrow margin of defeat was perhaps deceiving; Kilgore had been a steadfast opponent: he was not making an abrupt, intoxicated decision. Ralph Flanders, a Vermont Republican who initially voted to substitute the George resolution and then switched to oppose final passage, was extremely loyal to Eisenhower and responded predictably to the administration's appeal. At least two other senators, Republican Frank Barrett of Wyoming and Democrat John Sparkman of Alabama, although they thought it politically advantageous to support the amendment, had each indicated a willingness to switch if his vote was needed to defeat it. The administration, having finally abandoned its long quest for a harmless compromise, could probably have rallied other support as well, if necessary. The truest measure of desire to restrict presidential treaty-making authority appears to have been the 42 votes cast for Bricker's resolution on February 25 rather than the 60 votes cast for the weaker George substitute on the final roll call two days later.[125] That final vote, however, provides a measure of the broader desire, especially on the part of southern Democrats, to protect existing state racial and social arrangements against perceived threats from federal and UN sources.

Had the Bricker amendment or the George substitute achieved a two-thirds endorsement from the Senate, would it have surmounted the other Article V obstacles to adoption? If one chooses to speculate, it is helpful to recall the circumstances that produced the near-success in the Senate. Disaffection with executive power led 32 of 47 Republican senators, over two-thirds of the party's members, to abandon their president. Twenty-eight Democrats joined in, eighteen of them southerners concerned about the treaty power's threat to state control over racial policy. In the House of Representatives, not only were Republicans more likely to support Eisenhower, but also southern Democrats were proportionally fewer. In other words, the House would have had difficulty duplicating the coalition formed in the Senate, just as in 1945 the Senate had failed to mirror the action of the House in endorsing Hatton Sumner's resolution. State ratification would have been problematic as well, given the international situation and civil rights concerns present in various northern states. The Eisenhower administration could be counted on to campaign against the measure, reinforcing remaining respect for Roosevelt's and Truman's international leadership. In the face of such formidable obstacles, ratification by three-fourths of the states would have been difficult to achieve, although, given the appeal of enhanced state power, perhaps not so great a challenge as winning House approval.

John Bricker kept pressing for an amendment limiting presidential authority in foreign affairs, but he never again came nearly as close to success as in February 1954. The Eisenhower administration recognized the concerns of Bricker's supporters as well as advocates of the George resolution and moved to defuse their complaints. In spring 1954 the president refused to aid the French in Vietnam without congressional approval, and the following year he took the same stance regarding Formosa. Eisenhower also

declined to submit the UN Genocide and Human Rights Conventions to the
Senate for ratification in 1955. In a variety of other ways as well, he displayed a strong reluctance to press states to desegregate or to embark on any
social reform against their will. These actions, whatever their other attrib-
utes, undercut the image of a potential threat of autonomous presidential action in foreign affairs or an imposition on unwilling states of new social
requirements.

Democrats regained control of Congress in the November 1954 elections. At that time a dozen senators who had supported the George resolution were defeated as compared to only three opponents. When John Bricker
himself lost a reelection race in 1958, the last strenuous advocate of constitutional reform of the treaty power left the Senate.[126]

THROUGHOUT THE TWO DECADES after the 1937 Court fight, amendments
provided a means for opponents to strike back at the New Deal. One com-
mentator on the adoption of the Twenty-second Amendment wrote, "It's as
if vengeance finally has been achieved against Franklin D. Roosevelt."[127]
Some measures, indeed those that obtained the most support, were rooted in
sincere efforts to alter governmental practice, but others appeared essentially
symbolic gestures. In either case, these amendments allowed their backers to
take stands against behaviors identified with Roosevelt: running four times
for president, championing improved treatment of powerless groups, or
making important international decisions in conference with foreign leaders.
At the same time, none of these amendments required the direct overturning
of a specific, popular Roosevelt initiative. No wonder Republicans and
southern Democrats, disgruntled with New Deal reforms and worried particularly about further changes in race relations, other domestic social
arrangements, and the extent of federal power, found themselves drawn to
measures such as the Bricker amendment, which would limit presidential authority, and the Twenty-second Amendment, which could prevent another
incumbent from accumulating the power Roosevelt had wielded. The wave
of Republican-initiated anti-FDR measures, already ebbing when they began
to challenge a popular Republican president, subsided further once the Democrats regained a congressional majority in November 1954.

Less than three months after the near-passage of the substitute Bricker
amendment in the Senate, the Supreme Court announced a decision that,
among other things, reminded the country that constitutional amendments
had consequences. Speaking for a unanimous Court, Chief Justice Earl Warren based his decision in *Brown v. Board of Education of Topeka,* invalidat-

ing school segregation and foreseeably all racial segregation laws, squarely upon the Fourteenth Amendment.[128] The Civil War amendment whose racial objectives had long been treated as something of an inconvenience and whose plain words had been creatively avoided, provided the basis for a momentous Court ruling. The Fourteenth Amendment's promise of equal protection of the laws, due process of law, and protection against state abridgment of the privileges and immunities of citizens provided the launching platform for profound social change. From the moment that Warren finished speaking on May 17, 1954, no doubt could remain that a constitutional amendment, even one slow to have its intended effect, possessed enormous power to reshape the United States, perhaps in unanticipated fashion at unexpected times. In a written constitution, even long-ignored provisions needed to be taken seriously. Inattentiveness to amendments, noticeably widespread during recent years when they seemed largely aimed at marginal adjustment of past circumstances, abruptly vanished.

15

"NOT PERFECT, BUT BETTER THAN NO SOLUTION"

Amendments to Solve Immediate Problems

Since the adoption of the Bill of Rights in 1791, only the 1860s and 1910s produced an outburst of constitutional alteration comparable to the activity that occurred during the 1960s. Between 1961 and 1971, the Constitution acquired four amendments. During the same decade, several other attempts at amendment made considerable headway, even though each ultimately fell short of its goal. Altogether, these achievements and failures amounted to an extraordinary eruption of Article V activity. The reform flurry provided a second twentieth-century demonstration, fifty years after the first, that in some political climates amendments could be adopted in numbers without enervating struggle or traumatic results. As a result, Article V gained in stature as a device for responding to the most important contemporary issues: race, state versus federal authority, religion, and political discontent.

Rulings of the Supreme Court provoked, at least in part, almost all of the amending initiatives of the 1960s, including three of the four successful ones. *Brown v. Board of Education* encouraged the Twenty-third Amendment, granting presidential voting rights to residents of the District of Columbia, and the Twenty-fourth, banning poll taxes. Later, a complicated voting-rights decision led quickly to the era's final Article V reform, the Twenty-sixth Amendment, lowering the minimum voting age to eighteen. None of these amendments strove to overturn Court decisions but instead sought to expand on their implications or, in the final case, to reduce complications that a ruling had created. The only clear exception to this pattern of judicially inspired constitutional change was the Twenty-fifth Amendment, a reaction to the assassination of President John F. Kennedy and long-standing concerns about presidential disability and succession. Each of the four amendments represented a focused response to a particular problem of government rather than a broad declaration of fundamental principle.

Although the constitutional reform mechanism remained perpetually in motion during this era, the results, taken as a whole, proved modest. The four amendments adopted were narrowly drawn reforms that produced only marginal change. Unlike the three earlier periods of great Article V activity, each of which generated fundamental reforms that reverberated throughout the whole society, the 1960s produced amendments that solved problems of limited scope and, as a result, drew more notice from persons involved in political or governmental affairs than from the general public. The four amendments directly affected only select populations—citizens of the District of Columbia, the five states with poll taxes, and the eighteen-to-twenty-one-year-old age group—or uncommon circumstances—the death or disqualification of a president. Though certainly not an insignificant decade in terms of amending achievement, the 1960s might nevertheless be better characterized as a time of constitutional refinement rather than restructuring. Fundamental questions of the nature and extent of the federal government's responsibility raised during the New Deal remained in dispute, not settled by explicit and authentic acts of constitutional amendment.

THE *BROWN V. BOARD OF EDUCATION* decision brought the issue of race once again to the center of the American political stage. Race had been woven into the fabric of American constitutionalism from the 1787 provisions on representation and slavery to the adoption of the Civil War amendments. Later, racial fears influenced southern state legislatures to resist direct election of senators and woman suffrage, favor national prohibition, and support the presidential two-term limit. The post-*Brown* reform of American race relations law that culminated in the 1964 Civil Rights Act produced formal constitutional change as well. This time amendments possessed a vastly less sweeping character than those of the first Reconstruction but nevertheless once again provoked southern opposition.

Two constitutional amendments, each with racial connotations, were adopted within a decade of *Brown*. Each had substantive importance, but additionally both carried symbolic weight, especially together. By helping to shape notions that racial reform could be achieved and injustice remedied through the construction of new laws, they influenced the course of federal civil rights initiatives. Also, by demonstrating that Article V majorities could be assembled for civil rights measures in the face of southern opposition, they strengthened the belief of sympathetic politicians that the time had arrived when reform could be achieved. The climactic 1964 victory in the fierce struggle to overcome southern resistance to major civil rights legislation was rooted, at least in part, in recent constitutional amending experience.

The systematic denial of black citizens' voting rights throughout the South since the 1870s reflected the loose wording of the Fifteenth Amendment and northern acceptance of southern white manipulation of the franchise through literacy tests, poll taxes, and white-only party primary elections. Challenged by the National Association for the Advancement of Colored People (NAACP) for twenty years, the white primary was finally declared unconstitutional by the Supreme Court in 1944. The poll tax became a target of growing criticism during the 1930s as its burden on poor farmers and workers, white as well as black, became evident. The practice of levying a tax at every election and requiring registered voters to pay all arrears for elections missed before being allowed to cast a ballot helped to reduce participation to less than 5 percent of blacks throughout the South. An economic barrier rather than simply a racial obstacle, the poll tax nevertheless notably obstructed the enfranchisement of southern blacks, the most impoverished Americans.[1]

Franklin Roosevelt briefly attacked the poll tax in 1938, but, more important, white liberals, southern as well as northern, began to mobilize against it during the New Deal. Aided by the atmosphere of wartime, legislation banning poll taxes won House approval by a 254 to 84 margin in October 1942; however, a Senate filibuster could not be overcome. A second effort in 1944 met the same fate as once again a few northern Republicans and Democrats joined southerners in refusing to cut off debate. In the latter year a bill to provide military personnel with absentee ballots was adopted with a specific prohibition on the application of poll taxes to these votes. Southerners did not resist this limited and temporary measure.

Much resistance to poll tax legislation stemmed from the belief that each state retained power to determine voter qualifications. Article I, section 2 of the Constitution stipulated that suffrage standards for the most numerous branch of the state legislature established eligibility to participate in federal elections. Poll tax reformers argued that this provision was superseded by the Fourteenth Amendment's ban on a state abridging "the privileges or immunities of citizens." The Supreme Court, however, generally continued to uphold state authority over suffrage. Southerners eager to erect obstacles to federal intervention and wider reform argued that constitutional change offered the proper means to eliminate the poll tax nationally. Northern states' rights proponents agreed, as did even some advocates of poll tax abolition, despite the challenge of the Article V process. Each group acknowledged that although the Fifteenth and Nineteenth Amendments had struck down voting requirements based on race or gender they otherwise preserved state authority over suffrage. By 1944 both Franklin Roosevelt and the Republican party platform were endorsing a constitutional amendment as the way to deal with poll taxes.

When the poll tax ban resurfaced in the Republican-controlled Eightieth Congress, a filibuster once again blocked its path. This time southerners signaled their willingness to accept the substitution of an amendment resolution, apparently believing ratification could be defeated and, in any case, that an amendment represented a less sweeping threat to state regulation of suffrage than a legislative alternative. Republican leaders, who had pushed through the presidential term-limit amendment a year earlier, rejected the compromise, apparently fearing that to do otherwise would cost them a chance to win black votes in the 1948 election. In 1949, when the measure came up again, the only substantive result was a Republican and southern Democrat tightening of the cloture rule to require two-thirds of the entire Senate, not just those present and voting, to cut off debate. For the time being, despite rising agitation for black voting, the attack on the poll tax appeared rebuffed.

Announcement of the *Brown* decision forced Congress to begin grappling with civil rights issues in ways it had avoided since the passage of the Fourteenth and Fifteenth Amendments. Much debate revolved around the constitutional question of federal versus state authority to set the terms of race relations. States' rights proponents such as Senator Harry Byrd of Virginia who called for massive resistance to federal school desegregation orders echoed the arguments of John C. Calhoun 125 years earlier. Just as a general turned president reluctantly upheld federal authority against local recalcitrance in Charleston in 1832, so too did a general turned president in Little Rock in 1957. As the new era of reconstruction began, members of Congress looked for means of addressing issues of race. Various agendas surfaced, as did differing calculations of political possibilities. Inevitably, constitutional amendment was seized upon as a device for shaping and advancing, or, possibly, for retarding and deflecting change.

When the Founders created a separate federal enclave under the control of Congress so that the seat of government would not be hostage to any state, they probably did not anticipate that it would ever have any sizable permanent population. Neither could they predict that a large number of black citizens would gather within the borders of the District of Columbia. Nevertheless, by 1950 the District contained 802,172 residents, making it more populous than thirteen individual states. Due to significant immigration during World War II, the proportion of D.C. residents who were black had reached 35 percent, or 281,000.[2] District inhabitants lacked any voice in federal elections, representation in Congress, or local self-government. James Madison had indicated in the *Federalist* that "a municipal legislature for local purposes, derived from their own suffrage, will of course be allowed them," and such had been the case until the 1870s when a public works scandal led Congress to assume authority over the District government.[3] Three quarters of a century later the District still lacked control over its own affairs or even an elected representative to the Congress that governed it.[4] Amendment proposals to give District residents congressional representatives, a presidential vote, and access to federal courts had been put before Congress since 1888. Calls for District representation increased during the 1950s. With Republicans and Democrats attracting nearly equal numbers of voters in balloting for national convention delegates, the District's only political contest other than school board elections, both parties thought they could win elections there and thus became sympathetic to reform.[5]

Meanwhile, national consciousness and concern mounted over other denials of the franchise. Literacy tests were widespread and, although unevenly applied so as to discriminate against blacks, plausibly defensible. The poll tax, on the other hand, appeared increasingly vulnerable. Since the 1930s its use had actually declined in states not noted for encouraging black voting. Alabama reduced the cumulative feature of its poll tax, and Florida, Georgia, Louisiana, North Carolina, South Carolina, and Tennessee dispensed with theirs.[6] By 1960 only five states retained the device.

Amendments aimed at ameliorating racial discrimination stood little chance of winning the approval of the conservative, southern-dominated Senate Judiciary Committee chaired by James Eastland of Mississippi. If District of Columbia enfranchisement or poll tax prohibition were to move forward, they needed to avoid the bottleneck of the Judiciary Committee. Therefore, both proposals were introduced on the Senate floor in February 1960 as additions to a measure that had emerged from committee because of the cold war anxieties of the moment. Concerned about the possibility of a nuclear attack on Washington and the legislative disruption that the death of numerous congressmen would cause, Tennessee senator Estes Kefauver, chairman of the Senate Judiciary Subcommittee on Constitutional Amendments, had offered an amendment resolution providing for gubernatorial appointment of replacements until elections could be held. Democratic senator Spessard Holland of Florida, long an advocate of constitutional abolition of the poll tax in order to limit federal incursion into state suffrage regulation, attached his amendment to Kefauver's. Republican Kenneth Keating of New York did likewise with an amendment providing the District of Columbia with seats in the House of Representatives and presidential electoral votes on the same population basis as states. The Senate promptly approved the entire package 70 to 18 with the provision that any one of the three amendments could be ratified independently.[7]

Congressman Emanuel Celler of New York, chairman of the Committee on the Judiciary, saw no prospect that the House of Representatives would embrace the Senate resolution. Celler, a veteran Democratic legislator of strong liberal inclinations and cautious political instincts, recognized and perhaps even exaggerated southern strength in his committee and the House. He set aside the Senate package of amendments in favor of a single, narrowly drawn proposal to give the District of Columbia three presidential electoral votes, no more than the least populous state. Critics pointed out that this not only avoided consideration of full home rule for the District but also dropped the provision for District representatives in the House and reduced the number of electors to which the District would be entitled on the basis of population. Stewart Udall of Arizona regarded it not as a generous proposal but as a minimum one. Celler defended his plan, saying, "I knew it would be very, very difficult to get such a three-pronged constitutional amendment through the House, much less through my Committee on the Judiciary, and I reasoned that it would be better not to have such a broad target at which opponents could aim their shafts of opposition."[8] Celler's approach reversed the tactics of architects of the Fourteenth Amendment to include a variety of civil rights provisions in one measure in order to protect controversial features with more widely accepted ones. His powerful position and his announcement that he would support Senator Holland's quest for abolition of the poll tax in the next session of Congress did not end the grumbling but did enable Celler to prevail. On June 14, 1960, the House substituted his measure for the Senate bill and then approved the District of Columbia presidential voting amendment without a roll-call vote.[9]

Senators were unhappy with Celler's changes and the House action but, facing the imminent end of the session due to the upcoming political conventions and election campaign, chose to capitulate. "We all recognize the practical situation which exists," admitted South Dakota senator Francis Case, a cosponsor of Keating's original amendment. Ruefully observing that the District's population entitled it to four or five electoral votes and ignoring invidious comparisons with the three-fifths compromise in the original Constitution regarding the representation of slaves, Senator Keating decided that "three-fourths citizenship or three-fifths citizenship is better than no citizenship at all." On June 16, 1960, the Senate approved the Celler amendment without a roll-call vote and sent it to the states for ratification.[10]

Few state legislatures were in session and ready to act on the proposed amendment immediately. Hawaii, just admitted to statehood in 1959 and acutely aware of the importance of federal electoral participation, ratified within a week. Massachusetts, in August, provided the only additional ratification before the November 1960 election. Thereafter, however, as newly chosen legislatures began convening, the pace quickly accelerated. New Jersey approved the amendment on December 19, 1960. Seven states ratified in January 1961, thirteen in February, and sixteen in March, completing the process. Not one state outside the former Confederacy failed to ratify. Among the eleven states of the Old South, however, only Arkansas formally considered the matter, and it promptly rejected the amendment. Despite this solid regional resistance, ratification was completed in less than ten months, and residents of the District of Columbia were at least partially enfranchised.[11]

The separate effort on behalf of a poll tax amendment did not follow immediately. Although John Kennedy had signed on as a cosponsor of an anti-poll tax amendment in 1959, his administration chose to pursue other civil rights initiatives during its first year in office.[12] Not until March 14, 1962, did Holland, again avoiding the trap of the Committee on the Judiciary, offer his amendment resolution as a substitute for a minor bill already before the Senate, one making Alexander Hamilton's home a national monument. Southerners led by Georgia Democrat Richard Russell complained that this tactic improperly joined unrelated measures, but to no avail. For ten days senators debated the merits of Holland's proposal, an alternative put forth by Republican Jacob Javits of New York that simply legislated a federal poll tax ban, and the southern preference for doing nothing. As in earlier poll tax debates, the central issue was federal versus state authority to determine voting requirements.

The apparent slowness of the amending process concerned impatient advocates of the Javits solution. Ratification of an amendment would take time and indeed was not ensured, given the three-fourths state approval requirement. Congressional legislative action, on the other hand, could be taken quickly. To the contrary, Holland supporters argued, legislation would inevitably be challenged in court, might be long delayed by the judicial process, and, ultimately, would most likely be found unconstitutional. Amendment offered a far more certain route and not necessarily a long one. Of the seven most recent amendments, four had been ratified within a matter of months and only the Twenty-second, which required forty-seven months, took much more than a year.[13]

Southern senators did not mount a serious filibuster against the poll tax amendment resolution. After eleven days of debate they allowed it to come to a vote on March 27, 1962. With the Alexander Hamilton monument provision removed and the Javits alternative tabled 59 to 34, the Holland amendment won approval 77 to 16. All but one of the negative votes on the resolution came from southerners whose states retained or had only recently abandoned the poll tax. Even with this predictable opposition, civil rights proponents had reason to be pleased. The margin of victory in the Senate stood well above the two-thirds requirement of Article V.[14] Since this was not only by far the greatest victory margin yet achieved in the Senate for civil rights legislation but also in excess of the margin needed to end a southern filibuster, the prospect of reformers finally overcoming the most effective southern device to block change brightened considerably.

The House of Representatives had proved the obstacle to a poll tax amendment when first approved by the Senate in 1960. Now the House Rules Committee, chaired by conservative Virginian Howard Smith, kept the measure from coming to the floor from March until August. Finally, Emanuel Celler, keeping his two-year-old promise to work for the amendment, employed a rarely used parliamentary device. On August 27 he asked for consideration of the amendment under a suspension of the rules. If approved by a two-thirds vote of the House, this maneuver would compel a vote on the measure but prohibit any revision of the resolution and allow only forty minutes of debate. Celler argued that, under the circumstances, this method offered the best means of ensuring congressional passage of the amendment. Changes might strengthen the measure but would probably provoke opposition in the Senate that would have to approve them. He wanted results, not debate, a law, not a filibuster, Celler declared. Smith complained bitterly about the "farce" of suspending the rules, never before used, he said, "with the utmost disrespect" to deal with a constitutional amendment. Other southern opponents raised the specter of further consolidation in federal hands of control over voting rights. Liberal northern Republicans Charles Goodell and John Lindsay, unhappy at this use of the amending mechanism, divided over whether to support the measure. Nevertheless, when the brief debate concluded, the House voted 294 to 86 to submit the Holland amendment for ratification.[15]

Ratification of the poll tax amendment followed closely the pattern of the District of Columbia amendment, though at a somewhat slower pace. Every state of the former Confederacy declined to take action, except Mississippi, which formally rejected it in December 1962, and Tennessee, which provided the sole southern ratification in March 1963. Every other state, with the exception of Arizona and Wyoming, ratified between November 1962 and March 1964.[16]

As with the Twenty-third Amendment, adoption of the Twenty-fourth had limited substantive effect. It only ended the imposition of poll taxes in federal elections in five states. Yet it had great symbolic importance. The first amendment since the Fifteenth ninety-six years earlier to address black circumstances outside the District of Columbia, the Twenty-fourth Amendment was completed just as the Senate took up consideration of an administration-supported, House-approved civil rights bill during the first months of Lyndon Johnson's presidency. The Article V majorities forged for the poll tax amendment gave encouragement to the bill's supporters who patiently waited out a determined southern filibuster of unprecedented length throughout spring 1964. They then rallied the two-thirds majority to cut off debate and adopt the landmark Civil Rights Act of 1964. With the political balance now tipped toward federal action to ensure the franchise, the Voting Rights Act of 1965 followed a year later. In short order, entrenched obstacles to electoral participation by blacks, Hispanics, and other minorities were swept aside and a significant reordering of American politics took place.[17] Once again constitutional amendment had defined, authoritatively if incompletely and imperfectly, an American consensus on the responsibilities of government.

THE ASSASSINATION of President Kennedy instantly brought to the forefront of public consciousness an old constitutional concern: executive succession. Kennedy was the eighth of thirty-five presidents to die in office, causing, at least momentarily, a sense of uncertainty about the transfer of power and the stable functioning of government. Moreover, no fewer than sixteen vice-presidents had failed to complete their terms; eight moved up, seven died, and John C. Calhoun resigned, leaving the vice-presidency, the only constitutionally designated successor to the presidency, vacant for over thirty-eight years altogether. Furthermore, several chief executives had experienced periods during which illness or wounds left them unable to discharge their duties. Each of these occasions raised questions about the simple declaration in Article II of the Constitution that, in the event of presidential removal, resignation, death, or disability, the powers and duties of the office passed to the vice-president and that the Congress could determine who should act as chief executive if the elected vice-president too departed or was disabled.[18]

During the first unscheduled transfer of presidential power, Vice-President John Tyler established the precedent of doing nothing until his incapacitated predecessor expired. No crisis occurred during the month that William Henry Harrison lay dying of pneumonia in 1841. Nevertheless, some observers asked, what if during such a time immediate presidential action was required? James Garfield's eighty-day losing battle with gunshot wounds, Woodrow Wilson's nineteen-month enfeeblement following a stroke, and Franklin Roosevelt's weakness during his final months renewed concern. In the midst of cold war tensions, even the relatively brief illnesses of Dwight Eisenhower caused anxiety. Although vice-presidents joked that the only real responsibility of their office was to monitor the president's health, no formal procedure existed for determining presidential disability. In 1841 Vice-President Tyler declared that he was the president rather than merely serving as acting president. That practice had continued, raising the issue of whether a recovered predecessor could reclaim the office. If so, how?

Laws that Congress adopted in 1792, 1886, and 1947 stipulating the order of succession in the absence of a vice-president left other aspects of a transfer of power unresolved. The specter of nuclear attack while a president lay incapacitated increased concern about the disability problem in the 1950s, and a search for solutions soon began. Following Eisenhower's 1955 heart attack and again after his briefly disabling stroke in 1957, Attorney General Herbert Brownell proposed a constitutional amendment to clarify the declaration and termination of presidential disability. The measure, particularly its feature allowing a president to declare independently that a disability was ended, quickly ran afoul of congressional criticism. Eisenhower and Vice-President Richard Nixon settled for a private agreement on handling a disability. During the early 1960s Republican senator Kenneth Keating of New York, assisted by Democratic senator Estes Kefauver of Tennessee, fashioned a bipartisan proposal for an amendment authorizing Congress to deal with the issue through ordinary legislation, hardly a change from the original constitutional provision.[19] However, with the sudden death of Kefauver, chairman of the Senate Judiciary Subcommittee on Constitutional Amendments, in August 1963, Keating's initiative stalled.[20] Three months later the Kennedy assassination finally catalyzed the development and adoption of a presidential disability and succession amendment.

Upon Kefauver's death, Judiciary Committee chairman James Eastland considered disbanding his subcommittee. Birch Bayh, an ambitious thirty-five-year-old Democratic senator from Indiana in office less than a year and, in his own words, "eager to have an area of specific responsibility and authority," hurried to ask Eastland to assign the committee to him. Although his only experience with constitutional issues had been as a law student in the late 1950s, Bayh saw an opportunity to end his status as the only Judiciary Committee Democrat without his own subcommittee. Granted his request, Bayh was still trying to find office space and staff seven weeks later on November 22. Circumstance and ambition then merged. Bayh worried, as did many Americans, about new president Lyndon Johnson's serious heart attack eight years earlier and the frailty of the people next in line to succeed, seventy-one-year-old Speaker of the House John McCormack and eighty-six-year-old president pro tempore of the Senate Carl Hayden. A Judiciary Committee discussion on December 4 made Bayh aware also that opinions remained divided on how to deal with presidential disability. The neophyte subcommittee chairman used an airplane flight to Chicago that same afternoon to draft his own constitutional amendment to set forth specific procedures for vice-presidential replacement and presidential disability.[21]

Urged on by his staff "to get to work before some other senator took the initiative," Bayh held a press conference on December 9 to announce that his subcommittee would address the disability and succession problem. At another press conference three days later, he unveiled his draft amendment; the following day he enlisted the cooperation of the American Bar Association. From then on, Bayh was ever the driving force for obtaining an amendment, willing to compromise on the substance of his plan but insistent that reform be written into the Constitution. The Indiana senator understood, as did his allies Robert Kennedy of New York and Philip Hart of Michigan, that leaving the matter to ordinary legislation could conceivably allow Congress to label a president disabled and remove him or her from office by a simple majority vote. Therefore Bayh repeatedly argued for a constitutional solution requiring a two-thirds vote to declare a president disabled against his will so as to put presidential replacement beyond the reach of a self-serving congressional majority.[22]

Bayh's draft amendment dealt with the succession issue in a new manner by directing that a president nominate a replacement vice-president within thirty days and both houses of Congress confirm the choice by majority vote. If the presidency and vice-presidency both became vacant, the succession would pass to the secretary of state and then other cabinet members rather than, as the 1947 law stipulated, to congressional leaders. Bayh treated presidential disability as Eisenhower and Nixon had agreed: the president, if possible, or otherwise the vice-president could declare a president disabled, allowing the vice-president to act as president until the president declared the disability ended. This arrangement allowed a resumption of power once the disability was past.[23]

A dozen American Bar Association leaders reviewed the plan with Bayh in January 1964. Attention focused on the complex problem of declaring and then terminating a presidential disability if a chief executive, conceivably one who had become mentally ill, contended that none existed. Rather than leaving such a decision to the president, as the Eisenhower-Nixon agreement specified, the ABA group preferred to let Congress, or a commission that it would establish, make the final determination. They agreed also with Bayh's judgment that the provision changing the line of succession from Congress to the cabinet should be dropped. Fear that an offended Speaker McCormack would block the amendment outweighed, in their estimate, the remote possibility of simultaneous presidential and vice-presidential vacancies. After extensive discussion and editing of language, the ABA conferees and Bayh accepted the revised plan. The following month, the bar association's House of Delegates, which had earlier backed the Keating plan to delegate authority to Congress, endorsed the new approach.[24]

Bayh used hearings of his subcommittee to draw attention to the succession and disability problem as well as to the ABA's support for his proposed solution. In response to Senator Keating's continuing argument that such complex matters were better dealt with by legislation than a detailed, specific, and inflexible constitutional amendment, Bayh insisted that "a constitutional gap" existed. "We must fill this gap," he said, "if we are to protect our Nation from the possibility of floundering in the sea of public confusion and uncertainty which ofttimes exists at times of national peril and tragedy." The appearance of former vice-president Richard Nixon on the final day of hearings gained much more press notice than the preceding extended debate among legal experts over disability determination and vice-presidential selection. Not surprisingly, Nixon agreed with other witnesses on the importance of having a vice-president at all times, though he preferred to reconvene the electoral college to select a replacement. Most significantly, he asserted that it was better for Congress to decide a dispute over presidential disability than to leave the determination to the vice-president. Overall, Nixon effectively reinforced Bayh's appeal for an amendment.[25]

Using television appearances and magazine articles to gain notice for his proposal while public attention was focused on the Senate's civil rights filibuster and hearings in the House concerning prayer in schools, Bayh pressed on throughout spring 1964. Senator Keating conceded that if the Senate preferred the Indianan's measure to his own, it was better than more delay in resolving disability issues. Both House Judiciary Committee chairman Celler and former president Eisenhower expressed minor differences but general approval of the Bayh plan at an ABA conference on May 25. Two days later, the subcommittee approved a further refined amendment.[26]

Bayh's persistence kept the amendment moving forward. His role became clear when progress stopped while he was absent from the Senate during June and July. He, his wife, and Senator Edward Kennedy suffered injuries in a light plane crash in which the pilot and another passenger were killed. Upon his recuperation, the full Judiciary Committee took up and approved the amendment resolution August 4. Bayh then pressed for an early

Senate vote to sustain an image of legislative progress although there was no possibility of the House taking up the measure before adjournment. His doggedness resulted in a voice vote of approval on September 28 and, after Senator John Stennis objected to approving a constitutional amendment without a roll call and only nine senators on the floor, reapproval by 65 to 0 the following day.[27]

The election of 1964 filled the vacant vice-presidency and eased tension over Lyndon Johnson's potential successor, but it did not distract the junior senator from Indiana from his goal of achieving a constitutional amendment. Bayh and his staff successfully lobbied presidential assistants Bill Moyers and Ramsey Clark to have Lyndon Johnson mention the succession and disability problem in his State of the Union address and embrace Bayh's solution three weeks later.[28] The very next day, Attorney General Nicholas Katzenbach added his endorsement, saying that the measure represented "as formidable a consensus of considered opinion on any proposed amendment to the Constitution as one is likely to find. It may not satisfy in every respect the views of all scholars and statesmen who have studied the problem. . . . But, it . . . would responsibly meet the pressing need." Shortly thereafter, a unanimous Senate approved for a second time.[29]

The complex disability provisions of Bayh's amendment stirred lengthy debate in the Senate. Everett Dirksen tried unsuccessfully to revive the proposal to delegate authority to Congress rather than spell out a disability procedure in an amendment. Alternatives to specific features continued to be discussed during House hearings and floor debate on the measure. The House approved the amendment 368 to 29 on April 13 but only after altering several procedures for resolving disputes over presidential disability.[30]

Reconciliation of differences between the House and Senate versions of the amendment took two months and involved strenuous negotiations. The House sought time limits on congressional deliberations over disability disputes, and the Senate resisted any abridgment of its rule of unlimited debate. Bayh's unflagging determination to achieve an acceptable amendment led him to fashion a compromise conceding most of the House points. Senator Sam Ervin, a staunch Bayh supporter throughout, helped sell the compromise to their Senate colleagues. On July 6, by a vote of 68 to 5, the Senate duplicated the action of the House one week earlier in approving the conference version of the amendment.[31]

Ratification of the presidential disability and succession amendment was almost an afterthought to its champion.[32] Early in his campaign, Bayh had polled state legislative leaders about his proposal and found little opposition. Once Congress completed action, Bayh and his staff corresponded with governors and state legislative leaders but relied on their allies in the American Bar Association as "support creators" among "grass roots opinion leaders."[33] The ABA, in Bayh's words, "began to bombard the state legislators with information."[34] Ratification proceeded at a steady pace and with no significant resistance. Thirty-two state legislatures completed action within a year. After a six-month delay because of the 1966 elections, seven more states approved during the first six weeks of 1967, making the amendment effective as of February 10. The North Dakota legislature, maneuvering to be the state to complete the process, ratified, then declared its vote invalid on a technicality, saw two other states act before it could do so again, and abandoned the process in frustration. Eight more states added their endorsement by May 1967, but North Dakota joined South Carolina and Georgia as the only states never to ratify.[35] Lyndon Johnson, told that a president had absolutely no constitutional role in the amending process but determined to take part nevertheless, staged a televised White House rose garden ceremony to sign, merely as a witness, a proclamation that the administrator of General Services had received notice of the state ratification that put the amendment into effect.[36]

The Twenty-fifth Amendment encountered little outright opposition during the three years it required for adoption. Yet doubts kept surfacing about almost every provision of this longest and most technical of all constitutional amendments. Methods of dealing with disputed disability or transfer of executive power provoked debate time and again. Uncertainty persisted about the wisdom of casting any arrangements in the inflexible form of an amendment. Bayh himself confessed that only "the most likely eventualities" were covered, explaining "the more complicated you make a constitutional amendment, quite frankly, the more contingencies for which you provide, the more difficult it is to get it passed."[37] Still, Bayh and his ABA allies, convinced that a constitutional amendment offered the best prospect for a clear and unchallengeable remedy to most potential crises, won over legislators in both houses of Congress and the states as well.

The impossibility of constructing a flawless amendment was acknowledged time after time as the Twenty-fifth Amendment evolved. "The absolutely perfect solution," Walter Lippmann concluded, "will never be found," and, furthermore, "is not necessary."[38] The risks of anticipating problems were quickly illustrated. Although most attention during its development focused on disability provisions, the amendment was first used to guide two vice-presidential replacements, those of Spiro Agnew and Gerald Ford. Assumed to be highly unlikely, the departure of both a vice-president and a president during the same term occurred within a decade.[39] Ironically,

the amendment would not be invoked during the 1980s during the first instances akin to those envisioned by the drafters of provisions for voluntary
and involuntary declarations of presidential disability. The architects of the
disability and succession amendment had not anticipated the political considerations that prevailed during Ronald Reagan's presidency, the desire of a
White House staff and a cooperative vice-president to maintain an image of
presidential control regardless of circumstances. The Twenty-fifth Amendment, Birch Bayh told his colleagues, "we admit is not perfect, but [it] is better than no solution at all."[40]

THE FINAL EPISODE in this era of almost constant Article V activity recapitu-
lated elements of events that had already transpired. Another long-dormant
issue suddenly seemed to demand action. Again state and federal authority
clashed. Once more, a search for relief from a Supreme Court decision precipitated the resort to a constitutional solution. On this occasion, however,
legislators who now had acquired a decade of amending experience, with
the substantial unsuccessful initiatives to be discussed in the next chapter as
well as the three already ratified reforms, achieved extraordinarily rapid results. The adoption of the Twenty-sixth Amendment, lowering the voting
age to eighteen, in little more than five months revealed how little time constitutional alteration actually required.

The voting age amendment illuminated the Article V process in another
important respect. Its adoption took place despite clear evidence of considerable public opposition. This aversion went beyond one region or group; it
stood revealed in state referendum defeats in no fewer than ten states. No
amendment proposal since national prohibition repeal in 1933 had faced a
test at the ballot box. With the exception of the school prayer amendment,
few, if any, even achieved widespread public visibility. In contrast, voting age
reduction questions appeared on the ballot in sixteen states in 1969 and
1970, meeting rejection more often than not. When Congress and state legislatures nevertheless rapidly and overwhelmingly approved the voting age
amendment, its adoption challenged the prevailing belief that only constitutional changes enjoying enormous popular acceptance stood any chance of
being approved.

The post–World War II baby boom generation was beginning to mature
by the mid-1960s. This extraordinarily large age cohort made its influence
felt throughout the economy and culture. Its presence was particularly noticeable on college campuses that it attended in higher percentages than any preceding generation. Although half of the boomers did not go to college, those

who did clustered together and enjoyed disproportionate influence in shaping their generation's identity. Coming of age during the civil rights struggles and directly affected by a large military draft for which many regarded as at best a dubious war in Vietnam, the most politically sensitive of this generation quickly developed a political voice. Dissatisfied with a wide variety of social, economic, political, and diplomatic conditions, the cohort's most vocal members began insisting on political change. Rallies and demonstrations for social reform and an end to the Vietnam War spread from campuses to city streets and, most memorably, to the Democratic National Convention in Chicago in August 1968. The fact that this political energy appeared to flow from a group too young to vote was not lost on nervous older observers.

Lowering the voting age from twenty-one, the traditional British age of legal adulthood, had been discussed during every war in which the United States asked younger men to fight. World War II produced the strongest "old enough to fight, old enough to vote" argument and generated several congressional resolutions to grant suffrage to eighteen-year-olds. Republican senator Arthur Vandenburg of Michigan and two West Virginia Democrats, Senator Harley Kilgore and Representative Jennings Randolph, were outspoken proponents of the reform. The House Judiciary Committee held hearings on a voting age amendment in October 1943 but took no further action. In an August 1943 referendum, Georgia became the only state to reduce its voting age to eighteen during the war; for a dozen years it remained the only state with a sub-twenty-one suffrage. The Korean War generated more discussion of the issue, but no immediate action. In 1952 both Oklahoma and South Dakota rejected voting age reduction in referendums. Kentucky joined Georgia in 1955, and two new states, Alaska in 1956 and Hawaii in 1959, were admitted to the Union with nineteen- and twenty-year-old suffrage respectively. Otherwise suffrage at twenty-one remained the norm throughout the United States.[41]

As the Vietnam War with its military draft, for which all males became eligible at eighteen, grew increasingly controversial, discussion of voting age reduction began anew. Several state legislatures proposed a lower voting age, only to have it rejected in referendums in Michigan in 1966, New York (as part of a new state constitution) in 1967, and Hawaii, Maryland, Nebraska, North Dakota, and Tennessee in 1968.[42] Although there is no evidence that voters were otherwise ready to grant the suffrage to eighteen- to twenty-year-olds, resentment against several years of campus demonstrations, sporadic urban rioting, and antiwar protest undoubtedly did more to persuade older citizens not to lower the voting age than it did to convince them that younger people possessed the requisite political maturity.

The next two years saw even more state consideration of suffrage age as legislatures put the issue on numerous referendum ballots. In November 1969 voters in New Jersey and Ohio rejected suffrage at eighteen and nineteen. The following year produced the first approvals of voting age reduction since Kentucky had done so in 1955. Alaska, which already allowed nineteen-year-olds to vote, agreed to lower the threshold by one more year. Then in November, Massachusetts by a 2-to-1 majority and Minnesota and Montana by razor-thin margins approved nineteen-year-old voting. At the same election, Maine and Nebraska adopted twenty-year-old suffrage. While this represented the best showing ever for lower eligibility age, on the same day voters in nine states rejected it. Connecticut, Florida, Hawaii, and Michigan turned down eighteen-year-old suffrage proposals, and Colorado, New Jersey, South Dakota, Washington, and Wyoming refused to allow nineteen-year-olds ballot access. The defeats were all by substantial margins, and in Michigan the lower age proposal lost by more than 500,000 votes out of 2.5 million cast. On balance, voting age reduction appeared to lack majority support, much less a broad consensus.[43]

Undaunted by the first of these results and well aware that autumn 1969 had produced the largest demonstrations against the Vietnam War yet seen, Senator Birch Bayh convened hearings of the Subcommittee on Constitutional Amendments in February 1970 to consider the eighteen-year-old voting age amendment reintroduced by Jennings Randolph of West Virginia, long since moved from the House to the Senate. Bayh, who himself had advocated a lower voting age since his first term in the Indiana general assembly in 1954, began by asserting that people were maturing earlier. He equated maturity with length of schooling rather than with entry into the adult world of work. His concern for the unsettled contemporary political climate was evident in his question, "Can we in good conscience expect youth to work within the system when we deny them that very opportunity?"[44]

Dr. Walter Menninger, a prominent Kansas psychologist who had served on the National Commission on the Causes and Prevention of Violence, reinforced Bayh's opening remarks. Created by Lyndon Johnson following a series of disturbing urban riots, the commission concluded, among other things, that an earlier voting age would reduce the frustration among young people that was driving them to violence. Menninger argued that suffrage would offer "a direct, constructive, and democratic channel for making their views felt and for giving them a responsible stake in the future of the nation." Among the evidence he presented were lyrics from the Beatles song "Revolution" that included the line, "You say you'll change the constitution" and the reprise, "Don't you know it's gonna be alright, alright, alright." During the three days of hearings nearly every speaker shared Menninger's view that suffrage would go a long way toward curing youthful discontent.[45]

The Nixon administration, through the testimony of Deputy Attorney General Richard Kleindienst, endorsed the eighteen-year-old suffrage amendment, reminding senators that the Constitution left control over voting to the individual states, except as qualified by the Fifteenth, Nineteenth, and Twenty-third Amendments.[46] Whether persuaded that this position reflected an administration belief that an amendment would take a long time to achieve and thus be unlikely to expose it to younger voters, whether concerned with House Judiciary Committee chairman Emanuel Celler's longstanding and potentially fatal opposition to a voting age amendment, or whether simply impatient to respond to young people as soon as possible, the Senate abruptly switched course. On March 4, Senate majority leader Mike Mansfield proposed legislation amending the 1965 Voting Rights Act to protect the right to vote of all citizens eighteen and over. Senators Mansfield and Edward Kennedy argued that a 1966 Supreme Court decision, *Katzenbach v. Morgan,* upholding other blanket protections of voting rights under the 1965 act permitted it to be used to lower the voting age. Within nine days, the Senate embraced Mansfield's proposal and approved renewal of the amended Voting Rights Act by 64 to 17. The House quickly concurred, with Celler unwilling to slow the passage of the overall act to fight over a voting age provision he was convinced would be found unconstitutional anyway.[47]

President Nixon, who shared Celler's view that the voting age mandate unconstitutionally invaded the realm of state authority, nevertheless signed the 1970 Voting Rights Act on June 22. As with Celler, the desire to appear supportive of expanded voting rights, not to mention the legislation's other features protecting older citizens from being denied ballot access, outweighed doubts about federal constitutional authority. Nixon too believed that the courts would invalidate the eighteen-year-old suffrage edict. He was vindicated the very next day as a federal district judge ruled that the law's voting age provision was contrary to the Tenth Amendment reserving rights to the states.

By October the Supreme Court heard arguments on the constitutional question of state versus federal authority over suffrage. On December 21 the Court announced a decision in the case of *Oregon v. Mitchell* that upset all predictions. Four justices concluded with Mansfield and Kennedy that Congress had power to act in this area. Four others held with Celler and Nixon that it did not. Given the even division, the view of the ninth justice, Hugo

Black, proved decisive. Black and consequently the Court ruled that Congress had authority to stipulate the voting age for federal elections but that states retained the power to determine the age for their own contests.[48]

Though in keeping with previous Court judgments, *Oregon v. Mitchell* created the prospect of immense electoral complications. Eighteen- to twenty-year-olds would soon be voting in federal contests but, unless states individually changed their suffrage requirements, would be barred from participating in simultaneous state balloting. A nightmare of election-day confusion, extra expense, and tangles loomed large unless Congress either withdrew the eighteen-year-old voting provision from the Voting Rights Act or moved ahead with a constitutional amendment to define voting age on a national basis. Withdrawal would anger young people who would inevitably become voters within a short while; thus it was politically unpalatable and extremely unlikely. Amendment, on the other hand, would have to be completed before the next federal election in 1972 if *Oregon v. Mitchell*'s consequences were to be avoided. Faced with this dilemma, Congress not only responded with decisiveness but also with what passed in the Capitol for lightning speed.

Senator Randolph reintroduced his amendment resolution with eighty-six cosponsors on January 25, 1971. Senator Bayh on February 12 released a report detailing the potential electoral horrors created by *Oregon v. Mitchell*.[49] His subcommittee endorsed the Randolph resolution on March 2, and the full Judiciary Committee did likewise March 4. Bayh's report to the Senate on the resolution reiterated every justification for constitutional amendment offered at the 1970 hearings.[50] No mention was made of using the Article V state convention ratification process to carry out a public referendum on the amendment similar to 1933 on prohibition repeal. Bayh later said that he gave some thought to convention ratification but feared losing some marginal Senate and House support if the familiar amending process was changed.[51] Slowed only briefly by Senator Edward Kennedy's attempt to attach a provision for congressional representation for the District of Columbia, the voting age amendment was approved by the Senate 94 to 0 on March 10. Thirteen days later, the House concurred 401 to 19. Congressman Celler abandoned his objections in the face of what he considered impending electoral chaos, and only a few lonely voices were raised in opposition. Less than two months after Senator Randolph resubmitted his amendment resolution, it was on the way to state legislatures for ratification.[52]

Almost every state legislature was in session during spring 1971. Catalyzed as well by the specter of electoral confusion, legislators rushed to ratify the remedy. Five states ratified on the very day the amendment passed

Congress. Two of them, Connecticut and Washington, were states where only months before voters in state referendums had rejected lowering the voting age. This pattern continued throughout the spring. Within three-and-a-half months, the necessary thirty-eight states had completed ratification. Included among them were eight of the ten where voters had rejected suffrage age reduction in 1969 or 1970.[53] Curiously, in contrast to the vociferous protests of the 1920s when legislatures ratified national prohibition despite referendum disapproval, no significant public outcry arose regarding this apparent flouting of the popular will. Instead, the fastest ratification of an amendment on record, one taking a mere 101 days, went smoothly.

Ohio, which in 1919 insisted on its right of referendum on ratification of federal constitutional amendments, only to have the Supreme Court disagree in *Hawke v. Smith,* ironically became the state to complete ratification of the Twenty-fifth Amendment. In doing so, it demonstrated how concerns about the amending process had shifted in a half century. In 1969 Ohio voters rejected by a vote of 1,274,334 to 1,226,592 a state constitutional amendment to lower the voting age to nineteen. When the general assembly considered the federal amendment in June 1971, no one mentioned *Hawke v. Smith,* and only two legislators complained that ratification might ignore the people's wishes. After the senate ratified the amendment 30 to 2, the house recognized that Ohio had an opportunity to beat Oklahoma in a race for the distinction of being the thirty-eighth and final state needed to ensure enactment. House leaders thereupon called a special evening session, cut off debate after only ten minutes when they learned that the Oklahoma legislature had itself gone into session, and hurriedly obtained ratification by a vote of 81 to 9. Like other state legislatures, Ohio saw amendment as a solution to the headache of dual voting. Despite the expressed preferences of citizens already casting ballots, holding out for higher state suffrage for its own elections seemed foolish with federal voting at eighteen inevitable. The decade of constitutional reform ended without a whimper of complaint.[54]

THE LESSONS of the constitutional amending battles of the 1960s were not lost on advocates of progressive reform. Senator Birch Bayh, for one, clearly anticipated using Article V further to achieve desired goals. The Senate Subcommittee on Constitutional Amendments provided a stage for making statements of commitment to one reform principle or another that would undoubtedly be noticed. Amendment offered the undeniable lure of obtaining a sweeping national solution at one stroke, overcoming pockets of resistance that could foil state-by-state reform efforts for years, if not forever, and winning a victory virtually impossible to reverse.

The amending successes of the 1960s fostered the belief that the Article V process could be completed quickly and easily, especially once the hurdles of congressional committee resistance and obstructionist tactics on the House and Senate floor had been overcome. Four new amendments stood as silent testimony. Their relatively noncontroversial nature, their appearance as easy solutions to vexing problems, and their uncontested ratifications by states often at odds with centralized federal power were easy to overlook. The failure of other amendment attempts during this period should have provided reminders that Article V changes were still as difficult as the Founders had intended. In the 1960s' wave of amending successes that lesson was easy to ignore.

16

"To Set Out on a Vast Uncharted Sea"

Failed Quests to Alter Original Agreements

During the 1960s, the same decade that saw the extraordinary addition of four amendments to the Constitution, several other amending attempts made considerable headway as well. Launched from various points on the political compass, they ultimately failed. Opponents found ways to undermine or block even measures that appeared to have broad political and public support. Together with the four completed amendments, these noteworthy but unsuccessful initiatives served as a reminder of Article V's demanding procedural and consensual requirements. The miscarried attempts also called attention to an unused provision of the amending system to give states alternative means to initiate amendments if Congress proved unresponsive to political discontent. Thus the stillborn amendments as well as the more heralded live births contributed significantly to the constitutional history of the 1960s.

Disagreement with Supreme Court rulings was the engine driving several of the amendment proposals that stalled short of their goal. Alteration of the Constitution offered the ultimate antidote to unpalatable judicial decisions. Reaction against *Brown v. Board of Education* prompted an attempt to secure a trio of amendments to enhance state power to resist the federal judiciary. Later, Court rulings on the apportionment of legislative districts to ensure voter equality led to the pursuit of an amendment to block their implementation. Likewise, decisions declaring school prayer and Bible reading violations of the First Amendment generated demands for a reversing amendment. Unhappiness with a major Supreme Court decision almost inevitably provoked discussion of overturning it through Article V; these cases stirred serious attempts to do so. In a sense, the amending process worked to confirm judicial rulings when efforts to reverse them failed.

Not all unsuccessful amendment attempts during the 1960s reflected distaste for judicial rulings. A proposal to discard the electoral college system in favor of direct popular choice of presidents, an old idea suddenly popular in the aftermath of the 1968 election, came close to winning congressional approval. This episode reversed the usual alignment of political power in the decade's amending activity. Forces normally successful in Article V undertakings were stymied by those who lost on other occasions. The direct election amendment's failure underscored the capacity of skilled and determined parliamentarians to frustrate the amending process when they could appeal to residual doubts about the wisdom of change.

The failed amending efforts of the 1960s sought to alter well-established constitutional arrangements. Some had been honored only in the breech until the Supreme Court called for their full implementation; others had functioned continuously since 1789. In either case, proposals for their reform confronted the enduring sense that the Constitution was fundamentally sound and worries that change might imperil the federal system, civil liberties, and other vaguely understood but nevertheless valued elements of the American governmental structure. The inherently conservative nature of constitutionalism revealed itself again as reform proposals from across the political spectrum failed to survive the Article V process.

UNHAPPINESS WITH extensions of federal power, especially those requiring states to reform their racial practices, led states' rights defenders to seek constitutional change in the 1960s. The New Deal and the *Brown* decision had reawakened the dispute over state versus federal authority that reached back to the Articles of Confederation. The movement for a poll tax amendment further revived the debate. The Supreme Court's March 1962 *Baker v. Carr* decision, declaring state legislative apportionment subject to judicial review, enlarged the controversy still more.[1] The Court ruling precipitated attempts to reassert state power through three amendments to the Constitution.

The Council of State Governments, an organization established in 1933 to promote cooperation among governors, legislators, judges, and other state officials, had become a forum for states' rights advocacy by the late 1950s. One of the council's many subsidiary groups, the Conference of State Chief Justices, launched a tirade against criminal procedure decisions by the Supreme Court that, the conference said in 1958, overstepped federal authority. Four months after the *Baker v. Carr* ruling, the southern regional branch of the council called for constitutional amendment to prohibit federal interference in state apportionment. The next month 750 legislators from forty-six states attending the annual meeting of the council's National Legislative Conference resolved to study cooperative state action to secure constitutional reform.[2]

By December 1962 the council's Committee on Federal-State Relations set three amendments before a General Assembly of the States meeting in Chicago. The first would change Article V so that further constitutional amendments could be proposed for ratification by action of two-thirds of the state legislatures and without any involvement of either Congress or a federal convention. The second would eliminate federal judicial authority over the apportionment of state legislatures. The third would establish a Court of the Union, composed of the chief justices of each state, with authority to review Supreme Court decisions regarding federal-state relations. Together, proponents said, these three states' rights amendments would reverse the trend toward centralization of power in federal hands. "The problem is not possible of solution by mere protests, resolutions and reports," declared one enthusiastic Mississippi state legislator. "Only a solution based on reform at the most basic level will have any probability of success."[3]

The Committee on Federal-State Relations proposed that state legislatures seek a federal convention to secure adoption of the three states' rights amendments unless Congress itself approved them prior to January 1, 1965. This strategy employed the largely forgotten provision of Article V stipulating that if the legislatures of two-thirds of the states requested a constitutional convention, Congress must convene one. In 1912, the one time that the volume of such state petitions approached the required number, Congress, rather than allow a constitutional convention to be held, itself submitted for ratification the amendment for direct election of senators that states were seeking. The Committee on Federal-State Relations clearly hoped to bring about similar congressional action but presented the Article V alternative as an option. This effort represented an innovative and aggressive approach to seeking a constitutional amendment. Almost all state delegations to the 1962 General Assembly hastily approved.

Half of the states' legislatures considered the trio of amendments in 1963. Though not accorded the immediate and overwhelming endorsement their proponents sought, the states' rights amendments did receive significant support. Legislatures in sixteen states approved one or another of the three amendments and called for their consideration by a federal constitutional convention. Twelve legislatures and one house of eight others voted for the proposed reform of Article V. Thirteen and one house of five others endorsed the antireapportionment amendment. Five legislatures and one house of five others approved the Court of the Union. Arkansas, South Carolina, and Wyoming embraced the three amendments, and seven other states endorsed two.[4]

The convention calls, not to mention the states' rights amendments themselves, lacked wide notice at first. Chief Justice Earl Warren called attention to them in a May 22, 1963, speech to the American Law Institute in Washington. Warning that the amendments "could radically change the character of our institutions" yet had received "very little public mention," he urged the bar to oppose the Constitution's being "changed unwittingly." Otherwise, he warned, "Used unwisely by an uninformed public, [Article V] could soon destroy the foundations of the Constitution."[5] Thereafter, opposition came quickly from, among others, the American Bar Association Board of Governors, the American Civil Liberties Union, the AFL-CIO, and the U.S. Conference of Mayors as well as a number of city and state bar associations.[6] Historian Henry Steele Commager used the forum of the *New York Times Magazine* to label the amendments "gestures toward constitutional anarchy." He worried particularly about state legislatures acquiring the ability to bypass Congress entirely in amending the Constitution.[7] New York attorney William Fennell put the issue in the harshest terms of the day, writing, "The threat to our institutions posed by this 'counterrevolution' of the right is as real and as dangerous as the threat of Communism."[8]

Yale law professor Charles L. Black, Jr., became a vigorous and influential critic of the three states' rights amendments, characterizing them as "radical in the extreme" and aimed "not at the preservation but at the subversion of a balance in federal-state relations." The proposals appeared to him to be "collectively one more attempt, so late in the day, at converting the United States into a confederation." The first, wrote Black, would eliminate any obligation to discuss constitutional change in a nation forum. The Constitution would become amendable by state legislatures, many of them heavily malapportioned, unchecked by either Congress or even state governors. In the worst case, Black hypothesized, legislative majorities representing 38 percent of their states' populations could combine to form a constitutional majority of states containing less than 40 percent of the nation's citizens. Such a coalition could impose fundamental reform approved by only 15 percent of all Americans. The other two amendments would perpetuate this imbalance and further undermine traditional principles of equality and republicanism. Black concluded grimly, "That these proposals should be thrust forward as a means of *restoring a balance* between nation and state benumbs comment."[9]

Hostile reactions to the states' rights amendments stalled their momentum. Between May and July, the legislatures of Louisiana, New Jersey, North Carolina, Ohio, Oregon, and Pennsylvania tabled or rejected them. Moreover, they found little support in Congress when introduced in February by South Carolina senator Strom Thurmond and in March by Florida congressman Sydney Herlong. Failing to achieve the simultaneous state endorsements that might have forced a constitutional convention or moved Congress to act, the Council of State Governments' amendment package soon faded from view. Even the council's National Legislative Conference backed away from the amendments at its August 1963 meeting.[10]

With the collapse of the Council of State Governments' initiative, attention narrowed to the issue of apportionment. In 1964, four years after it began dealing with the distribution of voting power by banning racial gerrymandering[11] and two years after *Baker v. Carr,* the Supreme Court clarified its position in a series of related decisions. A ruling in *Wesberry v. Saunders* that dealt with congressional districts,[12] followed by *Reynolds v. Sims* and five other cases involving state legislative districts,[13] mandated that states draw boundaries so as to give all voters equal influence. The Court displayed a firm commitment to a principle of "one man, one vote" as well as its expectation that states would comply promptly. White southerners and rural dwellers throughout the country realized that they were about to lose their favored political position unless action was taken to preserve the status quo.

The Alabama legislature in August 1964 asked Congress to propose an amendment empowering a state to use "any criteria as in its wisdom may be in its individual best interest" in apportioning one house of its legislature. Virginia made a similar appeal in December, adding the stipulation that state apportionment on a basis other than population should be approved by popular vote. Eight more states made the same request the next year. Eleven legislatures followed the lead of Oklahoma in January 1965 in calling on Congress to convene a constitutional convention to propose an amendment along the same lines.[14] Although these state initiatives differed in requests for congressional or convention action under Article V, they provided a measure of the widespread reaction to the Court's apportionment decisions.

Meanwhile, after announcement of the "one man, one vote" rulings, Representative William Tuck of Virginia introduced legislation to deny the judiciary jurisdiction over apportionment. In the House, where the *Wesberry* decision threatened many members' safe seats, Tuck's measure won quick approval by 218 to 175. The bill died in the Senate, however, apparently not from outright opposition so much as the realization that it had come too late. It would not reverse the Court's decisions but, quite the contrary, permit them to stand without possibility of reversal. Instead, senators gave bipartisan support to a plan to defer until 1966, the date by which states would be required to comply with the reapportionment mandate. Liberals, willing to give states a reasonable opportunity to conform but not inclined to encourage delay, blocked this measure.[15]

Frustrated by these Senate actions, Republican minority leader Everett Dirksen was determined to pursue the quest to protect state control of apportionment. Dirksen disagreed with the *Reynolds v. Sims* ruling that every voter must be accorded equal weight in legislatures. He objected to what he considered a denial of a sovereign right in a republic, the right of a majority to choose its system of representation. The Republican leader, his thinking shaped by his central Illinois perspective on Chicago, believed that legitimate rural interests were being sacrificed to those of more populous urban areas. Having played a key role in ending the filibuster against the 1964 Civil Rights Act and thereby ensuring its passage, Dirksen did not appear to be operating with the racial motivation of some of his colleagues. He argued that the creators of the Constitution recognized factors other than population in the apportionment of legislative power, pointing to the granting of two Senate seats to every state regardless of population. Why, he asked, should states not have the same right to choose how to apportion their own legislatures? The only way to preserve such an option in the aftermath of *Reynolds v. Sims,* he recognized, was to obtain a constitutional amendment.[16] "Everett was deadly serious about it," an opponent acknowledged.[17]

In January 1965, Dirksen, with thirty-seven cosponsors, proposed an amendment permitting states to apportion a unicameral legislature or one house of a bicameral legislature, if they chose to do so by popular vote, on a basis other than population. Although the Senate Judiciary Committee received considerable mail in support of Dirksen's measure, some of it handwritten by rural people, committee members such as Paul Douglas of Illinois and Birch Bayh of Indiana criticized it for allowing malapportioned rural-dominated legislatures to draw up plans for their own perpetuation. William Proxmire of Wisconsin and Joseph Tydings of Maryland were particularly vehement in their objections to Dirksen's effort to place in the Constitution a system by which a minority could perpetuate its disproportionate power free of judicial review.[18]

Six months later, Dirksen circumvented his adversaries in the Judiciary Committee by attaching his proposal to a measure already on the floor, a routine minor bill proclaiming National American Legion Baseball Week. He reminded his liberal opponents that they had used the same tactic to achieve the District of Columbia and poll tax amendments. Dirksen's resolution, not nearly as severe as the failed Council of State Governments' anti-reapportionment measure to begin with, was now further softened to call for the amendment to be ratified by legislatures apportioned on the basis of population equality according to the most recent census. Thereafter, legislative reapportionment would be required after each decennial census, though states could continue to give weight to nonpopulation factors in the makeup of one house.

Senator Dirksen showed colleagues his desk stacked "so high you could barely see him" with postcards he claimed to be getting from amendment supporters throughout the country. Liberals, believing that the Republican leader had himself solicited this show of support, were unimpressed.[19] When the Dirksen amendment came to a vote on August 4, 1965, after two weeks of debate, southern Democrats and rural state senators of both parties joined in its support. The vote of 57 to 39 in favor of the amendment was, however, seven votes short of the two-thirds required for passage. Despite this substantial margin of defeat, Dirksen immediately renewed the battle, deadlocking other Senate work for a month until he extracted a Judiciary Committee promise that his amendment would be considered again the following spring. Assisted by experienced Republican lobbyists, Dirksen sought to convince senators to change their minds. On April 20, 1966, however, the Senate, this time by a virtually unaltered 55 to 38 tally, again declined to approve the Dirksen amendment.[20]

Reverting to the tactic of avoiding congressional involvement in the amendment process and building on the effort pursued by the Council of State Governments since 1963, Dirksen, assisted by a San Francisco public relations firm, encouraged every state legislature that had not already done so to adopt a resolution calling for a constitutional convention as provided for in Article V. The Founders, he said, had ensured that Congress could not deny the people the right to propose an amendment when they felt one was needed.[21] Quickly and quietly, states' rights proponents across the country acted upon Dirksen's suggestion. Before long, a constitutional amendment of unconventional nature and great consequence appeared imminent.

For years Congress routinely received state petitions, printed them in the *Congressional Record,* filed them with its judiciary committees and then forgot them. In March 1967 a front-page *New York Times* story startled Congress with a report that, with the just-completed actions of Colorado, Indiana, Illinois, and North Dakota, thirty-two states had requested a constitutional convention. The *Times* exaggerated in claiming that the convention campaign was "nearing success." Buried deep in the story was the acknowledgment that five of the state petitions asked for adoption of something other than the Dirksen amendment. Furthermore, the report revealed that the Georgia and New Mexico petitions were never officially sent to the Congress.[22] Nevertheless, congressional speeches and press editorials at once began either applauding or warning that if only two more states took action, the two-thirds threshold of Article V would be met. Congress was about to be compelled to call a convention that in turn could propose any amendments it chose, or so it appeared.

Senators opposed to the Dirksen initiative responded quickly. William Proxmire of Wisconsin pointed out that twenty-six of the thirty-two petitions came from malapportioned state legislatures and thus were of dubious standing. Joseph Tydings of Maryland, a member of the Subcommittee on Constitutional Amendments, challenged the validity of the state petitions on a number of grounds. They had not been submitted simultaneously, he pointed out. Furthermore, the petitions were dissimilar since they specifically requested different types of amendments. He echoed Proxmire's contention that most were void since they came from malapportioned legislatures under court order to redistrict. Tydings expressed the hope that "Congress will not be moved to lay open our sacred Constitution to amendment on the defective and self-serving petitions of 25 rotten borough legislatures which are no longer even in existence."[23]

Dirksen scoffed at such objections. Neither the drafters of Article V nor the Congress in 180 years ever talked about the form of petitions, he pointed out; content and purpose were what mattered. All of the petitions in question called for the convening of a constitutional convention simply to propose amendments to deal with apportionment of state legislatures. No more need existed for petitions to be simultaneous than for amendment ratifications to be so; the Court had already ruled in *Dillon v. Gloss* that, in the absence of any Article V specification, a "reasonable time" should apply. If these petitions were invalid because they had been adopted by malapportioned legislatures, then, Dirksen slyly suggested, all other acts of those bodies were equally invalid. Dismissing every other objection as well, Dirksen concluded that the ultimate safeguard of Article V was that no amendment, whether proposed by Congress or convention, could become part of the Constitution unless ratified by three-fourths of the states.[24]

As the implications of an unrestricted constitutional convention called under the terms of Article V began to sink in, even states' rights conservatives began to worry. North Carolina senator Sam Ervin, a literal reader of the Constitution and one of the most vigorous opponents of civil rights legislation during the previous decade, concluded that an uncontrolled constitutional convention could conceivably change the entire structure and mandate of American government, just as the 1787 Philadelphia convention had done. From the perspective of the late 1960s as blacks, women, and other groups capable of mustering substantial support pressed for fundamental reform, an unrestrained constitutional convention posed as many threats as rewards to Ervin and others who thought in similar terms. The Supreme Court's apportionment decisions might be "officious meddling," but to Ervin even greater horrors could lie waiting in a constitutional convention. Foe as well as friend took Ervin seriously, regarding him as the most knowledgeable senator on constitutional matters. Those of contrary political views fully shared Ervin's nervousness, fearing that a constitutional convention might dismantle the Bill of Rights, reverse recent steps toward implementation of equal protection of the law, and otherwise run amok.

Senator Ervin responded to the perceived peril in August 1967 by proposing a Federal Constitutional Convention Act. The measure proposed guidelines for state petitions and constitutional conventions under Article V, something Congress had never established, Ervin pointed out. Under its terms, petitions would have to specify the amendments sought, and states would retain the right to rescind them. Congress would be obliged to act only if uniform petitions were adopted by two-thirds of the states within a four-year period. Congress would have to call a convention within one year, but it would set the time and place as well as specify the means of ratification. Although states could determine the means of choosing their delegates, each state would be granted as many delegates as it had representatives and senators. Perhaps most important from Ervin's point of view, the convention could not propose amendments that differed in their general nature from those stated in the call for the convention. Finally, in an attempt to settle a long dispute, the measure specified that states retained the right to change their position, to ratify a previously rejected amendment or rescind an earlier ratification, until three-fourths of the states had ratified. Although not brought to a vote during Dirksen's crusade, the Ervin bill served as an effective reminder of the uncertainties of the Article V process once it was set in motion.[25]

As the number of state requests for a constitutional convention increased, so too did legislative reapportionments to comply with the *Reynolds v. Sims* mandate. The nondisruptive experience of implementing the Court's ruling, resulting changes in the distribution of legislative power, and rising apprehension about a constitutional convention slowed and then stopped Dirksen's crusade. Rural conservatives obtained legislative approval of a convention petition in Iowa in May 1969, but the seventeen other states that had not previously acted remained silent. Less than two months later, North Carolina rescinded its petition with one opponent explaining, "That Democratic convention in Chicago would look like a religious service compared to what a constitutional convention would be."[26] In August, Oklahoma declared its convention application no longer in force, and a federal judge in Utah ruled the state's application invalid because adopted by a malapportioned legislature.[27]

Already stalled, the antireapportionment amendment effort collapsed entirely after Dirksen's death in September 1969. Republicans who considered the measure unwise but had not wished to oppose their Senate leader no longer felt inhibited.[28] In November, the Wisconsin general assembly defeated a petition resolution by more than a 3-to-2 margin.[29] No additional petitions were filed, and during the next four years, Idaho, Dirksen's home state of Illinois, Kansas, and Texas formally withdrew theirs.[30] Experience with an initially much-derided judicial decision and contemplation of the potential consequences of attacking it finally took the wind out of an attempt that for most of the 1960s was a significant campaign for constitutional amendment. The "one man, one vote" principle, at first so much resisted in some quarters, rapidly became embedded in the national sense of democratic values.

Although the antireapportionment crusade expired, questions it raised about the amending process, in particular the conduct and consequences of a constitutional convention demanded by two-thirds of the states, remained very much alive. Everett Dirksen sought to minimize those concerns in his quest to advance his own amending agenda, but others such as Sam Ervin regarded them with alarm. Ervin's attempt to restrict the amending mechanism won unanimous Senate approval in 1971 and 1973 but died in the House Judiciary Committee.[31] Any sense of urgency about a constitutional convention faded, at least for the time being, along with the antireapportionment amendment, but uncertainties about Article V did not.

HOSTILE REACTION to another cluster of early 1960s Supreme Court rulings stirred an additional initiative to amend the Constitution. Senate Republican minority leader Dirksen once again took up a battle that others had started to restore practices the Court had disallowed. Not as well organized, able to agree on language, or tactically clever as the attempt to overturn the apportionment decisions, the campaign to return prayer to public school classrooms came nowhere near success. Indeed, the arguments that its advocates advanced appeared to increase doubts among legislators as to whether this constitutional change was wise. Nevertheless, demands for a school prayer amendment continued to reverberate from pulpits, pews, editorial pages, and public platforms.

Before the 1960s, the nation's religious culture faced few judicial challenges. Protestantism, the dominant faith, enjoyed a central and comfortable place in American public life. Roman Catholicism had gradually achieved general social approval, although the Know Nothing movement of the 1850s, the Ku Klux Klan of the 1920s, and widespread resistance to electing a Catholic president in 1960 provided continuing reminders that Catholics were not universally welcome. Judaism, a much smaller but growing presence, gained grudging and at best partial acceptance from the larger Christian society. Other religious groups and, even more, the nonreligious were generally ignored and sometimes, as Mormons and Jehovah's Witnesses well knew, treated disrespectfully. Public discourse and policy regarding religious observance, holy days, and other customs as well as a few minor and unsuccessful late-nineteenth-century constitutional amendment attempts casually accepted as standard the beliefs and practices of mainstream Christianity. During the cold war hysteria of the 1950s a closer than ever identification developed between American patriotism and the Christian church. Widespread support existed for Billy Graham, the most prominent evangelist of the day, who earnestly preached, "If you would be a loyal American, then become a loyal Christian."[32]

For over a century and a half, the Supreme Court interpreted in narrow terms the First Amendment stricture that "Congress shall make no law respecting an establishment of religion or prohibiting the free exercise thereof," going so far in 1892 as to say that "this is a Christian nation."[33] Justices generally gave priority to the free exercise clause and regarded the establishment clause as merely prohibiting government from favoring one Christian denomination over another, rather than providing equal standing to non-Christian religions or to nonbelief. Congress's minting of money proclaiming "In God we trust" as well as its 1954 addition of "one nation, *under God*" to the Pledge of Allegiance stood unchallenged as acts inconsistent with the establishment clause.

In 1961 the Court, which earlier confined itself to protecting the rights of religious minorities, took a step away from its traditional tacit acceptance of Christian dominance when it invalidated a Maryland law requiring a state employee to declare his belief in God. Justice Hugo Black wrote that this law put the power of the state "on the side of one particular sort of believer—those who are willing to say they believe 'in the existence of God.'"[34] Black's opinion specifically acknowledged the equal legal standing with theistic religions of nontheistic belief systems such as Buddhism, Taoism, Ethical Culture, and Secular Humanism as well as agnostic or atheistic disbelief.

In 1962 the Court took its new view of religion considerably further when it found that a state-composed prayer to "almighty God," used daily in the Hyde Park, New York, public schools intruded on the free exercise of religion and was "wholly inconsistent with the Establishment Clause." Writing for the Court in *Engel v. Vitale,* Justice Black explained, "It is neither sacrilegious nor antireligious to say that each separate government in this country should stay out of the business of writing or sanctioning official prayers and leave that purely religious function to the people themselves and to those the people choose to look to for religious guidance."[35] The following year Bible reading and recitation of the Lord's Prayer at the start of the school day were likewise ruled unconstitutional. The justices agreed in *Abington School District v. Schempp* and *Murray v. Curlett* that "such an opening exercise is a religious ceremony and was intended by the state to be so." They held that the establishment clause could not be avoided by making participation in such school exercises voluntary. Furthermore, the free exercise clause "never meant that a majority could use the machinery of the state to practice its beliefs."[36]

Far more than the state oath case, the school prayer and Bible reading decisions upset many American Christians. Typically they dismissed the subtleties of a ruling that repeatedly honored the place of religion in society and made clear that the justices were merely insisting upon the separation of church and state. Instead, angry Christians registered their fury at having practices that they regarded as modest and appropriate religious rituals banned from the schoolhouse. Unhappiness appeared greatest in the South and East where school prayer was much more common that in the Midwest and West.[37] One outraged Catholic law professor from New York wrote that the "Court paid an eccentric deference to the inflated scruples of a small minority, preferring them over the views of the vast majority who seek to extend to God a simple obeisance in accord with our national tradition."[38]

Demands for constitutional change were not blunted by President Kennedy's widely publicized press conference observation that besides the need to support Supreme Court decisions "even when we may not agree with them," there was "a very easy remedy." "That is," he said, "to pray ourselves. And I would think that it would be a welcome reminder to every American family that we can pray a good deal more at home, we can attend our churches with a good deal more fidelity, and we can make the true meaning of prayer much more important in the lives of all of our children."[39] Kennedy's gentle suggestion that religious activity could go on without state support failed to assuage many people offended by the Court's ruling.

House Judiciary Committee chairman Emanuel Celler received, and for twenty-two months resisted, a flood of calls from congressmen, clergy, governors, and citizens for an amendment to reverse *Engel v. Vitale* and, later, the *Abington* and *Murray* rulings. Finally, faced with a petition to discharge the bill from committee that had gathered 157 of the 218 required signatures, Celler reluctantly agreed to hold hearings. By April 22, 1964, when the hearings began, 117 representatives had introduced 154 resolutions proposing thirty-five different constitutional amendments. Congressman Frank Becker of New York, chairman of an informal fifty-nine-member caucus that drew up the most widely supported resolution and circulated the discharge petition, led a long parade of representatives and other witnesses before the committee to demand prompt action.[40]

At first Chairman Celler simply allowed amendment advocates to vent their unhappiness with the ending of traditional school religious rituals. Then he and other committee members gradually began raising questions about how a school prayer amendment would be worded and how it would work. Congressman Joel Broyhill, who represented the northern Virginia district nearest Washington, drew some of the most pointed queries. Would the proposed amendment override states' rights by, for instance, invalidating a Wisconsin law banning school prayers? Would it prevent judicial review of a prayer designed by the religious majority in a school district? Could a Catholic majority, for example, insist on the Hail Mary or a reading from the Catholic Bible as opposed to the Protestant King James version? Unable to answer, a discomfited and testy Broyhill pointed out that he was not a lawyer and confessed that he could not "tell these legal brains here how they should dot these 'i's' and cross the 't's.' " Nevertheless, he thought there should be some way to return to the pre-1962 situation.[41]

As the hearings proceeded, Celler brought forth statements from national and local religious groups opposed to an amendment. On April 24, for instance, he began the day by presenting a Baptist editorial worrying about religious minorities having their views overridden, a Lutheran statement finding school prayer of dubious value, and a Lansing, Michigan, Council of Churches' proclamation that worship and religious instruction belonged in churches, homes, and voluntary associations. The few House members willing to testify that they thought a prayer amendment was a bad idea received the chairman's full attention. Celler told Representative B. F. Sisk, a California Democrat who vigorously opposed the amendment, "We had a procession of Congressmen on the other side and I wanted to say you are very much like a breath of cool air in the heat of summer." For his part, Sisk blamed right-wing Christian extremists, stirred up through the radio network of fundamentalist minister Carl McIntyre, for a crusade to limit American freedom of religion. He expressed concern that a religious majority in a school district, whether Armenian Apostolic, Unitarian, Catholic, Buddhist, or Protestant, might impose its preferences on all local minorities. The prayer amendment, said Sisk, was a dangerous tinkering with the First Amendment, and he vowed to do all he could to block it.[42]

After four days, attention shifted from the testimony of congressmen to that of religious leaders. With a few notable exceptions, such as Catholic Bishop Fulton J. Sheen, most church leaders spoke against an amendment and for prayer as a family and church responsibility. Edwin Tuller, general secretary of the American Baptist Convention and spokesman for the National Council of Churches, endorsed the Supreme Court's ruling. He characterized prayer vague enough to be nonsectarian as meaningless and prayer specific enough to shape thought as unacceptably sectarian. Routine formal collective prayer rituals could replace devotion with hypocritical conformity, he said, adding, "An amendment to permit compulsory Bible reading and prayer in the public schools is not only a danger to the freedom of non-believers, it is also a threat to the religious well-being of the believer."[43]

As the hearings went forward, proponents of the prayer amendment continued to stress the importance of religion in American life while opponents emphasized the problem with finding any language that would protect diverse beliefs. A young associate professor from the University of Chicago Divinity School, Martin Marty, caught the committee's attention with a map showing that one denomination was dominant in most U.S. counties. The identity of the denomination varied, with Baptists strong in the South, Lutherans in the Northwest, and Roman Catholics in the urban Northeast. Furthermore, some very large national denominations, the Episcopalians and Presbyterians, for instance, seldom dominated any locality. Religious decisions by local majorities, Marty implied, not only ran against the grain of American religious pluralism but also would work against the interests of nearly every denomination somewhere in the country.[44] By the time the hearings concluded, such testimony produced mounting awareness of the prayer amendment's liabilities and waning congressional enthusiasm for a vote on the issue.

The school prayer amendment hearings consumed eighteen days from April to June 1964. They provided, among other things, a counterpoint to the Senate filibuster against the civil rights bill going on simultaneously. The intensity of the two debates was equivalent, as was the vehemence of denunciation of the Court by those who preferred the pre-*Brown* or pre-*Engel* status quo. As southern rhetoric against the civil rights bill eventually exhausted itself, so too did the ardent defense of school prayer. Representatives appeared to conclude, in the latter case, that it was best to do nothing. Once the prayer amendment hearings were over, the Judiciary Committee took no more action, Becker's discharge petition attracted no more support, and the issue stalled in the House. It was far from dead, however.

The Supreme Court's position on schoolhouse religion held a high place among the concerns of Senator Barry Goldwater's conservative supporters, who dominated the Republican National Convention of 1964. They insisted that the party platform endorse a school prayer amendment. Even after his party lost the 1964 election by a wide margin, Senator Everett Dirksen kept the prayer issue alive by introducing an amendment resolution to allow administrators of schools and other public buildings to permit voluntary prayer but prohibiting them from prescribing the form or content of the prayer.

The Senate Judiciary Subcommittee on Constitutional Amendments held six days of hearings on the Dirksen amendment in August 1966. Subcommittee chairman Birch Bayh appeared more confident of defeating the amendment than his House counterparts two years earlier. Rather than allowing amendment advocates to speak first, Bayh invited testimony from religious leaders opposed to any tampering with the First Amendment. Routine school prayer would have "no significant effect" on piety, began Jesuit Father Robert Drinan, Dean of the Boston College Law School. He disparaged the amendment campaign as "the obvious and sometimes truly pathetic desire of Congressmen to be identified in the popular mind with those individuals who want more godliness in our schools and more fervor in our public piety." Drinan suggested that submitting the amendment question to a popular vote, as Dirksen and his allies asked, might sacrifice constitutional protection of religious minorities to the power of an overbearing majority. A series of legal authorities and mainstream religious leaders agreed. When given an opportunity to reply, only Dirksen's subcommittee ally, Nebraska senator Roman Hruska, and spokesmen for evangelical and fundamentalist denominations dissented.[45]

Faced with an unsympathetic Judiciary Committee, Dirksen resorted to the familiar tactic of substituting his proposal for a minor bill already on the floor, this time a resolution proclaiming National UNICEF Day. After three days of repeating arguments made in committee, or previously in the House, the Senate voted on Dirksen's amendment on September 21, 1966. Although the resolution carried 49 to 37, the majority fell twelve votes short of the necessary two-thirds for adoption. Since Dirksen and Hruska argued that supporting the measure merely gave the people an opportunity to decide the issue and since the possibility of passage by two-thirds seemed remote, a yes vote was relatively easy to cast. Opponents faced a greater challenge making a case that the Dirksen amendment threatened religious freedom, but, among others, Sam Ervin of North Carolina, a constitutional conservative from a state with a dominant Christian culture, steadfastly so argued. Although Ervin and his liberal and conservative allies did not persuade a majority, they did keep the high-water mark of support for a school prayer amendment well below Article V minimum requirements for fundamental constitutional change.[46]

In an attempt to salvage the prayer amendment, Representative Chalmers Wylie, an Ohio Republican, was able in 1971 to persuade a House majority to petition for discharge of an amendment resolution from committee. Compelled to vote, the House registered a 240 to 162 majority in favor of the measure. The tally fell a substantial twenty-eight votes short of the two-thirds required for passage.[47] Confirming the absence of supermajority support, the House vote put an end to agitation for the prayer amendment for the time being.

Although no school prayer amendment emerged from either the House or Senate in the decade after *Engel v. Vitale,* the discussion of one in both bodies contributed to a public perception that the school prayer question remained unresolved. Especially in the South and East where schoolhouse Bible reading and prayer had been much more common than in the Midwest and West, the practice continued.[48] Even where schools complied with the Court decisions, resentment toward the rulings remained high.[49] Much of the public neither understood nor accepted the judicial reasoning behind *Engel* and the other cases. Such persons failed to perceive possible negative consequences of a prayer amendment as did those who closely followed the 1964 House Judiciary hearings. To the legally and constitutionally unsophisticated, the Supreme Court had suppressed rather than protected free religious expression. Therefore, the desire for a constitutional amendment to permit school prayer remained undiminished in some circles, ready to resurface at any time.

FOLLOWING HIS EXTRAORDINARY SUCCESS as a first-term senator in winning congressional approval of the Twenty-fifth Amendment, Birch Bayh encouraged the Subcommittee on Constitutional Amendments to address other areas of potential constitutional improvement. Attention naturally turned first to a provision of the Constitution long and frequently criticized, the electoral college system for choosing the president and vice-president. The winner-take-all treatment of a state's electoral votes that created the possibility of a candidate's losing the national popular vote but winning in the electoral college provoked many complaints over the years, as did the procedure for Congress choosing a president in the absence of an electoral college majority. Such critiques tended to overshadow justifications of the electoral sys-

tem on the grounds that it encouraged a moderate, national two-party political system rather than a fragmented, ideological multiparty alternative and
that it usually strengthened the sense of support for presidents who gained
narrow but nonetheless determinative popular victories.[50] The young Indiana senator, already experienced in the related area of presidential replacement, lost little time in taking up the cause of electoral college reform.

Suggestions for improving or abolishing the electoral system had been
advanced ever since 1796. The Twelfth Amendment, adopted after the 1800
election, modified the system for resolving cases where no candidate received
an electoral majority, linked presidential and vice-presidential contests, and
encouraged the rise of political parties. It did not, however, resolve all the
controversies surrounding the electoral system. When the four-way contest
of 1824 denied anyone an electoral college majority and allowed the House
of Representatives to select second-place popular-vote winner John Quincy
Adams as president, when a few disputed popular votes determined the fate
of several states' electoral votes and thus a close national contest in 1876,
when Benjamin Harrison lost the popular vote but won in the electoral college in 1888, or whenever a successful candidate lacked an absolute majority, as did Woodrow Wilson in 1912 or Harry Truman in 1948, reform
proposals poured forth. The hairbreadth and controversial victory of John
Kennedy over Richard Nixon in 1960 renewed concern. The next year proposals for presidential election reform received consideration from Senator
Estes Kefauver's Subcommittee on Constitutional Amendments along with
poll tax abolition and the eighteen-year-old vote. Altogether between 1796
and 1966 over 500 amendment resolutions were introduced in Congress to
reform the method of choosing the nation's executives.[51]

Ideas for changing the federal electoral system varied considerably. The
first proposal to eliminate the electoral college and use the result of a popular
vote to cast each state's electoral votes under the existing formula appeared
in 1826. This so-called automatic system would reaffirm a state-by-state
winner-take-all approach. Even earlier in 1800 Representative John Nicholas
of Virginia had proposed an amendment requiring that each congressional
district serve as the arena for an automatic winner-take-all count. Several
states preferred the existing option of a district to a statewide tally and used
it until the 1830s. In 1848, the proportional division of electoral votes
among various candidates began to be advocated as a substitute for the winner-take-all approach. The simple alternative to these various continuations
of the electoral college, a national direct election that would equalize every
vote cast, was suggested as early as 1826.[52]

Proposals for federal electoral reform did not address issues of who should vote for president but how votes should be counted. By the early nineteenth century, the right of each state's legal voters, not their legislators, to choose the state's electors and the obligation of those electors to cast their ballots for candidates to whom they had pledged their support was generally accepted. Entitlement to the suffrage was handled separately, legislatively in most cases and through amendments for minorities, women, and eighteen-year-olds. Much in dispute, however, was whether votes should be aggregated on a district, state, or national basis. A district system would protect smaller political subdivisions from being submerged in the state tally, whereas a statewide winner-take-all system would enhance the unitary political influence of each state. A direct national election or its functional equivalent, proportional voting, would reduce the exaggerated power of district or state majorities and give a voice in the national outcome to minorities within every political subdivision. The winner-take-all formulas of the existing electoral college, the automatic system, and, to a lesser extent, the district system maintained the power of individual states in the federal balance. The proportional and direct election methods shifted that balance and enhanced the role of national political parties, arguably ideologically differentiated ones even more so than the traditional American moderate type. No wonder that appeals for one or another of these measures, not to mention hybrid variations on them, continued to pile up. How the vote was counted could not only determine the winner of a close contest but also dramatically influence contending political interests in less visible but no less important ways.

Constantly under discussion, electoral reform proposals tended to divide rather than unite politicians, who paid far more attention to them than did the broader public. Before the Civil War, electoral reform ran afoul of sectional conflict. Thereafter the South continued to look upon the existing system as protective of state power and the white majority's interests. The automatic plan represented the slightest change from the status quo. Brought to a vote in the Senate in 1934, it achieved a majority but less than two-thirds and failed to arouse any passionate support; it did not reach the floor again. Direct election never gained serious consideration, even in the 1920s when forceful advocate Senator George Norris saw it as a logical extension of the march toward democracy embodied in the direct senatorial election and woman suffrage amendments. Proportional and district plans failed as well. In 1950 some Republican senators proposed proportional distribution as a means of strengthening minority parties within states; others opposed it for weakening the federal system. A district plan was put forth in the 1950s as a means of maintaining rural influence in the face of growing urban population concentrations.[53] Any reform that would alter the political influence of states faced a daunting challenge when the approval of two-thirds of their congressional representatives and three-quarters of their state legislatures was needed.

By the mid-1960s Senator Bayh believed that recent changes in thinking about apportionment and voting rights had created a new atmosphere for an electoral reform amendment.[54] In 1965 he embraced the automatic plan that Lyndon Johnson favored as a means of dealing with unreliable electors who might cast ballots at variance with the popular mandate, and early in 1966 his subcommittee held hearings to consider it. Then on May 18 a Gallup poll reported that 63 percent of Americans, many of whom were no doubt bewildered by the electoral college and unfamiliar with the complex, sophisticated arguments for either its modification or retention, favored its replacement with a simple direct national election. On the same day Bayh announced he was switching his support to direct election of the president. After conferring with an American Bar Association panel as he had on presidential disability and succession, Bayh altered his position further, embracing the ABA recommendation for a runoff election rather than a congressional choice if no presidential candidate received 40 percent of the total vote. Bayh and the bar panel agreed that this method provided the best means of avoiding the splintering of political parties that critics feared would result from direct election.[55] Marshaling generally supportive testimony from over fifty witnesses during eighteen days of hearings that began in February 1967, Bayh and the ABA contended that their direct election amendment, if not perfect, at least was consistent with "one man, one vote" and thus was the best available solution to an issue that needed attention.[56]

The forty-six electoral votes won by Alabama governor George Wallace in his 1968 presidential campaign stirred concerns that a strong third-party candidate in a contest where the two leading contenders were evenly balanced might deny either an electoral vote majority. A shift of 40,000 votes in three states could have prevented Richard Nixon's electoral college victory, Bayh pointed out. Such a situation required that the election be settled in the House of Representatives where each state would cast one vote and evenly divided delegations would have no voice at all. In such circumstances, a candidate unable to claim victory might yet decide the winner, as Henry Clay had done in 1825. The potential loomed large for an angry ideologue such as Wallace to barter his support for acceptance of some racist, radical, or reactionary demand.

The 1968 election also cast a spotlight upon Dr. Lloyd W. Bailey, a John Birch Society member who, chosen as a North Carolina Nixon elector, cast his vote for Wallace. Declaring that the United States was "dangerously close" to becoming a democracy instead of a republic, Bailey said that he had only agreed to join a Richard Nixon slate, not to surrender his right to exercise an elector's judgment with a binding pledge to vote for Richard Nixon. The appearance of a "faithless elector," although the first in eight years and only the sixth out of 15,783 since 1820, coincided with apprehensions about the House making a presidential choice.[57] Bayh's amendment suddenly attracted far more enthusiasm from mainstream politicians.

In the first six weeks of 1969 both houses of Congress considered and rejected proposals to invalidate Dr. Bailey's vote and opened hearings on Bayh's direct election amendment. Familiar and well-rehearsed arguments were repeated and masses of statistical evidence presented to demonstrate that the existing electoral system nearly produced deadlock or a minority president in 1960 and 1968 while direct election avoided such outcomes. The new Nixon administration, in a letter signed by the president as well as in testimony to the House Judiciary Committee by Attorney General John Mitchell, expressed preference for the proportional system but, in many respects, little relish for any reform. This attitude seemed to increase House Judiciary chairman Emanuel Celler's enthusiasm for the Bayh-ABA direct election amendment. Discarding his earlier ambivalence, he proceeded to win a 29 to 6 Judiciary Committee endorsement, surmount the resistance of Rules Committee chairman William Colmer, and bring the amendment to the floor in September. Celler began the debate by declaring, "The electoral college system turned out, contrary to the spirit and words of the Founding Fathers, to be a historical blunder, a real genuine blunder." He continued, "Whatever the advantage—to large States or to small States—neither can be justified because it rests on the notion of voter inequality." After six days of discussion most members of the House were persuaded, and the amendment won an overwhelming 339 to 70 victory. A Gallup poll shortly after the vote indicated that 81 percent of the public approved the plan. On September 30 President Nixon endorsed the direct election amendment, though without much fervor.[58]

Direct national presidential elections faced greater obstacles in the Senate where the unequal distribution of state power was incorporated into the design of the body by the Founders and reflexively defended by many members, especially those from small, rural, or southern states. James Eastland, chairman of the Judiciary Committee, was one such senator, and he had a number of allies. Eastland put off consideration of the amendment on the excuse of having to deal with the controversial Supreme Court nominations of Clement Haynsworth and G. Harold Carswell. Only by threatening to delay a confirmation vote on Carswell was Bayh eventually able to compel Eastland to agree to committee action on the amendment.[59]

Senator Sam Ervin then stepped forward to block the path of the direct election amendment. With Eastland's cooperation, Ervin was able to arrange more Judiciary hearings to raise questions about the measure. Bayh received notice only at the last moment, causing him to complain publicly about "blatant disregard for senatorial courtesy."[60] Ervin called a long list of witnesses who argued that the electoral college preserved a political role for small states that would be lost in a consolidated national popular vote. After the Judiciary Committee nevertheless narrowly voted down automatic, district, and proportionate alternatives and approved the direct election amendment, Eastland and Ervin stalled. They took two-and-a-half months to prepare a minority report to the full Senate to accompany the majority report that Bayh produced in five weeks. By delaying floor debate until the Senate was rushing to adjourn and then conducting what Ervin termed "extensive discussion" of the measure, these experienced and shrewd parliamentarians gained valuable strategic advantages.[61]

Although Bayh thought he had sixty to sixty-two votes for the direct election amendment when it came to the floor September 8, 1970, the senator from Indiana did not have nearly enough votes to cut off Ervin and other senators who wanted to prevent a vote.[62] Some of Ervin's allies, Republicans Carl Curtis and Roman Hruska of Nebraska and Strom Thurmond of South Carolina, proved melodramatic as well as loquacious. Yet they succeeded in focusing attention on their contention that the amendment represented a serious threat to federalism. Asserting that thirty-four states would lose voting power under a single national tally, Hruska termed the measure "the most mischievous and dangerous constitutional amendment that has ever received serious consideration by the Congress." Warming to his subject, he claimed that to adopt the amendment "would be to set out on a vast uncharted sea, with no guarantee that the slightest political breeze might not capsize and destroy our ship of state."[63]

The filibuster led an unhappy Bayh to call for cloture to cut off debate. He declared that "at a time when our very system of government is being sorely tested" and after the detailed scrutiny his measure had received for months, if not years, it would be "unconscionable to suggest that the Senate does not have the courage to stand up and vote on the merits of an issue like this." An attempt to obtain cloture drew the support of a 54 to 36 majority on September 17, well short of the two-thirds approval required. Bayh then indicated his readiness to accept drastic changes to gain support. He was willing to alter one of the amendment's most controversial features, the runoff election if no candidate obtained 40 percent in initial balloting, limiting a runoff to the two leading contestants and thereby eliminating all but the principal parties. When this concession weakened enthusiasm for the amendment and yet failed to reduce opposition, a second cloture vote lost 53 to 34 on September 29. The embattled senator pressed on, but as it became clear that a third attempt would fare no better, Bayh felt compelled to withdraw his measure.[64]

September 1969 proved in retrospect to be the high-water mark for the direct election amendment. At that point the measure appeared to enjoy extensive political and public support. A year later the anxiety induced by the 1968 election was fading and reservations about changing the electoral system were increasing. Alternative reform proposals, offered as compromise solutions, added an element of confusion. Senator Hruska proved to be far from alone in his reluctance to set out on uncharted seas. Observers following the debate asked serious questions: Would the knowledge that their vote would finally count in a presidential election bring many new voters to the polls who had previously been discouraged about their minority status within a state's electorate? Would a direct national election splinter the existing political parties that were, after all, coalitions of state parties, and substitute a new, more ideologically defined party system? Would third party movements be encouraged or stymied beyond reason? Would national voting mean federal voter registration and election supervision? Would the likelihood of vote fraud increase, or would its influence and thus the incentive for it be lessened? Would small states, big states, rural states, or urban states, not to mention minorities of the general population concentrated in one location, lose political advantages they perceived the current system provided? Would the insistence on equally weighted national voting even lead to an attempt to undo the Constitution's most glaring inequality, two Senate votes for every state, large or small? The likelihood that the existing political system would be upset in unpredictable ways kept the direct election amendment from achieving two-thirds Senate support, and in the words of a *New York Times* editorial, rendered presidential election reform out of the question "within the foreseeable future."[65]

Bayh reintroduced the direct election amendment in every Congress of the 1970s and devoted substantial amounts of his own and his staff's time in its behalf.[66] Never again, however, could he recapture the feeling of urgency that the 1968 election had evoked. Furthermore, doubts about the measure remained unresolved and objections strong. Hearings in 1973 roused little interest.[67] In 1975, even with Senator Ervin retired and the cloture rule altered to allow sixty votes to cut off debate, the Judiciary Committee failed to advance the measure.

Bayh regarded the 1976 election as the closest brush with electoral disaster yet, telling his colleagues that a switch of 9,245 votes in Ohio and Hawaii, which barely reduced Jimmy Carter's 1.7 million-vote popular majority, would have denied him an electoral college victory.[68] The Indiana senator held new hearings on direct election in January 1977.[69] President Carter became the first chief executive to embrace direct election with enthusiasm, but at the same time, in his usual well-intentioned but unfocused fashion, he endorsed other electoral reforms, election-day voter registration and public financing of congressional campaigns as well. Simultaneously occupied with many other concerns, Carter did not lobby Congress for the amendment. Despite the efforts of the American Bar Association, the League of Women Voters, the U.S. Chamber of Commerce, and organized labor as well as Bayh's committee staff, the amendment gained no ground.[70] Senate majority leader Robert Byrd refused to bring it to the floor because Bayh could not show that he had the votes to cut off the inevitable filibuster.[71]

The retirement of Judiciary Committee chairman James Eastland and other opponents of direct election revived Bayh's hopes in 1979. He quickly won pledges that in return for more hearings, no filibuster would be undertaken to prevent a Senate vote on the amendment. In the hearings, however, Senator Thurmond argued vigorously that thirty-one states would lose influence under a direct election system. More distressing to Bayh and his staff, black and Jewish leaders asserted that their constituencies, clustered in a few urban sites, would likewise lose political influence.[72] When the amendment came to the floor, Thurmond and others pressed for an immediate vote. Bayh decided that, given the legislative history of the measure, he could not object even though he had not fully presented his case to the entire Senate. On July 10 the direct election amendment received a bare majority of 51 to 48. With several former liberal supporters swayed by minority group concerns, Article V's two-thirds requirement was further out of reach than a decade earlier.[73] This defeat, followed by Bayh's own reelection loss the following year, signaled the death knell of the direct election amendment.

Even if direct election had passed Congress in the late 1960s or 1970s, states remained unlikely to embrace it. Elaborate arguments by reform advocates did not put to rest suspicion that small, rural states would draw little attention from presidential candidates and thus lose influence. Other doubts about direct election persisted as well. Skepticism was stronger in 1979 than a decade before. The Article V ratification formula prevented constitutional amendment unless embraced by a predominant number of the very states that saw themselves being damaged by this particular change. Senate obstructionists in 1970 received the credit for derailing the direct election amendment, but they merely articulated the broad-based concerns that almost certainly would have prevented its ratification.

THE FOUR ARTICLE V successes between 1960 and 1971 are, quite understandably, better remembered than the defeated apportionment, school prayer, and direct election amendments of the same period. Yet the latter, particularly school prayer restoration, stirred as much if not more interest at the time. Furthermore, direct election, according to public opinion surveys, was the most widely approved amendment proposal of the era. Momentary popularity, it is well to note, did not ensure success for the apportionment, prayer, or direct election proposals. Resistance to their adoption proved formidable and ultimately insurmountable. The four amendments that were adopted may have stimulated less passionate support but at the same time they generated fewer objections.

The Article V process worked smoothly when amendment proponents had the support of congressional leaders and did not face significant legislative or popular opposition. In some cases, these conditions reflected broad agreement; in others, general indifference. Yet when all the conditions were met in the 1960s, in other words, when an active or at least a passive constitutional consensus existed, amendments were promptly approved by Congress and ratified by the states. When substantial doubt remained, even though widespread popular and legislative support was present, the demanding requirements of Article V simply could not be met. The innovative use of parliamentary maneuvers and state constitutional convention petitions enlivened and enlightened amendment politics in the 1960s but did not reshape their essential nature. As the Founders had intended, the fundamental terms of the Constitution continued to be set, not by mere majorities, but by supermajority consensus. Constitutional change did not require unanimity, but it did demand acceptance by most substantial elements of the political culture.

Both thwarted and successful constitutional changes remain imperfectly understood aspects of the history of the 1960s. The difficulty of achieving reforms that altered the constitutional structure in major ways was, in reality, far greater than the challenge of adopting comparatively modest measures through the identical Article V process. Misjudging the strength of the American constitutional status quo would continue to mislead amendment seekers in the years ahead.

17

Amendments as Tests of National Consensus

I n the first two centuries of the U.S. Constitution's evolution, the explicit and authentic act of reform that took the most steps along the path toward adoption and yet failed to reach its goal was an amendment declaring that women should be regarded as the legal equals of men. Endorsed by Congress in 1972, the equal rights amendment gained ratification by thirty-five state legislatures, only to fall three shy of Article V's required approval by three-fourths of the states. Almost overlooked in the uproar surrounding the final stages of the battle over the ERA was another amendment granting the District of Columbia representation in Congress as well as the right to participate in federal elections and the constitutional amending process. This amendment gained congressional sanction in 1978. During the next seven years, however, it secured fewer than half the necessary state ratifications. Side by side, the two amendment failures of the 1970s and early 1980s caught by surprise reformers who had come to believe that congressional approval was the principal barrier to constitutional change.[1] These two amending experiences enhanced the image of the Article V process as a formidable obstacle. Especially among proponents of the long-sought, nearly won ERA, a system designed to guarantee a high degree of consensus among states as well as within Congress for formal revision of the fundamental law generated great frustration.

The issue of equal legal treatment of men and women first arose during consideration of the Fourteenth Amendment in 1867 but was brushed aside by a Congress preoccupied with former slaves. The equal rights amendment had been continuously before Congress since 1923, yet not until the 1970s did it acquire a broad enough base of support to gain a realistic chance of being added to the Constitution. Then it became one of the most widely debated, bitterly contested amendment proposals of all time. Representation for the District of Columbia had an even longer history, having been urged as early as 1818 by President James Monroe.[2] The Twenty-third Amendment, which in 1964 granted District residents a role in presidential elections, albeit a disproportionately small one, accelerated appeals for full participation of the District in national representative government. By the

1970s a critical mass of congressional support for the District's cause had been assembled, but state legislative support remained notably absent.

Together, the equal rights and D.C. representation amendments brought questions about the Article V process, both old and new, before a suddenly attentive mass audience. The battle over the ERA stirred serious consideration of the symbolic as well as the substantive purpose of constitutional amendments, the degree of consensus appropriate for declarations of constitutional principle, and the manner in which the amending process should function. The D.C. amendment drew attention to another quandary: do those persons granted authority under the Constitution have a duty in the name of equity to share it with the excluded and powerless when to do so is consistent with professed ideals but against both tradition and political self-interest? In other words, does an obligation ever exist to change the Constitution?

The sound and fury of the immediate contests aside, a further question, perhaps the most important one, hovered over these amending episodes: what is the consequence of failure in a substantial endeavor to achieve amendment? The equal rights amendment experience suggested that an amendment might not itself need to be completed in every instance in order to achieve its essential purpose. The effect of the ERA campaign on legal and political thought and behavior regarding women was extraordinary. On the other hand, the rejection of the D.C. amendment appeared to some observers to mark a significant backward step in American race relations. Because of the predominantly black population of the nation's capital, the ratification defeat seemed to represent a rejection of racial accommodation rather than just a denial of a few congressional seats to unrepresented citizens. The manner in which amendment proposals failed, not just the circumstances in which they were approved, could be regarded as statements of American constitutional values, reflections of core beliefs.

FOR MORE THAN SIX DECADES, a proposed constitutional declaration of gender equality stirred lively, sometimes shrill, and always contentious national discussion of the respective roles of men and women in American society. With the possible exceptions of slavery abolition, national prohibition, and woman suffrage, no amendment proposal ever drew more people into a consideration of the society's basic social arrangements. Whether they defended or denigrated traditional gender relationships, by the 1970s few Americans remained unaware of or indifferent to this proposed constitutional change.

The equal rights amendment, rooted in nineteenth-century women's initiatives, made its first formal appearance soon after the 1920 adoption of the Nineteenth Amendment enfranchised women. Winning the vote satisfied most suffragists, who then either joined the nonpartisan League of Women Voters seeking good government reform, took up social-betterment agendas, or followed conventional paths of political partisanship or noninvolvement. The National Woman's party (NWP), on the other hand, wanted to achieve full legal equality for women and, based on its recent experience, regarded constitutional amendment as a direct, manageable, and effective means to do so. The NWP quickly found itself at odds with most of its former allies in the suffrage crusade. The prevailing view, one articulated in the campaign for national prohibition as well, held that women, fragile and defenseless, deserved special protection as wives and mothers both in the home and when they ventured outside the domestic sphere into the workplace or other venues. Indeed, in contending that women faced special circumstances and needed to be protected, the majority of feminists in the 1920s stood closer to many suffrage opponents than to the advocates of equal rights who sought no special treatment for females.[3]

Following the lead of Alice Paul, the National Woman's party in 1921 began objecting to state legislation in Wisconsin and elsewhere that affirmed equality for women but retained protective laws. The next year, the NWP challenged the protectionist League of Women Voters, National Consumers' League, and National Council of Catholic Women; it argued that special treatment implied subordinate status and was inconsistent with true equality. The NWP began composing an equal rights amendment in September 1921 and unanimously endorsed it at a convention in Seneca Falls, New York, in July 1923. What better way, members felt, to raise consciousness about women's unsatisfactory legal status and to avoid slow and uncertain piecemeal reform of the thousands of federal and state laws that restricted women? This first equal rights amendment, drafted by Paul and introduced in Congress in December 1923 by Republican senator Charles Curtis, simply declared, "Men and women shall have equal rights throughout the United States and every place subject to its jurisdiction."[4]

To many people concerned with women's condition, equal rights seemed to be the worst possible reform, one exactly contrary to their goal of protecting females and improving their status. In 1905 the Supreme Court had struck down general employment regulations in *Lochner v. New York,* but only three years later in *Muller v. Oregon* it approved special protective laws on the basis of woman's distinctive "physical structure and the functions she performs in consequence thereof."[5] National Consumers' League leader

Florence Kelly, for example, divided her energy between advocating the child labor amendment and excoriating the ERA. Senator Thomas Walsh, a frequent Kelly ally, wrote a constituent, "We have passed all manner of laws in the various states to protect women—factory laws, for instance, hours of labor, etc. I can see no sense in a constitutional amendment that will wipe these laws off the statute books. Away back in 1843, the English Parliament passed a law prohibiting the employment of women in underground mines. Many of our states have similar laws. I wonder if you really want these abrogated."[6] Advocates of the protectionist viewpoint dominated one-day Senate hearings on the ERA in 1929 and again in 1931.[7]

Those few feminists in the 1920s who did not regard the equal rights amendment as wrongheaded often considered it meaningless. Specific reforms seemed more consequential and worth fighting for than an abstract declaration of principle. Even NWP leader Harriet Stanton Blatch at first termed ERA "much like the cure-all theory of patent medicine."[8] Attitudes began to shift, however, when courts in Massachusetts and Virginia upheld laws restricting jury service to males, declaring that the equal protection terms of the Fourteenth Amendment did not extend to women even though they were now enfranchised. For the most part, however, reformist women and their male supporters devoted their attention to such protective measures as the Sheppard-Towner maternal and infant health act and the child labor amendment. After a decade, the ERA had made no progress, and even the National Woman's party, fighting division in its already thin ranks, turned much of its attention to other matters.[9]

The New Deal revived interest in the situation of women but primarily from a protectionist viewpoint. Eleanor Roosevelt, Secretary of Labor Frances Perkins, Democratic National Committee vice-chairman Mollie Dewson, and their associates concentrated on improving women's economic and social situation. By the late 1930s, encouraged by the shift in the Supreme Court, New Deal reformers renewed efforts to protect all workers, not just women and children. Passage of the Fair Labor Standards Act superseded the campaign for the child labor amendment. In this climate, equal rights for women seemed less a threat to their welfare, and support for the equal rights amendment began to grow, at least outside the administration. The 65,000-member National Federation of Business and Professional Women endorsed a version of ERA in 1937; over the next few years, the General Federation of Women's Clubs, the National Association of Women Lawyers, and the National Education Association followed suit. Four days of Senate hearings in February 1938 reflected the fuller and more balanced consideration being given equal rights; the League of Women Voters offered as strong a protectionist argument as ever, but the National Woman's party received as much attention.[10] Congressional judiciary committees reported the ERA to the floor for the first time, though without recommendation, in the Senate in 1938 and the House the following year. Influential women's leaders in the U.S. Department of Labor Women's Bureau, the League of Women Voters, and elsewhere continued to maintain that women needed protection and prevented further progress of the equal rights movement. When the Republican party, seeing ERA as hostile to government regulation of business, endorsed the amendment in its 1940 platform, women's protection advocates, who leaned strongly toward the Democrats, saw less reason than ever to reconsider their views.[11]

World War II altered the circumstances of millions of American women. The departure of men for military service disrupted family life. Entry into the wage-earning work force led to confrontation with discrimination. Women were denied access to job security and seniority since they were supposedly working only "for the duration" until men returned. Protective labor laws imposed other limitations. Wartime experiences caused many women to reevaluate their status. Not coincidentally, support for the equal rights amendment surged. The Senate Judiciary Committee voted for it 9 to 3 in May 1942; a year later the endorsement reached 12 to 4 after the National Woman's party agreed to revise its 1923 language to clarify the amendment and render it parallel to the Nineteenth Amendment. The new proposal read, "Equality of rights under the law shall not be denied or abridged by the United States, or by any State, on account of sex." Forty-two representatives cosponsored the amendment in the House in 1943, but protectionist opposition within the Judiciary Committee blocked its progress. By 1944, despite the continuing hostility of the Women's Bureau, the Democratic party, mindful of the 50 percent wartime increase in the number of working women, recommended the ERA in its platform.[12]

As the war ended, prospects for the equal rights amendment improved. The House Judiciary Committee, over strenuous protectionist objections, endorsed the measure for the first time on July 12, 1945.[13] During Senate hearings in September, the Women's Bureau and the National Woman's Trade Union League rallied protectionists, particularly organized labor, to paint a bleak picture of ERA's consequences for women. In response a National Woman's party speaker likened her opponents to the felon's son who objected to abolishing capital punishment on the grounds that "if it was good enough for my father, it is good enough for me!"[14] After the Judiciary Committee again solidly endorsed the ERA, the Senate narrowly approved it on July 10, 1946. The 38 to 35 majority fell well short of the required two-thirds but represented a significant achievement for the amendment in its first congressional floor test.[15]

While the question of protecting women or granting them full equality remained the center of debate, it often camouflaged other more convoluted issues. Protectionism was an umbrella that covered not only individuals such as Eleanor Roosevelt who sincerely desired to advance women's status but also traditionalist men and women who felt females needed to be sheltered because they were innately inferior to men. The usual liberal-versus-conservative alignments broke down over the issues of defending women's individual freedom or using government to alter their social conditions. The 1946 Senate vote reflected this complexity. Almost two-thirds of the minority Republicans, in the midst of a vigorous anti–New Deal campaign, voted for the amendment, but less than one-third of the Democratic majority, the center of women's protection sentiment, did so. Southern Democratic senators voted no for another reason: they feared the possible implications of the ERA in empowering black women in their states.[16]

The progress of the ERA stirred opponents into action. One adversary with long experience in amendment battles was upstate New York Republican congressman James W. Wadsworth, a prominent foe of woman suffrage and national prohibition during his two terms in the Senate from 1915 through 1927. His unbending aversion to domestic federal reform activity had been evident in his leadership of the Association Against the Prohibition Amendment and the American Liberty League as well as his service in the House of Representatives beginning in 1933. Professing sympathy with protectionists from the League of Women Voters and the National Council of Catholic Women, Wadsworth pursued a shrewd strategy to attract yet divide those interested in women's situation and thus thwart the ERA.[17] He advanced a proposal to create a federal commission to study the status of women and to devise a national policy that "in law and its administration no distinctions on the basis of sex shall be made except such as are reasonably justified by differences in physical structure, biological, or social function."[18] Equal rights advocates and even a few Women's Bureau protectionists saw the claim of justifiable gender distinctions in Wadsworth's vague proposal as detrimental and dangerous. On the other hand, politicians from conservative Senate Republican majority leader Robert Taft to liberal Democratic representatives Emanuel Celler and Helen Gahagan Douglas embraced it as a means of displaying concern for their female constituents while defending protectionism and blocking the equal rights amendment. The Women's Bureau embraced but the National Woman's party adamantly opposed the proposal that came to be referred to as the women's status bill.[19]

Wadsworth's suggestion that it would be possible to end gender distinctions except when they benefited women did not bear immediate fruit. When the ERA again came before the Senate in January 1950, the women's status bill was voted down. However, immediately thereafter Democratic senator Carl Hayden of Arizona, a traditionalist in his gender views and an ally of the Women's Bureau protectionists, offered essentially the same idea more cleverly packaged. Hayden proposed an addition to the ERA resolution, a rider providing that "the provisions of this article shall not be construed to impair any rights, benefits, or exemptions conferred by law upon persons of the female sex." Although equal rights advocate Claude Pepper of Florida rose immediately to argue that the Hayden rider destroyed the essence of the ERA, its language appealed to his colleagues. Senators realized that the rider allowed them to go on record for equal rights and protection at the same time. Some clearly saw it as a convenient mask for their outright opposition to the amendment.[20] Hayden's measure was approved 51 to 31, and then the Senate endorsed the ERA 63 to 19.[21] Caught by surprise, ERA supporters were unable to block Senate action but soon made it clear that they preferred no amendment at all to this one. Because Chairman Celler, a committed protectionist, refused to allow the ERA out of the House Judiciary Committee, a petition compelling the amendment's discharge had been prepared; but faced with the Hayden rider, equal rights proponents decided not to file it. Instead, ERA was allowed to die in committee.[22] Protectionism again emerged victorious.

Given past Republican support for the ERA, the party's 1952 election triumph was expected to boost the amendment's prospects. But in July 1953 the Senate again attached the Hayden rider by a 58-to-25 vote before approving the measure 73 to 11.[23] Once more equal rights advocates chose not to have the House take up a measure that declared gender distinctions sometimes justified. Although both Republican and Democratic party platforms continued to pledge support for women's equal rights, the disputed understanding of what the term really meant remained an obstacle. When the amendment returned to the floor of the Senate in 1960, the Hayden rider won yet another victory without even a roll-call vote, and the amendment was sent back to the Judiciary Committee. The argument that women needed protection continued to thwart the advocates of unqualified gender equality.[24]

Senator John Kennedy typified the male politicians of the 1950s who found gender rights an awkward, if secondary issue. He sought women's votes by expressing concern for their problems but made no particular effort to consult or understand them. He was satisfied with the traditional protectionist position of most liberal Democrats, repeatedly declaring that he sup-ported equality but desired to spare women from harm.[25] In his policies and practices as president, Kennedy continued this paternalistic pattern of not taking women entirely seriously. He employed the old suggestion of the Women's Bureau and other ERA opponents to deal with the gender ques-tion. In December 1961, he appointed a President's Commission on the Sta-tus of Women to study the matter, loading it with people who could be expected to confirm the position with which he was comfortable.[26]

Most of the twenty-six men and women Kennedy named to the commis-sion were protectionists opposed to ERA, including chair Eleanor Roosevelt; executive vice-chair Esther Peterson, head of the Women's Bureau; and Edith Green, Democratic representative from Oregon, who chaired the critical committee on civil and political rights. Although only one open advocate of ERA was appointed, other commissioners and committee members voiced support for other means of attaining true gender equality. Black attorney Pauli Murray, for one, argued that the Fourteenth Amendment already guar-anteed women equal protection of the law. The Supreme Court, Murray contended, had erred in creating a separate but equal category for women with its 1908 *Muller v. Oregon* decision just as it had earlier done for blacks in *Plessy v. Ferguson*. Murray believed the reconsideration of the equal pro-tection clause that produced the *Brown v. Board of Education* decision could also resolve the gender issue. Perhaps equality could be achieved with-out constitutional amendment.[27]

The presidential commission, gathering overwhelming evidence of Amer-ican women's second-class economic, social, and legal status, adopted Mur-ray's position as a means of securing gender equality without necessarily sacrificing protections for women. The commission report took the position that "equality of rights under the law for all persons, male or female, is so basic to democracy and its commitment to the ultimate value of the individ-ual that it must be reflected in the fundamental law of the land." Embracing Murray's belief that the Fifth and Fourteenth Amendments supported the principle of gender equality, however, the commission concluded that a new amendment "need not be sought in order to establish that principle." With some commissioners hopeful of a judicial solution but most still opposed to the ERA, this report was a delicate compromise. The few amendment sup-porters managed to avoid an outright denunciation of the ERA with the ar-gument that it should be retained as a last resort in case judicial remedies failed.[28]

Although the October 1963 report of the President's Commission on the Status of Women represented, in effect, a standoff on the equal rights amendment, concurrent developments began improving its prospects. In May Congress had already adopted an equal pay act sought by the Women's Bureau. Though its sponsors encountered considerable resistance to the measure's modest requirement that women be given equal pay for equal work, a much lower standard than the "equal pay for comparable work" alternative, the law at least endorsed the principle of equality.[29] Published even earlier in the same year, Betty Friedan's *The Feminine Mystique* was attracting a wide readership. The book stirred many middle-class women to reconsider their circumstances in light of Friedan's assertion that they led a soothing but not fully adult life in "a comfortable concentration camp." Contemporaneously, the spreading campaign for black civil rights also led many women to contemplate their own situation. Those sharing in the risks of marches, sit-ins, and voter registration drives began reacting to the second-class treatment they received from their male counterparts. Stokely Carmichael provoked their anger with his comment that "the only position for women in [the Student Non-Violent Coordinating Committee] is prone." Female civil rights workers thought about how they had become the typists, coffee-makers, and sexual recreation of the movement but were not allowed a role in policy discussions. Women found themselves pushed forward only when violence was expected; putting them in the front rows of demonstrators was considered a means of highlighting southern brutality for a national television audience. As the civil rights movement asserted that blacks were entitled to equal protection of the laws under the Fourteenth Amendment, growing numbers of women began reassessing their own social and legal status.[30]

In the midst of these developments, an unexpected source supplied new momentum to the cause of women's equality. Trying to load down the proposed 1964 civil rights bill with features, defensible in themselves, that would impair its chances of passage, House Rules Committee chairman Howard Smith, long a supporter of the National Woman's party, proposed adding sex to the list of characteristics to be federally protected against discrimination. Many of his male colleagues laughed at the old Virginian's wit and guile, while Emanuel Celler, a leader of the civil rights forces as well as a steadfast protectionist opponent of ERA, fumed. Led by Democrat Martha Griffiths of Michigan, most of the few female representatives saw an opportunity and seized it. On the floor of the House, vocal male support for the sex provision came almost entirely from members who, like Smith, eventually voted against the overall bill. Meanwhile the bill's proponents divided. Most liberal Democrats voted no, fearful of undermining civil rights advances for blacks or undercutting women's protection. Republicans and eleven of the twelve women members joined anti–civil rights Democrats in an odd 168 to 133 majority for the change. The House then passed the civil rights bill 290 to 130. When the Civil Rights Act of 1964 ultimately survived a Senate filibuster intact, Smith's mischievous contribution remained in Title VII, the equal employment opportunity section of the law. Smith proved to be a hero of sorts for the women's movement. Even though the federal government, in particular the newly created Equal Employment Opportunity Commission, did not rush to enforce the Title VII ban on workplace sex discrimination, an important shift had occurred in the contest between protection and equality.[31]

In October 1966 Betty Friedan, Martha Griffiths, and other women impatient with the lack of change wrought by the President's Commission on the Status of Women and the Equal Employment Opportunity Commission, formed the National Organization for Women (NOW), which initially represented a female elite of government, business, labor, and university officials. Its members held much more moderate views than did the feminist groups emerging simultaneously from the civil rights movement, college campuses, and middle-class suburbs. At first NOW concerned itself with employment and economic conditions rather than with the sexual freedom issues that were drawing substantial attention from younger, more militant women. Yet intensive discussion of the nature of women's problems rapidly drew moderates and radicals together. Disenchantment with protectionism was becoming more widespread: either it did not work, or it did and thus relegated women to diminished status. NOW founders shared a conviction that the time had come to insist on nothing less than full equality for women.[32]

At its October 1967 national conference, the one-year-old National Organization for Women voted overwhelmingly to endorse the equal rights amendment. At the same time, NOW agreed to address a more extensive agenda of women's concerns. Most notably, it would seek repeal of laws that limited women's control over their own bodies, abortion prohibitions in particular. The venerable Alice Paul, delighted with having new allies in her ongoing crusade for the ERA, nonetheless disapproved of NOW's advocacy of a wider women's rights program. Any distraction from the single issue of constitutional amendment would complicate matters, she worried. A series of demands, Paul believed, "gets the men all mixed up."[33] Yet NOW had seized the leadership for an ERA campaign within the new, more assertive, and rapidly growing women's movement.

Propelled by their own discontents and the widespread desire for change within a deeply troubled American society during the late 1960s, women's rights advocates moved to disassociate themselves from protectionism and pursue absolute equality. Hopes for judicial relief continued to be frustrated as the Supreme Court in 1969 ruled that laws discriminating between sexes needed only to bear "some rational relationship to a legitimate state end" and could be set aside under the Fourteenth Amendment "only if no grounds can be conceived to justify them."[34] Frustrated feminists captured attention by interrupting Senate hearings on the eighteen-year-old vote in February 1970 to demand immediate consideration of the ERA.[35] A sympathetic Birch Bayh then arranged subcommittee hearings in early May during which formerly protectionist women's groups and labor organizations joined the National Woman's party, NOW, and others to advocate ERA passage. The hearings, however, went largely unnoticed by the public in the days immediately after U.S. military forces invaded Cambodia, protests erupted across the country, and national guardsmen shot students at Kent State University in Ohio.[36]

The same concern with angry, vocal, and energetic constituents that began to move voting age reduction rapidly ahead seized Congress on the issue of women's rights. The staunchly protectionist chairman of the House Judiciary Committee, Emanuel Celler, had steadfastly refused to hold hearings on the ERA, much less permit it to come the floor. By summer 1970, however, Martha Griffiths found a majority of her House colleagues agreeable to a discharge petition to break Celler's hold on the amendment. Celler, almost alone, warned about "the most disastrous consequences" of the amendment. He argued that "physical, emotional, psychological and social differences exist and dare not be disregarded." Griffiths's ally, Republican congresswoman Florence Dwyer of New Jersey, reassured the House that the ERA would not "obliterate the differences between male and female." Those distinctions should not, however, serve as "a subterfuge for denying the human and civil rights that belong to all of us." The ERA would dignify, not downgrade, the roles of wife and mother, Dwyer insisted. Women, "like their male counterparts, should be judged by the law as individuals, not as a class of inferior beings." On August 10, 1970, after only one hour of debate, the House by the extraordinary margin of 333 to 22 discharged a bill from committee for only the twenty-fourth time in sixty years. The amendment was then approved 352 to 15.[37]

In the Senate as in the House, few agreed with Celler; however, those who did were concentrated in the Judiciary Committee. Senior committee member Sam Ervin was a particularly shrewd and experienced defender of the constitutional and social status quo; he had helped derail the Dirksen school prayer as well as the Bayh direct presidential election amendments and, less successfully, contested all civil rights reforms. Ervin had never concealed his strong traditionalist attitudes toward women, in 1960 opposing the ERA even with the Hayden rider attached.[38] In September 1970 he arranged Judiciary Committee hearings as a forum for anti-ERA sentiment largely absent from Bayh's May subcommittee hearings or House consideration. The North Carolinian's prize witness was Harvard law professor Paul Freund, who had argued for more than twenty years that the Fifth and Fourteenth Amendments should be sufficient to guarantee women legal equality and that protective discrimination was not unfair. Ervin drew particular attention to Freund's judgment that the ERA would abolish gender distinctions in military service. The hearings managed to plant doubts about the ERA, even though they did not block its progress.[39]

Bayh's ally, Senate majority leader Mike Mansfield, brought the House-approved ERA directly to the floor rather than permitting the Judiciary Committee to bury it. However, Ervin's September filibuster against the direct presidential election amendment postponed consideration of the ERA. Then with Senate adjournment fast approaching, Ervin was able to thwart an amendment proposal for the second time in as many months. When the Senate took up the amendment on October 7, the North Carolinian launched a lengthy discussion of its flaws. He immediately claimed, incorrectly, that this was the first amendment proposal since the Civil War not to include a time limit on ratification. He sought to sow further doubts by proposing a series of amendments to prevent women from being "robbed" of existing rights and to prevent their being drafted for military service. Ervin had identified a sensitive issue that made proponents of equality uncomfortable and brought out strong protectionism. The Selective Service had become increasingly unpopular as the Vietnam War dragged on. In a close 36-to-33 vote on October 13, senators agreed to exempt women from the draft.[40]

The military draft exemption struck ERA proponents as the equivalent of the Hayden rider, an acknowledgment that women were different, in need of protection, and legally subordinate. With its adoption, ERA supporters again considered themselves effectively stymied and, disheartened, abandoned the fight for the moment. Later the same day Tennessee Republican senator Howard Baker was able, with no advance notice, to weigh down the resolution with language first offered by his father-in-law Everett Dirksen that "nothing contained in this Constitution shall abridge the right of people lawfully assembled, in any public building which is supported in whole or in part through the expenditure of public funds to participate in nondenominational prayer." The Baker motion passed 50 to 20 with little debate in the absence of Bayh and many other liberals who supported ERA and opposed school prayer.[41]

The following day, Senator Bayh reappeared, seeking to salvage the situation. He proposed a revised amendment, with a seven-year ratification time limit, stipulating, "Neither the United States nor any State shall, on account of sex, deny to any person within its jurisdiction the equal protection of the laws." Bayh clearly hoped to defuse Ervin's objections by adding the time limit and recasting the ERA along the lines of the Fourteenth Amendment. Extension of the equal protection clause to women had not been accomplished through the courts and remained the principal goal of the ERA, he said. Professor Freund's concerns about the possible elimination of even reasonable gender distinctions had not been overcome during Senate debate. Therefore, said Bayh, his revised language faced "the cold facts of life" of resistance to the current ERA terminology and offered a solution "insuring the equal protection of the laws to those who have been discriminated against on account of sex, while recognizing the need for a flexible standard in cases where different treatment under the law may be justified." Bayh's effort to compromise with protectionism in order to obtain passage of some sort of women's rights amendment forecast continuing difficulties for the ERA. Although several senators publicly embraced Bayh's solution, the Ninety-first Senate adjourned without taking any further action.[42]

As soon as the next Congress convened in January 1971, Congresswoman Griffiths reintroduced the ERA. To meet objections raised the previous year, she incorporated the second and third sections of Bayh's October revision, accepting language that gave enforcement authority to Congress but made no mention of concurrent state power and that delayed the effective date of the amendment until two years after ratification. She kept the wording of the crucial first section as it had stood since 1943, however; ERA advocates would not accept even the slight compromise with protectionism that Bayh suggested. During March and April hearings in Celler's Judiciary Committee, conservative Republican Charles Wiggins of California brought forth a provision in the Wadsworth-Hayden-Ervin tradition sparing women from military service and retaining any law "which reasonably promotes the health and safety of the people."[43] The protectionist argument by ERA opponents continued when the amendment finally came to the floor on October 12. Yet with Griffiths calling it "the old Hayden rider" and urging its defeat, Wiggins's motion failed 265 to 87, a sure sign of congressional conversion. The House then adopted the equal rights amendment 354 to 24.[44]

Senator Ervin continued to resist the ERA by seeking allowances for distinctions based on "physiological or functional differences." He appealed on the floor of the Senate for protection of wives, mothers, widows, and women in general. He proposed modifications of the ERA to maintain state laws banning homosexuality, requiring fathers to pay child support, and seg-regating males and females in prisons and public rest rooms. Ervin was rais-ing phony issues, Senator Bayh retorted; the ERA would not jeopardize the right of economic dependents to continued support, nor would it infringe rights to privacy recognized by the Supreme Court. None of the North Car-olinian's reservations was shared by more than eighteen senators, most by fewer than a dozen. Thus ERA supporters did not take his arguments too se-riously. Yet Ervin was sowing seeds of doubt that would germinate later. Having disposed of his objections, the Senate, eager to respond to the in-creasingly loud demands of the women's movement for full female equality, approved the equal rights amendment, unchanged from the House-passed language, by 84 to 8 on March 22, 1972.[45]

The upheaval in thinking about women's situation in the early 1970s be-came evident in more than just the emergence of a vocal women's movement and congressional adoption of the ERA. The Supreme Court, in a series of cases that the Women's Rights Project of the formerly protectionist Ameri-can Civil Liberties Union brought before it, began reconsidering the law on women's equality. In a 1971 case the Court ruled that an employer willing to hire a man with preschool children, but not a woman, was engaging in sex discrimination under Title VII.[46] Later the same year justices unanimously overturned as contrary to the Fourteenth Amendment's equal protection clause a long-standing policy of automatically favoring males to females as the executors of wills.[47] Five more years and several more cases were re-quired before Women's Rights Project attorney Ruth Bader Ginsburg per-suaded the Court to forgo the "rational basis" test for differential treatment and apply "heightened scrutiny" to claims of justified gender distinction, a notable step forward if not the "strict scrutiny" applied in racial discrimina-tion cases.[48] Nevertheless, the Court started down a path of rooting out gen-der discrimination before Congress approved the equal rights amendment.

Also, while the equal rights amendment was still making its way through Congress, the Supreme Court in December 1971 heard arguments and reached a tentative decision in the most tradition-shattering women's rights case of the era, *Roe v. Wade*. Negotiations dragged on over the details of Justice Harry Blackmun's opinion in an effort to assemble as many justices as possible behind it, and the seating of two new justices led to reargument of the case in October 1972. Thus the *Roe* decision was not announced until January 1973. Five of the seven justices present, however, had come to view a woman's right to an abortion as undeniable when they first discussed *Roe* in conference just before the end of 1971. In ruling that when it came to de-cisions regarding their own bodies, women possessed a right to private, personal choice as well as equal protection of the law under the Ninth and Fourteenth Amendments, the Court had clearly heeded the argument of the women's movement. The Court was also most likely anticipating that a new constitutional amendment would soon give added force to its ruling.[49]

By the time the Court announced the *Roe* decision on January 22, 1973, the ERA had been before the states for ten months. Twenty-two of the thirty-three state legislatures meeting in 1972 had ratified it, most with little opposition and many with minimal discussion. In fact, Hawaii had acted within an hour of the Senate vote, five other states during the following two days, and twenty within three months. In the two months after the *Roe* decision, eight more states endorsed the amendment.[50] The pace of ratification was not as fast as the seven months taken by the District of Columbia electoral vote amendment, much less the three months for eighteen-year-old suffrage; but at the time it seemed in stride with the seventeen months needed for the poll tax amendment or the nineteen for presidential succession reform, and it was certainly ahead of the forty-seven months for the presidential two-term limit.

With thirty state ratifications in a year, most with little debate or dissent, and only eight more necessary for the ERA's adoption, few proponents doubted that the amendment would soon be implanted in the Constitution. During 1972 opposition had come mainly from the John Birch Society and George Wallace's American party, extremely conservative groups whose complaints about the federal government did not seem to be winning enough adherents to pose a threat. In reality, however, prospects for the ERA were rapidly turning quite bleak. National Woman's Political Caucus executive director Doris Meissner acknowledged as early as January 1973, "The momentum for passage of the amendment has sort of worn out because it has already gone through in most of the states where it was a natural." She worried about difficulty ahead "because there's a natural backlash setting in towards the gains that women are making."[51] She proved prescient.

Of the twenty states not to ratify by March 1973, only five would eventually do so. Indeed, before the year ended each of the other fifteen had displayed a desire to avoid or defeat ratification. By that time all had taken negative legislative action, either in committee proceedings or floor votes, and not one would ever reverse itself.[52] Only thirteen state refusals were needed to deny an Article V ratification majority. Battles would rage for another eight-and-a-half years, and often the political balance appeared nearly even, but, significantly, not a single state among the fifteen ever changed its initial position. Furthermore, before 1973 was over the fifteen were arguably joined by Nebraska, which ratified a day after Congress approved the amendment but less than a year later voted to rescind its action. During the next five years, Tennessee, Idaho, and Kentucky likewise backed away from the amendment.[53] If these rescissions were recognized, a matter that remained in dispute, state support for ratification never exceeded the thirty-state level achieved by March 1973. In any case, with fifteen states manifesting opposition to the equal rights amendment even before public discussion became particularly heated or rescission efforts began, its fate thereafter was, to say the least, precarious.

Neither Bayh nor Griffiths had anticipated any difficulty in securing state ratification of the ERA. "Maybe some other folks thought of it," Bayh later recalled; "I didn't." His experience with the Twenty-fifth and Twenty-sixth Amendments and the direct presidential election proposal accustomed him to think of Congress as the great obstacle to constitutional change. The long congressional struggle, with its rapid shift in the final stages toward support for the ERA, seemed to portend the same result in this case. In Bayh's experience, once Congress approved an amendment, state legislators needed merely to be informed in order for ratification to proceed. Private organizations such as the ABA, the AFL-CIO, NOW, and other women's organizations would do what little was needed to ensure completion of the process in the states.[54] Griffiths had confidently declared to the House just before it approved the measure, "Personally I have no fear but that this amendment will be ratified as quickly as was the 18-year-old vote."[55]

Expecting easy ratification, neither of the amendment's floor leaders objected to the addition of a seven-year time limit. Most, though not all (and, ironically, neither women suffrage nor child labor) amendments had included such a provision since Warren Harding had first proposed one on the national prohibition amendment. Since precedent existed for a time limit and its elimination might offend an undecided senator, Bayh thought it should be included. Griffiths accepted it as "customary," although she acknowledged that it made some women nervous. Neither appeared aware of the time limit's origins as a device to frustrate ratification. Thus neither shared the gloomy forecast of eighty-seven-year-old Alice Paul, active in amendment politics at the time of the Harding proposal, that it gave opponents employing delaying tactics an advantage that rendered the equal rights amendment "dead on arrival."[56]

Sam Ervin began forging alliances with opponents of ERA outside Congress as the amendment neared passage in the Senate. By February 1972 he was in contact with Phyllis Schlafly, a southern Illinois lawyer long active in right-wing Republican party politics and publisher of a widely distributed, reactionary political newsletter. By her own admission, she had become sen-

sitized to the ERA only during the previous two months.[57] She was beginning to organize a campaign against ratification and wanted to hold a September workshop in St. Louis for state anti-ERA leaders. Ervin and Schlafly
arranged mass mailings of his Senate speeches against ERA to state legislators and to her supporters. His senatorial franking privilege and her address
list of conservative contacts enabled the two collaborators to mount very
quickly an effective challenge to ERA with limited resources and, at least at
first, few allies.[58] Schlafly displayed considerable skill in attracting public attention, especially after she established her STOP ERA organization in October 1972. The very fact that she was a woman opposing ERA gained her the
spotlight, and her capacity for articulating claims, however dubious, with
drama and conviction persuaded many listeners of her views. Yet Schlafly's
declarations as to the effects of the amendment, though expressed in her
own apocalyptic terms, remained essentially those of Sam Ervin, as she herself acknowledged.[59]

Ervin and Schlafly framed their objections to ERA in protectionist language. STOP ERA, for instance, was an acronym for Stop Taking Our Privileges. The senator and his ally contended that women were especially
vulnerable and required extraordinary defense. An amendment eliminating
gender distinctions would, they argued, strip away safeguards for women and
expose them to peril. Ervin and Schlafly expressed concern about females
being forced by employers to work longer hours, lift greater weights, and give
up gender-related privileges. Courts were already invalidating protectionist
labor laws as Title VII equal employment opportunity violations, so warnings
that ERA would do so were, at minimum, misplaced. Still, the complaints captured the attention of lower-class working women long schooled in the advantages of protectionism. Such women, especially if middle-aged or older, could
not see any benefit to themselves in eventual access to better jobs that employment equality would presumably provide more well-educated women.[60]

Anti-ERA arguments centered on issues of women's place in family and
society. Senator Ervin warned that ERA would amount to a war on traditional homemakers, and Schlafly carried his alarmist message to a wide audience. Not only would women be obliged to serve and die in the military,
the two charged, they would be driven out of the home into the work force.
Although ERA supporters argued that individual circumstances and abilities
determined such matters for men and should for women as well, the Ervin-
Schlafly contentions struck a chord with many women, especially those of
lower economic and social status, who did not embrace the reasoning of the
women's movement. The quickly developing logic of feminism, which by the
early 1970s asserted a range of women's rights including abortion and les-

bianism, appalled conservative men and women. Schlafly articulated and in-creased their fears with repeated claims that ERA would terminate men's obligations to support their families, eliminate alimony and widows' bene-fits, sanction homosexual marriage and child-rearing, and give constitutional protection to abortion. *Roe v. Wade* provided an ever-present reminder that modern notions of women's rights posed a challenge to traditional beliefs. The image of wholesale male and female abandonment of the family may have been incongruous in a society with one of the highest marriage rates in the world, but it captured the attention of people already concerned about declining birth rates, increasing divorce, and the implications of rapidly emerging feminism.

Recent experience with dramatic social change as the result of constitu-tional reform enhanced apprehensions about the ERA in some circles. Sepa-rate public restrooms for blacks and whites were among the Jim Crow institutions to fall as the Fourteenth Amendment's equal protection guaran-tee was implemented in *Brown v. Board of Education* and subsequent deci-sions. Sam Ervin, no admirer of racial desegregation, sought to link blacks' and women's rights in terms that white southerners would appreciate. In the Senate, he raised a specter of mixed-gender public rest rooms ("unisex toi-lets" was his phrase) that others thereafter endlessly invoked. Despite re-peated reassurances that ERA would not abridge rights to personal privacy, the image of sexual encounters in public bathrooms remained prominent, es-pecially in the South, among amendment critics.[61]

Enough unresolved anxiety about the implications of the equal rights amendment existed to thwart its ratification in conservative states in 1973. Thereafter, as public discussion increased, as rhetoric on both sides grew more heated, as disputes over the consequences of ERA stood unsettled, and opinion remained divided among both women and men, already hesitant state legislators became ever more disinclined to take the plunge into the un-known that to them ratification represented. Phyllis Schlafly, calling atten-tion to the amendment's provision of congressional authority to implement equal rights for women "by appropriate legislation," alleged that 70 percent of all state legislative power would thereby be transferred to the federal gov-ernment.[62] The claim, unsubstantiated, insupportable, and on its face ludi-crous, nevertheless raised apprehensions and reinforced legislative reluctance to approve the amendment.[63] The degree of state legislative consensus that the designers of Article V felt essential for constitutional amendment simply never existed in the 1970s on the issue of the ERA.

Supporters of the ERA appeared unprepared for the vehement reaction against it. Particularly at the outset of the ratification debate, they failed to convey calm and compelling explanations of the amendment to counter criticism, enlighten journalists, and reassure state legislators. The extraordinary growth of the women's movement since the mid-1960s spawned a rich variety of viewpoints as to the proper role for women in American society and how it should be achieved. Protectionism had not disappeared. At the same time, new feminist agendas ranged from political empowerment, allowing women a full voice in national decisions, to economic equalization, permitting them complete access to the capitalistic system, to social liberation in sexuality, childbearing and, at the radical extreme, withdrawal from male society into lesbianism. Divided into a variety of moderate to radical factions, feminists found it difficult to agree on the meaning of the ERA, much less offer a cogent explanation as to why protectionism should be abandoned.[64]

Under the circumstances, mounting an effective campaign in support of the amendment proved difficult. A pro-ERA Florida state legislator, Elaine Gordon, later bemoaned amendment supporters' initial lack of political experience. "We all tried to tell them how the process worked and the importance of things like raising money, but they didn't believe us," she said. "They thought that just being right would be enough."[65] A year passed before major supportive organizations formed a coordinating committee, and almost four years elapsed before ERAmerica, a well-financed body with no agenda other than ratification and a broad base of labor, professional, civic, and feminist support, took the field. Furthermore, the most prominent feminist organization, NOW, experienced constant internal turmoil; its national leadership was effectively immobilized between 1974 and 1977 and thereafter was often at odds with other organizations and leaders of grass-roots political campaigns in some states, such as Virginia. Even in the later stages of the struggle, differences of philosophy and tactics divided groups working for ratification.[66]

Efforts by ERA proponents in various crucial states proved ineffectual, though often by only the narrowest of margins, in winning over legislators whose conservatism had been reinforced by vocal anti-ERA women. For instance, in North Carolina, a state initially expected to ratify, letter writing and demonstrations stirred by STOP ERA's state leader, a John Birch Society member, offset modest, amateurish lobbying by overconfident advocates of the amendment, leaving it two votes short of ratification in 1973. Better organized but still subdued pro-ERA efforts in 1975 and 1977 failed to enlist the general public. Finally turning to direct electoral campaigns to defeat legislative opponents and install supporters, ERA forces became entangled in complex political crosscurrents. They lost as often as they won and continued to fall just short of victory in the North Carolina general assembly.[67]

Similar patterns unfolded in the border states of Missouri and Oklahoma, the western troika of Utah, Arizona and Nevada, and every other southern state except Tennessee and Texas. Stalemate developed in these conservative states as anemic initial campaigns for ratification failed to convince cautious legislators and stronger subsequent campaigns proved unable to gain ground once resistance had been aroused.[68]

The state of Illinois became a notable battlefield in the ratification struggle. Phyllis Schlafly built her most powerful STOP ERA organization in her own state.[69] She was able to arouse substantial antagonism to ERA in her home territory of southern Illinois, but she confronted a proamendment majority similar to that present in every other northern industrial state. In 1970, however, Illinois had adopted a new state constitution that provided for a three-fifths affirmative vote in each house of the legislature for the ratification of a federal amendment. The supermajority provision was challenged and sustained at every session of the general assembly considering ERA. Although debatable in light of the Supreme Court's 1920 *Hawke v. Smith* decision, the three-fifths provision was upheld by a three-judge federal court in February 1975.[70] As a result, despite supportive majorities in the assembly, ratification repeatedly failed. In a state with vocal opposition to the amendment, the 60 percent threshold proved too great a hurdle for ERA to surmount. Consequently, Illinois was the only state outside the southern, midwestern, border, or southwestern regions not to approve the equal rights amendment.

By 1977 the pressures that the seven-year ratification time limit created began to weigh on ERA supporters and encourage their opponents. Indiana ratified in January, the first such state to do so since 1975. Still, three additional ratifications were needed from legislatures that in some cases would meet only once more before the March 1979 deadline. Amendment proponents, in particular NOW president Eleanor Smeal, began advocating congressional extension of the time limit. Quickly determining that legal justification existed, ERA leaders in the Senate were nevertheless at first reluctant to take such a step. After further setbacks in unratified states, however, Smeal and several congresswomen convinced Don Edwards, chairman of the House Judiciary Subcommittee on Civil and Constitutional Rights, that more time was needed. After New York congresswoman Elizabeth Holtzman proposed a seven-year extension, Edwards opened hearings during the same month that 20,000 women were gathering in Houston and urging action to complete ratification. The federally sponsored National Woman's Conference provided the decade's greatest outpouring of ERA support, but it also provoked a highly visible counter-rally by Schlafly and her followers. By November 1977 no aspect of the women's movement, certainly not an attempt to enhance the prospects of the equal rights amendment, failed to stir opposition.[71]

Proponents of extending the ratification deadline believed that, in addition to support for the ERA by a lopsided majority of the American people, they had a strong constitutional argument. Article V made no mention of time limits on amendment ratification. The Supreme Court in *Dillon v. Gloss* had ruled the first legislative restriction, the seven years allowed the prohibition amendment, constitutionally permissible.[72] In *Coleman v. Miller,* however, the Court found nothing sacred about seven years. It was up to Congress to decide, as a political matter, a reasonable period for ratification.[73] Since the approval period for ERA had been made a part of the resolution transmitting it to the states rather than the language of the amendment itself, a common arrangement since the Twenty-third Amendment, changing that limit would not alter one word upon which thirty-five states had agreed. Extension was legitimate, its defenders concluded, because all the misinformation circulating about the ERA had prevented the amendment from receiving proper consideration.[74]

Opponents of extension disparaged it on various grounds. Several House Judiciary Committee members argued that state ratifications should be reasonably contemporaneous, attributing this notion to the Framers of Article V even though it had first been articulated by Justice Van Devanter in *Dillon v. Gloss.* Congressman Jack Brooks, a cosponsor of Martha Griffiths's ERA resolution in 1971, considered extension "a gross political misjudgment," one that would undermine the integrity of the amending process.[75] Senator Jake Garn of Utah likened it to adding a period to a sporting contest at the last minute because the favored team was losing at the end of regulation play. Furthermore, he complained, the new rules allowed only the trailing team to score. If unratified states were to be given an opportunity to reconsider, so too should states that had approved the amendment.[76] Four state legislatures had voted to rescind their ERA ratification and others were discussing it, but the legitimacy of rescission remained doubtful. Congress ignored Fourteenth Amendment rescissions in 1868 and took no action on the Wadsworth-Garrett proposal to sanction them in the 1920s. Sam Ervin's proposal to allow rescission as a general practice had passed the Senate in 1971, failed subsequently in the House of Representatives but retained some support. Despite frequent references to James Madison's declaration that "the Constitution requires an adoption in toto and for ever" and other justifications for ratification being an irreversible commitment, the appearance of deliberations resuming after a defeat of ratification but stopping once an amendment gained approval remained troublesome. Even Birch Bayh's Senate staff, dedicated ERA supporters, were prepared to concede that the Senate sitting at the time ratification was completed would have authority to accept rescissions. Questions regarding the legitimacy of constitutional amending practices wove the extension and rescission issues together.[77]

House Judiciary Committee hearings on ratification extension in November 1977 did not resolve either issue, nor did additional testimony in May 1978. In Washington in July on the first anniversary of Alice Paul's death, at least 40,000 ERA supporters marched to the Capitol, chanting, "One, two, three four, we need three states more; five, six, seven, eight, Congress must extend the date!"[78] Early the next month Senate hearings replayed the arguments for extending the limit. Faced with a fast-approaching deadline and resistance in the House Judiciary Committee, ERA proponents finally triumphed by compromising on the length of extension. They held their ground that rescission was a separate question that Congress did not need to address until a claim was made that three-fourths of the states had ratified. Accepting extension as ordinary congressional action requiring a mere majority rather than an Article V measure necessitating two-thirds approval, the House endorsed a three-year, three-month extension on August 15, 1978, by a vote of 233 to 189. The Senate agreed to the measure by 60 to 36 on October 6.[79] Although a majority of the members of Congress still supported ERA, these sharply reduced victory margins suggested either discomfort over the modification of ratification arrangements, declining enthusiasm for the amendment, or both.

The adoption of the extension did not end the controversy. Phyllis Schlafly railed against it as "wrong, illegal, immoral, unprecedented, and unconstitutional."[80] Utah's Senator Jake Garn, a steadfast ERA opponent, quickly wrote to the 7,172 state legislators questioning the constitutionality of the resolution "purporting to extend the period for ratification" and suggesting that they were just as free to rescind previous actions.[81] During the next three months, measures were introduced in at least a dozen states challenging the extension by one means or another. The South Dakota legislature in March 1979 adopted a resolution declaring ERA null and void after the original ratification deadline. Several legislatures considered similar proclamations, and others proposed to rescind their state's prior approval. Although only the South Dakota effort succeeded, several others gained enough support to suggest considerable resentment over the extension.[82]

The questions swirling around extension and rescission remained unanswered in any definitive fashion. Amendment foes mounted a legal challenge in an Idaho federal district court. Equal rights proponents sought unsuccessfully to disqualify Judge Marion Callister on the grounds that he was an elder of the anti-ERA Mormon church and thus unable to render an impartial decision. Refusing to step aside, Callister ruled rescission valid and extension unconstitutional. The Supreme Court, presented with briefs arguing that the judge's opinion ran counter to *Coleman v. Miller,* stayed the ruling and, after the June 30, 1982, ratification deadline passed, declared it moot.[83]

To the very end advocates continued to agitate furiously but futilely for the ERA. Thousands marched in mass demonstrations. State legislators received individual appeals. In Illinois a group of ardent feminists vowed to fast until the legislature ratified. Organizations sympathetic to the amendment joined an economic boycott started by NOW in 1977, refusing to hold meetings in unratified states. The boycott drew criticism as misdirected toward urban areas generally supportive of ERA and counterproductive. At the same time, the flurry of efforts brought ERA agonizingly close to victory in Oklahoma, Virginia, North Carolina, Florida, and Illinois. Yet the amendment failed to achieve the one success that supporters believed might turn momentum in their favor.[84]

Opponents of ERA remained steadfast in their traditionalist and protectionist views, if anything stiffening their resistance as they observed feminist desperation. STOP ERA mounted effective counterdemonstrations and lobbying efforts, especially in Illinois and North Carolina, in the final frenzied months of the struggle. Phyllis Schlafly drew attention to her own role in the anti-ERA campaign with public appearances, press releases, and on the day the battle ended a lavish "Over the Rainbow" party at Washington's Shoreham Hotel. After a band played "Ding, Dong, the Witch Is Dead" and "I Enjoy Being a Girl," a parade of leading conservatives including Senator Jesse Helms, direct-mail fund-raiser Richard Viguerie, author George Gilder, and the Reverend Jerry Falwell applauded the victory. "We have overcome one of the most powerful propaganda campaigns in the history of politics," declared Alabama senator Jeremiah Denton. An exultant editor of *Conservative Digest,* John Loften, proclaimed, "We're here to celebrate a death, to dance on a grave." The hyperbole reached its peak as the principal speaker, Schlafly herself, took credit for "the most remarkable political victory of the 20th century." Anointed by journalists as "the principal architect of the defeat," Schlafly made no mention of her debt to the retired Sam Ervin nor to the fact that her opponents had won a majoritarian if not an Article V victory. Instead, in her hubris, she talked of future campaigns against sex education, feminist influence in school textbooks, and, returning to her pre-ERA preoccupation with national security, nuclear disarmament. On her way to the Shoreham dinner, she told a *New York Times* reporter, "The atomic bomb is a marvelous gift that was given to our country by a wise God."[85]

In reality, the battle for the equal rights amendment had long been lost. Schlafly had played an important role as a publicist, but Ervin's arguments, traditional gender beliefs, and legislative caution deserve as much or more credit for the outcome. With a few, ultimately unimportant exceptions, states remained frozen in positions they had taken by 1973. The 1980 presidential election sounded the amendment's death knell. Ronald Reagan won on a conservative Republican platform that abandoned the party's forty-year tradition of endorsing the ERA. In contrast, the Democratic platform not only embraced the amendment but, at the insistence of feminists, declared that the party would not aid candidates who did not support the ERA and urged national organizations not to hold meetings in unratified states. "Pro-family," anti-ERA voices within the Republican party perhaps claimed too much credit for Reagan's 51 percent of the vote in a three-way contest with two pro-ERA opponents, a Democratic incumbent widely perceived as inept and an independent Republican. Nevertheless, the election returns discouraged legislators in conservative states from any last-minute conversion that would have lifted the amendment over the final few obstacles to ratification.[86]

Their defeat baffled and embittered many ERA advocates. Throughout the battle, public opinion polling continually indicated a majority of Americans favored the amendment. Results from various polls taken from 1970 to 1982 showed, one careful political scientist concluded, that "on average" 57 percent of Americans supported ratification and only 32 percent opposed it.[87] Further analysis, however, clarified that opposition clustered in rural areas among politically conservative, religious fundamentalist, white, middle-class, middle-aged, married women who did not work outside the home, and their husbands. Resistance to ERA was greatest among women certain that gender distinctions benefited them and conservatives of both sexes who equated ERA with abortion rights, lesbianism, women in the military, and other prospects they found distasteful. These groups were politically influential in the states that did not ratify. Such resistance was alien to the experience of younger, better-educated, culturally more liberal urban women, more likely to be single and employed, who rallied to the cause of gender equality. Their ranks produced the 210,000 who in the course of fifteen years joined the National Organization for Women.[88]

Although thirty-five states endorsed the ERA, the fifteen that did not contained over 28 percent of the nation's population. Thus the extra weight given rural states in the federal system did not distort the outcome. The non-ratifying states represented not just the one-quarter of the states that Article V allowed to block an amendment, but more than one-quarter of the nation's population.[89] It proved easier for disappointed ERA advocates to blame defeat on the misogyny of a few legislators, the distortions of Phyllis Schlafly, or behind-the-scenes influence of various economic interests than on the persistence of significant numbers of Americans, female as well as male, who still held traditionalist or protectionist views of women.[90] In any case, the process for achieving constitutional change demanded a consensus beyond what the proponents of reformed gender relationships could fashion.

By 1982 changes were occurring in women's social, political, and legal status that raised questions, even among some supporters, about further need for the equal rights amendment. The protracted and extensive discussion of women's rights appeared to be having a significant effect on American gender attitudes and practices. The Supreme Court had begun substantiating Pauli Murray's twenty-year-old argument that the Fourteenth Amendment's equal protection clause provided a legal tool for dealing with gender discrimination. Attitudes and practices had begun to shift regarding women's place in the economy and society. Indeed, within a few years many of Ervin and Schlafly's worst fears, such as women in military combat and public toleration of lesbianism, would begin to be realized, even without the amendment. Yet a specific constitutional statement of women's equality of rights remained important, for symbolic if not practical reasons, to many people who had long sought it.

Two weeks after the ERA ratification deadline passed, the amendment was reintroduced in Congress, unchanged, with more than 50 Senate and 200 House sponsors. These proponents made no modification whatsoever in the resolution, altering none of the amendment's language and not even removing the seven-year ratification time limit. They apparently believed that any revision might be read as weakness rather than willingness to reassure those with doubts about the amendment. Despite the resistance to ratification by over one quarter of state legislatures and evidence from opinion polls that support for the amendment was substantially greater among the public, the resolution did not opt for Article V's alternative method of ratification by state conventions. The relevant example of national prohibition, where the Eighteenth Amendment ratified by state legislatures was reversed by the Twenty-first Amendment ratified by popularly elected conventions, did not lead to any shift in tactics. Having sensed that the controversial 1978 time-limit extension had cost support, NOW leaders did not wish to be accused of again switching tactics for political advantage, even when doing so was both constitutionally authorized and precedented. Apprehensions about losing referendum contests to better-financed anti-ERA forces may also have weighed on their minds.[91]

The equal rights amendment remained, to both supporters and opponents, a token worthy of their attention. The president of the National Woman's party admitted to being momentarily depressed by the latest setback in a campaign that her organization had initiated fifty-nine years earlier but claimed to be encouraged by signs of growing female political power.[92] Some feminists maintained that the ERA remained much needed in a practical sense. Others thought that alive, even if unratified, it could become a rallying point and an organizing tool, as NOW and other organizations had already discovered. Still others wished to turn to more substantive, if narrower goals, such as economic equity, rather than concentrating on a measure that might not in the end produce practical gains. Some, noting that the coalition built around the Nineteenth Amendment had steadily grown during the struggle but shattered once suffrage was obtained and then taken a half century to reassemble, worried about a repeat performance.[93]

On the other side of the issue, conservatives found value in sounding alarms about the ERA. Utah Republican Orrin Hatch, an ERA foe who had become chairman of the Senate subcommittee on the Constitution, moved to hold the earliest hearings on the resubmitted amendment in May 1983 so that negative testimony could be heard first. Hatch's aggressive challenge to the amendment caught its ill-prepared Senate sponsor, Democrat Paul Tsongas of Massachusetts, by surprise. Hatch and Tsongas engaged in a testy exchange of hostile questions and uncertain responses that symbolized but did not advance the decade-old debate. Seven more days of hearings that Hatch arranged over the next year shed little new light on the amendment but demonstrated its continuing importance in partisan posturing.[94]

After both proponents and adversaries rehearsed old arguments in an active lobbying effort, the House of Representatives brought the resubmitted amendment to a vote on November 15, 1983. Although a 278-to-147 majority endorsed a new ERA, a six-vote switch would have been needed to attain the two-thirds required for passage.[95] The resolution would continue to be introduced in subsequent Congresses, but during the next dozen years it did not again come to a floor vote. In December 1993 frustrated ERA proponents launched a campaign to win three more state ratifications on the basis that the ratification time limit was itself invalid; this move appeared more an act of desperation than a realistic reading of Article V precedents.[96] Although its influence in enhancing the status of women would continue to be felt, the equal rights amendment itself appeared as dead as opponents proclaimed it when the ratification time limit expired in June 1982.

THE SAME POLITICAL CURRENTS that lifted and then deserted the ERA carried forward and then marooned an amendment to make inhabitants of the District of Columbia full participants in federal political life. From the moment of the Twenty-third Amendment's adoption in 1961, discontent festered over its limited grant of political power to District residents. A measure that had begun as a proposal for D.C. representation, proportional to its population, in the House of Representatives and presidential elections had been reduced to a mere three electoral votes and no congressional seats. Accepted as the best that could be obtained from Congress at the time, the amendment had within ten months won ratification from every state outside the old Confederacy. The surprisingly easy adoption of the Twenty-third Amendment immediately raised the question of whether a fuller measure of power for the District could have been obtained and should have been sought.

During the 1960s surge of concern with suffrage and political rights for the formerly disenfranchised, the District of Columbia's situation became a sensitive matter, especially given D.C.'s increasingly black population. Advocates of democratic participation rejected the traditional view that residents of the nation's capital should be denied a political voice in order to keep the national government free of any local pressures. Precedent existed for a frequently mentioned solution, return to Maryland of all but the nonresidential core area of official and monumental Washington. Retrocession in 1846 had restored to Virginia the portion of the original District across the Potomac River. But difficulties with public services, taxation, the dispersion of federal facilities, and the resistance of Maryland officials raised serious doubts about retrocession as a workable remedy. Reformers chose instead to seek improvement of the District's status.

Ever since 1818, constitutional amendments had been proposed to provide the District with congressional representation. In 1967 the latest of nearly 150 such propositions would have granted the District seats in Congress as if it were a state while retaining the Twenty-third Amendment and congressional authority over other District affairs. Congressman Richard Poff of Virginia asserted that such a measure would require ratification not just by three-fourths of the states but by every one. Article V provided that "no state without its consent shall be deprived of its equal suffrage in the Senate." Poff argued that giving a nonstate seats in the Senate without unanimous state approval would violate this requirement. His contention helped stall for the moment an amendment with, at best, uncertain prospects. Instead Lyndon Johnson replaced the long-standing Board of Commissioners with a presidentially appointed mayor and city council. Congress in turn granted the District a nonvoting delegate in the House of Representatives in

1970 and supplanted the appointed city government with an elected one by passing limited home-rule legislation in December 1973. For the time being, any role for the District in national affairs remained constitutionally restricted to the provisions that the Twenty-third Amendment allowed, an arrangement increasingly viewed as insufficient and unjust.[97]

Walter Fauntroy, the District's House delegate, took up the plea for a congressional representation amendment, and in July 1975 the House Judiciary Subcommittee on Civil and Constitutional Rights held hearings. Congressman Herman Badillo of New York, observing that Article V had never blocked the admission of new states, effectively contradicted Poff's objections. This amendment, Badillo asserted, would merely reduce slightly the proportional power, not the equality of each state.[98] Two years later, after another hearing, the subcommittee unanimously endorsed a revised amendment that would treat the District in presidential elections, Article V activities, and Congress as if it were a state yet retain congressional authority over other District affairs.

The House Judiciary Committee endorsed the D.C. representation amendment 27 to 6 eleven days after President Jimmy Carter urged its passage in his January 20, 1978, State of the Union speech. Before doing so, however, the committee made an important, if technical, change in reaction to the appeals then being made to extend ERA ratification. The committee moved the proposed seven-year ratification time limit from the transmission resolution, where it had been placed in amendments since the Twenty-third, to the language of the amendment itself. "It is the committee's view," the House was told, "that the state legislatures must know that they shall have a time certain in which to ratify the proposed amendment. . . . The effect of placing this time limit in the text of the amendment prohibits subsequent Congresses from deciding to extend the time allowed for ratification."[99] Clearly unhappy with the demands for ERA extension, the Judiciary Committee wished to avoid further such problems. Scarcely more than a month later, on March 2, House members approved the D.C. representation amendment in a 289-to-127 roll call.[100]

Senators Edward Kennedy and Birch Bayh had been calling for passage of a District representation amendment since 1973 and urged adoption of the House resolution when it came before the Senate in summer 1978. Senator Orrin Hatch sought to thwart them by raising once again the claim that unanimous consent of the states would be required to reduce their equal vote in the Senate. With a national election less than three months away, however, efforts to block the amendment proved futile. Most Republican and southern Democratic conservatives voted against the amendment, but a few broke ranks to join a bipartisan moderate and liberal majority supporting it. Usually staunch conservatives such as Barry Goldwater of Arizona and Strom Thurmond of South Carolina faced difficult reelection campaigns and increasingly influential minority constituencies at home. Howard Baker of Tennessee and Robert Dole of Kansas harbored presidential ambitions. Perhaps these senators, as well as others, perceived that the amendment stood little chance of ratification and thus a vote for it was a harmless, politically shrewd gesture. In any case they provided crucial votes as the Senate approved the D.C. representation amendment 67 to 32 on August 15.[101]

Despite its strong congressional endorsement, the D.C. representation amendment appeared from the outset to be in trouble in the states. North Carolina senator Jesse Helms, an outspoken opponent, declared that the ratification battle would make the ERA struggle "look like a cakewalk."[102] His prediction was soon vindicated. Unlike every other amendment during the previous half century, few states rushed to embrace the D.C. representation amendment. After seven months only five states had given their approval, and eight had rejected it; most simply took no action. Some journalists were already prepared to write its obituary.[103] The Pennsylvania legislature, which defeated ratification in November 1978, provided a clue to the measure's problems. In the lower house 81 of 83 Republican members voted against ratification. This almost unanimous partisan opposition reflected the conservative response in legislatures nationwide. The problem, as Edward Kennedy bluntly put it, was that the amendment suffered from the "four too's." State legislators perceived the District to be "too liberal, too urban, too black, and too Democratic."[104]

The social and political character of the District of Columbia had been changing since the late 1950s when it was both racially and politically balanced. By 1980 many middle-class whites had relocated to the nearby suburbs of Maryland and Virginia, reducing the population of the District 15 percent in only a decade. Seven of every ten who remained were black, and many were poor.[105] Moreover, since 1964 when they began participating in presidential elections under the Twenty-third Amendment and especially since 1974 when home rule allowed them to began choosing their own leaders, D.C. voters had shown an overwhelming preference for the Democratic party. Subsequently the mayor's endorsement of the ERA boycott and the city council's adoption of strict gun control as well as liberal abortion and welfare laws reinforced the District's image as a bastion of urban Democratic liberalism sensitive to the needs of minorities.

Adoption of the D.C. representation amendment would, it was widely believed, result in the addition of two black liberal Democrats to the Senate of the United States. Far more than the addition of two or three representatives to the 435-member House, those Senators could alter the existing balance in the 100-seat upper chamber. Conservative legislators in rural states viewed the prospect with particular distaste. Two more certain votes for civil rights, social welfare, and other liberal measures could dramatically shift the political tide in the Senate. In the face of such a prospect, few legislatures in the South, Midwest, or West saw any political advantage in ratification.

Birch Bayh realized the opposition to the D.C. amendment and knew it would be difficult to ratify. As in the past, he counted on interested parties to carry the battle forward in the states. Within the District two groups, the National Coalition for Self-Determination for the District of Columbia and the D.C. Voting Rights Service Corporation, formed to lobby for ratification. The former was an ethnically and politically diverse coalition of civic, religious, labor, and business leaders; the latter was established by three powerful black political leaders: Walter Washington, the first elected mayor; Sterling Tucker, president of the city council; and Walter Fauntroy, the nonvoting delegate to the House of Representatives. Competition between the two groups undermined their efforts. Furthermore, in the early months of the campaign Fauntroy's sudden descent on state legislatures considering the amendment and his strident calls for racial justice appeared to stir more antagonism than sympathy. Within two years the Service Corporation collapsed; the Self-Determination Coalition kept up a brave front to mask its discouraging prospects. In 1980 the Republican party withdrew its previous platform support for the amendment while the Democrats endorsed it as before. The Republicans' national victory that November provided another ominous sign. By mid-1981 Bayh, who had himself been defeated for reelection to the Senate, could not see much prospect of its ever achieving ratification.[106]

When the time limit for ratification of the D.C. representation amendment expired on August 22, 1985, only sixteen states had given it their approval.[107] All were states with sizable urban and black populations and Democratically controlled legislatures. Not one ratification came from a state legislature where Republicans held a majority of the seats. Pleas that the amendment be ratified as a matter of democratic principle and fairness to two-thirds of a million citizens failed to sway legislators and their constituents, who focused on its political liabilities. As time expired, District of Columbia mayor Marion Barry declared ratification by state legislatures "an insurmountable obstacle."[108]

As it became evident that amendment was unlikely, District residents grew frustrated with the Article V process. Some began to advocate that Congress simply ignore the Founders' intentions and the Constitution's specific provisions regarding the federal district. Instead, they urged Congress to grant statehood to all but a nonresidential central core of 3,000 acres of land and federal buildings, pointing out that Congress had the constitutional authority to admit states to the Union by a majority vote. Though leaving unresolved many issues involving the complex financial relationship between the city and the federal government, such an approach avoided the Article V obstacle. In 1980 proponents managed to place a statehood referendum on the November ballot and won 60 percent support. In 1982 elected delegates drew up a constitution for the state of New Columbia.[109] In the waning months of the amendment campaign, the House of Representatives held hearings on the statehood plan.[110] Three years of strenuous effort by the District's nonvoting congressional delegate, Eleanor Holmes Norton, finally brought the statehood proposal to a vote in the House in November 1993. The measure lost by a wide margin, 153 to 277, as old arguments against the D.C. representation amendment merged with new objections to the statehood plan itself and the circumvention of Article V. Despite a last-minute declaration from President Bill Clinton that "it is fundamentally unfair that residents of the District are denied full representation and participation in our national life," only 151 of 258 Democrats voted for statehood. Meanwhile, with one Texas Republican asserting, "The District hasn't even shown the ability to govern itself as a city, let alone as a state," all but one of his 175 partisan colleagues voted against the measure.[111]

After the failure of the statehood initiative, proposals were advanced to retrocede to Maryland all of the District except the approximately 3,000 acres of monumental Washington—the Capitol, mall, adjacent federal buildings, and White House. This solution, while it would enfranchise District residents as Maryland citizens, completely ignored the Twenty-third Amendment. That incomplete and imperfect 1961 constitutional reform erected an unforeseen obstacle to retrocession as a politically acceptable answer to the District's problems, but one that could not be circumvented or ignored. Retrocession would leave, by the terms of the Twenty-third Amendment, three electoral votes in the hands of the District's remaining legal residents—quite possibly only the individuals living at 1600 Pennsylvania Avenue. As frustrating as the constitutional amending process seemed to those who felt, with good reason, that it prevented an end to the District of Columbia's colonial status, its citizens being taxed and called to military service without representation, it remained the most satisfactory route to reform. As long as the path was blocked, the District would continue to be, as one resident journalist wryly noted, "the hole in the doughnut of democracy."[112]

* * *

THE SHIFTING American political balance in the 1970s, clearly evident in the November 1972 presidential election in which Richard Nixon, a foe of liberal domestic reform, soundly defeated George McGovern, one of its most outspoken advocates, altered the course of constitutional amending efforts. In the 1960s an Article V consensus could repeatedly be assembled to give the District of Columbia a limited role in presidential elections, end poll taxes, revise presidential succession arrangements, and expand the franchise to eighteen-year-olds. Even a few months before the 1972 election such a consensus could be built in Congress to approve the equal rights amendment, a much more consequential amendment than any of those during the previous decade. After the election results were known, however, the momentum for ERA ratification quickly dissipated. Two-and-a-half months later the announcement of the Supreme Court's *Roe v. Wade* decision provoked considerable angry opposition. Many critics of *Roe* accurately perceived the successful demand for abortion rights as an outgrowth of the recent upsurge of feminism and concluded that ERA would bring other changes they regarded as distasteful. The swing of the political pendulum to the right quickly dashed prospects that states already possessed of conservative tendencies would ratify.

During the 1970s liberal views lingered longer in Congress than in state legislatures. Consequently, supporters of greater political rights for the District of Columbia were able to win an amending majority in the Congress. Yet the two-thirds support for the D.C. representative amendment on Capitol Hill only translated into approval of the measure by about one-third of state houses. The relative conservatism of state legislators on gender issues was even more pronounced on racial matters. This is not to say that the entire country had turned misogynist or racist, but the political balance had shifted enough so that by a narrow margin in the first instance and an overwhelming one in the second, reform amendments failed to meet the Article V standard.

Declaring support for or opposition to the equal rights or D.C. representation amendment provided public figures a means of indicating general positions on gender and race. The outcome of the two amending efforts highlighted the possibilities of striking a pose on an issue without having to bear responsibility for a substantive measure. Article V requirements made it quite likely that no amendment of any sort could be adopted in a contentious political climate of relatively balanced power. Therefore, it was not surprising that a bevy of amendments, designed as much to articulate a position as to achieve adoption, would flourish in the 1980s when striking a constitutional posture became a popular means of dealing with besetting problems of government.

18

Amendment Politics in
a Conservative Era

A mendments to the Constitution were frequently proposed during the conservative ascendancy that began in the 1980s, but by the end of 1995 none had been adopted. As in the late nineteenth century, contending political parties were closely balanced. So too were the forces of American federalism, the centripetal power of the federal government and the centrifugal strength of the states. Each of these equilibriums inhibited agreement on amendments. Unlike a century earlier, however, when the view prevailed that the Constitution neared perfection, toward the end of the twentieth century discontent festered and serious reform schemes proliferated. Yet divisions within society together with the requirements of Article V frustrated every attempt to bring about fundamental change. Consensus on the direction constitutional reform should take, essential for Article V action, remained absent. Therefore the amending process, although it vexed many advocates of constitutional reform, functioned exactly as the Founders had intended. Article V stood as a barrier to change sought by minorities or even slight majorities of citizens or states but not widely agreed upon throughout the nation.

Disenchantment with contemporary government stimulated a steady stream of amendment proposals, several of which received serious congressional attention. Unhappiness with federal fiscal practice led to repeated calls for an amendment requiring a balanced annual federal budget. Less strident and persistent but nevertheless noteworthy appeals arose for an amendment authorizing presidents to veto individual items in complex pieces of legislation. Discontent with Supreme Court rulings stirred fervent demands for amendments to prohibit abortions, permit school prayers, and punish the burning of the American flag. None of these propositions proved capable of withstanding the careful scrutiny or achieving the broad support that Article V demanded.

Despite or perhaps because of the lack of achievement, constitutional amendments remained prominent on political agendas throughout the period. Various interest groups saw that proposing a constitutional amendment provided a means of putting before the American public their views on the nature of government. An amendment made a terse statement of principle as to how government should operate. Advancing one could provoke intense discussion and ignite passionate enthusiasm. Suggesting an addition to the nation's basic charter offered a vivid symbol of a precept its proponents considered vital. To advocate constitutional change was to assert that government ought to function according to some fundamental value not currently being observed.

To late-twentieth-century proponents of government restructuring, amendments possessed an additional attraction: they could cut through the usual impediments to change. Much of the appeal of an amendment lay in its capacity to redefine governmental practice instantly and in sweeping fashion. Presidents and legislators could be compelled to observe new guidelines. Contrary judicial rulings, often a source of unhappiness, could be overridden. Dramatic reform could be obtained as had been the case with the Civil War and Progressive Era amendments. Therefore, crusades for constitutional alteration and reactions to them reflected contemporary constitutional thinking as well as the role that the amending process had come to play in American political culture.

THE MOST WIDELY DISCUSSED constitutional reform proposal of the 1980s and early 1990s required that the annual expenditures of the federal government not exceed revenues for the year. The balanced budget amendment became closely identified with the conservative ideology of Ronald Reagan, although his adherents held widely divergent views on it and, indeed, some support for the measure came from decidedly anti-Reagan quarters. Often dismissed as a political gimmick to distract attention from the actual budgetary practices of the Reagan administration, the proposed balanced budget amendment did address fundamental issues of fiscal practice unattended since the 1930s.

As the national government substantially augmented its authority in domestic and international affairs during the New Deal and World War II, the annual federal budget grew twenty-fold. Indeed deficit spending became synonymous in some minds with the administration of Franklin Roosevelt. Previously, federal spending and debt had remained comparatively tiny except briefly during wartime. A unified federal budget was not even developed until the 1920s and then was constructed without distinction between capital and operating expenditures. This accounting method, a contrast to most state and local governmental budgeting for roads, bridges, and school buildings as well as private spending on houses and automobiles, called maximum attention to momentary debt and paid minimum notice to the multi-year benefits of (and appropriately distributed payments for) some current initiatives. Thus the extraordinary growth in government spending during the New Deal to produce benefits that would be reaped in years ahead created an exaggerated image of federal budget deficits that critics would point to as evidence of imprudence and irresponsibility.

Substantial budgetary imbalance in the 1930s and 1940s resulted not only from depression and wartime spending but from changes in economic thinking as well. Federal spending increased under circumstances that made prompt equivalent revenue collection virtually impossible. Furthermore, annual budget balancing lost favor to long-term economic stabilization through government fiscal manipulation. British economist John Maynard Keynes posited that cyclical economic declines could be checked through increased government expenditure and lower taxes while excessive, inflationary growth could likewise be moderated through reduced spending and higher taxation. Keynes assumed that the ultimate governmental objective of a balance between tax revenues and expenditures would be achieved over the course of a natural economic cycle, not the brief, artificial calendar of a fiscal year.

However sound otherwise, Keynes's theory did not anticipate the inherent political difficulties of central economic management in a democratic republic. Maintaining a balance between revenues and appropriations had been an accepted constitutional responsibility of Congress, though not an articulated mandate, for a century and a half. Once the connection between annual spending and taxation was loosened, however, elected officials found it much easier to authorize expenditures and reduce taxes than to lower spending or increase levies. In Keynesian terms, additional taxes should be imposed and government spending diminished to balance accounts when the nation's economy was surging, but politically this proved difficult. A balanced federal budget, either in annual terms or in longer cycles, turned out to be virtually unreachable in the post-Keynes era, whether because of economic sluggishness, national security apprehensions, or political distaste. As federal deficits became endemic, a search for constitutional solutions began.

Whether or not balanced budgets are economically important, and the debate on that issue is unsettled and ongoing, they have long had great weight as political symbols.[1] Alexander Hamilton was willing to incur debt to build a strong economy and national government, provoking Thomas Jefferson's 1798 wish for a constitutional amendment to prohibit federal borrowing. Jefferson, however, quickly abandoned this view when the opportunity arose to purchase the Louisiana Territory. Not until 1936 was a budget-restraining amendment first placed before Congress. At the height of New Deal legisla-

tive activity, Minnesota congressman Harold Knutson, a Republican, unsuccessfully proposed setting a peacetime per capita limit on federal debt.[2] Two
years later the American Taxpayers Association proposed an amendment to
limit federal taxes to 25 percent of income and, when Congress showed no
interest, encouraged states to petition for a constitutional convention.

During the post–World War II conservative resurgence, income tax limitation and required annual budget balancing stood out among suggestions
for restraining the federal government through constitutional amendment.
The most discussed proposal, submitted in 1954 by Republican senator
Styles Bridges of New Hampshire and Democrat Harry Byrd of Virginia, required the president each year to present an estimate of expected revenues
and a proposed balanced budget; Congress could not adjourn for more than
three days until adopting such a budget, unless three-fourths of the members
agreed otherwise. Nebraska Republican senator Carl Curtis, like Bridges and
Byrd a critic of federal spending on social programs, offered an amendment
similar in most respects but authorizing Congress to levy an added tax to reduce existing debt. The Eisenhower Treasury Department, hardly a bastion
of Keynesian enthusiasm, recommended against adopting such "relatively inflexible" budgeting methods.[3] Neither measure achieved substantial support,
and both faded from view, although every Congress thereafter witnessed the
introduction of at least a few balanced budget amendment resolutions.[4]

The 1960s brought increases in federal spending for both military and
domestic social purposes together with a modest tax reduction, one of the
most popular initiatives of the Kennedy administration. Budgetary imbalances grew precipitously as the Vietnam War escalated. First Lyndon Johnson and later Richard Nixon avoided seeking tax increases to pay for the
war's rising costs, not wishing to provide opponents further ammunition.
Various groups, each with its own political agenda, began showing interest
in constitutionally required, annually balanced budgets. Since they tended to
be lumped together as "balanced budget advocates," their dissimilar objectives often remained obscure.

In 1969 a number of libertarians, unhappy with recent developments in
particular but philosophically opposed to government in general, formed
the National Taxpayers Union (NTU). This Washington-based body regarded government as a hobble on individualism and taxes as the lifeblood
of government. The NTU's newsletter, *Dollars and Sense,* attacked government not merely for liberal social programs but for everything from Defense Department waste to corporate bailouts, rail and postal subsidies, and
tax-supported municipal trash collection. Assuming that Congress would
be unwilling to levy taxes if required to do so to fund all appealing spend-

ing programs, the union embraced a balanced budget amendment as a means of shrinking the federal government. By the late 1970s it claimed 100,000 members.[5]

Others of a libertarian bent soon took up the cause. In 1973 Jack Kemp, a young Republican congressman from Buffalo, New York, proposed a constitutional amendment limiting federal tax receipts and expenditures to a percentage of the previous year's national income.[6] The measure would force federal spending gradually to decline in proportion to the nation's overall economy. Kemp believed that increasing the profitability of private business was necessary to provide incentives for expansion. In his view, existing opportunities for enrichment offered insufficient motivation for investment that would eventually benefit the entire society. He became a vocal and energetic promoter of balanced and shrinking federal budgets as a means of achieving his objectives.

Concurrently some of California governor Ronald Reagan's libertarian-minded advisers also took up the balanced budget cause. They, too, aimed at restricting the government's resources in order to reduce its role in American life. Lewis Uhler, a one-time John Birch Society member who headed Reagan's tax reduction task force, subsequently, in 1975, established the National Tax Limitation Committee (NTLC). Within four years Uhler enlisted prominent economists Milton Friedman and William Niskanen, law professor Robert Bork, and over 300,000 paid members. The NTLC advocated an amendment that not only required a balanced budget but specifically limited tax increases to the rate of gross national product growth or, if inflation exceeded 3 percent, three-fourths of such growth. The NTLC plan gained a bipartisan cadre of congressional sponsors by the end of the decade. Under its provisions, if inflation continued as expected, federal spending would decline as a portion of gross national product.[7] Martin Anderson and David Stockman, both to become influential advisers during the early Reagan presidency, independently developed similar views about constricting the federal government. Anderson by 1979 was advocating a single constitutional amendment that would limit federal spending, require a balanced budget, prohibit wage and price controls, authorize the president to veto individual items in appropriations bills, and require a two-thirds congressional vote to approve expenditures.[8] Stockman, too, wanted to achieve permanent structural change in government and saw budget reduction as a promising path to his goal.[9]

Other Republicans embraced the balanced budget cause, not in a deliberate and systematic effort to stifle government, but as a device to ensure fiscal responsibility regardless of the level of government activity. They tended not to think of the federal budget as an economic policy statement in which one legitimate option might be inflation as a form of taxation and another might be shifting to future beneficiaries the costs of programs whose results would not be achieved for years to come. Instead, they regarded the federal budget as akin to the family checkbook where failure to limit household spending to income courted disaster in short order. This family analogy, formulated in terms of the need to live within the bounds of current resources, ignored the reality that large-scale borrowing, especially for home mortgages, was a central feature of American family economies.

Annual federal budget balancing, the fiscally conservative view held, would remedy inflation and require Congress to confront the costs of new programs. Indeed, under some circumstances, budget balancing might reasonably compel tax increases, a notion anathema to libertarians. In 1975 Senate veteran Carl Curtis, bemoaning "the rapidly deteriorating fiscal integrity of our nation" and declaring the Byrd-Bridges plan of preventing congressional adjournment no longer adequate in an era of almost continuous sessions, offered a complicated amendment proposal that mandated an immediate surtax to cover estimated federal revenue shortages for the year. This "pay as we go" amendment was hardly in keeping with the libertarian idea of absolutely capping taxes, much less a device certain to reduce government. Instead it reflected Curtis's simple distaste for "spendthrift politicians," the cost of interest on the federal debt, and the current high inflation, which he blamed largely on federal budgetary imbalances. Faced with the choice of spending restraint or tax increases, Curtis believed Congress would normally, though not invariably, opt for the former. Thirteen of his Senate colleagues as well as other witnesses agreed with Curtis that only a constitutional requirement would give Congress the needed discipline to check its spending habits.[10]

Not all who advocated a balanced budget amendment by the mid-1970s were libertarians eager to dismantle government or traditional conservatives happy to dispense with one or another federal social program but primarily concerned with overall fiscal restraint. Paul Simon of Illinois, a liberal Democrat, supported the Curtis proposal as a means of ensuring that Congress would reestablish the linkage between authorizing expenditures and providing adequate revenues. Although he did not say so at the hearing, Simon elsewhere suggested that he regarded a balanced budget requirement as a device to restrain presidents from proposing more politically popular spending than they were prepared to advocate funding through taxes. Greater fiscal responsibility could reduce military spending and possibly free resources for other purposes. At the very least, it avoided diversion of public funds into debt service. Simon's belief in the amendment, although not widely shared by those pursuing similar social reform agendas, would endure. Testifying in its behalf as a freshman representative in 1975, he remained a principal sponsor as an experienced senator in the 1990s.[11]

None of the various rationales moved Congress to embrace a balanced budget amendment in the mid-1970s. Chairman Birch Bayh allowed Senate Constitutional Amendments Subcommittee conservatives to hold 1975 hearings on the Curtis proposal but did not himself attend. Congressional inaction led proponents to revive the tactic of employing the alternative Article V route to amendment. Urged on by the National Taxpayers Union, the Maryland and Mississippi legislatures in 1975 requested a constitutional convention to propose a balanced budget amendment. The NTU campaign went ahead quietly and quickly as legislators found convention calls both painless and popular. By March 1978 twenty-two states had filed Article V petitions. In June, when California voters approved a state property tax reduction measure known as Proposition 13, a sense of popular discontent with increasing rates of inflation and government spending at all levels spurred further interest in a balanced federal budget requirement in state capitols from California to Arkansas to New Hampshire.[12]

Advocacy of a balanced federal budget became increasingly attractive to politicians in the midst of the stagnant but inflationary economy of the late 1970s. Ironically, specific steps to achieve a balanced budget, whether tax increases or spending reductions, did not have equivalent popularity. Public opinion surveys repeatedly showed two-thirds or more (sometimes substantially more) of Americans favoring a balanced federal budget. Whether or not they understood the implications of such a measure was doubtful, however. One early 1979 poll probed further and found that substantial majorities opposed reductions in every major area of federal spending.[13] The opportunity symbolically to embrace the balanced budget principle without having to explain how one would implement it, much less immediately do so, attracted a variety of politicians to the cause of constitutional amendment. Most notable among them was Ronald Reagan's successor as California governor, Jerry Brown, who decided to make the balanced budget amendment a centerpiece of his second inaugural address in January 1979.

Endorsement of the convention petition drive by Brown, a Democrat, albeit a frequently unconventional one, drew press attention and, in the words of the National Taxpayer Union's leader, "Blew our cover!" Congressional Democrats began saying that a good way to start balancing the federal budget would be to eliminate federal revenue sharing with the states. Meanwhile their Republican counterparts suggested that Congress submit an amendment limiting federal spending as a means to avoid an unpredictable constitutional convention. Citizens for the Constitution, an organization to oppose the state petition drive, sprang quickly to life, declaring, "The last President who used the balanced budget as a fiscal remedy was Herbert Hoover," and "The same folks who brought you the 'Great Depression' of the 1930's, now want to rewrite your Constitution." Headed by Massachusetts lieutenant governor Thomas P. O'Neill III, son of Speaker of the House "Tip" O'Neill, and supported by organized labor as well as the Carter administration, the ad hoc coalition lobbied strenuously to defeat petition resolutions in the Montana senate and the Massachusetts house. In February California held the first state legislative hearings on the amendment and a constitutional convention but then proceeded no farther. The Ohio legislature killed the convention petition as well. Although New Hampshire submitted the thirtieth convention request, by mid-1979 the state initiative was confronting significant resistance.[14]

The prospect of a constitutional convention, a phenomenon unknown since 1787 (unless one counted the irregular Civil War–eve gathering of state representatives in Washington at the invitation of Virginia), generated considerable anxiety among political leaders. Although lawyers debated whether such a convention could be confined to the subject for which it was ostensibly called, politicians and historians easily recalled that, once assembled, the 1787 body had acknowledged no restrictions on its mandate. From President Jimmy Carter, who proclaimed a convention "extremely dangerous" because "completely uncontrollable," to conservative Republican senator Barry Goldwater, who labeled convention calls "foolhardy," a wide spectrum of national figures denounced the petition drive.[15] Expressions of concern about a balanced budget amendment itself took second place to apprehensions regarding the unpredictable possibilities of a constitutional convention.

Birch Bayh's staff at the Senate Judiciary Subcommittee on the Constitution carefully examined the state petitions. Some proposed very strict budget balancing requirements; others permitted exceptions under various circumstances. Most had been formally filed with Congress, but, as it turned out, at least six had not and Indiana's had been filed by mistake, not actually having been adopted by the state legislature. Another half-dozen petitions requested submission of a balanced budget amendment but failed to specify that this be done by convention.[16] The review suggested that considerably fewer than the reported number of petitions could pass the test of asking for the same thing and doing so in a proper fashion, but Bayh's staff did not relax. Acknowledging the political appeal of a balanced budget requirement, the staff assembled arguments against it. They focused on its adverse effect on efforts to remedy economic recession. With the economy in decline, federal revenues shrinking, and required outlays for unemployment compensation and public assistance increasing, Congress would be compelled to reduce other expenditures and perhaps raise taxes as well rather than prime the pump of recovery. "In this situation," a staff memo concluded, "the budget might end up chasing the economy down its own slide."[17]

Meanwhile, the Carter White House staff consulted with Harvard law professor Laurence Tribe about dealing with a possible constitutional convention. Tribe thought the balanced budget amendment a bad idea on various grounds but counseled the administration not to take the antidemocratic position of resisting the right of the people to alter their Constitution. Though he provided a long list of unsettled questions about the operation of a convention, he urged emphasis instead on "the folly of engraving the policy of fiscal austerity in the Constitution." Point to slavery and prohibition, he advised, as the only specific policies endorsed in the Constitution, both unwisely so. Tribe argued that if a balanced budget was desirable, it was nevertheless too complex a matter to deal with in constitutional generalities. "Needlessly amending the Constitution injures our political system at its core. Once the amendment device had been transformed into a fuzzy substitute for the more focused legislative process, not only would the lawmaking function of Congress be eroded, but the Constitution itself would lose its unique significance as the ultimate expression of fundamental and enduring national values." To Tribe, unless the Constitution became "easier to alter than it has ever been or should ever become, it will remain the least appropriate instrument for American economic policy" with its need for "flexibility and rapid responsiveness to changing circumstances."[18]

Such economic and constitutional arguments failed to persuade advocates who sought the balanced budget amendment precisely because it would impose a particular economic policy upon the government and significantly restrict presidential and congressional discretion. The National Taxpayers Union kept up its petition drive, undaunted by questions about the validity of petitions or their continued vitality once the Congress to which they were addressed had adjourned. The Supreme Court's 1939 *Coleman v. Miller* ruling that the validity of a state act under Article V was a political question for Congress, not the courts, to decide, established a legal basis for ignoring disputed state petitions. Yet should the Congress come to believe that an overwhelming majority of states and constituents desired a balanced budget amendment, it would be unlikely to withstand the demand regardless of technicalities. A similar petition drive had broken Senate resistance to the Sixteenth Amendment, motivating senators to approve an amendment on their own rather than risk a convention that might propose a radically different measure, not to mention other reforms. The perception of a wide-spread desire for amendment, even in the absence of a completed convention application, had been sufficient to produce congressional action in 1912 and might well suffice again.

Even though federal spending remained relatively steady throughout the 1970s, rising inflation, declining public economic confidence, and spreading disenchantment with government by the end of the decade added force to the balanced budget campaign. Despite the resistance of subcommittee liberals, Republicans and conservative Democrats on the Senate Judiciary Subcommittee on the Constitution adopted a balanced budget amendment resolution by a vote of 5 to 2 in December 1979. Three months later the full Judiciary Committee narrowly defeated the resolution, 9 to 8, as one Republican, Charles Mathias of Maryland, joined eight Democrats in voting against it. Disappointed Republican senator Alan Simpson of Wyoming warned his colleagues that the issue was far from dead. He disparaged the ability of Congress to discipline itself on spending and said the only way to balance the budget was "to shrivel the pie so we don't have so much pie to play with."[19]

Ronald Reagan's 1980 presidential campaign further strengthened the balanced budget crusade. Deriding government as oversized, inefficient, and corrupt, itself the problem rather than a problem solver, Reagan built on resentments toward federal civil rights and social welfare reforms of the 1960s, the Vietnam War, the scandals of the Nixon administration, and the perceived ineptitude of its successors. Reagan's call for tax cuts to free investment capital and thereby stimulate growth, lately termed supply-side economics, seemed at odds with his pledges to reduce inflation and to increase military spending. Yet he repeatedly offered assurances that he intended to be a fiscally conservative president, underscoring such statements with enthusiastic endorsements of the balanced budget amendment. His message exuded responsibility and rectitude: "Balancing the budget is like protecting your virtue: all you have to do is learn to say no."[20]

In 1980 the Democratic party platform and its presidential candidate opposed the balanced budget amendment. Such a position was consistent with the Democrats' economic approach of the previous half century but awkward to defend in light of a poorly performing economy and a $60 billion annual deficit. The Carter administration struggled to produce a balanced budget for the election year but found itself unable to keep pace with the falling revenues and rising costs of a deteriorating economic climate. Ultimately the administration proved unwilling to sacrifice other objectives in order to achieve the illusive goal. Thus balanced budget advocates hailed the election verdict of 1980, complex and ambiguous though the reasons for

Reagan's 51 percent victory might have been, as demonstrating a public preference for their position.

The first months of the Reagan presidency further invigorated the balanced budget amendment campaign. Libertarian expectations of reducing government grew apace. At the same time, the new administration and Congress engaged in the very sort of political performance that had helped fuel demands for a constitutional balanced budget requirement. Together they demonstrated the relative political ease of approving tax cuts and spending increases and the comparative difficulty of endorsing levies to pay the government's bills. Although the new president endorsed the balanced budget principle in his inaugural address, his first legislative requests were for a 10 percent tax cut each of the next three years and a large increase in defense spending. Reagan's electoral victory, his confident rhetoric, and even the sympathy generated by the attempt on his life ten weeks into his term made a politically popular vote to reduce taxes even simpler for members of Congress. They found it just as easy to support the request for a larger military budget. The inevitable consequences of these actions appalled Reagan's libertarian-minded budget director, David Stockman. Without the difficult additional step of reducing other government spending, the federal deficit would skyrocket, he predicted.[21] It did. Whether Reagan blindly maintained his long-standing single-minded determination to reduce taxes he considered too high, unwisely embraced unsound economic advice, or deliberately executed a libertarian plan to make federal spending on domestic social programs virtually impossible, his initiatives rapidly accelerated the growth of the federal debt. Either to excuse their own 1981 fiscal decisions or to check a president from putting them in a politically difficult situation, more and more members of Congress began finding merit in a constitutionally required balanced budget.

Orrin Hatch, who became chairman of the Senate Judiciary Subcommittee on the Constitution when the Republicans acquired a Senate majority in 1981, quickly convened hearings on balanced budget proposals. With Democratic liberal Birch Bayh defeated for reelection and the more conservative Dennis DeConcini of Arizona now the subcommittee's ranking minority member, Hatch enjoyed a congenial forum. Rather than question state petitions as Bayh and his staff had done, Hatch argued that they made prompt congressional action imperative. He treated existing petitions as valid and noted that in their current session one house of four more legislatures had already adopted petitions. To avoid a constitutional convention, he urged adoption of a "consensus" amendment that he, DeConcini, and Judiciary chairman Strom Thurmond had fashioned; it required Congress to balance each year's budget unless war was declared or three-fifths of Congress approved additional expenditures. Furthermore, federal tax revenues could not increase as a portion of national income without specific congressional authorization. Hatch presented this amendment as a modest proposal "to restore accountability and honesty to a decisionmaking process that is today characterized by illusion and legerdemain," one that would merely reduce access to borrowing and tax increases. Yet the consensus amendment's restraint on tax levies positioned it much closer to the version of budget balancing sought by libertarians eager to shrink government than to the more neutral alternative preferred by "pay as you go" advocates of fiscal responsibility. The enthusiastic witnesses Hatch paraded before the subcommittee, conservative economists, bankers, and attorneys as well as spokesmen for the National Taxpayers Union and National Tax Limitation Committee, underscored the government reduction agenda of the amendment.[22]

After his subcommittee and the Judiciary Committee approved the consensus amendment in May 1981, Hatch justified it to the Senate as a reasonable solution to greater pressures on Congress to authorize spending than to provide sufficient tax revenue. In light of the concurrent Reagan tax cut and spending proposals, the argument may have represented a sincere concern. It disregarded, however, any Keynesian justification for longer budgetary cycles. It ignored the case for temporary deficit spending to stimulate an ailing economy and meet welfare needs that would increase precisely at the moment that declining employment reduced income tax revenues. Nor, of course, did it advance any argument on behalf of ongoing budget deficits. None of the phalanx of conservative economists quoted in support of the balanced budget–tax limitation amendment thought budgetary flexibility worthy of mention, much less referred to it in positive terms. Instead, they drew attention to "bracket creep," the gradual increase of tax rates as inflation moved incomes to higher levels. This rise represented, critics charged, an additional tax that Congress did not have to justify imposing.[23]

Ronald Reagan's central economic message in the early 1980s was that U.S. taxation and government spending were high and getting higher. The balanced budget–tax limitation amendment campaign rested firmly on this premise. The comparatively low taxes that Americans paid and the relatively modest progressivity of U.S. tax rates as judged by the standards of other advanced industrial nations went unnoted. So, too, did universal availability of pensions, health care, and other social services in more heavily taxed but nevertheless thriving capitalist nations from Japan to Canada to Germany and other Western European democracies. The repeated libertarian assertion that Americans were too heavily taxed by too big a government became widely accepted. Similarly, the image of a burdensome U.S. debt obscured the higher per capita national indebtedness of thriving Japan and Western Europe.[24] Furthermore, Reagan's rhetorical skill in blaming Congress for unbalanced budgets based upon his own tax reduction and spending proposals underscored the prevalence of political posturing over fiscal realism in the balanced budget campaign.

Over a year passed before the consensus amendment came to the Senate floor. By summer 1982, however, Reagan's supply-side economic theories had failed to produce the predicted new tax revenues from tax cuts, and the administration had set forth the first federal budget with a deficit in excess of $100 billion. Both the executive branch and legislators were eager to demonstrate before the fall elections that they were seeking remedies. Presidential aides stressed to reporters the difficulty of campaigning for a balanced budget amendment after submitting a prodigiously unbalanced budget, though in fact doing so provided an easy means of symbolically embracing principles being violated in practice. Reagan demonstrated this maneuver by proclaiming in a White House rose garden press conference that "Americans understand that the discipline of a balanced budget amendment is essential to stop squandering and overtaxing" and then ignoring questions about his apparent inconsistency.[25] A week later he told 5,000 supporters at a noon rally on the Capitol steps, an event crafted for television, that the amendment was needed "to bring to heel a federal establishment which has taken too much power from the states, too much liberty with the Constitution and too much money from the people."[26] Presumably, this federal establishment did not include Reagan's own administration.

Many members of Congress were ready to embrace the amendment as a way of demonstrating that they opposed deficits. Supporting the amendment was attractive although, or perhaps because, any need actually to balance the budget would await ratification. Sensing that the drive for the amendment was gathering momentum, opponents began warning that it might lead to dishonest revenue forecasts, requirements for individual or business payment instead of government funding for such items as universal health care, and other deceptive and regressive budgetary practices.[27] Such arguments failed to slow the amendment's progress in the Senate, where on August 4, 1982, with every member voting, the balanced budget amendment won approval 69 to 31.[28]

The political pressures of the moment led some senators who had earlier opposed it to support the measure. In 1979 Democratic majority leader Robert Byrd of West Virginia had stated unequivocally that the amendment "would not be in the nation's best interest," and influential Democrat

William Proxmire of Wisconsin sternly warned that the nation could be "locked into a rigid budgetary straitjacket that could plague our nation with years of deepening recession." In 1982, however, both men voted for the amendment. Republican John Tower of Texas did not even wait three years to retreat. After declaring that the measure "should not really be in the fundamental law of this land," Tower immediately bowed to popular opinion. He would vote to submit the amendment to the states, he said, to provide "a referendum of the people as they are represented in their respective state legislatures." Having thus taken political refuge in Article V, Tower then further exposed his waffling by announcing that "if invited by any state legislature in the country, I would be deeply delighted to testify against [the amendment's] ratification."[29]

The nation's governors were not impressed by the Senate's action. Meeting a week later in Afton, Oklahoma, the National Governors' Association discussed the amendment in a twenty-one-hour closed session. Arizona Democrat Bruce Babbitt emerged castigating "a sloppy piece of constitutional draftsmanship" and scornfully adding, "It's beginning to look like the constitution of a banana republic." A less predictable and thus more devastating evaluation came from Illinois Republican James Thompson. "The way you balance the budget is you balance the budget," he said. "It doesn't take a constitutional amendment. It just takes guts."[30]

As the half-passed amendment resolution moved to the Democratically controlled House of Representatives, different concerns emerged from those that prevailed in the Republican-dominated Senate. Not wishing to appear fiscally irresponsible but seeking to render the amendment harmless, Democrats on a Judiciary subcommittee struck out the tax limitation section that Republican congressman Henry Hyde of Illinois called "the heart of the bill." The Democrats also shifted budget balancing responsibility from an annual basis to a far more flexible "fixed period" and reduced the majority required to approve an unbalanced budget from three-fifths of the body to three-fifths present and voting. The revisions gave Democrats a measure they could endorse during the fall election campaign without furthering the libertarian goals of the amendment's original sponsors. At the same time, the changes reduced Republican enthusiasm for immediate passage of the resolution.[31] Stalled for the moment, the amendment died altogether when the November 1982 election increased the Democratic majority in the House by twenty-six.

The 1982 Senate approval of the consensus amendment turned out to be the high point of the congressional balanced budget campaign during the 1980s, though far from its final gasp. A rapidly deteriorating economy increased political resistance to the economic policies of the Reagan administration, not to mention called attention to the rising costs of unemployment relief at the very time tax revenues were declining. However, though enthusiasm for the balanced budget amendment slipped slightly in Congress, the state response was more complicated. In March 1983 Missouri became the thirty-second state to request a constitutional convention for the purpose of proposing a balanced budget amendment.[32] With only two more state petitions apparently needed to force a convention call, attention shifted from the amendment itself to questions concerning an Article V convention.

Ever since the 1960s, when Everett Dirksen nearly succeeded in persuading enough states to petition to force a convention for proposing an amendment to reverse the Supreme Court's "one man, one vote" legislative apportionment decision, Congress had actively discussed the prospects of such a convention. Debate centered on whether or not a convention could address topics beyond those for which it was called to deal, becoming, in the words of critics who feared the prospect, a "runaway convention." Senator Sam Ervin, convinced that no existing restraints limited such a convention and apprehensive that radical reform might result, proposed a Federal Constitutional Convention Procedures Act in August 1967. Ervin's measure, among other things, required state petitions to deal with the same subject in order to be counted among the two-thirds to compel a convention, limited their life span to four years and allowed states to withdraw them, restricted a convention's authority to those subjects addressed in the petitions, and provided that delegates be popularly elected, one from every House District and two at large from each state.[33] The Senate revised the bill, extending the life of a state petition to seven years and requiring a two-thirds vote of convention delegates to adopt an amendment, and then approved it 84 to 0 in October 1971.[34] Although again endorsed by the Senate in March 1973, this time by a unanimous voice vote, the Ervin bill made no progress in the House of Representatives. House Judiciary Committee chairman Emanuel Celler, convinced that Congress lacked the power to limit a convention called under Article V, refused to let the bill go forward. Following Ervin's retirement in 1978, his North Carolina colleague Jesse Helms took up the effort, and then, in 1981, Orrin Hatch became the bill's champion. In spring 1984, the balanced budget campaign enabled Hatch to gain the Judiciary Committee's attention.[35]

Like Ervin, Hatch wanted to limit the power of state petitions and any convention they might call into being. Constitutional scholars debated at great length without reaching consensus the question of whether a convention as a deliberative body could be so restricted.[36] Hatch opened the 1980 hearings contending that Article V provided symmetrical procedures for proposing amendments so that states would have "substantial, although not unlimited, autonomy." He acknowledged a convention as "a temporary and independent branch of the National Government" but then drew a disputable conclusion. "While [a convention] is free to act within its authority to propose amendments to the Constitution," Hatch contended, "it is also subject to checks and balances designed to ensure that its actions are contained within the proper and limited scope of its authority. In other words, as with any other institution of Government, the powers of the convention are defined and limited powers and subject to check by other institutions of Government."[37] The Utah senator denied that the balanced budget amendment prompted his efforts but left no doubt that restricting a constitutional convention to a single subject would undermine one of the most frequent objections to holding one.

Apprehensions about an impending convention prompted interest in Hatch's convention procedures proposal by, among others, Democratic senator Patrick Leahy of Vermont. He asked two constitutional scholars to rehearse arguments over whether a constitutional convention could be limited in the subjects it addressed or the procedures it chose. They could not agree.[38] While the Judiciary Committee then unanimously recommended the bill to the Senate, the central issue remained unresolved. Senator Leahy, along with Senators Charles Mathias of Maryland, Joseph Biden of Delaware, and Max Baucus of Montana, expressed concern about having no established convention procedures but doubted whether, once in session, a convention could be restricted.[39] Entangled in insoluble controversy, the procedures bill went no farther.

In summer 1984 the contrasting positions of the major political parties further confounded the balanced budget amendment and convention questions. The Republican platform pledged the party to work for an amendment, declaring, "If Congress fails to act on this issue, a constitutional convention should be convened to address only this issue in order to bring deficit spending under control." The Democratic platform decried "the artificial and rigid Constitutional restraint of a balanced budget amendment" and the attempt to call a constitutional convention. The mixed results of the national elections, a Reagan presidential victory but a renewed Democratic majority in the House and a reduced Republican margin in the Senate, offered no clear indication of voter preference.[40]

The prospect of an unpredictable constitutional convention generated nervousness. In September 1984 the Michigan senate approved a balanced budget amendment convention petition, but the measure then died in a house committee after a Republican legislator turned against it, saying she "realized I don't want the Constitution tampered with." Referendums on compelling legislators to petition for a convention failed to get on the 1984 ballot in California and Montana. Then a petition resolution failed after intense debate in the Republican-controlled Connecticut state senate in March 1985. Further state setbacks followed.[41] By August, a new Gallup poll registered a sharp decline in public support for the balanced budget amendment and a rise in uncertainty, though not clear-cut opposition.[42]

Reduced enthusiasm for a balanced budget amendment became evident when the issue again came before the Senate in March 1986. During the previous year differences among balanced budget advocates had surfaced in the Senate Judiciary Subcommittee on the Constitution as Chairman Orrin Hatch led a majority of members to endorse a version limiting spending increases to the previous year's rate of national income growth, thus preventing any overall expansion of government programs or services. Paul Simon of Illinois, now a senator, unsuccessfully fought this blanket restriction, warning that it could "create real mischief."[43] Despite losing the argument within the subcommittee, Simon nevertheless continued to support the amendment. Other senators, however, had more doubts about this latest libertarian-leaning balanced budget amendment. Although four years earlier the Senate had mustered more than the required two-thirds majority, now it failed to approve by a one-vote margin. In part, the 1986 defeat appeared to be due to the recent passage of ordinary legislation to limit deficits. The Balanced Budget and Emergency Deficit Control Act of November 1985, commonly known as the Gramm-Rudman-Hollings Act, prescribed gradual deficit reduction until achievement of a balanced federal budget in 1991. Perhaps a balanced budget could be realized without a constitutional amendment.

Enthusiasm for an amendment flagged further as the Reagan administration neared its end. The bicentennial of the 1787 convention reminded the Americans of the power such a body possessed. Support for another waned. Although during the bicentennial year Ronald Reagan vaguely endorsed a convention if necessary to obtain a balanced budget amendment, the Montana senate refused to accept its lower house's support for a petition.[44] In May 1988 Alabama formally withdrew its convention petition, ignoring White House appeals not to do so and overriding Governor Guy Hunt's veto of the measure. A wide spectrum of organizations, from the liberal People for the American Way to the Daughters of the American Revolution to the John Birch Society urged the Alabama action, as they had the Montana senate vote. Phyllis Schlafly was among those who thought a convention "a very bad idea," saying, "We have a wonderful Constitution that has lasted for 200 years, and we don't think anybody should play games with it." The

Alabama legislature had, she declared, dealt "a death blow" to the convention movement. Although NTU president James Davidson discounted apprehensions about a convention and decried Schlafly as "the Mad Hatter of American society," the divisions in conservative ranks did not bode well for the amendment campaign.[45]

Ronald Reagan's successor, George Bush, emulated his predecessor's advocacy of a balanced budget amendment with no greater success. Like Reagan, Bush proposed budgets with large deficits during each year of his presidency, renewing questions as to whether his calls for constitutional budgetary restraints amounted to anything other than posturing to offset images of profligacy. Whatever Bush's motives, the House of Representatives twice considered and twice narrowly rejected balanced budget amendments sponsored by conservative Democrat Charles Stenholm of Texas. In July 1990 the measure passed 279 to 150 but fell seven votes short of the two-thirds requirement, and in June 1992 it passed 280 to 153, nine short.[46] These amendment proposals slightly altered the language but retained the tenor of the Reagan-era libertarian measures that made it more difficult to increase taxes than to reduce spending. Congress would be required to estimate revenues, then confine expenditures to that level unless a majority of all members in each house of Congress (not just those present and voting) agreed in a recorded vote to increase federal taxes. Only a three-fifths majority could authorize deficit spending or increase the national debt ceiling. In May 1992, Stenholm thought he had 305 votes for his measure, and Paul Simon believed the Senate would likewise pass it. Yet opposition from Democratic leaders in both houses; outspoken criticism from a group of economists including seven Nobel laureates; the specter of deep budget cuts; the possibility that the judiciary would have to resolve presidential-congressional disagreements over revenue estimates, spending, or taxation; and the doubts of wavering representatives again thwarted the amendment.[47] One House member who initially cosponsored the resolution but ultimately turned against it revealed the cause of his apostasy. After asking Bush how he would balance the budget and receiving an evasive answer, frustrated South Carolina Democrat Robin Tallon exclaimed, "There was not the wisp of a plan between the President and Congress to actually make the hard choices, to do the heavy lifting, to balance the budget." A nonfunctioning symbolic amendment did not appeal to Tallon, so he, along with others, abandoned it.[48]

Efforts to constrain current federal spending became more determined after the 1992 election of Bill Clinton as president, leading at least two state legislatures to abandon petitions to force a constitutional convention.[49] However, perceptions of need for a balanced budget amendment persisted.

Explicit and Authentic Acts

Independent presidential candidate Ross Perot had made criticism of budgetary deficits and congressional gridlock centerpieces of his unexpectedly successful insurgent campaign in 1992. Clinton's first budget, combining substantial spending cuts with modest tax increases, significantly reduced but far from eliminated the annual deficit. Paul Simon, Stenholm's ally in 1990 and 1992, reemerged as chief advocate of a balanced budget amendment and obtained a Senate vote on it in March 1994. Conservatives from both major parties aided Simon. He also received backing from a few professed liberals who believed that continued federal deficits in good times as well as bad undermined the economic stimulus impact of Keynesian policies and blocked new government activities, however beneficial.[50]

In 1994 critics of Simon's views countered that government finances were now being dealt with more responsibly, that the economy was responding favorably, and that constitutionally requiring an annually balanced budget would hamstring the government in the future. Falling revenues in a recession would force spending reductions or tax increases precisely at the time when the reverse was needed to revive the economy. An amendment, they said, would shift spending responsibilities to state governments and business. It would also inhibit outlays for unanticipated natural disasters such as had just been approved to compensate victims of midwestern floods and a California earthquake, not to mention discourage funding of long-term projects with uncertain results, cancer research for instance. New federal undertakings, such as a national health care program, would become impossible. Worst of all, in the eyes of some critics, requiring a three-fifths vote to waive the balanced budget requirement would allow a 41 percent congressional minority to override a 59 percent majority. Rather than just restrain the budget, this amendment would fundamentally alter basic arrangements of constitutional authority and responsibility.[51]

On March 1, 1994, the Senate again defeated a balanced budget amendment, in this instance by a vote of 63 to 37. Although the positive vote was the smallest in a dozen years, it demonstrated the amendment's continuing appeal. Libertarian desires to shrink federal government, pay-as-you-go fiscal conservatism, and broad-based concern with striking a constitutional balance between the authority to spend and the less politically appealing obligation to raise revenues contributed to its enduring popularity. The relative ease of justifying to one's constituents a vote in favor of compelling a balanced budget, compared to the difficulty of explaining a contrary vote, no doubt played a role.[52] In any case, a sense of majority support for their objective salved the sting of defeat for amendment advocates and encouraged them to persist in their efforts to overcome Article V's obstacles to constitutional reform.

In September 1994 all but five of the 157 sitting Republican congressmen together with more than 185 candidates to join them gathered on the west steps of the Capitol building to call attention to a ten-point campaign platform they labeled a Contract with America. They declared that reintroduction of the balanced budget amendment would be among their highest legislative priorities.[53] In the following weeks, Republican office seekers continued to speak of their Contract despite the apparent lack of attention shown by the electorate and the scorn of critics who described it as a threadbare set of discredited ideas from the Reagan years. When Republicans won an unexpected and sweeping victory in the November 1994 election, gaining control of both houses of Congress for the first time in forty years, they regarded the result as a specific mandate to implement the Contract with America whether, in fact, their victory represented that or merely generalized discontent with Democratic incumbents.

The new House majority, dominated by libertarian conservatives, acted quickly on the balanced budget amendment. A week after Congress convened, a House committee cleared a balanced budget amendment with a provision that a three-fifths vote of Congress would be required to raise taxes. State governors immediately began to express concern that the measure's effect would be to shift governmental responsibilities to states without a commensurate transfer of resources. Two weeks later, the House adopted the amendment 312 to 132 after removing the three-fifths supermajority requirement to raise taxes but declaring three-fifths requisite to approve of an unbalanced budget. Given the speed and strength of the House action, together with a political atmosphere of conservative hubris after a midterm election not seen since 1947 when the Eightieth Congress rapidly adopted the Twenty-second Amendment, the balanced budget amendment was widely expected to be embraced quickly by the Senate.[54]

In the Senate, however, the amendment encountered lengthy and intense criticism that, among other things, raised alarms about the future of the Social Security system. Five senators, three Democrats and two Republicans who had voted against the amendment a year earlier but who faced reelection contests a year hence and no doubt were disquieted by the 1994 election, decided to support the resolution. But a number of others, including five who endorsed the amendment while running for reelection in 1994, decided that its perils outweighed its attractions. After protracted parliamentary maneuvering, the balanced budget amendment fell two votes short of adoption. The margin of defeat was really only one vote because a negative ballot was cast by majority leader Robert Dole so that he could ask for reconsideration at any time and maintain political pressure on his opponents.

Newly elected Republicans appeared particularly frustrated that a member of their party, five-term senator Mark Hatfield of Oregon, provided the margin of defeat by casting the lone Republican vote against the amendment. Hardly philosophical about Article V's demands for consensus on constitutional change, young Republicans sought, without immediate success, to punish Hatfield.[55]

Had the balanced budget amendment passed the Senate in March 1995, state ratification remained problematic. Although many legislatures were eager to approve the amendment as soon as possible, a number of smaller and poorer states easily sufficient to block ratification displayed concern that they would suffer from sharply curtailed federal spending.[56] As the 104th Congress turned its attention to cutting the current federal budget, debate continued as to the consequences of fundamental changes in the federal relationship and the first significant reduction since the 1930s in the central government's responsibility for domestic conditions. Under such circumstances, Article V's requirements for supermajority consensus stood athwart the road to constitutional redefinition.

As long as the political culture that had prevailed since the New Deal persisted, the balanced budget amendment was likely to keep resurfacing. For more than fifty years, it had retained an appeal despite substantive arguments against it and occasional admissions from supporters such as Stenholm that "they might be right."[57] It would quite likely continue to attract support because it conveyed fiscal integrity despite approval of spending in excess of tax revenues. The symbolic value of the balanced budget amendment kept it alive notwithstanding the observation of opponents such as Maryland senator Paul Sarbanes that "tampering with the Constitution is no way to restore a sense of fiscal responsibility to our system."[58]

The political effect of prolonged agitation over constitutional amendment was one of the few ramifications of the balanced budget amendment not specifically noted during the 1994 and 1995 debates. Nevertheless, fifteen years of constant discussion and repeated demonstrations of support for balanced budget–tax limitation amendments had evident consequences. The Clinton administration, the first since the 1960s with an interest in assuming further federal government social responsibilities, felt obliged to avoid any action that might increase, much less even temporarily further unbalance the federal budget, even if the result might ultimately benefit the nation. In seeking to reform health care in 1994, for instance, the Clinton administration steadfastly avoided policy options that might give the appearance of major spending or tax increases. Many liberal Democrats argued that a "single payer system" of government-provided universal health care funded by a general tax would be most equitable and economical, achieving efficiencies and cost controls by funneling health care spending through government rather than through business or individuals. Advocates of a single payer system pointed to Canada as a nearby example of high quality health care for every citizen at significantly lower per capita cost than the United States currently bore. The administration ignored its natural political allies, however, opting instead for a complicated proposal of employer mandates that would, whatever its other merits or flaws, require employers to provide medical coverage and keep revenues and expenditures for health care outside the federal budget. Health care reform, enormously complicated in any event, ran aground in 1994 on rocks cast up by the long debate over limiting and balancing the federal budget. Other issues of education, social welfare, and domestic policy would intensify the debate.

No OTHER AMENDMENT to overturn prevailing federal policies or practices gained the ongoing support that the balanced budget amendment enjoyed during the 1980s and early 1990s. It stood unrivaled as a unifier of discontent with contemporary government. Various groups embraced the balanced budget amendment as meeting their needs, undaunted by the clearly contrary goals of other supporters. No other constitutional reform emerging in this era appealed to such a broad spectrum of citizens, and thus none came anywhere near as close to winning congressional endorsement or state petition approval. Yet the very appearance of other proposals reflected the importance constitutional amendments had assumed as political icons.

On his third day in office, President Reagan welcomed to the White House representatives of groups seeking to outlaw abortion. Ever since the Supreme Court ruled in *Roe v. Wade* exactly eight years earlier that a woman's choice to have an abortion was a protected right of personal privacy, demands for the decision's reversal had been growing. After his inauguration, Reagan lost no time in meeting with leaders of the right-to-life movement whose cause he had embraced and who had helped him attain the presidency. While they spoke, some 60,000 supporters gathered on the Washington Mall to demonstrate their feelings on this emotional issue. The symbolic embrace of the right-to-life movement by the new president, and vice versa, brought an antiabortion constitutional amendment into the political spotlight.

When the *Roe v. Wade* ruling was announced, Senators James Buckley of New York and Jesse Helms of North Carolina had rushed to propose constitutional amendments overturning the decision by declaring that human life began at conception. This measure would, they believed, entitle a fetus to full legal protection. Sixteen days of hearings before Birch Bayh's Senate Subcommittee on Constitutional Amendments between March 1974 and July 1975 produced passionate objections to abortion from, among others, four cardinals of the Catholic church. Defenders of *Roe* were equally fervent. Harvard law professor Laurence Tribe tried to alert both sides that the Buckley and Helms amendments would not necessarily produce the intended result. To recognize fetal rights, Tribe argued, did not deny that pregnant women had rights as well, rights that the Court in *Roe* had found compelling until the fetus could survive outside the womb.[59] The House Judiciary Subcommittee on Civil and Constitutional Rights covered much the same ground in eight days of hearings during February and March 1976. Members of the subcommittee, particularly in their questioning of another Catholic cardinal, New York's Terrance Cooke, focused on the issue of women's rights versus fetal rights.[60] Once their hearings concluded, neither subcommittee took action on the amendment proposals.

From the outset antiabortionists sought as well to stop federal funding of abortion services, most of which benefited poor women. Requiring only a simple congressional majority rather than an Article V supermajority, this tactic appeared more immediately promising. Freshman Republican congressman Henry Hyde of Illinois championed legislation to ban funding in 1976. After the House passed the Hyde measure 207 to 167, the Senate balked until an exception was allowed for cases where a mother's life was endangered. Obtaining a congressional majority for a strong antiabortion statement, especially since it represented an unexpected reversal of earlier defeats, bolstered the image of the growing political strength of the antiabortion movement. The simultaneous and related rise of opposition to the equal rights amendment encouraged the belief that a constitutional amendment banning abortion might be attainable.

An antiabortion amendment became a factor in the presidential campaign of 1976. In the first Democratic primary contest in Iowa, Birch Bayh encountered a furious reaction when he ended two years of noncommitment by declaring opposition to an amendment. Hitherto obscure former Georgia governor Jimmy Carter won a surprising victory over Bayh and several others in Iowa after taking the ambiguous (critics said duplicitous) position that he personally opposed abortion but did not like the amendments put forth. He later added that he would not stand in the way of any amendment, technically just an acknowledgment that presidents had no role in the Article V process but an important political statement nonetheless. Meanwhile, in the closely fought Republican contest, Ronald Reagan embraced an antiabortion amendment. An embattled Gerald Ford, whose wife was on record supporting *Roe*, announced that he favored abortion only in cases of rape, incest, or danger to the mother's life and supported an amendment leaving the issue to state legislative decision. Although Ford narrowly defeated Reagan for their party's nomination, the Republic platform supported "a constitutional amendment to restore the protection of the right to life for unborn children." In the general election, the compromising positions of both Carter and Ford kept an amendment from becoming a major point of contention.[61]

The Carter administration made no attempt to resist congressional renewal of the Hyde ban on federal abortion funding. Meanwhile, state legislation to restrict abortion met an unfriendly reception in the Supreme Court. Abortion foes, assessing the situation, encouraged state legislatures to petition for a constitutional convention. This ploy, paralleling the balanced budget petition drive, generated twenty state petitions by 1980, scarcely enough to force a convention but plenty to maintain antiabortionist enthusiasm for a constitutional amendment.[62]

In 1980, abortion again became a factor in a national political campaign. More resolutely committed to women's rights than Carter, the Democratic convention declared that "reproductive freedom is a fundamental human right. We therefore oppose government interference in the reproductive decisions of Americans."[63] In sharp contrast, the Republican platform, with the enthusiastic support of its nominee, reiterated the party's 1976 commitment to "protection of the right to life of unborn children."[64] Antiabortionists perceived the 1980 Republican victory as confirmation that the country endorsed their views. Though this perception may have been an undue interpretation of an election in which unhappiness with Carter appeared to outpace enthusiasm for Reagan, it fueled new congressional initiatives.

Fervent antiabortionists, led by North Carolina senator John East, immediately sought to capitalize on the Republican victory while avoiding the rigors of constitutional amendment. East proposed a "human life" statute declaring a fetus to be a person from the moment of conception and thus eligible for Fifth and Fourteenth Amendment protection. The statute was correctly perceived as an effort to overturn judicial rulings on constitutional doctrine by mere majority vote of Congress rather than through the Article V process as the Founders had intended. Writing in the *New York Times,* constitutional scholars John Hart Ely and Laurence Tribe, who disagreed with each other on the merits of abortion, concurred that if such an approach prevailed, Americans could "skip all the bother and just let Congress redefine due process of law to include any law Congress or a state legislature approves."[65]

Utah senator Orrin Hatch, a long-standing abortion opponent, tried to fashion a solution able to withstand the scrutiny that quickly felled East's initiative. Moving beyond amendments offered by Jesse Helms and others that embodied East's human life doctrine but conceding the need for super-majority adoption and ratification, Hatch offered a plan ostensibly to make abortion a politically determined possibility rather than a judicially pro-tected right. He proposed an amendment that declared, "A right to abortion is not secured by this Constitution. The Congress and the several States shall have the concurrent power to restrict and prohibit abortions: Provided, That a law of a State which is more restrictive than a law of Congress shall gov-ern." Hatch sought to disarm criticism by presenting his amendment as a means of making abortion a question of states' rights and democratic will, but his characterization was immediately disputed. On the first day of hear-ings on the measure in October 1981, Laurence Tribe argued that the Con-stitution was meant to protect individual liberties from government interference and shifting democratic majorities. The Supreme Court had rec-ognized women's right to make a private decision regarding pregnancy, he said, and this amendment "would create an opportunity in every State to vote down the woman's liberty by a bare majority."[66]

The requirements of Article V rendered constitutional amendment im-possible without a national consensus that did not exist on the abortion issue. Surveys of public opinion indicated that nearly three-fourths of Ameri-cans agreed that women should have a legal right to abortion, although a substantial portion of this support was reluctant and qualified.[67] Opposition, on the other hand, remained absolute and passionate. A compromise on abortion, around which a constitutional consensus could assemble, appeared highly unlikely. Nevertheless, Vermont senator Patrick Leahy, in a clear ref-erence to the prohibition episode, worried at the outset of Hatch's hearings, "It is even possible for this process to produce unwise results if the atmos-phere of deliberation gives way to one of passion and pressure." More than seventy witnesses produced no consensus during nine days of testimony. Dis-agreement was particularly noticeable within the ranks of abortion oppo-nents. On the final day of hearings, militant antiabortionist Nellie Gray criticized the Hatch amendment for merely permitting rather than mandat-ing abortion bans. She reported that Hatch's measure had divided the prolife movement. Her ally, Paul Brown of the Life Amendment Political Action Committee, then urged Hatch to withdraw the amendment "for the good of prolife efforts."[68]

Orrin Hatch was able to win unanimous subcommittee approval of his proposed amendment the day the hearings adjourned, December 16, 1981.

Three months later, he obtained a less clear-cut 10-to-7 endorsement from the full Judiciary Committee.[69] Before the amendment resolution reached the floor, however, the Senate defeated a Jesse Helms bill to deny federal funds for any abortion-related service and to declare that life began at conception. The Helms bill failed by only a single vote, but fail it did, despite lobbying efforts on its behalf by both Ronald Reagan and George Bush. After the uncompromising antiabortion Helms bill lost, the Hatch amendment fared no better, going down to defeat 49 to 50.[70] The defeat was much more severe than it appeared.

The failure to achieve even a majority, much less the necessary two-thirds supermajority, for a relatively mild antiabortion amendment deflated the attempt to reverse *Roe v. Wade* through Article V action. Hatch found no support for his effort to revive the amendment in 1983.[71] Not only the Reagan administration but also its like-minded successor declined to invest more energy in pursuing a goal that appeared out of reach. Instead, they sought the more attainable but less irreversible objectives of denying federal funds for abortions and naming federal judges who might overturn *Roe.* Yet as decisions mounted in which even Reagan- and Bush-appointed judges upheld *Roe*'s central conclusion that women possessed a private right of choice concerning their own bodies, even though that right had to be weighed against the responsibilities of the state and the rights of spouses and fetuses, the significance of the 1982 defeat became ever clearer. A constitutional amendment proposal might rally a political movement, but failure to come within reach of an Article V supermajority could cause a substantial interest group to decline in stature.[72]

Ronald Reagan again struck the pose of constitutional reformer on May 17, 1982. Acknowledging his support among conservative Christians, he revived an amendment permitting prayer in public schools. Reagan appeared to have identified another popular position on a constitutional issue. A simultaneous public opinion survey indicated that more than four-fifths of the public had heard of the prayer amendment, three-fourths of those could offer arguments for and against it, and 79 percent favored it. Only the intensity of public sentiment was in doubt. When asked to identify the most important setting for religious and spiritual development of children, 86 percent named the home, 10 percent the church, and only 2 percent the school.[73]

Over a decade had passed since the most recent congressional defeat of a school prayer amendment. However, Senator Jesse Helms had begun exploring ways to circumvent the need for amendment. In 1979 he sought to attach to the legislation creating the Department of Education a provision that would strip the Supreme Court of jurisdiction over the school prayer issue. The Senate shifted the Helms measure to another bill and then let it die. A similar maneuver in the House passed 255 to 122 but was eliminated in a conference committee. The following year the House sought to stipulate that the Department of Education not use its funds to prevent implementations of programs of voluntary prayer. Although Helms repeatedly failed in his efforts to remove the Court's jurisdiction over school prayer, he did return the issue to the fore just as Reagan campaigned for the presidency as a restorer of traditional values.

The day after Reagan's 1982 prayer amendment appeal, Strom Thurmond and Orrin Hatch offered to the Senate the president's measure, which stipulated: "Nothing in this Constitution should be construed to prohibit individual or group prayer in public schools or other public institutions. No person shall be required by the United States or by any state to participate in prayer."

When Senate hearings on the prayer amendment began two months later, the same issues that had stymied its proponents in the 1960s quickly resurfaced. How was the character of prayer to be determined? How could a right be protected not to conform to whatever prayer ritual was established? The proposed amendment sought to resolve these questions by declaring prayer to be voluntary, but objections persisted that locally dominant sects would determine the nature of prayers and that children of other faiths or no faith would feel pressure to conform. North Carolina congressman Stephen Neal testified that silent prayer or meditation avoided these problems and for that "we do not need a constitutional amendment."[74]

The Reagan administration displayed less interest in resolving the complex constitutional questions raised by the prayer issue than in clarifying its support for school prayer. An assistant attorney general appeared before the Senate Judiciary Committee to testify, "I really see nothing wrong whatsoever with teaching minorities that they ought to respect the views of the majority in matters of prayer and other things."[75] This attitude came to trouble even Orrin Hatch, a principal Senate sponsor of the administration's amendment. Hatch, whose Mormon church was dominant in his home state of Utah but a minority almost everywhere else, eventually confessed his lack of enthusiasm for the Reagan prayer amendment. He embraced a Judiciary Committee compromise approving a narrowly drawn amendment authorizing only silent prayer or meditation in public schools.[76] The committee version of the amendment went to the Senate where, in the absence of enthusiasm or consensus among potential supporters, it died.

The Reagan administration gained its immediate political objective of displaying solidarity with school prayer advocates. Although it achieved no constitutional change, it stirred the Court to distinguish between the First Amendment free expression clause, said to allow student-initiated private prayer and Bible reading in schools, and the establishment clause, ruled to prohibit school endorsement or sponsorship of such activities. As a political symbol a school prayer amendment retained vitality, especially among Christian conservatives. While a new generation of Republican leaders spoke enthusiastically in 1995 of a "religious equality amendment," concerns about minority rights and other issues that had arisen every time school prayer came to the fore since the *Engel v. Vitale* decision remained formidable obstacles to any consensus on constitutional change.[77]

Ronald Reagan repeatedly showed that he understood the political appeal of amendments, even those with little or no chance of adoption. His Article V proposals established a pattern that his admirers would continue to emulate. Again and again, he embraced amendments whose simple solutions to vexing problems were more readily apparent than their other constitutional consequences. For instance, in his 1984 State of the Union address, Reagan advocated the item veto, an idea that had been around since the time of Ulysses Grant.[78] Since 1945, opinion surveys had repeatedly demonstrated that, when innocuously presented as a means of permitting a president to strike elements without blocking an entire bill, the item veto won strong popular support.[79] Authorizing presidents to veto individual provisions of multifaceted legislation appealed particularly to proponents of federal budget reduction.

Item veto supporters were at least indifferent to the challenge the device posed to Congress and in some instances enthusiastic about it. Consolidated bills had evolved as a means to reach budgetary agreements, first in order to assemble legislative majorities and then for Congress to obtain executive acceptance of its desires in return for granting presidential wishes. Attaching to presidentially favored bills measures that would otherwise be vetoed and thus need two-thirds support for adoption gave Congress leverage in disputes with the executive branch. Allowing a president to eliminate individual items from an omnibus bill would make any spending initiative not favored by the president highly unlikely, sharply shifting the constitutional balance of authority toward the White House.

Orrin Hatch obliged Reagan by holding Senate hearings on the item veto in April 1984 but gave congressional critics ample opportunity to make the case against the amendment. Oregon Republican Mark Hatfield took the lead, calling the item veto "more power than a good man would want, and more than a bad man should have." He decried the proposed shift from presidential power to control overall spending to an ability to "virtually dictate spending priorities on individual programs and activities." Hatfield worried that "with this power the President can frustrate a decision of the Congress on any individual program, be it for political or ideological reasons or simply because of personal bias." Oklahoma congressman Mickey Edwards agreed, saying, "The powers that are surrendered to one President remain to be used by others. Give to this President the power to strike from appropriations bills the domestic programs he thinks we can do without, and another President will use the same power to strike from defense appropriation bills the weapons systems he thinks we can do without."[80] No member of Congress challenged Hatfield and Edwards's characterization of the issue as a nonpartisan question of constitutional balance versus excessive presidential power.

That a majority, much less two-thirds, of Congress would voluntarily agree to enhance presidential authority and diminish its own could hardly be expected. Therefore, to propose the item veto, as Reagan, his two successors, and the 1994 Republican Contract with America did, made less sense as constitutional reform with a realistic chance of adoption than as a political tactic to gain popular support. By 1995 advocates had given up on seeking an amendment and turned instead to various schemes to put an item veto into effect through ordinary legislation. Even if such a measure were agreed upon, two centuries of legislative practice and congressional-executive relations suggested that it would be unlikely to endure for long. Simple change in governmental arrangements could be reversed as legislative majorities shifted, and the Article V consensus required to render an item veto more permanent appeared nowhere to be found.[81]

Another amendment discussed during the Reagan presidency, though not directly addressed until Republicans held a House majority in 1995, would limit congressional terms much as the Twenty-second Amendment limited presidential terms. Advocacy of restricting the number of terms served by representatives and senators appeared to grow out of frustration, particularly among Republicans, at the acknowledged high reelection rate and assumed electoral advantages of incumbents, notably Democrats, in the post–New Deal era. Though Republicans promised in their 1994 campaign Contract with America to vote on a term-limits amendment, not all specifically promised to vote in favor of it. Once again an amendment proposal served best as a campaign device. On closer examination, the consequences of amendment eroded support. The specter of less-experienced legislators being more susceptible to the influence of bureaucrats and lobbyists, voters losing their right to return satisfactory incumbents, and newly empowered Republicans being soon obliged to surrender positions of power caused Republican enthusiasm to dwindle. Four different term-limit amendments were brought to the House floor in March 1995. Three were soundly defeated. Only the least restrictive gained even a slim majority of 227 to 204, and it came nowhere close to achieving an Article V consensus. The defeat of the term-limit amendment was the first setback for the new Republican House leadership, a reminder that risks as well as benefits accompanied the use of amendment proposals as electoral campaign appeals.[82]

THE FINAL EXAMPLE of the 1980s politics of symbolism initiating efforts for constitutional reform was perhaps the most clear-cut. The quintessential American symbol, the United States flag, became its centerpiece. In a drive that some observers regarded as a patriotic crusade and others as a crass political maneuver playing on the overwhelming unpopularity of political protests involving flag burning, President George Bush and a phalanx of conservative members of Congress campaigned for a constitutional amendment to offer extraordinary protection to the national flag. The resulting controversy reflected the cultural divisions in the country. It also demonstrated the manner in which political leaders had learned to appeal to their constituents by proposing amendments.

The Supreme Court recognized the status of the American flag as a national symbol during World War II. The Court at first ruled that the state had the authority to compel school children to salute and pledge allegiance to the flag, notwithstanding claims by Jehovah's Witnesses that such rules violated their constitutionally protected religious freedom not to worship secular symbols.[83] Later in the war when tensions over loyalty had subsided, the Court reversed itself and acknowledged the right to abstain from flag pledges on religious grounds. Justice Robert Jackson, writing for the Court, declared, "If there is any fixed star in our constitutional constellation, it is that no official, high or petty, can prescribe what shall be orthodox in politics, nationalism, religion, or other matters of opinion or force citizens to confess by word or act their faith therein."[84]

A quarter century later attention shifted from the withholding of gestures of patriotic fealty to the national emblem to acts of disdain for it. In the midst of the unrest provoked by civil rights agitation and the Vietnam War, disfiguring, destroying, or showing contempt for the flag became acts of political expression. The Court, regarding such matters as symbolic speech protected by the First Amendment, overturned convictions of individuals for burning the flag, wearing it sewn to the seat of jeans, or altering it through the attachment of peace symbols.[85] Veterans' and conservative groups expressed acute unhappiness with such treatment of the flag, but years passed before calls arose for constitutional action.

During the 1988 presidential campaign, Republican candidate George Bush, in the midst of what at the time appeared to be a tight race with Democrat Michael Dukakis, criticized the Massachusetts governor's veto of a bill to require schoolchildren to pledge allegiance to the flag. Bush's attack played on popular sensibilities and ignored Dukakis's explanation that he felt obliged to heed the forty-year-old Supreme Court ruling against such requirements. Bush persisted, traveling to a New Jersey flag factory and declaring that voters should never doubt his love of the flag. This use of patriotic symbols appeared to help Bush overcome Dukakis's early lead and win a convincing victory.

Five months after Bush took office, the Supreme Court ruled on another flag case, this one involving a Texas law prohibiting "desecration of a venerated object." Gregory Lee Johnson and others had set an American flag on fire and chanted, "America, the red, white, and blue, we spit on you," at a political demonstration in Dallas during the 1984 Republican National Convention. The Court, by a 5-to-4 margin, agreed with the Texas Court of Criminal Appeals that the law was unconstitutional because Johnson's action involved protected symbolic expression. Justice William Brennan, writing for the majority, held, "If there is a bedrock principle underlying the First Amendment, it is that the Government may not prohibit the expression of an idea simply because society finds the idea itself offensive or disagreeable. . . . We do not consecrate the flag by punishing its desecration, for in doing so we dilute the freedom that this cherished emblem represents."[86]

Within a day of the _Johnson_ decision's announcement, the Senate, by a 97-to-3 vote, adopted a resolution expressing "profound disappointment."[87] Not to be outdone, Bush, in a White House news conference and a hastily arranged speech at the Iwo Jima Marine Memorial, called for a constitutional amendment to overturn the decision. The right to protest government action must be protected, he said, but flag burning "goes too far."[88] The proposed amendment would declare, "The Congress and the states shall have the power to prohibit the physical desecration of the flag of the United States." The Democratic leadership of Congress found itself caught between fear that opposing such a popular position might invite another severe defeat and distaste for action that would, thoughtful conservatives as well as liberals warned, alter the Bill of Rights.[89]

During the initial explosion of outrage over the _Johnson_ decision, Democratic leaders agreed to hold hearings in both House and Senate. By mid-July, as House hearings began, passions already appeared to be cooling while doubts grew about the wisdom of amendment. Still, fears lingered that opposing the flag-burning prohibition would be seen as unpatriotic and bear harmful political consequences. After four days of testimony, the House Judiciary Committee recommended a statute levying a $1,000 fine and a one-year prison sentence on "whoever knowingly mutilates, defaces, burns, maintains on the floor or ground, or tramples upon any flag of the United States." Senator Joseph Biden, chair of the Senate Judiciary Committee, crafted the flag-burning statute as an alternative to an amendment and presented it as a device to protect the flag physically without blocking political protest. Supported by Speaker Thomas Foley as a means to avert an amendment, the statute won House approval, 380 to 38, on September 12. Three weeks later the Senate, having conducted its own hearings, added "physically defiles" to the list of offenses and adopted the statute 91 to 9. The House quickly concurred in the changes. Despite widespread expectation that the measure would not survive Court review, it allowed nervous politicians to claim they had protected the flag yet defended the First Amendment.[90]

Although he signed the flag-burning statute, Bush disdained it as inadequate and continued to press for an amendment. Support for further action quickly eroded, however, as Congress perceived that the public had lost interest. Two Republican senators, John Danforth of Missouri and Warren Rudman of New Hampshire, reversed their initial endorsements of an amendment; Danforth proclaimed his earlier support for the amendment "just plain wrong," a "mistake of the heart." On October 19, the amendment carried by only 51 to 48, fifteen votes short of the necessary two-thirds. For the moment, the politically sensitive issue was put to rest, or so it appeared.[91]

The flag-burning statute faced challenges as soon as it took effect. In front of the Seattle Post Office and on the Capitol steps in Washington (where Gregory Lee Johnson took part in the demonstration and complained because he was not among those arrested), flags were set afire.[92] In both cases federal district judges quickly ruled the flag protection act unconstitutional.[93] The Supreme Court expedited an appeal, heard arguments on May 14, 1990, and on June 11 ruled that, like the Texas law, the federal statute "suppresses expression out of concern for its likely communicative effect." Every justice voted as he or she had in *Texas v. Johnson*. Once again Justice Brennan announced for the Court majority that the First Amendment fully protected flag burning. "Punishing desecration of the flag," he concluded, "dilutes the very freedom that makes this emblem so revered and worth revering."[94] Even though he dissented from the Court's ruling, Justice John Paul Stevens wrote disparagingly of "leaders who seem to advocate compulsory worship of the flag . . . or who seem to manipulate the symbol of national purpose into a pretext for partisan disputes about meaner ends."[95]

After the Supreme Court for a second time declared punishment of flag burning unconstitutional, flag protection advocates felt their only option was to seek constitutional revision. No political benefit derived from remaining silent. Republican political strategists expressed delight with the opportunity to use the flag as "a defining issue" in forthcoming contests against Democratic opponents. Within an hour of the decision's announcement, Bush again called for an amendment. Congressional leaders, caught once more in a familiar dilemma, agreed to prompt hearings and a floor vote on an amendment.[96] One uncomfortable congressman acknowledged the political risks of resisting amendment demands. "I saw what happened to Michael Dukakis," said Illinois congressman Richard Durbin, "so I understand the flag issues have real visceral appeal."[97]

Unexpectedly, flag burning failed to generate the political heat in 1990 that it had produced a year earlier. Instead a typical reaction was that of the president of the American Bar Association, who quickly asserted that a flag protection amendment "would erode the most basic right of freedom of expression and create a dangerous precedent."[98] Within a week nervous congressmen were reporting that the anticipated public outcry against the latest Court ruling had not materialized while arguments regarding the need to defend the Bill of Rights had been effective. Senate hearings elicited testimony that for the most part urged caution in tampering with the Constitution.[99] Democratic leaders quickly brought the amendment resolution to the House floor bearing a negative recommendation from the Judiciary Subcommittee on Civil and Constitutional Rights and no recommendation (after a close 19-to-17 vote) from the full Judiciary Committee.[100] An effort by amendment supporters to delay a vote was easily thwarted, after which the amendment resolution fell far short of two-thirds on a vote of 254 to 177. Five days later the Senate likewise defeated the amendment on a 58-to-42 vote.[101] Not even the president, who had displayed such concern for the flag, pursued the issue further, and the furor over constitutional reform to prohibit flag desecration promptly faded away.

Patriotic symbolism reemerged as a constitutional issue upon the 1994 election of a Republican congressional majority. In spring 1995 another flag amendment was thrust forward by Republicans responding to appeals from fraternal, religious, and military veterans' organizations. A series of representatives rose on the House floor to demand special protection for the national emblem, brushing off complaints that vague terminology "would open a Pandora's box of litigation" and undermine First Amendment free speech protections. The most cynical commentators characterized the amendment as a ploy to distract veterans while the new Congress enacted severe reductions in their benefits. Such arguments had no effect, as the House on June 28 approved the flag desecration amendment 312 to 120, with Republicans voting 219 to 12 in its favor and Democrats dividing 97 to 107.[102]

Earlier in the year in its defeat of the balanced budget amendment, the Senate had given evidence that it was less inflamed with passion for constitutional reform than the House of Representatives with its seventy-three freshmen Republican members. Nevertheless, voting against the flag desecration amendment appeared to carry substantial political risks. Republican leaders delayed a vote for more than five months while they sought to enlist the requisite support. The amendment's main champion, Judiciary Committee chairman Orrin Hatch, tried to overcome objections by offering to eliminate concurrent state enforcement power, but the ploy failed. Democratic senators John Glenn of Ohio and John Kerry of Nebraska, whose distinguished military service shielded them from political attacks on their patriotism, spoke out forcefully against the amendment as a threat to the First Amendment.[103] Equally important, four Republicans, led by Senator Mitch McConnell of Kentucky, joined the opposition to the amendment. Flag burning was not a serious enough problem to justify action that would "rip the fabric of the Constitution at its very center," declared McConnell.[104] On December 12, the Senate rejected the flag amendment on a vote of 63 to 37, the closest vote to date but still three votes shy of a two-thirds majority. Unhappy spokespersons for the Citizens' Flag Alliance, able to point to public opinion polls showing 79 percent approval of an amendment, vowed, "We'll be back."[105]

For the moment senatorial caution about constitutional change had again prevailed over popular sentiment. But once more legislators found it awkward to vote against an appealing symbolic amendment, even one with problematic consequences. As with the balanced budget amendment, senators appeared reluctant to support a controversial constitutional measure when their vote might be crucial; once the measure's defeat was assured, voting for it became easier. The extent of reservations about the flag desecration and balanced budget amendments may well have been greater than the vote tally reflected. Nevertheless, the appearance of near-success encouraged amendment proponents to renew their quests. In an era when complicated explanations for leaving governmental arrangements undisturbed tended to attract less sympathy than demands for change that could be expressed in a political campaign slogan or on an automobile bumper sticker, it seemed likely that even repeatedly defeated proposals of the 1980s and 1990s would be put forth again.

THE AMENDMENT PROPOSALS coming to the fore in the 1980s made good sense to their advocates, horrified their most staunch opponents, but failed to stir deep mass enthusiasm. Seldom, if ever, did a suggested amendment have a serious prospect of success. The political posturing that seemed so central to amendment undertakings offended both conservative and liberal admirers of American constitutionalism. The Reagan administration's early burst of amendment proposals provoked journalist George Will to write that the infrequency of amendment "pleases true conservatives to whom constitutional tinkering is an insect in the salad of life."[106] At the end of the decade, Senate Democratic majority leader George Mitchell, reacting to George Bush's endorsement of a flag-burning amendment in addition to his previously announced support for amendments to allow school prayer, require a balanced budget, create an item veto, and ban abortion, said, "One of the president's policies which I find most disturbing is the haste with which he is prepared to endorse amendments to the Constitution."[107] Partisanship may have been a factor in Mitchell's remark, but not so in Will's. Together they suggest notable discomfort with the almost casual willingness of contemporary politicians to suggest fundamental change in the design of government as a means of dealing with specific public policy issues. If the proponents of change were as serious as they seemed, they would appear to have little regard for existing constitutional arrangements; if they were not, the Constitution had become, in their eyes, little more than a dramatic prop in a quest to attract attention and popular support.

19

Amendments in Constitutional
Thought and Practice

A strange recapitulation of almost the entire sweep of U.S. constitutional amendment history occurred in 1992. An amendment resurfaced that had been first offered in the late eighteenth century, the era when the notion first emerged that written constitutions should be open to formal revision by, as George Washington put it, "an explicit and authentic act of the whole people." A constitutional amendment denying Congress authority to adjust its own salary was only the second it ever approved under Article V of the Constitution. Of well over 10,000 amendment resolutions set before Congress in the course of two centuries, this measure became one of only thirty-three to receive two-thirds approval from both the Senate and the House of Representatives. Even more distinctive, it remained one of only seven among those thirty-three not promptly ratified by three-fourths of the states. Two hundred and three years after its initial appearance, however, in an era when amendments had come to carry great symbolic weight, the Twenty-seventh Amendment gained the endorsement of the necessary proportion of the states. Congress then quickly cut through decades of debate over ratification procedure to certify the propriety of its incorporation into the Constitution. An amendment drafted by James Madison and approved by the First Congress in 1789 finally entered the Constitution five years after the bicentennial of the 1787 Philadelphia convention.

Ironically, this extraordinary Twenty-seventh Amendment drew less notice at the moment of its ratification than perhaps any other constitutional reform. The presidential election taking place simultaneously was much more immediate and exciting as well as, at least on its face, significant. The contest over whether George Bush, Bill Clinton, or Ross Perot would lead the nation for the next four years seemed vastly more important than whether or not members of Congress should have the power to raise their own salaries. Not surprisingly, few Americans even realized in spring 1992 that their nation's fundamental law had been altered. Those who did notice might well have wondered whether constitutional amending bore any importance. At most, the new feature of the fundamental law would only briefly delay until after the next biennial election increases in legislative compensation. In no respect did the new amendment produce revolutionary change in the structure or function of U.S. government.

A curiosity in its own right, the Twenty-seventh Amendment raised basic questions about the amending process itself. The fact that the work of James Madison and the First Congress could become effective after a lapse of more than 200 years gave an immediacy as well as a new dimension to the normally abstract question of what hold eighteenth-century constitutional ideas and practices retained over American government by the end of the twentieth century. Certainly the completion of the Twenty-seventh Amendment gave fresh meaning to William Faulkner's observation, "The past isn't dead, it isn't even past."

The Twenty-seventh Amendment, regardless of its anomalous nature or perhaps because of it, provides a good reason to reflect more generally on the role of constitutional amendment in the political culture of the United States. The process of amendment as well as formal constitutional changes themselves and, conversely, failed attempts to achieve amendment have notably shaped the nation's history. Article V bears a substantial responsibility for what some observers would laud as the stability and others castigate as the conservatism of American government.

THE FOUNDERS BELIEVED the members of Congress should receive a federal salary in order to avoid the model of the unpaid British Parliament that either limited officeholding to the wealthy or, scarcely better, allowed constituents to provide a stipend that could influence the judgment of the representative. The Philadelphia convention manifested less concern with the potential for abuse of salaries than with their absence or placement in state hands.[1] Attention shifted when states considered the Constitution. A bar on Congress's adjusting its own salary appeared among the long list of measures to restrain the new federal government proposed in state ratification conventions. Both the Virginia and New York conventions, two of the most important forums for debate over adoption of the new fundamental law, endorsed such a measure.[2] James Madison, initially reluctant to amend the Philadelphia document, became persuaded that it was vital to the successful launching of the new government. Although incorporating the salary adjustment ban into his list of amendments, he considered it a matter of relatively little importance. Madison doubted that legislatures would abuse the power to set their own compensation but conceded, "There is a seeming impropriety in leaving any set of men without control to put their hand into the public coffers, to take out money to put in their own pockets."[3] The principal objection to the measure, offered by Theodore Sedgwick of Massachusetts, was that "designing men" might keep congressional wages so low as to prevent men of ability but limited means from serving in Congress. Nevertheless, Madison's view that the amendment was probably unnecessary but that many people desired it carried the day.[4]

A mandate that increases in legislators' pay could not take effect until after an intervening election became the second of twelve amendments that Congress endorsed in September 1789.[5] The first state legislature to consider ratifying the twelve, New Jersey, singled out the pay raise amendment for rejection. Whether New Jersey legislators regarded the measure as a hobble on representative democracy, an undue restriction on legislative authority, an unwelcome obstacle to self-aggrandizement, a matter not appropriate to the Constitution, or objectionable for other reasons remains unclear. In any case, New Hampshire, New York, Pennsylvania, and Rhode Island soon followed suit in declining to approve it.[6]

Rather than creating the appearance of an unstable and thus unattractive Constitution, the availability of the amending process and its immediate use to adopt the Bill of Rights enhanced confidence in the new system of government. For instance, the reassurances that the package of amendments offered overcame Rhode Island's general resistance to the Constitution. In May 1790 a state convention ratified the Constitution, and only thirteen days later Rhode Island's assembly ratified eleven of the twelve proposed amendments. The proposed restriction on congressional pay increases once again stood alone in defeat.[7] Although the reason for the singular rejection is not altogether clear, Rhode Island's long-standing radical tradition and its resistance to elitism suggest that it would have been responsive to the Sedgwick argument against a device that might be used to discourage persons of modest means from serving in Congress. In any case, Rhode Island's level of comfort with the Constitution clearly increased as it exercised its right to select which amendments it wished to see added to the federal frame of government.

The proposed second amendment, alone among the twelve, did not appear within reach of enactment by 1790. Its fortunes declined further as the overall pace of ratification slowed. The Massachusetts and Connecticut assemblies, supportive of the individual rights provisions, bogged down in disputes over the first two amendments, and the two legislatures ended up taking no action at all. Once the amendments they unquestionably supported had been adopted, they considered further ratification unnecessary. Meanwhile, Virginia's upper and lower houses divided and proved unable to reach a decision, and Georgia refused its endorsement, regarding the amendments as undesirable. When Vermont ratified the federal Constitution in

January 1791 and the twelve amendments ten months later, it brought ten amendments within one state of ratification. The pay raise ban remained far short of the goal, however. Finally, on December 15 the Virginia House of Delegates ratified all twelve amendments. The action installed ten of the twelve amendments in the Constitution.

Except in Kentucky, further discussion of amendment ratification simply ceased. After embracing the Constitution to qualify for statehood in 1792, the Kentucky legislature endorsed the twelve congressionally approved amendments as one of its first orders of business as a state.[8] Still, its action left the pay raise amendment well below the Article V threshold. Kentucky's ratification appears not to have been officially reported to the Congress and therefore was almost totally overlooked.[9] It is difficult to imagine a clearer indication of how undefined the new process of constitutional change remained, particularly away from the center of national government, not to mention how imperfectly the Article V system functioned in its early years. No wonder the pay raise amendment slid so rapidly into obscurity.

Eighty-one years after Kentucky acted, the Ohio legislature rediscovered the 1789 amendment proposal. In obtaining statehood in 1803, Ohio merely embraced the Constitution as it stood, ignoring the unratified amendments proposed fourteen years earlier. In this respect Ohio replicated the pattern of every other state that entered the Union after Kentucky. In 1873, however, Ohioans became angry about a perceived congressional "salary grab." Just before its adjournment in March, the Forty-second Congress not only raised the compensation of future senators and representatives from $5,000 per year to $7,500 but also granted itself the same salary retroactively. The Ohio legislature quickly determined to ratify the pay raise amendment as one of several expressions of its displeasure. Questions arose as to whether ratification was still possible eight decades after the pay raise amendment had been brought forth, but such technical problems hardly deterred the disgruntled legislators.[10] The issue of how long an amendment continued to be eligible for ratification remained unresolved since no other state followed Ohio's lead. With no claim advanced that the amendment's ratification had been completed, no need or basis was thought to exist for a legal challenge to the validity of Ohio's action.

Over a century later displeasure with Congress, never totally absent from the American political conversation, surged again, fueled by perceptions that senators and representatives inappropriately earned much more than those whom they represented. Congress, given members' responsibility to maintain two residences, travel back and forth from their district to Washington on a frequent basis, and carry out endless public duties, paid itself a good

but hardly munificent salary during most of its history. During the inflationary 1970s and 1980s, it began to grant itself substantial increases to keep
pace with rising costs. Annual congressional salaries, which had been
$30,000 from 1965 to 1969 then rose to $42,500, inched up to $44,500 in
1975 before jumping to $57,500 in 1977. During each Congress of the
1980s emoluments increased significantly, reaching $96,600 for representa-
tives and $98,400 for senators by 1990. Then in the first Congress of the
new decade, those salaries leaped to $125,100.

As congressional wages climbed, so did interest in Madison's antique
amendment. No concern was manifested for Theodore Sedgwick's argument
that good salaries were needed to ensure that able individuals could serve in
Congress without being wealthy themselves or beholden to wealthy benefac-
tors. In 1978, the year that extension of the time limit for ratification of the
equal rights amendment was being debated, the Wyoming state legislature
provided the first ratification of the pay raise amendment in 105 years, declaring that Congress "upon proposing that amendment did not place any
time limitation on its final adoption." Furthermore, the resolution stated,
Congress had recently voted itself pay raises in which "the percentage increase in direct compensation and benefits was at such a high level, as to set
a bad example to the general population." Wyoming's act was as iconoclas-
tic as Ohio's and almost equally noninfluential, perhaps because at first it
followed the example of Kentucky. Notice of the Wyoming legislature's ratification action does not appear to have been officially sent to the federal
government until March 1985, seven years later.[11]

Not until five years after Wyoming endorsed the pay raise amendment
did a serious, coordinated campaign to secure its ratification get under way.
Then in 1982 Gregory Watson, a twenty-year-old University of Texas student, learned about Madison's unratified amendments while writing an un-
dergraduate paper on the equal rights amendment. Watson reasoned that
without a time limit on ratification such as ERA carried, the pay raise
amendment was still alive. At first he could not even convince his instructor.
Nevertheless, Watson began sending letters to state legislatures across the
country, calling attention to the amendment. He argued that it was both
possible and appropriate to ratify it. "The American people want a Congress
that is honest, that has integrity," he declared. "This amendment is one vehicle by which some degree of decorum can be restored."[12] Other voices, some
from within the Congress, joined in the campaign.[13]

State legislators began realizing that a vote to ratify the pay raise amendment was a painless way to demonstrate their fiscal responsibility. No program had to be cut, no service had to be reduced, no self-sacrifice was

involved. Discussion of two crucial but potentially embarrassing issues, the cost of campaigning and the operation of the current system of political fund-raising, could be avoided. Best of all, those affected by the pay raise limitation, members of Congress, would have a hard time exacting political retribution. In 1983 Maine ratified, and in 1984 Colorado did likewise. In its resolution of ratification the Colorado legislature declared that the amendment was still "meaningful and needed as part of the United States Constitution and that the present political, social, and economic conditions are the same or even more demanding today than they were when the proposed amendment was submitted for its adoption."[14]

Resentment of federal government spending and the allure of a simple means of chastising the people immediately responsible fueled growing interest in Madison's long-dormant proposal. As support in Congress for the balanced budget amendment began to wane, state legislative enthusiasm for the congressional pay raise amendment accelerated. In 1985 five legislatures ratified; three more followed suit in 1986, four in 1987, and three in 1988.[15] As had been the case with the wave of child labor amendment ratifications in the 1930s, the number of virtually simultaneous new ratifications of Madison's amendment provided substantial evidence that a broad desire existed for this constitutional change.

Idaho voters in a November 1988 referendum overwhelmingly endorsed the amendment, prompting legislative ratification and demonstrating in the only such test that popular support existed for the amendment. Ten years earlier, in the midst of the equal rights amendment controversy, the Idaho legislature had resolved that referendum approval must precede any ratification of a federal amendment. Designed to shape rather than overrule state legislative action, the Idaho approach varied slightly from that of Ohio sixty years earlier. Nevertheless, it appeared to ignore the Supreme Court's *Hawke v. Smith* and *U.S. v. Sprague* rulings that no limits could be placed on a congressional directive regarding Article V's ratification method. Disregarding the adverse recommendation of its own attorney general, Idaho proceeded with its referendum.[16] At least in Idaho, mounting eagerness to place constitutional decisions directly in the hands of the electorate mattered more than amending precedents.

Idaho was one of six states to ratify the pay raise amendment in 1989. By the end of that year supporters claimed a total of thirty-two ratifications. Had they known of Kentucky's 1792 ratification, they could have claimed thirty-three. Reacting to the impressive recent growth in the number of ratifications, Congress in 1989 adopted a statutory prohibition against same-term salary increases, an act designed to render constitutional amendment unnecessary. Nevertheless, the appeal to state legislators of voting for the Madison amendment appeared undiminished. After two more states ratified in 1990 and one in 1991, five states acted in the first week of May 1992 to more than complete the process. Michigan's action on May 7 was declared to be the thirty-eighth and final necessary ratification. If the Kentucky ratification had been recognized, however, the Twenty-seventh Amendment would have been declared completed two days earlier with the approval of Missouri.[17]

Discerning a pattern in the ratifications of the Twenty-seventh Amendment beyond the simple and obvious hostility to Congress that arose during the 1980s remains difficult. Notable among the nine states that did not ratify were several with large populations, full-time state legislatures, and Democratic majorities. Yet the small, conservative-leaning states of Mississippi, Nebraska, and Washington and the small liberal states of Rhode Island and Hawaii joined the large states of California, New York, Pennsylvania, and Massachusetts in declining to approve the amendment. Perhaps most interesting is that four states, Massachusetts, Rhode Island, New York, and Pennsylvania, that could have ratified in 1790 still chose not to do so more than two centuries later. Thus the pay raise amendment still could not achieve three-fourths endorsement among the original thirteen states despite the passage of time and the change of political circumstances.

The ratification of a two-century-old amendment was particularly remarkable considering when it occurred. Only ten years earlier the equal rights amendment had been declared no longer eligible for adoption a mere decade after being approved by Congress. Not surprisingly, questions posed during Reconstruction regarding the pay raise amendment's continuing viability arose again a century later. Why, if the pay raise amendment's vitality was already in doubt in 1873, was it installed into the Constitution 119 years later?

Article V specified no time limit on ratification of a constitutional amendment by the states. The drafters of Article V left no evidence that they thought in terms of restricting the rights of states to endorse at any time constitutional change approved by Congress. The sovereign right of the people to sanction constitutional change through the agency of a state legislature or convention was fundamental and unqualified. Before Warren Harding's 1917 attempt to derail the national prohibition amendment, no amendment that the Congress proposed ever contained any limitation. The ratification time limit issue arose only because clever politicians sought, in effect, to vote both yes and no on constitutional change. The stratagem was shrewd in theory but disastrous in practice, judged not only by the failure of Harding's maneuver but by the subsequent role of time-limit considerations in distracting attention from the substance of proposals such as the child labor and District of Columbia representation amendments and, above all, the equal rights amendment.

In 1922 the Supreme Court ruled that Congress possessed the power to set a limit on the prohibition amendment's ratification to ensure that states would take contemporaneous action. The notion of ratification within a confined time span being an essential characteristic of the amendment process was, like other aspects of amendment thought, a twentieth-century innovation not explicit in the thinking of the Founders. The idea of contemporaneity that arose with Warren Harding received its first judicial defense in Justice Van Devanter's *Dillon v. Gloss* decision. The Court's thinking appeared to be shaped by a sense of obligation to uphold the Eighteenth Amendment just overwhelmingly endorsed for addition to the Constitution.[18]

A later Court, bruised by its politically unpopular New Deal rulings, retreated somewhat from a dogmatic defense of ratification time limits. In the 1939 child labor amendment case of *Coleman v. Miller,* the Court held that the issue of whether widely separated ratifications of an amendment without a specific time limit were valid amounted to a political rather than a judicial question. In other words, certification of ratification was a matter for Congress, not the Court, to decide.[19] The difficulty for Congress of rendering a negative decision, in light of ratification by three-fourths of the states and absent a time limit, would not be revealed until the pay raise amendment resurfaced.

Most but not all amendments after national prohibition contained a time limit, either in the language of the amendment itself or, beginning in the 1960s, in the enabling resolution. Constitutionally no time limit was required, but increasingly one came to be expected as the notion took hold that ratifications always had been and therefore always should be contemporaneous. Opponents objected, for instance, to the absence of a ratification time limit from the proposed equal rights amendment. Without giving the matter much thought, ERA sponsors agreed, much to their later regret, to a seven-year limit. Even when extended thirty-nine months, this limit erected a fatal stumbling block to the ERA. Its expiration in June 1982, however, drew attention to the four nineteenth-century amendments approved by Congress, yet never approved by a sufficient number of states, that might still be ratified.[20] The concerted campaign to ratify the pay raise amendment began the same year.

In May 1992 when ratifications by three-fourths of the states (actually forty or four-fifths, not even counting Kentucky) were filed with the

Archivist of the United States, Congress, according to the *Coleman* ruling, possessed the authority to determine the validity of ratifications spread over two centuries. The decision had to be made against the backdrop of recently revealed irregularities in the operation of the House of Representatives bank as well as a general atmosphere of suspicion about political ethics. The situation inspired political posturing worthy of a body builders' competition. Recognizing that the pay raise amendment represented an outburst of anger at the Congress, that its rejection on a technicality after endorsement by so many states would be likely to provoke greater outrage, and that in any case it would only briefly delay pay raises, the House by 414 to 3 and the Senate by 99 to 0 declared the Twenty-seventh Amendment properly adopted.[21]

At the same time that it gave final sanction to the Twenty-seventh Amendment, the Senate received a reminder from former majority leader Robert Byrd that several other long-standing unratified amendments still technically remained before the states.[22] These included Madison's first amendment limiting the size of congressional districts to 50,000 residents, the 1810 amendment banning citizens from accepting foreign titles, the 1861 amendment guaranteeing the continuation of slavery in states where it then existed, and the 1924 child labor amendment. The West Virginia Democrat offered a resolution declaring the old amendments no longer eligible for ratification, but Byrd's proposal failed to stir his colleagues' interest. No action was taken to ensure that the Twenty-seventh Amendment would be the last of its kind.[23] None of the other amendments without stipulated ratification time limits seemed even a remote possibility for adoption, but then neither had the pay raise amendment for most of the nineteenth and twentieth centuries.

The substantive content of the proposal, not procedural precedents, thwarted challenges to the pay raise amendment and secured its final passage. The amendment could have easily been contested constitutionally but not politically, especially in the context of the moment. In failing to take action against the other old unratified amendments, the Congress appeared to assume that their substance gave them no likelihood of being likewise ratified. The bestowing of titles on American citizens, as Great Britain did with former presidents Ronald Reagan and George Bush, provoked mild amusement rather than outrage. Slavery had few serious proponents after the Civil War, and the Thirteenth Amendment specifically countermanded the 1861 proposal anyway. Child labor had been dealt with by other means. Congress ignored the possibility that anger against it could rise to the point that the public would consider ratifying Madison's first amendment. If another Gregory Watson–style movement got under way, Congress might find it awkward and embarrassing, if not impossible, to block the replacement of the existing body by a very different legislature. If constituencies were limited to 50,000 citizens, the nature of republican government in a nation of 250 million people would change dramatically. A representative would bear a very different relationship to 50,000 constituents than to the present average of nearly 600,000 and to 4,999 colleagues than to the current 434. Despite its experience with the pay raise amendment, Congress remained unconcerned that the other 1789 amendment could gain belated rapid state ratification. Probably they were correct, but the possibility that they were not was evident in the odd history of the Twenty-seventh Amendment. Most political leaders and the nation in general continued to be only vaguely aware of the Article V process and its use over two centuries. The history of formal change in the U.S. Constitution deserved closer attention.

THE CURIOUS SAGA of the Twenty-seventh Amendment raised anew some old questions about the amending process set forth in Article V of the Constitution. Although the issue of whether the procedures involved inherent time limits attracted most of the attention, the controversial Madison amendment also drew notice to the overall terms of Article V.[24] In particular, the pay raise measure renewed discussion of whether the Founders had established an amending method that was too difficult or too easy. Proponents of unattainable reforms and critics of changes achieved had disputed the merits of Article V since the nineteenth century. The lapse of more than two centuries in completing a relatively simple reform highlighted the obstacles to constitutional change, but at the same time the rapid, almost unnoticed adoption of the long-neglected amendment suggested that perhaps procedural difficulties had been exaggerated.

The notion of formal amendment, like the concept of written constitutionalism itself, was rooted in the idea that the sovereign people granted governments their power. While this bequest involved the right to make laws binding on all by the decision of a simple momentary majority, it did not include the right to change the parameters of governmental authority by the same means. A higher degree of consensus on the part of the sovereign people, or at least their elected representatives, was to be necessary to set or alter fundamental rules of government conduct. The community must be in general agreement regarding the system of governance to which it was committing itself. By 1776 American political thinkers had embraced this core constitutional belief, but they remained undecided about the proper means of achieving the desired consensus on the frame of government. Their first inclination was to require simple majority agreement within representative bodies designing constitutional mechanisms, the Confederation Congress and state assemblies, but unanimity among those bodies when they gave sanction to the establishment or alteration of a constitution.

The Constitution-makers of 1787 reached different conclusions. They held that a majority of delegates to a specially elected convention had to agree in order to bind each state to the new Constitution. For this fundamental act of self-government, permitting officials with general republican powers of legislation to make the decision was insufficient. The equation for further constitutional reform underwent additional revision. The Founders desired a rigorous but not unreachable standard for altering the terms of government. A new balance, more demanding in some respects and less strict in others, was established for achieving amendment. A greater degree of consensus for proposing amendments, two-thirds of Congress or of states seeking a constitutional convention, would be required to initiate reform, while a less than universal, although still very substantial level of agreement of three-fourths of the states could give sanction to changes.

The 1787 amending formula rested squarely on the belief that a constitution was a higher law requiring much more than simple majoritarian sanction and not to be undertaken lightly. At the same time, a few dissenters should not be able to prevent substantial supermajorities from determining how they wished to design and limit government. The critical factor in Article V was its definition of the size of supermajority necessary and sufficient to approve amendment. The two-thirds requirement was the most rigorous standard set for congressional action. Three-fourths state approval was even more demanding; it represented the highest level of consensus established anywhere in the Constitution. Both standards reflected the Founders' vision of federalism. General agreement on the basic structures and functions of central government was necessary, they believed, and objection by one-quarter of the states ought to be able to prevent changes in fundamental arrangements. They concluded, however, that smaller, isolated protestations should not be able to block action by a dominant consensus. Establishing lesser or greater consensus requirements would not only have altered the amending mechanism, it would have changed the fundamental character of American federalism.

In designing Article V, the Philadelphia convention not only gave respect to federalism; it also repeatedly acknowledged the ultimate authority of the people by devising mechanisms to give them a voice in constitutional matters. The Founders limited the independence of republican elites by ensuring that legislative assemblies could be circumvented by conventions. The power of the federal Congress was shackled by granting two-thirds of the states the right to force a constitutional convention. Early in the twentieth century state petitions for a convention to propose an amendment mandating direct election of senators pushed a reluctant Senate to endorse that significant reform itself. Other petitions later led Congress to give serious consideration to a reapportionment amendment in the 1960s and a balanced budget amendment in the 1980s.

With a different sort of convention, one with the specific but narrow power to ratify or reject proposed amendments, the Founders likewise restrained state legislatures. Congress was allowed to direct that amendments be submitted for ratification to state conventions rather than legislatures. As the conventions that ratified the Twenty-first Amendment eventually demonstrated, this device stood much closer to direct democracy than to republican decisionmaking. The electorate could choose convention delegates on the basis of their position on a single issue rather than leaving a critical constitutional decision to their judgment. Had the Founders required the use of convention ratification with every amendment as they had with the Constitution itself, this commitment to direct popular sanction would have been stronger, but the presence of the ratifying convention option in Article V does manifest the Founders' endorsement of popular participation in constitutional decisionmaking.

The two separate and distinct convention devices were not employed frequently. Indeed the convention method of ratification was used only once, and though a convention to propose amendments appeared several times on the verge of being convened, it never was in the two centuries after its singular employment in Philadelphia in 1787. Yet the mere availability of these alternative amending methods could move disinclined legislatures to act and thus render amendment more feasible. The apprehension aroused by the prospect of a convention empowered to propose changes in the Constitution testifies to the conservatism of the American political culture. While the work of the Philadelphia convention came to be greatly admired, confidence that its basic tenets would survive another such gathering appeared notably absent. When proposals to limit the power of conventions were confronted by the prospect that such bodies, once in session, could overturn any confinement, willingness to countenance this approach to amendment quickly faded. Not even the knowledge that convention-endorsed reforms would require state ratification could persuade the political culture that the possible rewards of a convention empowered to reconsider the Constitution outweighed its risks. Ratification conventions posed no such threat to topple a whole constitutional system, but they too were avoided. This neglect may have stemmed less from insecurity than from a simple lack of familiarity

with convention ratification, but it too marked the reluctance of later generations of political leaders to employ the Founders' devices for obtaining the
most direct possible popular involvement in constitutional revision.

Once the Constitution received popular sanction in ratifying conventions, the smooth and widely applauded use of Article V's most republican
method a dozen times in the next fifteen years fostered a lasting preference
for that approach to reform. The belief rapidly became entrenched that an
adequate amending mechanism had been established. Alternatives to amendment by congressional proposal and state legislative ratification, if not forgotten altogether, came to be thought of as inferior. At the same time, the
widespread conviction that a satisfactory Constitution had been created
tempered any felt need for frequent further amendment. Most problems of
constitutional interpretation and application could be resolved judicially.
Problems beyond the scope of judicial review also lay beyond the reach of
amendment built on supermajority consensus. Ultimately they proved solu-
ble only through the constitutional revolution achieved by the Civil War.

Over the course of the nineteenth century, satisfaction with Article V
gradually eroded, replaced by a sense that amendment was, under ordinary
circumstances, impossibly difficult. Early-twentieth-century reformers, including Theodore Roosevelt, Woodrow Wilson, and Robert La Follette, regarded the degree of required consensus as unreachable and the Constitution
as hopelessly inflexible. Progressive constitutional scholars J. Allen Smith
and Charles Beard concurred, attributing the difficulty of amendment to antidemocratic motivations of an economic elite that had designed the Constitution.[25] Judge Charles Amidon told an American Bar Association audience,
"There is a very general understanding that formal amendment is impossible." He observed, "A changeless constitution becomes the protector not
only of vested rights but of vested wrongs."[26] The 1912 Progressive platform
proposed reforming Article V to enable a democratic majority to revise the
Constitution more readily.[27] Then, however, a wave of progressive amendments forced reformers to reconsider their views of Article V.

The constitutional amendments of the 1910s and after provoked calls for
revision of the amending process from those who wanted reform to be made
more arduous. Opponents of recent or proposed amendments sought sanction through referendums to restrain or overturn state legislative ratification,
authorization of subsequent legislatures' rescission of ratification by an earlier body, and limitation on the authority of constitutional conventions.
Conservative constitutional sentiments linked the proposals of James
Wadsworth and Finis Garrett in the 1920s to those of Sam Ervin in the
1960s and Orrin Hatch in the 1980s. The failure of efforts either to relax or

stiffen Article V requirements may not have signaled absolute contentment with Article V as much as inability to construct a preferable alternative, in itself a noteworthy result.

Alternative models of amendment procedure were always available. The Founders of 1787 had the strict requirements of the Articles of Confederation system to consider. They also had before them the example of the 1776 Pennsylvania state constitution with its system of automatic and frequent constitutional review by an independent Council of Censors. The Founders opted for an amendment mechanism that favored greater stability but not immobility. The Pennsylvania process required, at the least, frequent formal reaffirmation of existing arrangements and thus raised the prospect of regular constitutional turmoil. The routine-review approach allowed every political generation to consider fully its own constitutional arrangements, a prospect attractive to some in the late eighteenth century but distasteful to most then and since. The Founders instead embraced the 1780 Massachusetts state model that did not encourage constitutional reform as a routine aspect of government yet would not place insurmountable obstacles in its path. Once chosen, the Article V system easily survived every effort to revise or replace it. In fact, proposals for change hardly ever attracted much notice, much less serious discussion. By the imperfect standards of a democratic republic, this acceptance amounted to general endorsement of the status quo.

The Article V procedure gained acceptance because it functioned well by the standards that its creators established. Those standards have not encountered substantial challenge. When Congress avoided conventions to propose amendments and neglected to use ratification conventions to obtain direct popular sanction of change, it exercised discretion allowed by the Founders. Congress's choices seldom occasioned comment, much less objection. Preempting convention petitions by acting on the requested amendment effectively disarmed criticism each time a petition drive reached the threshold of success. In 1933, when the only strenuous demand was raised for convention ratification, Congress hastened to comply. In the absence of such a request, however, Congress routinely reverted to more familiar legislative ratification. Inattention to the possibilities of Article V appears to be a much larger component of the history of American constitutional amending than deliberate efforts to manipulate the process.

Acceptance also greeted the balance struck by the Founders in their search for an amending formula that would recognize the need for both a popular and a federal consensus on constitutional matters. This reception occurred because the standards of supermajority consensus established in 1787 served to permit occasional, widely approved amendments while effectively discouraging more controversial, less thoroughly embraced changes in the frame of government. The degree of agreement deemed by the Founders necessary and sufficient to legitimize or prevent constitutional reform proved to be both required and achievable for the Article V system to work as it did. A lower threshold of consensus would have permitted considerably more reform; a higher one would have prevented almost all reform. A smaller proportion of the population was not able to manipulate the system to its benefit and a larger supermajority was not blocked. The notion endured that satisfactory constitutional terms could and should be set by this level of supermajority agreement. Therefore, no substantial national debate ever occurred as to whether two-thirds of Congress and three-fourths of the states represented precisely the right degree of consensus.

Despite concerns that a tiny fraction of the citizenry located in small states could block amendment or that the majority of Americans clustered in a few large states could have their interests overridden, in reality the amending process carried out the Founders' intentions. The distribution of population in ratifying and nonratifying states was, in the aggregate, close to the proportion that the Founders held to be satisfactory to establish or deny a supermajority consensus. In other words, although the least populated states could in theory block reform desired by the more populous, allowing less than 5 percent of the population to block constitutional change favored by an overwhelming majority of Americans, it has never happened. Nor have smaller states collectively imposed amendment upon the minority of states containing the bulk of the citizenry. Small states and their residents have theoretically enjoyed much greater influence on the amending process and in practice experienced a slight advantage. Nevertheless, amendments favored by supermajorities of the size dictated by the Founders, calculated on the basis of population as well as the numbers of states, have been adopted, and amendments not so favored have failed. The federal system has not significantly distorted the Article V consensus equation.[28]

With the exception of the Twenty-seventh Amendment and a handful of others, most amendments, once a consensus of either congressional or state support emerged, gained prompt approval at the other level of the federal system as well. Although protection of states' rights in a federal system was one of the concerns of the Founders, Article V never functioned to exaggerate small state influence either to block or compel amendment. Southern state opposition to amendment proved the most frequent obstacle to change, but it was effective only when the region was substantially united and supported by at least a few allies among states from other parts of the country. In the case of the equal rights amendment, for example, the South led the successful resistance to ratification but was joined by a few western and Mississippi Valley states. Notably, the combined population of the nonratifying states stood well in excess of that determined by the Founders to deny constitutional consensus. The architects of American federalism would have been pleased with outcomes that carried out their notion that constitutional declarations should be made only on the basis of a broad federal as well as a popular consensus.

Although it has inevitably disappointed advocates of change on some occasions and their opponents on others, Article V has functioned very much as the Founders desired. The amending mechanism has ensured constitutional stability unless a supermajority of approximately the proportion that the Founders intended could agree on the terms of reform. Thus the Founders' original intent regarding how an amending system should function has been realized. Whether that was beneficial needs to be judged against two centuries of performance. The historical record does not make it easy to render a judgment. Constitutional reforms of great consequence were achieved repeatedly, testifying to Article V's utility for transforming the nature of U.S. government. At the same time, various amendments widely thought to possess merit have failed to secure adoption, also a matter of great consequence. How one evaluates the desirability of amendments won and lost affects how one regards the amending system itself.

THE TWENTY-SEVENTH AMENDMENT stands as an exception to a pattern of highly meaningful amendments to the Constitution. James Madison correctly regarded it as less significant than the other eleven measures in the package he laid before the First Congress, and he could not know that it would also be less consequential than every other amendment adopted during the next 200 years. The practical impact of the Twenty-seventh Amendment on the structure and operation of government was minimal. Indeed, it merely obliged Congress to schedule its next pay increases to take effect after an intervening election no more than two years away, a predictable and satisfactory arrangement for the overwhelming proportion of members of Congress who would be returning. In a larger sense, however, its effect was to devalue the role of Article V in American constitutionalism.

In sharp contrast to the Twenty-seventh Amendment, some of the formal alterations in the terms of the Constitution have been profoundly important in shaping the structure and practice of American government. To use the terminology of Yale law professor Bruce Ackerman, they have been "transformative."[29] None possessed greater transformative power than the first, the substitution of the 1787 Constitution for the Articles of Confederation. Though not usually thought of as an amendment, the 1787 Constitution deserves such a label, given the understandings of amendment prevailing at the time. To use the definition of amendment the chairman of the Philadelphia convention later employed himself, the United States' first self-created instrument of government had been "changed by an explicit and authentic act of the whole people." A peaceful, deliberative, popularly sanctioned recasting of the terms of government to create "a more perfect Union," the 1787 Constitution departed from the established amending formula of the Articles of Confederation only by having a convention rather than the Confederation Congress draft the changes and by allowing a less-than-unanimous ratification put the new instrument into effect. However, the Congress did formally authorize and then approve the work of the Philadelphia convention. Furthermore, the thirteen Confederation states did ultimately ratify the new Constitution. No alteration of the nation's constitutional framework has lasted longer or had greater influence on the operation of American government.

The next act of amendment, the first using methods set forth in Article V of the 1787 Constitution, was also transformative. The adoption of the Bill of Rights reshaped a mere scheme of governmental structure into an instrument that protected basic individual rights against federal infringement. Though there was debate at the time as to whether the Constitution needed a Bill of Rights since states were thought to be the governments that would deal directly with individuals, there was no doubt that the prompt amendment of the new Constitution reformulated its essential contours. The magnitude of these amendments established that Article V could be used to alter the Constitution fundamentally as opposed to merely adjusting its details. At the same time, the placement of the Bill of Rights as an appendix to the Constitution rather than as a series of interwoven alterations and additions enhanced the image of the original Constitution, however much subsequently revised, as a sacrosanct, enduring design of government.

The amendments of the framework of federal government that soon followed lacked the stature of the 1787 Constitution itself or the Bill of Rights, but they were not inconsequential changes. The Eleventh Amendment strengthened the position of states within the federal relationship. Furthermore, it made clear that amendment could reverse an unpopular Supreme Court decision, thereby easing the acceptance of judicial review for the resolution of most of the inevitable disputes regarding constitutional law. The Twelfth Amendment redrew the electoral arrangements for the officers of the executive branch. In the process it replaced an administrative structure in which two national political parties would each have a voice with a single-party-controlled administration. National elections became more combative, winner-take-all contests as a result. Thereafter, Article V became an ever-present consideration in the half-century struggle to define a balance between federal power and states' rights, not to mention the growing fear of southern slave states that a diminished place in the federal Union might lead to the loss of their peculiar institution through constitutional change.

Another burst of transformative amendments occurred in the 1860s. The Civil War amendments completed and confirmed the evolution of the Constitution from a framework for a confederation of states into a design for a national government. The culmination of nineteenth-century sectional conflict also recast the Constitution in another way. Thereafter it no longer would be thought of as a confining set of specific authorizations but as a grant of authority adequate to sanction a broad range of reasonable government actions. Although the war itself effected these changes, the adoption of constitutional amendments, and particularly their grudging acceptance by the defeated Confederate states, gave explicit formal confirmation to the second American revolution.

The next wave of amendments also reconfigured the terms of government in basic ways. Not only did the Sixteenth Amendment again reverse a Supreme Court ruling, it also fundamentally altered the nation's approach to paying for government. In revising the tax system it shifted the costs of government to more affluent elements of society. The income tax amendment increased the federal government's potential fiscal resources, which in turn enhanced its capacity to undertake a vastly wider range of actions than ever before. The almost simultaneous Seventeenth Amendment transformed the U.S. Senate from an insulated, elitist body into a far more democratically responsive institution. Together with the Nineteenth Amendment, which doubled the size of the electorate through the enfranchisement of American women, and the Twentieth Amendment, ending lame duck sessions of Congress and ensuring an immediate response to the electoral will, these constitutional changes curtailed the power of a wealthy male elite and rendered Congress a legislative body more responsive to a heterogeneous political culture. The other amendments of the era, those establishing and then repealing national prohibition of alcoholic beverages, echoed these structural changes. Although the Twenty-first Amendment canceled the Eighteenth, the prohibition episode twice gave powerful testimony to the capacity of constitutional amendment to redirect suddenly and sharply the agenda of government.

Post–World War II amendments were relatively narrow in focus and effect, but they too had substantial impact upon the character of American government. By limiting presidents to only two terms, the Twenty-second Amendment notably reduced the political influence of every reelected incumbent. Compared to the second term accomplishments of Theodore Roosevelt, Woodrow Wilson, Franklin Roosevelt, and Harry Truman, those of Dwight Eisenhower, Richard Nixon, and Ronald Reagan consistently appeared unimpressive. Though this pattern may not be entirely explained by the adoption of the Twenty-second Amendment, the ineligibility of a leader of proven popularity to run for office again not only encouraged opponents but also preoccupied potential supporters with a succession contest. The restrictive amendment diluted the political power of the national official upon whom the greatest constitutional responsibility lay and in whose hands the only nationally based electoral mandate rested. The Twenty-third, Twenty-fourth, and Twenty-sixth Amendments expanded the electorate in symbolically if not numerically important ways. The poll tax ban, participation in presidential elections for the District of Columbia, and suffrage for eighteen-year-olds strengthened the claim and expectation that the entire adult society was able to engage in self-government. Finally, the Twenty-fifth Amendment established a procedure that would be used twice within a decade to fill vice-presidential vacancies, mitigate succession crises, and, as a consequence, install the first president not elected by the procedure established in 1787.

Measured against its predecessors, the Twenty-seventh Amendment looks trivial. Amendments prior to 1992 repeatedly transformed the government of the United States. They significantly altered the structure and operation of government, proclaimed the protection of individual right from government interference, expanded the electorate, or authorized the removal of property from private hands to achieve public purposes. Any comparison of the first twenty-six revisions of the Constitution with the twenty-seventh makes evident that before 1992 the Article V process of change regularly produced noteworthy reform of American government.

THE CONSTITUTION ALSO EVOLVED in the absence of "explicit and authentic acts" of amendment. Although some scholars argue that constitutional change by judicial review with legislative and electoral validation is as well sanctioned as reform through amendment, the historical evidence suggests otherwise. The failure to carry out the formal process of constitutional change has likewise had momentous consequence for American government. The adoption of the Twenty-seventh Amendment provides a striking reminder of this effect by calling attention to the last remaining unratified 1789 amendment, the measure limiting congressional district size that long languished beside the pay raise amendment. James Madison's first amendment, if ratified, would transform the current House of Representatives into a very different institution. Other congressionally approved but unratified amendments would likewise have had great impact if they had been adopted. The effect of the 1861 amendment protecting slavery in states where it then existed is incalculable. The equal rights amendment would have speeded, shaped, and deepened the evolution of gender relationships taking place in American society after the 1960s. The grant of full federal representation to the District of Columbia would have removed a remaining vestige of American racism and perhaps given the political balance in the country a slightly more liberal tilt. Yet these nonratified amendments do not represent the only or possibly even the most important instances of noteworthy nonamendment.

When James Madison, near the end of his second presidential term, sought an amendment to give the federal government explicit authorization to engage in domestic public works, activity previously regarded as a state responsibility, he wanted to erase any doubts about federal authority in this area. He remained unwilling to approve federal spending for internal improvements in the absence of such an amendment. Although constitutional views as strict as Madison's gradually faded after the departure from office of the last of the Founders, the question of federal domestic economic authority long remained insecurely settled. Yet the failure to amend the Constitution in this instance, though a restraining influence on federally financed national economic development, had far less consequence than the abandonment of amendment during the New Deal over a century later.

The New Deal sought to redefine permanently the basic responsibilities of the American federal government, but it did not follow the Founders' model of seeking to secure this revolutionary change by specifically articulating it and embedding it in a constitutional framework. The New Deal likewise ignored the pattern that the Civil War generation provided of using the Article V process to incorporate the fundamental changes achieved through blood and struggle into the Constitution. By this means a second American revolution had been rendered permanent. A new measure of federal authority and civil rights was secured in the 1860s, though admittedly full implementation would be long delayed. In contrast, the New Deal failed to revise the Constitution, settling instead for a new interpretation of its existing terms, initiated by the executive, endorsed by the legislature, and sanctioned by the judiciary.

One can reasonably argue that the circumstances of the third American constitutional revolution did transform the nation's understanding of the role of the federal government. A case can be made that the repeated electoral victories of Franklin Roosevelt and his legislative supporters gave an informal sanction to this constitutional transformation.[30] However, reflection ought to make clear that such changes fell considerably short of formal amendment in terms of effective force, clarity, and acceptance.

The decision of Franklin Roosevelt, in the face of direct and powerful challenges to the constitutionality of his first-term programs, to forgo a quest for amendment in favor of political maneuvers to influence the Supreme Court cost the third great revolution in American government the security and stability of its predecessors in the 1780s and the 1860s. An amendment giving explicit recognition to a federal responsibility for domestic social and economic welfare was within reach after the 1936 election, but Roosevelt, wary of the Article V process, chose instead to seek reform of the Court. It was a costly choice, not only in respect to its short-term political effect but also because it left the New Deal vision of government responsibility on a less firm foundation.

At least one member of Roosevelt's inner circle later came to regret the decision to forgo amendment in the New Deal's battle with the Court. Rexford Tugwell, one of FDR's most visionary as well as progressive advisers, served in a variety of positions concerned with economic planning and social welfare. In his biography of Roosevelt, Tugwell described an amendment as a "forthright and permanent cure" to the New Deal's constitutional problems, a means to "establish the missing principles by which the Court could be guided as it judged legislation in the industrial age." Yet he acknowledged that an amendment would have taken time and, although disappointed, accepted FDR's tactics.[31] Later in his life, however, as a fellow of the Center for the Study of Democratic Institutions in Santa Barbara, California, Tugwell devoted considerable energy to calling attention to the risks for a democratic republic when government slipped the bonds of constitutionalism.[32] He went so far as to devise a new Constitution for the United States, the discussion of which he hoped would focus attention on appropriate modern powers and restraints for government. He specifically accorded the federal government powers to stabilize and regulate the economy, promote education and social well-being, and "advance, through every agency of government, the excellence of national life." Given the perspective of forty years, Tugwell quite clearly regretted the failure to spell out the New Deal philosophy of government in constitutional terms.[33]

The consequence of this lapse of formal constitutional redefinition was reduced long-term impact for the innovations of the 1930s. During the next half century, there was no significant retreat from the New Deal's major legislative innovations. Political opinion, however, grew more divided on the question of the federal government's responsibility to seek further enhancement of the social and economic welfare of the nation's citizens. A disaffected minority did not gradually come to accept a new constitutional understanding as was the usual pattern after an amendment had been adopted; instead discontent with the principle in question increased. Only once, and then quite briefly during the early years of Lyndon Johnson's presidency, did a political consensus fully in tune with the New Deal philosophy of government have an unchallenged opportunity to expand the initiatives of the Roosevelt years.

When dissenters from the New Deal vision of a federal obligation to secure the society's welfare gained the presidency in 1968 and 1980 and obtained control of the House of Representatives in 1994, they had a far easier time than might otherwise have been the case turning the policies and practices of the United States in a contrary direction. The core New Deal principle, the ultimate responsibility of the federal government for ensuring society's well-being, though continuing to receive lip service, was abandoned by the courts as well as the executive and legislative branches in the face of political slogans calling for "a new federalism," "individual freedom," and "less government and lower taxes." For instance, a 1973 Supreme Court majority dominated by appointees of Richard Nixon rejected the plea of Hispanic Texans that the state's school-district-based property tax financing of public education discriminated against the poor. The Court said that a claim of a right to equal funding for education might well lead to similar claims for the ill-fed, ill-clothed, and ill-housed. The justices explicitly denied that the Constitution required the federal government to carry out the very social obligation that Franklin D. Roosevelt had proclaimed as its responsibility nearly forty years earlier.[34]

In the absence of their constitutional expression, the retreat from New Deal principles continued. By 1989 the Court, dominated by appointees of Ronald Reagan, refused to hold Winnebago County, Wisconsin, social workers liable in the death of a four-year-old boy when they failed to remove him from his father's custody even after he had been hospitalized several times as the result of that parent's beatings. Chief Justice William Rehnquist revealed how narrow had become the Court's view of government responsibility for society's general welfare when he declared for the 5-to-4 majority, "The State does not become a permanent guarantor of an individual's safety by having once offered him shelter."[35]

In April 1995, the Supreme Court, for the first time since the election of 1936, declared an act of Congress unconstitutional on the basis that it had exceeded the bounds of its power to regulate interstate commerce. A 1990 act making it a federal offense to take firearms into or near a school had nothing to do with economic activity that substantially affected interstate commerce, a five-member majority ruled in *U.S. v. Lopez*. Justice Stephen Breyer and three other justices held, to the contrary, that education was "inextricably intertwined with the Nation's economy" and that the Court should defer to Congress's view that a rational basis existed for connecting legislation to interstate commerce. The adequacy of the Constitution to authorize federal domestic actions was once more in question. Both sides rooted their argument in the 1930s as Chief Justice William Rehnquist's majority opinion took a narrow view of the New Deal's expansion of congressional regulatory power, and Breyer bewailed a return to pre-1937 views of the commerce clause and Congress's prerogative to address social conditions. Justice Clarence Thomas, in an extended concurrence, extolled a much more limited view of congressional authority than Rehnquist's. Demonstrating how little bound he felt by sixty years of New Deal jurisprudence, Thomas wrote, "If anything, the 'wrong turn' was the Court's dramatic departure in the 1930's from a century and a half of precedent." Though the long-term impact of *Lopez* remained to be seen, the decision gave further evidence that without explicit and authentic acts of amendment, any constitutional construction remained fundamentally insecure.[36] The failure of the New Deal to imbed its transformative ideas in the Constitution, as it might well have done, limited the durability of its conception of federal responsibility in the face of later onslaughts.

Conversely, the failure of numerous post–New Deal conservative efforts to amend the Constitution prevented the complete reversal of the third American revolution. The unsuccessful efforts of Representative Louis Ludlow and Senator John Bricker to confine executive authority in foreign affairs gave at least modest confirmation to the expansion of presidential diplomatic power in the era of the cold war. Repeated failure to overturn decisions of the post–New Deal Supreme Court regarding race, apportionment, school prayer, abortion, and flag burning also solidified liberal constitutional values. Various efforts to restrict federal fiscal authority, most notably the balanced budget amendment, which would have dismantled New Deal innovations in managing the national economy, fell short, although sometimes just barely short, of success. One can easily imagine a very different American government if these amendments had been achieved. But the fact that they have not won endorsement is an insufficient basis for claims that the New Deal truly transformed the American Constitution without explicit acts of amendment.

The core value of written constitutionalism has remained the same since its first proposal by the Levelers during the English Civil War: the powers of government must be defined so that those charged with carrying them out will be bound by them. Not only will legislators and executives then comprehend what they are to do and not do, they will also be unable to deviate legally from the prescription of their responsibilities established by consensus of the sovereign people. The failure to keep a constitution in tune with fundamental understandings of the obligations of government, whatever they may be, and the willingness to tolerate the resulting dissonance between principle and practice, inevitably undermines the objective of written constitutionalism.

Finally, the very triviality of the Twenty-seventh Amendment ought to serve as a reminder of the importance of amendment in the design and conduct of American constitutionalism. The pay raise amendment's lack of consequence underscores that, more often than not, when the Article V process has been employed, it has exercised transformative power over American government. On occasions when Article V might have been employed but was not, the direction of American government became less certain, the achievement of progress less secure against backlash. The adoption of a relatively insignificant constitutional reform should call attention to the place of amendment in authorizing as well as limiting the activities of government over the course of two centuries of U.S. history.

The architects of the Constitution intended change to come in the American government through an orderly process. Routine, modest, and unobjectionable revisions would be achieved by ordinary legislation or judicial elaboration. Fundamental recasting of government's authority or obligation, on the other hand, required deeper consideration, broader acknowledgment, and a greater degree of political consensus. This two-tiered approach, what Bruce Ackerman labels the dualist nature of U.S. constitutionalism, is the essential feature of a governmental system that the Founders wished to make stable but did not want to make static. They abhorred a structure of governance unresponsive to the popular will when a reasonable degree of consensus for change existed. For the American constitutional system to work as they intended, use of the amending system would be essential as notions of government evolved. Government based on informal, unarticulated understandings would cease to be constitutional. It would no longer be government limited and directed by an expression of the sovereign power of the people.

George Washington described his view of the proper role of amendment in the nation's development in his enthusiastic endorsement of the 1787 Constitution when it was less than a decade old. In his Farewell Address, the first president assured the country that appropriate, deliberative, popularly sanctioned action had produced a Constitution that was a decided improvement over the Articles of Confederation. "This Government," he said, "the offspring of our own choice, uninfluenced and unawed, adopted upon full investigation and mature deliberation, completely free in its principles, in the distribution of its powers, uniting security with energy, and containing within itself a provision for its own amendment, has a just claim to your confidence and your support." The Constitution deserved to be sustained, Washington continued, because of its provision for further revision as well as the methods of its adoption. "Respect for its authority, compliance with its laws, acquiescence in its measures, are duties enjoined by the fundamental maxims of true liberty. The basis of our political system is the right of the people to make and to alter their constitutions of government." Washington placed the right to amend the Constitution on an equal footing with the right of the sovereign people to establish the terms of their government in the first place.[37]

The retiring first president then articulated the central tenet of the Founders' constitutional faith. Washington declared, "The constitution which at any time exists till changed by an explicit and authentic act of the whole people is sacredly obligatory upon all. The very idea of the power and the right of the people to establish government presupposes the duty of every individual to obey the established government."[38] In Washington's view, the capacity of the sovereign people to set and, equally important, to change the terms of their governance gave the government, once established, a legitimate claim to respect and obedience. Were government to lose touch with the power that originally gave it authority, it would lose its legitimacy. The fact that an effective provision existed for revising the frame of government meant that each generation could be regarded as reapproving the Constitution. If they chose not to amend it, they were nevertheless engaging in an act of endorsement just as much as if they made Article V alterations or embraced an entirely new Constitution. In Washington's view the availability of a process for "an explicit and authentic act" of amendment produced the "sacred obligation" to respect the Constitution while at the same time imposing upon the government limits that demanded observance.

Washington's contemporaries and colleagues in establishing the U.S. government shared these views. Delegates to the Philadelphia convention, whether enthusiasts for the Constitution such as James Madison and

Alexander Hamilton or critics such as George Mason, applauded Article V. Thomas Jefferson, too, perceived the crucial function of amendment in keeping a constitution from becoming outmoded. "I am certainly not an advocate for frequent and untried changes in laws and constitutions," he asserted. "I think moderate imperfections had better be borne with; because, when once known, we accommodate ourselves to them, and find practical means of correcting their ill effects." Yet he was quick to add, "But I know also that laws and institutions must go hand in hand with the progress of the human mind. As that becomes more developed, more enlightened, as new discoveries are made, new truths disclosed and manners and opinions change with the change of circumstances, institutions must advance also, and keep pace with the times." In Jefferson's judgment, "We might as well require a man to wear still the coat which fitted him when a boy, as civilized society to remain under the regime of their barbarous ancestors." He disparaged a political system that did not make use of amendment. "Some men look at constitutions with sanctimonious reverence and deem them like the ark of the covenant, too sacred to be touched. They ascribe to the men of the preceding age a wisdom more than human, and suppose what they did to be beyond amendment."[39]

Even the great proponent of judicial review, John Marshall, acknowledged the higher standing of amendment. "The people made the constitution, and the people can unmake it," he wrote in 1821. "It is the creature of their own will, and lives only by their will."[40] Marshall was reiterating the late-seventeenth-century belief of the early advocate of constitutionalism, Algernon Sidney, that the people not only possessed a right to establish governments but also to change even just governments "to prevent or cure the mischiefs arising from them, or to advance a good that at the first was not thought on."[41]

To Sidney, as later to Jefferson and Marshall, no restraint should be placed on amendment other than the requirement that it reflect the sovereign will. Washington ultimately agreed, though he urged the nation to exercise caution and care in constitutional innovation. He asked his fellow citizens to remember that "time and habit are at least as necessary to fix the true character of government as of other human institutions." The first president concluded that "experience is the surest standard by which to test the real tendency of the existing constitution of a country."[42]

Certainly subsequent developments would suggest that Americans affirmed Sidney's belief that amendments could depart from established principles just as they heeded Washington's advice not to rush ahead to make constitutional change. Amendments to the U.S. Constitution proved to be rare, but when they did occur they often brought about fundamental alterations in the character of American government. Indeed, although the original 1787 frame of government established notable principles of federalism, separation of powers, and checks and balances, subsequent amendments, especially those guaranteeing individual rights and broad democratic participation, gave the Constitution many of its most profoundly important features.

The power of amendment, in the eyes of eighteenth-century constitutionalists, was the means of keeping a constitutional system stable by keeping it vital. The belief is as central to constitutionalism now as it was then. If a society perceives that different arrangements are more suitable for its present and future, then it is appropriate for it to make those desired changes. Moreover, if the desire is for a government of defined directions and limits, then it is well to heed the history of written constitutions and their amendment. That history points to the value of defining the further course of government by "explicit and authentic acts of the whole people." No political culture desiring to be self-governing can ignore the observation of George Washington that constitutional government is "the offspring of our own choice."

NOTES

PREFACE

1. John R. Vile, *The Constitutional Amending Process in American Political Thought* (New York: Praeger, 1992), 115.

2. Bruce Ackerman, *We the People: Foundations* (Cambridge: Harvard University Press, 1991), esp. 50–54, 268–69.

3. Quoted in Gordon S. Wood, *The Creation of the American Republic, 1776–1787* (Chapel Hill: University of North Carolina Press, 1969), 614.

4. David E. Kyvig, *Repealing National Prohibition* (Chicago: University of Chicago Press, 1979).

5. Herman V. Ames, *Proposed Amendments to the Constitution of the United States During the First Century of Its History,* part 2 of *Annual Report of the American Historical Association for the Year 1896* (Washington, D.C.: GPO, 1897), esp. 300–302.

6. Michael A. Musmanno, *Proposed Amendments to the Constitution* [1889–1929], 70th Cong., 2d sess., House Doc. 551 (Washington, D.C.: GPO, 1929).

7. Lester B. Orfield, *The Amending of the Federal Constitution* (Ann Arbor: University of Michigan Press, 1942).

8. Russell L. Caplan, *Constitutional Brinksmanship: Amending the Constitution by National Convention* (New York: Oxford University Press, 1988).

9. Charles Leedham, *Our Changing Constitution* (New York: Dodd, Mead, 1964).

10. Clement E. Vose, *Constitutional Change: Amendment Politics and Supreme Court Litigation Since 1900* (Lexington, Mass.: Lexington Books, 1972).

11. Alan P. Grimes, *Democracy and the Amendments to the Constitution* (Lexington, Mass.: Lexington Books, 1978).

12. Mary Frances Berry, *Why ERA Failed: Politics, Women's Rights, and the Amending Process of the Constitution* (Bloomington: Indiana University Press, 1986).

13. Michael Kammen, *A Machine That Would Go of Itself: The Constitution in American Culture* (New York: Knopf, 1986).

14. Richard B. Bernstein with Jerome Agel, *Amending America: If We Love the Constitution So Much Why Do We Keep Trying to Change It?* (New York: Times Books, 1993).

15. Bruce Ackerman, "Discovering the Constitution," *Yale Law Journal* 93 (1984): 1058.

1. THE RISE OF CONSTITUTIONALISM

1. George Washington, Farewell Address, September 17, 1796, in *A Compilation of the Messages and Papers of the Presidents, 1789–1897,* ed. James D. Richardson, 20 vols. (New York: Bureau of National Literature, 1897), 1: 209.

2. Ibid., 212.

3. George Washington to David Humphreys, October 10, 1787, in *The Records of the Federal Convention of 1787,* ed. Max Farrand, 4 vols. (New Haven: Yale University Press, 1937), 3: 103–4.

4. Washington, Farewell Address, in Richardson, ed., *Messages and Papers of the Presidents,* 1: 200.

5. Euripides, *Suppliants,* quoted in Francis D. Wormuth, *The Origins of Modern Constitutionalism* (New York: Harper, 1949), 11.

6. *The Laws,* quoted in George H. Sabine, *A History of Political Theory,* 3d ed. (New York: Holt, Rinehart and Winston, 1961), 69–70.

7. Ibid., 69.

8. J. C. Holt, *Magna Carta* (Cambridge: Cambridge University Press, 1965), 327. The impact of Magna Carta is well explored in A. E. Dick Howard, *The Road from Runnymeade: Magna Carta and Constitutionalism in America* (Charlottesville: University Press of Virginia, 1968).

9. Edmund S. Morgan, *Inventing the People: The Rise of Popular Sovereignty in England and America* (New York: W. W. Norton, 1988), 39.

10. The literature on the Levelers is immense. This discussion draws heavily on Morgan, *Inventing the People,* Sabine, *History of Political Theory,* and Wormuth, *Origins of Modern Constitutionalism.*

11. Quoted in Wormuth, *Origins of Modern Constitutionalism,* 105.

12. Quoted in ibid., 107–8.

13. Algernon Sidney, *Discourses Concerning Government,* 3d ed. (London: A. Millar, 1751), 136.

14. Ibid., 119.

15. An excellent modern edition is John Locke, *Two Treatises of Government,* ed. Peter Laslett (Cambridge: Cambridge University Press, 1963).

16. Charles M. Andrews, *The Colonial Period of American History: The Settlements,* 3 vols. (New Haven: Yale University Press, 1934–1937), 1: 180–205. A useful brief summary of the seventeenth-century rise of representative assemblies in the American colonies is Michael Kammen, *Deputyes & Libertyes: The Origins of Representative Government in Colonial America* (New York: Knopf, 1969).

17. Andrews, *Colonial Period of American History,* 1: 249–99.

18. Ibid., 1: 368–99, 430–61.

19. *The History of the Colony and Province of Massachusetts Bay,* ed. Lawrence S. Mayo, 3 vols. (Cambridge, Mass.: Harvard University Press, 1936), 1: 38–39, quoted in Wesley Frank Craven, *The Colonies in Transition, 1660–1713* (New York: Harper and Row, 1968), 5.

20. Andrews, *Colonial Period of American History,* 2: 100–109, 131–39.

21. Ibid., 2: 25–26, 40–47.

22. Donald Lutz, *The Origins of American Constitutionalism* (Baton Rouge: Louisiana State University Press, 1988), 27, 46–49; Craven, *Colonies in Transition,* 46–53.

23. Craven, *Colonies in Transition,* 88–91, 99–102, 195–98.

24. George Dargo, *Roots of the Republic: A New Perspective on Early American Constitutionalism* (New York: Praeger, 1974), 61–63.

25. Kingsley Martin, *French Liberal Thought in the Eighteenth Century,* 3d ed. (New York: Harper and Row, 1962), 147–69; Sabine, *History of Political Theory,* 542–60.

26. Sabine, *History of Political Theory,* 575–96.

27. Anne M. Cohler, *Montesquieu's Comparative Politics and the Spirit of American Constitutionalism* (Lawrence: University Press of Kansas, 1988); Paul Merrill Spurlin, *Rousseau in America, 1760–1809* (University: University of Alabama Press, 1969).

28. Charles H. McIlwain, *Constitutionalism: Ancient and Modern* (Ithaca, N.Y.: Cornell University Press, 1947), 3.

29. Emmerich de Vattel, *The Law of Nations; or, Principles of the Law of Nature Applied to the Conduct and Affairs of Nations and Sovereigns,* ed. Joseph Chitty (Philadelphia: T. and J. W. Johnson, 1883), 77.

30. Bernard Bailyn, *The Ideological Origins of the American Revolution* (Cambridge: Harvard University Press, 1967), 176–81; Gerald Stourzh, "*Constitution:* Changing Meanings of the Term from the Early Seventeenth to the Late Eighteenth Century," in *Conceptual Change and the Constitution,* ed. Terence Ball and J. G. A. Pocock (Lawrence: University Press of Kansas, 1988), 35, 45–46.

31. McIlwain, *Constitutionalism: Ancient and Modern,* 2.

32. Morgan, *Inventing the People,* 153.

33. A good summary of American constitutional thought by 1776 can be found in Paul K. Conkin, *Self-Evident Truths: Being a Discourse on the Origins and Development of the First Principles of American Government—Popular Sovereignty, Natural Rights, and Balance and Separation of Powers* (Bloomington: Indiana University Press, 1974), 1–47.

34. *The Papers of Daniel Webster: Speeches and Formal Writings,* vol. 1, *1800–1833,* ed. Charles M. Wiltse and Alan R. Berolzheimer (Dartmouth, N.H.: Dartmouth College Press, 1986), 325.

35. Joseph Story, *Commentaries on the Constitution of the United States,* 3 vols. (Boston: Hilliard, Gray, 1833), 1: 198–99.

36. Ibid., 200–203.

37. Garry Wills called attention to the importance of Lincoln's view in *Inventing America: Jefferson's Declaration of Independence* (Garden City, N.Y.: Doubleday, 1978), xiv–xvi, and *Lincoln at Gettysburg: The Words That Remade America* (New York: Simon & Schuster, 1992), 131–47.

2. THE EMERGENCE OF THE AMENDING COROLLARY

1. John M. Murrin, "The British and Colonial Background of American Constitutionalism," in *The Framing and Ratification of the Constitution,* ed. Leonard W. Levy and Dennis J. Mahoney (New York: Macmillan, 1987), 30.

2. Edward S. Corwin, *The "Higher Law" Background of American Constitutional Law* (Ithaca, N.Y.: Cornell University Press, 1955), 85–87; Gordon S. Wood, *The Creation of the American Republic, 1776–1787* (Chapel Hill: University of North Carolina Press, 1969), 260–61.

3. Corwin, *"Higher Law" Background of American Constitutional Law,* 61–89.

4. Willi Paul Adams, *The First American Constitutions: Republican Ideology and the Making of the State Constitutions in the Revolutionary Era,* trans. Rita and Robert Kimber (Chapel Hill: University of North Carolina Press, 1980), 49–59.

5. Quoted in ibid., 61.

6. Ibid., 5.

7. Quoted in Wood, *Creation of the American Republic,* 128.

8. Jere R. Daniell, *Experiment in Republicanism: New Hampshire Politics and the American Revolution, 1741–1794* (Cambridge: Harvard University Press, 1970), 109–12; Adams, *First American Constitutions,* 68–69.

9. Adams, *First American Constitutions,* 70–71; Elisha P. Douglas, *Rebels and Democrats: The Struggle for Equal Political Rights and Majority Rule During the American Revolution* (Chicago: Quadrangle, 1955), 40–42.

10. Adams, *First American Constitutions,* 74.

11. [Anonymous], "The Alarm: or, an Address to the People of Pennsylvania on the

Late Resolve of Congress" (1776), in *American Political Writing During the Founding Era, 1760–1805,* ed. Charles S. Hyneman and Donald S. Lutz (Indianapolis: Liberty Press, 1983), 1: 322, 326.

12. Adams, *First American Constitutions,* 77.

13. Douglas, *Rebels and Democrats,* 61.

14. Adams, *First American Constitutions,* 138.

15. Wood, *Creation of the American Republic,* 307.

16. Ibid., 78–79; Douglas, *Rebels and Democrats,* 260–74.

17. Adams, *First American Constitutions,* 75–76, 80–81.

18. Ibid., 81–82; Douglas, *Rebels and Democrats,* 132.

19. Adams, *First American Constitutions,* 82–83.

20. Ibid., 83–86.

21. Douglas, *Rebels and Democrats,* 162–63.

22. Ibid., 164; Adams, *First American Constitutions,* 88–89.

23. Douglas, *Rebels and Democrats,* 164.

24. Ibid., 169; Adams, *First American Constitutions,* 90.

25. Douglas, *Rebels and Democrats,* 176–78; Adams, *First American Constitutions,* 91.

26. Douglas, *Rebels and Democrats,* 188–89; Adams, *First American Constitutions,* 91–92.

27. Adams, *First American Constitutions,* 92.

28. Ronald M. Peters, Jr., *The Massachusetts Constitution of 1780* (Amherst: University of Massachusetts Press, 1978), 174.

29. Adams, *First American Constitutions,* 93; Douglas, *Rebels and Democrats,* 189.

30. Andrew C. McLaughlin, *The Foundations of American Constitutionalism* (New York: New York University Press, 1932), 98.

31. Edmund S. Morgan, *Inventing the People: The Rise of Popular Sovereignty in England and America* (New York: W. W. Norton, 1988), 250–60.

32. Daniell, *Experiment in Republicanism,* 164–79.

33. Quoted in Wood, *Creation of the American Republic,* 382.

34. Quoted in Adams, *First American Constitutions,* 141–43.

35. Douglas, *Rebels and Democrats,* 294.

36. Adams, *First American Constitutions,* 140.

37. Lewis H. Meader, "The Council of Censors," *Pennsylvania Magazine of History and Biography* 22 (1898): 267–69; J. Paul Selsam, *The Pennsylvania Constitution of 1776* (Philadelphia: University of Pennsylvania Press, 1936), 199–200.

38. Selsam, *Pennsylvania Constitution of 1776,* 200.

39. Donald S. Lutz, *Popular Consent and Popular Control: Whig Political Theory in the Early State Constitutions* (Baton Rouge: Louisiana State University Press, 1980), 44. The history of the Vermont council was significantly different from its Pennsylvania counterpart. In Vermont the council continued to operate until 1869, proposing various amendments that were subsequently adopted by convention. It was generally regarded as functioning successfully in that small, homogeneous state (ibid., 142–43).

40. Ibid., 145.

41. Adams, *First American Constitutions,* 141.

42. Lutz, *Popular Consent and Popular Control,* 141.

43. Quoted in Adams, *First American Constitutions,* 141.

44. Peter S. Onuf, "The First Federal Constitution: The Articles of Confederation," in Levy and Mahoney, eds., *The Framing and Ratification of the Constitution,* 84; Richard B. Morris, *The Forging of the Union, 1781–1789* (New York: Harper and Row, 1987), 80–82; Jack N. Rakove, *The Beginnings of National Politics: An Interpretive History of the Continental Congress* (New York: Knopf, 1979), 136–44.

45. Morris, *Forging of the Union,* 82–83.

46. Merrill Jensen, *The Articles of Confederation* (Madison: University of Wisconsin Press, 1940), 126–39; Morris, *Forging of the Union*, 84–90.

47. Rakove, *Beginnings of National Politics*, 163.

48. June 23, 1777, quoted in ibid., 177.

49. June 26, 1777, quoted in ibid.

50. Jensen, *Articles of Confederation*, 187.

51. Quoted in ibid, 189.

52. Rakove, *Beginnings of National Politics*, 189.

53. Quoted in Morris, *Forging of the Union*, 61.

54. Rakove, *Beginnings of National Politics*, 288.

55. Quoted in ibid.

56. Merrill Jensen, *The New Nation: A History of the United States During the Confederation, 1781–1789* (New York: Knopf, 1950), 59; Morris, *Forging of the Union*, 246.

57. Jensen, *New Nation*, 57–65.

58. Ibid., 74–76.

59. Ibid., 402–4.

60. To be added to the Articles of Confederation were Articles Fourteen, giving Congress power to regulate interstate and foreign trade; Fifteen, requiring states that failed to pay requisitions within a time fixed by Congress to pay a 10 percent per year surcharge; Sixteen, giving Congress power to assess and collect taxes in states that failed to take action to meet requisitions after a majority of the states had done so; Seventeen, awarding interest to any state paying more than its share of a requisition and charging interest to states paying less than their share; Eighteen, making a congressional requisition of revenue for no more than fifteen years binding on all states once approved by eleven; Nineteen, allowing Congress to define treasonable offenses against the United States and to establish federal courts to which could be appealed all state court cases involving interpretation of treaties, regulation of trade and commerce, collection of federal revenue, and cases in which the United States was a party; and Twenty, disqualifying from further federal or state officeholding anyone who accepted election as a delegate to Congress and then failed to attend or withdrew without permission (ibid., 419–20).

61. Ibid., 419–21.

62. Resolution of Congress, February 21, 1787, in Max Farrand, ed., *The Records of the Federal Convention of 1787*, 4 vols. (New Haven: Yale University Press, 1937), 3:14.

63. *Pennsylvania Gazette*, March 24, 1779, quoted in Meader, "Council of Censors," 286.

64. Meader, "Council of Censors," 287.

65. Ibid., 287–95. The Council of Censors never again functioned as designed. In 1790 the Pennsylvania legislature, ignoring the 1776 constitution, itself called a constitutional convention and then ratified a new instrument that provided for a two-house legislature, created a stronger executive, and eliminated the Council of Censors. By 1790 radical democrats had lost a power struggle in Pennsylvania to those who declared in the new constitution that all power to reform government rested with the people but who substituted legislative action for direct popular consent (Lutz, *Popular Consent and Popular Control*, 140–41).

3. DEVISING THE AMERICAN AMENDING SYSTEM

1. There are several reliable descriptions of the events of the Philadelphia convention. The relatively brief account in Richard B. Morris, *The Forging of the Union 1781–1789* (New York: Harper and Row, 1987), is perhaps the best of those occasioned by the constitutional bicentennial, and Clinton Rossiter, *1787: The Grand Convention* (New York: Macmillan, 1966), is a fine earlier treatment. Carl Van Doren, *The Great Rehearsal*

(New York: Viking, 1948), and Catherine Drinker Bowen, *Miracle at Philadelphia: The Story of the Constitutional Convention, May to September 1787* (Boston: Little, Brown, 1966), continue to merit attention. Leonard W. Levy and Dennis J. Mahoney, eds., *The Framing and Ratification of the Constitution* (New York: Macmillan, 1987), brings together a great deal of modern scholarship.

2. Max Farrand, ed., *The Records of the Federal Convention of 1787*, 4 vols. (New Haven: Yale University Press, 1937), 1:28.

3. Ibid., 1: 18–19.

4. Ibid., 1: 20–22.

5. Morris, *Forging of the Union*, 278.

6. Charles Pinckney, "Observations of the Plan of Government submitted to the Federal Convention in Philadelphia, on the 28th of May 1787," in Farrand, ed., *Records of the Federal Convention of 1787*, 3: 106–23. Pinckney's pamphlet was published shortly after the convention adjourned and was purported to be the speech he intended to give on May 29. He was unable to do so because of insufficient time; it may well have been altered somewhat in the course of the convention.

7. Farrand, ed., *Records of the Federal Convention*, 1: 24–26.

8. Ibid., 1: 33.

9. Ibid., 1: 33–39.

10. Ibid., 1: 122–23.

11. Ibid., 1: 123, 209.

12. Ibid., 1: 176–88.

13. Ibid., 1: 242–45.

14. Ibid., 1: 246, 249, 257. These June 15 notes of Robert Yates may simply be a misplaced summary of the argument that Lansing made at length on June 16, according to both Madison's and Yates's notes.

15. Ibid., 1: 283, 294, 295, 301.

16. Ibid., 1: 26; 2: 88–89.

17. Ibid., 2: 90–91.

18. Ibid., 2: 92.

19. Ibid., 2: 92–93.

20. Ibid., 2: 123.

21. Ibid., 1: 93–94; 2: 90–91.

22. Spaight to James Iredell, August 12, 1787, in ibid., 3: 68.

23. Farrand, ed., *Records of the Federal Convention*, 2: 189.

24. Ibid., 2: 468–69.

25. Ibid., 2: 469.

26. Ibid., 2: 469, 475–77.

27. Ibid., 2: 475–77.

28. Ibid., 1: 22.

29. Ibid., 2: 189.

30. North Carolina Delegates to Governor Richard Caswell, August 7, 1787, in ibid., 3: 68.

31. Farrand, ed., *Records of the Federal Convention*, 2: 478.

32. Van Doren, *Great Rehearsal*, 159. He also declared it "in the long run one of the most practical."

33. Farrand, ed., *Records of the Federal Convention*, 2: 559–62.

34. Ibid., 2: 562–63.

35. Ibid., 2: 93, 604, 631–32.

36. Ibid., 2: 632.

37. Ibid., 2: 633.

38. Randolph explained his position in some detail in a letter to the speaker of the Virginia House of Delegates, October 10, 1787; see ibid., 3: 123–27.

39. Farrand, ed., *Records of the Federal Convention,* 2: 646–49.

40. Ibid., 1: 22, 121–23; 3: 595–609.

41. Ibid., 1: 202–3.

42. Ibid., 1: 227, 242–47, 282–311, 322; 2: 84, 188, 467–68. Hamilton gave a document to Madison near the end of the convention that delineated the constitution he would have preferred to see. It contained a provision that called for amendments to be proposed by two-thirds of both houses of Congress and ratified by legislatures or conventions in two-thirds of the states. It is not clear when or how Hamilton reached this view of the amending process, but there is no evidence that it was a part of his June 18 presentation. Ibid., 3: 619–30.

43. Ibid., 2: 557–58.

44. Ibid., 2: 559.

45. Ibid.

46. Ibid., 2: 629.

47. Ibid., 2: 629–30.

48. Ibid., 2: 630.

49. Ibid.

50. Ibid.

51. Ibid., 2: 630–31.

52. Ibid., 2: 662–63. Article I, section 9, clause 1: "The Migration or Importation of such Persons as any of the States now existing shall think proper to admit, shall not be prohibited by the Congress prior to the Year one thousand eight hundred and eight, but a Tax or duty may be imposed on such Importation, not exceeding ten dollars for each Person." Article I, section 9, clause 4: "No Capitation, or other direct, Tax shall be laid, unless in Proportion to the Census or Enumeration herein before directed to be taken" (ibid., 2: 656).

53. Gordon S. Wood, *The Creation of the American Republic 1776–1787* (Chapel Hill: University of North Carolina Press, 1969), and Donald S. Lutz, *Popular Consent and Popular Control* (Baton Rouge: Louisiana State University Press, 1980), offer illuminating discussions of these contending systems of political thought.

54. Morris, *Forging of the Union,* 299.

55. Farrand, ed., *Records of the Federal Convention,* 2: 583–84.

56. Morris, *Forging of the Union,* 299; Van Doren, *Great Rehearsal,* 176–78; Rossiter, *1787,* 236–37.

57. A survey of American journalism during 1787 and a provocative interpretation of its influence can be found in John K. Alexander, *The Selling of the Constitutional Convention: A History of News Coverage* (Madison, Wis.: Madison House, 1990).

58. Wood, *Creation of the American Republic,* 614.

4. AMENDING AND THE ADOPTION OF THE CONSTITUTION

1. A rich collection of private correspondence, newspapers and pamphlets, and official records having to do with these state proceedings appears in Merrill Jensen, ed., *The Documentary History of the Ratification of the Constitution,* vol. 3, *Ratification of the Constitution by the States: Delaware, New Jersey, Georgia, Connecticut* (Madison: State Historical Society of Wisconsin, 1978).

2. Harold Hancock, "Delaware Becomes the First State," in *The Constitution and the States: The Role of the Original Thirteen in the Framing and Adoption of the Federal Constitution,* ed. Patrick T. Conley and John P. Kaminski (Madison, Wis.: Madison House, 1988), 21–36; Gaspare J. Saladino, "Delaware: Independence and the Concept of a Commercial Republic," in *Ratifying the Constitution,* ed. Michael Allen Gillespie and Michael Lienesch (Lawrence: University Press of Kansas, 1989), 29–51.

3. Mary R. Murrin, "New Jersey and the Two Constitutions," in Conley and Kaminski, eds., *Constitution and the States*, 55–75; Sara M. Shumer, "New Jersey: Property and the Price of Republican Politics," in Gillespie and Lienesch, eds., *Ratifying the Constitution*, 71–89.

4. Edward J. Cashin, "Georgia: Searching for Security," in Gillespie and Lienesch, eds., *Ratifying the Constitution*, 93–116; Albert B. Saye, "Georgia: Security Through Union," in Conley and Kaminski, eds., *Constitution and the States*, ed. 77–92.

5. Robert Allen Rutland, *The Ordeal of the Constitution: The Antifederalists and the Ratification Struggle of 1787–1788* (Norman: University of Oklahoma Press, 1966), 82–86.

6. Jonathan Elliot, ed., *The Debates in the Several State Conventions on the Adoption of the Federal Constitution* 2d ed., 5 vols. (Philadelphia: Lippincott, 1836–1845) 2: 200.

7. Donald S. Lutz, "Connecticut: Achieving Consent and Assuring Control," in Gillespie and Lienesch, eds., *Ratifying the Constitution*, 117–37.

8. John Bach McMaster and Frederick D. Stone, eds., *Pennsylvania and the Federal Constitution, 1787–1788* (Philadelphia: Historical Society of Pennsylvania, 1888), 27–83; Merrill Jensen, ed., *The Documentary History of the Ratification of the Constitution*, vol. 2, *Ratification of the Constitution by the States: Pennsylvania* (Madison: State Historical Society of Wisconsin, 1976); Richard B. Morris, *The Forging of the Union, 1781–1789* (New York: Harper and Row, 1987): 300–302; Rutland, *Ordeal of the Constitution*, 50–54.

9. Elliot, ed., *Debates*, 2: 432–33.

10. Ibid., 2: 436.

11. Rutland, *Ordeal of the Constitution*, 58–59, 62–65; McMaster and Stone, eds., *Pennsylvania and the Federal Constitution*, 418–27.

12. The Massachusetts ratification convention was the first to maintain extensive records of its proceedings; they appear in Elliot, ed., *Debates*, 2: 1–183. Rutland, *Ordeal of the Constitution*, 66–114, provides an excellent narrative account of the convention. Detailed and still useful is Samuel Bannister Harding, *The Contest over the Ratification of the Federal Constitution in the State of Massachusetts* (New York: Longmans, Green, 1896).

13. Cecelia M. Kenyon, "Men of Little Faith: The Anti-Federalists on the Nature of Representative Government," *William and Mary Quarterly*, 3d series, 12 (1955): 3–46.

14. Rutland, *Ordeal of the Constitution*, 104–7. Michael Allen Gillespie, "Massachusetts: Creating Consensus," in Gillespie and Lienesch, eds., *Ratifying the Constitution*, 138–67, makes a strong argument that Hancock acted out of his own convictions that ratification was needed and this was the best means of achieving it.

15. Elliot, ed., *Debates*, 2: 83, 116.

16. Ibid., 2: 117, 122. They either misunderstood the three-fourths state ratification requirement, miscalculated, or assumed that Rhode Island would not ratify.

17. Ibid., 2: 122–41.

18. Ibid., 2: 178–83.

19. Philadelphiensis to the *Independent Gazetteer* [Philadelphia], February 21, 1788, in Cecelia M. Kenyon, ed., *The Antifederalists* (Indianapolis: Bobbs-Merrill, 1966), 79.

20. Rutland, *Ordeal of the Constitution*, 117–23; Jere Daniell, "Ideology and Hardball: Ratification of the Federal Constitution in New Hampshire," in Conley and Kaminski, eds., *Constitution and the States*, 181–94.

21. Rutland, *Ordeal of the Constitution*, 124–27.

22. See especially The Landholder to Luther Martin, *Maryland Journal*, February 29, 1788, in Max Farrand, ed., *The Records of the Federal Convention of 1787*, rev. ed., 4 vols. (New Haven: Yale University Press, 1937), 3: 271–75.

23. Luther Martin to The Landholder, *Maryland Journal*, March 21, 1788, in Farrand, ed., *Records of the Federal Convention*, 3: 286–95. For an analysis of Martin's opposition to the Constitution, see Peter S. Onuf, "Maryland: The Small Republic in the New Nation," in Gillespie and Lienesch, eds., *Ratifying the Constitution*, 171–200.

24. Elliot, ed., *Debates*, 2: 547–56; Rutland, *Ordeal of the Constitution*, 154–58.

25. Elliot, ed., *Debates*, 4: 253–340; Rutland, *Ordeal of the Constitution*, 162–68.

26. Elliot, ed., *Debates*, 1: 325–27; Rutland, *Ordeal of the Constitution*, 210–12; Jean Yarbrough, "New Hampshire: Puritanism and the Moral Foundations of America," in Gillespie and Lienesch, eds., *Ratifying the Constitution*, 250–51.

27. The fullest compilation of debate over the Constitution during this period is John P. Kaminski and Gaspare J. Saladino, eds., *The Documentary History of the Ratification of the Constitution*, vol. 8, *Ratification of the Constitution by the States: Virginia* (Madison: State Historical Society of Wisconsin, 1988) and vols. 13–16, *Commentaries on the Constitution: Public and Private* (Madison: State Historical Society of Wisconsin, 1981–86).

28. *Federalist* no. *85*, in Edward Mead Earle, ed., *The Federalist* (New York: Modern Library, 1937), 567–75.

29. The Virginia convention had the additional virtue of having its debates well recorded; no other ratifying convention left such a full record of its deliberations. See Elliot, ed., *Debates*, 3: 1–663. A thoughtful summary of the Virginia deliberations is provided by Lance Banning, "Virginia: Sectionalism and the General Good," in Gillespie and Lienesch, eds., *Ratifying the Constitution*, 261–99. See also Alan V. Briceland, "Virginia: The Cement of the Union," in Conley and Kaminski, eds., *The Constitution and the States*, 201–23.

30. Edmund Randolph, "Letter on the Federal Convention, October 16, 1787," *Pamphlets on the Constitution of the United States*, ed. Paul Leicester Ford (Brooklyn, 1888), 259–76.

31. Elliot, ed., *Debates*, 3: 24–26.

32. Ibid., 3: 49–50.

33. Ibid., 3: 88–89.

34. Ibid., 3: 101–2.

35. Ibid., 3: 159.

36. Ibid., 3: 174.

37. Ibid., 3: 187, 191.

38. Ibid., 3: 303.

39. Ibid., 3: 315.

40. Ibid., 3: 586–87, 627, 629.

41. Ibid., 3: 591–96.

42. Ibid., 3: 622–52.

43. Ibid., 3: 653–62.

44. A thoughtful evaluation of New York antifederalism can be found in Linda Grant DePauw, *The Eleventh Pillar: New York State and the Federal Constitution* (Ithaca, N.Y.: Cornell University Press, 1966), esp. 170–79. See also John P. Kaminski, "New York: The Reluctant Pillar," in *The Reluctant Pillar: New York and the Adoption of the Federal Constitution*, ed. Stephen L. Schechter (Troy, N.Y.: Russell Sage College, 1985), 48–117; Cecil L. Eubanks, "New York: Federalism and the Political Economy of Union," in Gillespie and Lienesch, eds., *Ratifying the Constitution*, 300–340.

45. Elliot, ed., *Debates*, 2: 220–23.

46. Steven R. Boyd, *The Politics of Opposition: Antifederalists and the Acceptance of the Constitution* (Millwood, N.Y.: KTO Press, 1979), esp. 132–33.

47. Elliot, ed., *Debates*, 2: 322–25.

48. If debate did not cease altogether, it at least disappeared from the pages of the official record of proceedings. What had hitherto been a full transcript of debate became a lean record of formal motions and votes (ibid., 2: 205–414, esp. 406–13).

49. Ibid., 2: 410–12; DePauw, *Eleventh Pillar*, 217–45, clarifies the latter stages of the New York proceedings.

50. Ibid., 2: 412–13.

51. Ibid.

52. Ibid., 4: 4–7.

53. Ibid., 4: 176–77.

54. Ibid., 4: 208, 242–51; Michael Lienesch, "North Carolina: Preserving Rights," in Gillespie and Lienesch, eds. *Ratifying the Constitution,* 343–67; Alan D. Watson, "North Carolina: States' Rights and Agrarianism Ascendant," in Conley and Kaminski, eds., *Constitution and the States,* 252–68.

55. Rutland, *Ordeal of the Constitution,* 279–92.

56. Gordon S. Wood, *The Creation of the American Republic 1776–1787* (Chapel Hill: University of North Carolina Press, 1969), 614.

5. IMMEDIATE AMENDMENT AS THE CONSTITUTION'S PRICE AND PROOF

1. Considerable insight on the development of the U.S. Bill of Rights is available in Robert Allen Rutland, *The Birth of the Bill of Rights, 1776–1791,* rev. ed. (Boston: Northeastern University Press, 1983); Leonard W. Levy, *Legacy of Suppression: Freedom of Speech and Press in Early American History* (Cambridge: Harvard University Press, 1960), and *Origins of the Fifth Amendment: The Right Against Self-Incrimination* (New York: Oxford University Press, 1968); Bernard Schwartz, *The Great Rights of Mankind: A History of the American Bill of Rights* (New York: Oxford University Press, 1977); and Patrick T. Conley and John P. Kaminski, *The Bill of Rights and the States: The Colonial and Revolutionary Origins of American Liberties* (Madison, Wis.: Madison House, 1992).

2. Rutland, *Birth of the Bill of Rights,* 26–27.

3. Willi Paul Adams, *The First American Constitutions,* trans. Rita and Robert Kimber (Chapel Hill: University of North Carolina Press, 1980), 156–58.

4. Levy, *Origins of the Fifth Amendment,* 412.

5. Ibid.

6. Max Farrand, ed., *The Records of the Federal Convention of 1787,* rev. ed., 4 vols. (New Haven: Yale University Press, 1937), 1: 34, 49, 2: 119–20.

7. Ibid., 1: 493.

8. Ibid., 2: 587–88.

9. Ibid., 2: 633.

10. James Madison to Thomas Jefferson, October 24, 1787, in *The Papers of James Madison,* ed. William T. Hutchinson, Robert A. Rutland, et al. 17 vols. (Chicago: University of Chicago Press, 1977), 10: 215.

11. Jonathan Elliot, ed., *The Debates in the Several State Conventions on the Adoption of the Federal Constitution,* 2d ed., 5 vols. (Philadelphia: Lippincott, 1836–1845), 1: 494.

12. Rutland, *Birth of the Bill of Rights,* 124–25.

13. Ibid., 120–22.

14. Ibid., 127, 134–37.

15. Elliot, ed., *Debates,* 2: 435–36, 453–54.

16. John Bach McMaster and Frederick D. Stone, eds., *Pennsylvania and the Federal Constitution, 1787–1788* (Philadelphia: Historical Society of Pennsylvania, 1888), 418–27.

17. Rutland, *Birth of the Bill of Rights,* 142–43.

18. Elliot, ed., *Debates,* 2: 131.

19. Thomas Jefferson to James Madison, December 20, 1787, in Rutland et al., eds., *Papers of James Madison,* 10: 337.

20. Rutland, *Birth of the Bill of Rights,* 128–30, 148–49.

21. Elliot, ed., *Debates,* 2: 518–35.

22. Rutland, *Birth of the Bill of Rights,* 141–42, 155.

23. Elliot, ed., *Debates,* 1: 325–27.

24. A careful analysis of the transformation of Madison's attitudes can be found in Paul Finkelman, "James Madison and the Bill of Rights: A Reluctant Paternity," *Supreme Court Review* (1990): 301–47.

25. See Kenneth R. Bowling, "'A Tub to the Whale': The Founding Fathers and the Adoption of the Federal Bill of Rights," *Journal of the Early Republic* 8 (1988): 223–51, and Jack N. Rakove, "The Madisonian Theory of Rights," *William and Mary Law Review* 31 (1990): 245–66. For a dissenting opinion, consult Robert A. Rutland, "The Trivialization of the Bill of Rights: One Historian's View of How the Purposes of the First Ten Amendments Have Been Defiled," *William and Mary Law Review* 31 (1990): 287–94.

26. Elliot, ed., *Debates,* 3: 617–22.

27. James Madison to Thomas Jefferson, October 17, 1788, in Rutland et al., eds., *Papers of James Madison,* 11: 297–99.

28. Madison to George Eve, January 2, 1789, in ibid., 11: 405.

29. Madison revealed the strength of his sense of obligation in a letter to Richard Peters, August 10, 1789, in ibid., 12: 347.

30. George Washington, Inaugural Address, April 30, 1789, in *Creating the Bill of Rights: The Documentary Record from the First Federal Congress,* ed. Helen E. Veit, Kenneth R. Bowling, and Charlene Bangs Bickford (Baltimore: Johns Hopkins University Press, 1991), 231–32.

31. Rutland, *Birth of the Bill of Rights,* 198.

32. *Congressional Register,* May 5, 1789, and [New York] *Daily Advertiser,* May 6, 1789, in Veit et al., eds., *Creating the Bill of Rights,* 57–62.

33. James Madison to Thomas Jefferson, May 27, 1789, and *Congressional Register,* June 8, 1789, in ibid., 69, 240.

34. *Congressional Register,* June 8, 1789, in ibid., 70–95.

35. Ibid., 73, 78–80.

36. Ibid., 75.

37. Ibid., 95.

38. For the full text of Madison's June 8 proposal, see ibid., 11–14.

39. *Congressional Register,* June 8, 1789, in ibid., 11–14, 83–85.

40. Ibid., xv, 175, 245, 259, 276, 278.

41. *Congressional Register,* June 8, 1789, in ibid., 95.

42. Particularly insightful on Madison's approach to drafting his proposals is Levy, *Origins of the Fifth Amendment,* 422–24.

43. James Madison to Richard Peters, August 10, 1789, in Rutland et al., eds., *Papers of James Madison,* 12: 347.

44. *Congressional Register,* June 8, 1789, in Veit et al., eds., *Creating the Bill of Rights,* 79, 86.

45. *Gazette of the United States,* August 22, 1789, in ibid., 193; *Congressional Register,* August 18, 1789, in ibid., 197.

46. *Congressional Register,* July 21, 1789, in ibid., 97–103.

47. *Congressional Register,* August 13, 1789, in ibid., 112–17.

48. Ibid., 117.

49. Ibid., 118.

50. Ibid., 118–20.

51. Ibid., 120–21.

52. Ibid., 121–22.

53. Ibid., 128.

54. *Congressional Register,* August 19, 1789, in ibid., 197–98.

55. James Madison to Alexander White, August 24, 1789, in Rutland et al., eds., *Papers of James Madison,* 12: 352.

56. Ibid.

57. William L. Smith to Edward Rutledge, August 15, 1789, in Veit et al., eds., *Creating the Bill of Rights,* 278.

58. *Congressional Register,* August 14, 1789, in ibid., 137–39.

59. *Congressional Register,* August 19, 1789, in ibid., 198.

60. *Congressional Register,* August 14, 1789, in ibid., 139–49.

61. Ibid., 21, 26.

62. *Congressional Register,* June 8, 1789, in ibid., 84. A fuller discussion of the measure appears in chapter 19 of this volume.

63. *Congressional Register,* August 17, 1789, in ibid., 187.

64. *Congressional Register,* August 15, 1789, in ibid., 159–77.

65. *Congressional Register,* August 18, 1789, August 21, 1789, and August 22, 1789, in ibid., 193–95, 199–205, 208–13.

66. Ibid., 9.

67. Ibid., 9–10.

68. Ibid., 49–50.

69. William S. Price, Jr., "'There Ought to Be a Bill of Rights': North Carolina Enters a New Nation," in Conley and Kaminski, eds., *The Bill of Rights and the States,* 424–59.

70. Patrick T. Conley, "First in War, Last in Peace: Rhode Island and the Constitution, 1786–1790," in *The Constitution and the States: The Role of the Original Thirteen in the Framing and Adoption of the Federal Constitution,* ed. Patrick T. Conley and John P. Kaminski (Madison, Wis.: Madison House, 1988), 259–65; Elliot, ed., *Debates,* 1: 333–37.

71. Patrick T. Conley, "Rhode Island: Laboratory for the 'Lively Experiment,'" in Conley and Kaminski, eds., *Bill of Rights and the States,* 152–53.

72. Elliot, ed., *Debates,* 1: 339–40.

73. See esp. *Daily Advertiser,* August 15, 1789, in Veit et al., eds., *Creating the Bill of Rights,* 129–31.

74. Elliot, ed., *Debates,* 1: 339–40.

75. Bernard Schwartz, *The Bill of Rights: A Documentary History,* 2 vols. (New York: Chelsea House, 1971), 2: 1172–76.

76. Alan P. Grimes, *Democracy and the Amendments to the Constitution* (Lexington, Mass.: Lexington Books, 1978), 28, n.40.

77. *Documentary History of the Constitution of the United States of America, 1786–1870* (Washington, D.C.: Department of State, 1894), 2: 371–76.

78. Richard Henry Lee and William Grayson to the speaker of the Virginia House of Delegates, September 28, 1789, in Veit et al., eds., *Creating the Bill of Rights,* 299–300.

79. Richard Henry Lee to Patrick Henry, September 14, 1789, in ibid., 295–96.

80. Richard Henry Lee to Patrick Henry, September 27, 1789, in ibid., 299.

81. *Documentary History of the Constitution,* 2: 387–90.

6. AMENDMENTS AND THE JUDICIAL REVIEW ALTERNATIVE

1. Herbert V. Ames, *The Proposed Amendments to the Constitution,* in *Annual Report of the American Historical Association, 1896* (Washington, D.C.: GPO, 1897), 19–23, 307–65.

2. Michael Kammen, *A Machine That Would Go of Itself: The Constitution in American Culture* (New York: Knopf, 1986), 43–94.

3. George Athan Billias, "American Constitutionalism and Europe, 1776–1848," and Robert J. Kolesar, "North American Constitutionalism and Spanish America," in *American Constitutionalism Abroad: Selected Essays in Comparative Constitutional History,* ed. George Athan Billias (Westport, Conn.: Greenwood, 1990), 13–39 and 41–63.

4. Thomas Jefferson to James Madison, March 15, 1789, in Julian P. Boyd et al., eds., *The Papers of Thomas Jefferson,* 25 vols. (Princeton: Princeton University Press, 1958), 14: 659.

5. Clyde E. Jacobs, *The Eleventh Amendment and Sovereign Immunity* (Westport, Conn.: Greenwood, 1972), 1–46, 64.

6. *Chisholm v. Georgia,* 2 US (2 Dallas) 419 (1793); Jacobs, *Eleventh Amendment,* 46–55; John V. Orth, *The Judicial Power of the United States: The Eleventh Amendment in American History* (New York: Oxford University Press, 1987), 12–29.

7. Jacobs, *Eleventh Amendment,* 55–62.

8. Ibid., 64–67.

9. Ibid., 67.

10. Ibid., 67–74.

11. *Hollingsworth v. Virginia,* 3 US (3 Dallas) 378 (1798); David P. Currie, *The Constitution in the Supreme Court: The First Hundred Years, 1789–1888* (Chicago: University of Chicago Press, 1985), 21–22; Jacobs, *Eleventh Amendment,* 75–76.

12. John J. Turner, Jr., "The Twelfth Amendment and the First American Party System," *Historian* 35 (1973): 221–32; Tadahisa Kuroda, *The Origins of the Twelfth Amendment: The Electoral College in the Early Republic, 1787–1804* (Westport, Conn.: Greenwood, 1994), 7–114.

13. Kuroda, *Origins of the Twelfth Amendment,* 118–43.

14. Turner, "Twelfth Amendment," 232–35; Alan P. Grimes, *Democracy and the Amendments to the Constitution* (Lexington, Mass.: Lexington Books, 1978), 22–25.

15. Kuroda, *Origins of the Twelfth Amendment,* 147–51.

16. Ibid., 155–61, provides the most detailed account available.

17. Ames, *Proposed Amendments,* 188, 329–30.

18. For an interesting discussion of the larger topic of population distribution and the amending process, see Peter Suber, "Population Changes and Constitutional Amendments: Federalism Versus Democracy," *University of Michigan Journal of Law Reform* 20 (1987): 409–90.

19. Ames, *Proposed Amendments,* 307–65, provides a comprehensive list of amendments offered in the Congress and their disposition.

20. John C. Miller, *The Federalist Era, 1789–1801* (New York: Harper, 1960), 230; idem, *Crisis in Freedom: The Alien and Sedition Acts* (Boston: Little, Brown, 1951), 48–49; Ames, *Proposed Amendments,* 323.

21. Ames, *Proposed Amendments,* 46, 326; James M. Banner, Jr., *To the Hartford Convention: The Federalists and the Origins of Party Politics in Massachusetts, 1789–1815* (New York: Knopf, 1970), 102–3.

22. Banner, *To the Hartford Convention,* 299–306.

23. Ibid., 306–35.

24. Ames, *Proposed Amendments,* 46, 331–32; Banner, *To the Hartford Convention,* 341–42.

25. Ames, *Proposed Amendments,* 46. The eight disapprovals were spread from Ver-

mont, New York, New Jersey, and Pennsylvania to Virginia, Ohio, Tennessee, and Louisiana.

26. Banner, *To the Hartford Convention*, 342–50; Ames, *Proposed Amendments*, 46.

27. Ames, *Proposed Amendments*, 80–125, 330–40.

28. Ibid., 56–57.

29. Max Farrand, ed., *The Records of the Federal Convention of 1787*, rev. ed., 4 vols. (New Haven: Yale University Press, 1937), 1: 21, 97–111.

30. Charles F. Hobson, "The Negative on State Laws: James Madison, and the Crisis of Republican Government," *William and Mary Quarterly* 36 (1979): 215–35.

31. Farrand, ed., *Records of the Federal Convention*, 1: 109.

32. Quoted in Brinton Coxe, *An Essay on Judicial Power and Unconstitutional Legislation* (Philadelphia: Kay and Brother, 1893), 234, 241.

33. J. M. Sosin, *The Aristocracy of the Long Robe: The Origins of Judicial Review in America* (Westport, Conn.: Greenwood, 1989), 214–18.

34. The early development of judicial review has been widely examined. Useful discussions can be found in Robert Lowry Clinton, *Marbury v. Madison and Judicial Review* (Lawrence: University Press of Kansas, 1989), 1–77; Currie, *Constitution in the Supreme Court: The First Hundred Years*, 1–74; Sylvia Snowiss, *Judicial Review and the Law of the Constitution* (New Haven: Yale University Press, 1990), 1–108; Sosin, *Aristocracy of the Long Robe*; and Christopher Wolfe, *The Rise of Modern Judicial Review* (New York: Basic Books, 1986), 17–38.

35. Thomas Jefferson to James Madison, March 15, 1789, in Boyd et al., eds., *Papers of Thomas Jefferson*, 14: 659.

36. *Chisholm v. Georgia*, 2 US (2 Dallas) 433.

37. *Hylton v. United States*, 3 US (3 Dallas) 171 (1796).

38. *Ware v. Hylton*, 3 US (3 Dallas) 199 (1796).

39. An excellent summary of the immediate circumstances of the case is provided by Donald O. Dewey, *Marshall versus Jefferson: The Political Background of Marbury v. Madison* (New York: Knopf, 1970).

40. *Marbury v. Madison*, 5 US (1 Cranch) 177–78 (1803).

41. Dewey, *Marshall versus Jefferson*, 181–82.

42. James Bryce, *The American Commonwealth*, 3d ed. (New York: Macmillan, 1895), 256.

43. Contributions to this debate have come from, among others, Edward S. Corwin, *Court over Constitution: A Study of Judicial Review as an Instrument of Popular Government* (Princeton: Princeton University Press, 1938); William W. Crosskey, *Politics and the Constitution in the History of the United States* (Chicago: University of Chicago Press, 1953); Raoul Berger, *Congress v. the Supreme Court* (Cambridge: Harvard University Press, 1969); and Wolfe, *Rise of Modern Judicial Review*.

44. Dumas Malone, *Jefferson the President: First Term, 1801–1805* (Boston: Little, Brown, 1970), 311–32; Merrill D. Peterson, *Thomas Jefferson and the New Nation* (New York: Oxford University Press, 1970), 770–76.

45. Dumas Malone, his premier biographer, notes this in *Jefferson the Virginian* (Boston: Little, Brown, 1948), 235–36, 304–5, 381. Gordon Wood places him in the forefront of this important element of eighteenth-century republican thought in *Creation of the American Republic 1776–1787* (Chapel Hill: University of North Carolina Press, 1969), 128, 307, 342.

46. James Madison calls attention to this in *Federalist 49*, in Edward Mead Earle, ed., *The Federalist* (New York: Modern Library, 1937), 327.

47. Thomas Jefferson to James Madison, September 6, 1789, in Boyd et al., eds., *The Papers of Thomas Jefferson*, 15: 392–97.

48. Madison, *Federalist 49*, 327–32.

49. Malone, *Jefferson the President: First Term*, 330.

50. James Madison, Seventh Annual Message, December 5, 1815, in James D. Richardson, ed., *A Compilation of the Messages and Papers of the Presidents 1789–1897*, 20 vols. (New York: Bureau of National Literature, 1897), 2: 553.

51. James Madison, Eighth Annual Message, December 3, 1816, in ibid., 564.

52. James Madison, Veto Message, March 3, 1817, in ibid., 570.

53. Thomas Jefferson to George Ticknor, May ?, 1817, *The Writings of Thomas Jefferson*, ed. Paul Leicester Ford (New York: G. P. Putnam, 1899), 10: 81.

54. *McCulloch v. Maryland*, 17 US (4 Wheat.) 316, 407–8 (1819); italics Marshall's.

55. Ibid., 415, 421.

56. Dumas Malone, *The Sage of Monticello* (Boston: Little, Brown, 1981), 352–53.

57. Madison to Roane, September 2, 1819, quoted in Drew R. McCoy, *The Last of the Fathers* (New York: Cambridge University Press, 1989), 99–103.

7. STATES' RIGHTS AND CONSTITUTIONAL AMENDMENT

1. Abraham Lincoln, "Second Inaugural Address," in James D. Richardson, ed., *A Compilation of the Messages and Papers of the Presidents, 1789–1897*, 20 vols. (New York: Bureau of National Literature, 1897), 8: 3477.

2. An insightful consideration of Madison's thinking and actions is found in Charles F. Hobson, "The Negative on State Laws: James Madison and the Crisis of Republican Government," *William and Mary Quarterly* 36 (1979): 215–35.

3. Max Farrand, ed., *The Records of the Federal Convention of 1787*, rev. ed., 4 vols. (New Haven: Yale University Press, 1937), 1: 21.

4. Ibid., 1: 164–67.

5. Ibid., 1: 165–68, 318–19; 2: 27, 390, 440, 589.

6. Ibid., 1: 245; 2: 183, 603.

7. John C. Miller, *Crisis in Freedom: The Alien and Sedition Acts* (Boston: Little, Brown, 1951), 3–168.

8. A full and careful account of their collaboration is Adrienne Koch and Harry Ammon, "The Virginia and Kentucky Resolutions, An Episode in Jefferson's and Madison's Defense of Civil Liberties," *William and Mary Quarterly* 5 (1948): 145–76.

9. "Extracts from the Address to the People Which Accompanied the Foregoing [Virginia] Resolutions," January 23, 1799, in Jonathan Elliot, ed., *The Debates in the Several State Conventions on the Adoption of the Federal Constitution*, 2d ed., 5 vols. (Philadelphia: Lippincott, 1836–1845), 4: 531.

10. First Kentucky Resolution of 1798, in ibid., 4: 540.

11. Virginia Resolutions of 1798, in ibid., 4: 528.

12. Kentucky Resolution of 1799, in ibid., 4: 545.

13. Miller, *Crisis in Freedom*, 171.

14. Drew R. McCoy, *The Last of the Fathers: James Madison and the Republican Legacy* (New York: Cambridge University Press, 1989), 139–43.

15. James M. Banner, Jr., *To the Hartford Convention: The Federalists and the Origins of Party Politics in Massachusetts, 1789–1815* (New York: Knopf, 1970), 118–21.

16. Ibid., 306–50.

17. *McCulloch v. Maryland*, 17 US (4 Wheat.) 316 (1819).

18. William W. Freehling, *Prelude to Civil War: The Nullification Controversy in South Carolina, 1816–1836* (New York: Harper and Row, 1966), 164–73.

19. Quoted in ibid., 167–68.

20. "Extract from Report of Kentucky in reply to South Carolina—January 27, 1830," in *State Documents on Federal Relations*, no. 4, *The Tariff and Nullification, 1820–1833*, ed. Herman V. Ames (Philadelphia: University of Pennsylvania History Department, 1902), 26–27.

21. Richard E. Ellis, *The Union At Risk: Jacksonian Democracy, States' Rights, and the Nullification Crisis* (New York: Oxford University Press, 1987), 11, 48.

22. Herman V. Ames, *The Proposed Amendments to the Constitution*, in *Annual Report, American Historical Association, 1896* (Washington, D.C.: GPO, 1897), 282, 345; Freehling, *Prelude to Civil War*, 265; Ellis, *Union at Risk*, 106–12, 159, 123–60; McCoy, *Last of the Fathers*, 141–42.

23. Andrew Jackson, proclamation, December 10, 1832, in Richardson, ed., *Messages and Papers of the Presidents*, 3: 1205–6.

24. Freehling, *Prelude to Civil War*, 297.

25. Ames, *Proposed Amendments*, 327, 334, 339.

26. Ibid., 193, 349; William W. Freehling, *The Road to Disunion: Secessionists at Bay, 1776–1854* (New York: Oxford University Press, 1990), 342–45.

27. Ames, *Proposed Amendments*, 354.

28. Freehling, *Prelude to Civil War*, 170.

29. Harold M. Hyman and William M. Wiecek, *Equal Justice Under Law: Constitutional Development, 1835–1875* (New York: Harper and Row, 1982), 137–38.

30. Ames, *Proposed Amendments*, 194, 354–65.

31. Albert D. Kirwan, *John J. Crittenden: The Struggle for the Union* (Lexington: University of Kentucky Press, 1962), 367.

32. James Buchanan, "Fourth Annual Message," in Richardson, ed., *Messages and Papers of the Presidents*, 7: 3167.

33. Ibid., 7: 3168–70; Ames, *Proposed Amendments*, 194, 354–55.

34. Harold M. Hyman, *A More Perfect Union: The Impact of the Civil War and Reconstruction on the Constitution* (New York: Knopf, 1973), 40–41.

35. Quoted in Kenneth M. Stampp, *And the War Came: The North and the Secession Crisis, 1860–1861* (Baton Rouge: Louisiana State University Press, 1950), 123.

36. Ames, *Proposed Amendments*, 357; Kirwan, *Crittenden*, 375.

37. James M. McPherson, *Battle Cry of Freedom: The Civil War Era* (New York: Oxford University Press, 1988), 253; Kirwan, *Crittenden*, 379–82. Kirwan credits Lincoln with the December defeat of the Crittenden plan in the committee of thirteen (*Crittenden*, 389).

38. Stampp, *And the War Came*, 123–29; Kirwan, *Crittenden*, 391–92.

39. Ames, *Proposed Amendments*, 358; Kirwan, *Crittenden*, 392.

40. Kirwan, *Crittenden*, 394–95.

41. Ibid., 396–400.

42. Ibid., 401–4.

43. Robert G. Gunderson, *Old Gentlemen's Convention: The Washington Peace Conference of 1861* (Madison: University of Wisconsin Press, 1961); Jesse L. Keene, *The Peace Convention of 1861* (Tuscaloosa, Ala.: Confederate Publishing, 1961); Ames, *Proposed Amendments*, 364.

44. A useful legislative history of the Corwin amendment can be found in R. Alton Lee, "The Corwin Amendment in the Secession Crisis," *Ohio Historical Quarterly* 70 (1961): 1–26.

45. Ames, *Proposed Amendments*, 196, 363; Kirwan, *Crittenden*, 410–21.

46. Philip L. Martin, "Illinois' Ratification of the Corwin Amendment," *Journal of Public Law* 15 (1966): 187–91; Ames, *Proposed Amendments*, 196–97, 363. The Illinois constitutional convention acted on the basis that for the moment it possessed the state's legislative powers. Although this assertion was never tested in court because the ratification process was not completed, it runs counter to later Supreme Court decisions in *Hawke v. Smith*, 253 US 221 (1920) and *United States v. Sprague*, 282 US 716 (1931) that Congress had specific and sole power to authorize state legislative or convention ratification.

47. Quoted in Jesse T. Carpenter, *The South as a Conscious Minority, 1789–1861: A Study in Political Thought* (New York: New York University Press, 1930), 157.

48. Don E. Fehrenbacher, *The Dred Scott Case: Its Significance in American Law and Politics* (New York: Oxford University Press, 1978), 547–48.

49. Arthur Bestor, "The American Civil War as a Constitutional Crisis," *American Historical Review* 69 (1964): 334, 341; Fehrenbacher, *Dred Scott Case,* 549–50.

8. THE SECOND AMERICAN CONSTITUTIONAL REVOLUTION

1. A contemporary articulation of this argument appeared in Timothy Farrar, "The Adequacy of the Constitution," *New Englander* 21 (1862): 52–73. It is thoroughly and well examined in Harold M. Hyman, *A More Perfect Union: The Impact of the Civil War and Reconstruction on the Constitution* (New York: Knopf, 1973), and Hyman and William M. Wiecek, *Equal Justice Under Law: Constitutional Development, 1835–1875* (New York: Harper and Row, 1982).

2. A useful discussion of congressional actions can be found in Herman Belz, *A New Birth of Freedom: The Republican Party and Freedmen's Rights, 1861–1866* (Westport, Conn.: Greenwood, 1976), 3–16.

3. An insightful, if brief, discussion of Lincoln's thinking regarding the necessity of amendment is contained in Garry Wills, *Lincoln at Gettysburg: The Words that Remade America* (New York: Simon and Schuster, 1992), 137–47.

4. Abraham Lincoln, Annual Message to Congress, December 1, 1862, in Roy P. Basler, ed., *The Collected Works of Abraham Lincoln,* 9 vols. (New Brunswick, N.J.: Rutgers University Press, 1953–1955), 5: 527–31.

5. Belz, *New Birth of Freedom,* 9.

6. James G. Randall, *Constitutional Problems Under Lincoln* (New York: D. Appleton, 1926), 373.

7. Herman V. Ames, *The Proposed Amendments to the Constitution,* in *Annual Report, American Historical Association, 1896* (Washington, D.C.: GPO, 1897), 214.

8. Ibid., 214–15.

9. Ibid., 214–17, 367–68; Earl M. Maltz, *Civil Rights, the Constitution, and Congress, 1863–1869* (Lawrence: University Press of Kansas, 1990), 14–25; Alan P. Grimes, *Democracy and the Amendments to the Constitution* (Lexington, Mass.: Lexington Books, 1978), 35–37.

10. Basler, ed., *Collected Works of Abraham Lincoln,* 8: 107.

11. Ames, *Proposed Amendments,* 217–18; Maltz, *Civil Rights, the Constitution, and Congress,* 17–18; Grimes, *Democracy and the Amendments,* 38.

12. James M. McPherson, *Battle Cry of Freedom: The Civil War Era* (New York: Oxford University Press, 1988), 839–40.

13. *Hollingsworth v. Virginia,* 3 US (3 Dallas) 378 (1798).

14. Andrew C. McLaughlin, *A Constitutional History of the United States* (New York: Appleton-Century-Crofts, 1935), 635.

15. Grimes, *Democracy and the Amendments,* 35.

16. McLaughlin, *Constitutional History of the United States,* 636.

17. Phillip S. Paludan, *A Covenant with Death: The Constitution, Law, and Equality in the Civil War Era* (Urbana: University of Illinois Press, 1975), 214.

18. Reconstruction, its constitutional aspect in particular, has received a great deal of scrutiny. Noteworthy studies include Horace E. Flack, *The Adoption of the Fourteenth Amendment* (Baltimore: Johns Hopkins University Press, 1908); Jacobus tenBroek, *The Antislavery Origins of the Fourteenth Amendment* (Berkeley: University of California Press, 1951); Joseph B. James, *The Framing of the Fourteenth Amendment* (Urbana: University of Illinois Press, 1956); W. R. Brock, *An American Crisis: Congress and Recon-*

Explicit and Authentic Acts

struction, 1865–1867 (New York: St. Martin's Press, 1963); Michael Les Benedict, *A Compromise of Principle: Congressional Republicans and Reconstruction, 1863–1869* (New York: W. W. Norton, 1974); Joseph B. James, *The Ratification of the Fourteenth Amendment* (Macon, Ga.: Mercer University Press, 1984); Michael Kent Curtis, *No State Shall Abridge: The Fourteenth Amendment and the Bill of Rights* (Durham, N.C.: Duke University Press, 1986); Eric Foner, *Reconstruction: America's Unfinished Revolution, 1863–1877* (New York: Harper and Row, 1988); William E. Nelson, *The Fourteenth Amendment: From Political Principle to Judicial Doctrine* (Cambridge: Harvard University Press, 1988); and Maltz, *Civil Rights, the Constitution, and Congress.*

19. Benedict, *Compromise of Principle,* 136–61; Maltz, *Civil Rights, the Constitution, and Congress,* 50–52; Ames, *Proposed Amendments,* 373.

20. Ames, *Proposed Amendments,* 220, 371.

21. *Congressional Globe,* 39th Cong., 1st sess., 157–58.

22. Benedict, *Compromise of Principle,* 162–66.

23. James, *Framing of the Fourteenth Amendment,* 100–102, 172; Maltz, *Civil Rights, the Constitution, and Congress,* 79–81.

24. Ames, *Proposed Amendments,* 219–26, provides a bare-bones account, while Benedict, *Compromise of Principle,* 169–83, Curtis, *No State Shall Abridge,* 57–130, Foner, *Reconstruction,* 252–60, James, *Framing of the Fourteenth Amendment,* 81–116, Maltz, *Civil Rights, the Constitution, and Congress,* 79–120, and Nelson, *Fourteenth Amendment,* 40–90, set forth differing interpretations at length.

25. Nelson, *Fourteenth Amendment,* 61. This view is amplified by Robert J. Kaczorowski, "Searching for the Intent of the Framers of the Fourteenth Amendment," *Connecticut Law Review* 6 (1972–1973): 368–98.

26. Maltz, *Civil Rights, the Constitution, and Congress,* 114–15.

27. The fullest rendering of this revisionist view can be found in Raoul Berger, *Government by Judiciary: The Transformation of the Fourteenth Amendment* (Cambridge: Harvard University Press, 1977); see also Alexander M. Bickel, "The Original Understanding and the Segregation Decision," *Harvard Law Review* 69 (1955): 1–65. The argument for the contrary, more expansive interpretation is well put in Curtis, *No State Shall Abridge.* A useful analysis of the controversy that adds weight to Curtis's conclusion can be found in Richard L. Aynes, "On Misreading John Bingham and the Fourteenth Amendment," *Yale Law Journal* 103 (1993): 57–104.

28. Foner, *Reconstruction,* 255.

29. James, *Framing of the Fourteenth Amendment,* 117–31.

30. Ibid., 132–52.

31. James, *Ratification of the Fourteenth Amendment,* 6–7.

32. Ibid., 6–18.

33. Ibid., 19–26.

34. James, *Framing of the Fourteenth Amendment,* 172–76; idem, *Ratification of the Fourteenth Amendment,* 33–36.

35. Benedict, *Compromise of Principle,* 210–12.

36. Quoted in James, *Ratification of the Fourteenth Amendment,* 177.

37. Ames and others disagree on the dates of state action. Joseph James's close examination of state legislative records lends weight to his account (ibid., 58–155).

38. Ibid., 58–155.

39. Ibid., 55–58, 73–74, 156–77, 182–98; Ames, *Proposed Amendments,* 377.

40. The complex evolution of this act is well described in Benedict, *Compromise of Principle,* 210–43.

41. James, *Ratification of the Fourteenth Amendment,* 181–87.

42. Ibid., 233–74.

43. Quoted in ibid., 266.

44. Quoted in ibid., 250.

45. Quoted in ibid., 262.

46. Ibid., 282–86.

47. James, *Ratification of the Fourteenth Amendment,* 294–97. By the time Seward issued a formal proclamation on July 28, he was able to add Georgia to the list of ratifying states.

48. *Coleman v. Miller,* 307 US 433 (1939).

49. For an extreme example, see the popular older account of Claude G. Bowers, *The Tragic Era: The Revolution After Lincoln* (Cambridge, Mass.: Houghton Mifflin, 1929). Bowers, the 1928 Democratic National Convention keynote speaker, had political reasons for so portraying Republican politics; they are explored in David E. Kyvig, "History as Present Politics: Claude Bowers' *The Tragic Era,*" *Indiana Magazine of History* 63 (1977): 17–31.

50. William Gillette, *The Right to Vote: Politics and the Passage of the Fifteenth Amendment* (Baltimore: Johns Hopkins University Press, 1965).

51. Benedict, *Compromise of Principle,* 325–27.

52. Ibid., 77–79, 121; Maltz, *Civil Rights, the Constitution, and Congress,* 8–11, 36–37.

53. Gillette, *Right to Vote,* 25–26, focuses on the overall results, while Benedict, *Compromise of Principle,* 116, stresses the Republicans' preference.

54. Maltz, *Civil Rights, the Constitution, and Congress,* 118–20.

55. Ibid., 134–35.

56. Ames, *Proposed Amendments,* 230.

57. Maltz, *Civil Rights, the Constitution, and Congress,* 121–41.

58. Quoted in ibid., 143.

59. Benedict, *Compromise of Principle,* 325–27; Maltz, *Civil Rights, the Constitution, and Congress,* 143–44.

60. Ames, *Proposed Amendments,* 283–90.

61. Quoted in Maltz, *Civil Rights, the Constitution, and Congress,* 144.

62. The convoluted legislative history of the amendment resolution receives detailed treatment and different interpretation in Ames, 229–35, Benedict, *Compromise of Principle,* 331–35, Gillette, *Right to Vote,* 46–78, and Maltz, *Civil Rights, the Constitution, and Congress,* 145–56.

63. *Congressional Globe,* 40th Cong., 3d sess., 1626. Earl Maltz concludes that because broader terms were discussed but not adopted, the Fifteenth Amendment should be interpreted narrowly. Yet even his own account implies that the bulk of the Fortieth Congress favored some sort of broader protection and that only the impending end of the session terminated the search for more satisfactory language in order that a fundamental declaration on suffrage could be adopted (see Maltz, *Civil Rights, the Constitution, and Congress,* 145–56).

64. Ames, *Proposed Amendments,* 388–89.

65. Ibid., 385–86, 389; Ralph R. Martig, "Amending the Constitution—Article V: The Keystone of the Arch," *Michigan Law Review* 35 (1937): 1277–78.

66. Gillette, *Right to Vote,* 98–103.

67. Ibid. provides a chronology and legislative voting analysis of ratification, 84–86, and offers the fullest summary of state actions, 101–58.

68. As with the Fourteenth Amendment, the Congress refused to recognize the rescission as legitimate.

69. *Texas v. White,* 74 US (7 Wall.) 700 (1869) at 729; Currie, *The Constitution in the Supreme Court: The First Hundred Years, 1789–1888* (Chicago: University of Chicago Press, 1985), 311–16.

70. *Slaughter-House Cases,* 83 US (16 Wall.) 36 (1873); Currie, *Constitution in the Supreme Court,* 342–51; Nelson, *Fourteenth Amendment,* 155–64.

71. *U.S. v. Reese*, 92 US 214 (1876); Currie, *Constitution in the Supreme Court*, 393–95.

72. *U.S. v. Cruikshank*, 92 US 542 (1876).

73. *U.S. v. Harris*, 106 US 629 (1883).

74. *Civil Rights Cases*, 109 US 3 (1883); an excellent discussion of these cases can be found in Alan F. Westin, "The Case of the Prejudiced Doorkeeper," in *Quarrels That Have Shaped the Constitution*, ed. John A. Garraty, rev. ed. (New York: Harper and Row, 1987), 139–56.

75. *Hall v. DeCuir*, 95 US 485 (1878) and *Louisville, New Orleans & Texas Railway v. Mississippi*, 133 US 587 (1890).

76. *Plessy v. Ferguson*, 163 US 537 (1896); a thorough and thoughtful examination of the case and its social, intellectual, political, and legal context can be found in Charles A. Lofgren, *The Plessy Case: A Legal-Historical Interpretation* (New York: Oxford University Press, 1987).

77. *Williams v. Mississippi*, 170 US 213 (1898).

78. *Strauder v. West Virginia*, 100 US 303 (1880); *ex parte Virginia* 100 US 339 (1880); *Neal v. Delaware*, 103 US 370 (1881); Donald G. Nieman, *Promises to Keep: African-Americans and the Constitutional Order, 1776 to the Present* (New York: Oxford University Press, 1991), 97–98.

79. *Munn v. Illinois*, 94 US 113 (1877); C. Peter McGrath, "The Case of the Unscrupulous Warehouseman," in Garraty, ed., *Quarrels That Have Shaped the Constitution*, 119–38.

80. *Santa Clara County v. Southern Pacific Railway Co.*, 118 US 394 (1886); Howard Jay Graham, "The 'Conspiracy Theory' of the Fourteenth Amendment," *Yale Law Journal* 47 (1938): 371–403 and 48 (1938): 171–94; Loren P. Beth, *The Development of the American Constitution, 1877–1917* (New York: Harper and Row, 1971), 172–73.

9. RESURRECTING THE AMENDING REMEDY

1. Michael Kammen, *A Machine That Would Go of Itself: The Constitution in American Culture* (New York: Knopf, 1986), 142, 162–63.

2. Arthur W. Machen, Jr., "The Elasticity of the Constitution," *Harvard Law Review* 14 (1900): 209.

3. Walter Clark, "Inevitable Constitutional Changes," *North American Review* 163 (1896): 462.

4. Herman V. Ames, *The Proposed Amendments to the Constitution*, in *Annual Report, American Historical Association, 1896* (Washington, D.C.: GPO, 1897), 277–78, 396; Michael A. Musmanno, *Proposed Amendments to the Constitution*, 70th Cong., 2d sess., House Doc. 551 (Washington, D.C.: GPO, 1929), 182.

5. Lawrence B. Goodheart, "The Ambiguity of Individualism: The National Liberal League's Challenge to the Comstock Law," in *American Chameleon: Individualism in Trans-National Context*, ed. Richard O. Curry and Lawrence B. Goodheart (Kent, Ohio: Kent State University Press, 1991), 135.

6. Musmanno, *Proposed Amendments*, 183–85.

7. Ames, *Proposed Amendments*, 272, 396, 407–21; Leonard J. Arrington and Davis Bitton, *The Mormon Experience: A History of the Latter-day Saints* (New York: Knopf, 1979), esp. 161–84; Richard S. Van Wagoner, *Mormon Polygamy: A History*, 2d ed. (Salt Lake City: Signature, 1989); Gustive O. Larson, *The "Americanization" of Utah for Statehood* (San Marino, Calif.: Huntington Library, 1971); and Edwin Brown Firmage and Richard Collin Mangrum, *Zion in the Courts: A Legal History of the Church of Jesus Christ of Latter-day Saints, 1830–1900* (Urbana: University of Illinois Press, 1988).

8. Musmanno, *Proposed Amendments*, 212; Russell L. Caplan, *Constitutional Brinksmanship* (New York: Oxford University Press, 1988), 66.

9. Ames, *Proposed Amendments*, 248–49, 402.

10. Ibid., 36–38, 416, 418.

11. Musmanno, *Proposed Amendments*, 5–6.

12. Ames, *Proposed Amendments*, 301–2.

13. Quoted in ibid., 302.

14. William P. Potter, "The Method of Amending the Federal Constitution," *University of Pennsylvania Law Review and American Law Register* 57 (1909): 603; Joseph R. Long, "Tinkering with the Constitution," *Yale Law Review* 24 (1915): 574; Seba Eldridge, "Need for a More Democratic Procedure of Amending the Constitution," *American Political Science Review* 10 (1916): 683–88.

15. James Bryce, *The American Commonwealth*, 3d ed. (New York: Macmillan, 1895), 371.

16. Potter, "Method of Amending," 590, 606.

17. Henry Bournes Higgins, "The Rigid Constitution," *Political Science Quarterly* 20 (1905): 208.

18. John W. Burgess, "Present Problems of Constitutional Law," *Political Science Quarterly* 19 (1904): 548.

19. Frederic Bruce Johnstone, "An Eighteenth Century Constitution," *University of Illinois Law Review* 7 (1912): 274.

20. Monroe Smith, "Shall We Make Our Constitution Flexible?" *North American Review* 194 (November 1911): 657.

21. Potter, "Method of Amending," 608; Smith, "Shall We Make Our Constitution Flexible," 663.

22. Long, "Tinkering with the Constitution," 573.

23. *Hylton v. U.S.*, 3 US (3 Dallas) 171 (1796).

24. *Springer v. U.S.* 102 US 586 (1880). Nineteenth-century judicial treatment of the federal taxing power is well summarized in Carl Brent Swisher, *American Constitutional Development* (Boston: Houghton Mifflin, 1943), esp. 439; Sidney Ratner, *American Taxation* (New York: W. W. Norton, 1942); and Loren P. Beth, *The Development of the American Constitution, 1877–1917* (New York: Harper and Row, 1971), 154. A revisionist account that argues support for an income tax was more widespread and less contentious than hereinafter portrayed is Robert Stanley, *Dimensions of Law in the Service of Order: Origins of the Federal Income Tax, 1861–1913* (New York: Oxford University Press, 1993).

25. William L. Wilson, "The Income Tax on Corporations," *North American Review* 158 (January 1894): 1.

26. Allan Nevins, *Grover Cleveland* (New York: Dodd, Mead, 1933), 667; Paolo Coletta, *William Jennings Bryan: Political Evangelist, 1860–1908* (Lincoln: University of Nebraska Press, 1964), 56–57; Louis W. Koenig, *Bryan* (New York: G. P. Putnam, 1971), 129.

27. Alan P. Grimes, *Democracy and the Amendments to the Constitution* (Lexington, Mass.: Lexington Books, 1978), 68–74, provides a good description of the debate and passage of the act.

28. Benjamin R. Twiss, *Lawyers and the Constitution* (Princeton: Princeton University Press, 1942), 111–14, 215.

29. *Pollock v. Farmers' Loan and Trust Co.* file, Records of the Supreme Court, National Archives, Washington D.C.; Arnold M. Paul, *Conservative Crisis and the Rule of Law* (New York: Harper and Row, 1969), 172; Gerald G. Eggert, "Richard Olney and the Income Tax Cases," *Mississippi Valley Historical Review* 48 (1961): 26–29; Edward B. Whitney, "The Income Tax and the Constitution," *Harvard Law Review* 20 (1907): 285.

30. Philip B. Kurland and Gerhard Casper, eds., *Landmark Briefs and Arguments of the Supreme Court of the United States: Constitutional Law*, vol. 12, *Pollack v. Farmers'*

Loan and Trust Co. (1895) (Washington, D.C.: University Publications of America, 1975–), 312–15, 359–439, 464–67.

31. Ibid., 445; Paul, *Conservative Crisis,* 189; Eggert, "Richard Olney and the Income Tax Cases," 31–33; Swisher, *American Constitutional Development,* 448.

32. Guessing the identity of the switching justice became a favorite occupation of journalists and scholars. So much effort was spent on trying to decide whether Justice Shiras, Gray, or Brewer switched sides that the more important issue of public response to the outcome of the case may have been overshadowed. See Edward S. Corwin, *Court over Constitution* (Princeton: Princeton University Press, 1938), 194–96; George Shiras 3rd, *Justice George Shiras, Jr., of Pittsburgh* (Pittsburgh: University of Pittsburgh Press, 1953), 170–83; Willard L. King, *Melville Weston Fuller: Chief Justice of the United States, 1888–1910* (New York: Macmillan, 1950), 218–20.

33. Stanley, *Dimensions of Law,* 136–75.

34. *Pollock v. Farmers' Loan and Trust Company,* 157 US 429 (1895) and 158 US 601 (1895); Swisher, *American Constitutional Development,* 450.

35. Long, "Tinkering with the Constitution," 576.

36. Sylvester Pennoyer, "The Income Tax Decision and the Power of the Supreme Court to Nullify Acts of Congress," *American Law Review* 29 (1895): 550–58.

37. Quoted in Long, "Tinkering with the Constitution," 576; Elmer Ellis, "Public Opinion and the Income Tax, 1860–1900," *Mississippi Valley Historical Review* 27 (1940): 240–41; Beth, *Development of the Constitution,* 40–45; Nevins, *Grover Cleveland,* 670; Alan F. Westin, "The Supreme Court, the Populist Movement and the Campaign of 1896," *Journal of Politics* 15 (1953): 23; Musmanno, *Proposed Amendments,* 212.

38. Kammen, *A Machine That Would Go of Itself,* 191–92; Paul, *Conservative Crisis,* 221–23; Corwin, *Court over Constitution,* 209; Walter Clark, "Inevitable Constitutional Changes," *North American Review* 163 (October 1896): 462–69; Harold M. Bowman, "Congress and the Supreme Court," *Political Science Quarterly* 25 (1910): 20–34; L. B. Boudin, "Government by Judiciary," *Political Science Quarterly* 26 (1911): 238–70; and Burgess, "Present Problems"; Clark, "Changes"; Johnstone, "Eighteenth Century Constitution"; Higgins, "Rigid Constitution"; and Potter, "Amending the Constitution."

39. Paul, *Conservative Crisis,* 225; Ratner, *American Taxation,* 216; Westin, "Supreme Court, the Populist Movement and the Campaign of 1896," 30–39; Koenig, *Bryan,* 234.

40. Ratner, *American Taxation,* 229–46.

41. John D. Buenker, *The Income Tax and the Progressive Era* (New York: Garland, 1985), 1–57; Coletta, *Bryan: Political Evangelist,* 333; Koenig, *Bryan,* 381; Gabriel Kolko, *The Triumph of Conservatism* (New York: Free Press, 1963), 112; Jacob Tanger, "The Amending Procedure of the Federal Constitution," *American Political Science Review* 10 (1916): 696; Henry F. Pringle, *Theodore Roosevelt,* 2d ed. (New York: Harcourt Brace, 1956), 336; Ratner, *American Taxation,* 261–69.

42. Ratner, *American Taxation,* 270–303, provides the best account of the congressional battle of 1909. Unless otherwise noted, it is the basis for this paragraph and those that follow. Buenker, *Income Tax,* 58–137, provides another valuable perspective. Bowman, "Congress and the Supreme Court," 20–34, considered and found legitimate legislative action directly challenging the *Pollock* decision.

43. Beveridge to Chas. F. Remy, June 21, 1909, Albert J. Beveridge Papers, Library of Congress (LC).

44. Dolliver to La Follette, October 13, 1909, Robert La Follette Papers, LC.

45. Root, speech of July 1, 1909, Elihu Root Papers, LC.

46. Ratner, *American Taxation,* 307.

47. *New York Times,* July 22, 1909, 1, 2.

48. The most detailed description of state ratification is provided by Buenker, *Income Tax,* 138–337.

49. Charles Evans Hughes to the Legislature, January 5, 1910, Senate Journal 1910, Appendix, page 54, in U.S. Department of Justice, *The 16th Amendment: Governors* (Washington, GPO, 1938), 28–35.

50. Dwight W. Morrow, "The Income Tax Amendment," *Columbia Law Review* 10 (1910): 379–415; Arthur C. Graves, "Inherent Improprieties in the Income Tax Amendment to the Federal Constitution," *Yale Law Journal* 19 (1910):505–32; Twiss, *Lawyers and the Constitution*, 225.

51. "Message of the Governor of New Jersey," February 7, 1910, Senate Doc. 265, 61st Cong, 2d sess., 1910.

52. William E. Borah, "Income Tax," speech of February 10, 1910, William E. Borah Papers, LC.

53. Root to Frederick M. Davenport, February 17, 1910, Senate Doc. 398, 61st Cong., 2d sess., 1910.

54. Borah, February 10, 1910, speech, Borah Papers.

55. Buenker, *Income Tax*, 196–237.

56. See, for example, Senator Norris Brown of Nebraska, "Shall the Income Tax Be Ratified," *Editorial Review*, April 1910, 354–62.

57. *Flint v. Stone Tracy Co.*, 220 US 107 (1911).

58. Ratner, *American Taxation*, 295; Swisher, *American Constitutional Development*, 533–34.

59. *Brushaber v. Union Pacific Railroad Co.*, 240 US 1 (1916); see also Frank Warren Hackett, "The Constitutionality of the Graduated Income Tax Law," *Yale Law Journal* 25 (1916): 427–42.

60. Long, "Tinkering with the Constitution," 577; the same view was expressed by Gordon E. Sherman, "The Recent Constitutional Amendments," *Yale Law Journal* 23 (1913): 145.

61. Ames, *Proposed Amendments*, 61–62, 340, 353–54, 356, 383.

62. The evolution of the Senate and its image during the late nineteenth century is well described in David J. Rothman, *Politics and Power: The United States Senate, 1869–1901* (Cambridge: Harvard University Press, 1966).

63. George H. Haynes, *The Senate of the United States: Its History and Practice*, 2 vols. (Boston: Houghton Mifflin, 1938), 1: 86–92.

64. Quoted in Rothman, *Politics and Power*, 243.

65. Haynes, *Senate of the United States*, 1: 97; *Congressional Record*, 52d Cong., 2d sess., 617–18; Ames, *Proposed Amendments*, 61–62; Musmanno, *Proposed Amendments*, 219.

66. Haynes, *Senate of the United States*, 1: 97–98.

67. Caplan, *Constitutional Brinksmanship*, 63–64; Philip L. Martin, "The Application Clause of Article Five," *Political Science Quarterly* 85 (1970): 616–22.

68. Haynes, *Senate of the United States*, 1: 100–103; Grimes, *Democracy and the Amendments*, 76.

69. Haynes, *Senate of the United States*, 1: 105 and 1: 131–35.

70. Larry J. Easterling, "Sen. Joseph L. Bristow and the Seventeenth Amendment," *Kansas Historical Quarterly* 41 (1975): 491–93.

71. Ibid., 493–503.

72. *Congressional Record*, 52d Cong., 2d sess., 618.

73. Elihu Root, "Direct Election of Senators," speech of February 10, 1911, Root Papers.

74. Easterling, "Bristow and the Seventeenth Amendment," 494–500.

75. Grimes, *Democracy and the Amendments*, 77–82; Easterling, "Bristow and the Seventeenth Amendment," 503–6.

76. Easterling, "Bristow and the Seventeenth Amendment," 507–9.

77. Caplan, *Constitutional Brinksmanship*, 65.

78. *The Constitution of the United States of America: Analysis and Interpretation*, 99th Cong., 1st sess. (Washington, D.C.: GPO, 1987), 34.

79. Long, "Tinkering with the Constitution," 577–88; see also Sherman, "Recent Constitutional Amendments."

10. AN ERA OF CONSTITUTIONAL ACTIVITY AND FAITH

1. William Rorabaugh, *The Alcoholic Republic* (New York: Oxford University Press, 1979), 225–33.

2. The best general history of American prohibition can be found in Jack S. Blocker, Jr., *American Temperance Movements: Cycles of Reform* (Boston: Twayne, 1989).

3. Jack S. Blocker, Jr., *Retreat from Reform: The Prohibition Movement in the United States, 1890–1913* (Westport, Conn.: Greenwood, 1976), 39–153, provides the most detailed look at the Prohibition party. Ruth Bordin, *Woman and Temperance: The Quest for Power and Liberty, 1873–1900* (Philadelphia: Temple University Press, 1981), offers a shrewd and balanced assessment of the WCTU.

4. A splendid portrait of the league can be found in K. Austin Kerr, *Organized for Prohibition: A New History of the Anti-Saloon League* (New Haven: Yale University Press, 1985). Much older but also valuable is Peter H. Odegard, *Pressure Politics: The Story of the Anti-Saloon League* (New York: Columbia University Press, 1928).

5. Blocker, *Retreat to Reform*, 154–234; Kerr, *Organized for Prohibition*, 139–41.

6. *Leisy v. Hardin*, 135 US 100 (1890): *Rhodes v. Iowa* 170 US 412 (1898). These cases are well discussed in Richard F. Hamm, *Shaping the Eighteenth Amendment: Temperance Reform, Legal Culture, and the Polity, 1880–1920* (Chapel Hill: University of North Carolina Press, 1995), 64–68, 176–82.

7. Hamm, *Shaping the Eighteenth Amendment*, 203–26.

8. Herman V. Ames, *The Proposed Amendments to the Constitution*, in *Annual Report, American Historical Association, 1896* (Washington, D.C.: GPO, 1897), 272–73; Michael A. Musmanno, *Proposed Amendments to the Constitution*, 70th Cong., 2d sess., House Doc. 551 (Washington, D.C.: GPO, 1929), 230–31.

9. Cited in Kerr, *Organized for Prohibition*, 141.

10. Quoted in ibid., 141.

11. Ibid., 143; James H. Timberlake, *Prohibition and the Progressive Movement, 1900–1920* (Cambridge: Harvard University Press, 1966), 169–71.

12. Associated Press dispatch, September 24, 1930, quoted in Charles Merz, *The Dry Decade* (Garden City, N.Y.: Doubleday, Doran, 1931), 297.

13. *Congressional Record*, 63d Cong., 3d sess., 509–12, 519–24, 540–58, 616.

14. See Kerr, *Organized for Prohibition*, 160–84.

15. Odegard, *Pressure Politics*, 163.

16. *Clark Distilling Co. v. Western Maryland Railway Co.*, 242 US 311, argued May 10 and 11, 1915, reargued November 8 and 9, 1916, decided January 8, 1917, by a vote of 7 to 2. See Hamm, *Shaping the Eighteenth Amendment*, 224–25.

17. Timberlake, *Prohibition and the Progressive Movement*, 176–78.

18. *Congressional Record*, 63d Cong., 3d sess., 609–11.

19. Ibid., 5648.

20. *Congressional Record*, 65th Cong., 1st sess., 5648–66; Odegard, *Pressure Politics*, 172.

21. Odegard, *Pressure Politics*, 155, 172–74.

22. *The Constitution: Analysis and Interpretation*, 35; Merz, *Dry Decade*, 316.

23. The literature on the rise and spread of prohibition sentiment is large. Blocker, *American Temperance Movements*, and Timberlake, *Prohibition and the Progressive*

Movement, are particularly insightful, but one should not overlook Andrew Sinclair, *Prohibition: The Era of Excess* (Boston: Little, Brown, 1962); Robert A. Hohner, "The Prohibitionists: Who Were They?" *South Atlantic Quarterly* 68 (1969): 491–505; Norman H. Clark, *Deliver Us from Evil: An Interpretation of American Prohibition* (New York: W. W. Norton, 1976); Mark Edward Lender and James Kirby Martin, *Drinking in America: A History* (New York: Free Press, 1982), and a series of studies that concentrate on individual states: Gilman M. Ostrander, *The Prohibition Movement in California, 1848–1933* (Berkeley: University of California Press, 1957); Norman H. Clark, *The Dry Years: Prohibition and Social Change in Washington* (Seattle: University of Washington Press, 1965); Paul E. Isaac, *Prohibition and Politics: Turbulent Decades in Tennessee, 1885–1920* (Knoxville: University of Tennessee Press, 1965); C. C. Pearson and J. Edwin Hendricks, *Liquor and Anti-Liquor in Virginia, 1619–1919* (Durham, N.C.: Duke University Press, 1967); Jimmie L. Franklin, *Born Sober: Prohibition in Oklahoma, 1907–1959* (Norman: University of Oklahoma Press, 1971); Lewis L. Gould, *Progressives and Prohibitionists: Texas Democrats in the Wilson Era* (Austin: University of Texas Press, 1973); Larry Engelman, *Intemperance: The Lost War Against Liquor* (New York: Free Press, 1979), on Michigan; and Robert S. Bader, *Prohibition in Kansas: A History* (Lawrence: University Press of Kansas, 1986).

24. Blocker, *Retreat from Reform,* 237–40.

25. *Congressional Record,* 66th Cong., 1st sess., 7610–11, 7633–34.

26. Ida Husted Harper, *Life and Work of Susan B. Anthony,* 3 vols. (Indianapolis: Hollenback, 1898–1908), 1: 64–68; Bordin, *Woman and Temperance,* 5, 68–70, 87–102; Ellen Carol Dubois, *Feminism and Suffrage: The Emergence of an Independent Women's Movement in America, 1848–1869* (Ithaca, N.Y.: Cornell University Press, 1978), 40–52.

27. Jack S. Blocker, Jr., *"Give to the Winds Thy Fears": The Women's Temperance Crusade, 1873–74* (Westport, Conn.: Greenwood, 1985), illuminates this turning point.

28. A clear picture of the centrifugal forces in the nineteenth-century women's movement is presented in William L. O'Neill, *Everyone Was Brave: The Rise and Fall of Feminism in America* (Chicago: Quadrangle, 1969). Also valuable on the complexity of women's rights thought is Aileen S. Kraditor, *The Ideas of the Woman Suffrage Movement, 1890–1920* (New York: Columbia University Press, 1965).

29. Eleanor Flexner, *Century of Struggle: The Woman's Rights Movement in the United States* (Cambridge: Harvard University Press, 1959), 222.

30. Alan P. Grimes, *The Puritan Ethic and Woman Suffrage* (New York: Oxford University Press, 1967).

31. Ames, *Proposed Amendments,* 230, 237–38, 373, 384–86; Musmanno, *Proposed Amendments,* 247–48; Flexner, *Century of Struggle,* 262.

32. An admiring and insightful study is Christine A. Lunardini, *From Equal Suffrage to Equal Rights: Alice Paul and the National Woman's Party, 1910–1928* (New York: New York University Press, 1986). Also helpful is Loretta Ellen Zimmerman, "Alice Paul and the National Woman's Party, 1912–1920" (Ph.D. diss., Tulane University, 1964).

33. *Congressional Record,* 63d Cong., 2d sess., 5108.

34. *Congressional Record,* 63d Cong., 3d sess., 1483–84.

35. Thomas J. Walsh to Rose E. Rust, March 24, 1916, and to M. M. Dean, May 24, 1916, Thomas J. Walsh Papers, LC.

36. Flexner, *Century of Struggle,* 267–68.

37. Carrie Chapman Catt, *Woman Suffrage by Federal Constitutional Amendment* (New York: National Woman Suffrage Publishing Company, 1917), 6–11.

38. Flexner, *Century of Struggle,* 279–82.

39. The antisuffrage argument is explored in Kraditor, *Ideas of the Woman Suffrage Movement,* 12–37. The most detailed study of this underexamined subject is Jane Jerome Camhi, "Women Against Women: American Antisuffragism, 1880–1920" (Ph.D. diss.,

Tufts University, 1973); see also Clement E. Vose, *Constitutional Change: Amendment Politics and Supreme Court Litigation Since 1900* (Lexington, Mass.: Lexington Books, 1972), 47–53.

40. Vose, *Constitutional Change,* 49.

41. Camhi, "Women Against Women," 135–54, quotation on 154.

42. Pennsylvania Association Opposed to Woman Suffrage, *Defeats and Failures of Woman Suffrage* (Philadelphia, 1915), in Walsh Papers.

43. Mrs. Walter D. Lamar, *The Vulnerability of the White Primary* (Macon, Ga., n.d.), pamphlet in Georgia State Library quoted in A. Elizabeth Taylor, "The Last Phase of the Woman Suffrage Campaign in Georgia," *Georgia Historical Quarterly* 43 (1959): 16.

44. Quoted in Taylor, "Last Phase of the Woman Suffrage Campaign in Georgia," 18.

45. National Association Opposed to Woman Suffrage, *To Uphold and Defend the Constitution of the United States Against all Foreign and Domestic Enemies* (n.p., 1917), Walsh Papers.

46. Ibid., 160–67; Flexner, *Century of Struggle,* 295–305; Vose, *Constitutional Change,* 50–52.

47. "Joint Resolution Depriving Each State of the Right to Regulate Suffrage: Brief in Opposition," in Everett P. Wheeler to Thomas J. Walsh, January 29, 1919, Walsh Papers.

48. Quoted in Camhi, "Women Against Women," 162–63 (italics theirs).

49. Timberlake, *Prohibition and the Progressive Movement,* 179; Flexner, *Century of Struggle,* 296–98.

50. Woodrow Wilson, Address to the National American Woman Suffrage Association, Atlantic City, N.J., September 8, 1916, in *The Papers of Woodrow Wilson,* ed. Arthur S. Link, 69 vols. (Princeton: Princeton University Press, 1982) 38: 161–64.

51. Christine A. Lunardini and Thomas J. Knock, "Woodrow Wilson and Woman Suffrage: A New Look," *Political Science Quarterly* 95 (1980–1981): 655–63.

52. Lunardini, *From Equal Suffrage to Equal Rights,* 104–39; Zimmerman, "Alice Paul and the National Woman's Party," 223–44.

53. Woodrow Wilson, statement, January 9, 1918, printed in *New York Times,* January 10, 1918, in Link, ed., *Wilson Papers,* 45: 545.

54. Wilson to Joseph P. Tumulty, January 23, 1918, in ibid., 46: 79–81.

55. Lunardini and Knock, "Woodrow Wilson and Woman Suffrage," 663–66; Flexner, *Century of Struggle,* 277–93; *Congressional Record,* 65th Cong., 2d sess., 810.

56. Kenneth R. Johnson, "White Racial Attitudes as a Factor in the Arguments Against the Nineteenth Amendment," *Phylon* 31 (1970): 33.

57. Woodrow Wilson, Address to the Senate, September 30, 1918, in Link, ed., *Wilson Papers,* 51: 158–61. The only cabinet absentee was Secretary of State Robert Lansing who, along with his wife, opposed woman suffrage.

58. William Gibbs McAdoo, *Crowded Years* (Boston: Houghton Mifflin, 1931), 498.

59. *Congressional Record,* 65th Cong., 2d sess., 10929–30, 10987.

60. Flexner, *Century of Struggle,* 310.

61. *Congressional Record,* 65th Cong., 3d sess., 3062.

62. *Congressional Record,* 66th Cong., 1st sess., 93–94, 567–70, 616–35.

63. Flexner, *Century of Struggle,* 222–82, 315–16; Zimmerman, "Paul and the Woman's Party," 162–93.

64. *The Constitution: Analysis and Interpretation,* 36; A. Elizabeth Taylor, "The Woman Suffrage Movement in Texas," *Journal of Southern History* 17 (1951): 215.

65. Quoted in Taylor, "Last Phase of the Woman Suffrage Campaign in Georgia," 27.

66. Carol E. Hoffecker, "Delaware's Woman Suffrage Campaign," *Delaware History* 20 (1983): 165–66.

67. Flexner, *Century of Struggle,* 319–20.

68. Descriptions of the Tennessee ratification struggle can be found in David Morgan,

Suffragists and Democrats: The Politics of Woman Suffrage in America (East Lansing: Michigan State University Press, 1972), 149–51, and, in greater detail, in A. Elizabeth Taylor, *The Women Suffrage Movement in Tennessee* (New York: Bookman, 1957), 104–24, and in Carol Lynn Yellin, "Countdown in Tennessee, 1920," *American Heritage* 30 (December 1978): 12–35. Two days after Tennessee acted, the North Carolina House of Representatives, refusing to concede, rejected the Nineteenth Amendment 47 to 41. A good description of the suffrage debate in North Carolina is provided by Donald G. Mathews and Jane Sherron De Hart, *Sex, Gender, and the Politics of ERA: A State and the Nation* (New York: Oxford University Press, 1990), 4–27.

69. *New York Times,* January 17, 1920, 1.

70. Kraditor, *Ideas of the Woman Suffrage Movement,* 51–54.

11. SECOND THOUGHTS ABOUT AMENDMENT

1. W. F. Dodd, "Amending the Federal Constitution," *Yale Law Journal* 30 (1921): 353.

2. Charles Evans Hughes, "Liberty and Law," ABA presidential address, September 2, 1925, *American Bar Association Journal* 11 (1925): 563.

3. See, for example, George D. Skinner, "Intrinsic Limitations on the Power of Constitutional Amendment," *Michigan Law Review* 18 (1919): 213–25; William L. Marbury, "The Limitations upon the Amending Power," *Harvard Law Review* 33 (1919), 223–35; and Charles Willis Needham, "Changing the Fundamental Law," *University of Pennsylvania Law Review* 69 (1921): 223–36. A balanced consideration of enthusiasms and fears can be found in Margaret C. Klinglesmith, "Amending the Constitution of the United States," *University of Pennsylvania Law Review* 73 (1925): 355–79.

4. George W. Knepper, *Ohio and Its People* (Kent, Ohio: Kent State University Press, 1989), 335, 342, 349, 351.

5. Ohio, *Annual Report of the Secretary of State, 1920,* 313–14. States' rights appear to have been a consideration with at least some voters for at the same election they chose to retain the state prohibition law, 496,786 to 454,933.

6. Emphasis added.

7. *Hawke v. Smith,* appellate case file 27337, Records of the Supreme Court of the United States, Record Group 267, National Archives.

8. Ibid.

9. William Howard Taft, "Can Ratification of an Amendment to the Constitution Be Made to Depend on a Referendum?" *Yale Law Journal* 29 (1920): 822–23; John B. Meers, "The California Wine and Grape Industry and Prohibition," *California Historical Society Quarterly* 46 (1967): 26–27; Norman C. Clark, *The Dry Years: Prohibition and Social Change in Washington* (Seattle: University of Washington Press, 1965), 142.

10. Elizabeth Flexner, *Century of Struggle: The Woman's Rights Movement in the United States* (Cambridge: Harvard University Press, 1959), 320–21.

11. *Hawke v. Smith,* 253 US 221, 227–30 (1920).

12. *National Prohibition Cases,* 253 US 350 (1920).

13. A. Elizabeth Taylor, *The Woman Suffrage Movement in Tennessee* (New York: Bookman, 1957), 104–7.

14. *New York Times,* June 3, 1920, 10.

15. Will Rogers, *Rogers-isms: The Cowboy Philosopher on Prohibition* (New York: Harper, 1919), 24.

16. *American Mercury* 12 (November 1927): 287.

17. Edward S. Corwin, "Constitutional Law in 1919–1920," *American Political Science Review* 14 (1920): 651.

18. *National Prohibition Cases,* 253 US 350, 354–57.

19. Ibid., 361–67; Philip C. Jessup, *Elihu Root,* 2 vols. (New York: Dodd, Mead, 1938), 2:478; quotation in Nicholas Murray Butler, *Across the Busy Years,* 2 vols. (New York: Scribner's, 1939–1940), 2: 333–34. Root's oral argument does not appear in the official report of the case.

20. Dodd, "Amending the Federal Constitution," 322.

21. Jessup, *Root,* 2: 476–80.

22. *National Prohibition Cases,* 253 US 350, 382–88.

23. *Dillon v. Gloss,* 256 US 368 (1921).

24. William L. Marbury laid out the essentials of his argument in "The Nineteenth Amendment and After," *Virginia Law Review* 7 (1920): 1–29.

25. *Myers v. Anderson,* 238 US 368 (1915); Clement E. Vose, *Constitutional Change: Amendment Politics and Supreme Court Litigation Since 1900* (Lexington, Mass.: Lexington Books, 1972), 38–40.

26. *Leser v. Garnett,* 258 US 130 (1922); see also Vose, *Constitutional Change,* 57–63.

27. Herman V. Ames, *The Proposed Amendments to the Constitution,* in *Annual Report, American Historical Association, 1896* (Washington, D.C.: GPO, 1897), 285–94; Ralph R. Martig, "Amending the Constitution—Article V: The Keystone of the Arch," *Michigan Law Review* 35 (1937): 1280.

28. Michael A. Musmanno, *Proposed Amendments to the Constitution,* 70th Cong., 2d sess., House Doc. 551 (Washington, D.C.: GPO, 1929), 191–99: Lester B. Orfield, "The Reform of the Federal Amending Power," *North Carolina Law Review* 10 (1931): 19–26.

29. David P. Thelen, *Robert M. La Follette and the Insurgent Spirit* (Boston: Little, Brown, 1976): 172–73, 180.

30. Charles Warren, *Congress, the Constitution, and the Supreme Court* (Boston: Little Brown, 1925), 138–39.

31. Martin L. Fausold, *James W. Wadsworth: The Gentleman from New York* (Syracuse, N.Y.: Syracuse University Press, 1975).

32. A description and defense of the Wadsworth-Garrett resolution is provided in George Stewart Brown, "The 'New Bill of Rights' Amendment," *Virginia Law Review* 9 (1922): 14–24.

33. Justin Miller, "Amendment of the Federal Constitution: Should It Be Made More Difficult?" *Minnesota Law Review* 10 (February 1926): 185–90.

34. James W. Wadsworth, Jr., to John A. Richardson, July 3, 1923, Wadsworth Papers, LC.

35. James W. Wadsworth, Jr., "Amending the Constitution," speech of February 12, 1923, Wadsworth Papers.

36. U.S. Senate, Committee on the Judiciary, *Proposal and Ratification of Constitutional Amendments: Hearings,* 67th Cong., 4th sess., 1923.

37. James W. Wadsworth to John A. Dutton, November 20, 1923, Wadsworth Papers; Orfield, "Reform of the Federal Amending Power," 37; Fausold, *Wadsworth,* 143.

38. *Congressional Record,* 68th Cong., 1st sess., 4929–45, 4995–5009; Orfield, "Reform of Federal Amending Power," 38. When Wadsworth returned to Congress after his election to the House in 1932, he attempted to raise the amendment procedure issue once again but with no success (Constitutional Amendment, 1935, file, Wadsworth Papers).

39. U.S. House of Representatives, Committee on the Judiciary, *Proposal and Ratification of Amendments to the Constitution of the United States: Hearings,* 68th Cong., 1st sess., 1924.

40. J. Stanley Lemons, *The Woman Citizen: Social Feminism in the 1920s* (Urbana: University of Illinois Press, 1973), 241–42.

41. Finis J. Garrett, "Amending the Federal Constitution," *Tennessee Law Review* 7 (1929): 286–309.

42. Useful considerations of the feminist divergence can be found in Nancy F. Cott, *The Grounding of Modern Feminism* (New Haven: Yale University Press, 1987); Susan D. Becker, *The Origins of the Equal Rights Amendment: American Feminism Between the Wars* (Westport, Conn.: Greenwood, 1981); Lemons, *Woman Citizen;* William L. O'Neill, *Everyone Was Brave: The Rise and Fall of Feminism in America* (Chicago: Quadrangle, 1969).

43. *Muller v. Oregon,* 208 US 412 (1908).

44. Christine A. Lunardini, *From Equal Suffrage to Equal Rights: Alice Paul and the National Woman's Party, 1910–1928* (New York: New York University Press, 1986): 150–68.

45. Ethel M. Smith and Elizabeth Eastman to Thomas J. Walsh, February 3, 1925, Thomas J. Walsh Papers, LC; Florence Kelley, "Twenty Questions About the Proposed Equal Rights Amendment of the Woman's Party, 1923–1924," Walsh Papers; Becker, *Origins of the Equal Rights Amendment,* 207–24. See also U.S. Senate, Committee on the Judiciary, *Equal Rights Amendment: Hearings,* 70th Cong., 2d sess., 1929.

46. A detailed study of child labor and the legislation and litigation it generated is Stephen B. Wood, *Constitutional Politics in the Progressive Era: Child Labor and the Law* (Chicago: University of Chicago Press, 1968).

47. *Hammer v. Dagenhart,* 247 US 251 (1918); Wood, *Constitutional Politics in the Progressive Era,* 47–176.

48. Stephen Wood, the closest student of the child labor controversy during the 1920s, thinks an amendment campaign launched in 1918 might well have succeeded (Wood, *Constitutional Politics in the Progressive Era,* 188).

49. *Bailey v. Drexel Furniture Company,* 259 US 20 (1922); Wood, *Constitutional Politics in the Progressive Era,* 185–294.

50. Summaries of the campaign for a child labor amendment can be found in Clarke A. Chambers, *Seedtime of Reform: American Social Service and Social Action, 1918–1933* (Minneapolis: University of Minnesota Press, 1963), 29–46, and Walter I. Trattner, *Crusade for the Children: A History of the National Child Labor Committee and Child Labor Reform in America* (Chicago: Quadrangle, 1970), 163–86.

51. Richard B. Sherman, "Rejection of the Child Labor Amendment," *Mid-America* 45 (1963): 4–7; Trattner, *Crusade for the Children,* 163–66.

52. Chambers, *Seedtime of Reform,* 33–37.

53. Sherman, "The Rejection of the Child Labor Amendment," 4–5; Trattner, *Crusade for the Children,* 163–65.

54. *Congressional Record,* 68th Cong., 1st sess., 9859, 10141–42, 7294–95.

55. Chambers, *Seedtime of Reform,* 37–38.

56. Minutes of the All Day Meeting of the Emergency Conference on Ratification of the Child Labor Amendment, September 23, 1924, National Child Labor Committee (NCLC) Papers, LC.

57. Confidential Summary of the Situation Concerning the Ratification of the Child Labor Amendment, October 22, 1924, NCLC Papers; Katherine T. Balch to Thomas J. Walsh, February 19, 1924, Walsh Papers; Sherman, "Rejection of the Child Labor Amendment," 10–12; Trattner, *Crusade for the Children,* 175–76.

58. Bentley W. Warren, "A Statement from Sentinels of the Republic in Opposition to a Child Labor Amendment to the Federal Constitution, February 19, 1924, William Borah Papers, LC.

59. Quoted in Lemons, *Woman Citizen,* 220.

60. "Resolution drawn by the Secretary of State of Georgia and adopted by the legislature July 2 and 3, 1924," Walsh Papers.

61. Vose, *Constitutional Change,* 249.

62. Committee for the Ratification of the Child Labor Amendment, Minutes, November 7 and 21, 1924, NCLC Papers.

63. Jeannette H. Mann to Thomas J. Walsh, January 22, 1925, Walsh Papers.

64. Maley O. Hudson, "Is the Child Labor Amendment Properly Drawn?" National Child Labor Committee pamphlet, Walsh Papers; Lemons, *Woman Citizen,* 220–21.

65. *The Pilot,* reprinted articles of October 4 and 11, 1924, Walsh Papers.

66. National League of Women Voters, "Why a Federal Child Labor Law Can Be Secured Only Through a Constitutional Amendment," November 28, 1924, Walsh Papers; Ethel M. Smith, legislative secretary, National Women's Trade Union League of America, to Thomas J. Walsh, December 11, 1924, Walsh Papers; Florence Kelley to Thomas J. Walsh, December 31, 1924, Walsh Papers; Jeannette H. Mann to Thomas J. Walsh, January 22, 1925, Walsh Papers; Trattner, *Crusade for the Children,* 175–76; Chambers, *Seedtime for Reform,* 40–41.

67. Trattner, *Crusade for the Children,* 177–78.

68. Status of Ratification, February 21, 1925, NCLC Papers.

69. Organizations Associated for Ratification of the Child Labor Amendment, press release, January 29, 1925, NCLC Papers.

70. Robert von Moschzisker, "Dangers in Disregarding Fundamental Conceptions when Amending the Federal Constitution," *Cornell Law Quarterly* 11 (1925): 10.

71. NCLC, Twenty-fifth Anniversary Conference transcript, December 16–17, 1929, NCLC Papers.

72. The most careful and reliable evaluation of 1920s drinking patterns is John C. Burnham, "New Perspectives on the Prohibition 'Experiment' of the 1920s," *Journal of Social History* 2 (1968): 51–68. See also David E. Kyvig, *Repealing National Prohibition* (Chicago: University of Chicago Press, 1979), chap. 2, and Jack S. Blocker, *American Temperance Movements: Cycles of Reform* (Boston: Twayne, 1989), chap. 4.

73. A detailed history of the Association Against the Prohibition Amendment (AAPA) can be found in Kyvig, *Repealing National Prohibition.* See also Robert F. Burk, *The Corporate State and the Broker State: The Du Ponts and American National Politics, 1925–1940* (Cambridge: Harvard University Press, 1990), chaps. 3–7.

74. Quoted in Dayton E. Heckman, "Prohibition Passes: The Story of the Association Against the Prohibition Amendment" (Ph.D. diss., Ohio State University, 1939), 256–57.

75. *New York Times,* April 7, 1922, 1, 2.

76. Samuel Harden Church, "The Paradise of the Ostrich," *North American Review* 221 (June 1925): 626.

77. Archibald E. Stevenson, *States' Rights and National Prohibition* (New York: Clark Boardman, 1927), 126.

78. Clarence Darrow, "The Ordeal of Prohibition," *American Mercury* 2 (August 1924): 419.

79. William Green to William H. Stayton, June 24, 1925, Samuel Gompers Letterbooks, LC; Walter Lippmann, "Our Predicament Under the Eighteenth Amendment," *Harper's Magazine,* December 1926, 39.

80. *New York Times,* May 12, 1922, 18.

81. U.S. House of Representatives, Committee on the Judiciary, *Proposed Modification of the Prohibition Law to Permit the Manufacture, Sale, and Use of 2.75 Per Cent Beverages: Hearings,* 68th Cong., 1st sess., serial 39, 1924.

82. U.S. Senate, Committee on the Judiciary, *The National Prohibition Law: Hearings Before the Subcommittee on Bills to Amend the National Prohibition Act,* 69th Cong., 1st sess., 1926.

83. Kyvig, *Repealing National Prohibition,* 54–64.

84. Arthur T. Hadley, "Law Making and Law Enforcement," *Harper's Magazine,* November 1925, 641–46.

85. Lippmann, "Our Predicament Under the Eighteenth Amendment," 51–56. He did

not easily abandon the idea; see Lippmann, "The Popular Dogma of Law Enforcement," *Yale Review* 19 (1929): 1–13.

86. Clarence Darrow and Victor S. Yarros, *The Prohibition Mania* (New York: Boni and Liveright, 1927); Brand Whitlock, *The Little Green Shutter* (New York: D. Appleton, 1931); John A. Ryan, *Declining Liberty and Other Papers* (New York: Macmillan, 1927). See also Jerome D. Greene, "The Personal Problem," *Atlantic Monthly* 138 (October 1926): 527–28, and unsigned editorials, "Nullification by Consent," *New Republic* 47 (June 16, 1926): 101–2, and "Enforcement, Repeal, and Nullification," *World's Work* 53 (November 1926): 5–6.

87. Robert C. Binkley, "The Ethics of Nullification," *New Republic* 58 (May 1, 1929): 297–300; Wainwright Evans, "The Sanctity of the Law," *Outlook and Independent* 152 (June 19, 1929): 283–86, 317.

88. Darrow, "Ordeal of Prohibition," 419–27; idem, "Tyranny and the Volstead Act," *Vanity Fair* 28 (March 1927): 45–46, 116; idem, "Our Growing Tyranny," *Vanity Fair*, 29 (February 1928): 39, 104; Charles Merz, *The Dry Decade* (Garden City, N.Y.: Doubleday, Doran, 1931), 36–46; Peter H. Odegard, *Pressure Politics: The Story of the Anti-Saloon League* (New York: Columbia University Press, 1928). For Mencken's views, see Andrew C. McLaughlin, "Satire as a Weapon Against Prohibition, 1920–1928: Expression of a Cultural Conflict" (Ph.D. diss., Stanford University, 1969), chapter 2.

89. For a summary of referendums through 1929, see Merz, *Dry Decade,* 334. For later referendums, see Association Against the Prohibition Amendment, *32 Reasons for Repeal* (Washington, D.C.: AAPA, 1932), 34.

90. Marbury, "Limitations upon the Amending Power," 223–35; Justin DuPratt White, "Is There an Eighteenth Amendment?" *Cornell Law Quarterly* 5 (1920): 113–27; Everett V. Abbot, "Inalienable Rights and the Eighteenth Amendment," *Columbia Law Review* 20 (1920): 183–95; Charles K. Burdick, "Is Prohibition Lawful?" *New Republic,* April 21, 1920, 245–48; D. O. McGovney, "Is the Eighteenth Amendment Void Because of Its Contents?" *Columbia Law Review* 20 (1920): 499–518; George Stewart Brown, "Irresponsible Government by Constitutional Amendment," *Virginia Law Review* 8 (1922): 157–66.

91. Selden Bacon, *The X Amendment, Its Supreme Importance and Its Effects on the XVIII Amendment* (New York, 1938), Eleutherian Mills Historical Library pamphlet collection, Wilmington, Del. See also Selden Bacon, "How the Tenth Amendment Affected the Fifth Article of the Constitution," *Virginia Law Review* 16 (1930): 771–91.

92. Kyvig, *Repealing National Prohibition,* 138–39.

93. *United States v. Sprague,* 44 F. (2d) 967 (1930); Joseph P. Pollard, *The Road to Repeal: Submission to Conventions* (New York: Brentano's, 1932), 154–56.

94. *New York Times,* December 17, 1930, 1, 22–23.

95. *United States v. Sprague,* 282 US 716, 730 (1931); Pollard, *Road to Repeal,* 177–81.

96. *United States v. Sprague,* 44 F. (2d) 967 (1930).

97. Selden Bacon to William H. Stayton, December 29, 1930, Pierre S. Du Pont Papers, Eleutherian Mills Historical Library, Wilmington, Del.

98. The most straightforward discussions appear in Bruce Williams, "The Popular Mandate on Constitutional Amendments," *Virginia Law Review* 7 (1921): 280–301, and George Stewart Brown, "The People Should Be Consulted as To Constitutional Changes," *American Bar Association Journal* 16 (1930): 404–6.

12. ALTERING ESTABLISHED CONSTITUTIONAL PROVISIONS AND PRACTICES

1. Thomas J. Walsh to James F. O'Conner, January 22, 1926, Thomas J. Walsh Papers, LC.

2. U.S. House of Representatives, Committee on Elections, *Proposed Constitutional Amendments: Hearings,* 70th Cong., 1st sess., 1927, 2.

3. Herman V. Ames, *Proposed Amendments to the Constitution,* in *Annual Report, American Historical Association, 1896* (Washington, D.C.: GPO, 1897), 36; Michael A. Musmanno, *Proposed Amendments to the Constitution,* 70th Cong., 2d sess., House Doc. 551 (Washington, D.C.: GPO, 1929), 1–9, 23–44.

4. John P. Robinson, Norris's secretary, to Lorraine Leuck, February 18, 1938, George W. Norris Papers, LC.

5. A detailed biography of George Norris is Richard Lowitt, *George W. Norris,* 3 vols. (Syracuse, N.Y.: Syracuse University Presss, 1963; Urbana: University of Illinois Press, 1971–1978).

6. Musmanno, *Proposed Amendments,* 27–30.

7. George W. Norris to Francis M. W. Price, March 19, 1924, Norris Papers.

8. George W. Norris to Christian A. Herter, February 1, 1925, Norris Papers.

9. George W. Norris to Frank A. Harrison, June 28, 1926, Norris Papers.

10. Levi Cooke, statement of January 18, 1926, in U.S. House of Representatives, Committee on Elections, *Proposed Amendments to the Constitution of the United States Fixing Commencement of Terms: Hearings,* 69th Cong., 1st sess., 1926, 314.

11. *Congressional Record,* 70th Cong., 1st sess., 4413, 4429–30.

12. George W. Norris to A. S. Goss, March 25, 1928, Norris Papers.

13. *Congressional Record,* 71st Cong., 3d sess., 5906–7.

14. *Cleveland Plain Dealer,* February 26, 1931.

15. "Lame Duck Nuisance," *Nation* 131 (November 19, 1930): 543; *Lincoln* [Nebraska] *Star,* November 18, 1930.

16. *Congressional Record,* 72d Cong., 1st sess., 1383, 3827, 4060.

17. John P. Robertson to Arthur W. Gosling, January 17, 1933, Norris Papers; Richard Lowitt, *George W. Norris: The Persistence of a Progressive, 1913–1933* (Urbana: University of Illinois Press, 1973), 518.

18. *The Constitution of the United States: Analysis and Interpretation,* 99th Cong., 1st sess. (Washington, D.C.: GPO, 1987), 36–37.

19. William H. Stayton to Halbert L. Hoard, May 8, 1926, Halbert L. Hoard Papers, Wisconsin State Historical Society, Madison, Wis.

20. U.S. House of Representatives, Committee on the Judiciary, *The Prohibition Amendment: Hearings,* 71st Cong., 2d sess., 1930, 135–37.

21. For a discussion of the background and ideas of Du Pont and Raskob as well as Murphy and others with whom they associated, see David E. Kyvig, *Repealing National Prohibition* (Chicago: University of Chicago Press, 1979), chap. 5. Also instructive is Robert F. Burk, *The Corporate State and the Broker State: The Du Ponts and American National Politics, 1925–1940* (Cambridge: Harvard University Press, 1990), chaps. 3–4.

22. Executive Committee of the Board of Directors, *Report to the Directors, Members and Friends of the Association Against the Prohibition Amendment for the Year 1928* (Washington, D.C.: AAPA, 1929), 7.

23. *United States v. Lanza,* 260 US 377 (1922).

24. *Carroll et al. v. United States,* 267 US 132 (1924).

25. *Olmstead et al. v. United States,* 277 US 438 (1928).

26. Forrest Revere Black, *Ill-Starred Prohibition Cases: A Study in Judicial Pathology* (Boston: Richard G. Badger, 1931).

27. U.S. National Commission on Law Observance and Enforcement, *Report on the Enforcement of the Prohibition Law of the United States,* 71st Cong., 3d sess., House Doc. 722, 1931; see also Kyvig, *Repealing National Prohibition,* 111–15.

28. National Commission on Law Observance and Enforcement, *Report on Enforcement of Prohibition,* 45, 135–36, 156, 162.

29. Pierre S. du Pont to Henry Curran, January 21, 1931, Pierre S. du Pont Papers, Eleutherian Mills Historical Library, Wilmington, Del.

30. For a detailed picture, see David E. Kyvig, "Women Against Prohibition," *American Quarterly* 28 (Fall 1976): 465–82.

31. James W. Wadsworth, Jr., "The Reminiscences of James W. Wadsworth" (Oral History Research Office, Columbia University, 1952), 358.

32. Kyvig, *Repealing National Prohibition,* 117, 130–35.

33. On final passage of the Eighteenth Amendment in 1917, the partisan division in Congress was almost even. In the Senate, 29 Republicans and 36 Democrats supported the resolution while 8 Republicans and 12 Democrats opposed it. In the House 137 Republicans, 141 Democrats, and 4 independents voted "yea" while 62 Republicans, 64 Democrats, and 2 independents voted "nay."

34. *New York Times,* February 12, 1930, 2; March 13, 1930, 6; March 14, 1930, 22; March 31, 1930, 4; April 5, 1930, 18; and May 22, 1930, 2; U.S. Senate, Committee on the Judiciary, *Lobbying and Lobbyists: Partial Report,* 71st Cong., 2d sess., Senate report 43, pt. 8, 1930.

35. John J. Raskob to members of the Democratic National Committee, April 4, 1931, John J. Raskob Papers, Eleutherian Mills Historical Library.

36. *New York Times,* July 1, 1926, 2; Musmanno, *Proposed Amendments,* 237.

37. U.S. House of Representatives, Committee on the Judiciary, *The Prohibition Amendment: Hearings,* 71st Cong., 2d sess., 1930.

38. *New York Times,* March 15, 1932, 1, 12.

39. U.S. Senate, Committee on the Judiciary, *Modification or Repeal of National Prohibition: Hearings Before a Subcommittee,* 72d Cong., 1st sess., 1932, 17–18, 152–59.

40. "Why Not Count Noses—Wet or Dry?" *World's Work* 59 (March 1930): 40; "Vox Pop: Can It Bring Repeal?" *World's Work* 61 (January 1932): 28; "Repeal the Eighteenth Amendment," *Nation* 134 (May 4, 1932): 502.

41. Henry H. Curran to Republican National Convention delegates, May 28, 1932, Irénée Du Pont Papers, Eleutherian Mills Historical Library.

42. *New York Times,* June 27, 1932, 1, 10, 11.

43. *Official Report of the Proceedings of the Twentieth Republican National Convention, 1932* (New York, 1932), 119–21.

44. *Official Report of the Proceedings of the Democratic National Convention, 1932* (n.p., n.d.), 146–50, 192.

45. *Time,* July 18, 1932.

46. *Congressional Record,* 72d Cong., 2d sess., 4144.

47. *New York Times,* November 10, 1932, 10; [Jouett Shouse], *Annual Report of the President of the Association Against the Prohibition Amendment for 1932* (Washington, D.C.: AAPA, 1933), 8–12.

48. James M. Beck, press release, November 13, 1932, James M. Beck Papers, Princeton University Library, Princeton, N.J.

49. *Congressional Record,* 76th Cong., 2d sess., 6–12; *New York Times,* December 6, 1932, 1.

50. *Congressional Record,* 76th Cong., 2d sess., 4005; John J. Blaine to J. J. Seelman, January 30 and February 15, 1933, John J. Blaine Papers, Wisconsin State Historical Society, Madison, Wis.

51. Everett Somerville Brown, comp., *Ratification of the Twenty-first Amendment to the Constitution of the United States: State Convention Records and Laws* (Ann Arbor: University of Michigan Press, 1938), 4; [Jouett Shouse], *Annual Report of the President of the Association Against the Prohibition Amendment for the Year 1933* (Washington, D.C.: AAPA, 1934), 12–15.

52. *New York Times,* February 14, 1933, 2.

53. *Congressional Record,* 72d Cong., 2d sess., 4169, 4179, 4231, 4516.

54. Clement E. Vose, *Constitutional Change: Amendment Politics and Supreme Court Litigation Since 1900* (Lexington, Mass.: Lexington Books, 1972), 112–15.

55. Brown, comp., *Ratification of the Twenty-first Amendment,* 5, 515; *New York Times,* February 26, 1933, 1, 30.

56. The most reliable account is Clement E. Vose, "Repeal as a Political Achievement," in *Law, Alcohol, and Order: Perspectives on National Prohibition,* ed. David E. Kyvig (Westport, Conn.: Greenwood, 1985), 97–121. For an alternative version, see Noel T. Dowling, "A New Experiment in Ratification," *American Bar Association Journal* 19 (1933): 383–87.

57. Joseph H. Choate, Jr., to Arthur K. Stebbins, January 28, 1933, Voluntary Committee of Lawyers Papers, Collection on Legal Change, Wesleyan University, Middletown, Conn.

58. A full account is in Vose, "Repeal as a Political Achievement," 97–121.

59. Ibid., 112–13.

60. Brown, comp., *Ratification of the Twenty-first Amendment,* 515–700; draft bill, Voluntary Committee of Lawyers Papers, Collection on Legal Change.

61. Brown, comp., *Ratification of the Twenty-first Amendment,* 518.

62. Ibid., 214–33.

63. [Shouse], *Annual Report for 1933,* 18–22, an analysis of the vote within each state is on 22–27.

64. Brown, comp., *Ratification of the Twenty-first Amendment,* 5–9.

65. The lengthiest ratification would not be completed until 1992 when the second of James Madison's initial twelve amendments was ratified 203 years after being proposed and 201 years after three through twelve were ratified as the Bill of Rights.

66. Brown, comp., *Ratification of the Twenty-first Amendment,* 432, 280, 196.

67. Ibid., 330.

68. *State Board of Equalization of California v. Young's Market Co.,* 299 US 59, 62 (1936).

69. Joe de Ganahl, "The Scope of Federal Power over Alcoholic Beverages Since the Twenty-first Amendment," *George Washington Law Review* 8 (1940): 819–34, 875–903.

70. *California v. LaRue,* 409 US 109 (1972).

13. FORGOING AMENDMENT IN THE THIRD AMERICAN CONSTITUTIONAL REVOLUTION

1. The phrase is that of Bruce Ackerman, whose *We the People: Foundations* (Cambridge: Harvard University Press, 1991) well states this constitutional view of the New Deal.

2. A clear and eloquent summary is offered by William E. Leuchtenburg, *The Supreme Court Reborn: The Constitutional Revolution in the Age of Roosevelt* (New York: Oxford University Press, 1995).

3. *Panama Refining v. Ryan,* 293 US 388, *Retirement Board v. Alton R. Co.,* 295 US 330, *Louisville Joint Stock Bank v. Radford,* 295 US 555, *Humphrey's Executor v. U.S.,* 295 US 602, and *Schechter v. U.S.,* 295 US 495 (all 1935).

4. Franklin D. Roosevelt, *Public Papers and Addresses* 4 (New York: Random House, 1938): 221.

5. Most notable were *U.S. v. Butler,* 297 US 1, *Carter v. Carter Coal Co.,* 298 US 238, and *Morehead v. New York ex rel. Tipaldo,* 298 US 587 (all 1936).

6. Charles Grove Haines, "Judicial Review of Acts of Congress and the Need for Constitutional Reform," *Yale Law Journal* 45 (1936): 847.

7. See Leuchtenburg, *Supreme Court Reborn,* chap. 4.

8. For this second phase, see ibid., chap. 5.

9. James T. Patterson, *Congressional Conservatism and the New Deal: The Growth of the Conservative Coalition in Congress, 1933–1939* (Lexington: University of Kentucky Press, 1967), 125–27.

10. W. T. Dickerson to FDR, February 21, 1937, President's Personal File (PFF), Franklin D. Roosevelt Library (FDRL); George W. Norris, "Government by Injunction," speech, March 12, 1937, George W. Norris Papers, LC; Martin L. Sweeney, "The Supreme Court Issue," radio address, March 12, 1937, CBS, *Congressional Record,* March 15, 1937; Ernest C. Carman, *Shall the Constitution Be Amended—Yes* (n.p., March 24, 1937), Office File (OF), FDRL; Jerome Frank to Thomas Corcoran, May 28, 1937, Thomas G. Corcoran Papers, LC.

11. Roosevelt, *Public Papers,* 6 (New York: Macmillan, 1941): 59.

12. Kenneth S. Davis, *FDR: The Beckoning of Destiny* (New York: G. P. Putnam, 1971), 257, 265; Frank Freidel, *Franklin D. Roosevelt: A Rendezvous with Destiny* (Boston: Little, Brown, 1990), 19.

13. Joseph P. Lash, *Eleanor and Franklin* (New York: W.W. Norton, 1971), 290–91.

14. For a detailed examination of the battle within the Democratic party, see David E. Kyvig, *Repealing National Prohibition* (Chicago: University of Chicago Press, 1979), 143–59.

15. AAPA president Jouett Shouse, who had earlier been John Raskob's executive director of the Democratic National Committee, now became Liberty League president with Raskob and Pierre Du Pont in the background as active if unofficial advisers. AAPA founder William Stayton became league secretary, and board member Grayson Murphy served as treasurer. The league executive committee was dominated by former AAPA leaders or friends: Shouse, James Wadsworth, Irénée Du Pont, Pauline Sabin, John W. Davis, Al Smith, Mrs. Henry B. Joy, and Mrs. James Ross Todd (Minutes of American Liberty League executive committee, August 23 and September 4, 18, and 24, 1934, James W. Wadsworth, Jr., Papers, LC). A detailed examination of the Liberty League is contained in Robert F. Burk, *The Corporate State and the Broker State: The Du Ponts and American National Politics, 1925–1940* (Cambridge: Harvard University Press, 1990), 122–253.

16. Jouett Shouse, *The Return to Democracy,* NBC radio speech, July 1, 1935, reprinted as a pamphlet (Washington, D.C.: American Liberty League, 1935), is a good example of the league's arguments. See also Frederick Rudolph, "The American Liberty League, 1934–1940," *American Historical Review* 56 (1950): 19–33, and George Wolfskill, *The Revolt of the Conservatives: A History of the American Liberty League, 1934–1940* (Boston: Houghton Mifflin, 1962), 65–67, 102–18.

17. Roosevelt, *Public Papers,* 5: 14.

18. Ibid., 234.

19. Wolfskill, *Revolt of the Conservatives,* 212–19; David E. Kyvig, "Objection Sustained: Prohibition Repeal and the New Deal," in *Alcohol, Reform, and Society,* ed. Jack S. Blocker (Westport, Conn.: Greenwood, 1979), 211–12.

20. Franklin D. Roosevelt to Lewis M. Herman, September 7, 1935, and to Herbert S. Houston, July 31, 1936, PPF; James A. Farley diary, December 30, 1935, January 16 and 19, March 24, and April 20, 1936, James A. Farley Papers, LC.

21. Roosevelt, *Public Papers,* 6:152.

22. Harold L. Ickes diary, January 11, 1935, Harold L. Ickes Papers, LC. The most detailed contemporary account of the Court fight, Joseph Alsop and Turner Catledge, *The 168 Days* (Garden City, N.Y.: Doubleday, Doran 1938), dated Roosevelt's and Cummings's inquiries as beginning in summer 1936 (see pp. 20–28), and thus overlooked the period when amendments were being most seriously considered.

23. A summary of many of the proposals advanced for resolving the problem can be found in Jane Perry Clark, "The Recent Proposals for Constitutional Amendment," *Wisconsin Law Review* 12 (1937): 313–36. Perhaps the most intriguing was a 1936 congressional proposal to alter Article I, section 8, by simply replacing the commas after Excises with a semicolon. This punctuation change, it was argued, would broaden Congress's power to provide for the general welfare (ibid, 332).

24. Michael Kammen, *A Machine That Would Go of Itself: The Constitution in American Culture* (New York: Knopf, 1986), 261.

25. George Norris to Judge Arthur G. Wray, February 21, 1930, Norris Papers; Norris to FDR, February 1, 1935, in FDR to Homer Cummings, February 11, 1935, Homer Cummings Papers, University of Virginia Library.

26. Cummings diary, May 27, 1935, Cummings Papers. Characteristically, he provided no details other than that he had spent two hours at the White House discussing amendments with FDR, Richberg, and Solicitor General Stanley Reed.

27. Edward Costigan to FDR, May 29, 1935, PPF.

28. FDR to Marvin McIntyre, June 11, 1935, PPF.

29. Jack Garrett Scott to Tom Corcoran, September 2, 1935, Corcoran Papers.

30. Felix Frankfurter to FDR, May 23, 1935, Felix Frankfurter Papers, LC. See also Frankfurter to National Consumer's League, September 16, 1936, Mary W. Dewson Papers, FDRL.

31. FDR to James T. Soutter, June 10, 1935, PPF.

32. FDR notation to Marvin McIntyre on Karl L. Gauck to FDR, June 8, 1935, PPF.

33. James W. Wadsworth, "The Blessings of Stability," Institute of Public Affairs, University of Virginia, July 12, 1935, James W. Wadsworth Papers, LC.

34. Charlton Ogburn to FDR, August 7, 1935, OF. The correspondence does not make clear what sort of amendment Ogburn then had in mind.

35. FDR to Ogburn, August 14, 1935, OF.

36. Ickes diary, November 13, 1935, and December 27, 1935.

37. Ogburn to FDR, January 9, 1936, OF.

38. Ogburn to Cummings, February 3, 1936, and Cummings to Ogburn, February 10, 1936, Cummings Papers.

39. Cummings to FDR, February 7, 1936, Cummings Papers.

40. Undated memo, Cummings to FDR, Cummings Papers. See also Homer Cummings, "The Nature of the Amending Process," *George Washington Law Review* 6 (1938): 247–58.

41. Cummings to FDR, January 29, 1936, Cummings Papers.

42. Donald R. Richberg, "Undermining the Constitution," *Vital Speeches of the Day* 2 (January 13, 1936): 238–44.

43. Donald R. Richberg, "The Constitution, the New Deal and 1936," address at luncheon of Penn Athletic Club, January 9, 1936, speech file, Donald R. Richberg Papers, LC.

44. Donald R. Richberg, "Constitutional Difficulties of Self-Government," Boston, February 16, 1936, *Congressional Record*, February 27, 1936.

45. Donald R. Richberg, "Should We Amend the Constitution?" *Missouri Bar Journal* 7 (1936): 45–53.

46. Donald R. Richberg, "The Need for Constitutional Growth by Construction or Amendment," speech to Kentucky Bar Association, April 3, 1936; "What About the Constitution?" speech to meeting of Sons of the American Revolution, Washington, December 16, 1936, speech file, Richberg Papers.

47. Richberg to J. R. Brackett, Associated Press, June 3, 1936; "Social Welfare and the Constitution," speech to American Association for Labor Legislation and American Political Science Association, Chicago, December 30, 1936, speech file, Richberg Papers.

48. Cummings to FDR, June 20, 1936, Cummings Papers; Richberg to Marvin McIntyre, June 16, 1936, Richberg Papers.

49. National Consumers' League, *Clarifying the Constitution by Amendment* (New York, December 15, 1936), Cummings Papers.

50. Summary of meeting of Minimum Wage Conference, November 27, 1936; Elmer F. Andrews, New York state industrial commissioner, to Joseph M. Tone, commissioner, Connecticut Department of Labor and Factory Inspection, December 22, 1936; Anderson to members of the New York State Minimum Wage Conference, January 26, 1937, Dewson Papers.

51. Dewson to Stanley Reed, December 10, 1936; to James Thompson, New Orleans, December 12, 1936; to J. C. Pryor, Burlington, Iowa, January 13, 1937; to James M. Langley, Concord, N.H., January 26, 1937, Dewson Papers.

52. Cummings diary, November 15, 1936.

53. Ibid., December 24, 1936.

54. Ibid., December 26, 1936, January 7, 24, 30, February 2, 3, and 4, 1937.

55. Roosevelt, *Public Papers,* 5: 639; 6: 76.

56. Ickes diary, February 6, 1937.

57. FDR to Felix Frankfurter, February 9, 1937, Frankfurter Papers. Thomas Corcoran, speaking for FDR, had told Ickes essentially the same thing January 8, 1937 (Ickes diary).

58. FDR to Charles Burlingham, February 23, 1937, President's Secretary's File, FDRL.

59. Roosevelt, *Public Papers,* 6:126–27, 131.

60. Ibid., 131–32.

61. Dewson to Mrs. Anna Dickie Olesen, March 4, 1937, Dewson Papers; Ogburn to FDR, February 6, 1937, PPF; William Green to George W. Norris, February 23, 1937, Norris Papers; Ickes diary, February 6, 11, and 14, 1937, Ickes Papers.

62. Farley diary, February 11 and 15, 1937, Farley Papers; Thomas G. Corcoran, New Deal files, Corcoran Papers.

63. New York newspaper editorials in March 1936 repeatedly decried the arrogance and obstructionism of Senate Judiciary Committee chairman William T. Byrne (National Child Labor Committee scrapbooks, NCLC Papers, LC).

64. Cummings to Alexander Holtzoff, July 13, 1937, Cummings Papers.

65. Cummings to Holtzoff, July 22, 1937, Cummings Papers; see also Cummings, "Nature of the Amending Process," 347–58.

66. Roosevelt, *Public Papers,* 6: 366.

67. Norris to Jerome F. Heyn, April 3, 1937, Norris Papers.

68. Norris to Green, February 26, 1937, Norris Papers.

69. Ickes diary, February 6, 1937.

70. Clark to William Borah, February 23, 1937, Borah Papers, LC, quoted in Patterson, *Congressional Conservatism,* 89–90.

71. Special Committee of the American Bar Association, "The Federal Child Labor Amendment," *American Bar Association Journal* 21 (1935): 12.

72. Child Labor Amendment Conference minutes, January 27, 1934, NCLC Papers; Walter I. Trattner, *Crusade for the Children: A History of the National Child Labor Committee and Child Labor Reform in America* (Chicago: Quadrangle, 1970), 189–90.

73. Quoted in Trattner, *Crusade for the Children,* 193.

74. Roosevelt, "Annual Message to Congress," January 3, 1934, *Public Papers,* 3: 10.

75. [Miriam Keller, NCLC president], speech to Florida PTA, December 1935, NCLC Papers.

76. Minutes of conferences on the Child Labor Amendment, January 27, 1934, April 10, 1935, April 3, 1936, December 9, 1936, April 9, 1937, NCLC Papers.

77. Trattner, *Crusade for the Children,* 201.

78. Ibid., 201–2.

79. Ibid., 197.

80. Quoted in ibid., 199.

81. Special Committee of the ABA, "Federal Child Labor Amendment," 12–13.

82. James W. Wadsworth to Herbert L. Satterlee, January 22, 1935; to Nicholas Murray Butler, January 28, May 8 and 11, 1935, April 15, 1937, and September 30, 1939; and to Vincent H. Dowling, March 24, 1937; "Amending the Constitution" [January 18, 1938], Wadsworth Papers.

83. *Coleman v. Miller,* 307 US 433 (1939).

84. *Chandler v. Wise,* 307 US 474 (1939).

85. Committee for Ratification of the Child Labor Amendment, Minutes, March 3, 1938, NCLC Papers.

86. *Coleman v. Miller,* 307 US 450.

87. Ibid., 453–54.

88. Ibid., 457–59.

89. *Chandler v. Wise,* 307 US 474.

90. *Coleman v. Miller,* 307 US 459. Noel T. Dowling, "Clarifying the Amending Process," *Washington and Lee Law Review* 1 (1940): 215–23, provides a useful analysis of the decision. Vigorous arguments that *Coleman* was wrongly decided and that final review of the amending process should remain with the Court, not the Congress, are found in Homer Clark, "The Supreme Court and the Amending Process," *Virginia Law Review* 39 (1953): 621–52, and Walter Dellinger, "The Legitimacy of Constitutional Change: Rethinking the Amendment Process," *Harvard Law Review* 97 (1983): 386–432.

91. Trattner, *Crusade for the Children,* 203–7.

92. National Child Labor Committee, "Child Labor in 1939," NCLC Papers.

93. Minutes, Conference on Child Labor Amendment, March 15, 1939, NCLC Papers.

94. *U.S. v. Darby,* 312 US 100 (1941).

14. ATTEMPTED COUNTERREVOLUTION BY AMENDMENT

1. See especially Manfred Jonas, *Isolationism in America, 1935–1941* (Ithaca, N.Y.: Cornell University Press, 1966), 139–68; also Charles Chatfield, *For Peace and Justice: Pacifism in America, 1914–1941* (Knoxville: University of Tennessee Press, 1971), 144–45.

2. Ernest C. Bolt, Jr., *Ballots Before Bullets: The War Referendum Approach to Peace in America, 1914–1941* (Charlottesville: University Press of Virginia, 1977), 1–92; Chatfield, *For Peace and Justice,* 26, 35; Walter R. Griffin, "Louis Ludlow and the War Referendum Crusade, 1935–1941," *Indiana Magazine of History* 64 (1968): 270–71.

3. Bolt, *Ballots Before Bullets,* 99–151; Griffin, "Ludlow and the War Referendum," 271.

4. Bolt, *Ballots Before Bullets,* 153–57; Griffin, "Ludlow and the War Referendum," 267–73.

5. Ludlow to Sumners, April 3, 1935, quoted in Griffin, "Ludlow and the War Referendum," 274, n. 20.

6. Ludlow to Franklin D. Roosevelt, January 21, 1935, PPF, FDRL.

7. Ludlow to Roosevelt, December 21, 1936, OF, FDRL.

8. Franklin D. Roosevelt to Ludlow, December 29, 1936, OF, FDRL.

9. Bolt, *Ballots Before Bullets,* 159–61.

10. Chatfield, *For Peace and Justice,* 283.

11. George Gallup and Saul Forbes Rae, *The Pulse of Democracy* (New York: Simon and Schuster, 1940), 315.

12. Bolt, *Ballots Before Bullets,* 162–63.

13. Ibid., 155.

14. *New York Times,* December 18, 1937, 3.

15. Bolt, *Ballots Before Bullets* 164–67.

16. Louis Ludlow, press release, December 22, 1937, OF, FDRL; Chatfield, *For Peace and Justice,* 281–86; Bolt, *Ballots Before Bullets,* 157–72; Wayne S. Cole, *Roosevelt and the Isolationists, 1932–45* (Lincoln: University of Nebraska Press, 1983), 256–57.

17. Bolt, *Ballots Before Bullets,* 170.

18. *Congressional Record,* 75th Cong., 3d sess., 278.

19. Griffin, "Ludlow and the War Referendum," 284.

20. *Congressional Record,* 75th Cong., 3d sess., 130–31.

21. Ibid., 192.

22. Ibid., 193–95.

23. Franklin D. Roosevelt to William Bankhead, January 6, 1938, OF, FDRL; *Congressional Record,* 75th Cong., 3d sess., 277.

24. *Congressional Record,* 75th Cong., 3d sess., 278–82.

25. Ibid., 277, 281.

26. James A. Farley to Franklin D. Roosevelt, January 10, 1938, President's Secretary's File, FDRL. In a nine-page memorandum Farley described his conversation with each of the seventy-eight congressmen and listed thirty-two others he tried unsuccessfully to reach.

27. *Congressional Record,* 75th Cong., 3d sess., 282–83.

28. Griffin, "Ludlow and the War Referendum," 285; Bolt, *Ballots Before Bullets,* 175. Among those signers who reversed themselves to support the administration were freshman Lyndon B. Johnson and his Texas colleague Maury Maverick. Those who did not included the usually reliable New Deal supporter Jerry Voorhis of California.

29. Stephen Early to Franklin D. Roosevelt, January 24, 1938; Early to Cordell Hull, January 25, 1938; Early to James Dunn, February 14, 1938; Hatton Sumners to Early, February 28, 1938, miscellaneous correspondence, 1938–1941, War Referendum file, OF; Henry Morgenthau, Jr., diary, March 3, 1938, FDRL.

30. Richard Dean Burns and W. Addams Dixon summarize a wide range of public discussion casting the issue in terms of representative prerogative versus popular determination in "Foreign Policy and the 'Democratic Myth': The Debate on the Ludlow Amendment," *Mid-America* 47 (1963): 288–306.

31. *Congressional Record,* 75th Cong., 3d sess., 277.

32. Louis Ludlow, "Who Shall Say When We Shall Go to War?" *Good Housekeeping* 108 (March 1939): 167, quoted in Griffin, "Ludlow and the War Referendum," 279.

33. *Congressional Record,* 75th Cong., 3d sess., 278–82.

34. Hadley Cantril and Mildred Strunk, eds., *Public Opinion, 1935–1946* (Princeton: Princeton University Press, 1951), 1025–26.

35. Bolt, *Ballots Before Bullets,* 175–79.

36. Bill file, S.J. Res. 84, 76th Cong., 1st sess., Record Group 46, National Archives; Griffin, "Ludlow and the War Referendum," 285–88; Bolt, *Ballots Before Bullets,* 175–83.

37. James C. Schneider, *Should America Go to War? The Debate over Foreign Policy in Chicago, 1939–1941* (Chapel Hill: University of North Carolina Press, 1989).

38. Cole, *Roosevelt and the Isolationists,* 253–62, Chatfield, *For Peace and Justice,* 281–86, and Bolt, *Ballots Before Bullets,* passim, regard the amendment more seriously than do Jonas, *Isolationism in America,* 158–67, Robert Divine, *The Illusion of Neutrality* (Chicago: University of Chicago Press, 1962), 219–21, or Robert Dallek, *Franklin D. Roosevelt and American Foreign Policy, 1932–1945* (New York: Oxford University Press, 1979), 154–56. None of them places the Ludlow amendment in the context of other constitutional debates in the 1930s.

39. Frederick D. Zucker, "The Adoption of the Twenty-Second Amendment" (Ph.D. diss., Pennsylvania State University, 1958), 10–30.

40. The best study of Roosevelt's third term election is Herbert S. Parmet and Marie B. Hecht, *Never Again: A President Runs for a Third Term* (New York: Macmillan, 1968). Roosevelt's November 2, 1940, Cleveland speech is quoted on 268.

41. Ibid., 187.

42. Zucker, "Adoption of the Twenty-Second Amendment," 30–33.

43. Parmet and Hecht, *Never Again,* 269.

44. James L. Wick to Robert A. Taft, June 1, 1944, Robert A. Taft, Jr., Papers, LC; Zucker, "Adoption of the Twenty-Second Amendment," 33–39.

45. Alan P. Grimes, *Democracy and the Amendments to the Constitution* (Lexington, Mass.: Lexington Books, 1978), 114–15; Stephen W. Stathis, "The Twenty-Second Amendment: A Practical Remedy or Partisan Maneuver?" *Constitutional Commentary* 7 (1990): 62–64.

46. Zucker, "Adoption of the Twenty-Second Amendment," 45–46.

47. Wick to Taft, June 1, 1944, Taft Papers; Susan M. Hartmann, *Truman and the 80th Congress* (Columbia: University of Missouri Press, 1971), 3–26.

48. *Congressional Record,* 80th Cong., 1st sess., 872; Zucker, "Adoption of the Twenty-Second Amendment," 53–79.

49. *New York Times,* January 9, 1947, 15.

50. *Congressional Record,* 80th Cong., 1st sess., 857–58.

51. Grimes, *Democracy and the Amendments,* 117.

52. *Congressional Record,* 80th Cong., 1st sess., 844–54.

53. Zucker provides a good overview of public attention in "Adoption of the Twenty-Second Amendment," 120–29. See also Paul and George Willis, "The Politics of the Twenty-Second Amendment," *Western Political Quarterly* 5 (1952): 477.

54. *Congressional Record,* 80th Cong., 1st sess., 1773.

55. Paul H. Appleby, "Roosevelt's Third Term Decision," *American Political Science Review* 46 (1952): 754.

56. *Congressional Record,* 80th Cong., 1st sess., 845.

57. Ibid., 871.

58. Ibid., 1807.

59. Ibid., 1800–1807. The frustration of a leading scholar of convention ratification with this lack of understanding on the senators' part is evident in Everett S. Brown, "The Term of Office of the President," *American Political Science Review* 41 (1947): 447–50.

60. *Congressional Record,* 80th Cong, 1st sess., 1773, 1800–1803.

61. Ibid., 1862.

62. Ibid., 1862–63, 1938, 1955–59.

63. Ibid., 1978; Zucker, "Adoption of the Twenty-Second Amendment," 136.

64. *Congressional Record,* 80th Cong., 1st sess., 2389–92.

65. Zucker, "Adoption of the Twenty-Second Amendment," 173.

66. These eighteen, in order of ratification, were Maine, Michigan, Iowa, Kansas, New Hampshire, Delaware, Illinois, Oregon, Colorado, California, New Jersey, Vermont, Ohio, Wisconsin, Pennsylvania, Connecticut, Missouri, and Nebraska.

67. Zucker, "Adoption of the Twenty-Second Amendment," 179, 187–88.

68. Ibid., 179.

69. Ibid., 179–81.

70. Ibid., 179, 220–21.

71. Ibid., 179, 222.

72. Ibid., 181, 222–26.

73. Ibid., 181, 212–18.

74. Quoted in ibid., 192, 195–96.

75. Neither the official nor the personal presidential files in the Harry S Truman Library, Independence, Missouri, contain comments of substance, in sharp contrast to Truman's Post-Presidential Files. Sabath's remark appears in *Congressional Record*, 80th Cong., 1st sess., 841.

76. "The Two-Term Limit," *Nation* 172 (March 10, 1951): 216–17.

77. Stathis, "Twenty-Second Amendment," 72–73.

78. Harry S Truman, "Excerpt from Statement before the Subcommittee on Constitutional Amendments of the Senate Committee on the Judiciary on Repeal of the 22nd Amendment," May 4, 1959, Post-Presidential Files, Truman Library.

79. U.S. Senate, Committee on the Judiciary, *Presidential Terms of Office: Hearings*, 86th Cong., 1st sess. (Washington, D.C.: GPO, 1959), 10–13.

80. Harry S Truman to Bernard Fensterwald, Jr., May 29, 1959, Post-Presidential Files, Truman Library.

81. Stathis, "Twenty-Second Amendment," 74–75.

82. Ibid., 77–81.

83. Clinton Rossiter, quoted in ibid., 87.

84. Russell L. Caplan, *Constitutional Brinksmanship: Amending the Constitution by National Convention* (New York: Oxford University Press, 1988), 69; Frank E. Packard, "Problems Arising from an Attempt to Amend the Constitution by Convention Concerning the Limiting of Income Tax Rates to 25 Percent," *Nebraska Law Review* 31 (1952): 408.

85. Caplan, *Constitutional Brinksmanship*, 69. For a strong argument that several of these state convention applications were defective and ought to be ignored, see Bernard Fensterwald, Jr., "The States and the Amending Process—A Reply," *American Bar Association Journal* 46 (1960): 717–21.

86. Packard, "Problems Arising from an Attempt to Amend the Constitution," 407–8; Homer Clark, "The Supreme Court and the Amending Process," *Virginia Law Review* 39 (1953): 621–22; Clement E. Vose, "Conservatism by Amendment," *Yale Review* 46 (1956): 184.

87. U.S. Senate, Committee on the Judiciary, Subcommittee on Constitutional Amendments, *Balancing of the Budget: Hearings*, 84th Cong., 2d sess., 1956.

88. Vose, "Conservatism by Amendment," 180.

89. Quoted in ibid., 180. See also Neal R. Peirce and Lawrence D. Longley, *The People's President: The Electoral College in American History and the Direct Vote Alternative*, rev. ed. (New Haven: Yale University Press, 1981), 136–38.

90. Peirce and Longley, *People's President*, 146–50.

91. Ibid., 151–53; Vose, "Conservatism by Amendment," 180.

92. William Logan Martin, "The Amending Power: The Ebinger Proposal," *American Bar Association Journal* 40 (1954): 767–71, 802–3; Frank W. Grinnell, "The Controversial Reed-Walter Amendment to Change the Amending Process in the Federal Constitution," *Massachusetts Law Quarterly* 40 (1955): 25–26; James P. Murtagh, "Procedure for Amending the Constitution and the Reed-Walter Amendment," *Pennsylvania Bar Association Quarterly* 27 (1955): 90–101.

93. Vose, "Conservatism by Amendment," 176–90.

94. *Missouri v. Holland*, 252 US 416 (1920). A good discussion of this case is provided by Charles A. Lofgren, "Missouri v. Holland in Historical Perspective," *Supreme Court Review* 1975: 77–122.

95. *U.S. v. Curtiss-Wright Export Corporation*, 299 US 304. See Robert A. Divine, "The Case of the Smuggled Bombers," in *Quarrels That Have Shaped the Constitution*, ed. John A. Garraty, rev. ed. (New York: Harper and Row, 1987), 253–65.

96. *U.S. v. Belmont*, 301 US 324. A further Supreme Court decision in *U.S. v. Pink*, 315 US 204 (1942) held that the Roosevelt-Litvinov agreements on property distribution, though never ratified by Congress, overrode a specifically contrary New York state statute.

97. Edwin Borchard, "The Proposed Constitutional Amendment on Treaty Making," *American Journal of International Law* 39 (1945): 537–41; *Congressional Record,* 79th Cong., 1st sess., 4341–68.

98. Duane Tananbaum, *The Bricker Amendment Controversy: A Test of Eisenhower's Political Leadership* (Ithaca, N.Y.: Cornell University Press, 1988): 1–15.

99. U.S. Senate, Committee on the Judiciary, *Treaties and Executive Agreements: Hearings,* 83d Cong., 1st sess., 1953, 136–37.

100. Clarence Manion, 1952 campaign radio address in Manion to Robert A. Taft, November 25, 1953, Taft Papers; Athan G. Theoharis, *The Yalta Myths: An Issue in U.S. Politics, 1945–1955* (Columbia: University of Missouri Press, 1970), 39–153.

101. A clear statement of his viewpoint can be found in John W. Bricker, "Socialism by Treaty," a speech to the Conference of American Small Business Organizations, Washington, D.C., April 22, 1952, constitutional amendment files, John W. Bricker Papers, Ohio Historical Society, Columbus, Ohio.

102. Tananbaum, *Bricker Amendment Controversy,* 20–31.

103. Walter F. George to Bricker, September 20, 1951, and nineteen other senators, September 22 to October 9, 1951, constitutional amendment files, Bricker Papers.

104. Tananbaum, *Bricker Amendment Controversy,* 32–43.

105. Truman's action as well as the political and judicial response is well discussed in Maeva Marcus, *Truman and the Steel Seizure Case: The Limits of Presidential Power* (New York: Columbia University Press, 1977).

106. Eberhard P. Deutsch, "The Need for a Treaty Amendment," *American Bar Association Journal* 38 (1952): 735–38, 793–96; Clarence Manion, undated 1952 radio campaign speech, in Manion to Robert A. Taft, November 25, 1952, Taft Papers; Tananbaum, *Bricker Amendment Controversy,* 42–65.

107. Frank E. Holman to Bricker, December 17, 1952, and January 12, 1953, constitutional amendment files, Bricker Papers.

108. Tananbaum, *Bricker Amendment Controversy,* 68–69, 82.

109. Ibid., 92.

110. Ibid., 55–60.

111. John W. Bricker, interview with Alfred E. Eckes, March 14, 1974, Former Members of Congress Oral History Project, LC.

112. Dwight D. Eisenhower, news conference of March 19, 1953, *Public Papers of the Presidents of the United States, 1953* (Washington, D.C.: GPO, 1960), 109–10.

113. Eisenhower, news conference of March 26, 1953, *Public Papers, 1953,* 132.

114. Tananbaum, *Bricker Amendment Controversy,* 72–79, 87–90.

115. Alexander Wiley to Frank E. Holman, June 9, 1953, and Lyndon B. Johnson to F. F. Nine, July 14, 1953, constitutional amendment files, Bricker Papers.

116. Tananbaum, *Bricker Amendment Controversy,* 113–32.

117. Eisenhower, news conference of July 1, 1953, *Public Papers, 1953,* 469–70.

118. Tananbaum, *Bricker Amendment Controversy,* 97–111; Gary W. Reichard, *The Reaffirmation of Republicanism: Eisenhower and the Eighty-Third Congress* (Knoxville: University of Tennessee Press, 1975), 58–68, provides useful insight into administration negotiations with Bricker throughout the controversy as well as analysis of the divisions within Republican congressional ranks.

119. John W. Bricker to Frank E. Holman, July 23, 1953, constitutional amendment files, Bricker Papers.

120. Eisenhower, news conference of January 13, 1954, *Public Papers, 1954,* 52–53.

121. Quoted in *New York Times,* January 27, 1954, 1.

122. Tananbaum, *Bricker Amendment Controversy,* 133–56.

123. *Congressional Record,* 83d Cong., 2d sess., 1740, 2262, 2374–75; Tananbaum, *Bricker Amendment Controversy,* 161, 169–83.

124. Eisenhower, news conference of March 3, 1954, *Public Papers, 1954*, 296.

125. Tananbaum, *Bricker Amendment Controversy*, 179–89.

126. Ibid., 191–215.

127. *Washington Star*, March 2, 1951, A–11.

128. *Brown v. Board of Education of Topeka*, 347 US 483 (1954).

15. AMENDMENTS TO SOLVE IMMEDIATE PROBLEMS

1. A detailed discussion of the poll tax battles of the 1940s can be found in Steven F. Lawson, *Black Ballots: Voting Rights in the South, 1944–1969* (New York: Columbia University Press, 1976), 1–85.

2. U.S. Bureau of the Census, *Historical Statistics of the United States: From Colonial Times to 1957* (Washington, D.C.: GPO, 1960), 12.

3. *Federalist 43*, in Edward Mead Earle, ed., *The Federalist* (New York: Modern Library, 1937), 280.

4. A brief history of the District of Columbia's legal status can be found in Philip G. Schrag, *Behind the Scenes: The Politics of a Constitutional Convention* (Washington, D.C.: Georgetown University Press, 1985), 10–15.

5. Herman V. Ames, *The Proposed Amendments to the Constitution*, in *Annual Report, American Historical Association, 1896* (Washington, D.C.: GPO, 1897), 181; Clement E. Vose, "When District of Columbia Representation Collides with the Constitutional Amendment Institution," *Publius* 9 (1979): 114–16.

6. Lawson, *Black Ballots*, 59, 77, 84.

7. Alan P. Grimes, *Democracy and the Amendments to the Constitution* (Lexington, Mass.: Lexington, Books, 1978), 125–28.

8. *Congressional Record*, 86th Cong., 2d sess., 12556.

9. Ibid., 12551–71; Grimes, *Democracy and the Amendments*, 128–30.

10. *Congressional Record*, 86th Cong., 2d sess., 12850–58; Grimes, *Democracy and the Amendments*, 130.

11. *The Constitution of the United States: Analysis and Interpretation*, 99th Cong., 1st sess. (Washington, D.C.: GPO, 1987), 40.

12. S.J. Res. 126, August 6, 1959, with Kennedy's name handwritten in the margin as a last-minute added sponsor, Pre-Presidential Papers, John. F. Kennedy Papers, John F. Kennedy Presidential Library, Boston.

13. *The Constitution: Analysis and Interpretation*, 33–39.

14. *Congressional Record*, 87th Cong., 2d sess., 5101–5.

15. Ibid., 17651–70.

16. *The Constitution: Analysis and Interpretation*, 41.

17. An account of the fight over the civil rights bill from the viewpoint of a participating Republican congressman is Charles Whalen and Barbara Whalen, *The Longest Debate: A Legislative History of the 1964 Civil Rights Act* (Cabin John, Md.: Seven Locks Press, 1985).

18. Useful histories of these episodes are provided by Ruth C. Silva, *Presidential Succession* (Ann Arbor: University of Michigan Press, 1951) and John D. Feerick, *From Failing Hands: The Story of Presidential Succession* (New York: Fordham University Press, 1965).

19. U.S. Senate, Committee on the Judiciary, Subcommittee on Constitutional Amendments, *Presidential Inability: Hearings*, 88th Cong., 1st sess., 1963, 12.

20. John D. Feerick, *The Twenty-fifth Amendment: Its Complete History and Earliest Applications* (New York: Fordham University Press, 1976), 51–57.

21. Birch Bayh, *One Heartbeat Away: Presidential Disability and Succession* (Indi-

anapolis: Bobbs-Merrill, 1968), 1–32; Birch Bayh, interview with author, July 8, 1981, tape in possession of author.

22. Bayh, *One Heartbeat Away*, 30–42; Bayh interview, July 8, 1981.

23. Bayh, *One Heartbeat Away*, 32–33.

24. Ibid., 43–63.

25. U.S. Senate, Committee on the Judiciary, Subcommittee on Constitutional Amendments, *Presidential Inability and Vacancies in the Office of Vice President: Hearings,* 88th Cong., 2d sess., 1964, 3, 234–52; Bayh, *One Heartbeat Away*, 52–87.

26. Bayh, *One Heartbeat Away*, 95–128.

27. *Congressional Record,* 88th Cong., 2d sess. 23002, 23056–61; Bayh, *One Heartbeat Away*, 129–59. As recently as 1960 both the Senate and the House of Representatives had approved the Twenty-third Amendment without a roll call.

28. Bayh, *One Heartbeat Away*, 161–79.

29. U.S. Senate, Committee on the Judiciary, Subcommittee on Constitutional Amendments, *Presidential Inability and Vacancies in the Office of Vice President: Hearings,* 89th Cong., 1st sess., 1965, 11–12; *Congressional Record,* 89th Cong., 1st sess., 3286.

30. U.S. House of Representatives, Committee on the Judiciary, *Presidential Inability and Vice Presidential Vacancy: Hearings,* 89th Cong., 1st sess., 1965; *Congressional Record,* 89th Cong., 1st sess., 7968–69.

31. *Congressional Record,* 89th Cong., 1st sess., 15596.

32. In his account of the amendment's adoption, *One Heartbeat Away,* Bayh devoted 333 pages to congressional approval and a seven-page epilogue to ratification.

33. Bayh interview, July 8, 1981.

34. Bayh, *One Heartbeat Away,* 108–9, 175, 336.

35. *The Constitution: Analysis and Interpretation,* 42–43; Feerick, *Twenty-fifth Amendment,* 112.

36. Bayh, *One Heartbeat Away,* 341–42.

37. Ibid., 227.

38. *New York Herald Tribune,* June 9, 1964, 20, quoted in Feerick, *Twenty-fifth Amendment,* 218.

39. Feerick, *Twenty-fifth Amendment,* 117–86, provides a detailed examination of the use of the new procedures as Gerald Ford and Nelson Rockefeller replaced the resigned Spiro Agnew and Richard Nixon. The author, an ABA lawyer, was involved in the drafting of the amendment.

40. Bayh, *One Heartbeat Away,* 192.

41. Although flawed in style, analysis, documentation, and, occasionally, statements of fact, Wendell W. Cultice, *Youth's Battle for the Ballot: A History of Voting Age in America* (Westport, Conn.: Greenwood, 1992), is the only comprehensive study of voting age reform.

42. Ibid., 86–91.

43. Though Cultice, *Youth's Battle for the the Ballot,* 144–59, considers the 1970 referendums a strong showing for suffrage age reduction, the numbers he presents seem to suggest a different conclusion.

44. U.S. Senate, Committee on the Judiciary, Subcommittee on Constitutional Amendments, *Lowering the Voting Age to 18: Hearings,* 91st Cong., 2d sess., 1970, 2; Bayh interview, July 8, 1981.

45. U.S. Senate, *Hearings, Lowering the Voting Age,* 21–27 and passim.

46. Ibid., 78–80.

47. Cultice, *Youth's Battle for the Ballot,* 116–38.

48. *Oregon v. Mitchell,* 400 US 112 (1970).

49. U.S. Senate, Committee on the Judiciary, Subcommittee on Constitutional Amendments, *Lowering the Voting Age to 18—A Fifty-State Survey of the Costs and Other Problems of Dual-Age Voting,* 92d Cong., 1st sess., 1971.

50. U.S. Senate, Committee on the Judiciary, *Lowering the Voting Age to 18: Report on S.J. Res. 7,* 92d Cong., 1st sess., 1971.

51. Bayh interview, July 8, 1981.

52. *Congressional Record,* 92d Cong., 1st sess., 5830, 7569–70.

53. *The Constitution: Analysis and Interpretation,* 44.

54. *Akron Beacon Journal,* July 1, 1971; *Cincinnati Enquirer,* July 1, 1971; *Cleveland Plain Dealer,* June 30, 1971, *Columbus Citizen Journal,* July 1, 1971. For a fuller discussion of this topic, see David E. Kyvig, "Amending the U.S. Constitution: Ratification Controversies, 1917–1971," *Ohio History* 83 (1974): 156–69.

16. FAILED QUESTS TO ALTER ORIGINAL AGREEMENTS

1. *Baker v. Carr,* 369 US 186 (1962).

2. Greater detail on these developments is available in Paul Oberst, "The Genesis of the Three States-Rights Amendments of 1963," *Notre Dame Lawyer* 39 (1964): 648–53.

3. Frank E. Shanahan, Jr., "Proposed Constitutional Amendments: They Will Strengthen Federal-State Relations," *American Bar Association Journal* 49 (1963): 632.

4. Reports of state legislative action on the states' rights amendments are fragmentary and not always in agreement. William G. Fennell, "The States Rights Amendments— Debates of the 'Founding Fathers' Cast Doubts on Current Proposals," *New York State Bar Association Journal* 35 (1963): 466–67, appears the most thorough, though it is sometimes at odds with Oberst, "Genesis of the Three States-Rights Amendments," 654.

5. *New York Times,* May 23, 1963, 1.

6. Oberst, "Genesis of the Three States-Rights Amendments," 653.

7. Henry Steel Commager, "To Form a Much Less Perfect Union," *New York Times Magazine,* July 14, 1963, 5, 40–42.

8. Fennell, "States Rights Amendments," 472.

9. Charles L. Black, Jr., "Proposed Constitutional Amendments: They Would Return Us to Confederacy," *American Bar Association Journal* 49 (1963): 637–40. Black also published "The Proposed Amendment of Article V: A Threatened Disaster," *Yale Law Journal* 72 (1963): 957–66.

10. Oberst, "Genesis of Three States-Rights Amendments," 654–55.

11. *Gomillion v. Lightfoot,* 364 US 339 (1960).

12. *Wesberry v. Saunders,* 376 US 1 (1964).

13. *Reynolds v. Sims,* 377 US 533; *WMCA v. Lomenza,* 377 US 633; *Maryland Committee for Fair Representation v. Tawes,* 377 US 656; *Davis v. Mann,* 377 US 678; *Roman v. Sincock,* 377 US 697; *Lucas v. Forty-Fourth General Assembly of Colorado,* 377 US 713 (all 1964).

14. Apportionment, 87th–91st Congress, Memorials from State Legislatures, Record Group 46, National Archives, Washington, D.C. Congressional action was requested by Alabama, Virginia, Arizona, Idaho, Texas, Nevada, Maryland, North Carolina, Florida, and Mississippi. Convention calls came first from Oklahoma, Kansas, and Arkansas, followed by Kentucky, Louisiana, Missouri, Montana, Nebraska, New Mexico, South Carolina, South Dakota, and Tennessee.

15. William F. Swindler, *Court and Constitution in the 20th Century: The New Legality, 1932–1968* (Indianapolis: Bobbs-Merrill, 1970), 325.

16. A good summary of his thinking is found in Everett McKinley Dirksen, "The Supreme Court and the People," *Michigan Law Review* 66 (1968): 837–56.

17. Birch Bayh, interview with author, July 8, 1981.

18. Bill File, S.J. Res. 2, 89th Cong., 1st sess., Records of the Senate, Record Group 46, National Archives, Washington, D.C.; *Congressional Record,* 89th Cong., 2d sess., 5153–58.

19. Bayh interview, July 8, 1981.

20. An extremely detailed account of congressional treatment of the Dirksen amendment in 1964 and 1965 can be found in Edward Keynes, "The Dirksen Amendment: A Study of Legislative Strategy, Tactics and Public Policy" (Ph.D. diss., University of Wisconsin, 1967); see also *Congressional Record*, 89th Cong., 1st sess., 17843–19373 passim; and 2d sess., 3831–32, 5153–58, 8583.

21. Dirksen, "Supreme Court and the People," 862.

22. *New York Times*, March 18, 1967, 1, 12.

23. *Congressional Record*, 90th Cong., 1st sess., 7551–52, 7573–74.

24. Dirksen, "Supreme Court and the People," 864–73.

25. Sam J. Ervin, Jr., "Proposed Legislation to Implement the Convention Method of Amending the Constitution," *Michigan Law Review* 66 (1968): 875–902. Extensive commentary on the Ervin bill is found in Paul G. Kauper, "The Alternative Amendment Process: Some Observations," *Michigan Law Review* 66 (1968): 903–20, and Arthur Earl Bonfield, "The Dirksen Amendment and the Article V Convention Process," *Michigan Law Review* 66 (1968): 949–1000. See also Wilbur Edel, *A Constitutional Convention: Threat or Challenge?* (New York: Praeger, 1981), 87–97.

26. *Wall Street Journal*, June 2, 1969, 1.

27. Apportionment, 87th–91st Congress, Memorials from State Legislatures; Philip L. Martin, "The Application Clause of Article Five," *Political Science Quarterly* 85 (1970): 626.

28. *Wall Street Journal*, June 5, 1969, 1, 33.

29. *New York Times*, November 5, 1969, 37.

30. Apportionment, 87th–91st Congress, Memorials from State Legislatures, Record Group 46, National Archives; state petitions and memorials to Congress requesting a constitutional convention on the subject of apportionment, undated memorandum, U.S. Senate, files of the Subcommittee on the Constitution.

31. Edel, *Constitutional Convention*, 101–12.

32. Quoted in Stephen J. Whitfield, *The Culture of the Cold War* (Baltimore: Johns Hopkins University Press, 1991), 81.

33. *Holy Trinity Church v. United States*, 143 US 457, 471 (1892).

34. *Torcaso v. Watkins*, 367 US 488, 490 (1961).

35. *Engel v. Vitale*, 370 US 421, 424, 435 (1962).

36. *Abington School District v. Schempp* and *Murray v. Curlett*, 374 US 203 (1963).

37. Kenneth M. Dolbeare and Phillip E. Hammond, *The School Prayer Decisions: From Court Policy to Local Practice* (Chicago: University of Chicago Press, 1971).

38. Charles E. Rice, *The Supreme Court and Public Prayer: The Need for Restraint* (New York: Fordham University Press, 1964), ix.

39. John F. Kennedy, press conference of June 27, 1962, *Public Papers of the Presidents of the United States: John F. Kennedy, 1962* (Washington, D.C.: GPO, 1963), 511.

40. U.S. House of Representatives, Committee on the Judiciary, *School Prayers: Hearing*, 88th Cong., 2d sess., 1964.

41. Ibid., 385–98.

42. Ibid., 441–43, 533–45.

43. Ibid., 654–59.

44. Ibid., 1746–52.

45. U.S. Senate, Committee on the Judiciary, Subcommittee on Constitutional Amendmens, *Dirksen School Prayer Amendment August 1966: Hearings*, 89th Cong., 2d sess., 1966. Drinan's testimony appears on 7–22.

46. *Congressional Record*, 89th Cong., 2d sess., 23063–556 passim. For a summary of his views, see Sam J. Ervin, Jr., *Preserving the Constitution: The Autobiography of Senator Sam Ervin* (Charlottesville, Va.: Michie, 1984), 237–48.

47. *Congressional Record,* 92d Cong., 1st sess., 39886–958.

48. Dolbeare and Hammond, *School Prayer Decisions.*

49. William K. Muir, Jr., *Prayer in the Public Schools: Law and Attitude Change* (Chicago: University of Chicago Press, 1967).

50. A balanced and useful discussion of the strengths and weaknesses of the electoral system is Wallace S. Sayre and Judith H. Parris, *Voting for President: The Electoral College and the American Political System* (Washington, D.C.: Brookings Institution, 1970).

51. An excellent survey of electoral reform proposals and their fate in Congress is found in Neal R. Peirce and Lawrence D. Longley, *The People's President: The Electoral College in American History and the Direct Vote Alternative,* rev. ed. (New Haven: Yale University Press, 1981), 131–67; U.S Senate, Committee on the Judiciary, Subcommittee on Constitutional Amendment, *Nomination and Election of President and Vice President and Qualifications for Voting: Hearings,* 87th Cong., 1st sess., 1961.

52. Herman V. Ames, *The Proposed Amendments to the Constitution,* in *Annual Report, American Historical Association, 1896* (Washington, D.C.: GPO, 1897), 80–95.

53. Peirce and Longley, *People's President,* 137–58. See chapter 14 of this volume.

54. Bayh interview, July 8, 1981.

55. Peirce and Longley, *People's President,* 159–70.

56. U.S. Senate, Committee on the Judiciary, Subcommittee on Constitutional Amendment, *Election of the President: Hearing,* 89th Cong., 2d sess., and 90th Cong., 1st sess., 1967.

57. Lawrence D. Longley and Alan G. Braun, *The Politics of Electoral College Reform* (New Haven: Yale University Press, 1972), 29, 139.

58. Ibid., 140–56; U.S. Senate, Committee on the Judiciary, Subcommittee on Constitutional Amendments, *Electing the President: Hearings,* 91st Cong., 1st sess., 1969; U.S. House of Representatives, Committee on the Judiciary, *Electoral College Reform: Hearings,* 91st Cong., 1st sess., 1969; *Congressional Record,* 91st Cong., 1st sess., 24963–6007.

59. Longley and Braun, *Politics of Electoral College Reform,* 157–58.

60. U.S. Senate, Committee on the Judiciary, *Electoral College Reform: Supplemental Hearings,* 91st Cong., 2d sess., 1970, 7.

61. Longley and Braun, *Politics of Electoral College Reform,* 159–60.

62. Bayh interview, July 8, 1981.

63. *Congressional Record,* 91st Cong., 2d sess., 30822, 30836.

64. Ibid., 31753, 32357, 34031–33, 34034, 34935–37; Tom Wicker, "Sabotaging the System," *New York Times,* September 29, 1970, 43; U.S. Senate, Committee on the Judiciary, *Direct Popular Election of the President and Vice President of the United States: Report,* 96th Cong., 1st sess., 1979, 3; Longley and Braun, *Politics of Electoral College Reform,* 160–74.

65. *New York Times,* September 29, 1970, 42; Mary Medved to Nels Ackerson, memorandum review 1970 Senate floor debate of SJR1, May 19, 1977, U.S. Senate, Subcommittee on the Constitution, office files.

66. Subcommittee on the Constitution, office files, U.S. Senate, Subcommittee on the Constitution, *Direct Popular Election: Report.*

67. U.S. Senate, Subcommittee on the Constitution, *Direct Popular Election: Report.*

68. Birch Bayh to senators not sponsoring SJR1, June 8, 1977, Subcommittee on the Constitution, office files.

69. U.S. Senate, Committee on the Judiciary, *The Electoral College and Direct Election: Hearings,* 2 vols., 95th Cong., 1st sess., 1977.

70. Nels J. Ackerson to Bayh, December 19, 1977, Subcommittee on the Constitution, office files.

71. Peirce and Longley, *People's President,* 198–200.

72. U.S. Senate, Committee on the Judiciary, Subcommittee on the Constitution, *Direct Popular Election of the President and Vice President of the United States,* 96th Cong., 1st sess., 1979; Subcommittee on the Constitution, office files.

73. Subcommittee on the Constitution, office files; Peirce and Longley, *People's President,* 204–5.

17. AMENDMENTS AS TESTS OF NATIONAL CONSENSUS

1. Birch Bayh, interview with author, July 8, 1981.

2. Herman V. Ames, *The Proposed Amendments to the Constitution,* in *Annual Report, American Historical Association, 1896* (Washington, D.C.: GPO, 1897), 177.

3. An overview of women's rights activity and thought in the 1920s can be gained from Susan D. Becker, *Origins of the Equal Rights Amendment: American Feminism Between the Wars* (Westport: Greenwood, 1981); Nancy F. Cott, *The Grounding of Modern Feminism* (New Haven: Yale University Press, 1987); Peter Geidel, "The National Woman's Party and the Origins of the Equal Rights Amendment, 1920–1923," *Historian* 42 (1980): 557–82; and J. Stanley Lemons, *The Woman Citizen* (Urbana: University of Illinois Press, 1973).

4. Becker, *Origins of the Equal Rights Amendment,* 17–19.

5. *Lochner v. New York,* 198 US 45 (1905); *Muller v. Oregon,* 208 US 412 (1908).

6. Thomas J. Walsh to Louise F. Lusk, January 20, 1932, Thomas J. Walsh Papers, LC.

7. U.S. Senate, Committee on the Judiciary, *Equal Rights Amendment: Hearing,* 70th Cong., 2d sess., 1929; U.S. Senate, Committee on the Judiciary, *Equal Rights: Hearing,* 71st Cong., 3d sess., 1931.

8. Quoted in Becker, *Origins of the Equal Rights Amendment,* 77.

9. Ibid., 77–127.

10. U.S. Senate, Committee on the Judiciary, *Equal Rights for Men and Women: Hearings,* 75th Cong., 3d sess., 1938.

11. Becker, *Origins of the Equal Rights Amendment,* 202–27; Cynthia Harrison, *On Account of Sex: The Politics of Women's Issues, 1945–1968* (Berkeley: University of California Press, 1988), 10–16.

12. Harrison, *On Account of Sex,* 3–19.

13. U.S. House of Representatives, Committee on the Judiciary, *Equal Rights Amendment: Report,* 79th Cong., 1st sess., Report 907, 1945.

14. U.S. Senate, Committee on the Judiciary, *Equal Rights Amendment: Hearing,* 79th Cong., 1st sess., 1945, 8.

15. *Congressional Record,* 79th Cong., 2d sess., 9405.

16. Harrison, *On Account of Sex,* 20–22.

17. James W. Wadsworth to Mrs. Charles E. Henning, president of the New York League of Women Voters, March 24, 1944, and Wadsworth to Cecilia M. Yowman, president, Rochester Diocesan Council, National Council of Catholic Women, October 1, 1945; Wadsworth Papers, LC.

18. James W. Wadsworth to Jane H. Todd, president of the Federation of Women's Republican Clubs, March 20, 1947, Wadsworth Papers.

19. Jane H. Todd to James W. Wadsworth, March 18, 1947, and Wadsworth to W. G. Andrews, April 16, 1947, Wadsworth Papers; Harrison, *On Account of Sex,* 26–29.

20. Robert A. Taft to Mrs. T. J. Fitzgerald, May 22, 1946, and unidentified Taft aide to Phoebe C. Munnecke, July 30, 1952, Robert A. Taft, Jr., Papers, LC.

21. *Congressional Record,* 81st Cong., 2d sess., 870–73.

22. Harrison, *On Account of Sex,* 31–32.

23. *Congressional Record,* 83d Cong., 1st sess., 8973–74.

24. *Congressional Record,* 86th Cong., 2d sess., 15683–86; Harrison, *On Account of Sex,* 35–38.

25. John F. Kennedy to Alma Lutz, February 11, 1957, and Kennedy to Adele E. Moroney, February 4, 1958, Kennedy Prepresidential Papers, JFK Library.

26. Harrison, *On Account of Sex,* 69–88, 109–15.

27. Ibid., 69–88, 109–28.

28. U.S. President's Commission on the Status of Women, *American Women: Report* (Washington, D.C.: GPO, 1963), 44–45: Harrison, *On Account of Sex,* 69–88, 130–34.

29. Harrison, *On Account of Sex,* 89–105.

30. An insightful memoir and history of these developments is Sara Evans, *Personal Politics: The Roots of Women's Liberation in the Civil Rights Movement and the New Left* (New York: Knopf, 1979); the Carmichael quotation is on 87.

31. The best account is found in Harrison, *On Account of Sex,* 176–91.

32. Ibid., 192–204.

33. Ibid., 205.

34. *McDonald v. Board of Elections,* 394 US 802 (1969).

35. *New York Times,* February 18, 1970, 20.

36. U.S. Senate, Committee on the Judiciary, Subcommittee on Constitutional Amendments, *The Equal Rights Amendment: Hearings,* 91st Cong., 2d sess., 1970.

37. *Congressional Record,* 91st Cong., 2d sess., 28000–28004; 28036–37; Gilbert Y. Steiner, *Constitutional Inequality: The Political Fortunes of the Equal Rights Amendment* (Washington, D.C.: Brookings, 1985), 15.

38. *Congressional Record,* 86th Cong., 2d sess., 15683.

39. U.S. Senate, Committee on the Judiciary, *Equal Rights 1970: Hearings,* 91st Cong., 2d sess., 1970; Freund's testimony is on 71–86.

40. *Congressional Record,* 91st Cong., 2d sess., 35449, 36451.

41. Ibid., 36478–505.

42. Ibid., 36863–66; Birch Bayh to Dr. Bernice Sandler, Women's Equity Action League, October 29, 1970, ERA Files, Senate Judiciary Subcommittee on the Constitution.

43. U.S. House of Representatives, Committee on the Judiciary, *Equal Rights for Men and Women 1971: Hearings,* 92d Cong., 1st sess., 1971.

44. *Congressional Record,* 92d Cong., 1st sess., 35784–815.

45. *Congressional Record,* 92d Cong., 2d sess., 9080–9106, 9314–25, 9517–40, 9598.

46. *Phillips v. Martin Marietta Corporation,* 400 US 542 (1971).

47. *Reed v. Reed,* 404 US 71 (1971).

48. *Frontiero v. Richardson,* 411 US 677 (1973); *Stanton v. Stanton,* 421 US 7 (1975); *Craig v. Boren,* 429 US 190 (1976).

49. *Roe v. Wade,* 410 US 113 (1973). The Court's deliberations, insofar as they are known, as well as other aspects of the case are well presented in David J. Garrow, *Liberty and Sexuality: The Right to Privacy and the Making of Roe v. Wade* (New York: Macmillan, 1994), especially 473–599.

50. U.S. Senate, Committee on the Judiciary, Subcommittee on Constitutional Amendments, *Constitutional Amendments: Annual Report, 1976,* 95th Cong., 1st sess., 1977, 5; Janet K. Boles, *The Politics of the Equal Rights Amendment: Conflict and the Decision Process* (New York: Longman, 1979), 2–3, provides additional information on legislative votes.

51. *New York Times,* January 15, 1973, 1, 12.

52. By the end of 1973, the ERA had been turned down in house or senate committees in Arizona, Florida, Georgia, and Mississippi; it had been defeated on the floor of the senate in Alabama, Arkansas, Missouri, Nevada, and North Carolina and of the house in Illinois (three times), Louisiana, Missouri, Oklahoma, South Carolina, Utah, and Vir-

ginia. None of these states subsequently ratified. The best summary of state legislative actions can be found in U.S. Senate, Committee on the Judiciary, Subcommittee on the Constitution, *The Impact of the Equal Rights Amendment: Hearings*, 98th Cong., 1st and 2d sess., 1984, 92–93. Boles, *Politics of the Equal Rights Amendment*, 142–78, offers details on the resistance to ratification in the Georgia and Illinois legislatures; Jane J. Mansbridge, *Why We Lost the ERA* (Chicago: University of Chicago Press, 1986), 165–77, adds insight on Illinois; and Donald G. Mathews and Jane Sherron DeHart, *Sex, Gender, and the Politics of ERA: A State and the Nation* (New York: Oxford University Press, 1990), do likewise for North Carolina.

53. U.S. Senate, Subcommittee on the Constitution, *The Impact of the Equal Rights Amendment*, 92–93. Acting governor Thelma Stovell vetoed the Kentucky legislature's 1978 rescission action. The question of the validity of an executive veto of a legislative act of amendment was wrapped in the larger, and unsettled, question of rescission. Nevertheless, the Kentucky legislature's action buoyed the rescission campaign.

54. Bayh interview, July 8, 1981.

55. *Congressional Record*, 92d Cong., 1st sess., 35814.

56. Bayh interview, July 8, 1981; *Congressional Record*, 92d Cong., 1st sess., 35814; Amelia R. Fry, "Alice Paul and the ERA," in *Rights of Passage: The Past and Future of the ERA*, ed. Joan Hoff-Wilson (Bloomington: Indiana University Press, 1986), 8.

57. Carol Felsenthal, *The Sweetheart of the Silent Majority: The Biography of Phyllis Schlafly* (Garden City, N.Y.: Doubleday, 1981), 240.

58. The Ervin-Schlafly relationship is examined in Mathews and DeHart, *Sex, Gender, and the Politics of ERA*, 50–51.

59. U.S. House of Representatives, Committee on the Judiciary, Subcommittee on Civil and Constitutional Rights, *Equal Rights Amendment Extension: Hearings*, 95th Cong., 2d sess., 1978, 255. This is evident though scarcely acknowledged in the admiring biography by Felsenthal, *Sweetheart of the Silent Majority*, 232–76. Crediting Schlafly, rather than Ervin, with leadership of the anti-ERA movement is common; see, for instance, Rosalind Rosenberg, *Divided Lives: American Women in the Twentieth Century* (New York: Hill and Wang, 1992), 222–27, and Winifred D. Wandersee, *On the Move: American Women in the 1970s* (Boston: Twayne, 1988), 178–82.

60. The anti-ERA argument is elaborated most fully and fairly in Mathews and DeHart, *Sex, Gender, and the Politics of ERA*. See also Boles, *Politics of the Equal Rights Amendment*; Mansbridge, *Why We Lost the ERA*; Steiner, *Constitutional Inequality*; Mary Frances Berry, *Why ERA Failed* (Bloomington: Indiana University Press, 1986); Pamela Johnston Conover and Virginia Gray, *Feminism and the New Right: Conflict over the American Family* (New York: Praeger, 1983); and Myra Marx Ferree and Beth B. Hess, *Controversy and Coalition: The New Feminist Movement* (Boston: Twayne, 1985).

61. Mathews and DeHart, *Sex, Gender, and the Politics of ERA*, 165–66.

62. Felsenthal, *Sweetheart of the Silent Majority*, 235–36.

63. Schlafly's Washington political director considered the argument particularly influential with state legislators (Noreen Barr, interview with author, August 4, 1982, tape recording in possession of author).

64. Excellent surveys of feminism during these years are found in Rosenberg, *Divided Lives*, and Wandersee, *On the Move*.

65. Quoted in Anastasia Toufexis, "What Killed Equal Rights?" *Time* 120 (July 12, 1982): 33.

66. Mary Ann Fowler, Virginia ERA leader, interview with author, August 4, 1982, and Elizabeth Chittick, president, National Women's party, interview with author, August 10, 1982, tape recordings in possession of author; Berry, *Why ERA Failed*, 66.

67. Mathews and DeHart, *Sex, Gender, and the Politics of ERA*, 57–123.

68. Boles, *Politics of the ERA,* 72–98. A useful state study is Joan S. Carver, "The Equal Rights Amendment and the Florida Legislature," *Florida Historical Quarterly* 60 (1982): 455–81.

69. Barr, interview with author, August 4, 1982.

70. *Dyer v. Blair,* 390 F. Supp. 1291 (S.D. Ill. 1975).

71. Barbara [Dixon] to Senator [Birch Bayh], May 9 and August 22, 1977, Eleanor Cutri Smeal to Don Edwards, November 1, 1977, and press clippings of Bayh news conference, November 9, 1977, ERA files, U.S. Senate Judiciary Subcommittee on the Constitution; U.S. House of Representatives, Subcommittee on Civil and Constitutional Rights, *Equal Rights Amendment Extension: Hearings.* An overview of the Houston conference can be found in Wandersee, *On the Move,* chapter 9.

72. *Dillon v. Gloss,* 256 US 368 (1921).

73. *Coleman v. Miller,* 307 US 433 (1939).

74. U.S. House of Representatives, Committee on the Judiciary, *Proposed Equal Rights Amendment Extension: Report,* 95th Cong., 2d sess., 1978, 1–12. The subsequent August 2–4, 1978, Senate hearings were dominated by proextension witnesses who made the same argument at greater length; see U.S. Senate, Committee on the Judiciary, Subcommittee on the Constitution, *Equal Rights Amendment Extension: Hearings,* 95th Cong., 2d sess., 1978.

75. U.S. House of Representatives, Committee on the Judiciary, *Proposed Equal Rights Amendment Extension: Report,* passim (Brooks's comment appears on page 19).

76. U.S. Senate, Subcommittee on the Constitution, *Equal Rights Amendment Extension,* 21. Syndicated columnist George F. Will offered this sports analogy in a radio debate with Representative Patricia Schroeder, and it was often repeated during the extension discussion (National Public Radio, "National Town Meeting: ERA: Symbol or Substance," June 29, 1978).

77. Barb [Dixon] and Mary [Jolly] to Senator [Bayh], September 13, 1978, and Sheila Greenwald to ERAmerica ratified state contacts, December 1, 1978, ERA files, U.S. Senate Judiciary Subcommittee on the Constitution. A helpful but inconclusive examination of rescission is available in Samuel S. Freedman and Pamela J. Naughton, *ERA: May a State Change Its Vote?* (Detroit: Wayne State University Press, 1978).

78. *Washington Post,* July 10, 1978, 1, 10–11.

79. *Congressional Record,* 95th Cong., 2d sess., 26264–65, 34314–15.

80. Quoted in *U.S. News & World Report* 88 (April 2, 1979): 10.

81. Jake Garn to Legislators, November 3, 1978, in Mary [Jolly] to Nels [Ackerson], November 14, 1978, ERA files, U.S. Senate Judiciary Subcommittee on the Constitution.

82. Pat Antonisse and David Abrams to ERAmerica Corporate Board, February 14, 1979, ERA files, Senate Judiciary Subcommittee on the Constitution; U.S. Senate, Subcommittee on the Constitution, *The Impact of the Equal Rights Amendment: Hearings,* 93.

83. *Idaho v. Freeman,* 529 F. Supp. 1107 (1981); Nathan Lewin, "Judgment Time for the ERA," *New Republic* 186 (February 10, 1982): 8–13; Berry, *Why ERA Failed,* 73.

84. Mathews and DeHart, *Sex, Gender, and the Politics of ERA,* 91–123; Berry, *Why ERA Failed,* 70–85; U.S. Senate, Subcommittee on the Constitution, *The Impact of the Equal Rights Amendment: Hearings,* 92–93.

85. Eagle Forum press release and "Over the Rainbow" dinner program, June 30, 1982; *Washington Post,* July 1, 1982, C1, 6; *New York Times,* July 1, 1981, A12; Toufexis, "What Killed Equal Rights?" 32–33.

86. Useful insights on the election can be found in Gerald Pomper et al., *The Election of 1980: Reports and Interpretations* (Chatham, N.J.: Chatham House, 1981).

87. Mansbridge, *Why We Lost the ERA,* 14–28, 201–18. Even in June 1982 a Gallup poll showed 56 percent for ERA and 34 percent opposed, and a CBS News poll found 52 percent approval and 36 percent opposition; *New York Times,* July 1, 1982, A12.

88. Valuable insights are provided in Val Burris, "Who Opposed the ERA? An Analysis of the Social Bases of Antifeminism," *Social Science Quarterly* 64 (1983): 305–17; David W. Brady and Kent L. Tedin, "Ladies in Pink: Religion and Political Ideology in the Anti-ERA Movement," *Social Science Quarterly* 56 (1976): 564–75; and Mathews and DeHart, *Sex, Gender, and the Politics of ERA,* 152–80, 212–25.

89. A useful discussion of ratification mathematics can be found in Peter Suber, "Population Changes and Constitutional Amendments," *University of Michigan Journal of Law Reform* 20 (1987): 424–25, 479–80.

90. See particularly Toufexis, "What Killed Equal Rights?" 32–33.

91. *Washington Post,* July 15, 1982, A5; Walter Dellinger, "Another Route to the ERA," *Newsweek* 100 (August 2, 1982): 8; Fowler, interview with author, August 4, 1982.

92. Chittick, interview with author, August 10, 1982.

93. *Washington Post,* July 7, 1982, C1, and August 27, 1982, A2; Riane Eisler and Allie C. Hixson, *The Equal Rights Amendment: Fact and Action Guide* (n.p.: National Women's Conference Center, 1986).

94. U.S. Senate, Committtee on the Judiciary, Subcommittee on the Constitution, *The Impact of the Equal Rights Amendment;* Tsongas's testimony appears on 14–42.

95. *Congressional Record,* 98th Cong., 1st sess., 32684–85. Berry, *Why ERA Failed,* 102–7, provides a summary of the 1983 congressional debate over ERA.

96. Associated Press, December 11, 1993, and Cong. Robert E. Andrews to Colleagues, February 4, 1994, in Allie Hixson to author, March 28, 1994.

97. U.S. House of Representatives, Committee on the Judiciary, *D.C. Representation in Congress: Hearings,* 90th Cong., 1st sess., 1967; Clement E. Vose, "When District of Columbia Representation Collides with the Constitutional Amendment Institution," *Publius* 9 (1979): 108–11.

98. U.S. House of Representatives, Subcommittee on Civil and Constitutional Rights, Committee on the Judiciary, *Representation of the District of Columbia in the Congress: Hearings,* 94th Cong., 1st sess., 1975, 10.

99. U.S. House of Representatives, Committee on the Judiciary, *District of Columbia Representation in Congress: Report,* 95th Cong., 2d sess., report 95–886, 1978, 7.

100. *Congressional Record,* 95th Cong., 2d sess., 5272–73.

101. Ibid., 27249–60.

102. Quoted in *Time* 117 (September 4, 1978): 15.

103. *U.S. News & World Report* 88 (April 2, 1979): 10.

104. Quoted in *Newsweek* 92 (September 4, 1978): 20.

105. U.S. Bureau of the Census, Department of Commerce, *Statistical Abstract of the United States 1987* (Washington, D.C.: GPO, 1986), 20.

106. "D.C.'s Amendment at Two," *Washington Post,* August 22, 1980, 14; Joseph L. Rauh, Jr., and Harold Himmelman, "D.C. Voting Rights: We Won't Give Up the Fight," *Washington Post,* August 22, 1980, 15; Rauh, "D.C. Voting Rights: 'Shall We Give Up? Nonsense!'" *Washington Post,* August 22, 1982, C8; Bayh, interview with author, July 8, 1981.

107. They were Connecticut, Delaware, Hawaii, Iowa, Louisiana, Maine, Maryland, Massachusetts, Michigan, Minnesota, New Jersey, Ohio, Oregon, Rhode Island, West Virginia, and Wisconsin.

108. Quoted in *New York Times,* August 22, 1985, B13.

109. Philip G. Schrag, *Behind the Scenes: The Politics of a Constitutional Convention* (Washington, D.C.: Georgetown University Press, 1985).

110. *New York Times,* August 22, 1985, B13.

111. *Washington Post,* November 19, 1993, C1, 7; November 20, 1993, A1, 9; November 21, 1993, A1, 24; and November 22, 1993, A1, 12; *New York Times,* November 22, 1993.

112. Steve Twomey, "The 51st State," *Washington Post Magazine,* July 4, 1993, 11. This magazine section was entirely devoted to the statehood issue; it provides a useful summary of the contemporary debate.

18. AMENDMENT POLITICS IN A CONSERVATIVE ERA

1. A well-developed argument that discounts the economic importance of budget balancing and finds the American concern with it both unusual and politically symbolic is James D. Savage, *Balanced Budgets and American Politics* (Ithaca, N.Y.: Cornell University Press, 1988).

2. U.S. Senate, Committee on the Judiciary, *Balanced Budget–Tax Limitation Constitutional Amendment: Report,* 97th Cong., 1st sess., 1981, 17.

3. U.S. Senate, Committee on the Judiciary, Subcommittee on Constitutional Amendments, *Balancing of the Budget: Hearings,* 84th Cong., 2d sess., 1956.

4. U.S. Senate, Committee on the Judiciary, *Balanced Budget–Tax Limitation Constitutional Amendment: Report,* 18.

5. Robert Kuttner, *Revolt of the Haves: Tax Rebellions and Hard Times* (New York: Simon and Schuster, 1980), 280–81.

6. U.S. Senate, Committee on the Judiciary, *Balanced Budget–Tax Limitation Constitutional Amendment: Report,* 19.

7. Ibid., 277–86.

8. Martin Anderson, *Revolution* (San Diego, Calif.: Harcourt Brace Jovanovich, 1988), 120.

9. David A. Stockman, *The Triumph of Politics: How the Reagan Revolution Failed* (New York: Harper and Row, 1986), esp. 51–54.

10. U.S. Senate, Committee on the Judiciary, Subcommittee on Constitutional Amendments, *Balancing the Budget: Hearings,* 94th Cong., 1st sess., 1975, esp. 3–13.

11. Ibid., 182–85; *Washington Post,* April 30, 1992, A1, 14; Michael Kinsley, "The Liberal Case for a Budget Amendment," *Washington Post,* May 14, 1992, A23; Paul Simon, "Why We Need the Balanced Budget Amendment," *Washington Post,* November 25, 1993, A30.

12. Russell L. Caplan, *Constitutional Brinksmanship: Amending the Constitution by National Convention* (New York: Oxford University Press, 1988), 79; Kuttner, *Revolt of the Haves,* 282.

13. ABC News–Harris Survey, February 8, 1979; Associated Press–NBC News poll, *Washington Star,* February 13, 1979; surveys of June 16–19, 1978, and February 2–5, 1979, George H. Gallup, *The Gallup Poll* (Wilmington, Del.: Scholarly Resources, 1979–80), 1978: 198–99, and 1979: 81. A Gallup survey of May 14–17, 1982, confirmed these results (Gallup, *Gallup Poll,* 1982: 124–27).

14. Citizens for the Constitution brochures, Linda Rogers-Kingsbury office files, U.S. Senate Judiciary Subcommittee on the Constitution; Caplan, *Constitutional Brinksmanship,* 79–82; Kuttner, *Revolt of the Haves,* 282–89.

15. Caplan, *Constitutional Brinksmanship,* 81–82.

16. Linda [Rogers-Kingsbury] to Senator [Bayh], July 19, 1978, and petition files, Linda Rogers-Kingsbury office files, U.S. Senate Judiciary Subcommittee on the Constitution.

17. Balanced Budget Group to Senator [Bayh], January 16, 1979, Linda Rogers-Kingsbury office files, U.S. Senate Judiciary Subcommittee on the Constitution.

18. Laurence H. Tribe to Timothy E. Kraft, assistant to the president, January 17, 1979, Linda Rogers-Kingsbury office files, U.S. Senate Judiciary Subcommittee on the Constitution.

19. *Washington Post,* March 19, 1980, A12.

20. Quoted in Elizabeth Drew, *Portrait of an Election: The 1980 Presidential Campaign* (New York: Simon and Schuster, 1981), 113.

21. William Greider, "The Education of David Stockman," *Atlantic Monthly* 248 (December 1981): 27–54; Stockman, *Triumph of Politics,* 269–76.

22. U.S. Senate, Subcommittee on the Constitution, Committee on the Judiciary, *Balanced Budget–Tax Limitation Constitutional Amendment: Hearings,* 97th Cong., 1st sess., 1981, esp. Hatch's statement on 3–6.

23. *Washington Post,* May 8, 1981, A3, and May 20, 1981, A7; U.S. Senate, Committee on the Judiciary, *Balanced Budget–Tax Limitation Constitutional Amendment: Report,* 3, 5–8, 26–33.

24. Savage, *Balanced Budgets and American Politics,* 2.

25. *Washington Post,* July 13, 1982, A3.

26. *Washington Post,* July 20, 1982, A1, 6.

27. *Washington Post,* July 25, 1982, A6.

28. *Congressional Record,* 97th Cong., 2d sess., 19229.

29. *Washington Post,* August 8, 1982, C5–7.

30. *Washington Post,* August 10, 1982, A5.

31. *Washington Post,* August 19, 1982, A9.

32. U.S. Senate, Committee on the Judiciary, *Constitutional Convention Implementation Act of 1984: Report,* 98th Cong., 2d sess., 1984, 57.

33. Sam J. Ervin, Jr., "Proposed Legislation to Implement the Convention Method of Amending the Constitution," *Michigan Law Review* 66 (1968): 875–902.

34. "Proposed Legislation on the Convention Method of Amending the United States Constitution," *Harvard Law Review* 85 (1972): 1612–48.

35. U.S. Senate, Committee on the Judiciary, *Constitutional Convention Implementation Act of 1984: Report,* 13–15; Caplan, *Constitutional Brinksmanship,* 76–77.

36. Among the most substantive discussions are Paul G. Kauper, "The Alternative Amendment Process: Some Observations," *Michigan Law Review* 66 (1968): 903–20; Arthur Earl Bonfield, "The Dirksen Amendment and the Article V Convention Process," *Michigan Law Review* 66 (1968): 949–1000; Charles L. Black, Jr., "Amending the Constitution: A Letter to a Congressman," *Yale Law Journal* 82 (1972): 189–215; William W. Van Alstyne, "Does Article V Restrict the States to Calling Unlimited Conventions Only? A Letter to a Colleague," *Duke Law Journal* (1978): 1295–1306; Walter Dellinger, "The Recurring Question of the 'Limited' Constitutional Convention," *Yale Law Journal* 88 (1979): 1623–40; Gerald Gunther, "The Convention Method of Amending the United States Constitution," *Georgia Law Review* 14 (1979): 1–25.

37. U.S. Senate, Committee on the Judiciary, Subcommittee on the Constitution, *Constitutional Convention Procedures: Hearings,* 98th Cong., 2d sess., 1985, 2.

38. Ibid., 21–54.

39. U.S. Senate, Committee on the Judiciary, *Constitutional Convention Implementation Act of 1984: Report,* 62–78.

40. Caplan, *Constitutional Brinksmanship,* 83.

41. Ibid., 86.

42. In June 1983, 53 percent of respondents had heard or read about the amendment; 71 percent favored it, 21 percent opposed it, and 8 percent offered no opinion. By August 1985, 57 percent knew about it, 49 percent favored, 27 percent opposed, and 24 percent remained neutral. Two years later the 1985 pattern persisted (Gallup, *Gallup Poll,* 1983:126; 1985: 211–12; 1987: 184).

43. *Washington Post,* May 16, 1985, A4.

44. Caplan, *Constitutional Brinksmanship,* 85–89.

45. *Washington Post,* May 9, 1988, A6.

46. *Congressional Record,* 101st Cong., 2d sess., July 17, 1990, H4870; 102d Cong., 2d sess., June 11, 1992, H4670–71.

47. Editorial, *New York Times,* May 10, 1992, E16; *Washington Post,* June 3, 1992, A4; June 6, 1992, A12; June 11, 1992, A6–8; Roy L. Ash, "The I.O.U.S.A. Amendment," *Washington Post,* June 11, 1992, A27.

48. Michael Ross, "Amendment Tough Choices for Lawmakers," *Los Angeles Times,* June 12, 1992, 1, quoted in Richard B. Bernstein, with Jerome Agel, *Amending America* (New York: Times Books, 1993), 183–85.

49. *Washington Post,* February 10, 1993, A22.

50. Paul Simon, "Why We Need the Balanced Budget Amendment," *Washington Post,* November 25, 1993, A30; George F. Will, "Political-Class Bloat," *Washington Post,* November 12, 1993, A25.

51. *Washington Post,* February 13, 1994, A5, and February 16, 1994, A8; Lloyd N. Cutler, "An Unbalanced Constitution," *Washington Post,* February 16, 1994, A19; American Association of Retired Persons, *AARP Bulletin* 35 (February 1994): 1, 3, 17; "Simon's Simple Pie," *New Yorker* 70 (February 28, 1994): 6–8: *Congressional Record,* 103d Cong., 2d sess., February 22–March 1, 1994, S1590–2158.

52. *Congressional Record,* 103d Cong., 2d sess., March 1, 1994, S2158–59.

53. *Washington Post,* September 28, 1994, A1, 4.

54. *Congressional Record,* 104th Cong., 1st sess., H700–72; *Washington Post,* January 12, 1995, A8; January 27, 1995, A1, 4.

55. *Congressional Record,* 104th Cong., 1st sess., S3314; *New York Times,* February 27, 1995, A9; February 28, 1995, A1, 10; March 1, 1995, A1, 12–13; March 2, 1995, A1, 12–13; March 3, 1995, A1, 10–11; *Washington Post,* March 3, 1995, A1, 16; March 8, 1995, A1, 7; March 9, 1995, D1, 4.

56. *Washington Post,* November 19, 1994, A11; January 12, 1995, A9; March 1, 1995, A12.

57. *Washington Post,* June 6, 1992, A14.

58. *New York Times,* May 17, 1992, A4, 2.

59. U.S. Senate, Committee on the Judiciary, Subcommittee on Constitutional Amendments, *Abortion: Hearings,* 93d Cong., 2d sess., and 94th Cong., 1st sess., 1974–1976. The testimony of Cardinals John Krol of Philadelphia, Timothy Manning of Los Angeles, Humberto Medeiros of Boston, and John Cody of Chicago, the first prelates of their rank ever to come before a congressional committee, appears in part 1, 153–80; Tribe's is in part 3, 347–53.

60. U.S. House of Representatives, Committee on the Judiciary, Subcommittee on Civil and Constitutional Rights, *Proposed Constitutional Amendments on Abortion: Hearings,* 94th Cong., 2d sess., 1976; Cooke's testimony appears on 308–17.

61. Laurence H. Tribe, *Abortion: The Clash of Absolutes,* rev. ed. (New York: W. W. Norton, 1992), 147–49.

62. Ibid., 150–59; U.S. Senate, Committee on the Judiciary, *Constitutional Convention Implementation Act of 1984: Report,* 56–57.

63. "The 1980 Democratic Platform," *Congressional Quarterly Weekly Report* 38 (August 5, 1980): 2405.

64. "The 1980 Republican Platform," *Congressional Quarterly Weekly Report* 38 (July 18, 1980): 2034.

65. "Let There Be Life," *New York Times,* March 17, 1981, A17.

66. U.S. Senate, Committee on the Judiciary, Subcommittee on the Constitution, *Constitutional Amendments Relating to Abortion: Hearings,* 97th Cong., 1st sess., 1983, 72–92.

67. *Washington Post,* June 8, 1981, A1, 4.

68. U.S. Senate, Committee on the Judiciary, Subcommittee on the Constitution, *Constitutional Amendments Relating to Abortion: Hearings,* 3, 1173, 1214.

69. U.S. Senate, Committee on the Judiciary, *Human Life Federalism Amendment: Report,* 97th Cong., 2d sess., 1982, 7; *Washington Post,* March 11, 1982, A1, 9.

70. Tribe, *Abortion,* 164.

71. U.S. Senate, Committee on the Judiciary, Subcommittee on the Constitution, *Legal Ramifications of the Human Life Amendment: Hearings,* 98th Cong., 1st sess., 1983.

72. Tribe, *Abortion,* 167–228.

73. Gallup, *Gallup Poll,* 1982: 121.

74. U.S. Senate, Committee on the Judiciary, *Proposed Constitutional Amendment to Permit Voluntary Prayer: Hearings,* 97th Cong., 2d sess., 1982; Neal's testimony is on 227–28.

75. U.S. Senate, Committee on the Judiciary, Subcommittee on the Constitution, *Voluntary School Prayer Constitutional Amendment: Hearings,* 98th Cong., 1st sess., 1984, 12.

76. U.S. Senate, Committee on the Judiciary, *School Prayer Constitutional Amendment: Report,* 98th Cong., 2d sess., 1984.

77. *Board of Education v. Mergens,* 496 U.S. 226 (1990); Frank Rich, "The God Patrol," *New York Times,* July 12, 1995, A15.

78. Ronald Reagan, address before a joint session of Congress, January 25, 1984, *Public Papers of the Presidents of the United States: 1984* (Washington, D.C.: GPO, 1986), 89; Herman V. Ames, *The Proposed Amendments to the Constitution,* in *Annual Report, American Historical Association, 1896* (Washington, D.C.: GPO, 1897), 132–33, 394, 398.

79. Gallup, *Gallup Poll,* 1987: 184.

80. U.S. Senate, Committee on the Judiciary, Subcommittee on the Constitution, *Line-Item Veto: Hearings,* 98th Cong., 2d sess., 1984, 18–19, 24.

81. *Washington Post,* March 13, 1995, A11; March 17, 1995, A7; March 22, 1995, A4; March 24, 1995, A1, 6.

82. *Congressional Record,* 104th Cong., 1st sess., H3889–965; *Washington Post,* November 30, 1994, A1, 21; *New York Times,* March 30, 1995, A1, 9.

83. *Minersville v. Gobitis,* 310 US 586 (1940). An excellent summary of the relationship between the First Amendment and the flag from 1940 to 1990 is Murray Dry, "Flag Burning and the Constitution," *Supreme Court Review* 1990: 69–103.

84. *West Virginia State Board of Education v. Barnette,* 319 US 624 (1943).

85. *Street v. New York,* 394 US 576 (1969); *Smith v. Goguen,* 415 US 566 (1974); *Spence v. Washington,* 418 US 405 (1974).

86. *Texas v. Johnson,* 491 US 397 (1989).

87. *Washington Post,* June 23, 1989, A1, 8; June 24, 1989, A17.

88. George Bush, *The Public Papers of the Presidents of the United States: 1989* (Washington, D.C.: GPO, 1990), 805, 831–33.

89. *Washington Post,* June 28, 1989, A1, 4–5; July 1, 1989, A4; July 13, 1989, A4.

90. U.S. House of Representatives, Committee on the Judiciary, Subcommittee on Civil and Constitutional Rights, *Statutory and Constitutional Responses to the Supreme Court Decision in Texas v. Johnson: Hearings,* 101st Cong., 1st sess., 1989; U.S. Senate, Committee on the Judiciary, *Hearings on Measures to Protect the Physical Integrity of the American Flag: Hearings,* 101st Cong., 1st sess., 1989; *Washington Post,* July 14, 1989, A7; September 13, 1989, A1, 6; October 13, 1989, A21.

91. *Washington Post,* October 18, 1989, A5; October 19, 1989, A9; October 20, 1989, A1, 14; *Congressional Record,* 101st Cong., 1st sess., S13733.

92. *Washington Post,* November 1, 1989, A5.

93. *Washington Post,* February 22, 1990, A5; and March 6, 1990, A4.

94. *United States v. Eichman,* 496 US 310 (1990).

95. Ibid., 319.

96. *Washington Post,* June 12, 1990, A1, 7; Bush, *Public Papers of the Presidents, 1990* (Washington, D.C.: GPO, 1991), 809–12.

97. *Washington Post,* June 13, 1990. A9.

98. *Washington Post,* June 15, 1990, A6–7.

99. U.S. Senate, Committee on the Judiciary, *Measures to Protect the American Flag: Hearings,* 101st Cong., 2d sess., 1990.

100. *Washington Post,* June 14, 1990, A4; June 19, 1990, A8; June 20, 1990, A14.

101. *Congressional Record,* 101st Cong., 2d sess., H4087–88, S8736–37.

102. *Congressional Record,* 104th Cong., 1st sess., H6403–46; *New York Times,* June 29, 1995, A1. Vermont independent Bernard Sanders voted no.

103. *New York Times,* December 13, 1995, C18.

104. Quoted in *New York Times,* December 9, 1995, A8.

105. *New York Times,* December 13, 1995, A1, C18.

106. George R. Will, "The Folly of a Constitutional Convention," *Washington Post,* May 21, 1981, A27.

107. *Washington Post,* October 13, 1989, A21.

19. AMENDMENTS IN CONSTITUTIONAL THOUGHT AND PRACTICE

1. Richard B. Bernstein, "The Sleeper Wakes: The History and Legacy of the Twenty-Seventh Amendment," *Fordham Law Review* 61 (1992): 499–508.

2. Helen E. Veit, Kenneth R. Bowling, and Charlene Bangs Bickford, eds., *Creating the Bill of Rights* (Baltimore: Johns Hopkins University Press, 1991), 21, 26.

3. *Congressional Register,* June 8, 1789, in ibid., 84.

4. *Congressional Register,* August 14, 1789, in ibid., 149–50.

5. Ibid., 47–50.

6. Jonathan Elliot, ed., *Debates in the Several State Conventions on the Adoption of the Federal Constitution,* 2d ed., 5 vols. (Philadelphia: Lippincott, 1836–1845), 1: 339–40.

7. Patrick T. Conley, "Rhode Island: Laboratory for the 'Lively Experiment,'" in *The Bill of Rights and the States,* ed. Patrick T. Conley and John P. Kaminski (Madison, Wis.: Madison House, 1992), 152–53.

8. Kentucky, Acts passed at the General Assembly, June 27, 1792, Kentucky Department for Libraries and Archives, Frankfort, Kentucky.

9. No formal designation of where states should send ratification notices was made until 1818. Prior to that time, states normally notified Congress or the secretary of state. From 1818 to 1951 the secretary of state bore formal responsibility for gathering ratifications. From 1951 until 1984, the administrator of General Services assumed the obligation, and thereafter the duty belonged to the archivist of the United States (Don W. Wilson, archivist of the United States, "List of State Ratifications of the Constitutional Amendment relating to Compensation of Members of Congress as Proposed September 25, 1789," *Congressional Record,* 102d Cong., 2d sess., S6829–31). Although none of these federal officials acknowledged Kentucky's action, an Ohio state senator somehow knew of it in spring 1873, as Professor G. Wallace Chessman of Denison University called to my attention.

10. G. Wallace Chessman, "State Senator Samuel Knox and Ohio's Approval of Old Article the Second in May 1873," Presentation, Ohio Academy of History, April 23, 1994.

11. Thyra Thomson, Wyoming secretary of state, to John E. Byrne, director of the Federal Register, March 19, 1985, in Wilson, "List of State Ratifications," S6836.

12. Quoted in *New York Times,* May 8, 1992, A8; see also *Washington Post,* May 8, 1992, A1, 8; "The Man Who Would Not Quit," *People* 58 (June 1, 1992): 72; Bernstein, "Sleeper Wakes," 536–37.

13. Editorial, [Newark, Ohio] *Advocate,* August 4, 1991; William L. Renfro, "Ratifying the Second Amendment," *Vital Speeches of the Day* 58 (May 1, 1992): 429–530.

14. Wilson, "List of State Ratifications," S6837.

15. Ibid., S6831.

16. Bernstein, "Sleeper Wakes," 539.

17. Wilson, "List of State Ratifications," S6831. The archivist listed forty states as having ratified by May 15. Subsequently, California on June 26, 1992, and Rhode Island on June 10, 1993, added their endorsement, according to Sandra Jablonski, head of the legal services staff, Office of the Federal Register, National Archives and Records Administration, in a telephone conversation with the author on June 9, 1994. At that point Kentucky's ratification was still unknown to the Archives.

18. *Dillon v. Gloss,* 256 US 368 (1921).

19. *Coleman v. Miller,* 307 US 433 (1939).

20. *New York Times,* June 29, 1982, 18.

21. *Congressional Record,* 102d Cong., 2d sess., S6948, H3505–6.

22. Ibid., S6831.

23. Deb Wood, aide to Robert Byrd, phone conversation with Sandra Jablonski, Office of the Federal Register, conveyed to author, June 10, 1994.

24. Richard B. Bernstein, with Jerome Agel, *Amending America* (New York: Times Books, 1993), the writing of which was being completed just as the Twenty-seventh Amendment was being adopted, is evidence of this.

25. J. Allen Smith, *The Spirit of American Government* (New York: Macmillan, 1907), 40–46; Charles A. Beard, *An Economic Interpretation of the Constitution of the United States* (New York: Macmillan, 1913), 160–61.

26. Charles F. Amidon, "The Nation and the Constitution," *Green Bag* 19 (1907): 597–98.

27. Charles E. Merriam, *American Political Ideas: Studies in the Development of American Political Thought, 1865–1917* (New York: Macmillan, 1920), 221.

28. Peter Suber, "Population Changes and Constitutional Amendments," *University of Michigan Journal of Law Reform* 20 (1987): 409–90.

29. Bruce Ackerman, *We the People: Foundations* (Cambridge: Harvard University Press, 1991).

30. Ibid.

31. Rexford G. Tugwell, *The Democratic Roosevelt* (Garden City, N.Y.: Doubleday, 1957), 390–91.

32. Rexford G. Tugwell, *The Compromising of the Constitution (Early Departures)* (Notre Dame, Ind.: University of Notre Dame Press, 1976).

33. Rexford G.Tugwell, *The Emerging Constitution* (New York: Harper's Magazine Press, 1974), appendix.

34. *Rodriguez v. San Antonio Independent School District,* 411 US 1 (1973).

35. *DeShaney v. Winnebago County Department of Social Services,* 480 US 189 (1989).

36. *U.S. v. Lopez,* 115 S.Ct. 1624 (1995).

37. George Washington, Farewell Address, in *A Compilation of the Messages and Papers of the Presidents, 1789–1897,* ed. James D. Richardson, 20 vols. (New York: Bureau of National Literature, 1897), 1:209.

38. Ibid.

39. Thomas Jefferson to Samuel Kerchaval, July 12, 1816, in *The Writings of Thomas Jefferson,* ed. Albert Ellery Bergh, 20 vols. (Washington, D.C.: Thomas Jefferson Memorial Association, 1907), 15: 40–41.

40. *Cohens v. Virginia,* 19 US (6 Wheat.) 264, 389 (1821).

41. Algernon Sidney, *Discourses Concerning Government,* 3d ed. (London: A. Millar, 1751), 136

42. Washington, Farewell Address, in Richardson, ed., *Messages and Papers of the Presidents,* 1: 210.

BIBLIOGRAPHY

ARCHIVES AND MANUSCRIPT COLLECTIONS

Aldrich, Nelson W., Papers. Library of Congress, Washington, D.C.

Association Against the Prohibition Amendment, Papers. Library of Congress.

Baker, Newton D., Papers, Library of Congress.

Beck, James M., Papers. Princeton University Library, Princeton, New Jersey.

Beveridge, Albert J., Papers. Library of Congress.

Black, Hugo L., Papers. Library of Congress.

Blaine, John J., Papers. Wisconsin State Historical Society, Madison, Wisconsin.

Borah, William E., Papers. Library of Congress.

Bricker, John W., Papers. Ohio Historical Society, Columbus, Ohio.

Butler, Nicholas Murray, Papers. Columbia University Library, New York.

Catt, Carrie Chapman, Papers. Library of Congress.

Celler, Emanuel, Papers. Library of Congress.

Coolidge, Calvin, Papers. Library of Congress.

Corcoran, Thomas G., Papers. Library of Congress.

Cummings, Homer, Papers. University of Virginia Library, Charlottesville, Virginia.

Dewson, Mary W., Papers. Franklin D. Roosevelt Library, Hyde Park, New York.

Du Pont, Irénée, Papers. Eleutherian Mills Historical Library, Wilmington, Delaware.

Du Pont, Pierre S., Papers. Eleutherian Mills Historical Library, Wilmington, Delaware.

Eisenhower, Dwight D., Papers. Dwight D. Eisenhower Library, Abilene, Kansas.

ERAmerica Papers, Library of Congress.

Farley, James A., Papers. Library of Congress.

Frankfurter, Felix, Papers. Library of Congress.

Gompers, Samuel, Letterbooks. Library of Congress.

Harding, Warren, Papers. Ohio Historical Society, Columbus, Ohio.

Hoard, Halbert L., Papers. Wisconsin State Historical Society, Madison, Wisconsin.

Holmes, John Haynes, Papers, Library of Congress.

Hoover, Herbert, Papers. Herbert Hoover Presidential Library, West Branch, Iowa.

Hughes, Charles Evans, Papers. Library of Congress.

Hull, Cordell, Papers. Library of Congress.

Ickes, Harold L., Papers. Library of Congress.

Joy, Henry Bourne, Papers. Michigan Historical Collections, University of Michigan, Ann Arbor, Michigan.

Kennedy, John F., Papers. John F. Kennedy Presidential Library, Boston, Massachusetts.

La Follette, Robert M., Sr., Papers. Library of Congress.

League of Women Voters of the United States, Papers. Library of Congress.
Lodge, Henry Cabot, Papers. Massachusetts Historical Society, Boston, Massachusetts.
Longworth, Nicholas, Papers. Library of Congress.
National American Woman Suffrage Association, Papers. Library of Congress.
National Association for the Advancement of Colored People, Papers. Library of Congress.
National Child Labor Committee, Papers. Library of Congress.
Norris, George W., Papers. Library of Congress.
Raskob, John J., Papers. Eleutherian Mills Historical Library, Wilmington, Delaware.
Richberg, Donald R. Papers. Library of Congress.
Ritchie, Albert C., Papers. Maryland Historical Society, Baltimore, Maryland.
Roosevelt, Franklin D., Papers. Franklin D. Roosevelt Library, Hyde Park, New York.
Root, Elihu, Papers. Library of Congress.
Shouse, Jouett, Papers. University of Kentucky Library, Lexington, Kentucky.
Sutherland, George, Papers. Library of Congress.
Taft, Robert A., Papers. Library of Congress.
Truman, Harry S, Papers. Harry S Truman Presidential Library, Independence, Missouri.
United States Senate, Records. National Archives, Washington, D.C.
United States Supreme Court, Records. National Archives.
Voluntary Committee of Lawyers, Papers. Collection on Legal Change, Wesleyan University, Middletown, Connecticut.
Wadsworth, James W., Papers. Library of Congress.
Walsh, Thomas J., Papers. Library of Congress.
Williams, John Sharp, Papers. Library of Congress.
Women's Joint Congressional Committee, Papers. Library of Congress.
Women's Organization for National Prohibition Reform, Papers, in Alice Belin du Pont files, Pierre S. du Pont Papers. Eleutherian Mills Historical Library.

ORAL HISTORY INTERVIEWS

Barr, Noreen. Interview with author, August 4, 1982.
Bayh, Birch. Interview with author, July 8, 1981.
Bricker, John W. Interview with Alfred E. Eckes, March 14, 1974, Former Members of Congress Oral History Project, Library of Congress.
Chittick, Elizabeth. Interview with author, August 10, 1982.
Fowler, Mary Ann. Interview with author, August 4, 1982.
Wadsworth, James W., Jr. "The Reminiscences of James W. Wadsworth." Oral History Research Office, Columbia University, 1952.

COURT CASES

Abington School District v. Schempp, 374 US 203 (1963).
Bailey v. Drexel Furniture Company, 259 US 20 (1922).
Baker v. Carr, 369 US 186 (1962).

Board of Education v. Mergens, 496 U.S. 226 (1990).
Brown v. Board of Education of Topeka, 347 US 483 (1954).
Brushaber v. Union Pacific Railroad Co., 240 US 1 (1916).
California v. LaRue, 409 US 109 (1972).
Carroll et al. v. United States, 267 US 132 (1924).
Carter v. Carter Coal Co., 298 US 238 (1936).
Chandler v. Wise, 307 US 474 (1939).
Chisholm v. Georgia, 2 US (2 Dallas) 419 (1793).
Civil Rights Cases, 109 US 3 (1983).
Clark Distilling Co. v. Western Maryland Railway Co., 242 US 311 (1917).
Cohens v. Virginia, 19 US (6 Wheat.) 264, 389 (1821).
Coleman v. Miller, 307 US 433 (1939).
Craig v. Boren, 429 US 190 (1976).
Davis v. Mann, 377 US 678 (1964).
DeShaney v. Winnebago County Department of Social Services, 480 US 189 (1989).
Dillon v. Gloss, 256 US 368 (1921).
Dyer v. Blair, 390 F. Supp. 1291 (1975).
Engel v. Vitale, 370 US 421 (1962).
ex parte Virginia, 100 US 339 (1880).
Flint v. Stone Tracy Co., 220 US 107 (1911).
Frontiero v. Richardson, 411 US 677 (1973).
Gomillion v. Lightfoot, 364 US 339 (1960).
Hall v. DeCuir, 95 US 485 (1878).
Hammer v. Dagenhart, 247 US 251 (1918).
Hawke v. Smith, 253 US 221 (1920).
Hollingsworth v. Virginia, 3 US (3 Dallas) 378 (1798).
Holy Trinity Church v. United States, 143 US 457, 471 (1892).
Humphrey's Executor v. United States, 295 US 602 (1935).
Hylton v. United States, 3 US (3 Dallas) 171 (1796).
Idaho v. Freeman, 529 F. Supp. 1107 (1981).
Katzenbach v. Morgan, 384 US 641 (1966).
Leisy v. Hardin, 135 US 100 (1890).
Leser v. Garnett, 258 US 130 (1922).
Lochner v. New York, 198 US 45 (1905).
Louisville, New Orleans & Texas Railway Co. v. Mississippi, 133 US 587 (1890).
Louisville Joint Stock Bank v. Radford, 295 US 555 (1935).
Lucas v. Forty-Fourth General Assembly of Colorado, 377 US 713 (1964).
Marbury v. Madison, 5 US (1 Cranch) 137 (1803).
Maryland Committee for Fair Representation v. Tawes, 377 US 656 (1964).
McCulloch v. Maryland, 17 US (4 Wheat.) 316, 407–8 (1819).
McDonald v. Board of Elections, 394 US 802 (1969).
Minersville v. Gobitis, 310 US 586 (1940).
Missouri v. Holland, 252 US 416 (1920).
Morehead v. New York ex rel. Tipaldo, 298 US 587 (1936).
Muller v. Oregon, 208 US 412 (1908).
Munn v. Illinois, 94 US 113 (1877).

Murray v. Curlett, 374 US 203 (1963).

Myers v. Anderson, 238 US 368 (1915).

National Prohibition Cases, 253 US 350 (1920).

Neal v. Delaware, 103 US 370 (1881).

Olmstead et al. v. United States, 277 US 438 (1928).

Oregon v. Mitchell, 400 US 112 (1970).

Panama Refining v. Ryan, 293 US 388 (1935).

Phillips v. Martin Marietta Corporation, 400 US 542 (1971).

Plessy v. Ferguson, 163 US 537 (1896)

Pollock v. Farmers Loan and Trust Company, 157 US 429 and 158 US 601 (1895).

Reed v. Reed, 404 US 71 (1971).

Retirement Board v. Alton R. Co. 295 US 330 (1935).

Reynolds v. Sims, 377 US 533 (1964).

Rhodes v. Iowa, 170 US 412 (1898).

Rodriguez v. San Antonio Independent School District, 411 US 1 (1973).

Roe v. Wade 410 US 113 (1973).

Roman v. Sincock, 377 US 697 (1964).

Santa Clara County v. Southern Pacific Railway Co., 118 US 394 (1886).

Schechter v. United States, 295 US 495 (1935).

Slaughter-House Cases, 83 US (16 Wall.) 36 (1873).

Smith v. Goguen, 415 US 566 (1974).

Spence v. Washington, 418 US 405 (1974).

Springer v. United States, 102 US 586 (1880).

Stanton v. Stanton, 421 US 7 (1975).

State Board of Equalization of California v. Young's Market Co., 299 US 59, 62 (1936).

Strauder v. West Virginia, 100 US 303 (1880).

Street v. New York, 394 US 576 (1969).

Texas v. Johnson, 491 US 397 (1989).

Texas v. White, 74 US (7 Wall.) 700 (1869).

Texas Railway v. Mississippi, 132 US 587 (1890).

Torcaso v. Watkins, 367 US 488, 490 (1961).

United States v. Belmont, 301 US 324 (1937).

United States v. Butler, 297 US 1 (1936).

United States v. Cruikshank, 92 US 542 (1876).

United States v. Curtiss-Wright Export Corporation, 299 US 304 (1936).

United States v. Darby, 312 US 100 (1941).

United States v. Eichman, 496 US 310 (1990).

United States v. Harris, 106 US 629 (1883).

United States v. Lanza, 260 US 377 (1922).

United States v. Lopez, 115 S. Ct. 1624 (1995).

United States v. Pink, 315 US 204 (1942).

United States v. Reese, 92 US 214 (1876).

United States v. Sprague, 44 F. (2d) 967 (1930); 282 US 716 (1931).

Ware v. Hylton, 3 US (3 Dallas) 199 (1796).

Wesberry v. Saunders, 376 US 1 (1964).

West Virginia State Board of Education v. Barnette, 319 US 624 (1943).
Williams v. Mississippi, 170 US 213 (1898).
WMCA v. Lomenza, 377 US 633 (1964).

PUBLISHED DOCUMENTS

Ames, Herman V., ed. *State Documents on Federal Relations.* Philadelphia: University of Pennsylvania History Department, 1902.

Association Against the Prohibition Amendment. *32 Reasons for Repeal.* Washington, D.C.: AAPA, 1932.

Basler, Roy P., ed. *The Collected Works of Abraham Lincoln.* 9 vols. New Brunswick, N.J.: Rutgers University Press, 1953–1955.

Bergh, Albert Ellery, ed. *The Writings of Thomas Jefferson.* 20 vols. Washington, D.C.: Thomas Jefferson Memorial Association, 1907.

Boyd, Julian P., et al., eds. *The Papers of Thomas Jefferson.* 25 vols. Princeton: Princeton University Press, 1956–1992.

Boyd, Steven R. *Alternative Constitutions for the United States: A Documentary History.* Westport, Conn.: Greenwood, 1992.

Brown, Everett S., comp. *Ratification of the Twenty-First Amendment to the Constitition of the United States: State Convention Records and Laws.* Ann Arbor: University of Michigan Press, 1938.

Catt, Carrie Chapman. *Woman Suffrage by Federal Constitutional Amendment.* New York: National Woman Suffrage Publishing Company, 1917.

Congressional Globe, 1833–1873.

Congressional Record, 1873–1995.

The Constitution of the United States of America: Analysis and Interpretation. 99th Cong., 1st sess., Washington, D.C.: GPO, 1987.

Earle, Edward Mead, ed. *The Federalist.* New York: Modern Library, 1937.

Eliot, Jonathan, ed. *The Debates in the Several State Conventions on the Adoption of the Federal Constitution.* 2d ed. 5 vols. Philadelphia: Lippincott, 1836–1845.

Farrand, Max, ed. *The Records of the Federal Convention of 1787.* rev. ed. 4 vols. New Haven: Yale University Press, 1937.

Ford, Paul Leicester, ed. *Essays on the Constitution of the United States Published During its Discussion by the People, 1787–1788.* New York: Burt Franklin, 1970. Reprint of 1892 edition.

————, ed. *Pamphlets on the Constitution of the United States Published During its Discussion by the People, 1787–1788.* New York: Da Capo, 1968. Reprint of 1888 edition.

————, ed. *The Writings of Thomas Jefferson.* New York: G. P. Putnam, 1899.

Gallup, George H. *The Gallup Poll.* 3 vols. New York: Random House, 1971. 16 vols. Wilmington, Del.: Scholarly Resources, 1978–1992.

Hutchinson, William T., Robert A. Rutland, et al., eds. *The Papers of James Madison.* 17 vols. Chicago: University of Chicago Press, and Charlottesville: University Press of Virginia, 1962–1991.

Hutson, James H., ed. *Supplement to Max Farrand's The Records of the Federal Convention of 1787.* New Haven: Yale University Press, 1987.

Hyneman, Charles S., and Donald S. Lutz, eds. *American Political Writing During the Founding Era, 1760–1805.* 2 vols. Indianapolis: Liberty Press, 1983.

Jensen, Merrill, John P. Kaminski, and Gaspare J. Saladino, eds. *The Documentary History of the Ratification of the Constitution.* 10 vols. Madison: State Historical Society of Wisconsin, 1976–1993.

Kurland, Philip B., and Gerhard Casper, eds. *Landmark Briefs and Arguments of the Supreme Court of the United States: Constitutional Law.* Washington, D.C.: University Publications of America, 1975–.

Link, Arthur S., ed. *The Papers of Woodrow Wilson.* 69 vols. Princeton: Princeton University Press, 1966–1994.

Locke, John. *Two Treatises of Government.* Edited by Peter Laslett. Cambridge: Cambridge University Press, 1963.

McMaster, John Back, and Frederick D. Stone, eds. *Pennsylvania and the Federal Constitution, 1787–1788.* Philadelphia: Historical Society of Pennsylvania, 1888.

Official Report of the Proceedings of the Democratic National Convention, 1932. N.p., n.d.

Official Report of the Proceedings of the Twentieth Republican National Convention, 1932. New York, 1932.

Public Papers of the Presidents of the United States [1929–1993]. 71 vols. Washington, D.C.: GPO, 1974–1993.

Richardson, James D., ed. *A Compilation of the Messages and Papers of the Presidents, 1789–1897.* 20 vols. New York: Bureau of National Literature, 1897.

Roosevelt, Franklin D. *The Public Papers and Addresses of Franklin D. Roosevelt.* 13 vols. New York: vols. 1–5, Random House, vols. 6–9, Macmillan, vols. 10–13, Harper, 1938–1950.

Schwartz, Bernard. *The Bill of Rights: A Documentary History.* 2 vols. New York: Chelsea House, 1971.

U.S. Bureau of the Census. *Historical Statistics of the United States: From Colonial Times to 1957.* Washington, D.C.: GPO, 1960.

U.S. House of Representatives, Committee on Elections. *Proposed Amendments to the Constitution of the United States Fixing Commencement of Terms: Hearings.* 69th Cong., 1st sess., 1926.

———. *Proposed Constitutional Amendments: Hearings.* 70th Cong., 1st sess., 1927.

———. *Proposed Constitutional Amendments: Hearings.* 72d Cong., 1st sess., 1932.

———. *Proposed Constitutional Amendments Relating to the Fixing of the Time for the Commencement of the Terms of President, Vice President and Members of Congress, and Fixing the Time of the Assembling of Congress: Hearings.* 70th Cong., 1st sess., 1928.

———. *Proposed Constitutional Amendments Relating to Nominations and Elections of President, Vice President, U.S. Senators and Representatives: Hearings.* 67th Cong., 4th sess., 1923.

———. *Proposing an Amendment to the Constitution of the United States: Report.* 70th Cong., 1st sess., Report, 333, 1928.

———. *Terms of Office of President: Hearings.* 69th Cong., 2d sess., 1927.

U.S. House of Representatives, Committee on the Judiciary. *Constitutional Amendments to Balance the Federal Budget: Hearings.* 96th Cong., 1st and 2d sess., 1980.

——. *D.C. Representation in Congress: Hearings.* 90th Cong., 1st sess., 1967.

——. *District of Columbia Representation in Congress: Report.* 95th Cong., 2d sess., Report 95-886, 1978.

——. *Electoral College Reform: Hearings.* 91st Cong., 1st sess., 1969.

——. *Equal Rights Amendment: Report.* 79th Cong., 1st sess., Report 907, 1945.

——. *Equal Rights Amendment Extension: Hearings.* 95th Cong., 1st and 2d sess., 1978.

——. *Equal Rights for Men and Women 1971: Hearings.* 92d Cong., 1st sess., 1971.

——. *Presidential Inability and Vice Presidential Vacancy: Hearings.* 89th Cong., 1st sess., 1965.

——. *The Prohibition Amendment: Hearings.* 71st Cong., 2d sess., 1930.

——. *Proposal and Ratification of Amendments to the Constitituion of the United States: Hearings.* 68th Cong., 1st sess., 1924.

——. *Proposed Constitutional Amendments on Abortion: Hearings.* 94th Cong., 2d sess., 1976.

——. *Proposed Equal Rights Amendment Extension: Report.* 95th Cong., 2d sess., 1978.

——. *Proposed Modification of the Prohibition Law to Permit the Manufacture, Sale, and Use of 2.75 Per Cent Beverages: Hearings.* 68th Cong., 1st sess., serial 39, 1924.

——. *Representation of the District of Columbia in the Congress: Hearings.* 94th Cong., 1st sess., 1975.

U.S. House of Representatives, Committee on the Judiciary, Subcommittee on Civil and Constitutional Rights. *Equal Rights Amendment Extension: Hearings.* 95th Cong., 2d sess., 1978.

——. *Proposed Constitutional Amendments on Abortion: Hearings.* 94th Cong., 2d sess., 1976.

——. *Representation of the District of Columbia in the Congress: Hearings.* 94th Cong., 1st sess., 1975.

——. *Statutory and Constitutional Responses to the Supreme Court Decision in Texas v. Johnson: Hearings.* 101st Cong., 1st sess., 1989.

U.S. House of Representatives, Committee on Rules. *Amendment to Constitution Relating to Elections of Presidents, Etc.: Hearing.* 71st Cong., 3d sess., 1931.

——. *Constitutionality of Vote Adopting Prohibition and Suffrage Amendments: Hearings.* 65th Cong., 2d sess., 1918.

U.S. National Commission on Law Observance and Enforcement. *Report on the Enforcement of the Prohibition Law of the United States.* 71st Cong., 3d sess., House document 722, 1931.

U.S. President's Commission on the Status of Women. *American Women: Report.* Washington, D.C.: GPO, 1963.

U.S. Senate, Committee on the Judiciary. *Abortion: Hearings.* 93d Cong., 2d sess., and 94th Cong., 1st sess., 1974–1976.

——. *Balanced Budget–Tax Limitation Constitutional Amendment: Report.* 97th Cong., 1st sess., 1981.

——. *Congressional Tenure: Hearings.* 95th Cong., 2d sess., 1978.

——. *Constitutional Amendments Annual Report 1976.* 95th Cong., 1st sess., 1977.

———. *Constitutional Amendments: Hearings.* 82d Cong., 2d sess., 1952.
———. *Constitutional Convention Implementation Act of 1984: Report.* 98th Cong., 2d sess., 1984.
———. *Constitutional Convention Procedures: Hearing.* 96th Cong., 1st sess., 1980.
———. *Direct Popular Election of the President and Vice President of the United States: Report.* 96th Cong., 1st sess., 1979.
———. *Electing the President: Hearings.* 91st Cong., 1st sess., 1969.
———. *Election of the President: Hearings.* 89th Cong., 2d sess., and 90th Cong., 1st sess., 1968.
———. *The Electoral College and Direct Election: Hearings.* 2 vols. 95th Cong., 1st sess., 1977.
———. *Electoral College Reform: Supplemental Hearings.* 91st Cong., 2d sess., 1970.
———. *Equal Rights: Hearing.* 71st Cong., 3d sess., 1931.
———. *Equal Rights Amendment: Hearing.* 70th Cong., 2d sess., 1929.
———. *Equal Rights Amendment: Hearing.* 79th Cong., 1st sess., 1945.
———. *Equal Rights Amendment: Extension: Hearings.* 95th Cong., 2d sess., 1978.
———. *Equal Rights for Men and Women: Hearings.* 75th Cong., 3d sess., 1938.
———. *Equal Rights for Men and Women: Report.* 92d Cong., 2d sess., 1972.
———. *Equal Rights 1970: Hearings.* 91st Cong., 2d sess., 1970.
———. *Federal Constitutional Convention: Hearings.* 90th Cong., 1st sess., 1968.
———. *Federal Constitutional Convention Procedures Act: Report.* 92d Cong., 1st sess., 1971.
———. *Federal Constitutional Convention Procedures Act: Report.* 93d Cong., 1st sess., 1973.
———. *Four-Year U.S. House of Representatives Terms: Hearings.* 96th Cong., 1st sess., 1979.
———. *Hearings on Measures to Protect the Physical Integrity of the American Flag: Hearings.* 101st Cong., 1st sess., 1989.
———. *Human Life Federalism Amendment: Report.* 97th Cong., 2d sess., 1982.
———. *Lobbying and Lobbyists: Partial Report.* 71st Cong., 2d sess., Senate report 43 May 21, 1930.
———. *Lowering the Voting Age to 18: Hearings.* 91st Cong., 2d sess., 1970.
———. *Lowering the Voting Age to 18: Report.* 92d Cong., 1st sess., 1971.
———. *Marriage and Divorce (Amendment to the Constitution): Hearings.* 68th Cong., 1st sess., 1924.
———. *Measures to Protect the American Flag: Hearings.* 101st Cong., 2d sess., 1990.
———. *Modification or Repeal of National Prohibition: Hearings.* 72d Cong., 1st sess., 1932.
———. *The National Prohibition Law: Hearings.* 69th Cong., 1st sess., 1926.
———. *Nomination and Election of President and Vice President and Qualifications for Voting: Hearings.* 87th Cong., 1st sess., 1961.
———. *Presidential Terms of Office: Hearings.* 86th Cong., 1st sess., 1959.
———. *Proposal and Ratification of Amendments to the Constitution of the United States: Hearings.* 67th Cong., 4th sess., 1923.

———. *Proposed Constitutional Amendments to Balance the Federal Budget: Hearings.* 96th Cong., 1st sess., 1979.

———. *Proposed Constitutional Amendment to Permit Voluntary Prayer: Hearings.* 97th Cong., 2d sess., 1982.

———. *Ratification of Constitutional Amendments by Popular Vote: Hearings.* 75th Cong., 2d sess., 1938.

———. *School Prayer Constitutional Amendment: Report.* 98th Cong., 2d sess., 1984.

———. *Subcommittee on the Constitution Annual Report 1977.* 95th Cong., 2d sess., 1978.

———. *Treaties and Executive Agreements: Hearings.* 83d Cong., 1st sess., 1953.

———. *War Referendum: Hearings.* 76th Cong., 1st sess., 1939.

U.S. Senate, Committee on the Judiciary, Subcommittee on the Constitution. *Balanced Budget—Tax Limitation Constitutional Amendment: Hearings.* 97th Cong., 1st sess., 1981.

———. *Constitutional Amendments Relating to Abortion: Hearings.* 97th Cong., 1st sess., 1983.

———. *Constitutional Conventions Procedures: Hearings.* 98th Cong., 2d sess., 1985.

———. *Direct Popular Election of the President and Vice President of the United States.* 96th Cong., 1st sess., 1979.

———. *Equal Rights Amendment Extension: Hearings.* 95th Cong., 2d sess., 1978.

———. *The Impact of the Equal Rights Amendment: Hearings.* 98th Cong., 1st and 2d sess., 1984.

———. *Legal Ramifications of the Human Life Amendment: Hearings.* 98th Cong., 1st sess., 1983.

———. *Line-Item Veto: Hearings.* 98th Cong., 2d sess., 1984.

———. *Voluntary School Prayer Constitutional Amendment: Hearings.* 98th Cong., 1st sess., 1984.

U.S. Senate, Committee on the Judiciary, Subcommittee on Constitutional Amendments. *Abortion: Hearings.* 93d Cong., 2d sess., and 94th Cong., 1st sess., 1974–1976.

———. *Balancing the Budget: Hearings.* 84th Cong., 2d sess., 1956.

———. *Balancing the Budget: Hearings.* 94th Cong., 1st sess., 1975.

———. *Constitutional Amendments: Annual Report, 1976.* 95th Cong., 1st sess., 1977.

———. *Constitutional Amendments: Report.* 92d Cong., 1st sess., 1971.

———. *Dirksen School Prayer Amendment August 1966: Hearings.* 89th Cong., 2d sess., 1966.

———. *Electing the President: Hearings.* 91st Cong., 1st sess., 1969.

———. *Election of the President: Hearing.* 89th Cong., 2d sess., and 90th Cong., 1st sess., 1967.

———. *The Equal Rights Amendment: Hearings.* 91st Cong., 2d sess., 1970.

———. *Lowering the Voting Age to 18: Hearings.* 91st Cong., 2d sess, 1970.

———. *Lowering the Voting Age to 18—A Fifty-State Survey of the Costs and Other Problems of Dual-Age Voting.* 92d Cong., 1st sess., 1971.

———. *Nomination and Election of President and Vice President and Qualifications for Voting: Hearings.* 87th Cong., 1st sess., 1961.

———. *Presidential Inability: Hearings.* 88th Cong., 1st sess., 1963.
———. *Presidential Inability and Vacancies in the Office of Vice President: Hearings.* 88th Cong., 2d sess., 1964.
———. *Presidential Inability and Vacanices in the Office of Vice President: Hearings.* 89th Cong., 1st sess., 1965.
U.S. Senate, Committee on the Judiciary, Subcommittee on Separation of Powers. *Federal Constitutional Convention: Hearings.* 90th Cong., 1st sess., 1968.
Vattel, Emmerich de. *The Law of Nations; or, Principles of the Law of Nature Applied to the Conduct and Affairs of Nations and Sovereigns.* Edited by Joseph Chitty. Philadelphia: T and J. W. Johnson, 1883.
Veit, Helen E., Kenneth R. Bowling, and Charlene Bangs Bickford, eds., *Creating the Bill of Rights: The Documentary Record from the First Federal Congress.* Baltimore: Johns Hopkins University Press, 1991.
Wiltse, Charles M., and Alan R. Berolzheimer, eds., *The Papers of Daniel Webster.* Dartmouth, N.H.: Dartmouth College Press, 1986.

NEWSPAPERS

Akron Beacon Journal, 1971.
Cincinnati Inquirer, 1971.
Cleveland Plain Dealer, 1931, 1971.
Columbus Citizen Journal, 1971.
Lincoln [Nebraska] *Star,* 1930.
New York Times, 1918–1995.
Wall Street Journal, 1969.
Washington Post, 1980–1995.
Washington Star, 1951.

ARTICLES

Abbot, Everett V. "Inalienable Rights and the Eighteenth Amendment." *Columbia Law Review* 20 (1920): 183–95.
Ackerman, Bruce A. "Constitutional Politics/Constitutional Law." *Yale Law Journal* 99 (1989): 453–546.
———. "The Storrs Lectures: Discovering the Constitution." *Yale Law Journal* 93 (1984): 1013–72.
Albertsworth, E. F. "Streamlining the Constitution." *New York University Law Quarterly Review* 16 (1938): 1–18.
Almond, Michael A., and Ronald D. Rotunda. "Running Out of Time: Can E.R.A. Be Saved?" *American Bar Association Journal* 64 (1978): 1504–9.
Amar, Akhil Reed. "Philadelphia Revisisted: Amending the Constitution Outside Article V." *University of Chicago Law Review* 55 (1988): 1043–1104.
Amidon, Charles F. "The Nation and the Constitution." *Green Bag* 19 (1907): 597–98.
Apostel, Jane. "Why Women Should Not Have the Vote: Anti-Suffrage Views in the Southland in 1911." *Southern California Quarterly* 70 (1988): 29–42.
Appleby, Paul H. "Roosevelt's Third Term Decision." *American Political Science Review* 46 (1952): 754–65.

Armstrong, Walter P. "Bettering our Federal Government by Constitutional Amendment." *Mississippi Law Journal* 20 (1949): 296–303.

Arneson, Ben A. "Is It Easy to Amend the Constitution?" *American Law Review* 60 (1926): 600.

Aynes, Richard L. "On Misreading John Bingham and the Fourteenth Amendment." *Yale Law Journal* 103 (1993): 57–104.

Bacon, Selden. "How the Tenth Amendment Affected the Fifth Article of the Constitution." *Virginia Law Review* 16 (1930): 771–91.

Baker, John S. "The Federalist and the Bill of Rights." *Texas Tech Law Review* 21 (1990): 2425–42.

Baker, Paula. "The Domestication of Politics: Women and American Political Society, 1780–1920." *American Historical Review* 89 (1984): 620–47.

Ball, Norman T. "Ratification of Constitutional Amendment by State Conventions." *George Washington Law Review* 2 (1934): 216–21.

Banks, Margaret. "Drafting the American Constitution: Attitudes in the Philadelphia Convention Toward the British System of Government." *American Journal of Legal History* 10 (1966): 15–33.

Beard, Charles A. "The Supreme Court—Usurper or Grantee?" *Political Science Quarterly* 27 (1912): 1–35.

Bernstein, Richard B. "The Sleeper Wakes: The History and Legacy of the Twenty-Seventh Amendment." *Fordham Law Review* 61 (1992): 499–508.

Bestor, Arthur. "The American Civil War as a Constitutional Crisis." *American Historical Review* 69 (1964): 327–52.

Bickel, Alexander M. "The Original Understanding and the Segregation Decision." *Harvard Law Review* 69 (1955): 1–65.

Binkley, Robert C. "The Ethics of Nullification." *New Republic* 58 (May 1, 1929): 297–300.

Black, Charles L., Jr. "Amending the Constitution: A Letter to a Congressman." *Yale Law Journal* 82 (1972): 189–215.

———. "The Proposed Amendment of Article V: A Threatened Disaster." *Yale Law Journal* 72 (1963): 957–66.

———. "Proposed Constitutional Amendments: They Would Return Us to Confederacy." *American Bar Association Journal* 49 (1963): 637–40.

Blackman, Paul H. "Presidential Disability and the Bayh Amendment." *Western Political Quarterly* 20 (1967): 440–55.

Bonfield, Arthur Earl. "The Dirksen Amendment and the Article V Convention Process." *Michigan Law Review* 66 (1968): 949–1000.

———. "Proposing Constitutional Amendments by Convention: Some Problems." *Notre Dame Lawyer* 39 (1964): 659–79.

Borah, William E. "Income-Tax Amendment." *North American Review* 191 (1910): 755–61.

Borchard, Edwin. "The Proposed Constitutional Amendment on Treaty Making." *American Journal of International Law* 39 (1945): 537–41.

Boudin, L. B. "Government by Judiciary." *Political Science Quarterly* 26 (1911): 238–70.

———. "Truth and Fiction About the Fourteenth Amendment." *New York University Law Quarterly Review* 16 (1938): 19–82.

Boutwell, George S. "The Income Tax." *North American Review* 160 (May 1895): 589–601.

Bowling, Kenneth R. "'A Tub to the Whale': The Founding Fathers and the Adoption of the Federal Bill of Rights." *Journal of the Early Republic* 8 (1988): 223–51.

Bowman, Harold M. "Congress and the Supreme Court." *Political Science Quarterly* 25 (1910): 20–34.

Boyd, Stephen R. "Antifederalism and the Acceptance of the Constitution: Pennsylvania, 1787–1792." *Publius* 9 (1979): 123–37.

Bradford, M. E. "The Authoritative Constitution: A Reading of the Ratification Debates." *Texas Tech Law Review* 21 (1990): 2349–74.

Brady, David W., and Kent L. Tedin. "Ladies in Pink: Religion and Political Ideology in the Anti-ERA Movement." *Social Science Quarterly* 56 (1976): 564–75.

Breckenridge, Ralph W. "Is the Federal Constitution Adapted to Present Necessities, or Must the American People Have a New One?" *Yale Law Journal* 17 (1908): 347–64.

Brown, Barbara A., Thomas J. Emerson, Gail Falk, and Ann E. Freedman. "The Equal Rights Amendment: A Constitutional Basis for Equal Rights for Women." *Yale Law Journal* 80 (1971): 871–985.

Brown, Everett S. "The Ratification of the Twenty-First Amendment." *American Political Science Review* 29 (1935): 1005–17.

———. "The Term of Office of the President." *American Political Science Review* 41 (1947): 447–52.

Brown, George Stewart. "Irresponsible Government by Constitutional Amendment." *Virginia Law Review* 8 (1922): 157–66.

———. "The 'New Bill of Rights' Amendment." *Virginia Law Review* 9 (1922): 14–24.

———. "The People Should Be Consulted as to Constitutional Changes." *American Bar Association Journal* 16 (1930): 404–6.

Brown, Norris. "Shall the Income Tax Amendment Be Ratified?" *Editorial Review* (April 1910): 354–62.

Buenker, John D. "The Ratification of the Federal Income Tax Amendment." *Cato Journal* 1 (1981): 183–223.

———. "The Urban Political Machine and the Seventeenth Amendment." *Journal of American History* 56 (1969): 305–22.

———. "The Urban Political Machine and Woman Suffrage: A Study in Political Adaptability." *Historian* 33 (1971): 264–79.

Bullock, Charles J. "The Origin, Purpose and Effect of the Direct-Tax Clause of the Federal Constitution." *Political Science Quarterly* 15 (1900): 217–39, 452–81.

Burdick, Charles K. "Is Prohibition Lawful?" *New Republic* 22 (April 21, 1920): 245–48.

Burgess, John W. "Present Problems of Constitutional Law." *Political Science Quarterly* 19 (1904): 546–78.

Burnham, John C. "New Perspectives on the Prohibition 'Experiment' of the 1920s." *Journal of Social History* 2 (1968): 51–68.

Burns, Richard Dean, and W. Addams Dixon. "Foreign Policy and the 'Democratic Myth': The Debate on the Ludlow Amendment." *Mid-America* 47 (1965): 288–306.

Burris, Val. "Who Opposed the ERA? An Analysis of the Social Bases of Antifeminism." *Social Science Quarterly* 64 (1983): 305–17.

Cadwalader, T. F. "Wadsworth-Garrett Amendment." *American Bar Association Journal* 8 (1922): 777.

Caplan, Russell L. "The History and Meaning of the Ninth Amendment." *Virginia Law Review* 69 (1983): 223–68.

Carman, Ernest C. "Why and How the Present Method of Amending the Federal Constitution Should Be Changed." *Oregon Law Review* 17 (1938): 102–9.

Carson, Ralph M. "Disadvantages of a Federal Constitution Convention." *Michigan Law Review* 66 (1968): 921–30.

Carver, Joan S. "The Equal Rights Amendment and the Florida Legislature." *Florida Historical Quarterly* 60 (1982): 455–81.

Chafee, Zechariah, Jr. "Amending the Constitution to Cripple Treaties." *Louisiana Law Review* 12 (1952): 345–82.

———. "Stop Being Terrified of Treaties: Stop Being Scared of the Constitution." *American Bar Association Journal* 38 (1952): 731–34.

Chenery, William. "Child Labor—The New Alignment." *Survey* 53 (January 11, 1925): 379–82.

Church, Samuel Harden. "The Paradise of the Ostrich." *North American Review* 221 (June 1925): 626.

Clark, Donald C., Jr. "The Amending Process: Extending the Ratification Deadline of the Proposed Equal Rights Amendment." *Rutgers Camden Law Journal* 10 (1978): 91–108.

Clark, Homer. "The Supreme Court and the Amending Process." *Virginia Law Review* 39 (1953): 621–52.

Clark, Jane Perry. "The Recent Proposals for Constitutional Amendment." *Wisconsin Law Review* 12 (1937): 313–36.

Clark, Walter. "Inevitable Constitutional Changes." *North American Review* 163 (October 1896): 462–69.

———. "Some Defects in the Constitution of the United States." *American Law Register* 54 (1906): 263–88.

Codman, Julian. "Must Congress Enforce an Amendment?" *Independent* 116 (June 12, 1926): 683–84, 699.

Coleman, William C. "The Fifteenth Amendment." *Columbia Law Review* 10 (1910): 416–50.

Commager, Henry Steele. "To Form a Much Less Perfect Union." *New York Times Magazine,* July 14, 1963, 5, 40–42.

Corwin, Edward S. "Constitutional Law in 1919–1920." *American Political Science Review* 14 (1920): 635–58.

Corwin, Edward S., and Mary Louise Ramsey. "The Constitutional Law of Constitutional Amendment." *Notre Dame Lawyer* 26 (1951): 185–213.

"The Creation of the American Republic, 1776–1787: A Symposium of Views and Reviews." *William and Mary Quarterly* 44 (1987): 549–640.

Cronin, Thomas E. "The Direct Vote and the Electoral College: The Case for Meshing Things Up!" *Presidential Studies Quarterly* 9 (1979): 114–63.

Cross, Lawrence Delbert. "An Armed Community: The Origins and Meaning of the Right to Bear Arms." *Journal of American History* 71 (1984): 22–42.

Cuddihy, William, and B. Carmon Hardy. "A Man's House Was Not His Castle: Origins of the Fourth Amendment to the United States Constitution." *William and Mary Quarterly* 37 (1980): 371–400.

Cummings, Homer S. "The Nature of the Amending Process." *George Washington Law Review* 6 (1938): 247–58.

Darrow, Clarence. "Our Growing Tyranny." *Vanity Fair* 29 (February 1928): 39, 104.
———. "The Ordeal of Prohibition." *American Mercury* 2 (August 1924): 419–27.
———. "Tyranny and the Volstead Act." *Vanity Fair* 28 (March 1927): 45–46, 116.
Dellinger, Walter. "Another Route to the ERA." *Newsweek* 100 (August 2, 1982): 8.
———. "Constitutional Politics: A Rejoinder." *Harvard Law Review* 97 (1983): 446–50.
———. "The Legitimacy of Constitutional Change: Rethinking the Amendment Process." *Harvard Law Review* 97 (1983): 386–432.
———. "The Recurring Question of the 'Limited' Constitutional Convention." *Yale Law Journal* 88 (1979): 1623–40.
Deutsch, Eberhard P. "The Need for a Treaty Amendment: A Restatement and a Reply." *American Bar Association Journal* 38 (1952): 735–38, 793–96.
Dirksen, Everett McKinley. "The Supreme Court and the People." *Michigan Law Review* 66 (1968): 837–74.
Dixon, Robert G. "Article V: The Comatose Article of Our Living Constitution." *Michigan Law Review* 66 (1968): 931–48.
Dodd, W. F. "Amending the Federal Constitution." *Yale Law Journal* 30 (1921): 321–54.
Dow, David R. "When Words Mean What We Believe They Say: The Case of Article V." *Iowa Law Review* 76 (1990): 1–66.
Dowling, Noel T. "Clarifying the Amending Process." *Washington and Lee Law Review* 1 (1940): 215–23.
———. "A New Experiment in Ratification." *American Bar Association Journal* 19 (1933): 383–87.
Dresser, Robert B. "The Case for the Income Tax Amendment." *American Bar Association Journal* 39 (1953): 25–28, 84–87.
Dry, Murray. "Flag Burning and the Constitution." *Supreme Court Review* 1990: 69–103.
Dunker, William L. "Constitutional Amendments—The Justiciability of Ratification and Retraction." *Tennessee Law Review* 41 (1973): 93–112.
Easterling, Larry J. "Sen. Joseph L. Bristow and the Seventeenth Amendment." *Kansas Historical Quarterly* 41 (1975): 488–511.
Eggert, Gerald G. "Richard Olney and the Income Tax Cases." *Mississippi Valley Historical Review* 48 (1961): 24–41.
Eisenman, Susan G., Maryann B. Gall, and Nina R. Hatfield. "Toward Equality for Ohio Men and Women: The ERA and Legislative Response." *Ohio State Law Journal* 37 (1976): 537–38.
Ekirch, Arthur A. "The Sixteenth Amendment: The Historical Background." *Cato Journal* 1 (1981): 161–82.
Eldridge, Seba. "Need for a More Democratic Procedure of Amending the Constitution." *American Political Science Review* 10 (1916): 693–88.
Ellis, Elmer. "Public Opinion and the Income Tax, 1860–1900." *Mississippi Valley Historical Review* 27 (1940): 225–42.

"Enforcement, Repeal, and Nullification." *World's Work* 53 (November 1926): 5–6.

Ervin, Sam J. "Proposed Legislation to Implement the Convention Method of Amending the Constitution." *Michigan Law Review* 66 (1968): 875–902.

Evans, Wainwright. "The Sanctity of the Law." *Outlook and Independent* 152 (June 19, 1929): 283–86, 317.

Fairman, Charles. "The Retirement of Federal Judges." *Harvard Law Review* 51 (1938): 397–443.

Falk, Richard A. "The Relation of Law to Culture, Power, and Justice." *Ethics* 72 (1961): 12–27.

Farber, Daniel A., and John E. Muench. "The Ideological Origins of the Fourteenth Amendment." *Constitutional Commentary* 1 (1984): 235–79.

Farrar, Timothy. "The Adequacy of the Constitution." *New Englander* 21 (1862): 52–73.

Fasteau, Brenda Feigen, and Marc Feigen Fasteau. "May a State Legislature Rescind Its Ratification of a Pending Constitutional Amendment?" *Harvard Women's Law Journal* 1 (1978): 27–51.

Fennell, William G. "The States Rights Amendments—Debates of the 'Founding Fathers' Cast Doubts on Current Proposals." *New York State Bar Association Journal* 35 (1963): 465–72.

Fensterwald, Bernard, Jr. "The States and the Amending Process—A Reply." *American Bar Association Journal* 46 (1960): 717–21.

Ferrell, Ruth M. "The Equal Rights Amendment to the United States Constitution—Areas of Controversy." *Urban Lawyer* 6 (1974): 853–91.

Finch, George A. "Treaty-clause Amendment: The Case for the Association." *American Bar Association Journal* 38 (1952): 467–70, 527–30.

Finkelman, Paul. "James Madison and the Bill of Rights: A Reluctant Paternity." *Supreme Court Review* 1990: 301–47.

Forkosch, Morris D. "The Alternative Amending Clause in Article V: Reflections and Suggestions." *Minnesota Law Review* 51 (1967): 1053–85.

Foster, Edward. "The Balanced Budget Amendment and Economic Thought." *Constitutional Commentary* 2 (1985): 353–71.

Freund, Ernst. "The Prohibition Amendment and Consent Requirements and Time Limits." *American Bar Association Journal* 7 (1921): 656–58.

Freund, Paul A. "The Equal Rights Amendment Is Not the Way." *Harvard Civil Rights–Civil Liberties Law Review* 6 (1971): 235–42.

Frierson, William L. "Amending the Constitution of the United States: A Reply to Mr. Marbury." *Harvard Law Review* 33 (1920): 659–66.

Fuller, Paul. "Expansion of Constitutional Powers by Interpretation." *Columbia Law Review* 5 (1905): 193–214.

Ganahl, Joe de. "The Scope of Federal Power over Alcoholic Beverages Since the Twenty-First Amendment." *George Washington Law Review* 8 (1940): 819–34, 875–903.

Garrett, Finis J. "Amending the Federal Constitution." *Tennessee Law Review* 7 (1929): 286–309.

Gaugush, Bill. "Principles Governing the Interpretation and Exercise of Article V Powers." *Western Political Quarterly* 35 (1982): 212–21.

Geidel, Peter. "The National Woman's Party and the Origins of the Equal Rights Amendment, 1920–1923." *Historian* 42 (1980): 557–82.

Ginsburg, Ruth Bader. "Let's Have E.R.A. as a Signal." *American Bar Association Journal* 63 (1977): 70–73.

Goldstein, Robert J. "The Great 1989–1900 Flag Flap: An Historical, Political, and Legal Analysis." *University of Miami Law Review* 45 (1990): 19–106.

Goodheart, Lawrence B. "The Ambiguity of Individualism: The National Liberal League's Challenge to the Comstock Law." In *American Chameleon: Individualism in Trans-National Context*. Edited by Richard O. Curry and Lawrence B. Goodheart, 133–50. Kent, Ohio: Kent State University Press, 1991.

Graham, Howard Jay. "The 'Conspiracy Theory' of the Fourteenth Amendment." *Yale Law Journal* 47 (1938): 371–402; 48 (1938): 171–94.

Graves, Arthur C. "Inherent Improprieties in the Income Tax Amendment to the Federal Constitution." *Yale Law Journal* 19 (1910): 505–32.

Green, Elna C. "Those Opposed: The Antisuffragists of North Carolina, 1900–1920." *North Carolina Historical Review* 67 (1990): 315–33.

Greene, Jerome D. "The Personal Problem." *Atlantic Monthly* 138 (October 1926): 527–28.

Greider, William. "The Education of David Stockman." *Atlantic Monthly* 248 (December 1981): 27–54.

Griffin, Walter R. "Louis Ludlow and the War Referendum Crusade, 1935–1941." *Indiana Magazine of History* 64 (1968): 267–88.

Grinnell, Frank W. "The Controversial Reed-Walter Amendment to Change the Amending Process in the Federal Constitution." *Massachusetts Law Quarterly* 40 (1955): 25–26.

———. "Petitioning Congress for a Convention: Cannot a State Change Its Mind?" *American Bar Association Journal* 45 (1959): 1164–66.

———. "Procedure for Amending the Federal Constitution." *American Bar Association Journal* 28 (1942): 588–91.

Gunther, Gerald. "The Convention Method of Amending the United States Constitution." *Georgia Law Review* 14 (1979): 1–25.

Hackett, Frank Warren. "The Constitutionality of the Graduated Income Tax Law." *Yale Law Journal* 25 (1916): 427–42.

Hadley, Arthur T. "Law Making and Law Enforcement." *Harper's Magazine* (November 1925): 641–46.

Haines, Charles Grove. "Judicial Review of Acts of Congress and the Need for Constitutional Reform." *Yale Law Journal* 45 (1936): 816–56.

Hall, James Parker. "'An Eighteenth Century Constitution'—A Comment." *Illinois Law Review* 7 (1912): 285–90.

Hatch, Orrin G. "The Equal Rights Amendment Extension: A Critical Analysis." *Harvard Journal of Law and Public Policy* 2 (1979): 19–56.

Heckman, J. William, Jr. "Ratification of a Constitutional Amendment: Can a State Change Its Mind?" *Connecticut Law Review* 6 (1973): 28–35.

Henderson, Edith Guild. "The Background of the Seventh Amendment." *Harvard Law Review* 80 (1966): 289–337.

Hershey, Lenore. "Where Do Women Go from Here?" *Ladies Home Journal* 96 (February 1979): 79, 147–48.

Higgins, Henry Bournes. "The Rigid Constitution." *Political Science Quarterly* 20 (1905): 203–22.

Hobson, Charles F. "The Negative on State Laws: James Madison and the Crisis of Republican Government." *William and Mary Quarterly* 36 (1979): 215–35.

Hodes, William. "Women and the Constitution: Some Legal History and a New Approach to the Nineteenth Amendment." *Rutgers Law Review* 25 (1970): 26–53.

Hoffecker, Carol E. "Delaware's Woman Suffrage Campaign." *Delaware History* 20 (1983): 149–67.

Hohner, Robert A. "The Prohibitionists: Who Were They?" *South Atlantic Quarterly* 68 (1969): 491–505.

Hoober, John A. "Popular Prejudice and Constitutional Amendatory Conventions." *Yale Law Journal* 1 (1892): 207–15.

Hughes, Charles Evans. "Liberty and Law." *American Bar Association Journal* 11 (1925): 563–69.

Johnson, Kenneth R. "White Racial Attitudes as a Factor in the Arguments Against the Nineteenth Amendment." *Phylon* 31 (1970): 31–37.

Johnston, Henry Alan. "The Eighteenth Amendment Is Void." *Century Magazine* 115 (April 1928): 641–53.

Johnstone, Frederic Bruce. "An Eighteenth Century Constitution." *University of Illinois Law Review* 7 (1912): 265–84.

Jones, Francis R. "Pollack v. Farmers' Loan and Trust Company." *Harvard Law Review* 9 (1895): 198–211.

"Judge Clark and the Constitution." *New Republic* 65 (December 31, 1930): 178–79.

"Judge Clark Overruled." *Outlook and Independent* 157 (March 11, 1931): 359.

"Judge Clark's Decision." *Nation* 131 (December 31, 1930): 732.

Kaczorowski, Robert J. "Searching for the Intent of the Framers of the Fourteenth Amendment." *Connecticut Law Review* 6 (1972–1973): 368–98.

Katz, Stanley N. "The Origins of American Constitutional Thought." *Perspectives in American History* 3 (1969): 474–90.

Kauper, Paul G. "The Alternative Amendment Process: Some Observations." *Michigan Law Review* 66 (1968): 903–20.

Kefauver, Estes. "Proposed Changes in the Presidential Election System." *Vanderbilt Law Review* 1 (1948): 395–401.

Kenyon, Cecelia M. "Men of Little Faith: The Anti-Federalists on the Nature of Representative Government." *William and Mary Quarterly* 12 (1955): 3–46.

Klinglesmith, Margaret C. "Amending the Constitution of the United States." *University of Pennsylvania Law Review and American Law Register* 73 (1925): 355–79.

Koch, Adrienne, and Harry Ammon. "The Virginia and Kentucky Resolutions: An Episode in Jefferson's and Madisons's Defense of Civil Liberties." *William and Mary Quarterly* 5 (1948): 146–76.

Kurland, Philip B. "The Equal Rights Amendment: Some Problems of Construction: *Harvard Civil Rights–Civil Liberties Law Review* 6 (1971): 243–52.

Kyvig, David E. "Amending the U.S. Constitution: Ratification Controversies, 1917–1971." *Ohio History* 83 (1974): 156–69.

————. "Can the Constitution Be Amended: The Battle over the Income Tax, 1895–1913." *Prologue* 20 (1988): 181–200.

————. "Objection Sustained: Prohibition Repeal and the New Deal." In *Alcohol, Reform, and Society.* Edited by Jack S. Blocker, 211–12. Westport, Conn.: Greenwood, 1979.

————. "Raskob, Roosevelt, and Repeal." *Historian* 37 (1975): 469–87.

————."The Road Not Taken: FDR, the Supreme Court, and Constitutional Amendment." *Political Science Quarterly* 104 (1989): 463–81.

————. "Women Against Prohibition." *American Quarterly* 28 (Fall 1976): 465–82.

"Lame Duck Nuisance." *Nation* 131 (November 19, 1930): 543.

Lee, R. Alton. "The Corwin Amendment in the Secession Crisis." *Ohio Historical Quarterly* 70 (1961): 1–26.

Lenroot, Irvine L. "Congress and the Constitution." *Marquette Law Review* 7 (1923): 181–91.

Leuchtenburg, William. "FDR's Court-Packing Plan: A Second Life, a Second Death." *Duke Law Journal* 1985: 673–89.

Levinson, Sanford. "'Veneration' and Constitutional Change: James Madison Confronts the Possibility of Constitutional Amendment." *Texas Tech Law Review* 21 (1990): 2443–60.

Lewin, Nathan. "Judgement Time for the ERA." *New Republic* 186 (February 10, 1982): 8–13.

Lincoln, Alexander. "Ratification by Convention." *Massachusetts Law Quarterly* 18 (1933): 287–98.

Linder, Douglas. "What in the Constitution Cannot be Amended?" *Arizona Law Review* 23 (1981): 717–31.

Lippmann, Walter. "Our Predicament Under the Eighteenth Amendment." *Harper's Monthly Magazine* 154 (December 1926): 51–56.

————. "The Popular Dogma of Law Enforcement." *Yale Review* 19 (1929): 1–13.

Lofgren, Charles. "Missouri v. Holland in Historical Perspective." *Supreme Court Review* 1975: 77–121.

Long, Joseph R. "Tinkering with the Constitution." *Yale Law Journal* 24 (1915): 573–89.

Lunardini, Christine A., and Thomas J. Knock. "Woodrow Wilson and Woman Suffrage: A New Look." *Political Science Quarterly* 95 (1980–1981): 655–71.

Lutz, Donald S., "The Intellectual Background to the American Founding." *Texas Tech Law Review* 21 (1990): 2327–48.

————. "Toward a Theory of Constitutional Amendment." *American Political Science Review* 88 (1994): 355–70.

Machen, Arthur W., Jr., "The Elasticity of the Constitution." *Harvard Law Review* 14 (1900): 200–216, 273–85.

————. "Is the Fifteenth Amendment Void?" *Harvard Law Review* 23 (1910): 169–93.

McClain, Emlin. "Written and Unwritten Constitutions in the United States." *Columbia Law Review* 6 (1906): 69–81.

McCleskey, Clifton. "Along the Midway: Some Thoughts on Democratic Constitution Amending." *Michigan Law Review* 66 (1968): 1001–16.

McDonagh, Eileen L., and H. Douglas Price. "Woman Suffrage in the Progressive Era: Patterns of Opposition and Support in Referenda Voting, 1910–1918." *American Political Science Review* 79 (1985): 415–35.

McGovney, D. O. "Is the Eighteenth Amendment Void Because of Its Contents?" *Columbia Law Review* 20 (1920): 499–518.

McLaughlin, Andrew C. "The Court, the Corporation and Conkling." *American Historical Review* 46 (1940): 45–63.

MacLean, Judy. "Women Fight Back: ERA Extension Has Given the Feminist Movement a Second Wind." *Progressive* 43 (February 1979): 38–40.

Mambretti, Catherine Cole. "'The Burden of the Ballot': The Woman's Anti-Suffrage Movement." *American Heritage* 30 (December 1978): 24–25.

Marbury, William L. "The Limitations upon the Amending Power." *Harvard Law Review* 33 (1919): 223–35.

———. "The Nineteenth Amendment and After." *Virginia Law Review* 7 (1920): 1–29.

Marshall, Susan E. "In Defense of Separate Spheres: Class and Status Politics in the Antisuffrage Movement." *Social Forces* 65 (December 1988): 327–51.

———. "Ladies Against Women: Mobilization Dilemmas of Antifeminist Movements." *Social Problems* 32 (1985): 348–62.

Martig, Ralph R. "Amending the Constitution—Article V: The Keystone of the Arch." *Michigan Law Review* 35 (1937): 1253–85.

Martin, Philip L. "The Application Clause of Article Five." *Political Science Quarterly* 85 (1970): 616–28.

———. "Convention Ratification of Federal Constitutional Amendments." *Political Science Quarterly* 82 (1967): 61–71.

———. "Illinois' Ratification of the Corwin Amendment." *Journal of Public Law* 15 (1966): 187–91.

Martin, William Logan. "The Amending Power: The Background of the Income Tax Amendment." *American Bar Association Journal* 39 (1953): 21–24, 77–80, 124–27, 167–68.

———. "The Amending Power: The Ebinger Proposal." *American Bar Association Journal* 40 (1954): 767–71, 802–3.

Meader, Lewis H. "The Council of Censors." *Pennsylvania Magazine of History and Biography* 22 (1898): 265–300.

Meers, John B. "The California Wine and Grape Industry and Prohibition." *California Historical Society Quarterly* 46 (1967): 19–32.

Merritt, Schuyler. "The Erosion of the Constitution of the United States." *Connecticut Bar Journal* 2 (1928): 61–71.

Miller, Justin. "Amendment of the Federal Constitution: Should It Be Made More Difficult?" *Minnesota Law Review* 10 (February 1926): 185–206.

Morrow, Dwight W. "The Income Tax Amendment." *Columbia Law Review* 10 (1910): 379–415.

Moschzisker, Robert von. "Dangers in Disregarding Fundamental Conceptions When Amending the Federal Constitution." *Cornell Law Quarterly* 11 (1925): 1–19.

Murphy, Walter F. "Slaughter House, Civil Rights, and Limits on Constitutional Change." *American Journal of Jurisprudence* 32 (1987): 1–22.

Murtagh, James P. "Procedure for Amending the Constitution and the Reed-Walter Amendment." *Pennsylvania Bar Association Quarterly* 27 (1955): 90–101.

Musmanno, M. H. "The Difficulty of Amending Our Federal Constitution: Defect or Asset?" *American Bar Association Journal* 15 (1929): 505–8.

Needham, Charles Willis. "Changing the Fundamental Law." *University of Pennsylvania Law Review and American Law Register* 69 (1921): 223–36.

Nelson, William E. "Reason and Compromise in the Establishment of the Federal Constitution, 1787–1801." *William and Mary Quarterly* 44 (1987): 458–84.

Nelson, William T. "Changing Conceptions of Judicial Review: The Evolution of Constitutional Theory in the States, 1790–1860." *University of Pennsylvania Law Review* 120 (1972): 1166–85.

"No Eighteenth Amendment for Judge Clark." *Literary Digest* 107 (December 27, 1930): 6.

"Nullification by Consent." *New Republic* 47 (June 16, 1926): 101–2.

Oberst, Paul. "The Genesis of the Three States-Rights Amendments of 1963." *Notre Dame Lawyer* 39 (1964): 644–58.

Orfield, Lester B. "The Federal Amending Power: Genesis and Justiciability." *Minnesota Law Review* 14 (1930): 369–84.

———. "The Procedure of the Federal Amending Power." *Illinois Law Review* 25 (1930): 418–45.

———. "The Reform of the Federal Amending Power." *North Carolina Law Review* 10 (1931): 16–55.

———. "The Scope of the Federal Amending Power." *Michigan Law Review* 33 (1930): 550–85.

———. "Sovereignty and the Federal Amending Power." *Iowa Law Review* 16 (1931): 391–404, 504–22.

Packard, Frank E. "Problems Arising from an Attempt to Amend the Constitution by Convention Concerning the Limiting of Income Tax Rates to 25 Percent." *Nebraska Law Review* 31 (1952): 407–15.

Parrish, Michael E. "The Great Depression, the New Deal, and the American Legal Order." *Washington Law Review* 59 (1984): 723–50.

Pedrick, Willard H., and Richard C. Dahl. "Let the People Vote Ratification of Constitutional Amendments by Convention." *Arizona Law Review* 30 (1988): 2243–56.

Pennoyer, Sylvester. "The Income Tax Decision and the Power of the Supreme Court to Nullify Acts of Congress." *American Law Review* 29 (1895): 550–58.

Phillips, L. H., and C. J. Tilson. "Equal Rights Amendment to the Federal Constitution." *Connecticut Bar Journal* 20 (1946): 62–74.

Platz, William A. "Article Five of the Federal Constitution." *George Washington Law Review* 3 (1934): 17–49.

Pollard, Joseph Percival. "The Rebel on the Bench." *North American Review* 231 (March 1931): 227–34.

Potter, William P. "The Method of Amending the Federal Constitution." *University of Pennsylvania Law Review and American Law Register* 57 (1909): 589–610.

Potts, Louis W. "The Framers and the Amendment Process." *Mid-America* 71 (1989): 65–87.

Priest, Henry Samuel. "Prohibition and Respect for Law." *North American Review* 221 (June 1925): 596–601.

"Proposed Legislation on the Convention Method of Amending the United States Constitution." *Harvard Law Review* 85 (1972): 1612–48.

"Proposing Amendments to the United States Constitution by Convention." *Harvard Law Review* 70 (1957): 1067–76.

Quarles, James. "Amendments to the Federal Constitution." *American Bar Association Journal* 26 (1940): 617–20.

Rakove, Jack N. "The Madisonian Theory of Rights." *William and Mary Law Review* 31 (1990): 245–66.

Rapacz, Max P. "Effect of the Eighteenth Amendment upon the Amending Process." *Notre Dame Lawyer* 9 (1934): 313–16.

"Ratification of Child Labor Amendment by a State Legislature After Previous Rejection." *Yale Law Journal* 47 (1937): 148–51.

Reardon, Paul C. "The Massachusetts Constitution Marks a Milestone." *Publius* 12 (1982): 45–55.

Renfro, William L. "Ratifying the Second Amendment." *Vital Speeches of the Day* 58 (May 1, 1992): 429–530.

"Repeal the Eighteenth Amendment." *Nation* 134 (May 4, 1932): 502.

Rice, Charles, E. "Let Us Pray—An Amendment to the Constitution." *Catholic Lawyer* 210 (1964): 178–84, 193.

Richberg, Donald R. "Should We Amend the Constitution?" *Missouri Bar Journal* 7 (1963): 45–53.

———. "Undermining the Constitution." *Vital Speeches of the Day* 2 (January 13, 1936): 238–44.

Roll, Charles W., Jr., "We, Some of the People: Apportionment in the Thirteen State Conventions Ratifying the Constitution." *Journal of American History* 56 (1969): 21–40.

Rudolph, Frederick. "The American Liberty League, 1939–1940." *American Historical Review* 56 (1950): 19–33.

Rutland, Robert A. "The Trivialization of the Bill of Rights: One Historian's View of How the Purposes of the First Ten Amendments Have Been Defiled." *William and Mary Law Review* 31 (1990): 287–94.

Scheips, Paul J. "The Significance and Adoption of Article V of the Constitution." *Notre Dame Lawyer* 26 (1950): 46–67.

Schubert, Glendon Austin. "Politics and the Constitution: The Bricker Amendment During 1953." *Journal of Politics* 16 (1954): 257–98.

Seelander, Judith. "Feminist Against Feminist: The First Phase of the Equal Rights Amendment Debate, 1923–1963." *South Atlantic Quarterly* 81 (1982): 147–61.

Seligman, Edwin R. A. "The Income Tax." *Political Science Quarterly* 9 (1894): 610–48.

Shalhope, Robert E. "The Ideological Origins of the Second Amendment." *Journal of American History* 69 (1982): 599–614.

Shalhope, Robert E., and Lawrence Delbert Cross. "The Second Amendment and the Right to Bear Arms: An Exchange." *Journal of American History* 71 (1984): 587–93.

Shanahan, Frank E., Jr. "Proposed Constitutional Amendments: They Will Strengthen Federal-State Relations." *American Bar Association Journal* 49 (1963): 631–36.

Sherman, Gordon E. "The Recent Constitutional Amendments." *Yale Law Journal* 23 (1913): 129–57.

Sherman, Richard B. "The Rejection of the Child Labor Amendment." *Mid-America* 45 (1963): 3–17.

Silva, Edward T. "State Cohorts and Amendment Clusters in the Process of Federal Constitutional Amendments in the United States, 1969–1931." *Law and Society Review* 4 (1970): 445–66.

"Simon's Simple Pie." *New Yorker* 70 (February 28, 1994): 6–8.

Skinner, George D. "Intrinsic Limitations on the Power of Constitutional Amendment." *Michigan Law Review* 18 (1919): 213–25.

Smith, Monroe. "Shall We Make Our Constitution Flexible?" *North American Review* 194 (November 1911): 657–73.

Special Committee of the American Bar Association. "The Federal Child Labor Amendment." *American Bar Association Journal* 21 (1935): 12.

Stathis, Stephen W. "The Twenty-Second Amendment: A Practical Remedy or Partisan Maneuver?" *Constitutional Commentary* 7 (1990): 61–68.

Stevens, Daniel Norman. "Ratification of Proposed Federal Amendment After Prior Rejection." *Southern California Law Review* 11 (1938): 472–76.

Sturm, Albert L. "The Development of American State Constitutions." *Publius* 12 (1982): 57–98.

Suber, Peter. "Population Changes and Constitutional Amendments: Federalism Versus Democracy." *University of Michigan Journal of Law Reform* 20 (1987): 409–90.

Taft, Henry W. "Amendment of the Federal Constitution: Is the Power Conferred by Article V Limited by the Tenth Amendment?" *Virginia Law Review* 16 (1930): 647–58.

Taft, William Howard. "Can Ratification of an Amendment to the Constitution Be Made to Depend on a Referendum? *Yale Law Review* 29 (1920): 821–25.

Tanger, Jacob. "The Amending Procedure of the Federal Constitution." *American Political Science Review* 10 (1916): 689–99.

Taylor, A. Elizabeth. "The Last Phase of the Woman Suffrage Campaign in Georgia." *Georgia Historical Quarterly* 43 (1959): 11–28.

———. "The Woman Suffrage Movement in Texas." *Journal of Southern History* 17 (1951): 194–215.

Toufexis, Anastasia. "What Killed Equal Rights?" *Time* 120 (July 12, 1982): 33.

Tribe, Laurence H. "A Constitution We Are Amending: In Defense of a Restrained Judicial Role." *Harvard Law Review* 97 (1984): 433–45.

Tuller, Walter K. "A Convention to Amend the Constitution—Why Needed—How It May Be Obtained." *North American Review* 193 (1911): 369–87.

Turner, John J., Jr. "The Twelfth Amendment and the First American Party System." *Historian* 35 (1973): 221–37.

"The Two-Term Limit." *Nation* 172 (March 10, 1951): 216–17.

Van Alstyne, William W. "Does Article V Restrict the States to Calling Unlimited Conventions Only? A Letter to a Colleague." *Duke Law Journal* 1978: 1295–1306.

Vile, John R. "The Amending Process: Alternative to Revolution." *Southeastern Political Review* 11 (1983): 49–96.

———. "American Views of the Constitutional Amending Process: An Intellectual History of Article V." *American Journal of Legal History* 35 (1991): 44–69.

———. "Judicial Review of the Amending Process: The Dellinger-Tribe Debate." *Journal of Law and Politics* 3 (1986): 21–50.

———. "Legally Amending the United States Constitution: The Exclusivity of Article V's Mechanics." *Cumberland Law Review* 21 (1991): 271–307.

———. "Limitations on the Constitutional Amending Process." *Constitutional Commentary* 2 (1985): 373–88.

Vose, Clement E. "Conservatism by Amendment." *Yale Review* 46 (1956): 176–90.

———. "Repeal as a Political Achievement." In *Law, Alcohol, and Order: Perspectives on National Prohibition.* Edited by David E. Kyvig, 97–121. Westport, Conn.: Greenwood, 1985.

———. "When District of Columbia Representation Collides with the Constitutional Amendment Institution." *Publius* 9 (1979): 105–25.

"Vox Pop: Can It Bring Repeal?" *World's Work* 61 (January 1932): 28.

Wallace, Schuyler C. "Nullification: A Process of Government." *Political Science Quarterly* 45 (1930): 347–58.

Wechsler, Herbert. "Presidential Elections and the Constitution: A Comment on Proposed Amendment." *American Bar Association Journal* 35 (1949): 181–84, 270–74.

Weclew, Robert G. "The Constitution's Amending Article: Illusion or Necessity?" *DePaul Law Review* 18 (1968): 167–87.

Weinfield, Abraham C. "Power of Congress over State Ratifying Conventions." *Harvard Law Review* 51 (1938): 473–505.

Westin, Alan Furman. "The Supreme Court, the Populist Movement, and the Campaign of 1896." *Journal of Politics* 15 (1953): 3–41.

Wheeler, Wayne B. "Is a Constitutional Convention Impending?" *Illinois Law Review* 21 (1927): 782–803.

White, Justin DuPratt. "Is There an Eighteenth Amendment?" *Cornell Law Quarterly* 5 (1920): 113–27.

Whitney, Edward B. "The Income Tax and the Constitution." *Harvard Law Review* 20 (1907): 280–96.

"Why Not Count Noses—Wet or Dry?" *World's Work* 59 (March 1930): 40.

Williams, Bruce. "The Popular Mandate on Constitutional Amendments." *Virginia Law Review* 7 (1921): 280–301.

Williams, George H. "Article V of the Constitution." *Constitutional Review* 12 (1928): 69–83.

Williams, George Washington. "Are There Any Limitations upon the Power to Amend the United States Constitution?" *Temple Law Quarterly* 5 (1931): 554–61.

Willis, Hugh Evander. "The Doctrine of the Amendability of the United States Constitution." *Indiana Law Journal* 7 (1932): 457–69.

Willis, Paul G., and George L. "The Politics of the Twenty-Second Amendment." *Western Political Quarterly* 5 (1952): 469–82.

Wilson, William L. "The Income Tax on Corporations." *North American Review* 158 (January 1894): 1–7.

Wohlenberg, Ernest H. "Correlates of Equal Rights Amendment Ratification." *Social Science Quarterly* 60 (1980): 676–84.

Wolf, Peter H. "An Antireapportionment Amendment: Can It Be Legally Ratified?" *American Bar Association Journal* 52 (1966): 326–31.

Yellin, Carol Lynn. "Countdown in Tennessee, 1920." *American Heritage* 30 (December 1978): 12–23, 26–35.

Zuckert, Michael P. "Completing the Constitution: The Thirteenth Amendment." *Constitutional Commentary* 4 (1987): 259–83.

Zueblin, Charles. "Rejuvenating the Constitution." *Yale Law Journal* 25 (1916): 211–20.

BOOKS

Abbott, David W., and James P. Levine. *Wrong Winner: The Coming Debacle in the Electoral College.* New York: Praeger, 1991.

Ackerman, Bruce. *We the People: Foundations.* Cambridge: Harvard University Press, 1991.

Adams, Willi Paul. *The First American Constitutions: Republican Ideology and the Making of the State Constitutions in the Revolutionary Era.* Translated by Rita and Robert Kimber. Chapel Hill: University of North Carolina Press, 1980.

Alexander, John K. *The Selling of the Constitutional Convention: A History of News Coverage.* Madison, Wis.: Madison House, 1990.

Alsop, Joseph, and Turner Catledge. *The 168 Days.* Garden City, N.Y.: Doubleday, Doran, 1938.

Ames, Herman V. *The Proposed Amendments to the Constitution of the United States During the First Century of Its History,* in *Annual Report of the American Historical Association for the Year 1896.* Washington, D.C.: GPO, 1897.

Anastaplo, George. *The Amendments to the Constitution: A Commentary.* Baltimore: Johns Hopkins University Press, 1995.

———. *The Constitution of 1787: A Commentary.* Baltimore: Johns Hopkins University Press, 1989.

Anderson, Martin. *Revolution.* San Diego: Harcourt Brace Jovanovich, 1988.

Andrews, Charles M. *The Colonial Period of American History: The Settlements.* 3 vols. New Haven: Yale University Press, 1934–1937.

Arrington, Leonard J., and Davis Bitton. *The Mormon Experience: A History of the Latter-day Saints.* New York: Knopf, 1979.

Bader, Robert S. *Prohibition in Kansas: A History.* Lawrence: University Press of Kansas, 1986.

Bailyn, Bernard. *The Ideological Origins of the American Revolution.* Cambridge: Harvard University Press, 1967.

Baldwin, Leland D. *Reforming the Constitution: An Imperative for Modern America.* Santa Barbara, Calif.: ABC Clio, 1972.

Ball, Terence, and J. G. A. Pocock, eds. *Conceptual Change and the Constitution.* Lawrence: University Press of Kansas, 1988.

Banner, James M., Jr. *To the Hartford Convention: The Federalists and the Origins of Party Politics in Massachusetts, 1789–1815.* New York: Knopf, 1970.

Bayh, Birch. *One Heartbeat Away: Presidential Disability and Succession.* Indianapolis: Bobbs-Merrill, 1968.

Beard, Charles A. *An Economic Interpretation of the Constitution of the United States.* New York: Macmillan, 1913.

Beck, James M. *The Constitution of the United States.* New York: George H. Doran, 1922.

Becker, Carl. *The Declaration of Independence: A Study in the History of Political Ideas.* New York: Knopf, 1942.

Becker, Susan D. *The Origins of the Equal Rights Amendment: American Feminism Between the Wars.* Westport, Conn.: Greenwood, 1981.

Belz, Herman. *A New Birth of Freedom: The Republican Party and Freedmen's Rights, 1861–1866.* Westport, Conn.: Greenwood, 1976.

————. *Emancipation and Equal Rights: Politics and Constitutionalism in the Civil War Era.* New York: W. W. Norton, 1978.

Benedict, Michael Les. *A Compromise of Principle: Congressional Republicans and Reconstruction, 1863–1869.* New York: W. W. Norton, 1974.

Berger, Raoul. *Congress v. the Supreme Court.* Cambridge: Harvard University Press, 1969.

————. *Government by Judiciary: The Transformation of the Fourteenth Amendment.* Cambridge: Harvard University Press, 1977.

Bernstein, Richard B., with Jerome Agel. *Amending America: If We Love the Constitution So Much, Why Do We Keep Trying to Change It?* New York: Times Books, 1993.

Berry, Mary Frances. *Why ERA Failed: Politics, Women's Rights, and the Amending Process of the Constitution.* Bloomington: Indiana University Press, 1986.

Beth, Loren P. *The Development of the American Constitution, 1877–1917.* New York: Harper and Row, 1971.

Billias, George Athan, ed. *American Constitutionalism Abroad: Selected Essays in Comparative Constitutional History.* Westport, Conn.: Greenwood, 1990.

Black, Forrest Revere. *Ill-Starred Prohibition Cases: A Study in Judicial Pathology.* Boston: Richard G. Badger, 1931.

Block, Fred, Richard A. Cloward, Barbara Ehernreich, and Frances Fox Piven. *The Mean Season: The Attack on the Welfare State.* New York: Pantheon, 1987.

Blocker, Jack S., Jr. *American Temperance Movements: Cycles of Reform.* Boston: Twayne, 1989.

————. *"Give to the Winds Thy Fears": The Women's Temperance Crusade, 1873–74.* Westport, Conn.: Greenwood, 1985.

————. *Retreat from Reform: The Prohibition Movement in the United States, 1890–1913.* Westport, Conn.: Greenwood, 1976.

Boles, Janet K. *The Politics of the Equal Rights Amendment: Conflict and the Decision Process.* New York: Longman, 1979.

Bolt, Ernest C. *Ballots Before Bullets: The War Referendum Approach to Peace in America, 1914–1941.* Charlottesville: University Press of Virginia, 1977.

Bordin, Ruth. *Woman and Temperance: The Quest for Power and Liberty, 1873–1900*. Philadelphia: Temple University Press, 1981.

Bowen, Catherine Drinker. *Miracle at Philadelphia: The Story of the Constitutional Convention, May to September 1787*. Boston: Little, Brown, 1966.

Bowers, Claude G. *The Tragic Era: The Revolution After Lincoln*. Cambridge, Mass.: Houghton Mifflin, 1929.

Boyd, Steven R. *The Politics of Opposition: Antifederalists and the Acceptance of the Constitution*. Millwood, N.Y.: KTO Press, 1979.

Boyer, Paul. *Urban Masses and Moral Order in America, 1820–1920*. Cambridge: Harvard University Press, 1978.

Brant, Irving. *The Bill of Rights: Its Origins and Meaning*. Indianapolis: Bobbs-Merrill, 1965.

———. *James Madison*. 4 vols. Indianapolis: Bobbs-Merrill, 1941–1961.

———. *Storm over the Constitution*. Indianapolis: Bobbs-Merrill, 1936.

Brinkley, Alan. *The End of Reform: New Deal Liberalism in Recession and War*. New York: Knopf, 1995.

Brock, W. R. *An American Crisis: Congress and Reconstruction, 1865–1867*. New York: St. Martin's Press, 1963.

Bronner, Edwin B. *William Penn's "Holy Experiment": The Founding of Pennsylvania, 1681–1701*. New York: Temple University Publications, 1962.

Bryce, James. *The American Commonwealth*. 3d ed. New York: Macmillan, 1895.

Buechler, Steven M. *The Transformation of the Woman Suffrage Movement: The Case of Illinois, 1850–1920*. New Brunswick, N.J.: Rutgers University Press, 1986.

Buenker, John D. *The Income Tax and the Progressive Era*. New York: Garland, 1985.

———. *Urban Liberalism and Progressive Reform*. New York: Scribner's, 1973.

Burk, Robert F. *The Corporate State and the Broker State: The Du Ponts and American National Politics, 1925–1940*. Cambridge: Harvard University Press, 1990.

Butler, Nicholas Murray. *Across the Busy Years*. 2 vols. New York: Scribner's, 1939–1940.

Cannon, Lou. *President Reagan: The Role of a Lifetime*. New York: Simon and Schuster, 1991.

Cantril, Hadley, and Mildred Strunk, eds. *Public Opinion, 1935–1946*. Princeton: Princeton University Press, 1951.

Caplan, Russell L. *Constitutional Brinksmanship: Amending the Constitution by National Convention*. New York: Oxford University Press, 1988.

Carpenter, Jesse T. *The South as a Conscious Minority, 1789–1861: A Study in Political Thought*. New York: New York University Press, 1930.

Chambers, Clarke A. *Seedtime of Reform: American Social Service and Social Action, 1918–1933*. Minneapolis: University of Minnesota Press, 1963.

Chatfield, Charles. *For Peace and Justice: Pacifism in America, 1914–1941*. Knoxville: University of Tennessee Press, 1971.

Clancy, Paul R. *Just a Country Lawyer: A Biography of Senator Sam Ervin*. Bloomington: Indiana University Press, 1974.

Clark, Barbara Hinkson. *Chadha: The Story of an Epic Constitutional Struggle*. New York: Oxford University Press, 1988.

Clark, Norman H. *Deliver Us from Evil: An Interpretation of American Prohibition.* New York: W. W. Norton, 1976.
———. *The Dry Years: Prohibition and Social Change in Washington.* Seattle: University of Washington Press, 1965.
Clinton, Robert Lowry. *Marbury v. Madison and Judicial Review.* Lawrence: University Press of Kansas, 1989.
Cohler, Anne M. *Montesquieu's Comparative Politics and the Spirit of American Constitutionalism.* Lawrence: University Press of Kansas, 1988.
Cole, Wayne S. *Roosevelt and the Isolationists, 1932–45.* Lincoln: University of Nebraska Press, 1983.
Coletta, Paolo E. *William Jennings Bryan: Political Evangelist, 1860–1908.* Lincoln: University of Nebraska Press, 1964.
Conkin, Paul K. *Self-Evident Truths: Being a Discourse on the Origins and Development of the First Principles of American Government—Popular Sovereignty, Natural Rights, and Balance and Separation of Powers.* Bloomington: Indiana University Press, 1974.
Conley, Patrick T., and John P. Kaminski, eds. *The Bill of Rights and the States: The Colonial and Revolutionary Origins of American Liberties.* Madison, Wis.: Madison House, 1992.
———. *The Constitution and the States: The Role of the Original Thirteen in the Framing and Adoption of the Federal Constitution.* Madison, Wis.: Madison House, 1988.
Conover, Pamela Johnston, and Virginia Gray. *Feminism and the New Right: Conflict over the American Family.* New York: Praeger, 1983.
Corwin, Edward S. *Court over Constitution: A Study of Judicial Review as an Instrument of Popular Government.* Princeton: Princeton University Press, 1938.
———. *The "Higher Law" Background of American Constitutional Law.* Ithaca, N.Y.: Cornell University Press, 1955.
Cott, Nancy F. *The Grounding of Modern Feminism.* New Haven: Yale University Press, 1987.
Coxe, Brinton. *An Essay on Judicial Power and Unconstitutional Legislation.* Philadelphia: Kay and Brother, 1893.
Craven, Wesley Frank. *The Colonies in Transition, 1660–1713.* New York: Harper and Row, 1968.
Crosskey, William W. *Politics and the Constitution in the History of the United States.* 3 vols. Chicago: University of Chicago Press, 1953–1981.
Cultice, Wendell W. *Youth's Battle for the Ballot: A History of Voting Age in America.* Westport, Conn.: Greenwood, 1992.
Currie, David P. *The Constitution in the Supreme Court: The First Hundred Years, 1789–1888.* Chicago: University of Chicago Press, 1985.
———. *The Constitution in the Supreme Court: The Second Century, 1889–1986.* Chicago: University of Chicago Press, 1990.
Curtis, Michael Kent. *No State Shall Abridge: The Fourteenth Amendment and the Bill of Rights.* Durham, N.C.: Duke University Press, 1986.

Dallek, Robert. *Franklin D. Roosevelt and American Foreign Policy, 1932–1945.* New York: Oxford University Press, 1979.

Daniell, Jere N. *Experiment in Republicanism: New Hampshire Politics and the American Revolution, 1741–1794.* Cambridge: Harvard University Press, 1970.

Dargo, George. *Roots of the Republic: A New Perspective on Early American Constitutionalism.* New York: Praeger, 1974.

Darrow, Clarence, and Victor S. Yarros. *The Prohibition Mania.* New York: Boni and Liveright, 1927.

Davis, Kenneth S. *FDR: The Beckoning of Destiny.* New York: G. P. Putnam, 1971.

DePauw, Linda Grant. *The Eleventh Pillar: New York State and the Federal Constitution.* Ithaca, N.Y.: Cornell University Press, 1966.

Dewey, Donald O. *Marshall versus Jefferson: The Political Background of Marbury v. Madison.* New York: Knopf, 1970.

Divine, Robert A. *The Illusion of Neutrality.* Chicago: University of Chicago Press, 1962.

Dobyns, Fletcher. *The Amazing Story of Repeal: An Exposé of the Power of Propaganda.* Chicago: Willett, Clark, 1940.

Dodd, Walter Fairleigh. *The Revision and Amendment of State Constitutions.* Baltimore: Johns Hopkins University Press, 1910.

Dolbeare, Kenneth M., and Phillip E. Hammond. *The School Prayer Decisions: From Court Policy to Local Practice.* Chicago: University of Chicago Press, 1971.

Douglas, Elisha P. *Rebels and Democrats: The Struggle for Equal Political Rights and Majority Rule During the American Revolution.* Chicago: Quadrangle Books, 1955.

Drew, Elizabeth. *Portrait of an Election: The 1980 Presidential Campaign.* New York: Simon and Schuster, 1981.

Dubois, Ellen Carol. *Feminism and Suffrage: The Emergence of an Independent Women's Movement in America, 1848–1869.* Ithaca, N.Y.: Cornell University Press, 1978.

Edel, Wilbur. *A Constitutional Convention: Threat or Challenge?* New York: Praeger, 1981.

Eidelberg, Paul. *The Political Philosophy of the American Constitution: A Reinterpretation of the Intentions of the Founding Fathers.* New York: Free Press, 1968.

Eisler, Riane, and Allie C. Hixson. *The Equal Rights Amendment: Fact and Action Guide.* N.p.: National Women's Conference Center, 1986.

Eldot, Paula. *Governor Alfred E. Smith: The Politician as Reformer.* New York: Garland, 1983.

Ellis, Richard E. *The Jeffersonian Crisis: Courts and Politics in the Young Republic.* New York: Oxford University Press, 1971.

———. *The Union at Risk: Jacksonian Democracy, States' Rights, and the Nullification Crisis.* New York: Oxford University Press, 1987.

Elster, Jon, and Rune Slagstad, eds. *Constitutionalism and Democracy: Studies in Rationality and Social Change.* Cambridge: Cambridge University Press, 1988.

Ely, James W., Jr. *The Guardian of Every Other Right: A Constitutional History of Property Rights.* New York: Oxford University Press, 1992.

Engelman, Larry. *Intemperance: The Lost War Against Liquor.* New York: Free Press, 1979.

Epstein, Barbara Leslie. *The Politics of Domesticity: Women, Evangelism, and Temperance in Nineteenth-Century America.* Middletown, Conn.: Wesleyan University Press, 1981.

Ervin, Sam J., Jr. *Preserving the Constitution: The Autobiography of Senator Sam Ervin.* Charlottesville, Va.: Michie, 1984.

Evans, Sara. *Born for Liberty: A History of Women in America.* New York: Oxford University Press, 1989.

———. *Personal Politics: The Roots of Women's Liberation in the Civil Rights Movement and the New Left.* New York: Knopf, 1979.

Farrand, Max. *The Framing of the Constitution of the United States.* New Haven: Yale University Press, 1913.

Faulkner, Harold U. *Politics, Reform and Expansion, 1890–1900.* New York: Harper and Row, 1959.

Fausold, Martin L. *James W. Wadsworth: The Gentleman from New York.* Syracuse, N.Y.: Syracuse University Press, 1975.

Faux, Marian. *Roe v. Wade: The Untold Story of the Landmark Supreme Court Decision that Made Abortion Legal.* New York: Macmillan, 1988.

Feerick, John D. *From Failing Hands: The Story of Presidential Succession.* New York: Fordham University Press, 1965.

———. *The Twenty-fifth Amendment: Its Complete History and Earliest Applications.* New York: Fordham University Press, 1976.

Fehrenbacher, Don E. *Constitutions and Constitutionalism in the Slaveholding South.* Athens: University of Georgia Press, 1989.

———. *The Dred Scott Case: Its Significance in American Law and Politics.* New York: Oxford University Press, 1978.

Felsenthal, Carol. *The Sweetheart of the Silent Majority: The Biography of Phyllis Schlafly.* Garden City, N.Y.: Doubleday, 1981.

Ferree, Myra Marx, and Beth B. Hess. *Controversy and Coalition: The New Feminist Movement.* Boston: Twayne, 1985.

Firmage, Edwin Brown, and Richard Collin Mangrum. *Zion in the Courts: A Legal History of the Church of Jesus Christ of Latter-day Saints, 1830–1900.* Urbana: University of Illinois Press, 1988.

Flack, Horace Edgar. *The Adoption of the Fourteenth Amendment.* Baltimore: Johns Hopkins Press, 1908.

Flexner, Eleanor. *Century of Struggle: The Woman's Rights Movement in the United States.* Cambridge: Harvard University Press, 1959.

Foner, Eric. *Free Soil, Free Labor, Free Men: The Ideology of the Republican Party Before the Civil War.* New York: Oxford University Press, 1970.

———. *Reconstruction: America's Unfinished Revolution, 1863–1877.* New York: Harper and Row, 1988.

Franklin, Jimmie L. *Born Sober: Prohibition in Oklahoma, 1907–1959.* Norman: University of Oklahoma Press, 1971.

Freedman, Samuel S., and Pamela J. Naughton. *ERA: May a State Change Its Vote?* Detroit: Wayne State University Press, 1978.

Freehling, William W. *Prelude to Civil War: The Nullification Controversy in South Carolina, 1816–1836.* New York: Harper and Row, 1966.

———. *The Road to Disunion: Secessionists at Bay, 1776–1854.* New York: Oxford University Press, 1990.

Freeman, Jo. *The Politics of Woman's Liberation.* New York: McKay, 1975.

Freidel, Frank. *Franklin D. Roosevelt: A Rendezvous with Destiny.* Boston: Little, Brown, 1990.

Friedrich, Carl J. *Constitutional Government and Democracy: Theory and Practice in Europe and America.* Boston: Little, Brown, 1941.

———. *The Impact of American Constitutionalism Abroad.* Boston: Boston University Press, 1967.

Gallup, George, and Saul Forbes Rae. *The Pulse of Democracy.* New York: Simon and Schuster, 1940.

Garraty, John A., ed. *Quarrels That Have Shaped the Constitution.* Rev. ed. New York: Harper and Row, 1987.

Garrow, David J. *Liberty and Sexuality: The Right to Privacy and the Making of Roe v. Wade.* New York: Macmillan, 1994.

Gillespie, Michael Allen, and Michael Lienesch, eds. *Ratifying the Constitution.* Lawrence: University Press of Kansas, 1989.

Gillette, William. *The Right to Vote: Politics and the Passage of the Fifteenth Amendment.* Baltimore: Johns Hopkins University Press, 1965.

Goldstein, Joel K. *The Modern American Vice Presidency: The Transformation of a Political Institution.* Princeton: Princeton University Press, 1982.

Goodnow, Frank J. *Social Reform and the Constitution.* New York: Burt Franklin, 1911.

Gould, Lewis L. *Progressives and Prohibitionists: Texas Democrats in the Wilson Era.* Austin: University of Texas Press, 1973.

Green, Fletcher M. *Constitutional Development of the South Atlantic States, 1776–1860.* Chapel Hill: University of North Carolina Press, 1930.

Greene, Jack P. *Peripheries and Center: Constitutional Development in the Extended Politics of the British Empire and the United States, 1607–1788.* Athens: University of Georgia Press, 1986.

Griffith, Robert. *The Politics of Fear: Joseph R. McCarthy and the Senate.* Lexington: University of Kentucky Press, 1970.

Grimes, Alan P. *Democracy and the Amendments to the Constitution.* Lexington, Mass.: Lexington Books, 1978.

———. *The Puritan Ethic and Woman Suffrage.* New York: Oxford University Press, 1967.

Gunderson, Robert G. *Old Gentlemen's Convention: The Washington Peace Conference of 1861.* Madison: University of Wisconsin Press, 1961.

Gusfield, Joseph R. *Symbolic Crusade: Status Politics and the American Temperance Movement.* Urbana: University of Illinois Press, 1963.

Hall, Kermit L. *The Magic Mirror: Law in American History.* New York: Oxford University Press, 1989.

Hall, Kermit L., and James W. Ely, Jr., eds. *An Uncertain Tradition: Constitutionalism and the History of the South.* Athens: University of Georgia Press, 1989.

Hall, Kermit L., Harold M. Hyman, and Leon V. Sigal, eds. *The Constitutional Convention as an Amending Device.* Washington, D.C.: American Historical Association and American Political Science Association, 1981.

Hamm, Richard F. *Shaping the Eighteenth Amendment: Temperance Reform, Legal*

Culture, and the Polity, *1880–1920*. Chapel Hill: University of North Carolina Press, 1995.

Harding, Samuel Bannister. *The Contest over the Ratification of the Federal Constitution in the State of Massachusetts*. New York: Longmans, Green, 1896.

Harper, Ida Husted. *Life and Work of Susan B. Anthony*. 3 vols. Indianapolis: Hollenbeck, 1898–1908.

Harrison, Cynthia. *On Account of Sex: The Politics of Women's Issues, 1945–1968*. Berkeley: University of California Press, 1988.

Hartmann, Susan M. *Truman and the 80th Congress*. Columbia: University of Missouri Press, 1971.

Haynes, George H. *The Senate of the United States: Its History and Practice*. 2 vols. Boston: Houghton Mifflin, 1938.

Hoff-Wilson, Joan, ed. *Rights of Passage: The Past and Future of the ERA*. Bloomington: Indiana University Press, 1986.

Holt, J. C. *Magna Carta*. Cambridge: Cambridge University Press, 1965.

Horwitz, Morton J. *The Transformation of American Law, 1780–1860*. New York: Oxford University Press, 1977.

———. *The Transformation of American Law, 1870–1960: The Crisis of Legal Orthodoxy*. New York: Oxford University Press, 1992.

Howard, A. E. Dick. *The Road from Runnymeade: Magna Carta and Constitutionalism in America*. Charlottesville: University Press of Virginia, 1968.

Hyman, Harold M. *A More Perfect Union: The Impact of the Civil War and Reconstruction on the Constitution*. New York: Knopf, 1973.

Hyman, Harold M., and William M. Wiecek. *Equal Justice Under Law: Constitutional Development, 1835–1875*. New York: Harper and Row, 1982.

Irons, Peter. *Brennan vs. Rehnquist: The Battle for the Constitution*. New York: Knopf, 1994.

———. *The New Deal Lawyers*. Princeton: Princeton University Press, 1982.

Isaac, Paul E. *Prohibition and Politics: Turbulent Decades in Tennessee, 1885–1920*. Knoxville, University of Tennessee Press, 1965.

Jackson, Donald W. *Even the Children of Strangers: Equality Under the U.S. Constitution*. Lawrence: University Press of Kansas, 1992.

Jacobs, Clyde E. *The Eleventh Amendment and Sovereign Immunity*. Westport, Conn.: Greenwood, 1972.

James, Joseph B. *The Framing of the Fourteenth Amendment*. Urbana: University of Illinois Press, 1956.

———. *The Ratification of the Fourteenth Amendment*. Macon, Ga.: Mercer University Press, 1984.

Jensen, Merrill. *The Articles of Confederation*. Madison: University of Wisconsin Press, 1940.

———. *The New Nation: A History of the United States During the Confederation, 1781–1788*. New York: Knopf, 1950.

Jessup, Philip C. *Elihu Root*. 2 vols. New York: Dodd, Mead, 1938.

Jonas, Manfred. *Isolationsim in America, 1935–1941*. Ithaca, N.Y.: Cornell University Press, 1966.

Kammen, Michael. *Deputyes & Libertyes: The Origins of Representative Government in Colonial America*. New York: Knopf, 1969.

———. *A Machine That Would Go of Itself: The Constitution in American Culture*. New York: Knopf, 1986.

Kenne, Jesse L. *The Peace Convention of 1861*. Tuscaloosa, Ala.: Confederate Publishing, 1961.

Keller, Morton. *Affairs of State: Public Life in Late Nineteenth Century America*. Cambridge: Harvard University Press, 1977.

Kenyon, Cecelia M., ed. *The Antifederalists*. Indianapolis: Bobbs-Merrill, 1966.

Kenyon, Dorothy. *Changing the Constitution: A Study of the Amending Process*. Washington, D.C.: National League of Women Voters, 1926.

Kerr, K. Austin. *Organized for Prohibition: A New History of the Anti-Saloon League*. New Haven: Yale University Press, 1985.

Ketcham, Ralph. *James Madison: A Biography*. New York: Macmillan, 1971.

King, Willard L. *Melville Weston Fuller: Chief Justice of the United States, 1888–1910*. New York: Macmillan, 1950.

Kirwan, Albert D. *John J. Crittenden: The Struggle for the Union*. Lexington: University of Kentucky Press, 1962.

Knepper, George W. *Ohio and Its People*. Kent, Ohio: Kent State University Press, 1989.

Koenig, Louis W. *Bryan*. New York: G. P. Putnam, 1971.

Kolko, Gabriel. *The Triumph of Conservatism*. New York: Free Press, 1963.

Kraditor, Aileen S. *The Ideas of the Woman Suffrage Movement, 1890–1920*. New York: Columbia University Press, 1965.

Kull, Andrew. *The Color-Blind Constitution*. Cambridge: Harvard University Press. 1992.

Kuroda, Tadahisa. *The Origins of the Twelfth Amendment: The Electoral College in the Early Republic, 1787–1804*. Westport, Conn.: Greenwood, 1994.

Kuttner, Robert. *Revolt of the Haves: Tax Rebellions, and Hard Times*. New York: Simon and Schuster, 1980.

Kyvig, David E. *Repealing National Prohibition*. Chicago: University of Chicago Press, 1979.

Larson, Gustive O. *The "Americanization" of Utah for Statehood*. San Marino, Calif.: Huntington Library, 1971.

Lash, Joseph P. *Eleanor and Franklin*. New York: W. W. Norton, 1971.

Lawson, Steven F. *Black Ballots: Voting Rights in the South, 1944–1969*. New York: Columbia University Press, 1976.

Leder, Lawrence. *Liberty and Authority: Early American Political Ideology*. Chicago: Quadrangle Books, 1968.

Leedham, Charles. *Our Changing Constitution*. New York: Dodd, Mead, 1964.

Lemons, J. Stanley. *The Woman Citizen: Social Feminism in the 1920s*. Urbana: University of Illinois Press, 1973.

Lender, Mark Edward, and James Kirby Martin. *Drinking in America: A History*. New York: Free Press, 1982.

Leuchtenburg, William E. *The Supreme Court Reborn: The Constitutional Revolution in the Age of Roosevelt*. New York: Oxford University Press, 1995.

Levinson, Sanford. *Constitutional Faith*. Princeton: Princeton University Press, 1988.

————, ed. *Responding to Imperfection: The Theory and Practice of Constitutional Amendment.* Princeton: Princeton University Press, 1995.

Levy, Leonard W. *Legacy of Suppression: Freedom of Speech and Press in Early American History.* Cambridge: Harvard University Press, 1960.

————. *Original Intent and the Framer's Constitution.* New York: Macmillan, 1988.

————. *Origins of the Fifth Amendment: The Right Against Self-Incrimination.* New York: Oxford University Press, 1968.

————, ed. *Essays on the Making of the Constitution.* New York: Oxford University Press, 1969.

Levy, Leonard W., and Dennis J. Mahoney, eds. *The Framing and Ratification of the Constitution.* New York: Macmillan, 1987.

Liss, Peggy K. *Atlantic Empires: The Network of Trade and Revolution, 1713–1826.* Baltimore: Johns Hopkins University Press, 1983.

Livermore, Seward W. *Politics Is Adjourned: Woodrow Wilson and the War Congress, 1916–1918.* Middletown, Conn.: Wesleyan University Press, 1966.

Livingston, William S. *Federalism and Constitutional Change.* Westport, Conn.: Greenwood, 1974.

Lofgren, Charles A. *The Plessy Case: A Legal-Historical Interpretation.* New York: Oxford University Press, 1987.

Longley, Lawrence D., and Alan G. Braun. *The Politics of Electoral College Reform.* New Haven: Yale University Press, 1972.

Lowitt, Richard. *George W. Norris.* 3 vols. Syracuse: Syracuse University Press, 1963; Urbana: University of Illinois Press, 1971–1978.

Ludlow, Louis. *Hell or Heaven.* Boston: Stratford, 1937.

Lunardini, Christine A. *From Equal Suffrage to Equal Rights: Alice Paul and the National Woman's Party, 1910–1928.* New York: New York University Press, 1986.

Lurie, Jonathan. *Law and the Nation, 1865–1912.* New York: Knopf, 1983.

Lutz, Donald S. *The Origins of Modern Constitutionalism.* Baton Rouge: Louisiana State University Press, 1988.

————. *Popular Consent and Popular Control: Whig Political Theory in the Early State Constitutions.* Baton Rouge: Louisiana State University Press, 1980.

McAdoo, William G. *Crowded Years.* Boston: Houghton Mifflin, 1931.

McCloskey, Robert G., revised by Sanford Levinson. *The American Supreme Court.* 2d ed. Chicago: University of Chicago Press, 1994.

McCormick, Richard P. *Experiment in Independence: New Jersey in the Critical Period, 1781–1789.* New Brunswick, N.J.: Rutgers University Press, 1950.

McCoy, Drew R. *The Last of the Fathers: James Madison and the Republican Legacy.* New York: Cambridge University Press, 1989.

McDonald, Forrest. *Novus Ordo Seclorum: Intellectual Origins of the Constitution.* Lawrence: University Press of Kansas, 1985.

Macdonald, William. *A New Constitution for a New America.* New York: B. W. Huebsch, 1921.

McIlwain, Charles H. *Constitutionalism: Ancient and Modern.* Ithaca, N.Y.: Cornell University Press, 1947.

McLaughlin, Andrew C. *The Confederation and the Constitution, 1783–1789.* New York: Harper and Brothers, 1905.

———. *A Constitutional History of the United States.* New York: Appleton-Century-Crofts, 1935.

———. *The Foundations of American Constitutionalism.* New York: New York University Press, 1932.

MacNeil, Neil. *Dirksen: Portrait of a Public Man.* New York: World, 1970.

McPherson, James M. *Battle Cry of Freedom: The Civil War Era.* New York: Oxford University Press, 1988.

Main, Jackson, Turner. *The Anti-Federalists: Critics of the Constitution, 1781–1788.* Chapel Hill: University of North Carolina Press, 1961.

Malone, Dumas. *Thomas Jefferson and His Time.* 6 vols. Boston: Little, Brown, 1948–1981.

Maltz, Earl M. *Civil Rights, the Constitution, and Congress, 1863–1869.* Lawrence: University Press of Kansas, 1990.

Mansbridge, Jane J. *Why We Lost the ERA.* Chicago: University of Chicago Press, 1986.

Marcus, Maeva. *Truman and the Steel Seizure Case: The Limits of Presidential Power.* New York: Columbia University Press, 1977.

Martin, Kingsley. *French Liberal Thought in the Eighteenth Century: A Study of Political Ideas from Bayle to Condorcet.* 3d ed. New York: Harper and Row, 1962.

Mathews, Donald G., and Jane Sherron De Hart. *Sex, Gender, and the Politics of ERA: A State and the Nation.* New York: Oxford University Press, 1990.

Merriam, Charles Edward. *American Political Ideas: Studies in the Development of American Political Thought, 1865–1917.* New York: Macmillan, 1920.

———. *The Written Constitution and the Unwritten Attitude.* New York: R. R. Smith, 1931.

Merz, Charles. *The Dry Decade.* Garden City, N.Y.: Doubleday, Doran, 1931.

Meyer, Howard N. *The Amendment that Refused to Die.* Boston: Beacon, 1978.

Miller, Arthur Selwyn. *Social Change and Fundamental Law: America's Evolving Constitution.* Westport, Conn.: Greenwood, 1979.

Miller, John C. *Crisis in Freedom: The Alien and Sedition Acts.* Boston: Little, Brown, 1951.

———. *The Federalist Era, 1789–1801.* New York: Harper, 1960.

Morgan, David. *Suffragists and Democrats: The Politics of Woman Suffrage in America.* East Lansing: Michigan State University Press, 1972.

Morgan, Edmund S. *Inventing the People: The Rise of Popular Sovereignty in England and America.* New York: W. W. Norton, 1988.

Morris, Richard B. *The Forging of the Union, 1781–1789.* New York: Harper and Row, 1987.

Mowry, George E. *The Era of Theodore Roosevelt and the Birth of Modern America, 1900–1912.* New York: Harper and Row, 1958.

Muir, William K., Jr. *Prayer in the Public Schools: Law and Attitude Change.* Chicago: University of Chicago Press, 1967.

Murphy, Paul L. *The Constitution in Crisis Times, 1918–1969.* New York: Harper and Row, 1972.

Murphy, William P. *The Triumph of Nationalism: State Sovereignty, the Founding Fathers, and the Triumph of the Constitution.* Chicago: Quadrangle Books, 1967.

Musmanno, Michael A. *Proposed Amendments to the Constitution.* 70th Cong., 2d sess., House Doc. 551. Washington, D.C.: GPO, 1929.

Myers, Denys P. *The Process of Constitutional Amendment.* 76th Cong., 3d sess., Senate Doc. 314. Washington, D.C.: GPO, 1941.

Nedelsky, Jennifer. *Private Property and the Limits of American Constitutionalism: The Madisonian Framework and Its Legacy.* Chicago: University of Chicago Press, 1990.

Nelson, William E. *The Fourteenth Amendment: From Political Principle to Judicial Doctrine.* Cambridge: Harvard University Press, 1988.

Nevins, Alan. *Grover Cleveland.* New York: Dodd, Mead, 1933.

Newman, Roger K. *Hugo Black: A Biography.* New York: Pantheon, 1994.

Nieman, Donald G. *Promises to Keep: African-Americans and the Constitutional Order, 1776 to the Present.* New York: Oxford University Press, 1991.

Odegard, Peter H. *Pressure Politics: The Story of the Anti-Saloon League.* New York: Columbia University Press, 1928.

O'Neill, William L. *Everyone Was Brave: The Rise and Fall of Feminisim in America.* Chicago: Quadrangle, 1969.

Onuf, Peter S. *The Origins of the Federal Republic: Jurisdictional Controversies in the United States, 1775–1787.* Philadelphia: University of Pennsylvania Press, 1983.

Orfield, Lester B. *The Amending of the Federal Constitution.* Ann Arbor: University of Michigan Press, 1942.

Orth, John V. *The Judicial Power of the United States: The Eleventh Amendment in American History.* New York: Oxford University Press, 1987.

Ostrander, Gilman M. *The Prohibition Movement in California, 1848–1933.* Berkeley: University of California Press, 1957.

Palmer, Robert R. *The Age of the Democratic Revolutions.* 2 vols. Princeton: Princeton University Press, 1959–1964.

Paludan, Philip S. *A Covenant with Death: The Constitution, Law, and Equality in the Civil War Era.* Urbana: University of Illinois Press, 1975.

Parmet, Herbert S., and Marie B. Hecht. *Never Again: A President Runs for a Third Term.* New York: Macmillan, 1968.

Patterson, James T. *Congressional Conservatism and the New Deal: The Growth of the Conservative Coalition in Congress, 1933–1939.* Lexington: University of Kentucky Press, 1967.

Paul, Arnold M. *Conservative Crisis and the Rule of Law: Attitudes of Bar and Bench, 1887–1895.* New York: Harper and Row, 1969.

Paulson, Ross Evans. *Women's Suffrage and Prohibition: A Comparative Study of Equality and Social Control.* Glenview, Ill.: Scott, Foresman, 1973.

Pearson, C. C., and J. Edwin Hendricks. *Liquor and Anti-Liquor in Virginia, 1619–1919.* Durham, N.C.: Duke University Press, 1967.

Peirce, Neal R., and Lawrence D. Longley. *The People's President: The Electoral College in American History and the Direct Vote Alternative.* Rev. ed. New Haven: Yale University Press, 1981.

Peters, Ronald M., Jr. *The Massachusetts Constitution of 1780: A Social Compact.* Amherst: University of Masschusetts Press, 1978.

582 *Explicit and Authentic Acts*

Peterson, Merrill D. *Thomas Jefferson and the New Nation.* New York: Oxford University Press, 1970.

Phelps, Glenn A. *George Washington and American Constitutionalism.* Lawrence: University Press of Kansas, 1993.

Pocock, J. G. A. *The Machiavellian Moment: Florentine Political Thought and the Atlantic Republic Tradition.* Princeton: Princeton University Press, 1975.

Pole, J. R. *Political Representation in England and the Origins of the American Republic.* London: Macmillan, 1966.

Pollard, Joseph Percival. *The Road to Repeal: Submission to Conventions.* New York: Brentano's, 1932.

Pomper, Gerald et al. *The Election of 1980: Reports and Interpretations.* Chatham, N.J.: Chatham House, 1981.

Pringle, Henry F. *Theodore Roosevelt.* 2d ed. New York: Harcourt Brace, 1956.

Rakove, Jack N. *The Beginnings of National Politics: An Interpretive History of the Continental Congress.* New York: Knopf, 1979.

———. *James Madison and the Creation of the American Republic.* Glenview, Ill.: Scott, Foresman, 1990.

Randall, James G. *Constitutional Problems Under Lincoln.* New York: D. Appleton, 1926.

Ratner, Sidney. *American Taxation.* New York: W. W. Norton, 1942.

Reagan, Ronald. *An American Life.* New York: Simon and Schuster, 1990.

Reichard, Gary W. *The Reaffirmation of Republicanism: Eisenhower and the Eighty-third Congress.* Knoxville: University of Tennessee Press, 1975.

Reid, John Phillip. *Constitutional History of the American Revolution: The Authority of Rights.* Madison: University of Wisconsin Press, 1986.

Rice, Charles E. *The Supreme Court and Public Prayer: The Need for Restraint.* New York: Fordham University Press, 1964.

Richards, Leonard L. *The Life and Times of Congressman John Quincy Adams.* New York: Oxford University Press, 1986.

Rogers, Will. *Rogers-isms: The Cowboy Philosopher on Prohibition.* New York: Harper, 1919.

Root, Grace C. *Women and Repeal.* New York: Harper, 1934.

Rorabaugh, William. *The Alcoholic Republic.* New York: Oxford University Press, 1979.

Rosenberg, Rosalind. *Divided Lives: American Women in the Twentieth Century.* New York: Hill and Wang, 1992.

Rossiter, Clinton. *1787: The Grand Convention.* New York: Macmillan, 1966.

Rothman, David J. *Politics and Power: The United States Senate, 1869–1901.* Cambridge: Harvard University Press, 1966.

Rubin, Eva R. *Abortion, Politics, and the Courts: Roe v. Wade and Its Aftermath.* Westport, Conn.: Greenwood, 1982.

Rutland, Robert Allen. *The Birth of the Bill of Rights, 1776–1791.* Rev. ed. Boston: Northeastern University Press, 1983.

———. *The Ordeal of the Constitution: The Anti-federalists and the Ratification of 1787–1788.* Norman: University of Oklahoma Press, 1966.

———. *The Presidency of James Madison.* Lawrence: University Press of Kansas, 1990.

Ryan, John A. *Declining Liberty and Other Papers.* New York: Macmillan, 1927.

Sabine, George H. *A History of Political Theory.* 3d ed. New York: Holt, Rinehart and Winston, 1961.

Sarasohn, David. *The Party of Reform: Democrats in the Progressive Era.* Jackson: University Press of Mississippi, 1989.

Savage, James D. *Balanced Budgets and American Politics.* Ithaca, N.Y.: Cornell University Press, 1988.

Sayre, Wallace S., and Judith H. Parris. *Voting for President: The Electoral College and the American Political System.* Washington, D.C.: Brookings, 1970.

Schapsmeier, Edward L., and Frederick H. Schapsmeier. *Dirksen of Illinois: Senatorial Statesman.* Urbana: University of Illinois Press, 1985.

Schechter, Stephen L., ed. *The Reluctant Pillar: New York and the Adoption of the Federal Constitution.* Troy, N.Y.: Russell Sage College, 1985.

Schlesinger, Arthur M., Jr. *The Imperial Presidency.* Boston: Houghton Mifflin, 1973.

Schneider, James C. *Should America Go to War? The Debate over Foreign Policy in Chicago, 1939–1941.* Chapel Hill: University of North Carolina Press, 1989.

Schrag, Philip G. *Behind the Scenes: The Politics of a Constitutional Convention.* Washington, D.C.: Georgetown University Press, 1985.

Schwartz, Bernard. *The Great Rights of Mankind: A History of the American Bill of Rights.* New York: Oxford University Press, 1977.

Scott, Anne F., and Andrew M. *One Half the People: The Fight for Woman Suffrage.* Philadelphia: J. B. Lippincott, 1976.

Seligman, Edwin R. A. *The Income Tax.* 2d ed. New York: Macmillan, 1914.

Selsam, J. Paul *The Pennsylvania Constitution of 1776: A Study in Revolutionary Democracy.* Philadelphia: University of Pennsylvania Press, 1936.

Shiras, George, 3rd. *Justice George Shiras, Jr., of Pittsburgh: Associate Justice of the United States Supreme Court, 1892–1903.* Pittsburgh: University of Pittsburgh Press, 1953.

Sidney, Algernon. *Discourses Concerning Government.* 3d ed. London: A Millar, 1751.

Silva, Ruth C. *Presidential Succession.* Ann Arbor: University of Michigan Press, 1951.

Simister, Florence Parker. *The Fire's Center: Rhode Island in the Revolutionary Era, 1763–1780.* Providence: Rhode Island Bicentennial Commission, 1979.

Simpson, William. *Vision and Reality: The Evolution of American Government.* London: John Murray, 1978.

Sinclair, Andrew. *Prohibition: The Era of Excess.* Boston, Little, Brown, 1962.

Sindler, Allan P. *Unchosen Presidents: The Vice-President and Other Frustrations of Presidential Succession.* Berkeley: University of California Press, 1976.

Smith, David G. *The Convention and the Constitution: The Political Ideas of the Founding Fathers.* New York: St. Martin's, 1965.

Smith, Donald L. *Zechariah Chafee, Jr.: Defender of Liberty and Law.* Cambridge: Harvard University Press, 1986.

Smith, J. Allen. *The Spirit of American Government.* New York: Macmillan, 1907.

Smith, James Morton, ed. *The Constitution.* New York: Harper and Row, 1971.

Smith, Rodney K. *Public Prayer and the Constitution: A Case Study in Constitutional Interpretation.* Wilmington, Del.: Scholarly Resources, 1987.

Smith, Rogers M. *Liberalism and American Constitutional Law.* Cambridge: Harvard University Press, 1985.

Snowiss, Sylvia. *Judicial Review and the Law of the Constitution.* New Haven: Yale University Press, 1990.

Sosin, J. M. *The Aristocracy of the Long Robe: The Origins of Judicial Review in America.* Westport, Conn., Greenwood, 1989.

Spurlin, Paul Merrill. *Rousseau in America, 1760–1809.* University, Ala.: University of Alabama Press, 1969.

Stampp, Kenneth M. *And the War Came: The North and the Secession Crisis, 1860–1861.* Baton Rouge: Louisiana State University Press, 1950.

Stanley, Robert. *Dimensions of Law in the Service of Order: Origins of the Federal Income Tax, 1861–1913.* New York: Oxford University Press, 1993.

Stein, Charles W. *The Third-Term Tradition.* New York: Columbia University Press, 1943.

Steiner, Gilbert Y. *Constitutional Inequality: The Political Fortunes of the Equal Rights Amendment.* Washington, D.C.: Brookings, 1985.

Steuerle, C. Eugene. *The Tax Decade: How Taxes Came to Dominate the Public Agenda.* Washington, D.C.: Urban Institute Press, 1992.

Stevenson, Archibald E. *States' Rights and National Prohibition.* New York: Clark Boardman, 1927.

Stockman, David A. *The Triumph of Politics: How the Reagan Revolution Failed.* New York: Harper and Row, 1986.

Storing, Herbert J. *What the Anti-Federalists Were For.* Chicago: University of Chicago Press, 1981.

Story, Joseph. *Commentaries on the Constitution of the United States.* 3 vols. Boston: Hilliard, Gray, 1833.

Sutherland, Arthur E. *Constitutionalism in America: Origins and Evolution of Its Fundamental Ideas.* New York: Blaisdell, 1965.

Swindler, William F. *Court and Constitution in the 20th Century.* 2 vols. Indianapolis: Bobbs-Merrill, 1969–1970.

Swisher, Carl Brent. *American Constitutional Development.* Boston: Houghton Mifflin, 1943.

———. *Stephen J. Field: Craftsman of the Law.* Washington, D.C.: Brookings, 1930.

Tananbaum, Duane. *The Bricker Amendment Controversy: A Test of Eisenhower's Political Leadership.* Ithaca, N.Y.: Cornell University Press, 1988.

Taylor, A. Elizabeth. *The Woman Suffrage Movement in Tennessee.* New York: Bookman, 1957.

tenBroek, Jacobus. *The Antislavery Origins of the Fourteenth Amendment.* Berkeley: University of California Press, 1951.

Thelen, David P. *Robert M. La Follette and the Insurgent Spirit.* Boston: Little, Brown, 1976.

Theoharis, Athan G. *The Yalta Myths: An Issue in U.S. Politics, 1945–1955.* Columbia: University of Missouri Press, 1970.

Thorpe, Francis Newton. *The Story of the Constitution of the United States.* New York: Chautauqua Press, 1891.

Timberlake, James H. *Prohibition and the Progressive Movement, 1900–1920.* Cambridge: Harvard University Press, 1966.

Trattner, Walter I. *Crusade for the Children: A History of the National Child Labor Committee and Child Labor Reform in America.* Chicago: Quadrangle, 1970.

Trenholme, Louise. *The Ratification of the Federal Constitution in North Carolina.* New York: AMS Press, 1967.
Tribe, Laurence H. *Abortion: The Clash of Absolutes.* Rev. ed. New York: W. W. Norton, 1992.
Tugwell, Rexford G. *The Compromising of the Constitution (Early Departures).* Notre Dame, Ind.: University of Notre Dame Press, 1976.
———. *The Democratic Roosevelt.* Garden City, N.Y.: Doubleday, 1957.
———. *The Emerging Constitution.* New York: Harper's Magazine Press, 1974.
Twiss, Benjamin R. *Lawyers and the Constitution: How Laissez Faire Came to the Supreme Court.* Princeton: Princeton University Press, 1942.

Van Doren, Carl. *The Great Rehearsal: The Story of the Making and Ratifying of the Constitution of the United States.* New York: Viking Press, 1948.
Van Wagoner, Richard S. *Mormon Polygamy: A History.* 2d ed. Salt Lake City: Signature, 1989.
Vile, John R. *The Constitutional Amending Process in American Political Thought.* New York: Praeger, 1992.
———. *Rewriting the United States Constitution.* New York: Praeger, 1991.
Vose, Clement E. *Constitutional Change: Amendment Politics and Supreme Court Litigation Since 1900.* Lexington, Mass.: Lexington Books, 1972.

Wandersee, Winifred D. *On the Move: American Women in the 1970s.* Boston: Twayne, 1988.
Warren, Charles. *Congress, the Constitution, and the Supreme Court.* Boston: Little, Brown, 1925.
———. *The Making of the Constitution.* Boston: Little, Brown, 1928.
Weber, Paul J., and Barbara A. Perry. *Unfounded Fears: Myths and Realities of a Constitutional Convention.* New York: Greenwood, 1989.
Whalen, Charles, and Barbara Whalen. *The Longest Debate: A Legislative History of the 1964 Civil Rights Act.* Cabin John, Md.: Seven Locks Press, 1985.
White, G. Edward. *The Marshall Court and Cultural Change, 1815–1835.* Abridged ed. New York: Oxford University Press, 1991.
Whitfield, Stephen J. *The Culture of the Cold War.* Baltimore: Johns Hopkins University Press, 1991.
Whitlock, Brand. *The Little Green Shutter.* New York: D. Appleton, 1931.
Wiebe, Robert H. *Self-Rule: A Cultural History of American Democracy.* Chicago: University of Chicago Press, 1995.
Wills, Garry. *Explaining America: The Federalist.* Garden City, N.Y.: Doubleday, 1981.
———. *Inventing America: Jefferson's Declaration of Independence.* Garden City, N.Y.: Doubleday, 1978.
———. *Lincoln at Gettysburg: The Words that Remade America.* New York: Simon and Schuster, 1992.
Wolfe, Christopher. *The Rise of Modern Judicial Review.* New York: Basic Books, 1986.
Wolfskill, George. *The Revolt of the Conservatives: A History of the American Liberty League, 1934–1940.* Boston: Houghton Mifflin, 1962.

Wood, Gordon S. *The Creation of the American Republic, 1776–1787*. Chapel Hill: University of North Carolina Press, 1969.

———. *The Radicalism of the American Revolution*. New York: Knopf, 1992.

Wood, Stephen B. *Constitutional Politics in the Progressive Era: Child Labor and the Law*. Chicago: University of Chicago Press, 1968.

Woodward, Bob, and Scott Armstrong. *The Brethren: Inside the Supreme Court*. New York: Simon and Schuster, 1979.

Wormuth, Francis. *The Origins of Modern Constitutionalism*. New York: Harper, 1949.

DISSERTATIONS

Camhi, Jane Jerome. "Women Against Women: American Antisuffragism, 1880–1920." Ph.D. diss., Tufts University, 1973.

Heckman, Dayton E. "Prohibition Passes: The Story of the Association Against the Prohibition Amendment." Ph.D. diss., Ohio State University, 1939.

Keynes, Edward. "The Dirsken Amendment: A Study of Legislative Strategy, Tactics and Public Policy." Ph.D. diss., University of Wisconsin, 1967.

Louis, James P. "Woman Suffrage and Progressive Reform: The Fight for the Nineteenth Amendment, 1913–1920." Ph.D. diss., Harvard University, 1968.

McLaughlin, Andrew C. "Satire as a Weapon Against Prohibition, 1920–1928: Expression of a Cultural Conflict." Ph.D. diss., Stanford University, 1969.

Murdock, Catherine Gilbert. "Domesticating Drink: Women and Alcohol in Prohibition America, 1870–1940." Ph.D. diss., University of Pennsylvania, 1995.

Zimmerman, Loretta Ellen. "Alice Paul and the National Women's Party, 1912–1920." Ph.D. diss., Tufts University, 1964.

Zucker, Frederick D. "The Adoption of the Twenty-Second Amendment." Ph.D. diss., Pennsylvania State University, 1958.

INDEX